Fireworks® MX Bible

Fireworks® MX Bible

Joseph W. Lowery and Derren Whiteman

Wiley Publishing, Inc.

Best-Selling Books • Digital Downloads • e-Books • Answer Networks • e-Newsletters • Branded Web Sites • e-Learning

Fireworks® MX Bible

Published by
Wiley Publishing, Inc.
909 Third Avenue
New York, NY 10022
www.wiley.com

Copyright © 2002 by Wiley Publishing, Inc., Indianapolis, Indiana

Library of Congress Control Number: 2002107897

ISBN: 0-7645-3662-1

Manufactured in the United States of America

10 9 8 7 6 5 4 3 2 1

1B/SS/QY/QS/IN

Published by Wiley Publishing, Inc., Indianapolis, Indiana
Published simultaneously in Canada

For general information on our other products and services or to obtain technical support, please contact our Customer Care Department within the U.S. at 800-762-2974, outside the U.S. at 317-572-3993 or fax 317-572-4002.

Wiley also publishes its books in a variety of electronic formats.

Trademarks: Wiley, the Wiley Publishing logo, and related trade dress are trademarks or registered trademarks of Wiley Publishing, Inc., in the United States and other countries, and may not be used without written permission. PANTONE and other Pantone, Inc. trademarks are the property of Pantone, Inc. FreeHand 10 and Macromedia Flash MX Copyright © 1995-2000. Macromedia, Inc. 600 Townsend Street, San Francisco, CA 94103 USA. All Rights Reserved. Macromedia, Flash, Fireworks and FreeHand are trademarks or registered trademarks of Macromedia, Inc. in the United States and/or other countries. All other trademarks are the property of their respective owners. Wiley Publishing, Inc., is not associated with any product or vendor mentioned in this book.

About the Authors

Joseph Lowery has been writing about computers and new technology since 1981. He is the author of the current and previous editions of *Dreamweaver Bible* and *Fireworks Bible* as well as *Buying Online For Dummies* (all from Wiley Publishing, formerly Hungry Minds, Inc.). He recently co-wrote a book on Flash with designer Hillman Curtis and has also written books on HTML and using the Internet for business. His books are international best-sellers, having sold over 300,000 copies worldwide in ten different languages. Joseph is also a consultant and trainer and has presented at Seybold in both Boston and San Francisco, Macromedia UCON in the U.S. and Europe, and at ThunderLizard's Web World. As a partner in Deva Associates, Ltd., Joseph developed the Deva Tools for Dreamweaver set of navigational extensions. Joseph and his wife, dancer/choreographer Debra Wanner, have a daughter, Margot.

Derren Whiteman's online life began before the invention of the World Wide Web, when data moved across the Internet, and online communities were based around electronic bulletin board systems (BBS). He built Web sites "by hand" in the early days of the World Wide Web — because that was how you made them in those days — and later took up modern tools after joining *Mediafear*, a San Francisco-based Web design shop where he spent three years building dynamic Web sites for artists and musicians. Derren has also served as an information technology consultant and computer instructor, enabling individuals and small businesses to use technology to their greatest advantage.

Derren spends much of his time in technical publishing, helping to make today's Web-building tools accessible to everyone. He served as Technical Editor for versions 3 and 4 of Joseph Lowery's *Fireworks Bible* (Hungry Minds, Inc.) and *Dreamweaver 4 Bible* (Hungry Minds, Inc.). Other books that Derren worked on include *Mastering Dreamweaver 4 and Fireworks MX* (Sybex, Inc.), *Look & Learn Dreamweaver 4* (Hungry Minds, Inc.), and *From FrontPage to Dreamweaver* (Sams Publishing).

Derren is a Macromedia Certified Dreamweaver 4 Developer and a volunteer member of Team Macromedia for Fireworks (`http://www.macromedia.com/go/team`). He maintains a number of Web sites, including `FrancinePaul.com`, `Konis.com`, and of course, `Derren.com`. He makes his home in Toronto, Ontario, Canada.

Credits

Acquisitions Editor
Michael Roney

Project Editor
Martin V. Minner

Technical Editor
Kleanthis Economou

Copy Editors
Roxane Marini
Nancy Rapoport

Editorial Manager
Rev Mengle

**Vice President and
Executive Group Publisher**
Richard Swadley

**Vice President and
Executive Publisher**
Bob Ipsen

Executive Editorial Director
Mary Bednarek

Project Coordinator
Ryan Steffen

Graphics and Production Specialists
Beth Brooks, Melanie DesJardins,
Joyce Haughey, Clint Lahnen,
Kristin McMullan, Barry Offringa,
Brent Savage, Jeremey Unger

Quality Control Technicians
John Greenough, Susan Moritz

Permissions Editor
Laura Moss

Media Development Specialist
Angela Denny

Proofreading and Indexing
TECHBOOKS Production Services

Cover Image
Anthony Stuart

Foreword

The Fireworks engineering team saw the storm coming across the North Central Texas landscape. The Internet bubble had burst and companies were looking for ways to reduce costs while keeping quality high. The next release of Fireworks had to be really special; it wasn't enough to produce great looking, highly-optimized Web graphics or cutting-edge navigation elements. The process of production had become as important as the final output — the next generation of Fireworks needed to be easy to use, more powerful and open for enhanced teamwork.

A key goal was to streamline both the workspace and the workflow. For the workspace, we incorporated a Property inspector similar to the one found in Dreamweaver, but customized for a graphics application. The Property inspector makes it far easier to modify fill and stroke settings and much more without having to dig through a ton of panels. However, the Property inspector can't do it all, so we also enhanced the overall panel management with dockable, collapsible panel groups that are easy to find when you need them and get out of your way when you don't. Not coincidentally, you'll find the same polished user interface across the Studio MX line, including Macromedia Flash MX and Dreamweaver MX — a significant ease-of-use factor in and of itself.

We tried to improve the workflow with other enhancements to the workspace. One of the strengths of Fireworks is its ability to work both with vector-based and bitmap-based graphics; it hasn't, however, always been easy to move from one mode to another. To smooth out the workflow, Fireworks now switches modes automatically based on your selected tool, object, or layer; it's so effortless that we call it *modeless editing*. We think you'll also find our new on-screen text editing a great time-saver. Select the text tool, click anywhere on the canvas and begin typing to insert your text. Need to correct a word or change a font? Just double-click into the text and make your change.

One of the most popular features introduced in Fireworks 4 was our pop-up menu creator. We decided to ramp up the power on this feature and now in Fireworks MX you can make pop-up menus in either vertical or horizontal formats, with far greater control over positioning, appearance, and interactivity. Another new power-user feature that's getting rave reviews is the Data-Driven Graphics Wizard. This command — actually created by *Fireworks MX Bible* author Joseph Lowery — dissolves production roadblocks by combining Fireworks graphic templates with XML data files to output as many variations on a theme as required, with a fraction of the work.

The Data-Driven Graphics Wizard is, quite literally, the tip of an open architecture powerhouse as big as a proverbial iceberg. Starting in Fireworks MX, custom commands and panels can be constructed that leverage the JavaScript API of the Fireworks graphics engine with a Flash user interface. You'll find other examples of new Fireworks extensibility throughout the program as evidenced by the very handy Align panel and other extensions under the Commands menu. Like Dreamweaver and Flash, extensions are easily installed and removed through the Extension Manager.

The Web is continuing to evolve and Fireworks is keeping pace. In addition to outputting JavaScript and HTML for the majority of the world's code editors, Fireworks MX now speaks XHTML fluently. Moreover, the code output is compliant with Web accessibility standards, including Federal guideline Section 508. Fireworks is poised to help designers like yourself grow and move steadily forward.

Changes — whether they are the result of an economic downturn or the introduction of exhilarating new technologies — are often difficult to go through and made easier with the proper guide. In the book you hold in your hands, you'll find one of best roadmaps to the changes in Fireworks MX available. Joseph Lowery and Derren Whiteman provide details and examples essential for the Web graphics professional.

Our desire to make Fireworks better is ongoing and our mailbox never closes. If you have a suggestion for a new feature or a way to be more productive, feel free to drop us a line at `wish-fireworks@macromedia.com`. We're looking forward to hearing from you.

David Morris
Product Manager, Fireworks
Macromedia

Preface

Remember that burst of pleasure when you first realized how exciting the Web could be? I'll let you in on a little secret: Macromedia Fireworks makes creating graphics for the Web fun again. Images produced with Fireworks are as sophisticated and rich as those created with any other combination of programs, plus they're Web-ready — as optimized as possible and bundled with HTML and JavaScript code for amazing interactive effects.

I'll be the first to admit my bias. I'm a Dreamweaver power user, and it seems only natural to combine Macromedia's exciting Web-graphics solution with its premier Web-authoring tool. In fact, Macromedia encourages you to do so with its Studio MX offering. But while I'm confessing, let me also note that I have no patience for tools that don't do the job. The wonderful revelation about Fireworks is that this program eliminates production bottlenecks I didn't even know existed — all while producing stunning imagery that stays editable through revision after easy revision.

When I set out to write this book, I decided to really push Fireworks. Rather than using it merely to optimize a series of images (which it does superbly), or to create a compact animation (which it also does superbly) from work created in other programs, I used Fireworks exclusively for all image manipulation and creation. Consequently, both my productivity and my creativity went through the roof. *Fireworks MX Bible* was designed to give you all the information and techniques you need to achieve the same results.

—JL

Who Should Read This Book?

The Web is, without a doubt, one of the key phenomena of our time, and it has attracted an enormous amount of talent, both artistic and technical. After all, how often does a new mass medium appear? The range of Web designers extends from first-generation artists drawn to the exciting Internet possibilities, to print professionals who want to expand their creative horizons. *Fireworks MX Bible* talks to all those groups, offering solutions to everyday graphics problems, as well as providing a complete reference for the program.

What Hardware and Software Do You Need?

Fireworks MX Bible includes full coverage of Macromedia Fireworks MX. If you don't own a copy of the program, the CD-ROM that accompanies this book contains a fully functional, 30-day trial version. Written to be platform-independent, this book covers both Macintosh and Windows versions of Fireworks MX.

Fireworks for Windows requires a 300 MHz Pentium processor (Pentium II or higher recommended) and one of the following operating systems: Windows NT 4 (Service Pack 6 or later), Windows 98 SE, Windows Me, 2000, or XP.

Fireworks for Macintosh requires a Power Macintosh processor (G3 or higher recommended) and Mac OS 9.1 or a later version, including Mac OS X, version 10.1 or later.

On either platform, Fireworks also requires the following:

✦ 64MB of available RAM

✦ 80MB of available disk space

✦ 800×600-pixel, 256-color display (1,024×768 pixels or higher and millions of colors recommended)

✦ Adobe Type Manager 4, or a later version may be required if you work with Type 1 (PostScript) fonts. For Macintosh, this requirement applies only to OS 9.*x*)

Please note that these requirements are the minimum. As with all graphics-based design tools, more capability is definitely better for using Fireworks, especially in terms of RAM and processor speed.

How This Book Is Organized

Fireworks MX Bible can take you from raw beginner to full-fledged professional if read cover to cover. However, you're more likely to read each section as needed, taking the necessary information and coming back later. To facilitate this approach, *Fireworks MX Bible* is divided into seven major, task-oriented parts. When you're familiar with Fireworks, feel free to skip around the book, using it as a reference guide as you build your own knowledge base.

The early chapters present the basics, and all chapters contain clearly written steps for the tasks you need to perform. In later chapters, you'll encounter sections labeled "Fireworks Techniques." Fireworks Techniques are step-by-step instructions for accomplishing specific Web-design tasks — for example, using a mask to add an interesting border to an image. Naturally, you can also use Fireworks Techniques as steppingstones for your own explorations into Web-page creation.

If you're running Fireworks while reading this book, don't forget to use the CD-ROM. An integral element of the book, the CD-ROM offers a number of additional Fireworks textures, gradients, and HTML templates, in addition to trial programs from major software vendors.

Part I: Come See the Fireworks

Part I begins with an overview of the Fireworks philosophy and design. To get the most out of the program, you need to understand the key advantages it offers and the deficiencies it addresses. Part I takes you all the way from setting up documents to getting the most out of Fireworks.

The opening chapters give you a full reference to the Fireworks interface and all of its customizable features. Chapter 1 will be of special interest to users of previous versions of Fireworks; it's a complete guide to all the newly added features in Fireworks MX. Later chapters in Part I provide an overview of everything that Fireworks can do — this feature-rich program will often surprise you.

Part II: Mastering the Tools

The Fireworks approach to graphics is fundamentally different from any other tool on the market. Consequently, you'll need to travel the short learning curve before you can get the most out of Fireworks. The early chapters in Part II cover all the essentials, from basic object creation, to full-blown photo manipulation.

Color is a key component of any graphic designer's tool kit, and color on the Web requires special attention, as you'll see in Chapter 7. The object-oriented nature of Fireworks is explored in chapters on creating simple strokes and combining paths in a variety of ways to help you make more sophisticated graphics. Fireworks excels at creating graphical text for the Web — you'll see how in Chapter 10.

Part III: Achieving Effects

Fireworks graphics really begin to gain depth in Part III. The variety of fills and textures available — as well as the capability to add your own — are critical for the wide range of image production for which a Web designer is responsible. Chapter 12 explores the exciting world of Fireworks Live Effects and filters, which are exciting not just because they're easy to use and they look great, but also because of the positive impact that their always-editable nature will have on your workflow.

Most of the time, a graphic will actually contain a number of images. Chapter 13 explains the Fireworks methods for arranging and compositing multiple objects in order to achieve stunning results. The Fireworks mask-group feature, in particular, is an especially creative and powerful tool that takes the hard work out of alpha channels. Although Fireworks is a great drawing tool, it's also adept at handling bitmap imagery.

Part IV: Coordinating Workflow

Web design is an ongoing process, not a single event. Part IV is dedicated to helping you streamline your workflow, as you acquire images via scanning or importing, manipulate them in Fireworks, and then optimize them on export, either for the Web or for import into other creative tools, such as Macromedia Director or Flash.

Although it's true that Web graphic design is an art form, it's also a business — and one element of that business is applying a consistent look and feel to each element of a particular Web site. Fireworks styles enable you to save formatting instructions from one object and apply them to other objects again and again. The Library panel is a place to store *symbols,* objects you use frequently, such as logos and navigation buttons. Fireworks symbols further minimize repetitive work by linking similar objects so that changes need only be made once. Chapter 18 describes how Fireworks MX helps you update and maintain your graphics through the URL panel and the surprising Find and Replace feature. The final chapter in Part IV covers the greatly expanded Command feature set with it's new Flash movie interface capability and the History panel, useful for constructing simple reusable commands from your actions.

Part V: Entering the Web

Fireworks broke new ground as the first image editor to output HTML and JavaScript code. With its full-featured hotspots, image maps, and sliced images embedded in HTML tables, Fireworks is incredibly Web-savvy. Part V explains the basics of Web interactivity for those designers unfamiliar with the territory and also offers specific step-by-step instructions for linking JavaScript behaviors to graphics.

If you work with Dreamweaver (or work with someone who does), you'll want to check out Chapter 22 in order to get the most out of the integration possibilities between Fireworks and Dreamweaver.

Part VI: Animation

Animations have become important to the Web. Not only do they offer an alternative to static displays, but GIF animations are used extensively in the creation of banner ads. Animation in Fireworks MX is surprisingly full-featured and easy-to-use. We'll walk step by step through the creation of a banner ad and discover tweening, onion skinning, and other basic animation techniques.

Part VII: Programming with Fireworks

One of the most amazing things about Fireworks MX is the way it can be controlled by scripts written in JavaScript, the most common scripting language for Web authoring. Fireworks offers many ways to customize the way you work with the program. We'll look at each of them and discover the extensive Fireworks JavaScript API (Application Programming Interface). The final chapter explores the brave new world of Fireworks extensions and describes how you can use Flash to create user interfaces for such commands.

Part VIII: Appendixes

Appendix A is a Web primer, a place to get a good grounding on the ways of the Web. Appendix B is a handy reference guide to productivity-boosting keyboard shortcuts on both Macintosh and Windows systems. The material on the accompanying CD-ROM is detailed in Appendix C.

Conventions Used in This Book

The following conventions are used throughout this book.

Windows and Macintosh conventions

Because *Fireworks MX Bible* is a cross-platform book, it gives instructions for both Windows and Macintosh users when keystrokes for a particular task differ. Throughout this book, the Windows keystrokes are given first, and the Macintosh keystrokes are given second in parentheses, as in the following example:

To undo an action, press Ctrl+Z (Command+Z).

The first action instructs Windows users to simultaneously press Ctrl and Z, and the second action (in parentheses) instructs Macintosh users to press Command and Z together. In Fireworks for Windows, the keyboard shortcuts are displayed in the menus in plain English. In Fireworks for Macintosh, as in other Macintosh programs, the keyboard shortcuts are specified in the menus by using symbols that represent the modifier keys.

You'll notice that in most — but not all — keyboard shortcuts, the Windows Ctrl key corresponds to the Macintosh Command key, and the Windows Alt key corresponds to the Macintosh Option key.

Screen captures in odd-numbered chapters are of Fireworks for Windows running on Windows 98; in even-numbered chapters, they're of Fireworks for Macintosh running on Mac OS 9. In the rare event that a particular feature or example is markedly different on each platform, both are shown.

For the purposes of this book, *Windows* generally refers to Windows NT 4 (Service Pack 6 or later), Windows 98 SE, Windows Me, Windows 2000, or Windows XP. Similarly, *Macintosh* or *Mac OS* refers to Mac OS 9.1 or higher or OS X, version 10.1 or higher.

Keyboard combinations

When you are instructed to press two or more keys simultaneously, each key in the combination is separated by a plus sign. For example:

Ctrl+Alt+T (Command+Option+T)

The preceding line tells you to press and hold down the two modifier keys (either Ctrl+Alt or Command+Option, depending upon your platform), and then press and release the final key, T.

Mouse instructions

When instructed to *click* an item, move the mouse pointer to the specified item and click the mouse button once. A *double-click* means clicking the mouse button twice in rapid succession.

A *right-click* means clicking the secondary mouse button once. Macintosh users who use a one-button mouse can substitute a *Control-click* for a right-click. To do so, press and hold down Control on your keyboard, and click the mouse button once.

When instructed to select an item, you may click it once as previously described. If you are selecting text or multiple objects, you must click the mouse button once, hold it down, and then move the mouse to a new location. The item or items selected invert color. To clear the selection, click once anywhere in an empty part of the document background.

Menu commands

When instructed to select a command from a menu, you see the menu and the command separated by an arrow symbol. For example, when instructed to execute the Open command from the File menu, you see the notation File ➪ Open. Some menus use submenus, in which case you see an arrow for each submenu, as in Modify ➪ Transform ➪ Free Transform.

Typographical conventions

Italic type is used for new terms and for emphasis. **Boldface** type is used for text that you need to type directly from the computer keyboard.

Code

A special typeface indicates HTML or other code, as demonstrated in the following example:

```
<html>
<head>
<title>Have a Nice Day!</title>
</head>
<body bgcolor="#FFFFFF">
</body>
</html>
```

This code font is also used within paragraphs to designate HTML tags, attributes, and values, such as <body>, bgcolor, and #FFFFFF.

The (¬) character at the end of a code line means that you should type the next line of code before pressing Enter (Return).

Navigating through this book

Various signposts and icons are located throughout *Fireworks MX Bible* for your assistance. Each chapter begins with an overview of its information, and ends with a quick summary.

Icons are placed in the text to indicate important or especially helpful items. Here's a list of the icons and their functions:

Tips provide you with extra knowledge that separates the novice from the pro.

Notes provide additional or critical information, and technical data on the current topic.

Sections marked with a New Feature icon detail an innovation introduced in Fireworks MX.

Cross-Reference icons indicate places where you can find more information on a particular topic.

The Caution icon is your warning of a potential problem or pitfall.

The On the CD-ROM icon indicates the CD-ROM contains a related file.

Further information

You can find more help for specific problems and questions by investigating several Web sites. Macromedia's own Fireworks Web site is the best place to start:

```
http://www.macromedia.com/software/fireworks
```

I heartily recommend that you visit and participate in the official Fireworks newsgroup:

```
news://forums.macromedia.com/macromedia.fireworks
```

You're also invited to visit my Web site for book updates and new developments:

```
http://www.idest.com/fireworks
```

You can also e-mail me:

```
mailto:jlowery@idest.com
```

I can't promise instantaneous turnaround, but I answer all my e-mail to the best of my ability.

Acknowledgments

This is one of my favorite moments in writing a book: when I get to acknowledge and thank the many generous people who helped make this book possible. First and foremost among these folks is Derren Whiteman. For the past several editions, Derren had served as the unindicted co-conspirator for the *Fireworks Bible* in his role as technical editor. I'm extremely pleased to welcome him to the "indicted" ranks with the pleasures and privileges so associated. In other words, "Duck, Derren, duck!"

Seriously, Derren has provided an eagle eye for detail and a relentless drive for perfection all during the writing of the *Fireworks MX Bible*. I greatly value his expertise and sense of humor — it helped me keep mine despite a rather grueling production schedule.

I also owe a great debt of gratitude to Kleanthis Economou, who graciously accepted the technical editor chores for this edition. Not only is Kleanthis a terrific designer and Fireworks wizard in his own right — if you need any proof, just stop by www.projectfireworks.com — he's also a leader in the new Fireworks extension developer community. I'm honored to have him on-board.

The Fireworks community has grown considerably over the past year, and its generosity even more so. Special thanks to those designers who graciously allowed me to include their work on the CD-ROM: Kleanthis Economou, Massimo Foti, Linda Rathgeber, Eddie Traversa, Simon White, and others. I owe a debt of gratitude — and probably a drink or three — to another Fireworks community member, author Sandee Cohen. Sandee's work continues to inspire, and I wish her continued success.

Of course, I wouldn't be writing this book — and you certainly wouldn't be reading it — if it weren't for the fantastic vision of the Fireworks team. Fireworks is a marvelously complex program, and there is true glory in bringing it to life. A hearty thank you and a round of applause to you all: Jeff Ahlquist, Doug Benson, Brian Edgin, Andy Finnell, Rob McCullough, Randy Varnell, and Eric Wolff among many others. Finally, let me offer a special thanks to David Morris, Fireworks Product Manager, for his support and encouragement, as well as the openness and access he has granted me.

—JL

Contents at a Glance

Contents

Part I: Come See the Fireworks   1

Part IV: Coordinating Workflow   455

Chapter 14: Capturing and Importing 457

Come See
the Fireworks

◆   ◆   ◆   ◆

◆   ◆   ◆   ◆

Part I begins with an overview of the Fireworks philosophy and design. To get the most out of the program, you
need to understand the key advantages it offers and the deficiencies it addresses. Part I takes you all the way from setting
up documents to getting the most out of Fireworks.

The opening chapters provide a full reference to the Fireworks
interface and its customizable features. Chapter 1 will be of
special interest to users of previous versions of Fireworks; it's
a complete guide to all the newly added features in Fireworks
MX. Later chapters in Part I provide an overview of everything
Fireworks can do.

Welcome to Fireworks MX

Every Fourth of July, I sit with my friends and family on a neighbor's rooftop to watch the fireworks explode over Manhattan. Almost every apartment building roof around us holds a similar gathering. Everyone oohs and ahhs to his or her own view of the spectacular light show; some of the patterns and images are familiar, whereas others have never been seen before.

The World Wide Web has become a global light show, running around the clock. The graphics that fill Web pages explode with brilliance, intensity, and meaning, and are viewed by millions, each from his or her own perspective. The Web is still a relatively new medium, uniquely capable of both enlightening and entertaining; it's also an extremely voracious medium, as thousands upon thousands of new and updated Web sites emerge daily. In addition to content, the Web needs graphics: all manner of images, illustrations, logos, symbols, and icons. Some of the images are static, others are animated, and still others are interactive. Design has definitely entered a new frontier.

To contribute the most to this new medium, new tools are necessary. The Web is screen-, not print-based, and it has its own set of rules and guidelines. Though some print-oriented graphics tools have begun to extend themselves with the Internet in mind, a completely new tool was needed — a tool that did everything Web designers needed and did it efficiently, but with flair. A tool capable of creating graphics light enough to soar, yet powerful enough to brighten the night.

Enter Fireworks.

Mastering Fireworks MX — the Next-Generation Graphics Package

Fireworks is the premier Web graphics program from Macromedia. As a next-generation graphics package, Fireworks has definitely benefited from all the great computer graphics programs that came before it. But whereas much of Fireworks functions in a manner similar to other graphics tools — which significantly shortens the learning curve — the program is purely focused on the Web and offers many innovative Web-only features.

Fireworks was built from the ground up with the Web in mind. Before creating Fireworks, Macromedia examined the way graphic designers were working and found that most designers used a wide variety of tools to achieve their goals. Typically, an initial design was laid out in a vector drawing program such as FreeHand or Adobe Illustrator. But vectors aren't native to the Web, so the illustration was then ported to an image-editing program, such as Photoshop or Corel Photo-Paint. In these pixel-based programs, special effects, such as beveled edges, were laboriously added and text was merged with the bitmap before it was exported to an optimizing program. An optimizer, such as DeBabelizer, was necessary to ensure that Web-safe colors were used and that the file size was the smallest possible for the bandwidth-limited Internet. Next came integration into the Web: linking URLs, image maps, rollovers, slices, and more. A slew of small specialty programs filled these needs. Moreover, many designers were forced to learn HTML and JavaScript; because no program did everything that was needed, many tasks had to be done manually. Adding to the intense difficulty of mastering all the various programs was the problem of modifying an image. If a client wanted a change — and clients always want changes — the whole graphic had to be rebuilt from scratch.

Combining the best features

Fireworks offers a revolutionary way to create bitmap graphics for the Web. It combines the best features of all the various graphics programs:

✦ Vector drawing tools for easy layout and editing

✦ Sophisticated, bitmap-editing tools for working with existing graphics and scanned images

✦ Live effects for straightforward but spectacular special effects

✦ An export engine for file optimization to Web standards, with onscreen comparison views so that a Web designer can select the best image at the smallest size

✦ HTML and JavaScript output tied to the graphics themselves

Best of all, you can alter virtually every single aspect of a Fireworks graphic at any stage. In other words, in Fireworks everything is editable, all the time. Not only is this feature a tremendous time-saver, but it's also a major production enhancement — and the Web requires an extraordinary amount of material and maintenance. Not only are new sites and Web pages constantly going online, but existing pages also need continual updating. The underlying philosophy of Fireworks — everything editable, all the time — reflects a deep awareness of the Web designer's real-world situation.

Emphasizing vectors and incorporating bitmaps

If you're coming from a print background and you're used to working with tools like Photoshop, grasping certain Fireworks fundamentals is important. First, you should realize that Fireworks is not primarily an image-editing program, although it has excellent image-editing tools. Fireworks is fundamentally a vector-drawing program that outputs natural-looking bitmap images. After you get the hang of drawing with vectors — also known as *paths* and far more flexible than bitmaps — and applying bitmap strokes and fills, you'll never want to go back. With Fireworks, however, you can go home again; switching between vectors and bitmap graphics is handled naturally and intuitively by Fireworks.

Digging into screen orientation

Second, Fireworks, as a Web graphics engine, is screen — not print — oriented. The resolution of an image on a monitor is typically far lower than the resolution of the same image in print. Images are generally worked on and saved in their actual size; the technique of working with a larger image for fine detail and then reducing it to enhance the resolution won't work with Fireworks — in fact, it will backfire, and you'll lose the very detail you were trying to instill. However, you can zoom in (up to 6,400 percent) for detailed correction. Just keep in mind that, ultimately, all images are viewed at 100 percent in the browser.

Getting the most from this Internet-based program

This brings us to the final point for designers who are new to the Web: Fireworks is not just screen-based, it's Internet-based. Many Fireworks options are geared toward Web realities, such as the importance of a minimum file size, the limitations of Web-safe colors, and capabilities of the majority of browsers. Fireworks is extremely respectful of the Web environment and, when properly used, will help you conserve production, browser, and Internet resources.

 Cross-Reference For a visual explanation of what Fireworks makes possible, turn to the color insert.

Getting the Best of Both Pixels and Paths

Although the Web is almost always a bitmap-based medium, vectors — also called *paths* — are much easier to control and edit. Fireworks bases most of its graphics creation power on vectors, while offering a complete range of bitmap-editing options. By switching effortlessly between paths and pixels, Fireworks smoothly integrates them both.

Fireworks treats separate graphic elements as independent objects that you can easily manipulate, arrange, and align. The two primary types of objects you will work with in Fireworks are vector objects and bitmap objects. Fireworks' object orientation is also extremely useful for production work and greatly speeds up production time. A single vector object that defines the basic outline of a button, for example, can quickly be duplicated and positioned to build a navigation bar on which each button is identical, except for the identifying text. For all the variety in Figure 1-1, only three separate vector objects had to be drawn.

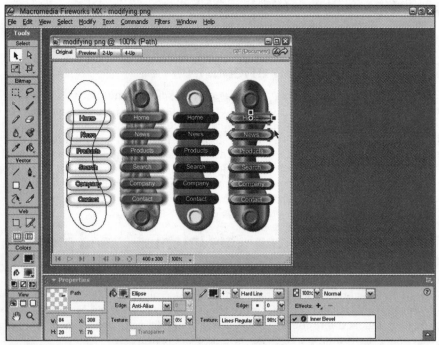

Figure 1-1: Reuse simple path shapes as you create and modify graphics in Fireworks.

Using vector tools with organic bitmaps

For ultimate flexibility, Fireworks separates the stroke, fill, and effects of its objects from the objects themselves. This enables the Web designer to create almost endless combinations for custom artwork, while keeping each element individual and editable. If the client loves the orange glow around a button, but wants the text to be centered instead of flush right, it's no problem in Fireworks. Changing one aspect of a graphic — without having to rebuild the image from scratch — is one of Fireworks' key strengths.

Although Fireworks depends on vector objects to create the underlying structure of its graphics, what goes on top of that structure (the stroke, fill, and effects) is displayed with pixels, as shown in Figure 1-2.

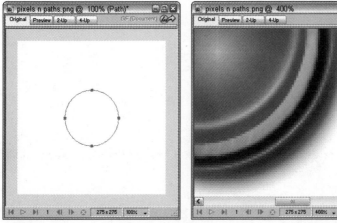

Figure 1-2: With no stroke, fill, or effect specified, a vector object's underlying path is clearly visible (left). After you apply a fill and/or stroke and/or effect, though, you can zoom in and see that Fireworks' visible elements are made up entirely of pixels (right).

Pixel components are calculated with numerous variables and, as a result, give an organic feel to Fireworks vector objects. Pixels are recalculated and reapplied each time the path structure is changed, as shown in Figure 1-3. This procedure eliminates the distortion that occurs with other programs that just reshape the pixels. In a sense, when you alter a path in Fireworks, the program quickly redoes all the work that you have done since you initially created the object.

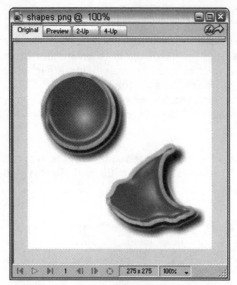

Figure 1-3: Change the shape of a Fireworks object and the bitmap fill, stroke, and other properties are recalculated and reapplied.

Cross-Reference   To find out more about strokes, see Chapter 8. You can find out more about fills in Chapter 11.

Exploring bitmap compatibility

As a next-generation graphics tool, Fireworks gracefully respects much of the imagery that has been previously created. With a full range of import filters, Fireworks can open and edit files from Photoshop, CorelDraw, FreeHand, and many more tools. Fireworks offers a full complement of bitmap selection tools, including Marquee, Lasso, and Magic Wand, as well as pixel-level drawing tools, such as Pencil and Eraser.

Filters are an important aspect of an image-editing program's feature set, and Fireworks is no slouch in that respect, either. In addition to various built-in filters, such as Gaussian Blur, Invert, and Sharpen, Fireworks is compatible with the Photoshop filter standard. Consequently, it works with any third-party plug-in that adheres to the standard, including Kai's Power Tools or Alien Skin's Eye Candy and Xenofex plug-ins. In fact, three of the Eye Candy 4000 filters, including the Alien Skin's Motion Trail filter shown in Figure 1-4, are included with Fireworks as Eye Candy 4000 LE (Limited Edition). What's more, you can easily include all the third-party plug-ins that you use in Photoshop by just editing a single preference.

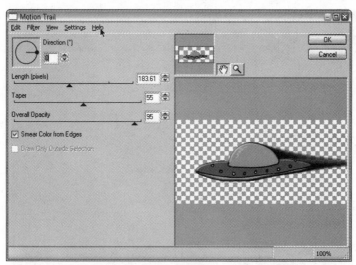

Figure 1-4: Alien Skin's Motion Trail filter is included with Fireworks as part of Eye Candy 4000 LE.

Cross-Reference   Want to know more about using third-party filters in Fireworks? Turn to Chapter 12.

Learning Live Effects

One of the most challenging aspects of Web graphics used to be special effects, such as applying beveled edges and drop shadows. Fireworks takes all the complex, painstaking layer and mask manipulation these effects used to require and replaces it with Live Effects. Live Effects provides almost one-step ease with sophisticated variations for such effects as Inner Bevel, Outer Bevel, Drop Shadow, Glow, and Emboss.

Not only are these effects straightforward to create in Fireworks, but they adapt to any changes made to the object itself — hence, the name Live Effects. This feature is important for modifying graphics, and it speeds up production work tremendously. You can even batch process a group of files, reducing them in size, and the effects are scaled and reapplied automatically.

In addition to working with Fireworks' built-in Live Effects, Fireworks will happily co-opt many Photoshop-compatible image filters that you may have installed as Xtras. These filters appear on the menu in the Effects section of the Property inspector, as shown in Figure 1-5, and are as "live" as any other Live Effect. In other words, you can apply Photoshop filters to vector objects while they remain editable, and the effects themselves can be edited, removed, or reordered at any time, too. What's more, you can name effect combinations and save them for later use.

Figure 1-5: The Effects feature enables you to apply, remove, and reorder Fireworks Live Effects, as well as Photoshop-compatible filters while maintaining the editability of all settings.

For detailed information on Live Effects, see Chapter 12.

Focusing on styles

Styles enable you to consistently apply the same look and feel to any number of objects. Fireworks styles quickly replicate strokes, fills, effects, and even text settings. Web designers can use styles to keep a client's Web site looking consistent across the board. Additionally, because styles can be exported as files and shared, a lead designer can create a base style for a Web graphic, which can then be applied on a production basis to the rest of the site.

Styles also provide a way to audition different looks for a single object because you can quickly and easily apply complex groups of settings one after the other, as shown in Figure 1-6.

Macromedia offers a huge range of prebuilt styles, in addition to the handful of styles that are available by default in the Styles panel. Find the prebuilt styles on the Fireworks CD-ROM, or at the Macromedia Exchange (www.macromedia.com/exchange).

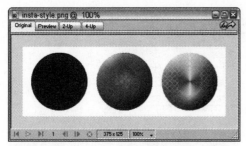

Figure 1-6: A basic geometric shape (left) quickly takes on a new life after styles are applied (center and right).

Cross-Reference

Styles are a major time- and work-saver; to find out more about them, see Chapter 16.

Looking at animation

Before Fireworks, one of the bevy of tools in a Web designer's arsenal was often a package to create animated GIFs (graphics stored in the Graphics Interchange Format), often specifically for creating banner ads. This type of separate program is no longer necessary: Fireworks enables Web designers to build, preview, and export animated GIFs in any size or shape. Naturally, you can take advantage of all the Fireworks vector and bitmap editing tools to create and edit your animation.

You can turn any Fireworks object into a symbol and store it in the Library. Copies of symbols are called *instances*. Multiple instances can be *tweened*—you make the beginning and end of an animation, and Fireworks extrapolates the middle for you—to create an animation in record time. Tweening can imply motion across the canvas or a change in an effect setting or other property. You could, for example, create an animated fade by tweening a fully opaque instance with one that's fully transparent.

In addition to basic frame-by-frame animation, Fireworks also offers special animated symbols with always-editable animation properties that make creating and editing animation in Fireworks a breeze (see Figure 1-7). The Animate Selection feature moves, rotates, scales, and fades any selected graphic over any number of frames to automate the animation creation process.

Cross-Reference

Animation is a specialized but integral aspect of Web graphics. To find out more about it, turn to Part VI.

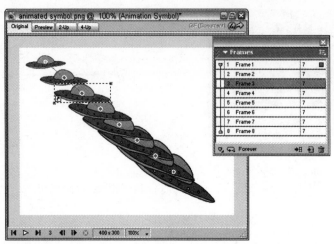

Figure 1-7: This single animation symbol is easily created and stretches across multiple frames of a Fireworks document.

Linking to the Web

What do you call a graphics program that doesn't just output graphics? In the case of Fireworks, I call it a major innovation, and a necessity for working Web artists. On the surface, a Web page appears to be composed of images and text, but underneath that, it's all code. Fireworks bridges the gap between the images of a Web page and its HTML and JavaScript code to create image maps, slices, rollovers, and much more. Fireworks even gives you the option of choosing different styles of code, depending on which Web authoring tool you use.

Fireworks is fully integrated with the Web in mind. Every aspect of the program, from Web-safe color pickers to export optimization, keeps the Internet target clearly in focus. Even functions common to other programs have been given a special Web-oriented twist. For example, the capability to output a graphic to print is invaluable to Web designers as a way to present comps to clients; in Fireworks, you can print an image the way it will appear on the Web, or at a higher print resolution — it's your choice.

Delving into hotspots and slices

Hotspots and *slices* are frequently used elements in Web page design. Until Fireworks came along, however, designers had to create them using a program outside their usual graphics tools, or designers had to tediously handcraft them individually. A hotspot is used as part of a Web page image map and is made of a series of *x, y* coordinates — elements definitely not in traditional visual artists' vocabulary. Fireworks enables you to draw out your hotspot, just as you would any other object, and it handles all the math output for you.

Slice is a general term for the different parts of a larger image that has been carved into smaller pieces for faster loading, or to incorporate a rollover. The separate parts of an image are then reassembled in an HTML table. If it sounds to you like an overwhelming amount of work, you're right — if you're not using Fireworks. Slicing an image is as simple as drawing slice objects, as shown in Figure 1-8, and choosing Export. Fireworks builds the HTML table for you. Additionally, Fireworks lets you optimize different slices, exporting one part as a JPEG (Joint Photographic Experts Group) image and another as a GIF (or whatever combination gives you the highest quality at the smallest file size).

Figure 1-8: You draw the slice objects and Fireworks will do the cutting — and add the HTML.

Explore more of what's possible with Fireworks hotspots and slices in Chapter 20.

Dissecting the URL panel

To take the fullest advantage of Fireworks HTML and JavaScript output, you need to attach hyperlinks or URLs to your images. You can import URLs from URL libraries, bookmark files, or HTML pages through the URL panel. Not only does this sidestep the drudgery of manually entering Web links, it also eliminates any typing errors you might otherwise have made in the process. After these URLs are in the URL panel, you can easily apply them to slices or to image map hotspots in order to Internet-enable navigation bar buttons.

Evaluating images with Behaviors

Static images are no longer enough on the Web; interactive images — images that react in some way when selected by the user — are a requirement for any state-of-the-art Web page. Fireworks handles this interactivity through a technique known as *Behaviors*. A Behavior is a combination of image and code: quite complex HTML and JavaScript code, to be exact. But when you apply a Behavior in Fireworks, all the code writing is handled for you.

A Fireworks Behavior can display a message when users pass their pointers over a particular image, or it can swap one image for another. Fireworks can even swap an image in one place if a graphic in another place is selected. Pop-up menu navigation systems are a snap with Fireworks' Set Pop-up Menu Behavior. Best of all, you can choose to output generic HTML code, or code that's optimized for your favorite

Web authoring tool. Fireworks includes application-specific output templates for Macromedia Dreamweaver, Adobe GoLive, and Microsoft FrontPage. If you have the need and the savvy, you can also create custom templates.

Cross-Reference   For more information about Behaviors, check out Chapter 21.

Optimizing for the Web

An overriding concern of many Web designers is file optimization: How do you get the best-looking image possible at the smallest size? Fireworks enables you to compare the results of up to four different file compression views simultaneously, right in the document window. Monitoring the way your work will look upon export is easy; just click one of the document window preview tabs, as shown in Figure 1-9.

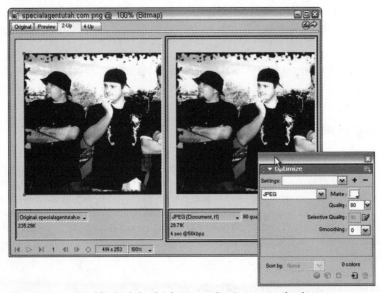

Figure 1-9: Quickly find the highest-quality image at the lowest possible size by comparing your original image with an optimized version, right in the workspace.

The Optimize panel contains the varied export options a Web artist requires, easily accessible at any time. And colors can be edited, locked, snapped to Web-safe, or made transparent with a click of the mouse in the Color Table panel. You'll also find animation timing controls in the Frames panel.

Cross-Reference   To get the most out of exporting in Fireworks, check out Chapter 15.

Integrating with Dreamweaver MX

Macromedia's Dreamweaver is a world-class Web authoring tool, now made even better through a tighter integration with Fireworks. Images placed in Dreamweaver pages are directly editable in Fireworks, as shown in Figure 1-10. Moreover, Dreamweaver contains commands that directly access Fireworks features or assist in importing Fireworks HTML code. In fact, the scriptability of Fireworks allows Dreamweaver commands to actually control Fireworks.

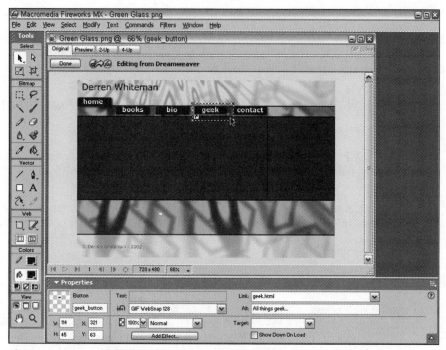

Figure 1-10: Send individual graphics or sliced images from Dreamweaver for editing in Fireworks with the click of a button.

The integration is not just apparent from the Dreamweaver side, either. Fireworks outputs standard Dreamweaver code or Dreamweaver Library code with Fireworks Behaviors that are editable within Dreamweaver, as if they were applied in Dreamweaver itself. The two programs are also moving closer to each other from a usability standpoint, with the most recent versions of both applications featuring a common user interface.

Cross-Reference For all the details on maximizing the Fireworks-Dreamweaver combination, see Chapter 22.

Stepping over to Flash MX

Dreamweaver isn't the only Macromedia product that integrates with Fireworks — Fireworks MX also works quite well with Flash MX, Macromedia's high-profile animation and application development tool. In addition to sharing a common panels and Property Inspector interface, Fireworks and Flash have a fairly porous barrier that permits graphic elements to travel from one to the other with minimum alteration. The connectivity between Fireworks and Flash enables a design to be comped in Fireworks using its enhanced drawing tools and brought into Flash for animation and compression.

Here are a few of the application-to-application moves possible:

✦ Copy a vector graphic in Fireworks and paste it directly in Flash — or vice versa.

✦ Import a PNG file from Fireworks directly into Flash. You can choose whether to keep the Fireworks objects, including text, editable or flatten them into a bitmap.

✦ Export any Fireworks file as a Flash player (or SWF) file. Animated sequences stretching over frames are automatically put into separated keyframes in Flash.

✦ Bitmaps created in Fireworks and imported into Flash can be sent back to Fireworks for editing — and then returned to Flash with all the changes intact.

Examining Production Tools

Although the Web offers plenty of room for creative expression, creating Web graphics is often — bottom line — a business. To succeed at such a business, you need a tool capable of high production output, and Fireworks certainly fits the bill. You can insert whole pages of URLs at a time, rescale entire folders of images, or update all the text embedded in a Web site's images.

Grasping batch processing

The large number of images in a typical Web page has made batch processing a virtual necessity. It's not at all uncommon for a client to request that thumbnail images of an entire product line be created for an online catalog. With batch processing, just point to the folder of full-size images and tell Fireworks whether to scale them to a particular pixel size or to a particular percentage.

Another great timesaver is the Find and Replace panel. Find and Replace in a graphics program? What use could that possibly have? Very far-reaching uses, to be frank. Fireworks can search and replace text, fonts, colors, or URLs in any Fireworks file or a group of files. What's more, you can even search for and snap non-Web-safe colors to their nearest Web-safe counterparts.

Cross-Reference Chapter 18 has everything you need to know about batch processing in Fireworks.

Using automation

Nothing eats up time and patience like having to do the same thing over, and over, and over again. Unfortunately, Web production features this kind of workflow all too often. The same steps are often required again and again. Chances are, if you have to do it more than once, you have to do it ten times.

In perhaps its simplest role, the History panel (see Figure 1-11) provides fine control over Undo steps, allowing you to reverse course at any time with pinpoint accuracy. Look a little deeper, though, and you'll notice that the History panel is also the heart of the Fireworks scripting and automation system.

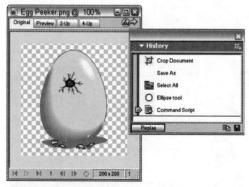

Figure 1-11: Is the History panel an enhanced Undo or a macro recorder? Both.

Select any step or group of steps in the History panel and you can instantly turn them into a command that's automatically added to the Commands menu. As useful as this feature is on its own, the History panel goes further still: Each step is actually represented by JavaScript code, which you can copy to the Clipboard and then paste into a text editor for refinement.

Cross-Reference Dive into Fireworks automation in Chapter 19.

Extending Fireworks with custom commands

The underlying architecture that makes it possible to repeat steps in the History panel form the foundation of Fireworks' extensibility layer. One manifestation of this extensibility is that commands from the History panel may be saved and replayed later. Furthermore, custom commands—a combination of JavaScript and Fireworks-specific code—may be created independently of the History panel and run at will; these scripts are saved as .jsf files. Found under the Commands menu, the simplest of these extensions range from converting an image to sepia tone to rearranging the panel sets.

New Feature

Fireworks MX offers much more than just Javascript commands, however. The biggest drawback to .jsf files was that the user interface was severely limited— typically, only a single text field was available for user input. With Fireworks MX, a new era in extensiblity dawns, born of the marriage of Fireworks and Flash technology. Now, Fireworks extensions employ Flash interfaces to gather user parameters and an extraordinary range of automation is possible. Certain extensions, such as the Align panel, have been incorporated into the standard Fireworks workflow while others, such as Arrowheads, shown in Figure 1-12, are available under the Commands menu. Even more extensions are available by visiting the Macromedia Web site by choosing Help ➪ Fireworks Exchange.

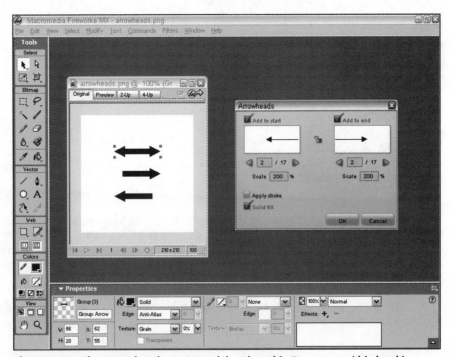

Figure 1-12: The Arrowheads command, by Kleanthis Economou (this book's technical editor), gets its sophisticated user interface from Flash, but works as a Fireworks command.

Learning What's New in Fireworks MX

With this version, Fireworks receives the full treatment: a major face-lift and deep enhancements under the hood. The improvements can be categorized into three areas: usability, graphics creation, and Web connectivity.

Looking at the user interface

User interface enhancements may not qualify as a "feature" for some people, but they can have an incredible impact on your day-to-day work in an application because changes are literally at your fingertips. Significant enhancements, such as those implemented in Fireworks MX, greatly increase productivity and workflow.

User interface enhancements include the following:

✦ Fireworks MX has a whole new look—complete with Property Inspector and docking panels, and what's more, it shares the interface with other Macromedia applications Dreamweaver MX and Flash MX.

✦ Speaking of new looks, Macintosh OS X and Windows XP users will appreciate the system native look and feel.

✦ Fireworks now supports multiple users—great for design teams working with a common set of preferences and extensions.

✦ The Tools panel is clearly divided now between bitmap and vector tools.

✦ Slices are easier to resize thanks to draggable slice guides.

✦ New view modes, selectable from the Tools panel, open up the display options. Now users can choose between the standard screen mode, full screen mode, and full screen mode with menus.

✦ Fireworks' zoom control has increased its flexibility; instead of the fixed magnification settings, zoom is now totally variable.

 Cross-Reference For details on all the user interface changes, see the rest of the chapters in Part I.

Exploring graphics creation

With each new release, Fireworks becomes a more focused drawing and bitmap-editing tool.

Graphics-creation enhancements include the following:

✦ Ever realize while you are drawing a new element that it really should be in a different place? Now you can suspend your drawing temporarily by holding down the spacebar and move your object wherever you like. In addition to working with drawing tools such as the rectangle, oval, and polygon, the space-bar move facility is available when cropping, slicing, or dragging out a marquee.

✦ Text — whether for logos, buttons, or body copy — is a key part of any Web designer's toolbox. Starting in Fireworks MX, you can enter text directly onto the canvas, or, if you prefer, use the Text Editor as before.

✦ If you're working with blocks of text, you'll really appreciate the new paragraph options such as first line indent and spacing control before or after paragraphs.

✦ A host of new bitmap editing tools are on board including Blur, Sharpen, Smudge, Dodge, and Burn.

✦ Transparency is now an option for gradients fills and can be applied to any color in the gradient range at any degree of opacity.

Discovering Web connectivity

When Fireworks first appeared, its capability to output HTML code was like a rocket taking off. Now, other applications have followed suit, but Fireworks has continued to build on its excellent history, bringing the two worlds of Web designers — graphics and code — closer together.

Web connectivity enhancements include the following:

✦ The popular Pop-up Menu Behavior has been greatly improved. In addition to vertical drop-down menus, horizontal flyout menus are also supported. Numerous parameters — such as cell padding, border color and width, and menu delay — greatly increase the designer's control over the final appearance and interactivity.

✦ It's not uncommon for Web designers to inherit a Web site designed by someone else and have to make modifications — without access to the source files. In these situations, Fireworks' new Reconstitute Table command is invaluable. Reconstitute Table takes a completed Web page and rebuilds each table of sliced graphics it finds. While this feature works with any HTML page, it really shines with Fireworks tables where even interactive Behaviors are rebuilt.

✦ Look out HTML, XHTML is coming fast — and Fireworks is ready now. XHTML is the next generation of HTML and offers increased connectivity to Web devices other than browsers, such as PDAs and wireless phones. Starting with this version, Fireworks is capable of exporting XHTML-compliant code.

✦ As XHTML crosses the browser barrier, UTF-8 spans international language borders. UTF-8 is a text encoding method that enables the display of multiple character sets in a single Web page. If you have a need to export text in Chinese, Portuguese, or another language, Fireworks has you covered.

Cross-Reference   Find out more about Web connectivity in Part V.

Summary

"Pick the right tool for the job," the saying goes — and Fireworks is definitely the right tool for the job of creating Web graphics. In many cases, it's the only tool you'll need to handle every aspect of this particular job: image creation, editing, optimization, and Web integration. It's no surprise that in the past, Web designers had to master many programs to even come close to what you can accomplish with Fireworks. If you're looking at Fireworks for the first time, keep these points in mind:

✦ Fireworks replaces an entire bookshelf of programs that Web designers had previously adapted for their use. With only one program to master, designers can work more efficiently and creatively.

✦ Fireworks is equally at home with vector objects or bitmap objects. Moreover, it combines vector structures with bitmap surfaces in order to make editing easier and the results cleaner.

✦ Fireworks works with Photoshop and many other existing file types — and can even use third-party Photoshop-compatible filters as Xtras or even as Live Effects.

✦ One of Fireworks' key capabilities is to connect you easily to the Web. To this end, Web-safe palettes are always available and HTML and JavaScript code — standard or custom — is just a click away.

✦ The more you work on the Web, the faster you realize just how much work there is to do. Fireworks is a terrific production tool and makes updating graphics, via search and replace operations or batch processing, an automated process instead of a manual drudge.

✦ Fireworks MX introduces a new user interface, ensuring a better experience for users of multiple Macromedia applications, such as Fireworks, Dreamweaver, and Flash.

In the next chapter, you take an extensive tour of the Fireworks user interface and all of its menu commands.

✦　　✦　　✦

Understanding the Interface

Fireworks was designed to meet a need among Web graphics artists: to simplify workflow. Before Fireworks, designers typically used different programs for object creation, rasterization, optimization, and HTML and JavaScript creation. Fireworks combines the best features of several key tools — while offering numerous innovative additions of its own — into a sophisticated interface that's easy to use and offers many surprising creative advantages. After you've discovered the power of Fireworks, designing Web graphics any other way is hard.

With Fireworks, the designer has tools for working with both vector objects and bitmap objects. You'll even find ways to combine the two different formats. When your document is ready to make the move to the Web, Fireworks acts as a bridge to the HTML environment by allowing you to create the necessary code in a point-and-click manner.

As with any truly powerful computer graphics program, examining all the tools and options that Fireworks has to offer at one time can be overwhelming. However, that's not how most artists work. You may find it easier to familiarize yourself with a new tool by carrying out a specific task. It's fine to go all the way through this chapter — which covers every element of the Fireworks interface — but you'll probably get the most value from the chapter elements, especially the menu-by-menu description of commands at the end of the chapter, by using them as a reference guide.

Examining the Fireworks Environment

Whether you start your graphics session by creating a new document or loading an existing one, you'll find yourself working within a complete environment that includes pull-down menus, one or more document windows, and a selection of floating panels, as shown in Figure 2-1. Each document window contains a single Fireworks file; the menus and floating panels affect the file in the active document window.

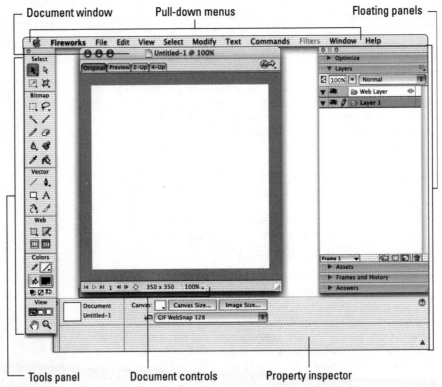

Figure 2-1: The Fireworks environment on both platforms includes menus, the Tools panel, the Property inspector, one or more document windows, and a variety of other floating panels.

Fireworks for Windows (see Figure 2-2) features the same interface elements as its Macintosh cousin, but also adds two toolbars and a context-sensitive status bar to the mix. The toolbars mimic commonly used functions from the menus, such as opening a document or arranging objects. The Windows version also uses a multiple document interface that contains all the documents and interface elements within the Fireworks application window. You can dock toolbars and panels to the application window, or float them as required, by dragging them toward or away from the edges of the application window.

We examine each element of the complete Fireworks environment throughout this chapter. Remember, you can refer to Figures 2-1 or 2-2 at any time if you find yourself losing track of a particular item.

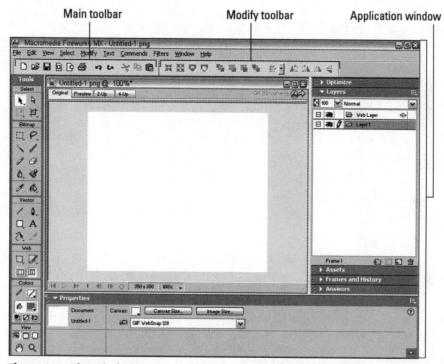

Figure 2-2: The Windows version of Fireworks has additional toolbars and uses a multiple document interface.

Understanding the Document Window

The document window is the central focus of your work in Fireworks. Each Fireworks document you open or create is contained within its own document window, with the filename and zoom setting displayed as the window's title. When your document has unsaved changes, Fireworks places an asterisk in the title bar of the document window, or a dot inside the Close button on Mac OS X. This asterisk is sometimes called a "dirty doc" indicator because it indicates that the document you are looking at has been "dirtied" since it was opened and needs to be saved to disk.

The Macromedia Common User Interface

The Web design workflow often involves more than one application. Many designers are working mainly in a combination of Fireworks and Dreamweaver, or Fireworks and Flash. Unfortunately, previous versions of many of Macromedia's own applications often featured wildly divergent user interface (UI) conventions, such as different keyboard shortcuts and different methods for hiding and showing floating panels. In short, Macromedia was not rewarding users for the time we spent learning one application's user interface. Beginning work in a second Macromedia application was often just like starting over. Moreover, different UI conventions made switching back and forth between two applications during the same session more trouble than it needed to be.

With more recent versions, however, Macromedia's applications have adopted interface elements from each other and now provide similar methods for accomplishing similar tasks no matter which Macromedia application you're using. Some of the common elements you'll notice if you switch between Fireworks and Dreamweaver are uniform keyboard shortcuts, customizable keyboard shortcuts, an optional launcher, located on each document window, for showing and hiding floating panels, and a Property inspector for modifying selections of objects. Focusing on the "cross-product UI" has also enabled Macromedia to shake out a few longstanding UI quirks and provide the user with a sleeker, more intuitive Fireworks experience.

You can open multiple documents and display them simultaneously, as shown in Figure 2-3. The menus and floating panels affect the file in the active document window.

Objects are created and edited on the *canvas* within the document window. The canvas is the active area of your document. To simplify editing at the edges of the canvas, it is surrounded by a gray canvas border. When you zoom in on the edge of a document, the canvas border provides some breathing room so that you can see what you're doing.

If you have multiple documents open and your workspace is getting cluttered, you can organize the document windows in three different ways:

✦ Choose Window ➪ Cascade to stack your open documents on top of each other in a diagonal, so that the title bar for each is visible.

✦ Select Window ➪ Tile Horizontal to see all open documents evenly distributed from top to bottom in the document window.

✦ Select Window ➪ Tile Vertical to view all open documents evenly distributed from left to right in the document window.

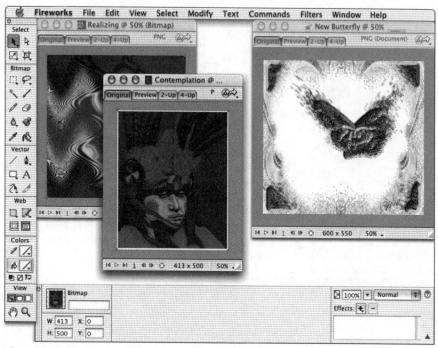

Figure 2-3: Each Fireworks file you open or create is contained within its own document window, and you can open multiple documents simultaneously.

You can also hide document windows that you're not currently using. Mac OS 9 users can click the Windowshade button on a document window to hide all but the title bar. Mac OS X users can click the Minimize Window button to minimize the document window to the Dock. Windows users can click the Minimize button on a document window to minimize its title bar to the bottom of the Fireworks application window. Windows users can also click Maximize to dock a document window to the application window, hiding all other windows. Clicking the document window's Restore button undocks it.

In addition to multiple document windows for multiple documents, Fireworks can also display multiple document windows for the same document. To open a new view of a selected document, choose Window ➪ New Window, or use the keyboard shortcut Ctrl+Alt+N in Windows (Command+Option+N for Macintosh). The new document window opens at the same magnification setting as the original document window but, as Figure 2-4 shows, you can easily zoom in for detail work on one view while displaying the overall effect in another.

Figure 2-4: Use the New Window command to open a new view of the same document if both pixel-level modifications and the big picture are required, such as when creating small icons.

Smart Maximize

A long-standing problem with applications that have customizable user interfaces is that it's difficult for the programmers to envision every possible way that users might set up their workspace. Too often, you can end up opening a document just to have its resize icon open underneath some portion of the UI. That's not the case with Fireworks. When you open a new document, Fireworks looks at the size of the document and determines the optimal magnification and window sizing to show you as much of your document as possible without hiding any portions of the document window under the panels or the Property inspector.

New Feature   Smart Maximize is new to Fireworks MX.

Document window controls

Fireworks enables you to control what you see in a document window in a number of ways. Tabs along the top of the document window enable you to preview your work in-place; you'll also find zoom and animation controls, and more (see Figure 2-5).

We'll look at each of the document window controls in turn.

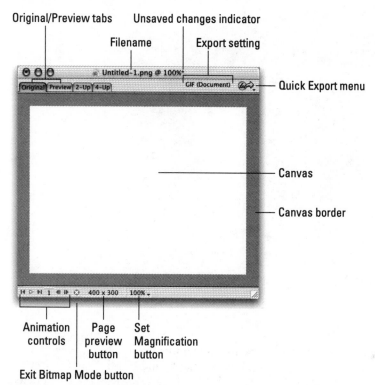

Original/Preview tabs   Unsaved changes indicator

Filename   Export setting

Quick Export menu

Canvas

Canvas border

Animation controls   Page preview button   Set Magnification button

Exit Bitmap Mode button

Figure 2-5: Fireworks document window controls enable you to alter how your document is presented in the document window.

Original/Preview tabs

When you open or create a document in Fireworks, the document window is set on the Original tab, so that you can interact with and edit the objects on the canvas. Choose one of the other tabs and Fireworks creates and displays a preview of your work as it will appear in your exported final output.

You can switch from Original to one of the preview modes at any time. Fireworks generates a preview based on the settings you select in the Optimize panel, as shown in Figure 2-6. Control of the export color palette is also available here.

Although the 2-Up preview gives you a side-by-side view of the Original and Preview views of a document, it only shows you half of each unless you manually expand your document window. If you have the screen real estate available, another way to get a side-by-side preview is to open a new document window for the same document (Window ⇨ New Window, as described previously) and set it to Preview.

Cross-Reference

For more on previewing and exporting, see Chapter 15.

Figure 2-6: A preview of your work is never more than a click away with Fireworks' in-place preview.

Quick Export menu

The upper right of the Fireworks document window features the Quick Export menu, which enables you to quickly export images and HTML from Fireworks to another application. With a single menu item, your Fireworks work is exported and opened in Dreamweaver, for example. Options for Macromedia and other applications are provided.

New Feature   The Quick Export menu allows you to export your document, or selected portions of it, with a minimal amount of fuss.

Cross-Reference   See Chapter 15 for more about exporting from Fireworks.

Animation controls

With these VCR-like buttons, you can play a frame-based animation straight through, using the timing established in the Frames panel. You'll also find buttons that enable you to move through the animation a frame at a time, or to go to the first or last frame.

Cross-Reference   See Chapter 23 for more about animation in Fireworks.

Exit Bitmap Mode button

Click this Stop button to quickly exit bitmap mode, and enter vector mode. When you're already in vector mode, the Stop button is grayed out.

 With the bitmap and vector tools listed separately in the Tools panel, Fireworks now switches into bitmap mode or vector mode as soon as you select a tool from the appropriate category. This seamless mode switching simplifies your workflow.

Page Preview

The Page Preview button displays the dimensions of your document in pixels. When you click the Page Preview button, the width, height, and print resolution of your document are displayed in a small pop-up window. Click anywhere outside or on the pop-up window to dismiss it.

Magnification settings

Whether you're working with pixels or vectors, a polished, finished graphic often demands close-up, meticulous work. Likewise, the designer often needs to be able to step back from an image in order to compare two or more large images for overall compatibility, or to cut and paste sections of a graphic. Fireworks offers a fast Magnification control with numerous keyboard shortcuts for rapid view changes.

Fireworks uses a series of zoom settings, from 6 percent to 6,400 percent, for its Magnification control. Because Fireworks always works with pixels (even when they're based on vectors), the magnification settings are predefined to offer the best image pixel to screen pixel ratio. When an image is viewed at 100 percent magnification, 1 screen pixel is used for each image pixel. Should you zoom in to 200 percent, 2 screen pixels are used for each image pixel. Zooming out reverses the procedure: At 50 percent, each screen pixel represents 2 image pixels. Fireworks' preset zoom method offers a full range of settings while maintaining an accurate view of your image.

Clicking the arrow button in the Set Magnification option list displays the available settings; alternatively you can choose View ⇨ Magnification and then choose a percentage. Highlight the desired zoom setting and release the mouse button in order to change magnifications. Fireworks also offers a variety of keyboard shortcuts to change the zoom setting, as detailed in Table 2-1. In addition to specifying a magnification setting, you can also have Fireworks fit the image in the current window. With this command, Fireworks zooms in or out to the maximum magnification setting possible — and still displays the entire image.

 Fireworks MX adds a new feature called Variable Zoom. This allows you to select the Zoom tool and then drag out an area to zoom into. When you release the mouse button, Fireworks zooms right into the selected area, filling your document window with a full view of your selection. Zooming is no longer limited to preset levels.

Table 2-1
Magnification Key Shortcuts

Magnification	Windows	Macintosh
50%	Ctrl+5	Command+5
100%	Ctrl+1	Command+1
200%	Ctrl+2	Command+2
300%	Ctrl+3	Command+3
400%	Ctrl+4	Command+4
800%	Ctrl+8	Command+8
1,600%	Ctrl+6	Command+6
Zoom In	Ctrl+Equals (=)	Command+Equals (=)
Zoom Out	Ctrl+Minus (–)	Command+Minus (–)
Fit Selection	Ctrl+Alt+Zero (0)	Command+Option+Zero (0)
Fit All	Ctrl+Zero (0) or double-click Hand tool	Command+Zero (0) or double-click Hand tool
Switch to Zoom tool temporarily	Hold down Ctrl+spacebar	Hold down Command+ spacebar

Launcher

The optional Launcher enables one-click access to commonly used floating panels. Users of Macromedia Dreamweaver will recognize the Launcher right away. Turned off by default, the Launcher is easily enabled via the Workspace: Show Tab Icons option in the General category of the Preferences. Enabling this preference also adds icons to your tabbed panels. If your document window is too narrow, you may not be able to see the whole Launcher. If so, resize your document window until it is wide enough to display the entire Mini-Launcher.

Clicking one of the buttons on the Launcher opens a panel if it is closed, brings a panel to the front if it is behind another panel, or closes a panel if it is open and already up front. To see what a Launcher button will do before you press it, hover your mouse cursor over it until a descriptive tooltip appears. From left to right, the Launcher buttons are for the Info, Color Mixer, Optimize, Layers, Library, Styles, and Behaviors panels. Unlike Dreamweaver, you cannot customize the Launcher to open any panels other than these, so you're stuck with the default panel selection.

New Feature

The Launcher now has a preference so that you can enable it or disable it depending on the way you work. It is disabled by default.

Cross-Reference

Floating panels are covered in more detail later in this chapter.

Display options

Most of the time, Fireworks designers work in Full Display mode. In fact, this practice is so common that many designers don't realize that another mode is even available. Toggling the View ⇨ Full Display command on and off controls whether the current document is in Full Display or Draft Display mode. Draft Display shows all vector objects with 1-pixel-wide outlines and no fill; bitmap objects are shown as rectangles with an "X" in the middle.

If you have a complex document with multiple layers that each contain multiple objects (see Figure 2-7), picking out the one object you would like to work on, or getting a feel for the true alignment of objects that have complex strokes or image filters applied, can sometimes be difficult.

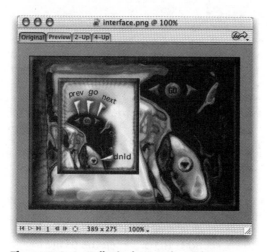

Figure 2-7: In Full Display mode, picking out individual objects can be difficult.

Looking at your document in Draft Display mode (see Figure 2-8) pares the view down to just the barest bones and enables you to pick out objects that are usually obscured by other objects in Full Display mode.

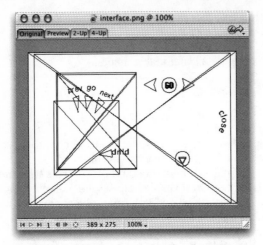

Figure 2-8: While you're in Draft Display mode, only the outlines of your objects are visible.

Exploring the Tools Panel

You can find all the Fireworks drawing and editing tools in the Tools panel. To "pick up" a tool, click its icon in the Tools panel. Your mouse cursor will change to reflect the tool that's currently active. Only one tool can be active at a time. Use the tool by clicking the canvas. Some tools, such as the Marquee tool, require that you click and drag to draw a selection. If you want to drag beyond the visible canvas area, the document window will scroll automatically to follow your cursor.

Note The preceding paragraph assumes that you have not enabled the Precise Cursors option in the Editing category of the Preferences.

New Feature Vector and Bitmap tools are now in their own sections on the Tools panel, which makes them easier to access and understand.

The Tools panel is broken down into six sections to help keep the usage of particular tools as clear as possible. Tools located in the Bitmap section work only on bitmaps, tools in the Vector section work only with vectors, and so on. The Eyedropper, Paint Bucket, and Gradient tools, which work with both vectors and bitmaps, have their own area between the Bitmap and Vector tool sections. Further, tools that are similar, such as the Lasso and Polygon Lasso, are grouped together into tool groups and accessed through a flyout. A tool group can be recognized by the small triangle in the lower-right corner of the button; clicking and holding the button causes the flyout to appear. After the tool group is visible, you can select any of the tools in the group by moving the pointer over the tool and releasing the mouse. Figure 2-9 shows a dissected Tools panel's anatomy in great detail.

Caution

On OS X, there is no visual divider separating the Eyedropper, Paint Bucket, and Gradient tools from the Bitmap tools. In Windows, and on OS 9, there is a divider that helps the user understand that those tools work with both bitmap and vector objects.

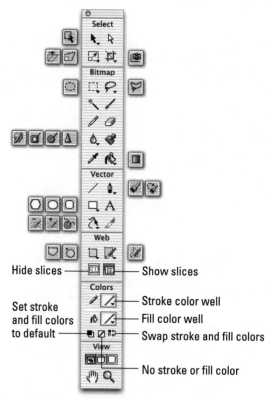

Figure 2-9: The Tools panel contains over 40 different creation and editing tools for both graphics and Web objects.

All but two of the tools have keyboard shortcuts. As befits a program that incorporates both bitmap and vector editing tools, these single-key shortcuts parallel the shortcuts for some of the pixel-based tools in Photoshop, and vector-based ones in FreeHand, where possible. If two or more tools share a keyboard shortcut (as with M for Marquee and Oval Marquee), the key acts as a toggle between the tools; the letter U toggles through the shape tools, for example. You can find the button for each tool, as well as its keyboard shortcut and a brief description of the tool, in Table 2-2. More detailed information on each tool is presented throughout this book when the tool is used for various operations.

New Feature Tool flyouts now include the tool's name and keyboard shortcut, which makes it easier than ever to become familiar with Fireworks tools.

Note In the tables throughout this chapter, commands or tools listed in **bold** text are new or have changed menu, or panel, locations in Fireworks MX.

Table 2-2
Fireworks Tools

Button	Name	Shortcut	Description
	Pointer	V or Zero	Selects and moves objects
	Select Behind	V or Zero	Selects and moves objects that are behind other objects
	SubSelection	A or 1	Selects an object within a group or points on a vector path
	Scale	Q	Resizes and rotates objects
	Skew	Q	Slants, rotates, and modifies the perspective of objects
	Distort	Q	Reshapes and rotates objects
	Crop	C	Increases or decreases canvas size
	Export Area	C	Exports a selected portion of a document
	Marquee	M	Selects a rectangular portion of a bitmap object
	Oval Marquee	M	Selects an elliptical portion of a bitmap object
	Lasso	L	Selects a freely drawn area of a bitmap object
	Polygon Lasso	L	Selects a polygon-shaped area of a bitmap object
	Magic Wand	W	Selects similarly colored areas of a bitmap object
	Brush	B	Draws strokes using the Stroke settings in the Property inspector

Button	Name	Shortcut	Description
	Pencil	B	Draws single-pixel freeform strokes
	Eraser	E	Deletes pixels from bitmap objects
	Blur	R	Blurs pixels that the cursor is dragged across
	Sharpen	R	Sharpens pixels that the cursor is dragged across
	Dodge	R	Lightens pixels that the cursor is dragged across
	Burn	R	Darkens pixels that the cursor is dragged across
	Smudge	R	Smudges pixels that the cursor is dragged across
	Rubber Stamp	S	Repeats a portion of a bitmap object
	EyeDropper	I	Picks up color from anywhere onscreen and applies it to the active color well
	Paint Bucket	G	Fills the selected area with color, patterns, or textures and enables fills to be adjusted
	Gradient	G	Fills the selected area with gradients and enables them to be edited
	Line	N	Draws straight lines
	Pen	P	Adds points to vector paths
	Vector Path	P	Draws freeform paths using the Stroke settings in the Property inspector
	Redraw Path	P	Redraws portions of a selected vector path
	Rectangle	U	Draws rectangles, rectangles with rounded corners, and squares
	Rounded Rectangle	U	Draws rectangles with a Roundness setting of 30 percent
	Ellipse	U	Draws ellipses and circles

Continued

	Table 2-2 *(continued)*		
Button	**Name**	**Shortcut**	**Description**
⬡	Polygon	U	Draws polygons and stars
A	Text	T	Inserts text objects
⟋	**Freeform**	O	Pushes or pulls a vector path with a variable-size cursor
⟲	Reshape Area	O	Reshapes an object's area with a variable-size cursor
+⟋	**Path Scrubber (+)**	n/a	Increases the stroke settings that are controlled by cursor speed or pen and tablet pressure
-⟋	**Path Scrubber (–)**	n/a	Decreases the stroke settings that are controlled by cursor speed or pen and tablet pressure
⟋	**Knife**	Y	Cuts the paths of vector objects
▢	**Rectangle Hotspot**	J	Draws an image-map hotspot area in a rectangular shape
◎	**Circle Hotspot**	J	Draws an image-map hotspot area in an elliptical shape
▽	**Polygon Hotspot**	J	Draws an image-map hotspot area in a polygonal shape
▨	**Slice**	K	Draws a slice object in a rectangular shape
▨	**Polygon Slice**	K	Draws a slice object in a polygonal shape
✋	Hand	H, or press and hold spacebar	Pans the view of a document
🔍	Zoom	Z	Increases or decreases the magnification level of a document by one setting per mouse click, or drag to select an area to zoom to

Tip Certain tools have keyboard shortcuts that enable you to temporarily replace the active tool. Press and hold Ctrl (Command) in order to switch to the Pointer temporarily, for example. You can also press and hold Ctrl+spacebar (Command+spacebar) in order to access the Zoom tool. Holding down the spacebar by itself temporarily retrieves the Hand tool.

Selecting the Proper View

Fireworks offers three different view modes depending on how you like to work. For most people, the Standard Screen mode is all you need for day-to-day work, but it's always good to know that other options are available to you. Your view choices are as follows:

✦ **Standard Screen mode:** This is the default mode that Fireworks starts up in. It shows you all of the standard interface elements and UI components that Fireworks has to offer.

✦ **Full Screen with Menus mode:** In this mode, your document is opened maximized, totally filling your screen so that you aren't bothered by document window edges.

✦ **Full Screen Mode:** This mode switches your entire screen black with the exception of your panels and your canvas. This blocks out the menus as well.

The Full Screen with Menus and Full Screen modes are new to Fireworks MX.

Simply choose the method of working that feels the best to you and stick with it. Or, switch between the different modes as needed depending on the project you're working on.

To get the most use out of the Full Screen with Menus and Full Screen modes, you can hide all the visible floating panels by pressing F4. Then you can open just the interface elements you really need, such as the Tools panel and the Property inspector, by choosing them from the Window menu.

On OS X, the Full Screen with Menus mode doesn't expand past the Dock. If you really wish to fill the entire screen, hide the Dock first by choosing Apple Menu ⇨ Dock ⇨ Turn Hiding On or by using the keyboard shortcut Command+Option+D.

Accessing Toolbars (Windows Only)

Some people hate toolbars, and some people love them. Either way, they're expected in Windows applications and are a welcome part of Fireworks for Windows for many users.

The two toolbars are Main and Modify. The Main toolbar contains common File and Edit menu functions. The Modify toolbar contains Modify menu functions, such as grouping, aligning, or rotating objects.

The toolbars are docked to the application window by default, but you can position them anywhere within the Fireworks window by undocking them. To detach a docked toolbar, click and drag the toolbar away from the application window. To dock a detached toolbar, drag the toolbar close to an edge of the Fireworks window until it snaps into position, or double-click its title bar.

Fireworks for Windows also has a context-sensitive status bar that runs along the bottom of the Fireworks window. We look at that in this section, as well.

Main toolbar

The Main toolbar, shown in Figure 2-10, displays a row of buttons that access the most commonly used menu functions. The Main toolbar enables you to perform several key file operations, such as creating a new document, opening or saving an existing document, and exporting or importing an image, all with just one click. The most often-used editing features — Undo, Redo, Cut, Copy, and Paste — are also located on the Main toolbar. Table 2-3 describes each button on the Main toolbar.

Figure 2-10: The Main toolbar gives Window users one-click access to many commonly used commands.

	Table 2-3 Main Toolbar	
Button	**Name**	**Description**
	New	Creates a new document
	Open	Opens an existing document
	Save	Saves the current document
	Import	Imports a file into the current document
	Export	Exports the current document
	Print	Prints the current document
	Undo	Undoes the last action
	Redo	Redoes the last action that was undone

Button	Name	Description
✂	Cut	Cuts the selected object to the Clipboard
🗐	Copy	Copies the selected object to the Clipboard
📋	Paste	Pastes the Clipboard into the current document

Modify toolbar

The Modify toolbar, shown in Figure 2-11, offers single-click access to four primary types of modifications:

✦ **Grouping:** Group or join two or more objects for easier manipulation. Buttons are also available for ungrouping and splitting combined objects.

✦ **Arranging:** Position objects in front of or behind other objects. Objects can also be moved on top of or underneath all other objects.

✦ **Aligning:** Align two or more objects in any of eight different ways, including centered vertically or horizontally.

✦ **Rotating:** Flip selected objects horizontally or vertically, or rotate them 90 degrees, either clockwise or counterclockwise.

Align pop-up

Figure 2-11: Group, arrange, align, or rotate selected objects with the Modify toolbar.

Instead of directly executing a command — like the other buttons on the Modify toolbar — the Align button opens a pop-up toolbar that contains a range of alignment buttons. In Fireworks, alignment commands — whether they're issued from this pop-up toolbar or from the Modify ⇨ Align submenu — align objects to a theoretical rectangle around the selection, not to the canvas as you might expect. For example, if you select a circle on the left side of the canvas and a bitmap object on the right, clicking the Align Left button causes the bitmap object to align along the left edge of the circle because it is the leftmost object in the selection. Table 2-4 details each button on the Modify toolbar.

Cross-Reference

Read more about aligning objects in Fireworks in Chapter 13.

Table 2-4
Modify Toolbar

Button	Name	Description
	Group	Groups selected objects
	Ungroup	Ungroups previously grouped objects
	Join	Joins the paths of two vector objects
	Split	Separates previously joined vector objects
	Bring Front	Positions the selected object on top of all other objects
	Bring Forward	Moves the selected object one step closer to the top
	Send Backward	Moves the selected object one step closer to the bottom
	Send to Back	Positions the selected object underneath all other objects
	Align Left	Aligns the selected objects to the left edge of the selection
	Center Vertical Axis	Centers the selected objects on a vertical line
	Align Right	Aligns the selected objects to the right edge of the selection
	Align Top	Aligns the selected objects along the top edge of the selection
	Center Horizontal Axis	Centers the selected objects on a horizontal line
	Align Bottom	Aligns the selected objects along the bottom edge of the selection
	Distribute Widths	Evenly distributes the selected objects horizontally
	Distribute Heights	Evenly distributes the selected objects vertically
	Rotate 90° CCW	Rotates the selected object 90 degrees counterclockwise
	Rotate 90° CW	Rotates the selected object 90 degrees clockwise

Button	Name	Description
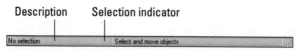	Flip Horizontal	Flips the selected object horizontally
	Flip Vertical	Flips the selected object vertically

Status bar

The status bar, shown in Figure 2-12, has two sections. The Selection Indicator displays the type of object or objects selected. If you're in bitmap mode, the status bar also displays the object type or selected object here as well. The Description indicator provides tooltips for each of the tools that are selected or moused over. The Status bar is not visible by default but its visibility is toggled by selecting View ➪ Status Bar.

Description   Selection indicator

| No selection | Select and move objects |

Figure 2-12: The status bar tells you what types of objects you have selected and offers context-sensitive tips.

The Property inspector

The Property inspector, shown in Figure 2-13, provides a central interface for altering the properties of selected objects or the currently selected tool. The Property inspector changes as you select different kinds of objects, exposing only the controls that are relevant to your current selection. As a result, this relatively small interface element packs a lot of power. You'll find yourself returning again and again to the Property inspector as you alter fills and strokes, add effects, or change text size or style.

Tip   The Property inspector replaces the Object, Stroke, Fill, Effect, and Tool Options panels from Fireworks 4.

Figure 2-13: The Property inspector, shown as it appears with a blank new document, offers one-stop shopping for all your tool options and settings.

Tool options

Many tools from the Fireworks Tools panel have configurable settings accessible through the Property inspector. The available tool options vary according to which tool is active. Some tools, such as the Rubber Stamp tool shown in Figure 2-14, provide numerous choices. Several tools — including the Hand, Zoom, Line, Pen, and Slice tools — have no options. Each tool's options are covered in the sections that follow.

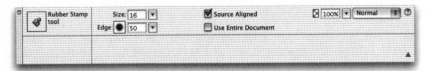

Figure 2-14: When the Rubber Stamp tool is selected, several options become available through the Property inspector.

Stroke settings

Any object created using one of the vector drawing tools — Line, Pen, Vector Path, Rectangle, Ellipse, or Text tool — is initially constructed with a path, the outline of the object. When a path is visible, it is said to be *stroked*. In Fireworks, strokes can be as basic as the 1-pixel Pencil outline, or as complex as the multicolored Confetti. The Stroke section of the Property inspector controls all the possible path settings and is a key tool in a graphic artist's palette.

Fireworks comes with a number of built-in stroke settings accessible through the Stroke section of the Property inspector, shown in Figure 2-15. You can also modify existing settings and save them as new strokes. Seven major options can affect the stroke:

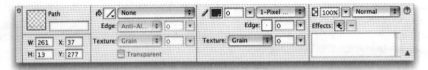

Figure 2-15: The Stroke section of the Property inspector controls the appearance of an object's outline or path.

✦ **Stroke category:** Fireworks provides 11 stroke categories from which to choose: Pencil, Basic, Airbrush, Calligraphy, Charcoal, Crayon, Felt Tip, Oil, Watercolor, Random, and Unnatural. To hide the path entirely, choose None.

✦ **Specific stroke:** After you've chosen a stroke category, a set of specific strokes, different for each category, is available. When you edit, rename, or save new strokes, the changes are reflected in the specific stroke option list.

✦ **Stroke color:** Selecting the Stroke color well displays the pop-up color picker and activates the Eyedropper, which you can use to select a color from one of the swatches or from anywhere on the screen. Click the Palette button to open your operating system's color picker(s).

✦ **Stroke edge:** Use the Stroke Edge slider to soften or harden the stroke. The higher the slider, the softer the stroke; when the slider is all the way to the bottom, the stroke has no softness.

✦ **Stroke size:** The Stroke Size slider determines the stroke size in pixels. You can increase the size by moving the slider up; you can also enter the value (from 1 to 100) directly in the Stroke Size text box. The size of the brush is previewed dynamically in the Property inspector.

✦ **Stroke texture:** In addition to color, size, and softness, you can also apply a texture to the stroke. Fireworks comes with 26 different textures, and you can also add your own.

✦ **Degree of stroke texture:** After a texture has been selected, you must specify how intensely you want the texture applied by using the Stroke Texture slider, or by entering a percentage value in the appropriate text box. The degree of stroke texture basically controls the opacity of the texture as it overlays the stroke.

If an object is selected, any changes made on the Property inspector are immediately applied to the object.

Cross-Reference Chapter 8 covers strokes in detail.

Fill settings

Just as the Stroke section of the Property inspector controls the outline of a drawn shape, the Fill section of the Property inspector controls the inside. Fills can be a solid color, a gradient, a pattern, or a Web Dither. All fills can have textures applied with a sliding scale of intensity; moreover, textured fills can even appear transparent.

Once you've chosen the type of fill from the Fill section of the Property inspector, shown in Figure 2-16, you can go on to pick a specific color, pattern, edge, or texture. Following are the key options for Fills:

Figure 2-16: The Fill section of the Property inspector offers many options to modify the interior of a drawn shape.

✦ **Fill category:** Select a fill category from these options: Solid (single color fill), Web Dither (two-color pattern), Pattern, or Gradient. The available standard gradients are Linear, Radial, Ellipse, Rectangle, Cone, Starburst, Bars, Ripples, Waves, Satin, and Folds.

✦ **Specific pattern or gradient color scheme:** If you choose Pattern or one of the gradient options, clicking the Fill color well gives you an option list with choices for each type of fill as well as a preview.

✦ **Fill edge:** The fill itself can have a hard edge, an antialiased edge, or a feathered edge.

✦ **Degree of feathering:** If you give the fill a feathered edge, you can specify the degree of feathering (the number of pixels affected) with this slider control, or by entering a value into the text box.

✦ **Fill texture:** The same textures available to the Stroke panel are available to a fill.

✦ **Degree of texture:** To make a texture visible, you must increase the degree of the texture's intensity by using the appropriate slider or text box. The higher the value, the more visible the texture.

✦ **Transparency of texture:** If the Transparency checkbox is selected, you can see through the lighter parts of the texture.

Cross-Reference   To delve deeper into fills, see Chapter 11.

Effect settings

In the early days of the Web, special graphics effects, such as drop shadows and beveled buttons, required many tedious steps in programs such as Photoshop. These days, Fireworks enables you to apply wondrous effects in a single step through the Effect section of the Property inspector. More importantly, like everything else in Fireworks, the effects are "live" and adapt to any change in the object. And you can easily alter them by adjusting values in the Property inspector.

The Add Effects menu, accessed by clicking the plus icon in the Effects section of the Property inspector, contains the actual effects, split into two groups. The top group consists of Fireworks built-in effects. The bottom group consists of Photoshop-compatible image filters from your Fireworks Filters folder and from another folder if you specified one in Fireworks' Preferences.

Note   The plug-ins on the Add Effects menu are only those that can be used as Live Effects. As not all filters work as Live Effects, if you don't see a particular set of installed plug-ins listed, check the Filters menu.

Choosing an effect from the Add Effects menu applies it to the current selection and adds it to the active list in the Effects section of the Property inspector. After an effect is in the active list, you can click the checkmark, or the X, beside it in order to enable or disable it.

Selecting the *i* button next to an applied effect's name enables you to modify its settings. Each Photoshop-compatible filter has its own unique dialog box. Many of Fireworks' built-in Live Effects open a small, pop-up editing window with their settings. Clicking anywhere outside the pop-up editing window dismisses it. An example of an effect with a pop-up editing window is Raised Emboss, shown in Figure 2-17.

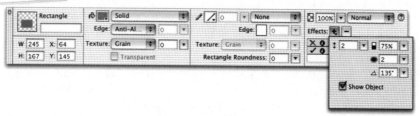

Figure 2-17: The settings for some Live Effects are displayed in unusual pop-up editing windows, lovingly referred to at Macromedia as Windoids, such as this one for Raised Emboss.

Effects can add serious pizzazz to your graphics in a hurry. Find out more about them—with details on how to get the most from each effect—in Chapter 12.

Managing the Floating Panels

Fireworks maintains a great deal of functionality in its floating panels. In all, the program offers 18 different panels for modifying everything from stroke colors to JavaScript behaviors. Toggling whether a particular panel is shown or hidden is as simple as choosing its name from the Window menu, or pressing its keyboard shortcut. Although an almost dazzling array of panels exists from which to choose, the effect is not overwhelming because panels are docked together into panel groups. When a panel is docked behind another one, click its tab to bring it to the front.

By default, Fireworks combines the floating panels into five different groups, but you can customize the groupings to fit the way you work. If you're working with dual monitors, you might want to display every panel separately, so that all 18 are instantly available. On the other hand, you could conserve maximum screen real estate by grouping all the panels into one supergroup with tabs visible for each individual panel. The middle ground, though, is probably the best for most people: some docked, some not, and commonly used panels always visible.

The more you work in Fireworks, the sooner you arrive at a panel configuration that's best for you. I tend to group my floating panels on the right side of the screen and use the left area as my workspace. After you come up with an arrangement you find useful, Fireworks allows you to save that arrangement as a Panel Layout Set and recall it for later use.

Grouping and moving panels

Grouping and ungrouping floating panels is a straightforward process. To separate a floating panel from its current group, click the panel's tab, open its Options menu, and choose Group Panel name with ➪ New Panel Group, where *Panel name* is the name of the panel you're trying to separate. As soon as you click New Panel Group, the panel is placed on the screen. The Options menu is dynamic for each panel you select. If you're trying to separate the Frames panel, then you select the Frames panel, click the Frames panel Options menu and choose Group Frames with ➪ New Panel Group.

Grouping one panel with another involves using the Options menu in the same manner. If you want to group the Frames panel with the Layers panel, simply select the Frames panel, click the Frames panel Options menu, and select Group Frames with ➪ Layers. A panel sitting by itself is simply referred to as a *panel*, while two or more panels grouped together are referred to as, surprisingly, a *panel group*.

In addition to the grouping feature, the floating panels also snap to the edges of the screen or to another floating panel. This snapping feature enables the designer to move panels out of the way quickly and to align them in a visually pleasing manner. It may seem like a minor detail, but when panels are snapped to an edge, the workspace appears less cluttered and more usable.

Just as individual panels can be moved around and grouped, so can panel groups. An arrangement of multiple panel groups is referred to as a *panel layout set*. To create a panel layout set, simply drag the panel, or panel group, by the Gripper, the square section on the left of the panel's title bar, referred to as the *Gripper bar*, and drag it over another panel or panel group. On Windows the Gripper is represented by 5 inlaid dots whereas the Macintosh Gripper appears as a grouping of 15 bumps similar to Braille. When your pointer moves over a different panel, or panel group, a thick line appears at either the top or the bottom, whichever you are closest to, of that panel or panel group. Release the mouse button and the panel, or panel group, being moved snaps in above or below the existing group.

The panel layout sets are easy to position around the screen. Just click the Gripper on the panel closest to the top of the screen, as described in the previous panel, and drag it to a new position. Likewise, you can easily resize and reshape any of the floating panels, panel groups, or layout sets. In Windows, position your pointer over any outer edge of the panel so that the cursor becomes a two-headed arrow and then drag the edge to alter the size or shape of the panel. On the Mac, drag the resize widget on the lower right corner of the panel in order to alter the size or shape of the panel, panel group, or layout set. Each of the panels has a minimum size that you'll "bump" into if you try to make the panel too small.

Panel Layout Sets

After you've discovered a particular arrangement of floating panels and panel groups that works for you, Fireworks allows you to save that Panel Layout Set using the Save Panel Layout command.

To save a panel configuration as a Panel Layout Set, follow these steps:

1. Create an arrangement of floating panels that you would like to save.

2. Choose Commands ➪ Panel Layout Sets ➪ Save Panel Layout. A JavaScript dialog box appears.

Cross-Reference

This is a JavaScript dialog box because all the items under Fireworks' Commands menu are built with Flash or XML and JavaScript. For more about the Commands menu, see Chapter 19.

3. Enter a name for your new Panel Layout Set. Click OK when you're done.

The arrangement of your floating panels is saved as a new Panel Layout Set and is added to the Commands ➪ Panel Layout Sets submenu.

To access a Panel Layout Set, choose Commands ➪ Panel Layout Sets and then the name of the Panel Layout Set that you want to access.

Caution

If you don't want to lose your current panel layout, save it before accessing a Panel Layout Set. A restored Panel Layout Set supercedes the current layout and this change can't be undone.

Hiding and revealing panels

The floating panels are extremely helpful for making all manner of alterations to your documents, but they can also get in the way, visually, as well as physically. When working on a large document at 100 percent magnification, I often hide most of the panels in order to better see and manipulate my work. Hiding — and revealing — all the floating panels is a one-key operation. With just a press of the Tab key, the floating panels all disappear, or, if they are already hidden, reappear.

Although the Tab key is extremely convenient, you can use a couple of other methods to hide and reveal panels:

✦ Choose View ➪ Hide Panels to toggle the panels off and on.

✦ Use the official keyboard shortcut, F4.

Cross-Reference

If there is another keyboard combination you prefer, you can customize the keyboard shortcut assignments in Fireworks. Learn more about customizable keyboard shortcuts in Chapter 3.

Collapsing panels

An alternative to hiding the panels is temporarily collapsing them. Clicking anywhere on the Gripper bar of a floating panel collapses its contents; clicking the Gripper bar again restores the panel to its original size.

Working with Dual Monitors

Fireworks works with dual monitors on Macintosh and on Windows systems that support the feature. You can set up this arrangement through the Displays System Preference on the Mac, and through the Display Control Panel on Windows. Traditionally, the best strategy for using two monitors is to keep your documents on one monitor and your floating panels on the other. This setup works especially well if you have one large monitor and one small one, for documents and panels, respectively.

Another advantage of dual monitors is the capability to continuously preview your work at a different screen resolution or color depth than the one that you typically work at. Most designers and graphic artists work at a high resolution and color depth, such as 1,600×1,200 with 32-bit color, whereas most Web surfers are using 800×600 or 1,024×768, with varying color depths. Work on one monitor, and preview your work in a browser window simultaneously on the other. Adjust the settings of the preview monitor in order to view your work at a wide range of resolution and color depth combinations. Continuously previewing your work as it will ultimately be displayed helps to avoid surprises and unnecessary revisions.

Examining common features

Although each floating panel does something different, they all share common interface elements. Many of the features, such as sliders and option lists, will be familiar to users of most any computer program. Some, such as color pickers, are more commonly found only in other graphics software. Figure 2-18 displays several different floating panels with different interface features highlighted.

The following is an overview of the most common Fireworks interface elements:

✦ **Tabs:** As mentioned previously, tabs appear when you dock a panel to one or more panels, thus creating a panel group.

✦ **Options menus:** All standard floating panels except for the Property inspector and Tools panel have a number of different options that you can access by selecting the Options menu button in the upper right of the panel. The third-party Flash panels in Fireworks are the exceptions to this rule as they do not have an Options menu.

✦ **Help button:** All standard floating panels except for the Tools panel have a context-sensitive Help button that opens the Fireworks help at the appropriate page to assist with the current operation. The third-party Flash panels in Fireworks are the exceptions to this rule as they do not have a Help button.

✦ **Option lists:** For many selections, Fireworks uses option lists. Click the arrow button of an option list to see the available choices. In some circumstances, as with patterns and textures, the option list displays a visual image, as well as a text listing of the options. This feature makes finding what you're looking for in Fireworks easy.

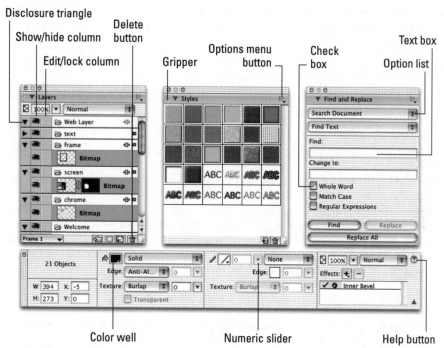

Figure 2-18: These floating panels exemplify many interface features found throughout Fireworks.

Tip

Windows users can type the first letter of an entry in an option list in order to jump to it. If multiple entries have the same first letter, pressing the letter again cycles through the entries.

✦ **Color wells:** Any color selection in Fireworks is handled through a color well that displays its currently selected color. Click the color well to pop up the color picker with the active swatch. All color pickers have an Eyedropper tool for choosing colors and a Palette button for opening your operating system's color picker(s). Most Fireworks color pickers also have a No Color button for deselecting any color.

✦ **Numeric sliders:** Any entry that requires a numeric value—whether it is a percentage, a hexadecimal value, or just a plain number—uses pop-up sliders. Selecting the arrow button next to a variable number, such as a stroke's tip size, pops up a sliding control. Drag the slider and the numbers in the text box increase or decrease in value. Release the mouse button when you've reached the desired value. You can also directly type a numeric value in the adjacent text box.

✦ **Disclosure triangle:** Some floating panels—Property inspector, Layers panel—have an additional section that you can reveal by selecting the expander arrow. The expander arrow is a small triangle on the floating panel that acts as a toggle. Select it once, and the panel expands to display the preview section; select it again, and the panel returns to its previous size.

✦ **Text boxes:** Enter values directly into text boxes. All Fireworks sliders have text boxes next to them so that you can quickly enter a number instead of using a mouse to move the slider.

✦ **Checkboxes:** You can enable an option by clicking the associated checkbox, or disable it by clicking it again in order to remove the checkmark.

Optimize panel

The Optimize panel enables you to specify export settings for the current document. Choose a file type and file type — specific settings, such as Quality for JPEG images, and palette for GIFs. Depending on which file format you choose, the available options change accordingly. The Optimize panel also displays the current export palette when working with 8-bit images, such as GIFs. This Color Table provides feedback that allows you to minimize the file size of exported GIF images by reducing the number of colors in their palette.

Figure 2-19 shows the Optimize panel set to GIF WebSnap 128.

The Color Table panel from Fireworks 4 has been merged with the Optimize panel in Fireworks MX to put all of your optimization needs in one place.

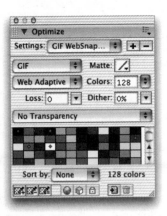

Figure 2-19: Choose export settings for your document in the Optimize panel.

The Optimize panel Options menu contains commands for fine-tuning your export settings. Table 2-5 details the commands.

Find more information about the Optimize panel in Chapter 15.

Table 2-5
Optimize Panel Options Menu Commands

Option	Description
Save Settings	Saves the current export settings
Delete Settings	Deletes the current saved export setting
Optimize to Size	Optimizes the current document to a particular export file size
Export Wizard	Starts the Export Wizard to assist in exporting a document
Interlaced	Toggles the interlaced option for formats that support it
Progressive JPEG	Toggles JPEG or Progressive JPEG
Sharpen JPEG Edges	Toggles sharpening of edges in exported JPEGs
Unlock All Colors	Unlocks all locked colors in the Optimize panel's color palette
Remove Unused Colors	Toggles whether or not Fireworks removes unused colors from the color palette on export
Replace Palette Entry	Opens your operating system's color picker(s) so that you can replace the selected palette entry with a different color
Make Transparent	Makes the selected color transparent
Show Swatch Feedback	Toggles between icons that indicate whether a color is locked, transparent, or has another attribute
Remove Edit	Restores selected color to what it was before editing
Remove All Edits	Restores all colors to what they were before editing
Load Palette	Loads a previously saved palette
Save Palette	Saves the current palette

Swatches panel

Whereas the Color Mixer defines the color universe, the Swatches panel identifies a more precise palette of colors. As the name implies, the Swatches panel contains a series of color samples, as you can see in Figure 2-20. You select a color by clicking on a swatch.

Tip

To reset a swatch palette after you've modified it or sorted it by color, select the palette again from the Swatches panel Options menu.

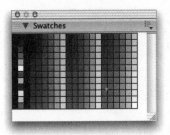

Figure 2-20: Palette management is coordinated through the Swatches panel.

A major feature of the Swatches panel is tucked away in its Options menu: palette management. With the commands in the Options menu, you can switch to standard palettes (such as the Windows or Macintosh system palettes), save and recall custom palettes, or access the current export palette. The Add Swatches command is especially useful; it can load palettes previously stored in the Photoshop color table file format, or pull the color information from a GIF file. Table 2-6 outlines all the Options menu commands.

Table 2-6
Swatches Panel Options Menu Commands

Option	Description
Add Swatches	Imports previously saved palettes from .aco or GIF files
Replace Swatches	Exchanges the current palette set for a previously saved one
Save Swatches	Stores the current palette set
Clear Swatches	Removes all palettes from the panel
Macintosh System	Switches to the Macintosh system palette
Windows System	Switches to the Windows system palette
Grayscale	Switches to a grayscale palette
Current Export Palette	Switches to the current export palette
Sort by Color	Sorts the swatches by color

Color Mixer panel

Web designers come from a variety of backgrounds: Some are well rooted in computer graphics, others are more familiar with print publishing, whereas an increasing number know only Web imagery. The Color Mixer lets you opt for the color model that you're most familiar with and that is best suited to your work.

The Color Mixer, shown in Figure 2-21, displays three different ways to choose colors:

✦ **Stroke and Fill color wells:** Select a color well to open the pop-up color picker and gain access to the system color picker(s) through the Palette button.

✦ **Color ramp:** The full-spectrum preview of the chosen color model is known as the color ramp. You can select any color by clicking it.

✦ **Color component sliders:** Like the color ramp, the color component sliders change according to the chosen color model. Four of the five color models — RGB, Hexadecimal, CMY, and HSB — display three different sliders, whereas Grayscale shows only one, K (black).

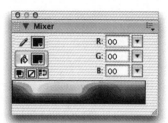

Figure 2-21: Select your stroke and fill colors from the color wells, the color ramp, or the color component sliders in the Color Mixer panel.

Like the Tools panel, the Color Mixer also features a Default Colors button for restoring the preset stroke and fill colors, and a Swap button for reversing the colors. Choose a color model by selecting it from the Options menu, detailed in Table 2-7.

Table 2-7
Color Mixer Panel Options Menu Commands

Option	Description
RGB	Changes the color mixer display to Red, Green, and Blue
Hexadecimal	Changes the color mixer display to Hexadecimal Red, Green, and Blue, the standard way to specify colors in HTML
CMY	Changes the color mixer display to Cyan, Magenta, and Yellow
HSB	Changes the color mixer display to Hue, Saturation, and Brightness
Grayscale	Changes the color mixer display to Grayscale, which is 256 shades of gray

Cross-Reference   A full understanding of the color possibilities and pitfalls is a must for any Web designer. Learn more about using the Color Mixer in Chapter 7.

Layers panel

Layers in Fireworks enable the creation of extremely complicated graphics, as well as compatibility with files stored in Photoshop format. Fireworks layers are like folders that can contain multiple objects, each with its own stacking order. Layers, in turn, have their own stacking order, and can be placed on top of, or beneath, other layers. Moreover, each layer can be hidden from view for easier editing of complex documents and can be locked to prevent accidental editing. Layers can be shared across frames, allowing you to instantly add a static element to every frame of an animation.

All Web objects, such as slices and hotspots, are stored in the Web Layer, which can be hidden or locked, or have its stacking order changed, but which cannot be deleted. The Web Layer is always shared across all frames.

The Layers panel, shown in Figure 2-22, is the central control center for layers. The layer list contains each layer's name, a thumbnail of its contents, as well as Expand/Collapse, Show/Hide, and Lock/Unlock columns. Create or delete layers with the New/Duplicate Layer and Delete Selection buttons. The Add Mask button adds a mask to the selected object or layer. The New Bitmap Image button creates an empty bitmap object as the next object on a layer.

Figure 2-22: Objects on a layer can be hidden or locked with a single click on the Layers panel.

A good portion of Fireworks' layer management is coordinated through the Layers panel Options menu commands, as described in Table 2-8.

Table 2-8 Layers Panel Options Menu Commands	
Option	**Description**
New Image	Creates a new, empty bitmap object the same size as the canvas of the current document
New Layer	Adds a new layer on top of all current layers
Duplicate Layer	Clones the current layer
Share this Layer	Enables all objects on the selected layer to be shared across all frames
Single Layer Editing	Restricts edits to the current layer
Delete Layer	Removes the current layer
Flatten Selection	Converts the currently selected objects, both vector and bitmap, into a single bitmap object
Merge Down	Merges a bitmap object with the bitmap that is directly beneath it in the stacking order
Hide All	Conceals all layers in the document
Show All	Reveals all layers in the document
Lock All	Prevents editing in the selected layer
Unlock All	Enables a locked layer to be edited
Add Mask	Adds a mask to the selected object
Edit Mask	Puts Fireworks in mask edit mode, so only the mask of the currently selected object can be modified in the document window
Disable Mask	Disables the currently selected object's mask
Delete Mask	Removes the currently selected object's mask
Thumbnail Options	Opens the Thumbnail Options dialog box, which offers a range of thumbnail sizes to choose from

Align panel

The Align panel is a very useful and flexible tool when it comes to arranging items in your document. It is a third-party Flash panel, written by Kleanthis Economou, that gives Fireworks users alignment options that are akin to those available in Flash MX. Rather than only being able to align objects in your document to each other, the Align panel enables you to align individual or multiple objects to the canvas, or even to paths. Shown in Figure 2-23, the Align panel adds tremendous alignment capabilities to Fireworks.

Figure 2-23: The Align panel takes Fireworks alignment options to a new level, enabling you to align to the canvas or even to points on a path.

New Feature   The Align panel is a new addition to Fireworks MX.

Cross-Reference   For more information on extensibility, and writing your own commands, see chapter 26.

Frames panel

Frames have two primary uses in Fireworks: rollovers and animations. When used to create rollovers, each frame represents a different state of the user's mouse with up to four frames being used. To create an animated GIF, each frame in Fireworks corresponds to one frame of the animation. You can use as many frames for your animation as necessary (although file size often dictates that the fewest frames possible is best).

By default, frame timing is set to 7 milliseconds. Double-click the frame timing setting to edit it in the pop-up dialog box. Double-click a frame's name to edit it in another pop-up dialog box.

The Frames panel, shown in Figure 2-24, is laid out like the Layers panel, with a list of frames featured prominently.

Figure 2-24: The Frames panel is Fireworks' center stage for creating rollovers and animated GIF images.

The Frames panel Options menu, detailed in Table 2-9, enables you to further control your interaction with frames.

Table 2-9 Frames Panel Options Menu Commands	
Option	**Description**
Add Frames	Opens the Add Frames dialog box
Duplicate Frame	Duplicates the current frame
Delete Frames	Deletes the current frame
Copy to Frames	Copies the selected object to a frame or a range of frames
Distribute to Frames	Distributes each selected object to a different frame, as determined by the stacking order of the objects
Auto Crop	Sets the frame disposal method to Auto Crop
Auto Difference	Sets the frame disposal method to Auto Difference
Properties	Opens the pop-up edit window for the current frame

History panel

The History panel, shown in Figure 2-25, allows precise control over Fireworks' multiple level Undo command. The Undo Marker points to your preceding step. To roll back to even earlier steps, slide the Undo Marker up one or more notches. The number of steps the History panel keeps track of is the number of Undo steps you have specified in Fireworks' Preferences.

Caution   The maximum number of Undo steps you can specify in Fireworks is 1,009.

Figure 2-25: The History panel contains a record of your actions that you can undo, repeat, or save as a command.

The capability to save or replay your steps makes the History panel more than just an enhanced Undo. Saving your previous steps as a command enables you to automate almost anything you do in Fireworks. If you have a project that requires you to tediously edit a number of objects in the same way, do it once and save the steps as a command that you can run on all the other objects.

The History panel Options menu contains the commands detailed in Table 2-10.

Table 2-10
History Panel Options Menu Commands

Option	Description
Replay Selected Steps	Replays the selected steps
Copy Steps	Copies the selected steps to the Clipboard
Save as Command	Saves the selected steps as a command
Clear History	Deletes all steps

Find out more about the History panel in Chapter 19.

Info panel

Often, checking an object's size or position when you're creating an overall graphic is necessary. The Info panel not only provides you with that feedback, but it also enables you to modify those values numerically for precise adjustments. The Info panel, shown in Figure 2-26, also lists the current pointer coordinates and the color values of the pixel found under the pointer, updated in real time. When you use a Transform tool, the Info panel keeps you advised of things such as rotation angle, enabling more accurate free transforms.

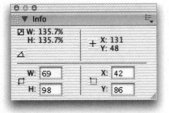

Figure 2-26: You can find any object's dimensions and position in the Info panel.

Be sure to press Enter (Return) after changing a value in the Info panel. You can press the Tab key to move from one value to another within the Info panel, but the values you enter won't take effect until you press Enter (Return).

You can alter the color model and measurement system shown in the Info panel by choosing another from the Info panel Options menu, detailed in Table 2-11.

| Table 2-11 | |
| **Info Panel Options Menu Commands** | |
Option	**Description**
Hexadecimal	Changes the color settings display to Hexadecimal Red, Green, and Blue
RGB	Changes the color settings display to Red, Green, and Blue
CMY	Changes the color settings display to Cyan, Magenta, and Yellow
HSB	Changes the color settings display to Hue, Saturation, and Brightness
Pixels	Changes the measurement display to pixels
Inches	Changes the measurement display to inches
Centimeters	Changes the measurement display to centimeters
Scale Attributes	Enables attributes to be scaled with the object

Behaviors panel

One of the key features of Fireworks that separates it from other graphics programs is its capability to output HTML and JavaScript code along with images. The code activates an image and makes it capable of an action, such as changing color or shape when the user passes the mouse over it. The code is known in Fireworks as a *Behavior.* A Behavior is actually composed of two parts: an action that specifies what is to occur, and an event that triggers the action.

Behaviors require a Web object, such as a slice or a hotspot, to function. After you've selected the desired Web object, you assign a Behavior by choosing the Add Action button (the plus sign) from the Behaviors panel. Fireworks comes with five main groups of Behaviors from which to choose: Simple Rollover, Swap Image, Set Nav Bar Image, Set Pop-up Menu, and Set Text of Status Bar.

All assigned Behaviors for a given Web object are listed in the Behaviors panel, as shown in Figure 2-27. The events, such as OnMouseOver or OnClick, are listed in the first column and the actions in the second. The third column, Info, offers specifics that identify the Behavior. To remove a Behavior, select it and then choose the Remove Action button (the minus sign). You can also delete a Behavior—or all the Behaviors for a Web object—through the Options menu commands listed in Table 2-12.

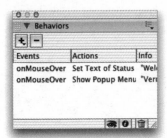

Figure 2-27: Use the Behaviors panel to generate HTML and JavaScript code at the click of a mouse.

Table 2-12
Behaviors Panel Options Menu Commands

Option	Description
Edit	Opens the dialog box for the selected Behavior
Delete	Removes the currently selected Behavior from its attached object
Delete All	Removes all Behaviors attached to the current object
Show All	Shows all Behaviors in a group
Ungroup	Ungroups a group of Behaviors

Cross-Reference Behaviors are a rich feature of Fireworks. To find out more about them, see Chapter 21.

URL panel

URLs are the life-blood of the Web. When a URL (Uniform Resource Locator, also known as a *link*) is attached to an image on a Web page, the user need only click once to jump to another section of the document, another page on the Web site, or another computer halfway around the world. For all their power, URLs can be difficult to manage; one typo in the often-complex string of letters and symbols can break a link.

The URL panel, shown in Figure 2-28, greatly eases the work required for managing URLs by listing all the Internet addresses inserted in the current session or loaded from an external file. You can easily assign URLs with a click of a listed item; more importantly, you can maintain a list of links for a particular Web site so that you don't have to re-enter them each time. To add the current URL to the Library, select the Add button (the plus sign).

Figure 2-28: Adding links to your Web objects is easy with the URL panel.

You can access most of Fireworks' URL management utilities through the URL panel Options menu, detailed in Table 2-13.

<table>
<tr><td colspan="2" align="center">Table 2-13
URL Panel Options Menu Commands</td></tr>
<tr><td>*Option*</td><td>*Description*</td></tr>
<tr><td>Add Used URLs to Library</td><td>Adds the list of current URLs to the URL Library</td></tr>
<tr><td>Clear Unused URLs</td><td>Removes all URLs from the current listing</td></tr>
<tr><td>Add URL</td><td>Adds a new URL to the URL Library</td></tr>
<tr><td>Edit URL</td><td>Opens the Edit URL dialog box</td></tr>
<tr><td>Delete URL</td><td>Removes the selected URL from the URL Library</td></tr>
<tr><td>New URL Library</td><td>Creates a new URL Library</td></tr>
<tr><td>Import URLs</td><td>Loads a new set of URLs from a previously stored URL Library, a bookmark file, or an HTML page</td></tr>
<tr><td>Export URLs</td><td>Stores the current URL Library</td></tr>
</table>

Styles panel

If you've ever spent hours getting just the right combination of stroke, fill, and effects for an object — and then find you need to apply the same combination to all the navigation buttons throughout a Web site — you'll greatly appreciate the Fireworks Styles feature.

In Fireworks, a *style* is a collection of attributes that you can apply to any object. The Styles panel is preset with a number of such designs, which appear as graphical buttons and text, with many more available on the Fireworks CD-ROM. To apply a style, select the object and then select the style; you can even select multiple objects (such as a row of navigation buttons) and apply the same style to them all with one click. Styles are a terrific time-saver and a great way to maintain a consistent look and feel.

The Styles panel, shown in Figure 2-29, is composed of a series of icons, each representing a different style. A style can have the following attributes: fill type, fill color, stroke type, stroke color, effect, text font, text size, and text color. In addition to the preset styles, you can also save your own combinations. Just highlight the object with the desired attributes and select the New Style button on the Styles panel. You can also accomplish this by choosing New Style from the Options menu. A full list of the Styles panel Options menu commands appears in Table 2-14.

Figure 2-29: Automate applying a consistent look and feel to your objects by using the Styles panel.

Table 2-14
Styles Panel Options Menu Commands

Option	Description
New Style	Creates a new style based on the current object
Edit Style	Opens the Edit Style dialog box
Delete Styles	Removes a selected style or styles
Import Styles	Loads a new set of styles after the currently selected style
Export Styles	Stores the currently selected style or styles
Reset Styles	Reloads the default configuration of styles
Large Icons	Displays the available styles with icons twice as large as normal

Cross-Reference
Find out more about creating and applying styles in Chapter 16.

Library panel

The Library panel contains Fireworks *Libraries:* collections of symbols that you can save and reopen as needed. Symbols are edited right in the Library. Dragging a symbol from the Library panel and dropping it into a document creates an *instance* of that symbol. Instances are copies of symbols that remain linked to the symbol and inherit changes to the symbol. Instances are similar to a Windows file shortcut or Mac alias—right down to the arrow badge—and can be animated, tweened, and edited as a group. You can save symbols in Symbol Libraries and use them again and again in multiple documents.

The commands detailed in Table 2-15 are located in the Library panel Options menu. Figure 2-30 shows the Library panel.

Figure 2-30: The Library panel enables you to store Libraries of symbols.

Table 2-15	
Library Panel Options Menu Commands	
Option	*Description*
New Symbol	Creates a new symbol
Duplicate	Duplicates the current symbol
Delete	Removes the current symbol from the Library and all its instances from the document
Edit Symbol	Opens the selected symbol in its own window for editing
Properties	Displays the Symbol Properties dialog box for the current symbol
Select Unused Items	Selects unused symbols in the Library

Continued

Table 2-15 *(continued)*	
Option	**Description**
Update	Updates symbols that were imported from external Libraries
Play	Consecutively displays all frames of a button
Import Symbols	Imports symbols from a saved Library
Export Symbols	Exports symbols to a saved Library

Find and Replace panel

Let's suppose you've just finished the graphics for a major Web site, chock-full of corporate logos, and you receive *the call*. You know, the one from the client who informs you that the company has just been acquired and instead of NewCo, Inc., it's now New2Co, Inc. Could you please redo all the graphics — by tomorrow?

Because Fireworks objects are always editable, the Find and Replace panel, shown in Figure 2-31, makes updating a series of Web graphics a snap. You can change all the graphics in a selection, a file, a frame, or a series of files. Moreover, Find and Replace can handle more than just text; you can also alter fonts, colors, and URLs, or even snap all the colors to their nearest Web safe neighbor.

Figure 2-31: Need to make global changes in text, font, color, or URLs? Pull up the Find and Replace panel and get the job done fast.

The Find and Replace feature works with the Project Log panel, which tracks changes made to your documents. You can enable Project Log tracking through the Options menu commands listed in Table 2-16, as well as specify replacement options for multiple file operations.

Table 2-16	
Find and Replace Panel Options Menu Commands	
Option	**Description**
Add Files to Project Log	Tracks changes made in a Find and Replace operation in the Project Log
Replace Options	Displays options for multiple-file Find and Replace operations

You can really ramp up your production level of Web graphics if you master the Find and Replace feature. To learn more about it, see Chapter 18.

Project Log panel

With the power inherent in Fireworks automation tools, such as Find and Replace and Batch Processing, you need a way to keep track of the many changes you may make. The Project Log panel, shown in Figure 2-32, details each change that has taken place and enables you to not only receive confirmation of the change, but also to easily open any file that was affected.

Figure 2-32: Use the Project Log to manage your Find and Replace and Batch Process operations.

In addition to listing documents altered during an automated process, you can use the Project Log to keep a number of files close at hand, ready to be opened at will. Through the Add Files to Log command, in the Options menu detailed in Table 2-17, files can be made accessible, but not immediately opened. The Options menu also enables you to quickly make changes to files in the Project Log and to re-export them using their previous settings.

To find out more about what's possible with the Project Log, turn to Chapter 18.

	Table 2-17	
	Project Log Options Menu Commands	
Option	**Description**	
Export Again	Exports selected files in the Project Log using their previous settings	
Add Files to Log	Includes additional graphic files in the Project Log without initially opening them	
Clear Selection	Removes the selected files from the Project Log	
Clear All	Removes all files from the Project Log	

Answers panel

The Answers panel, shown in Figure 2-33, is a Flash panel that dynamically interacts with Macromedia's Web site, allowing you to access a wide variety of information. The Answers panel initially contains links to the What's New file, the Readme file, and the Fireworks Tutorials. Along with these links you find a button labeled Update. Clicking the Update button checks the Macromedia Web site and refreshes the panel with an option list containing access to tech notes, a Web search for tech support issues, and a list of the newest extensions uploaded to the Fireworks exchange. To Update the information in the panel again, select Settings from the option list and then click Update Panel. The Answers panel Options menu has no special settings.

Figure 2-33: The Answers panel is your window to the Macromedia Web site. You can search for help, view top TechNotes, and even see recently uploaded extensions.

New Feature   The Answers panel is a new addition to Fireworks MX.

Using the Menus

You can also find many of the commands and options available in the various Fireworks panels in the menus. You'll also find, however, that many features are unavailable anywhere else. This section provides a reference to every menu item in Fireworks, along with its corresponding default keyboard shortcut, if available. Windows users won't see all of Fireworks' menus unless a document window is open.

Application menu (Mac OS X only)

The Application menu, also known as the Fireworks menu in this case, is an OS X only menu that contains commands for setting up an application and controlling how it interacts with the operating system. It is formally referred to the Application menu because it becomes the name of the application that is forefront in the OS. While in Fireworks, it's the Fireworks menu, while in Dreamweaver it's the Dreamweaver menu, and so forth. Table 2-18 lists the commands in the Fireworks menu.

Table 2-18
Fireworks Menu Commands (Mac OS X only)

Command	Description	Keystroke
About Fireworks	Displays the About Fireworks dialog box with information about the application and its authors	n/a
Keyboard Shortcuts	Displays the Keyboard Shortcuts dialog box, which enables you to modify keyboard shortcuts	n/a
Preferences	Displays the Preferences dialog box where you set user preferences	Command+U
Services	Displays a submenu of available system services	n/a
Hide Fireworks	Hides the Fireworks application and all of its windows	Command+H
Hide Others	Hides all running applications except for Fireworks	n/a
Show All	Shows all running applications	n/a
Quit Fireworks	Quits the Fireworks application	Command+Q

Note In the tables throughout this chapter, commands or tools listed in bold text are new or have changed menu, or panel, locations in Fireworks MX.

File menu

Placing basic computer operations — creating, saving, and printing files — in the File menu is standard practice. Fireworks follows this practice and also includes commands for importing and exporting. All File menu commands are listed in Table 2-19.

Table 2-19
File Menu Commands

Command	Description	Windows	Macintosh
New	Displays the New Document dialog box before creating a new document	Ctrl+N	Command+N
Open	Displays the Open dialog box before opening existing documents	Ctrl+O	Command+O
Open Recent ⇨ Your Recently Opened Documents	Displays a submenu of your recently opened documents	n/a	n/a
Reconstitute Table	Creates a Fireworks document with slice objects from an HTML table	n/a	n/a
Scan ⇨ Twain Acquire	Displays the interface dialog box for a twain source, such as a scanner, if one is available and has been selected, before acquiring an image	n/a	n/a
Scan ⇨ Twain Select	Displays the Select Source dialog box before allowing you to select a twain source to acquire an image from	n/a	n/a
Scan ⇨ Your Photoshop Acquire Plug-Ins (Macintosh only)	Lists currently installed Photoshop Acquire plug-ins — typically, each plug-in enables you to acquire an image from a corresponding device	—	n/a
Close	Closes the current document	Ctrl+W	Command+W
Save	Saves a document, or displays the Save As dialog box for an unnamed document	Ctrl+S	Command+S
Save As	Displays the Save As dialog box before saving a document	Ctrl+Shift+S	Command+Shift+S

Command	Description	Windows	Macintosh
Save a Copy	Displays the Save Copy As dialog box before saving a copy of a document	n/a	n/a
Revert	Replaces the current document with the previously saved version of the same document	n/a	n/a
Import	Displays the Import dialog box before importing a file into any open document	Ctrl+R	Command+R
Export	Displays the Export dialog box before exporting a document in the format specified in the Optimize panel	Ctrl+Shift+R	Command+Shift+R
Export Preview	Displays the Export Preview dialog box before exporting a document	Ctrl+Shift+X	Command+Shift+X
Update HTML	Places or updates Fireworks HTML code in another HTML file on the same computer	n/a	n/a
Export Wizard	Displays the Export Wizard before exporting a document	n/a	n/a
Batch Process	Displays the Batch Process dialog box before processing multiple image files	n/a	n/a
Preview in Browser ⇨ Preview in Primary Browser	Previews a document in your primary browser	F12	F12
Preview in Browser ⇨ Preview in Secondary Browser	Previews a document in your secondary browser	Shift+F12	Shift+F12
Preview in Browser ⇨ Set Primary Browser	Displays the Locate Browser dialog box before selecting a browser as your primary browser	n/a	n/a
Preview in Browser ⇨ Set Secondary Browser	Displays the Locate Browser dialog box before selecting a browser as your secondary browser	n/a	n/a
Page Setup	Displays the Page Setup dialog box (for printing)	n/a	n/a
Print	Displays the Print dialog box before printing a document	Ctrl+P	Command+P

Continued

Table 2-19 (continued)			
Command	*Description*	*Windows*	*Macintosh*
HTML Setup	Displays the HTML Setup dialog box	n/a	n/a
Exit (Windows only)	Quits Fireworks	Ctrl+Q	—

Edit menu

The Edit menu holds the standard editing commands, such as Undo, Cut, Copy, and Paste, as well as numerous commands specific to Fireworks graphics, such as Paste Inside and Crop Document. The Edit menu is detailed in Table 2-20.

Table 2-20 Edit Menu Commands			
Command	*Description*	*Windows*	*Macintosh*
Undo	Reverses the last action; the number of Undo steps is set in Preferences	Ctrl+Z	Command+Z
Redo	Redoes the last edit that was undone by Undo	Ctrl+Y	Command+Y
Insert ⇨ New Button	Displays the Button Editor before creating a new button	n/a	n/a
Insert ⇨ New Symbol	Displays the Symbol Properties dialog box before creating a new symbol	Ctrl+F8	Command+F8
Insert ⇨ Hotspot	Inserts a hotspot object	Ctrl+Shift+U	Command+Shift+U
Insert ⇨ Slice	Inserts a slice object	Alt+Shift+U	Option+Shift+U
Insert ⇨ Empty Bitmap	Inserts an empty bitmap object	n/a	n/a
Insert ⇨ Bitmap Via Copy	Creates a new bitmap of the selected pixels, leaving the original pixels in place	n/a	n/a
Insert ⇨ Bitmap Via Cut	Creates a new bitmap of the selected pixels, removing the original pixels from the document	n/a	n/a
Insert ⇨ Layer	Creates a new layer	n/a	n/a

Command	Description	Windows	Macintosh
Insert ⇨ Frame	Creates a new frame	n/a	n/a
Libraries ⇨ Animations	Imports sample animations included with Fireworks	n/a	n/a
Libraries ⇨ Bullets	imports sample bullets included with Fireworks	n/a	n/a
Libraries ⇨ Buttons	Imports sample buttons included with Fireworks	n/a	n/a
Libraries ⇨ Themes	Imports sample themes included with Fireworks	n/a	n/a
Libraries ⇨ Other	Displays the Open dialog box before importing a Library	n/a	n/a
Find and Replace	Displays the Find and Replace dialog box	Ctrl+F	Command+F
Cut	Moves the current selection to the system clipboard	Ctrl+X	Command+X
Copy	Copies the current selection to the system clipboard	Ctrl+C	Command+C
Copy as Vectors	Copies a Fireworks vector object from the current selection to the system clipboard as vector information	n/a	n/a
Copy HTML Code	Displays the Copy HTML Code Wizard, which guides you through the process of exporting images and copying HTML code to the system clipboard for pasting into an HTML editor, such as Macromedia Dreamweaver	Ctrl+Alt+C	Command+ Option+C
Paste	Copies the contents of the system clipboard to the current cursor position	Ctrl+V	Command+V
Clear	Removes the current selection from the document	Backspace	Delete
Paste as Mask	Copies the content of the clipboard as a mask	n/a	n/a

Continued

Table 2-20 *(continued)*

Command	Description	Windows	Macintosh
Paste Inside	Copies the contents of the system clipboard into a selected, closed path	Ctrl+Shift+V	Command+Shift+V
Paste Attributes	Copies the Fireworks-specific attributes of the contents of the system clipboard to a selected object	Ctrl+Alt+Shift+V	Command+Option+Shift+V
Duplicate	Creates a copy of the selected object, offset slightly from the original	Ctrl+Alt+D	Command+Option+D
Clone	Creates a copy of the selected object, directly on top of the original	Ctrl+Shift+D	Command+Shift+D
Crop Selected Bitmap	Displays crop handles around the selected bitmap object	n/a	n/a
Crop Document	Selects the Crop tool	n/a	n/a
Preferences	Displays the Preferences dialog box	Ctrl+U	Command+U
Keyboard Shortcuts	Displays the Keyboard Shortcuts dialog box before modifying keyboard shortcuts	n/a	n/a

Note   The last two menu items in Table 2-20 are only found on Windows and Mac OS 9. On Mac OS X, these items are in the Application menu, which is covered in Table 2-18.

View menu

The View menu commands, listed in Table 2-21, control a Web artist's views during the creation phase. In addition to numerous magnification commands, the View menu also contains helpful layout aids, such as Rulers, Grids, and Guides. You'll also find several features to help you see just the graphic when you need to have a clear, uncluttered perspective.

Table 2-21
View Menu Commands

Command	Description	Windows	Macintosh
Zoom In	Increases the magnification level of a document by one setting	Ctrl+ Equals (=)	Command+ Equals (=)
Zoom Out	Decreases the magnification level of a document by one setting	Ctrl+ Minus (–)	Command+ Minus (–)
Magnification ⇨ 6%	Sets the magnification level of a document to 6 percent	n/a	n/a
Magnification ⇨ 12%	Sets the magnification level of a document to 12 percent	n/a	n/a
Magnification ⇨ 25%	Sets the magnification level of a document to 25 percent	n/a	n/a
Magnification ⇨ 50%	Sets the magnification level of a document to 50 percent	Ctrl+5	Command+5
Magnification ⇨ 66%	Sets the magnification level of a document to 66 percent	n/a	n/a
Magnification ⇨ 100%	Sets the magnification level of a document to 100 percent	Ctrl+1	Command+1
Magnification ⇨ 150%	Sets the magnification level of a document to 150 percent	n/a	n/a
Magnification ⇨ 200%	Sets the magnification level of a document to 200 percent	Ctrl+2	Command+2
Magnification ⇨ 300%	Sets the magnification level of a document to 200 percent	Ctrl+3	Command+3
Magnification ⇨ 400%	Sets the magnification level of a document to 400 percent	Ctrl+4	Command+4
Magnification ⇨ 800%	Sets the magnification level of a document to 800 percent	Ctrl+8	Command+8
Magnification ⇨ 1600%	Sets the magnification level of a document to 1,600 percent	Ctrl+6	Command+6
Magnification ⇨ 3200%	Sets the magnification level of a document to 3,200 percent	n/a	n/a
Magnification ⇨ 6400%	Sets the magnification level of a document to 6,400 percent	n/a	n/a

Continued

Table 2-21 *(continued)*

Command	Description	Windows	Macintosh
Fit Selection	Sets the magnification level of a document so that all selected objects are visible	Ctrl+Alt+ Zero (0)	Command+ Option+ Zero (0)
Fit All	Sets the magnification level of a document so that all objects are visible	Ctrl+Zero (0)	Command+ Zero (0)
Full Display	Toggles Full Display	Ctrl+K	Command+K
Macintosh Gamma (Windows only)	Toggles the document display to simulate a typical Macintosh Gamma setting	n/a	—
Windows Gamma (Macintosh only)	Toggles the document display to simulate a typical Windows Gamma setting	—	n/a
Hide Selection	Hides selected objects	Ctrl+L	Command+L
Show All	Shows all hidden objects	Ctrl+Shift+L	Command+ Shift+L
Rulers	Toggles display of rulers	Ctrl+Alt+R	Command+ Option+R
Grid ⇨ Show Grid	Toggles display of the grid	Ctrl+Alt+G	Command+ Option+G
Grid ⇨ Snap To Grid	Toggles whether objects snap to the grid or not	Ctrl+Alt+ Shift+G	Command+ Option+ Shift+G
Grid ⇨ Edit Grid	Displays the Edit Grid dialog box	n/a	n/a
Guides ⇨ Show Guides	Toggles display of guides	Ctrl+Semi-colon (;)	Command+ Semicolon (;)
Guides ⇨ Lock Guides	Toggles whether or not guides can be edited and moved	Ctrl+Alt+ Semicolon (;)	Command+ Option+ Semicolon (;)
Guides ⇨ Snap to Guides	Toggles whether objects snap to Guides or not	Ctrl+Shift+ Semicolon (;)	Command+ Shift+ Semicolon (;)
Guides ⇨ Edit Guides	Displays the Edit Guides dialog box	n/a	n/a
Slice Guides	Toggles display of Slice Guides	Ctrl+Alt+ Shift+ Semicolon (;)	Command+ Option+Shift+ Semicolon (;)

Command	Description	Windows	Macintosh
Slice Overlay	Toggles display of the Slice Overlay	n/a	n/a
Hide Edges	Toggles display of selection borders	F9	F9
Hide Panels	Toggles display of all open panels	F4	F4
Status Bar (Windows only)	Toggles display of the status bar	n/a	—

Select menu

The Select menu, detailed in Table 2-22, contains commands for selecting objects as well as manipulating any selections you've already made.

Table 2-22			
Select Menu Commands			
Command	Description	Windows	Macintosh
Select All	Selects all objects in a document in vector mode, or all pixels in a bitmap object in bitmap mode	Ctrl+A	Command+A
Deselect	Deselects all objects or pixels	Ctrl+D	Command+D
Superselect	Selects the entire group to which the current (sub)selection belongs	n/a	n/a
Subselect	Selects an individual object within a group	n/a	n/a
Select Similar	Selects pixels that are similarly colored to the selection while in bitmap mode	n/a	n/a
Select Inverse	Selects all deselected pixels and deselects all selected pixels in bitmap mode	Ctrl+Shift+I	Command+ Shift+I
Feather	Displays the Feather Selection dialog box before feathering the edges of a pixel selection in bitmap mode	n/a	n/a
Expand Marquee	Displays the Expand Selection dialog box before expanding the current selection in bitmap mode	n/a	n/a

Continued

Table 2-22 *(continued)*			
Command	*Description*	*Windows*	*Macintosh*
Contract Marquee	Displays the Contract Selection dialog box before contracting the current selection in bitmap mode	n/a	n/a
Border Marquee	Displays the Select Border dialog box before selecting a border around the current selection in bitmap mode	n/a	n/a
Smooth Marquee	Displays the Smooth Selection dialog box before smoothing the edges of the current selection in bitmap mode	n/a	n/a
Save Bitmap Selection	Stores the current marquee selection for later recall	n/a	n/a
Restore Bitmap Selection	Recalls a stored marquee selection	n/a	n/a

Modify menu

After you've created your basic objects, you'll undoubtedly spend as much, if not more time, tweaking and modifying them in order to get them just right. The Modify menu commands, detailed in Table 2-23, are quite numerous and specific.

Table 2-23 **Modify Menu Commands**			
Command	*Description*	*Windows*	*Macintosh*
Canvas ➪ Image Size	Displays the Image Size dialog box before changing the size of a bitmap	n/a	n/a
Canvas ➪ Canvas Size	Displays the Change Canvas Size dialog box before changing the size of the canvas	n/a	n/a
Canvas ➪ Canvas Color	Displays the Canvas Color dialog box before changing the color of the canvas	n/a	n/a
Canvas ➪ Trim Canvas	Shrinks the canvas to fit snugly around all objects	Ctrl+Alt+T	Command+Option+T

Command	Description	Windows	Macintosh
Canvas ⇨ Fit Canvas	Shrinks or expands the canvas to fit snugly around all objects	Ctrl+Alt+F	Command+ Option+F
Canvas ⇨ Rotate 180°	Rotates the canvas 180 degrees	n/a	n/a
Canvas ⇨ Rotate 90° CW	Rotates the canvas 90 degrees clockwise	n/a	n/a
Canvas ⇨ Rotate 90° CCW	Rotates the canvas 90 degrees counterclockwise	n/a	n/a
Animation ⇨ Animate Selection	Displays the Animate dialog box before creating an animation symbol	Alt+Shift+F8	Option+ Shift+F8
Animation ⇨ Settings	Displays the Animate dialog box for the selected animation symbol	n/a	n/a
Animation ⇨ Remove Animation	Changes an animation symbol into a graphic symbol, removing the animation	n/a	n/a
Symbol ⇨ Convert to Symbol	Displays the Symbol Properties dialog box before converting an object to a symbol	F8	F8
Symbol ⇨ Edit Symbol	Displays the selected symbol in its own canvas for editing	n/a	n/a
Symbol ⇨ Tween Instances	Displays the Tween Instances dialog box before creating intermediate steps between two selected symbol instances	Ctrl+Alt+ Shift+T	Command+ Option+ Shift+T
Symbol ⇨ Break Apart	Breaks the link between the selected symbol and its instances	n/a	n/a
Pop-up Menu ⇨ Add Pop-up Menu	Displays the Add Pop-up Menu dialog box	n/a	n/a
Pop-up Menu ⇨ Edit Pop-up Menu	Displays the Edit Pop-up Menu dialog box	n/a	n/a
Pop-up Menu ⇨ Delete Pop-up Menu	Deletes an existing pop-up menu	n/a	n/a
Mask ⇨ Reveal All	Shows an object and its mask when editing a mask	n/a	n/a
Mask ⇨ Hide All	Shows only the mask when editing a mask	n/a	n/a

Continued

Table 2-23 *(continued)*

Command	Description	Windows	Macintosh
Mask ⇨ Paste as Mask	Copies the contents of the clipboard as a mask	n/a	n/a
Mask ⇨ Group as Mask	Groups one or more selected objects with the top object used as an alpha mask	n/a	n/a
Mask ⇨ Reveal Selection	Shows the area defined by a pixel selection	n/a	n/a
Mask ⇨ Hide Selection	Hides the area defined by a pixel selection	n/a	n/a
Mask ⇨ Disable Mask	Disables the selected object's mask	n/a	n/a
Mask ⇨ Delete Mask	Deletes the selected object's mask	n/a	n/a
Selective JPEG ⇨ Save Selection as JPEG Mask	Saves a selection as a selective JPEG mask	n/a	n/a
Selective JPEG ⇨ Restore JPEG Mask as Selection	Creates a selection that matches a selective JPEG mask	n/a	n/a
Selective JPEG ⇨ Settings	Displays the Selective JPEG Settings dialog box	n/a	n/a
Selective JPEG ⇨ Remove JPEG Mask	Removes a selective JPEG mask	n/a	n/a
Flatten Selection	Converts one or more selected objects into a single bitmap object	Ctrl+Alt+ Shift+Z	Command+ Option+ Shift+Z
Merge Down	Merges vectors or bitmaps onto a bitmap below	Ctrl+E	Command+E
Flatten Layers	Flattens visible layers into one layer, discarding hidden layers	n/a	n/a
Transform ⇨ Free Transform	Toggles the display of an object's transformation handles	n/a	n/a
Transform ⇨ Scale	Sets transformation handles to resize and rotate objects	n/a	n/a
Transform ⇨ Skew	Sets transformation handles to slant, change perspective, and rotate objects	n/a	n/a
Transform ⇨ Distort	Sets transformation handles to distort and rotate objects	n/a	n/a
Transform ⇨ Numeric Transform	Displays the Numeric Transform dialog box	Ctrl+Shift+T	Command+ Shift+T

Command	Description	Windows	Macintosh
Transform ⇨ Rotate 180°	Rotates an object 180 degrees	n/a	n/a
Transform ⇨ Rotate 90° CW	Rotates an object 90 degrees clockwise	Ctrl+9	Command+9
Transform ⇨ Rotate 90° CCW	Rotates an object 90 degrees counterclockwise	Ctrl+7	Command+7
Transform ⇨ Flip Horizontal	Flips an object horizontally	n/a	n/a
Transform ⇨ Flip Vertical	Flips an object vertically	n/a	n/a
Transform ⇨ Remove Transformations	Removes all transformations from an object	n/a	n/a
Arrange ⇨ Bring to Front	Moves an object to the front of a layer	Ctrl+Shift+ Up Arrow	Command+ Shift+Up Arrow
Arrange ⇨ Bring Forward	Moves an object in front of the object just in front of it	Ctrl+ Up Arrow	Command+ Up Arrow
Arrange ⇨ Send Backward	Moves an object in back of the object just behind it	Ctrl+ Down Arrow	Command+ Down Arrow
Arrange ⇨ Send to Back	Moves an object to the back of a layer	Ctrl+Shift+ Down Arrow	Command+ Shift+ Down Arrow
Align ⇨ Left	Aligns selected objects to the left edge of the selection	Ctrl+Alt+1	Command+ Option+1
Align ⇨ Center Vertical	Aligns selected objects to the vertical center of the selection	Ctrl+Alt+2	Command+ Option+2
Align ⇨ Right	Aligns selected objects to the right edge of the selection	Ctrl+Alt+3	Command+ Option+3
Align ⇨ Top	Aligns selected objects to the top edge of the selection	Ctrl+Alt+4	Command+ Option+4
Align ⇨ Center Horizontal	Aligns selected objects to the horizontal center of the selection	Ctrl+Alt+5	Command+ Option+5
Align ⇨ Bottom	Aligns selected objects to the bottom of the selection	Ctrl+Alt+6	Command+ Option+6
Align ⇨ Distribute Widths	Distribute selected objects horizontally throughout the selection	Ctrl+Alt+7	Command+ Option+7
Align ⇨ Distribute Heights	Distribute selected objects vertically throughout the selection	Ctrl+Alt+9	Command+ Option+9

Continued

Table 2-23 *(continued)*

Command	Description	Windows	Macintosh
Combine Paths ⇨ Join	Joins two or more selected paths or endpoints	Ctrl+J	Command+J
Combine Paths ⇨ Split	Splits an object into component paths	Ctrl+Shift+J	Command+Shift+J
Combine Paths ⇨ Union	Combines two or more selected closed paths into a single object	n/a	n/a
Combine Paths ⇨ Intersect	Combines overlapping parts of two or more selected closed paths	n/a	n/a
Combine Paths ⇨ Punch	Combines two or more selected closed paths by punching holes in the back object with the front object(s)	n/a	n/a
Combine Paths ⇨ Crop	Crops the back object of a selection with the front object of a selection of two or more closed paths	n/a	n/a
Alter Path ⇨ Simplify	Displays the Simplify dialog box before removing points from a path while keeping its overall shape	n/a	n/a
Alter Path ⇨ Expand Stroke	Displays the Expand dialog box	n/a	n/a
Alter Path ⇨ Inset Path	Displays the Inset dialog box before expanding or contracting one or more closed paths	n/a	n/a
Alter Path ⇨ Hard Fill	Removes antialiasing or feathering from the edges of a selection	n/a	n/a
Alter Path ⇨ Anti-Alias Fill	Antialiases the edges of a selection	n/a	n/a
Alter Path ⇨ Feather Fill	Feathers the edges of a selection	n/a	n/a
Group	Groups one or more selected objects	Ctrl+G	Command+G
Ungroup	Ungroups a Group or Mask Group	Ctrl+Shift+G	Command+Shift+G

Text menu

Text in a traditional graphics program plays a relatively small, but key role. In a Web graphics program such as Fireworks, text becomes more important because graphics are the only way to incorporate heavily styled text into Web pages. The Text menu commands, detailed in Table 2-24, offer many shortcuts that enable you to manipulate text objects without opening the Text Editor.

Table 2-24
Text Menu Commands

Command	Description	Windows	Macintosh
Font ⇨ Your Font List	Changes the selected text object's typeface or the default typeface if no text object is selected	n/a	n/a
Size ⇨ Other	Displays the Text Size dialog box	n/a	n/a
Size ⇨ Smaller	Decreases the font size by one point	Ctrl+Shift+ comma (,)	Command+ Shift+ comma (,)
Size ⇨ Larger	Increases the font size by one point	Ctrl+Shift+ period (.)	Command+ Shift+period (.)
Size ⇨ 8 to 120	Changes the selected text object's type size or the default type size if no text object is selected	n/a	n/a
Style ⇨ Plain	Removes bold, italic, and underline formatting from the selected text	n/a	n/a
Style ⇨ Bold	Makes the selected text bold	Ctrl+B	Command+B
Style ⇨ Italic	Italicizes the selected text	Ctrl+I	Command+I
Style ⇨ Underline	Underlines the selected text	n/a	n/a
Align ⇨ Left	Left-aligns the selected text	Ctrl+Alt+ Shift+L	Command+ Option+ Shift+L
Align ⇨ Centered Horizontally	Centers the selected text	Ctrl+Alt+ Shift+C	Command+ Option+ Shift+C
Align ⇨ Right	Right-aligns the selected text	Ctrl+Alt+ Shift+R	Command+ Option+ Shift+R

Continued

Table 2-24 *(continued)*			
Command	**Description**	**Windows**	**Macintosh**
Align ⇨ Justified	Justifies the selected text	Ctrl+Alt+ Shift+J	Command+ Option+ Shift+J
Align ⇨ Stretched	Force-justifies the selected text	Ctrl+Alt+ Shift+S	Command+ Option+ Shift+S
Align ⇨ Top	Aligns vertically flowing text to the top of the text block	n/a	n/a
Align ⇨ Centered Vertically	Aligns vertically flowing text to the vertical center of the text block	n/a	n/a
Align ⇨ Bottom	Aligns vertically flowing text to the bottom of the text block	n/a	n/a
Align ⇨ Justified Vertically	Justifies vertically flowing text to the top and bottom of the text block	n/a	n/a
Align ⇨ Stretched Vertically	Force-justifies vertically flowing text to the top and bottom of the text block	n/a	n/a
Editor	Displays the Text Editor dialog box	n/a	n/a
Attach to Path	Attaches the selected text block to a selected path	Ctrl+ Shift+Y	Command+ Shift+Y
Detach from Path	Detaches the selected text block from a path if it's attached to one	n/a	n/a
Orientation ⇨ Rotate Around Path	Orients attached text so that the bottom of each letter is closest to the path	n/a	n/a
Orientation ⇨ Vertical	Orients attached text so that the side of each letter is closest to the path	n/a	n/a
Orientation ⇨ Skew Vertical	Skews attached text vertically	n/a	n/a
Orientation ⇨ Skew Horizontal	Skews attached text horizontally	n/a	n/a
Reverse Direction	Reverses the direction of text attached to a path	n/a	n/a
Convert to Paths	Converts text objects into vector objects	Ctrl+ Shift+P	Command+ Shift+P

Command	Description	Windows	Macintosh
Check Spelling	Begins spell checking the current document	Shift+F7	Shift+F7
Spelling Setup	Opens a dialog box to set spell checking preferences	n/a	n/a

Commands menu

Commands enable the Fireworks user to extend the basic feature set; they are relatively easy to create because they're written in JavaScript. Table 2-25 details the commands that are included with Fireworks.

Table 2-25
Commands Menu Commands

Command	Description	Windows	Macintosh
Manage Saved Commands	Opens the Manage Saved Commands dialog box	n/a	n/a
Manage Extensions	Loads the Extension Manager to install, remove, or temporarily disable extensions	n/a	n/a
Run Script	Enables you to choose a scriptlet for Fireworks to run	n/a	n/a
Creative ⇨ Add Arrowheads	Adds arrowheads to an open path	n/a	n/a
Creative ⇨ Add Picture Frame	Creates a faux-wood picture frame around the current document	n/a	n/a
Creative ⇨ Convert to Grayscale	Converts the selection to grayscale	n/a	n/a
Creative ⇨ Convert to Sepia Tone	Converts the selection to a sepia tint	n/a	n/a
Creative ⇨ Fade Image	Applies one of eight preset alpha masks to your bitmap	n/a	n/a
Creative ⇨ Twist and Fade	Adds depth and rotation to objects	n/a	n/a
Data-Driven Graphics Wizard	Use an external XML file to insert variables into batched file processing	n/a	n/a

Continued

Command	Description	Windows	Macintosh
Table 2-25 *(continued)*			
Document ➪ Distribute to Layers	Distributes the selected objects in your document so that each one is on its own layer	n/a	n/a
Document ➪ Hide Other Layers	Hides all layers except the current layer	n/a	n/a
Document ➪ Lock Other Layers	Locks all layers except the current layer	n/a	n/a
Document ➪ Reverse Frames	Reverses the order of the frames in a document	n/a	n/a
Panel Layout Sets ➪ 1024×768/1152×768/ 1280×1024/800×600/ Your Panel Layout Sets	Arranges the floating panels to the right of the screen, sized for optimal viewing at various display resolutions, and lists panel layout sets created with the Commands ➪ Panel Layout Sets ➪ Save Panel Layout command	n/a	n/a
Panel Layout Sets ➪ Save Panel Layout	Displays a dialog box where you can name the current panel layout and save it so that it appears under Commands ➪ Panel Layout Sets	n/a	n/a
Reset Warning Dialogs	Resets all Warning dialog boxes that have a "Don't show this again" back to their default of appearing	n/a	n/a
Resize Selected Objects	Resizes selected objects graphically	n/a	n/a
Web ➪ Create Shared Palette	Creates a shared palette from multiple files	n/a	n/a
Web ➪ Select Blank ALT Tags	Selects all hotspots or slices that do not have alt text specified	n/a	n/a
Web ➪ Set ALT Tags	Displays a dialog box where you can specify alt text for a document's hotspots and slices	n/a	n/a

Filters

A *filter* is a plug-in that extends the capabilities of a program. With Fireworks, filters are primarily image filters and are, in most cases, the same plug-ins that are designed for use in Photoshop. As you can see in Table 2-26, Fireworks comes with four groups of its own filters, three Eye Candy 4000 filters, referred to as Eye Candy 4000 LE, plus Alien Skin Splat LE. Because Fireworks can read most Photoshop filters and plug-ins, you can greatly extend the available filters by assigning an additional Photoshop plug-ins folder in Fireworks Preferences.

Caution   Because all Fireworks filters are pixel-based image filters, any filter applied to a vector object first converts it into a bitmap object. Many filters are also available in the Effect section of the Property inspector as Live Effects, which work on both bitmap and vector objects without reducing editability.

Table 2-26
Filters Menu Commands

Command	Description	Windows	Macintosh
Repeat Filter	Repeats the most recently used Xtra	Ctrl+Alt+Shift+X	Command+Option+Shift+X
Adjust Color ⇨ Auto Levels	Autocorrects the selection's levels	n/a	n/a
Adjust Color ⇨ Brightness/Contrast	Displays the Brightness/Contrast dialog box before adjusting the selection's brightness and/or contrast levels	n/a	n/a
Adjust Color ⇨ Curves	Displays the Curves dialog box before adjusting the selection's color curves	n/a	n/a
Adjust Color ⇨ Hue/Saturation	Displays the Hue/Saturation dialog box before adjusting the selection's hue and saturation levels	n/a	n/a
Adjust Color ⇨ Invert	Changes each color in the selection to its mathematical inverse	Ctrl+Alt+Shift+I	Command+Option+Shift+I
Adjust Color ⇨ Levels	Displays the Levels dialog box before adjusting the selection's levels	n/a	n/a
Blur ⇨ Blur	Blurs the selection	n/a	n/a
Blur ⇨ Blur More	Blurs the selection across a larger radius than Blur	n/a	n/a
Blur ⇨ Gaussian Blur	Displays the Gaussian Blur dialog box before blurring the selection	n/a	n/a

Continued

Table 2-26 (continued)			
Command	**Description**	**Windows**	**Macintosh**
Other ➪ Convert to Alpha	Converts the selection into an alpha mask	n/a	n/a
Other ➪ Find Edges	Identifies edges in the selection	n/a	n/a
Sharpen ➪ Sharpen	Sharpens the selection	n/a	n/a
Sharpen ➪ Sharpen More	Sharpens the selection more than Sharpen	n/a	n/a
Sharpen ➪ Unsharp Mask	Displays the Unsharp Mask dialog box before sharpening the selection	n/a	n/a
Eye Candy 4000 LE ➪ Bevel Boss	Displays the Eye Candy 4000 Bevel Boss dialog box	n/a	n/a
Eye Candy 4000 LE ➪ Marble	Displays the Eye Candy 4000 Marble dialog box	n/a	n/a
Eye Candy 4000 LE ➪ Motion Trail	Displays the Eye Candy 4000 Motion Trail dialog box	n/a	n/a
Alien Skin Splat LE ➪ Edges	Displays the dialog for the Edges filter for Alien Skin's Splat!	n/a	n/a

Window menu

The Window menu commands, listed in Table 2-27, give you access to all of Fireworks' floating panels and toolbars. In addition, several commands help you work with multiple documents or multiple views of the same document.

Table 2-27 Window Menu Commands			
Command	**Description**	**Windows**	**Macintosh**
New Window	Creates a duplicate of the current document window	Ctrl+Alt+N	Command+ Option+N
Toolbars ➪ Main (Windows only)	Toggles display of the Main toolbar	n/a	—
Toolbars ➪ Modify (Windows only)	Toggles display of the Modify toolbar	n/a	—
Tools	Toggles display of the Tools panel	Ctrl+F2	Command+F2

Command	Description	Windows	Macintosh
Properties	Toggles display of the Property inspector	Ctrl+F3	Command+F3
Answers	Toggles display of the Answers panel	Alt+F1	Option+F1
Optimize	Toggles display of the Optimize panel	F10	F10
Layers	Toggles display of the Layers panel	F2	F2
Frames	Toggles display of the Frames panel	Shift+F2	Shift+F2
History	Toggles display of the History panel	Shift+F10	Shift+F10
Styles	Toggles display of the Styles panel	Shift+F11	Shift+F11
Library	Toggles display of the Library panel	F11	F11
URL	Toggles display of the URL panel	Alt+ Shift+F10	Option+ Shift+F10
Color Mixer	Toggles display of the Color Mixer	Shift+F9	Shift+F9
Swatches	Toggles display of the Swatches panel	Ctrl+F9	Command+F9
Info	Toggles display of the Info panel	Alt+ Shift+F12	Option+ Shift+F12
Behaviors	Toggles display of the Behaviors panel	Shift+F3	Shift+F3
Find and Replace	Toggles display of the Find and Replace panel	Ctrl+F	Command+F
Project Log	Toggles display of the Project Log panel	n/a	n/a
Align	Toggles display of the Align panel	n/a	n/a
Sitespring	Toggles display of the Sitespring panel	n/a	n/a
Cascade	Cascades the document windows	n/a	n/a
Tile Horizontal	Tiles the document windows horizontally	n/a	n/a
Tile Vertical	Tiles the document windows vertically	n/a	n/a
Your Open Documents List	Lists the currently open document windows	n/a	n/a

Help menu

Everyone needs help now and then, especially when working with a program as rich and deep as Fireworks. The Help menu provides quick access to the Fireworks help files, various online resources, and a number of key tutorials that explain the basics of the program.

The Macromedia and Fireworks Web sites offer a tremendous range of support options. If you're troubleshooting a problem, you should start with the searchable TechNotes, which cover virtually every aspect of working with Fireworks. You'll also find links to useful tutorials, articles on Web graphics design, and interviews with industry leaders in Fireworks' main Support section.

One of the most important resources is the Fireworks newsgroup, hosted by Macromedia. This discussion group, located at `<news://forums.macromedia.com/macromedia.fireworks>`, is an essential source for contacting other users of Fireworks. Fireworks support staff, as well as expert and novice users alike, frequent the newsgroup. Need a quick answer to a perplexing graphics problem? Can't figure out the final step in a procedure? Looking to have users with different systems and browsers check your site for compatibility? The Fireworks newsgroup can help in all of these areas and more.

The Help menu commands are detailed in Table 2-28.

Table 2-28			
Help Menu Commands			
Command	**Description**	**Windows**	**Macintosh**
About Balloon Help (Mac OS 9 only)	Describes Balloon Help	—	n/a
Show Balloons (Mac OS 9 only)	Toggles Balloon Help on or off	—	n/a
Fireworks Help (Mac only)	Opens the help files for Fireworks	—	Command+?
Welcome	Opens a dialog box allowing you to choose the What's New file, the Tutorial, and the Lessons	n/a	n/a
What's New	Opens a Flash panel that leads to a list of new features	n/a	n/a
Using Fireworks (Windows only)	Opens the help files for Fireworks	F1	—

Command	Description	Windows	Macintosh
Manage Extensions	Loads the Extension Manager to install, remove, or temporarily disable extensions	n/a	n/a
Fireworks Support Center	Connects to the Internet to view the Fireworks Support Center Web site	n/a	n/a
Macromedia Online Forums	Opens your Web browser and loads the page on Macromedia's Web site with online forum information	n/a	n/a
Online Registration	Connects to the Internet to register your copy of Fireworks with Macromedia	n/a	n/a
Print Registration	Prints the Fireworks registration form ready for you to mail to Macromedia	n/a	n/a
About Fireworks (Windows only)	Displays the About Fireworks dialog box	n/a	—

Tip   Mac OS 9 users can display the About Fireworks dialog box by choosing Apple Menu ➪ About Fireworks.

Summary

With a program as feature-laden as Fireworks, it's helpful to have an overview of what's possible. The Fireworks user interface is very flexible and customizable. The more familiar you become with the layout of the program, the smoother your workflow will become. When you're looking at the Fireworks interface, keep these points in mind:

✦ In some ways, Fireworks combines tools from several different types of applications: a bitmap graphics program, a vector drawing program, an image optimizer, and an HTML editor.

✦ The Macromedia Common UI streamlines the Fireworks interface and simplifies moving between multiple Macromedia apps.

✦ All the tools found in Fireworks' Tools panel have one-key shortcuts, such as V for the Pointer tool and Z for the Zoom tool.

✦ Customize your workspace in Fireworks by grouping, referred to as *docking*, the floating panels however you want, and then save that grouping as a Panel Layout Set.

✦ Many tools have special options you can access via the new Property inspector.

In the next chapter, you find out how to set up the Fireworks environment to suit your work style.

✦　　✦　　✦

Customizing Your Environment

You'll never find any two artists' studios that are exactly alike. And why should you? Creating—whether it's fine art, print images, or Web graphics—is a highly personal experience that requires the artist to be in comfortable, personalized surroundings. Fireworks reflects this attitude by enabling you to personalize numerous preferences to facilitate your workflow, from importing existing images through graphics editing all the way to exporting your final product. This chapter describes options Fireworks offers to custom-fit the program to your personal style.

Setting Preferences

Most, but not all, of Fireworks' customization options are handily grouped in the Preferences dialog box. Though you can adjust these preferences at any time, they are generally used to fine-tune the program's overall functions between sessions. Consequently, changes to a number of the options do not take effect until you restart Fireworks.

To access these program-wide settings, choose Edit ➪ Preferences (Fireworks ➪ Preferences on OS X). The Preferences dialog box opens with the first of its five categories displayed. The categories—detailed in the following sections—are labeled General, Editing, Launch and Edit, Folders, and Import. In Windows, move from category to category by selecting the various tabs. On the Mac, choose another option from the option list to move to another category.

Fireworks has an additional type of preference: the configuration and layout of the dockable floating windows. You can create your own combination of windows — Layers, Frames, Styles, and so on — by dragging and dropping their tabs on one another. For details on this aspect of customizing your workspace, see Chapter 2.

Learning general preferences

The General category of the Preferences dialog box, shown in Figure 3-1, is divided into three sections: Undo Steps, Color Defaults, and Interpolation.

The screenshots of the Preferences dialog box in Figures 3-1 through 3-6 show the default, freshly installed settings. If you're ever wondering what the default for a particular preference is, refer to these images.

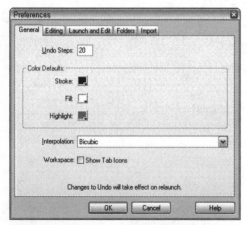

Figure 3-1: Set the number of Undo steps, change the color defaults, and specify the default interpolation method in the General panel of the Preferences dialog box.

Specifying undo levels

The capability to undo an action — whether it's a font color change, an image rotation, or an out-and-out deletion — is critical in computer graphics. Although some graphics programs only let you reverse or undo your last command, Fireworks not only gives you multiple undo levels, but the History panel provides a graphical way to interact with your previous steps. Of course, storing the changes that you make to a document in order to be able to undo that change requires a certain amount of memory. Rather than let an unlimited number of undo steps accumulate in the background until your computer starts to feel the strain, Fireworks allows you to specify the number of undo levels that you think strikes the best balance between usability and utility.

For more about the History panel, see Chapter 19.

By default, Fireworks prepares itself to keep track of 20 undo levels. You can change this by altering the Undo Steps value. The amount of memory needed to undo an operation depends on the type of operation. For example, rotating a 500×600-pixel photograph requires far more memory than changing the color of a straight line.

If you alter the number of Undo Steps, the new setting takes effect for both the Edit ➪ Undo menu command and the History panel after you restart Fireworks.

Indicating color defaults

Although the Web designer has a full palette from which to choose, Fireworks starts with just three basic colors:

✦ **Stroke:** The default Stroke color is applied to any path that is drawn or stroked with any of the drawing tools, such as the Pencil, Pen, Brush, or Rectangle.

✦ **Fill:** The default Fill color is applied to any object when a Solid fill-type is selected in the Fill window.

✦ **Highlight:** To show a selected object, Fireworks temporarily changes the outline of the object to the Highlight color. When the object is deselected (or another object is selected), the Highlight color is removed.

You make all default color changes through the Color Defaults section of the General category in the Preferences dialog box. To alter any of the Stroke, Fill, or Highlight colors, use their respective color wells, which display the standard Fireworks color picker. Choose any of the swatches shown, or use the Eyedropper tool to select an onscreen color. For a wider selection of colors, select the Palette icon to display your operating system's color picker(s).

You can alter both the Stroke and Fill colors by choosing their respective color well on the Tools panel, the Color Mixer, or any number of other windows. The Highlight color can only be changed through Preferences. All color changes take place immediately after the Preferences dialog box closes.

If you choose a gradient fill-type (such as Linear, Radial, or Cone) for an object, but no color combination, Fireworks uses the current Stroke and Fill selections to create the gradient.

Finding interpolation defaults

When you resize an image, Fireworks analyzes the original, and based on that analysis creates a new image with either more or fewer pixels. This process is called *interpolation*. Fireworks offers four interpolation methods: bicubic, bilinear, soft, and nearest neighbor. When you resize an image, you can choose any of these four, but the interpolation preference you set here determines the default in the Image

Size dialog box. Bicubic (the default) is the best general-purpose option. Unless you have a specific reason not to do so, I recommend leaving this preference at bicubic and modifying it as needed for special circumstances.

For more about interpolation methods and resizing images, see Chapter 6.

Toggling panel icon visibility

This option enables you to choose whether your tabbed panels simply display their names, or if they include the panel's icon as well. If the icon helps you to quickly identify the panel then select the Show Tab Icons checkbox. If you prefer the uncluttered workspace of the default option then simply leave this option blank.

Fireworks MX adds the option of showing or hiding the icons next to the names of the floating panels.

Adding preview icons when saving (Mac only)

Macintosh users have the choice of having Fireworks save their PNG source files with the Fireworks icon, or with a thumbnail of your document as a preview icon. The preview icon can be a great benefit if you're the kind of user who finds it easier to manage files by what your documents look like, rather than what you might have named them. If you'd prefer to have the regular Fireworks icon applied to your PNG files, rather than the default preview, then uncheck the Add Preview Icon checkbox.

Fireworks MX allows Mac users to choose either the Fireworks icon or a new preview icon that displays a thumbnail of your document, when you save your PNG files.

Understanding editing preferences

The Editing category of the Preferences, shown in Figure 3-2, enables you to customize the way tool cursors work, and presents options for working with bitmap images.

Using precise cursors

By default, when a particular drawing or selection tool is selected, the cursor changes into a representative shape. For example, select the Pencil tool and the cursor changes to a pencil shape. The Precise Cursors option replaces all the affected individual cursor shapes with a crosshair cursor.

If the Precise Cursors option is selected, the following tools use the crosshair cursor:

   ✦ All selection tools, including the rectangular and elliptical Marquee, and the Lasso, Polygon Lasso, and Magic Wand

   ✦ Drawing tools, such as the Line, Pen, Rectangle, Ellipse, Polygon, Pencil, and Brush

✦ Modification tools, such as Eraser and Paint Bucket

✦ All Web objects tools, including Hotspot Rectangles, Circle and Polygons, and the Slice tool

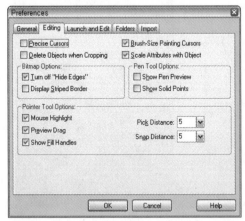

Figure 3-2: Customize your graphics creation style in the Editing category of the Fireworks Preferences dialog box.

The Precise Cursor is very useful for detail work where the tool-specific cursor might block the designer's view, as illustrated in Figure 3-3.

Tip

If you haven't enabled the Precise Cursors option in Preferences, the option can be toggled on or off with the Caps Lock key. Unless you find the standard cursors particularly distracting, I recommend keeping the Precise Cursors option disabled in Preferences and using the Caps Lock key whenever the crosshair cursor is needed.

Using the Delete Objects when Cropping preference

The Delete Objects when Cropping preference specifies that path or image objects outside of a cropped area should be deleted. Alternatively, you can choose to have cropping simply resize the canvas and leave your objects alone. If you prefer that way of working, be sure to uncheck this preference setting.

Using Brush-Size Painting Cursors

By default, Fireworks increases the size of the cursor to match the size of your painting stroke. For example, painting with the Brush tool and a Stroke setting of 20 displays a cursor that's twice as big as painting with a Stroke setting of 10. To paint with a standard-size cursor, uncheck this preference setting.

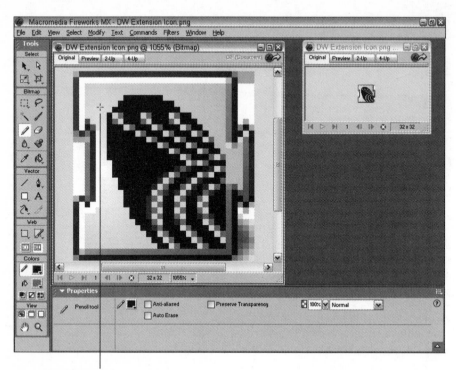

Pencil tool precise cursor

Figure 3-3: Use the Precise Cursors feature for close-up work where a standard cursor might hamper pixel-level accuracy.

Examining pixel-based image options

The Bitmap Options section of the Editing category affects only pixel-based bitmap images.

Hide Edges, found under the View menu, normally makes all the selection outlines vanish. When the Turn off "Hide Edges" option is enabled, the Hide Edges command is only temporary; making any selection causes the edges to reappear. In other words, the Hide Edges option means "hide edges until I make another selection." When Turn off "Hide Edges" is unchecked, the Hide Edges command hides edges until you choose it again and specifically ask to view selection borders. I've found that it's easy to lose track of selections if edges are hidden all the time, so I generally leave this option enabled.

Checking the Display Striped Border preference setting completely enables the barber-pole that surrounds bitmap images while you are working with bitmap tools. With this option enabled, you can quickly determine if you are working in Vector or Bitmap mode. If you're upgrading from an older version of Fireworks, where the Striped Border was always displayed during bitmap editing, you may find it helpful to enable this Preference while you're getting accustomed to the new interface.

Setting Pen tool preferences

The Show Pen Preview option enables you to set the Pen tool so that it shows you how and where the next path segment will be drawn. Not only is it very useful for ensuring that the lines you are drawing are straight, it also helps you to ensure that everything will be positioned where you want it on the canvas.

By default, the Pen tool's deselected points (the ones that you've already drawn) are displayed as hollow squares on the path, while the one in use is depicted by a solid square. The Show Solid Points option simply reverses this behavior by making the selected point hollow and the deselected points solid.

Setting your pointer options

The Mouse Highlight preference toggles whether or not moving your mouse over objects on the canvas highlights the bounding box for the various objects. You might want to disable the Mouse Highlight for documents that contain a lot of objects as the flashing of the highlight can become annoying. Keep in mind, however, that deselecting this option may make it difficult to select small objects on the canvas.

New Feature Fireworks MX lets you toggle whether or not the bounding boxes of items on the canvas light up when the mouse passes over them.

The Preview Drag preference is similar to the "Show window contents while dragging" option in Microsoft Windows. If you disable this option, you will see an outline of whatever you are dragging as opposed to moving the whole selection around. Preview Drag is enabled by default but you may want to uncheck it for those occasions where the preview of your selection makes exact positioning difficult.

New Feature Fireworks MX lets you decide whether you see the entire selection you are dragging, or just an outline.

Using Show Fill Handles

This setting toggles whether or not Fireworks shows the Fill Handles on an object that has a gradient fill applied. If you've already got a gradient fill tweaked just the way you want it, you may want to turn this option off to avoid accidentally modifying your fill by dragging one of the handles.

New Feature Fireworks MX lets you choose whether or not the fill handles are displayed for a gradient fill.

Using the Pick and Snap preference setting

As much as we would all like to have the steady hands of a surgeon and pixel-perfect mastery of the Fireworks tools, the reality is that "fuzzier" accuracy is often more productive. Missing an object by one pixel and coming away "empty handed" can be frustrating. The Pick preference setting tells Fireworks how close your cursor has to be to an object in order to select it successfully.

The Snap preference setting tells Fireworks how close an object has to be to a grid line or guide before it snaps to it. Once again, being slightly less accurate can result in a more productive Fireworks session.

The default setting for both Pick and Snap is five. Experimenting with these values is probably the best way to find out whether five or another value suits you best.

Learning Launch and Edit preferences

A common feature of the Web designer's workflow is to edit or optimize an image file that's already in an HTML page. A placed image may be too big in width or height, or even more commonly, too big in file size. Often, HTML editors such as Macromedia Dreamweaver or Adobe GoLive allow you to specify a default external image editor for image files. Of course, Fireworks is an excellent choice.

When you open an image for editing in Fireworks from an external application, Fireworks asks whether you would like to edit the actual GIF, JPEG, or PNG file from the page, or whether you want to use a Fireworks PNG file as a source for editing. Using an original Fireworks PNG file (if one is available) is always preferable because you'll maintain the highest quality possible, as well as retain vector information and editable text.

Under the Launch and Edit category of the Fireworks Preferences dialog box (see Figure 3-4), you can choose to always use a Fireworks PNG file, never use a Fireworks PNG file, or have Fireworks always ask. Additionally, you can specify a similar preference for optimizing an image in Fireworks when you use the Dreamweaver command Optimize Image in Fireworks.

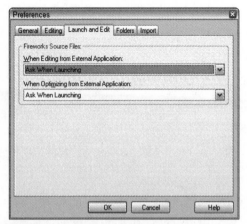

Figure 3-4: Customize how Fireworks interacts with other applications in the Launch and Edit category of the Fireworks Preferences dialog box.

Examining folder preferences

One of the features of a truly great software program is the capability for the user to extend its functionality. You can access additional resources in the Folders category of the Preferences dialog box, as shown in Figure 3-5.

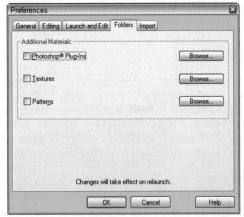

Figure 3-5: Access additional resources for Fireworks through the Folders category of Preferences.

Finding additional materials

Three key areas for expansion are detailed in the Additional Materials section of the Folders category.

✦ **Photoshop plug-ins:** Fireworks enables you to include additional image filters for applying effects to bitmap images. Fireworks works with Photoshop-compatible plug-ins, such as Alien Skin Eye Candy and Kai Power Tools.

✦ **A second Textures folder:** Textures are images that can be blended with other images to give the appearance of different surfaces. Textures are typically stored in the Configuration/Textures folder within the Fireworks program folder. Choose another folder here and Fireworks will use the textures from both folders.

✦ **A second Patterns folder:** Patterns are single images that repeat to fill a selected area. Find patterns in Configuration/Patterns within the Fireworks program folder, and specify an additional folder here.

Typically, designers use the Folder preferences to include resources that are currently available to another program, such as Photoshop. Fireworks has its own plug-ins (called Filters), Textures, and Patterns folders from which it works, but it is also willing to piggyback on another application to double the options that you have available when you're working in Fireworks.

Click the Browse button next to the Photoshop Plug-Ins, Textures, or Patterns checkboxes to navigate to a folder on your hard drive that contains the plug-ins, textures, or patterns that you want Fireworks to start using. Close the Preferences dialog box and restart Fireworks to complete the installation of these resources.

Patterns and textures add a great deal of richness to your graphics. For more details on how to apply them in Fireworks, see Chapter 11. For details on how to incorporate Photoshop plug-ins, turn to Chapter 12.

Discovering Import preferences

Photoshop is a well-established image-editing program that gains much of its power from its capability to layer one image on top of another, with varying degrees of opaqueness and transparency. Fireworks handles Photoshop 3, 4, 5, 6, and 7 files quite elegantly, keeping the layers separate and the text editable. You can specify import options each time you import a Photoshop document, but setting the defaults that suit you best in the Import preferences will save you time and trouble later on, as shown in Figure 3-6.

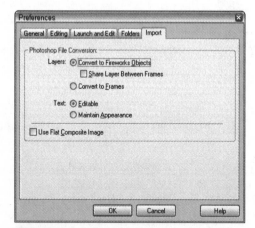

Figure 3-6: Specify the default options for importing Photoshop documents into Fireworks through the Import category of the Preferences dialog box.

By default, the Convert to Fireworks Objects option is selected and each layer of a Photoshop image becomes a Fireworks object on import. Check the Share Layer Between Frames option and Fireworks will share these layers across frames. Alternatively, you can choose to convert the Photoshop layers to Fireworks frames upon import by selecting Convert to Frames.

If you know that you'll never want to edit the text in an imported Photoshop document, or if you may not always have the matching fonts available, choose the Maintain Appearance option under Text to "flatten" editable text into bitmaps.

To load a flat, single-layer version of the graphic, choose the Use Flat Composite Image option. This is similar to flattening the layers of your Photoshop document in Photoshop.

Tip   If you know that your Photoshop document contains attributes that Fireworks doesn't support, such as Adjustment Layers, then you should import your file with the Use Flat Composite Image option checked.

Setting Up for Multiple Users

As more operating systems have developed multiple user capabilities, so has Fireworks. With multiple user support, you can ensure that each person using a particular computer will always have things set up exactly the way they want them. Gone are the days of setting up your panels just to find that someone used your computer afterwards and rearranged everything. Table 3-1 lists the default location of Fireworks user files on Windows and Table 3-2 lists the Macintosh locations.

New Feature   Fireworks MX now supports multiple users across both platforms and all operating system versions.

Table 3-1		
Default Windows User File Locations		
Operating System	*Multiple Users*	*Default Location*
Windows 98	No	C:\Windows\Application Data\Macromedia\Fireworks MX
Windows 98	Yes	C:\Windows\Profiles\<username>\Application Data\Macromedia\Fireworks MX
Windows ME	No	C:\Windows\Application Data\Macromedia\Fireworks MX
Windows ME	Yes	C:\Windows\Profiles\<username>\Application Data\Macromedia\Fireworks MX
Windows NT	—	C:\WinNT\Profiles\<username>\Application Data\Macromedia\Fireworks MX
Windows 2000	—	C:\Documents and Settings\<username>\Application Data\Macromedia\Fireworks MX
Windows XP	—	C:\Documents and Settings\<username>\Application Data\Macromedia\Fireworks MX

Table 3-2
Default Macintosh User File Locations

Operating System	Multiple Users	User Type	Default Location
Mac OS 9	No	—	Macintosh HD/System Folder/ Application Support/ Macromedia/Fireworks MX
Mac OS 9	Yes	Admin	Macintosh HD/System Folder/ Preferences/Macromedia/ Fireworks MX
Mac OS 9	Yes	User	Macintosh HD/Users/ <username>/Preferences/ Macromedia/Fireworks MX
Mac OS X	—	—	Macintosh HD/Users/ <username>/Library/ Application Support/ Macromedia/Fireworks MX

Adjusting the HTML Setup

Fireworks files are similar to those from a page layout program in one important way: Both are intended for publication. Although the page layout program outputs files intended for a printer or service bureau, Fireworks generates files to be published on the Web. Because of the increased variations possible with its HTML output, Fireworks allows you to set a range of properties for each document. You might think of the HTML Setup command as a "Printer Setup" for HTML.

The HTML Setup command enables you to set options for the kind of code that you create, and for both slicing and image map operations. Briefly, *slicing* cuts an image into smaller sections, which are placed in an HTML table, whereas an *image map* is a graphic with one or more hotspots. The parameters chosen through the HTML Setup command can be used for a single graphic or designated as the current default settings. Choose File ⇨ HTML Setup to set these parameters.

Understanding general options

The first tab of the HTML Setup dialog box (see Figure 3-7) deals with the actual code that you generate with Fireworks. Choose an HTML style that matches your favorite editor, from a list that includes Macromedia Dreamweaver, Adobe GoLive, and Microsoft FrontPage. Additionally, you may choose a generic option that's suitable for any editor.

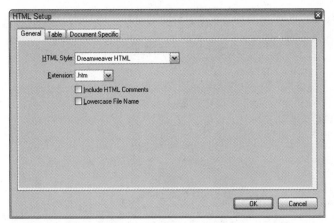

Figure 3-7: The General panel of the HTML Setup dialog box enables you to tailor HTML output to taste.

The Extension option enables you to choose a default filename extension for the HTML that you create. By default, Fireworks uses the DOS HTML filename extension of ".htm." You can change this to ".html" to suit your Web server, or to another extension, such as ".shtml," if that better serves your typical workflow.

Tip If none of the predefined filename extensions suits your needs, you can simply type one of your own.

The Include HTML Comments option tells Fireworks whether to include HTML comments in its output. Your personal preference or company policy dictates whether the comments that Fireworks provides are useful or a nuisance. I prefer to leave Fireworks' comments disabled and provide my own comments in my code.

Check the Lowercase File Name option and Fireworks-generated HTML will have a lowercase filename suitable for posting on the Web.

The Macintosh version of Fireworks also has an additional option on the General tab of the HTML Setup dialog box. The File Creator option list enables you to specify the Macintosh Creator Code that your HTML output file should have. The Creator Code tells the Macintosh operating system which application to use when opening the file. Choices include Dreamweaver, GoLive, BBEdit, and the two major browsers. You can also select the Other option and use an Open dialog box to navigate to a file and steal its Creator Code.

Discovering table options

Tables are a very important feature of almost any HTML page. Tables provide the layout structure and, quite often, unite separate image slices into a cohesive whole. The Table tab of the HTML Setup dialog box (see Figure 3-8) enables you to specify how you want Fireworks to build tables.

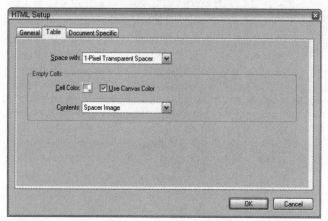

Figure 3-8: The Table tab of HTML Setup deals with table spacing and cell color.

Using spacer images

An unfortunate fact-of-Web-life has made a device known as a *spacer image* a necessity for many sliced images. When an image is sliced, each section is placed in a separate HTML table cell. Some browsers collapse the tables unless some content is included in each cell, rendering the image unattractive. Fireworks solves this problem by placing a one-pixel spacer image in each outside column and row, as shown in Figure 3-9. The spacer images serve to keep the graphic looking as designed, no matter what browser is used.

Learning spacer image options

A range of possibilities exists for using spacer images. Choose one of the options from the Space with option list:

✦ **Nested Tables — No Spacers:** Fireworks attempts to maintain the proper look by nesting tables. If you use this option, be sure to test your final output in all required browsers to make sure spacer images aren't required.

✦ **Single Table — No Spacers:** One table and no spacer images. As with the preceding option, comprehensive testing is required to make sure your output is acceptable.

✦ **One-Pixel Transparent Spacer:** This default method places transparent spacer images around the outside of your original image. Only one image file is added and used: a 1×1-pixel transparent GIF file called spacer.gif with a tiny file size of 43 bytes. The spacer.gif file only needs to be downloaded once but is used repeatedly and resized by the browser, when necessary.

You can also specify how Fireworks deals with empty table cells here. Generally, you'll want to leave these settings at their defaults: Fireworks fills each empty table cell with a spacer image and sets the background color to the same color as the canvas. If you prefer, Fireworks can place nonbreaking spaces into empty table cells. If you use this option, make sure to test it in all of your target browsers.

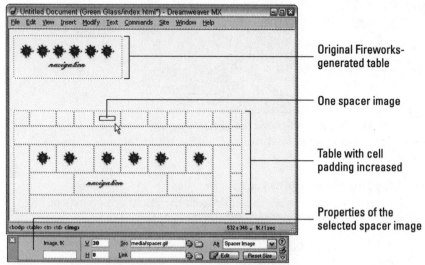

Figure 3-9: Opening this Fireworks-generated table in Dreamweaver and increasing the cell padding allows you to see the extra cells along the top and right side, each containing a spacer image. Note that in the Dreamweaver Property inspector the selected spacer image — which is really a 1×1-pixel GIF — is sized at 30×8.

Learning document-specific options

The final tab of the HTML Setup dialog box, shown in Figure 3-10, displays options that apply to the current document only, and specifies how you would like individual sliced images to be named. Numerous options under File Names enable you to build the perfect filename structure.

When Fireworks slices an image, each individual sliced section becomes a separate image file that must be stored using a unique name. Rather than asking the designer to name each section on export, Fireworks automatically generates a filename. The naming convention combines a number of identifiers, such as the document name, or the word "slice," with different numbering conventions. I find that the best way to work with the Slices option list is, initially, to set them all to None. Then, begin at the upper left and build the right filename by choosing options, noting each option's effect on the example filename that Fireworks displays.

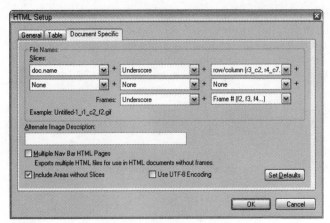

Figure 3-10: The Document Specific tab of HTML Setup handles the naming of sliced images.

Examining the Slices option lists

The following combinations are available from the Slices option lists on the Document Specific tab of the HTML Setup dialog box:

✦ **None:** Deactivates the particular option list's contribution to the final filename.

Caution Leaving all the File Names option lists set to None effectively turns off slice exporting, regardless of other Fireworks settings. Be sure to set at least one of the option lists to a naming convention.

✦ **doc.name:** Adds the filename of the current document to the final filename.

✦ **slice:** Adds the name "slice" to the output filename. When you create a new slice in Fireworks, by default its name is "slice" unless you explicitly change its name via the Property inspector or the Layers panel.

✦ **Slice # (1, 2, 3 . . .):** Adds an ascending number for each slice to the final filename.

✦ **Slice # (01, 02, 03 . . .):** Same as the preceding, but with a leading zero for numbers less than ten.

Tip Using the leading zero slice number creates filenames that sort properly in the Macintosh Finder or Windows Explorer. Without the leading zero, a list of files is sorted slice1.gif, "slice10.gif," "slice2.gif," and so on.

✦ **Slice # (A, B, C . . .):** Adds an ascending uppercase letter name for each slice to the output filename.

✦ **Slice # (a, b, c . . .):** Same as the preceding, but with lowercase letters.

✦ **Row Column (r3_c2, r4_c7 . . .):** Adds the number of the row and column of the HTML table used to display the slices; row numbers are prefaced with an "r" and columns with a "c." For example, a slice in row 1, column 1 would be called "r1_c1."

✦ **Underscore/Period/Space/Hyphen:** Adds an underscore, period, space, or hyphen to the output filename, respectively.

Both the numeric and alphabetical naming schemes follow the same pattern as they name objects in the HTML table. Objects are named row by row, left to right, as shown in Figure 3-11.

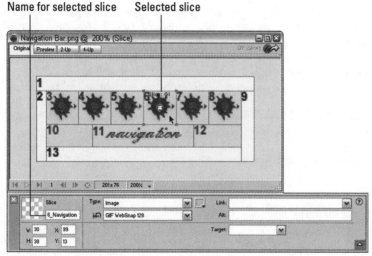

Figure 3-11: This figure depicts the slicing order as Fireworks moves top to bottom, left to right.

Slicing is one of Fireworks' richest features. For a complete discussion of slicing, see Chapter 20.

Adding frame-specific information

You can also add frame-specific information to a slice's filename, with the two Frames option lists. The following options are available:

✦ **None:** Deactivates the particular option list's contribution to the final filename.

✦ **Frame # (f1, f2, f3 . . .):** Adds an "f" (for frame), followed by an ascending number for each frame to the final filename.

✦ **Frame # (1, 2, 3 . . .):** Adds an ascending number for each frame to the final filename.

✦ **Rollover (over, down, overdown):** Describes the rollover function of a frame and adds that description to the output filename.

✦ **Abbreviated (o, d, od):** Same as the preceding, but with abbreviated descriptions of the rollover frames.

✦ **Underscore/Period/Space/Hyphen:** Adds an underscore, period, space, or hyphen to the output filename, respectively.

Once again, be sure to keep an eye on the example filename as you work with the File Names option lists. With a little experimentation, you can create very meaningful, readable filenames for your sliced output, simplifying the task of identifying individual slices later.

Under Alternate Image Description, you can provide a default alt property for the img tags in your HTML output. Alternate text allows text-only browsing, and simplifies browsing for visually impaired users, whose computers read alt text descriptions of the images in a page. Text that's entered here shows up in the Property inspector for every slice. Although providing specific alt text for most of your images is a good idea, having a meaningful default can save time and trouble.

Check Multiple Nav Bar HTML Pages in order to use Fireworks' Nav Bar functions in pages without HTML frames.

Cross-Reference   Find out more about using Nav Bars in Chapter 21.

Determining when slice objects aren't used

When you slice an image, you don't have to cover every portion of the canvas with a slice object. Although most of the time the entire graphic is translated into slices, you may prefer to store just the specifically sliced areas. If so, uncheck the Include Areas without Slices option.

Let's look at an example. Say that a designer uses a single canvas to create multiple, similar graphic elements that will ultimately be used on separate pages. If the Export Undefined Slices option is left selected (it's the default), the entire graphic will be exported in a single table with the individual elements in the same relative position to each other—however, the output would not be suitable for use on separate Web pages. If, on the other hand, the Include Areas without Slices option is deselected, the sliced objects are exported as separate files, using the naming convention described in the previous section.

Using UTF-8 encoding

UTF-8 stands for Unicode Transformation Format-8. The Use UTF-8 Encoding preference allows you to tell Fireworks to save the HTML page with a character set of UTF-8. The typical character set for North America is ISO-8859-1, which allows for the standard ASCII characters that exist in English. UTF-8 covers a much larger character set and allows for double-byte characters that are used in languages such as Japanese, Chinese, Korean, and Hebrew, just to name a few. In a nutshell, this means that if the user has the necessary fonts installed, you can set up your pages to display in multiple languages.

 New Feature   Fireworks now exports HTML with UTF-8 document encoding.

Finally, the Document Specific tab of the HTML Setup dialog box offers you the option of a Set Defaults button, which resets all the Document Specific options to their default settings. If you've made a mess of these settings and want to start over, you're never more than a click away.

Selecting Print Options

Although Fireworks is primarily a Web-oriented program, a printout of a graphic can be useful. Quite often, the designer is expected to present visual concepts to clients or other team members, and occasionally in a printed format.

Fireworks' Print feature is very straightforward and uses standards set on both Macintosh and Windows operating systems. The File ➪ Page Setup command opens a standard dialog box, shown in Figure 3-12, which enables the user to determine the page size, paper source, orientation, and margins. Clicking the Printer button opens the standard dialog box with printer-specific options. When you're ready to print the selected image, just choose File ➪ Print and select the number of copies and other choices.

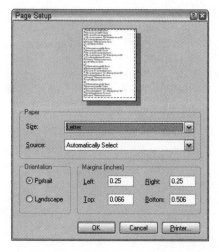

Figure 3-12: Use the Page Setup dialog box to establish your page size and orientation when printing from within Fireworks.

When Fireworks prints a selected image, the graphic is positioned in the center of the page at the preset resolution. You can change the resolution and the print size by selecting Modify ⇨ Image Size and entering new values in the appropriate text boxes in the Image Size dialog box.

Tip   If you often require printed proofs of Web designs, an excellent way to generate them is with Adobe Acrobat 4. Its Web Capture tool can grab a Web page or complete site from a local machine or the Web and turn it into a surprisingly good-looking PDF file, complete with navigable PDF bookmark links.

Personalizing Keyboard Shortcuts

Perhaps the most personal of all preference settings are keyboard shortcuts. If you cut your computer graphics teeth in Photoshop, it's likely that you have certain keyboard commands from Photoshop firmly "in your fingers," so that learning new keyboard shortcuts in Fireworks may be counter-productive. Similarly, if you spend the majority of your day using Macromedia Flash, you may not want to use completely different key shortcuts to access similar features in Fireworks. Enter customizable keyboard shortcuts.

Keyboard shortcuts in Fireworks — and in other Macromedia applications that conform to the Macromedia Common User Interface — are dictated by a saved key shortcut set. Fireworks starts out initially using the Macromedia Common key shortcut set. If you are just starting with Fireworks, or don't have a preference, using the Macromedia Common set prepares you for other Macromedia applications as you learn Fireworks.

In addition to the default Macromedia Common key shortcut set, Fireworks ships with four others that mimic the default keyboard shortcuts in other commonly used graphics applications: Fireworks 3, Photoshop, FreeHand, and Illustrator. These choices are excellent for users who already know the keyboard shortcuts from one of these applications.

Work with key shortcut sets in Fireworks by choosing Edit ⇨ Keyboard Shortcuts (Fireworks ⇨ Keyboard Shortcuts on OS X) to display the Keyboard Shortcuts dialog box (see Figure 3-13). Create or delete sets, edit a saved set, or even export a set as an HTML reference.

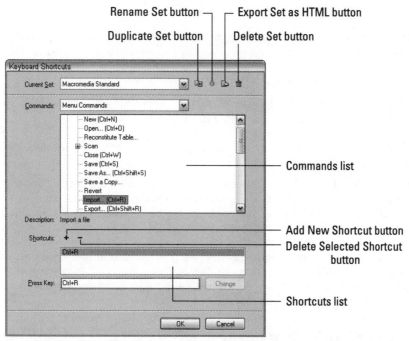

Figure 3-13: Use the Keyboard Shortcuts dialog box to work with keyboard shortcut sets.

Changing the current shortcut set

To change the current key shortcut set, follow these steps:

1. Choose Edit ⇨ Keyboard Shortcuts (Fireworks ⇨ Keyboard Shortcuts on OS X) to display the Keyboard Shortcuts dialog box.

2. Choose another set from the Current Set option list.

3. Click OK when you're done.

The newly selected keyboard shortcut set is immediately made active.

Working with custom keyboard shortcuts

Custom keyboard shortcut sets enable you to save time and trouble again and again, whether you're a keyboard shortcut power user, or just want to change one or two shortcuts that you find unproductive. Either way, the first step is to duplicate a default set and modify it further to suit your needs.

A shortcut key set consists of three kinds of shortcuts that you can modify:

✦ **Menu commands:** Key combinations that correspond exactly to a menu command, such as File ➪ Save. Menu command shortcuts must include either a function key (F1–F12) or the Ctrl (Command) modifier key, and can also include other modifier keys.

Tip   The modifier keys on Windows-based computers are Shift, Ctrl, and Alt. Macs have Shift, Command, Option, and Control modifier keys.

✦ **Tools:** A single letter or number key that makes a specific tool active. No modifier keys are allowed.

✦ **Miscellaneous:** Functions such as nudging an object a few pixels to the left or right. Miscellaneous shortcuts follow the same rules as Menu Commands (detailed earlier), but what makes them "miscellaneous" is that they don't have a corresponding menu command.

Each command, tool, or miscellaneous item can also have multiple keyboard shortcuts assigned to it, enabling you to leave default key commands in place and add an additional key command to an item, or access any particular command with a whole list of keyboard shortcuts.

Creating a custom keyboard shortcut set

To create a custom keyboard shortcut for a menu command, tool, or miscellaneous item, follow these steps:

1. Choose Edit ➪ Keyboard Shortcuts (Fireworks ➪ Keyboard Shortcuts on OS X) to display the Keyboard Shortcuts dialog box.

2. Choose the default set that most suits your needs from the Current Set option list. For example, if the Macromedia Standard set feels comfortable to you except for a few commands that you want to modify, choose the Macromedia Standard set as the basis for your new custom set.

3. Click the Duplicate Set button.

   Fireworks displays the Duplicate Set dialog box.

4. Enter a name for your new custom set.

5. Click OK when you're done.

Fireworks duplicates the current key shortcut set and gives it your custom name.

Modifying a custom keyboard shortcut set

To modify a custom keyboard shortcut set, follow these steps:

1. Choose Edit ➪ Keyboard Shortcuts (Fireworks ➪ Keyboard Shortcuts on OS X) to display the Keyboard Shortcuts dialog box.

2. Make sure that the custom keyboard shortcut set that you want to modify is the current set. If it is not, select it from the Current Set option list.

3. Choose the kind of shortcut you would like to modify — Menu Commands, Tools, or Miscellaneous — from the Commands option list.

   All the possible shortcut key combinations appropriate to the type of key shortcut you are modifying are displayed in the Commands list.

4. Select the command whose shortcut you want to modify from the Commands list.

   If the command already has a keyboard shortcut, it is displayed in the Shortcuts list.

5. If you want to add a new shortcut to the command, click the Add New Shortcut button.

6. Select the shortcut that you want to modify from the Shortcuts list.

7. If you want to delete the key shortcut, click the Delete Key Shortcut button.

8. Click inside the Press Key text box, and press a new shortcut to replace the selected key shortcut.

   The new keyboard shortcut appears in the Press Key text box.

   If the new keyboard shortcut conflicts with an existing one, Fireworks warns you with a text message directly below the Press Key text box. For example, if you try to assign Ctrl+E (Command+E) to File ⇨ Export, Fireworks will warn you that it is already assigned to the Merge Down command.

9. Click Change to update the keyboard shortcut.

   If the new shortcut conflicts with an existing one, Fireworks displays a warning dialog box. Click Reassign to overwrite the conflicting shortcut with your new one.

10. Click OK when you're done.

Renaming a shortcut set

To rename a shortcut set, follow these steps:

1. Choose Edit ⇨ Keyboard Shortcuts (Fireworks ⇨ Keyboard Shortcuts on OS X) to display the Keyboard Shortcuts dialog box.

2. Make sure that the custom keyboard shortcut set that you want to modify is the current set. If it is not, select it from the Current Set option list.

3. Click the Rename Set button.

Tip   Hover your mouse cursor over the buttons in the Keyboard Shortcuts dialog box to see tooltips that describe each function.

   Fireworks displays the Rename Set dialog box.

4. Enter a new name for the shortcut set and click OK.

Fireworks renames the current key shortcut set.

5. Click OK when you're done.

Deleting a shortcut set

To delete a shortcut set, follow these steps:

1. Choose Edit ➪ Keyboard Shortcuts (Fireworks ➪ Keyboard Shortcuts on OS X) to display the Keyboard Shortcuts dialog box.

2. Click the Delete Set button.

Fireworks displays the Delete Set dialog box (see Figure 3-14).

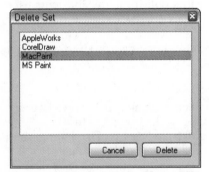

Figure 3-14: Choose a set to delete from the Delete Set dialog box.

3. Select the shortcut set you want to delete from the list.

Caution

Default sets are not shown in the Delete Set dialog box list and cannot be deleted.

4. Click Delete to delete the selected set, or Cancel to dismiss the Delete Set dialog box without deleting a shortcut set.

5. Click OK in the Keyboard Shortcuts dialog box when you're done.

Making a shortcut key reference

Fireworks can create an HTML file that details the contents of a shortcut key set, formatted as an HTML table. Creating a shortcut key reference makes learning new keyboard shortcuts, or studying the contents of a particular set in order to personalize it, easier.

To create an HTML shortcut key reference, follow these steps:

1. Choose Edit ➪ Keyboard shortcuts (Fireworks ➪ Keyboard Shortcuts on OS X) to display the Keyboard Shortcuts dialog box.

2. Click the Export Set as HTML button.

   Fireworks displays the Save dialog box.

3. Choose a folder and specify a filename for the HTML file. Click Save when you're done.

Fireworks exports an HTML file with your key shortcuts. Print the HTML file, or view it in a browser.

Summary

Setting your preferences not only allows you to work more comfortably, but also more effectively. Fireworks gives you control over many aspects of your graphics creation, output, and even printing. Here are a few key points to keep in mind about setting your Fireworks preferences:

✦ You can find most of the program's options by choosing Edit ➪ Preferences (Fireworks ➪ Preferences on OS X).

✦ Several preferences — such as other Photoshop plug-ins, Patterns, and Textures folders — require you to restart Fireworks before they take effect.

✦ You can turn the crosshair cursor on and off by pressing the Caps Lock key, but only if you do not choose the Precise Cursors option in the Editing category of the Preferences dialog box.

✦ The HTML Setup dialog box is similar to a Print Setup for your HTML output.

✦ Each document opened or created can have its own set of special properties that affect the HTML output for slices and image maps.

✦ Fireworks enables you to create and modify your own custom keyboard shortcut sets, and includes sets that correspond to commonly used graphics applications.

In the next chapter, you learn how to create new canvases for your Web graphic creations, as well as how to open existing works for modification.

✦   ✦   ✦

Setting Up Documents

♦ ♦ ♦ ♦

In This Chapter

Prepping a new canvas

Opening existing images

Bringing in multiple files

Saving your work

Adjusting canvas size and color

♦ ♦ ♦ ♦

Oil painters must complete a fairly involved set of preparation rituals even before they can begin to paint. Although Web artists don't have to stretch or prime their canvases, choosing certain options prior to undertaking a new work can save time down the line. Of course, one of the major benefits of electronic illustration in general, and Fireworks in particular, is that you can modify virtually anything at any stage.

This chapter covers all you need to know about "prepping your canvas" in Fireworks. How big should it be, and what kinds of things are you going to put on it? In addition, you discover how to open, save, and close Fireworks documents. We also look at how you can modify a canvas at any stage of the creative process.

Creating New Documents

Before you actually begin work, it's best to consider what you are aiming to create. The better you can visualize the final result, the fewer modifications you'll have to make along the way. This is not to say that trial and error is out of the question, but a little planning can save a lot of time and trouble later.

Exploring two approaches

A fundamental question that you have to answer before you even choose File ➪ New is what approach you're going to take in creating the multiple image files that typically make up Web pages. The two basic approaches are as follows:

✦ Create multiple small images in multiple Fireworks documents and assemble them into a Web page later in another application, such as Macromedia Dreamweaver.

✦ Populate one Fireworks canvas with a complete Web page design, including all the navigation elements, text, and images.

Before I started using Fireworks, I created Web page designs in Macromedia FreeHand, and then copied individual elements into separate Adobe Photoshop documents for touching up and final rendering. Later, I found myself replicating this workflow, but substituting Fireworks for Photoshop. Each of the images for the Web site lived in its own Fireworks document, as shown in Figure 4-1.

Figure 4-1: In a traditional workflow, each graphic is a separate document.

For many projects, though, your best option may be to create one large canvas, as shown in Figure 4-2, and populate it with your entire page design, either created from scratch or a mixture of from-scratch and imported elements. Fireworks allows you to happily draw, filter, effect, slice, specify hyperlinks, leave space for HTML text and finally, export the whole lot as HTML and JavaScript, along with GIF and JPEG images. And if, at any time, you want to export a single layer or slice all on its own, Fireworks enables you to do that, too.

Cross-Reference Turn to the color insert to see an example of a complete Web design in a single Fireworks document.

Whichever method you choose is a matter of personal preference, of course. I'll go on record as recommending the one-canvas approach. Fireworks excels at one-stop Web graphics, and an integrated approach takes full advantage of the variety of tools Fireworks places at your disposal.

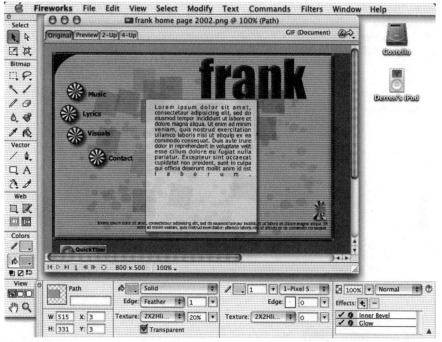

Figure 4-2: You can design and implement a complete Web page within one Fireworks document.

Understanding the canvas options

The "canvas" in Fireworks is a background for the visible area of a document. Fireworks gives you control over the following four basic elements of the canvas:

- ✦ **Width:** The horizontal dimension of a document, available in pixels, inches, or centimeters.

- ✦ **Height:** The vertical dimension of a document, also available in pixels, inches, or centimeters.

- ✦ **Resolution:** A print-style dots-per-inch (or centimeter) setting that Fireworks uses to translate inches or centimeters into pixels.

- ✦ **Canvas color:** The color of the underlying layer for your work. A transparent option is also considered a valid "color."

Discerning width and height

Although it may appear otherwise, all Web graphics files are ultimately rectangular. A document's width and height determine not only a document's size, but also its shape. Although the size of an image is theoretically unlimited, the Web designer must always consider file size as a vital factor and, everything else being equal, the larger the image, the bigger the file size. Typically, image dimensions are given in pixels, short for picture elements. Pixels are the red, green, and blue dots that make up a computer color monitor's screen. From time to time, it's helpful to switch to non-screen-based measurement systems, such as inches or centimeters, and Fireworks gives you that option. But Web design is a pixel-oriented world, and you'll find yourself primarily using them for measuring.

If you are building an entire page design in one Fireworks document, a typical size would be 600 pixels wide and 800 pixels tall for a page that is easily viewable at any display resolution and calls for an acceptable amount of scrolling at smaller resolutions (about two screen lengths). Another option is to make a page that's suitable for viewing on an 800×600 display with the browser filling the screen. If you start with a canvas that's 760×400 pixels (leaving space for browser toolbars), users won't have to scroll at all after they size their browser window correctly.

Tip   Don't be afraid to make your canvas a little bigger than you actually require. I find that a little elbow room is nice while drawing, especially when using a pen and tablet — you can experiment with strokes in the extra space before marking up your actual work. When you're done, delete the test strokes and choose Modify ➪ Canvas ➪ Trim Canvas to quickly get rid of the extra space and get your document ready for export.

Examining resolution

Even if you sized your canvas in inches or centimeters, the canvas itself is an online (onscreen) item, made up of pixels, and it has to have a pixel measurement, too. The (print) Resolution setting enables you to specify how Fireworks should make the translation from dots to inches. If you sized your canvas to 8.5 by 11 inches in order to print a standard letter-sized page at 150 dots per inch (dpi), then put 150 in the Resolution box, and you'll be able to print your document correctly when you're done.

If you're only using Fireworks to create online images — like most of us — the good news is that you can leave the Resolution setting at its default of 72 and continue to size your canvas and all of your objects in pixel measurements. As long as you leave the default at 72 for all the documents you make and work with, you can completely ignore it.

Cross-Reference   For more about online and print resolution settings, see Chapter 14.

Using canvas color

Canvas color is not only very important in Fireworks, but it's also very flexible. When you're creating Web graphics, the canvas color often needs to match the background color of a Web page. You don't have to match the colors when creating your new page, but if you can, you should in order to save a step or two in the near future. You can modify the canvas color at any point in Fireworks by choosing Modify ➪ Canvas ➪ Canvas Color, or by clicking the Canvas color well on the Property inspector.

Initially, you have three basic choices for a canvas color: white, transparent, or custom. Although white is not the default color for all browsers, it's a common default background in Web authoring tools and a popular choice on the Web in general. Naturally, transparent is not really a color — it's the absence of color. However, as many Web pages use an image or pattern for a background, designers often choose the transparent option to enable part of the background to be visible through their graphics. This enables graphics — which are always saved in a rectangular format — to appear nonrectangular. Fireworks includes many techniques for outputting a graphic with a transparent background, but many artists like to work with a transparent canvas regardless.

The third choice, marked custom color, is really all the colors. Selecting the Custom Color radio button enables you to choose a color from the 216 Web-safe colors that display the same way in the major browsers on Macintosh and Windows computers running at 8-bit color. You can also choose a color from your operating system's color picker(s), or use the Eyedropper to sample a color from anywhere on your display. The Custom Color option is great when you're trying to match a Web-page background.

 An understanding of color on the Internet is crucial for the Web graphics designer. See Chapter 7 for more information on using color in Fireworks.

Why 72?

The screen image on the original Macintosh computer was 512×342 pixels and 7.1×4.5 inches. This works out to 72 dots per inch (dpi) for every Mac of that time period because they all had the exact same display. If you wanted something to be exactly an inch wide on the screen (an inch on an onscreen ruler, for example) you would make it 72 pixels wide and it would work on all Macs. The number 72 is also convenient because there are 72 points (a standard typographical measure) in an inch, so one pixel could easily represent one point as well. Today, far too much variety exists in computer display resolutions and dimensions for there to be an actual, real-world common measurement, so 72 remains an arbitrary standard dpi setting. Although Windows and some Windows applications use 96, Fireworks uses the standard 72 on both platforms.

Determining your display's actual dpi involves measuring its visible height and width and then dividing those measurements by your display resolution. A display with a visible area of 12×9 inches, running at 1024×768, has a resolution of 85 dpi. An 85×85-pixel object on that display would be one inch square.

Discovering the steps to create a new document

To create a new document, follow these steps:

1. Choose File ➪ New or use the keyboard shortcut Ctrl+N (Command+N). Windows users can also click the New button on the Main toolbar. The New Document dialog box, shown in Figure 4-3, opens.

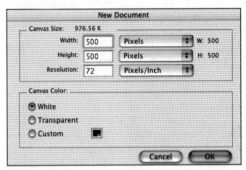

Figure 4-3: Set your document's dimensions, print resolution, and canvas color in the New Document dialog box.

2. To change the horizontal measurement of the canvas, enter a new value in the Width text box.

Tip

Press Tab when you're done to move on to the Height text box.

3. To change the vertical measurement of the canvas, enter a new value in the Height text box.

4. To enter a new resolution for the canvas, enter a value in the Resolution text box. The default resolution in Fireworks is 72 pixels per inch. Unless you have a specific reason to change it, leave it at 72.

5. To change the measurement systems used for Width, Height, or Resolution, select the arrow button next to the corresponding list box. You can choose Pixels, Inches, or Centimeters for both Width and Height; with Resolution, you can select either Pixels/Inch or Pixels/cm (centimeter).

Note

Whenever you switch Width or Height measurement systems, Fireworks automatically converts the existing values to the new scale. For example, if the new canvas was originally 144 pixels wide at 72 pixels per inch resolution, and the Width measurement system was changed to inches, Fireworks converts the 144 pixels to 2 inches. No matter which system you choose, Fireworks always displays the dimensions in pixels on the right side of the dialog box as W (width) and H (height).

6. Select a Canvas Color: White, Transparent, or Custom Color.

7. To choose a Custom Color, select the arrow button next to the color swatch and pick the desired color from the color palette.

8. For a more extensive color choice (beyond the 216 Web-safe colors in the display), either select the Palette button on the pop-up display or double-click the swatches to reveal the system color picker(s).

9. Click OK when you're done.

Tip

The New Document dialog box remembers your last settings the next time you create a new file, with one exception. If you've cut or copied a graphic to your system's Clipboard and you select File ➪ New, the dialog box contains the dimensions of the image on the Clipboard. This feature makes pasting an existing image into a new file easy.

Opening Existing Images

Your Fireworks documents will fall into two distinct categories. Sometimes you'll start from scratch in Fireworks, and sometimes you'll import work from another application just to prepare it for the Web. Because Fireworks is terrific at optimizing images for the Web, you're just as likely to find yourself opening an existing file as creating a new one.

Tip

Use a lossless file format such as PNG or TIFF to move images between applications. The GIF and JPEG formats are unsuitable for use as master copies because information — and quality — is thrown away when you create them in order to achieve a smaller file size.

Opening a regular PNG file is just like opening a Fireworks document. Opening a file of another type creates a new Fireworks document that will need to be saved as a Fireworks PNG-format document under a new name. Export GIF, JPEG, or other files from your Fireworks document as required.

Examining file formats

As probably anyone who's ever touched a computer graphic is aware, different computer programs, as well as platforms, store files in their own file format. Fireworks opens a wide range of these formats. With formats from advanced graphic applications, such as Photoshop, Fireworks retains as much of the special components of the image — such as layers and editable text — as possible. You can even open ASCII or RTF (Rich Text Format) files to import text into Fireworks.

Cross-Reference

Opening the native file formats of Macromedia FreeHand, Adobe Illustrator, or CorelDRAW causes Fireworks to display a dialog box for setting special options. The Vector File Options dialog box is described in Chapter 14.

Table 4-1 details formats supported by Fireworks.

Table 4-1 Supported Image Formats			
Format	**Filename Extension**	**Macintosh Type Code**	**Notes**
Fireworks File Format	.png	PNGf	A PNG file with Fireworks-only information such as vectors added. The default file format for Fireworks 3, 4, and MX.
Fireworks 4.0	.png	PNGf	Updated automatically when opened. Can be saved and then opened again in Fireworks 4.0.
Fireworks 3.0	.png	PNGf	Updated automatically when opened. Can be saved and then opened again in Fireworks 3.0.
Fireworks 2.0	.png	PNGf	Updated automatically when opened. Cannot be saved and then opened again in Fireworks 2.0.
Fireworks 1.0	.png	PNGf	Updated automatically when opened. Cannot be saved and then opened again in Fireworks 1.0. The Background is placed on its own layer.
Portable Network Graphic	.png	PNGf	Standard PNG documents that don't have extra Fireworks information.
Photoshop Document	.psd	8BPS	Version 3.0 or later only. Layers, editable text, and Layer Effects are preserved.
FreeHand 10 Document	.fh10	IPTC	The vector-based format of FreeHand 10.
FreeHand 9 Document	.fh9	AGD4	The vector-based format of FreeHand 9.
FreeHand 7 or 8 Document	.fh7 or .fh8	AGD3	The vector-based format of FreeHand 7 or 8.

Format	Filename Extension	Macintosh Type Code	Notes
Illustrator 7 Document	.ai or .art	UMsk	Adobe Illustrator 7's vector-based default format.
CorelDRAW 8 Document	.cdr	CDR8	CorelDRAW's vector-based format must have been saved without CorelDRAW's built-in bitmap or object compression to be opened in Fireworks.
GIF	.gif	GIFf	Graphics Interchange File Format. Static or animated. Each frame of an animated GIF is placed on its own frame in Fireworks.
JPEG	.jpg, .jpeg, or .jpe	JPEG	Avoid importing JPEG images due to their lossy compression scheme and low quality.
Targa	.tga	TPIC	Common UNIX image format.
WBMP	.wbm or .wbmp	WBMP	Wireless bitmap format. Used in wireless devices.
EPS	.eps	UMsk	Encapsulated PostScript format. Vectors are rasterized.
TIFF	.tif or .tiff	TIFF	Tag Image File Format. High-quality lossless compression similar to PNG.
ASCII Text	.txt or .text	TEXT	Plain text.
Rich Text Format	.rtf	RTF	Microsoft's styled text format, easily exported from Word and many other word processors.
Microsoft Bitmap	.bmp	BMP	Default image format for Windows 3+.
PICT (Macintosh only)	.pct , .pict, or .p	PICT	Default image format for Mac OS 1–9. Combination vector/bitmap format. Fireworks renders any vectors as bitmaps.

To open an existing file in Fireworks, follow these steps:

1. Choose File ➪ Open or use the keyboard shortcut, Ctrl+O (Command+O). Windows users can also select the Open button from the Main toolbar. The Open File dialog box appears, as shown in Figure 4-4.

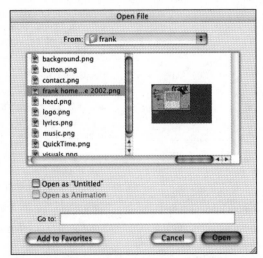

Figure 4-4: Preview files before opening them with the Fireworks Open File dialog box.

2. Select the desired file in the Open File dialog box. Fireworks identifies the file and displays a thumbnail of the image for certain file types in the Preview section of the dialog box.

Tip Windows users: To limit your view to a specific file format, click the arrow button next to the Files of Type option list and select a format. To choose from every file type, select All Files (*.*) from the Files of Type option list, or type an asterisk in the File Name text field. To choose from Fireworks-compatible files, select All Readable Files from the Files of Type option list.

3. To open a copy of the graphic, choose the Open as "Untitled" option.

4. Click OK when you're done. Fireworks opens the file, reducing the magnification, if necessary, so that the full image is displayed.

Tip You can also open files in Fireworks with the drag-and-drop method. In Windows, drop compatible image files on the Fireworks application icon, onto a shortcut to it, directly into the Fireworks window, or into an open document. On the Mac, you can drop image files on the Fireworks application, onto an alias of it, or onto the Fireworks icon in the floating Application Switcher (Mac OS 9), or the Dock (Mac OS X).

Opening Photoshop Files

Fireworks makes opening and working with Photoshop images relatively easy. When you open or import a Photoshop file, Fireworks displays a dialog box to enable you to adjust how the file will be converted. By default, Fireworks maintains Photoshop's layers and editable text, but you can also choose to flatten the file if you don't need to edit it in Fireworks. Photoshop masks created from grouped layers are converted to Mask Groups and Photoshop's Layer Effects are converted to editable Fireworks Live Effects.

 Fireworks MX enhances the way Photoshop 6/7 files are imported and exported.

 To get more information about the way Fireworks handles Photoshop 6/7 files, see Chapter 14.

Opening multiple images

It's the rare Web page that has but a single image on it. Most Web pages contain multiple graphics and, occasionally, a designer needs to work on several of them simultaneously. With the Open command, you can select as many files as you want to load into Fireworks, all at the same time. Hold down the Ctrl (Shift) key as you click on each file in turn in the Open File dialog box. When you're ready, click Open and Fireworks opens and displays all the files in a series of cascading windows.

 Macintosh users can also open multiple Fireworks documents by selecting a group of them in the Finder and either double-clicking them or choosing File ⇨ Open (or Command+O). Multiple image files that don't have a Fireworks Creator code can be selected as a group in the Finder and dropped on the Fireworks icon.

One significant advantage to being able to open multiple images is that you can create an animation by combining all the documents. When you choose the Open as Animation option in the Open File dialog box, Fireworks inserts each chosen file in a single graphic, but on an individual frame. Then, preview the animation using Fireworks VCR controls, or adjust the timing in the Export dialog box.

To open several files in one operation, follow these steps:

1. Choose File ⇨ Open or use the keyboard shortcut Ctrl+O (Command+O). The Open File dialog box appears, as shown in Figure 4-5.

2. Navigate to the folder containing the images to open.

3. To add a continuous range of files, select the first file, press and hold the Shift key, and then select the last file in the range.

4. To select a number of files that are not in a continuous range, press and hold the Ctrl (Command) key and click the files you want to open, one by one.

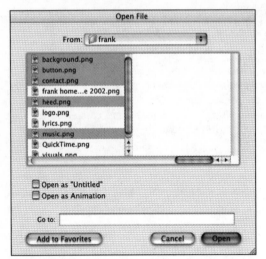

Figure 4-5: Select multiple files in the Open File dialog box by holding down the Ctrl (Command) key as you click each filename or icon.

5. To open all the files in the current folder, press Ctrl+A (Command+A).

Tip   If you're using Windows, you can open an entire folder of images by launching and minimizing Fireworks, dragging the folder onto Fireworks in the taskbar, and then releasing the folder on the Fireworks workspace once it has reopened. Fireworks opens all images in the selected folder and any existing subfolders.

6. To place the selected images in a series of frames, choose the Open as Animation option. Each image is placed in a separate frame of a single graphic, in the order listed.

7. To deselect a selected file, press and hold the Ctrl (Command) key and click the file.

8. Click the Open button to open your images.

Storing Files

Every computer graphics professional has one: a nightmare story about the system crash that erased all the intense, meticulous, time-consuming effort that went into an unsaved image. Saving your files is crucial in any graphics program, but it becomes even more important in Fireworks. To maintain the "everything's editable, all the time" capability, you must save your graphics in Fireworks' native format, PNG. Fireworks offers a very full-featured Export module to convert your graphics into whichever Web format you choose. However, a Fireworks file exported as a GIF or JPEG loses its all-encompassing editability — text can no longer be edited as text, vector-based objects are converted to bitmaps, effects are locked, and so on.

New
Feature

Fireworks MX stores a cached image of text for better support across different platforms and in circumstances where the font used may not be available.

To increase compatibility with file sharing and fonts, Fireworks stores a bitmap image of all fonts within the PNG file. If you create a document on one system, and then transfer it to another that lacks the fonts you used, Fireworks warns you that the font is not available and gives you the choice of maintaining the appearance of the font, or substituting it for another. If you choose to maintain the appearance, then you can edit other aspects of the file without affecting your text. The beautiful thing about this feature is that, when you return the document to the system that created it, the text is still editable, in the original font, despite the fact that other changes were made.

To keep the full range of Fireworks features active, it's essential that each file be saved, as well as exported. Fireworks uses standard commands to save: File ➪ Save, the keyboard shortcut Ctrl+S (Command+S), and, for Windows users, a Save button on the Main toolbar. When you select any of these methods to store your file the first time, the Save dialog box (see Figure 4-6) automatically opens.

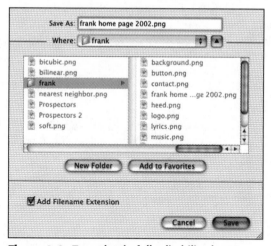

Figure 4-6: To maintain full editability, be sure to save every working graphic as a master Fireworks file, in addition to exporting it as a GIF, JPEG, or other format.

Cross-
Reference

To get all the details on exporting from Fireworks, see Chapter 15.

Saving a file after the initial save overwrites the existing file. If you would like to store multiple versions of the same file, Fireworks gives you two options: Save As and Save a Copy. Save As enables you to rename the file, and continue working with the newly saved file, while Save a Copy enables you to store a backup file in another folder (without saving the current document under its own name as well). Both are accessed in an identical manner. Choose File ➪ Save As or File ➪ Save a Copy to open the Save dialog box. Enter the new filename or navigate to a new folder in which to store the file (or both) and press the Save button.

Closing a file

When you're finished with a document but want to continue working in Fireworks, you can close the file in one of several ways:

✦ Choose File ➪ Close.

✦ Use one of the keyboard shortcuts, Ctrl+W (Command+W) or Ctrl+F4 (Windows only).

✦ Click the document window's Close button.

If the document has not been saved since the last modification, Fireworks asks whether you want to save the file before proceeding. You can identify documents that have not been saved (said to be "dirty") by the "dirty-dot" asterisk (see Figure 4-7) that Fireworks places in the title bar of document windows with unsaved changes. Document windows that don't have the asterisk in the title bar are exactly the same as the file saved on disk.

Dirty-dot asterisk

Figure 4-7: The "dirty-dot" asterisk enables you to identify documents with unsaved changes at a glance.

Reverting to a saved file

Part of the joy of computer graphics is the capability to try different approaches without fear of losing your earlier work. I'm a big fan of the Revert command, which enables you to completely alter a graphic and then restore it to its last-saved condition with one command. Among Revert, Undo, Save a Copy, and the History panel, you have a lot of options for safe creative experimentation.

The Revert command is very straightforward to use. After you've made some changes to your graphic and want to return to the original, choose File ➪ Revert. Fireworks asks for confirmation to revert to the last saved version of the file, and, when confirmed, replaces the onscreen image with the stored version.

Modifying Canvases

What do you mean, you want to change the size of your canvas? And its color, too? Are you saying you're not perfect and didn't predict needing these alterations? Don't worry, you're certainly not alone. In fact, most of my images undergo some degree of document surgery before they're done. It's the nature and the glory of computer graphics in general, and Fireworks in particular, to be very forgiving about changes.

In Fireworks, you can easily change the size of a complete image and its canvas, just the canvas dimensions, or the canvas color. It's very easy to expand the canvas in a particular direction, making it wider on the right, for example, either visually with the Crop tool, numerically with the command Modify ➪ Canvas ➪ Canvas Size, or via the Property inspector.

New Feature   Fireworks MX adds the ability to modify the canvas via its new Property inspector.

Altering the canvas size

Sometimes, the canvas is perfectly sized for all the objects it contains, but you may want to add another object, or apply a Glow or similar effect around an existing object, and there's no room. On the other hand, very often you start out with a canvas larger than necessary and you need to trim the canvas to fit the image. Whatever the situation, Fireworks has you covered.

Fireworks offers three different methods for enlarging or reducing the canvas: numerically, using a menu command; visually, using the Crop tool; or actually, according to the image, by trimming the canvas.

Specifying a new canvas size numerically

Quite often, I find myself needing to add a drop shadow and realize that I have to expand the canvas just a few pixels to the right and down for the effect to fit. With Fireworks, you can expand the canvas from the center out, or in any of eight specific directions. Naturally, only the size of the canvas is modified; the objects it contains don't change at all, except for their placement on the canvas.

The key concept to understand when you're resizing the canvas numerically is the anchor. The placement of the anchor (handled through the Canvas Size dialog box) determines how the canvas changes to meet the newly input dimensions. By default, the anchor is placed in the center of the canvas. If, for example, the canvas dimensions were increased by 100 pixels horizontally and 100 pixels vertically with a center anchor, the canvas edge would increase by 50 on all four sides. However, if the upper-left anchor was chosen and the same increase in dimensions entered, the canvas would increase by 100 pixels on the right and bottom border; because the upper-left is the anchor, the canvas in that corner does not change. You can think of the anchor as specifying where on the new canvas the old canvas should be.

To resize the canvas numerically, follow these steps:

1. Choose Modify ⇨ Canvas ⇨ Canvas Size or click on a blank portion of the canvas or workspace and click the Canvas Size button on the Property inspector. The Canvas Size dialog box opens, as shown in Figure 4-8.

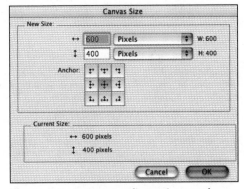

Figure 4-8: Enter new dimensions and select an anchor point in the Canvas Size dialog box to alter the canvas size.

2. To alter the dimensions of the canvas horizontally, enter a new value in the width (the horizontal double-headed arrow) text box.

3. To alter the dimensions of the canvas vertically, enter a new value in the height (the vertical double-headed arrow) text box.

Fireworks always displays the original canvas size in pixels in the Current Size section of the dialog box.

4. To alter the canvas size by inches or centimeters rather than the default pixels, select the arrow button next to the width and height drop-down lists and choose the desired alternative. The dimensions in pixels appear to the right of the height and width text boxes.

5. Choose one of the buttons inside the Anchor grid to determine how the canvas will expand or contract.

6. Click OK when you're done.

Using the Crop tool

Resizing the canvas numerically is great when you have to match a specific width or height for your image. Unfortunately, it can also take a lot of trial and error to get the tightest fit for an effect, like a glow or a drop shadow. The Crop tool provides a much faster method. Cropping is a familiar concept to anyone who has ever worked with photographs and needs to eliminate extraneous imagery. To *crop* means to cut off the excess. In addition to making the image smaller by cutting away the canvas, the Crop tool can expand the canvas as well.

The Crop tool works by enabling you to draw a rectangle with numerous sizing handles around an image. You then use these sizing handles to adjust the dimensions and shape of the cropped area. When the cropped region looks right, a double-click in the defined area completes the operation. The cropping border can stretch out past the edge of the canvas and, when double-clicked, the canvas is extended to the new cropped area.

Find the Crop tool in the Fireworks Tools panel, second from the top on the right. You can also use the keyboard shortcut by pressing C.

Using the Crop tool to extend the canvas, as shown in Figure 4-9, requires an additional step. When you first use the Crop tool and try to draw on the outside of the current canvas, you'll find that Fireworks snaps the cropping border to the edge of the canvas. As most designers are familiar with using the Crop tool to remove excess canvas, this starting point is convenient for most operations. To extend the cropping border, you then need to drag any of the sizing handles to a new position outside the canvas.

Changing canvas size for a single image

If your document only contains a single bitmap image, many times you'll want to adjust the size of an entire completed image either up or down to make it fit properly in a Web page. Fireworks allows you to make your adjustments either through specifying absolute pixel values or relative percentages with the Image Size command and automatically sizes the canvas appropriately, enabling you to work with single images as you would in Photoshop.

You can maintain the original proportions of your graphic or stretch it in one direction or another. The Image Size command enables you to resample your image, as well as resize it. *Resampling* refers to the process of adding or subtracting pixels when the image is resized. Resizing always works better with object-oriented (or vector-based) graphics than with bitmap graphics, especially when you're scaling to a larger size. However, Fireworks offers you a choice of interpolation methods to help create a scaled image that looks great.

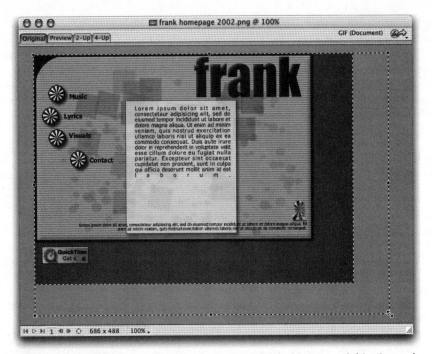

Figure 4-9: Adding some more canvas to the right and bottom of this Fireworks document is easy with the Crop tool.

Fireworks enables you to independently alter the onscreen pixel dimensions and the print size by changing the print resolution of the image. With this capability, you can print a higher or lower resolution of the image at the original image size. It does, however, proportionately alter the pixel dimensions of the image for onscreen presentation. In Figure 4-10, for example, the original image on the top is 1440×657 pixels — although it's been zoomed to a 25 percent view in Fireworks — with a print size of roughly 20×9 inches at 72 pixels per inch. The image on the bottom has been resized by setting the resolution to 18 pixels per inch (one-quarter of the original resolution) and is now only 360×164 pixels. The two images will print at the same size, though, with the resized one lacking one-quarter of the detail.

Note　Once again, if you're using Fireworks exclusively to create online images — as most of us are — stay entirely away from the Print Size settings and resize your images using the Pixel Dimensions settings in the Image Size dialog box.

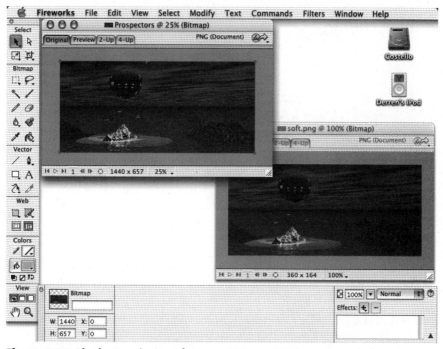

Figure 4-10: The bottom image, shown at 100 percent, was resampled at one-quarter the size of the original image, shown at 25 percent.

To alter the image size, follow these steps:

1. Choose Modify ➪ Canvas ➪ Image Size, or click on a blank portion of the canvas and click the Image Size button on the Property inspector. The Image Size dialog box opens, as shown in Figure 4-11.

2. To alter the dimensions of the image proportionately, enter a new value in width (the horizontal double-headed arrow) or height (the vertical double-headed arrow) text boxes.

Tip

If the default option, Constrain Proportions, is selected, changing one value causes the other to change as well.

Caution

It's better to select the entire value in the text boxes first and then enter in your new number. If you try to backspace through each digit, you'll encounter an alert when you delete the final number. Fireworks warns you that you're entering an invalid number because it interprets this as trying to reduce the dimensions below one.

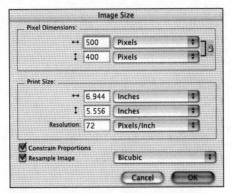

Figure 4-11: To proportionately enlarge or reduce your entire graphic, use the Image Size command.

3. To alter the dimensions by percentage rather than by pixel measurement, select the arrow button next to the width or height drop-down lists and choose Percent.

4. To use the print size as a guide for adjusting the image size, enter a value in the Print Size width and height text boxes.

5. To alter the print size by percentage or centimeters rather than the default inches, select the arrow button next to the Print Size width and height drop-down lists and choose the desired alternative.

6. To change the number of pixels per inch, enter a new value in the Resolution text box.

7. To disable the proportional sizing, deselect the Constrain Proportions option.

8. To change the print size but not the onscreen image, deselect the Resample Image option and choose new values for the Print Size width and height text boxes. When Resample Image is deselected, the Pixel Dimensions section becomes unavailable.

9. Choose an interpolation method from the interpolation method option list. Bicubic is the default and works well for most images.

Cross-Reference

A complete description of the various interpolation methods Fireworks offers is available in Chapter 6.

10. Click OK when you're done.

Trimming the canvas

What's the fastest, most accurate way to reduce the canvas to just the essential objects? Trim it, of course. If you've ever trimmed a real canvas with a razor-sharp matte knife, you know it's a very dramatic, fast operation. However, the Trim Canvas command is even faster — it handles four edges at once and there's no need to keep a supply of bandages.

The beauty of the Trim Canvas command is that it's all automatic — you don't even have to select any objects for Fireworks to trim to. Moreover, this feature even takes into account soft edges such as glows or drop shadows, so you can't accidentally truncate your effect. In fact, it's a great command to use in combination with other canvas expanders, such as the Crop tool or Canvas Size. Just open up the canvas more than you think necessary, make the alterations, and then choose Modify ➪ Canvas ➪ Trim Canvas. Presto! All the canvas edges are hugging the graphics as tightly as possible.

> **Note**   As the name indicates, Trim Canvas can only make your overall document size smaller; it can't expand it if part of the image is moved off the canvas. To expand the canvas to best fit all your artwork, you can use the Fit Canvas command. To access it choose Modify ➪ Canvas ➪ Fit Canvas

Picking a new canvas color

Although you set the canvas color when you create the document, you're by no means stuck with it. You can adjust the color at any point by choosing Modify ➪ Canvas ➪ Canvas Color or by selecting the Canvas color chip on the Property inspector. Using the menus, the Canvas Color dialog box opens. This replicates the Canvas Color section of the New Document dialog box. Again, you have three choices: White, Transparent, and Custom Color. Selecting the arrow button next to Custom Color has the same result as clicking the Canvas color chip on the Property inspector: it opens the color picker with the palette of 216 Web-safe choices (see Figure 4-12). For a wider color selection, click the Palette button on the color picker to display your operating system's color picker(s).

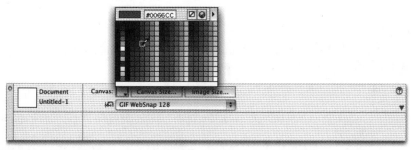

Figure 4-12: The color picker on the Property inspector is useful for quickly picking a Web-safe color for the canvas.

Tip   If you open a Photoshop or Fireworks 1.0 document, you may find that a solid-color Background layer is created. Hide this layer by clicking the Show/Hide Layer icon next to it in the Layers panel in order to see your document's actual canvas color.

Rotating the canvas

Although you can rotate objects with the Transform tools, the canvas itself always stays in the same place. If your canvas is not square, rotating a group of objects 90 degrees often leaves them hanging off the canvas. Instead of rotating objects, rotate the entire canvas by choosing Modify ➪ Canvas ➪ Rotate 180 degrees, Modify ➪ Canvas ➪ Rotate 90 degrees CW (clockwise), or Modify ➪ Canvas ➪ Rotate 90 degrees CCW (counterclockwise).

Tip   If you rotate any objects, and some portion of them ends up off of the canvas, you can use the Fit Canvas command, accessed via Modify ➪ Canvas ➪ Fit Canvas, to resize the canvas so that all objects are visible.

Summary

Setting up your document is the basis for all the work you do in Fireworks. Whether you're starting with the fresh slate of a new document, or opening an existing file, Fireworks gives you all the tools you need to build a solid foundation and modify it when necessary. When working with your objects, keep the following points in mind:

✦ The more you can visualize your graphics and thus design the canvas, the less time you'll spend making modifications.

✦ When you're creating a new document, Fireworks enables you to set the height, width, print resolution, and color of the canvas.

✦ Fireworks can open more than a dozen different file formats, including common ones such as TIFF, FreeHand, and Photoshop.

✦ You can open multiple files simultaneously.

✦ To get the most out of Fireworks, always save at least one version of your graphic in the native PNG format.

✦ You can alter the canvas size using any one of three different methods: Canvas Size, the Crop tool, or Trim Canvas.

✦ You can modify the canvas color or rotate the canvas at any time.

In the next chapter, you begin exploring the heart of Fireworks graphics: objects.

Mastering the Tools

T he Fireworks approach to graphics is fundamentally different from any other tool on the market. Consequently, you'll need to travel the short learning curve before you can get the most out of Fireworks. The early chapters in Part II cover all the essentials, from basic object creation, to full-blown photo manipulation.

Color is a key component of any graphic designer's tool kit, and color on the Web requires special attention, as you'll see in Chapter 7. The object-oriented nature of Fireworks is explored in chapters on creating simple strokes and combining paths in a variety of ways to help you make more sophisticated graphics. Fireworks excels at creating graphical text for the Web — you'll see how in Chapter 10.

Creating Vector Objects

Vector objects are the foundation of Fireworks. Don't get me wrong: All the other elements — bitmap objects, Web objects, Live Effects, and more — are vital, but vector objects are what give Fireworks its flexibility, precise control, and pervasive editability. They're what separate Fireworks from its contemporaries, such as Adobe Photoshop or ImageReady.

As you might suspect, a great number of Fireworks tools and features focus on vector objects. This chapter covers the basic vector operations — creation of the simple, geometric shapes and freeform lines and drawings — that draw special attention to one of the most difficult to master, but most rewarding concepts: Bézier curves.

Understanding Vector Objects in Fireworks

A Fireworks vector object is a free-floating vector-based graphic. Vector graphics are also called path-based, or simply *drawings*. Unlike bitmap objects that use rows of pixels to form mosaic-like images, vector objects use lines, or more accurately, the description of a line. Instead of plotting a series of pixels on the screen, a vector-based graphic basically says, "Start a line at position X, Y and draw it to position A, B." Or, "Draw a circle with a midpoint at C, D and make it 1.5 inches in diameter." Of course, you don't see all these instructions on the screen — it's all under the hood of the graphics engine — but it's what enables drawing programs, such as FreeHand and Adobe Illustrator, to maintain a smooth line, regardless of how the image is scaled.

Whereas Fireworks vector objects maintain the underlying path structure, their surfaces are composed of pixels. Although this may seem to be a contradiction, it's really at the heart of Fireworks' brilliance as a graphics tool. Whenever you modify a vector object — slanting a rectangle, for example — Fireworks first applies the modification to the path structure, and then reapplies the pixel surface. It is as if an image of a ballerina in a magazine suddenly is alive, leaping across the stage, and then it becomes an image again.

Examining Paths

Vector objects begin as *paths*. Paths are lines with at least two points. Whether you draw a squiggly line with the Pencil tool, or a multipoint star with the Polygon tool, the outline of your drawing is what is referred to as the path. Although Fireworks highlights selected paths for editing, by themselves paths are invisible and won't appear in your exported images at all (see Figure 5-1).

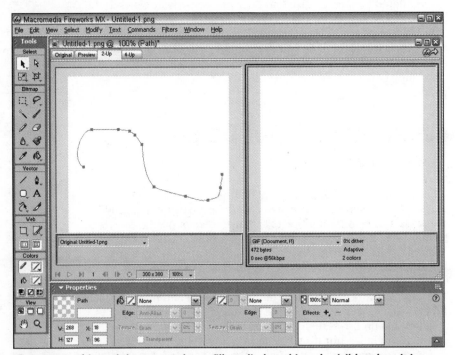

Figure 5-1: This path has no stroke or fill applied, and is only visible when it is selected for editing. The preview on the right shows that the path itself is invisible in Fireworks output.

Applying a stroke

To make a path visible, you have to apply a *stroke* to see the outline. You can quickly apply a stroke to a selected object by choosing a color from the Stroke color well, located on the Tools panel, or on the Property inspector. Performing this action via the Tools panel applies a 1-pixel Pencil stroke with a soft or *antialiased* edge. Selecting it from the Property inspector gives you whatever stroke settings were used last. Strokes can vary in category, color, width, softness, and texture, to name a few characteristics; several examples of different strokes are shown in Figure 5-2. You'll notice in the figure how, regardless of their different attributes, strokes always follow the path of the vector object.

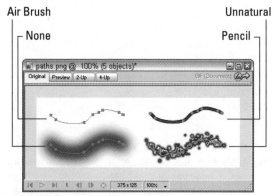

Figure 5-2: You can see the same path in each of these different strokes.

Cross-Reference Part of Fireworks' power is derived from the wide range of strokes possible. To find out more about strokes, see Chapter 8.

Looking at open and closed paths

The two types of paths are *open* and *closed*. The difference between the two is simple: A closed path connects its two endpoints (the start and finish of the line, also often referred to as origin and endpoints of a path), and an open path doesn't. Closed paths define different shapes, whether standard, such as a circle or polygon, or custom, such as a freeform drawing. Just as a stroke gives the outline of a path substance, a *fill* makes the interior of a path visible. As with strokes, fills come in different categories, colors, and textures. In addition, a *pattern* can be used as a fill. You can even change the softness of a fill's edge. As Figure 5-3 shows, regardless of what the interior fill is, it always follows the established path.

Pattern fill   Gradient fill

┌ Selected with no fill   Solid fill ┐

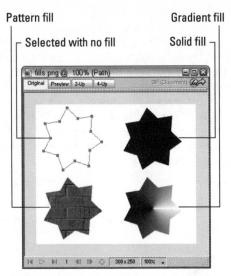

Figure 5-3: A vector object can be filled
with a solid color, a gradient, or a pattern.

Tip

Even though fills are most often applied to closed-path vector objects, it's perfectly
legal to apply a fill to an open-path vector object — although the results are not as
predictable. But then, that's one of the beauties of computer graphics — try it and if
you don't like it, undo it. This is one of the many features that sets Fireworks apart
from other vector drawing applications.

Grasping the center point

One common feature that all objects in Fireworks share is a *center point*. With vector objects, the location of the center point depends on whether the path is open or
closed. If the path is open, the center point is located in the center of the object's
bounding box. If the path is closed, it's located in the center of the object. Center
points are useful when you need to rotate an object. You can also adjust the center
point of an object when its transform handles are visible in order to rotate it around
a different axis, or control how its center aligns to other objects.

**Cross-
Reference**

Discover how to work with rotation in Chapter 9.

Examining direction

The final point to keep in mind about vector objects is that their paths all have
direction. Though it's more obvious with an object such as a line that you start
drawing at one point and finish at another, it's true even with rectangles and
ellipses. Generally, Fireworks draws vector objects in a clockwise direction, starting

at the upper-left corner of rectangles or squares and the left center of an ellipse or circle, as shown in Figure 5-4. Path direction becomes important when you begin attaching text to a path—wrapping a slogan around a circle, for example. Fireworks includes several tools for adjusting the path's direction.

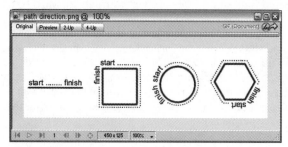

Figure 5-4: A path's direction determines how text is attached.

Starting from Shapes

Most Fireworks documents include many vector objects of different shapes, sizes, colors, and attributes. Drawing shapes sounds easy, but you must understand how to create each of the basic elements to get the greatest effect in the shortest amount of time.

Fireworks provides tools for creating a series of basic geometric shapes—rectangles, ellipses, and polygons—as well as those for drawing structured and freeform lines. All of these tools will be familiar to anyone who has worked with a vector drawing program in the last few years. In fact, many of the key shortcuts are industry-standard. This chapter, though, is written for a complete novice. Even if you've neve used a computer to draw before, you can have a full understanding of the basic tools in Fireworks after working your way through this chapter.

Tip If you have access to a graphics tablet, don't be afraid to use it here. Drawing is always easier with a pen and tablet than with a mouse.

The quickest way to create a Web page design, particularly the often-required navigational buttons, is to use one of Fireworks' shape-building tools. Although at first glance there only seem to be four such tools—the Rectangle, Rounded Rectangle, Ellipse, and Polygon—these tools each have options that enable them to produce a wide range of objects.

Tip It can be helpful to keep the Property inspector or the Info panel visible while you draw or edit vector objects. They both display the pixel width and height of new objects as they are drawn, making it easy to create a 50×50-pixel square, for example. The Property inspector and the Info panel also inform you of the canvas position of objects as you work with them.

Examining rectangles and squares

My dictionary defines a rectangle as "any four-sided figure with four right angles." A Web designer generally sees a rectangle as a basic building block for designs that are, after all, going to be viewed within the rectangular confines of a browser window. The Rectangle and Rounded Rectangle tools are very straightforward to use and offer a number of very useful options.

The two Rectangle tools are functionally the same. Anything you can do with one, you can do with the other. The difference between them is that the rectangles you draw with the Rounded Rectangle tool have rounded corners, whereas the Rectangle tool creates rectangles with perfectly square corners. You can even create a standard rectangle with the Rectangle tool, and then make it rounded by altering the Roundness setting in the Property inspector.

Creating rectangles

As with almost every other computer drawing tool on the planet, Fireworks creates rectangles using the familiar click-and-drag method. To draw a rectangle in Fireworks, follow these steps:

1. Select the Rectangle tool or use the keyboard shortcut, U.

2. Click once to select your originating corner and drag to the opposite corner to form the rectangle, as shown in Figure 5-5. As you drag your pointer, Fireworks draws a preview outline of the form.

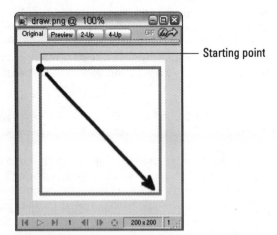

Starting point

Figure 5-5: Once you've selected your originating corner with the Rectangle tool, you can drag out a box shape in any direction, as indicated by the arrow.

3. Release the mouse button when the rectangle is the desired size and shape. If any stroke or fill has been previously set, these attributes are drawn when you release the mouse button.

Using keyboard modifiers

You can use three keyboard modifiers with the Rectangle or Rounded Rectangle tool: Shift, Alt (Option), and the spacebar in order to apply some very commonly required behaviors while drawing.

New Feature

Fireworks now has Spacebar Move! Without releasing the mouse button you can press and hold the spacebar to temporarily enable the hand tool while you're drawing. This allows you to pause drawing, move your shape, and then continue drawing instead of requiring you to start from scratch in a new position.

✦ **To create a square:** You can easily make your rectangle into a square by pressing Shift while you drag out your shape. Unlike some other graphics programs, you don't have to press Shift before you begin drawing; pressing Shift at any time while you're drawing causes Fireworks to increase the shorter sides to match the longer sides of the rectangle to form a square.

✦ **To draw from the center:** To draw your rectangle from the center instead of from the corner, press Alt (Option) when dragging out the shape. While Alt (Option) is held down, Fireworks uses the distance from your originating point to the current pointer position as the radius, rather than the diameter of the shape. As with Shift, you can press Alt (Option) at any time when drawing to change to a center origin, as shown in Figure 5-6.

✦ **Spacebar Move:** While not a typical keyboard modifier key, I've included it here because of the way it impacts your workflow. In those circumstances in which you begin drawing your rectangle, only to find that it's not quite where you want it, you can hold down the spacebar, reposition your work, release the spacebar, and continue dragging out your rectangle. This can be a huge time saver.

Tip

Of course, you can use Shift and Alt (Option) together to draw a square from the center. In fact, you can throw the spacebar into the mix if you find that you need to move your square before you're finished drawing it.

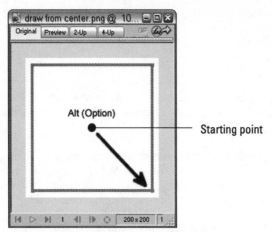

Figure 5-6: Holding down Alt (Option) while drawing a shape centers the shape around your starting point.

You can use the Info panel or the Property inspector to check the pixel placement of your rectangle as you are drawing. One section displays the Width and Height (marked with a W and H) dynamically, while another displays the X, Y coordinates of the upper-left point of the rectangle, even if it is being drawn from the center.

Working with rounded corners

The square and the circle are the most basic shapes, and are obviously useful for the Web designer in a number of ways. Fireworks also offers a pleasant and useful shape that's somewhere in between: the Rounded Rectangle. Whereas rectangles that are created with the Rectangle tool have perfectly square corners, the Rounded Rectangle tool creates rectangles with rounded corners. The most obvious use for rounded rectangles is more aesthetically pleasing square buttons. Rounding squares and rectangles used as design elements can also quickly lead to a better-looking graphic.

You can specify the degree of roundness that the Rounded Rectangle tool creates by selecting the tool and then changing the Roundness option on the Property inspector. Fireworks continues to use that setting for new Rounded Rectangles you create until you change it again. You can also alter the setting for any rectangle you've already created by changing the Roundness setting on the Property inspector when a rectangle is selected.

Select a rectangle to choose how rounded you want the corners to appear, by entering a value in the Rectangle Roundness text box or by using the Roundness slider. The Roundness scale is percentage-based: 0 represents a standard rectangle with perfectly square corners and 100 creates a fully rounded rectangle — also known as a circle. As Figure 5-7 shows, the higher the Rectangle Roundness value, the more rounded the rectangle's corners become.

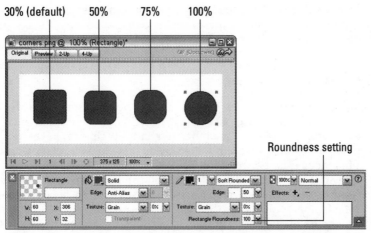

Figure 5-7: Select a rectangle and use the Rectangle Roundness setting in the Stroke section of the Property inspector to determine the degree of roundness for your rectangle or square's corners.

Exactly how Fireworks applies the Rectangle Roundness percentage is most easily explained with an example. Let's say you draw a rectangle 100 pixels wide by 50 pixels tall, and then give it a Rectangle Roundness value of 50 percent. As shown in Figure 5-8, Fireworks plots the points of the corner 50 pixels along the top edge (50% of 100 pixels = 50 pixels) and 25 pixels along the side edge (50% of 50 pixels = 25 pixels). The resulting arc makes the corner. If you created an ellipse with a horizontal diameter of 50 pixels and a vertical one of 25, it would fit right into the newly rounded corner.

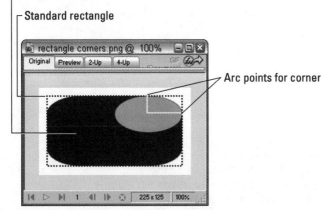

Figure 5-8: Fireworks draws the rounded corner of a rectangle according to a percentage formula.

Tip   While you are drawing your Rounded Rectangle, you can press the up or down cursor keys (or 1 and 2) on your keyboard to change the Rounded Rectangle percentage before you release the mouse button. Roundness adjustment on the fly!

Using ellipses and circles

In Fireworks, ellipses and circles are created in exactly the same manner as rectangles and squares. Clicking the mouse once sets the origin point, and then the shape is drawn out as you drag the pointer. Even the Shift and Alt (Option) keyboard modifiers and Spacebar Move function in the same way as they do with rectangles. In fact, only two differences exist between the Rectangle tools and the Ellipse tool. First, it's pretty obvious that no need exists for an ellipse function equivalent to the Roundness option for rectangles; ellipses are already rounded. Second — less apparent, but notable nonetheless — is the fact that the origin point of an ellipse or a circle never appears on its path. This fact is particularly important for novice designers who are trying to place an ellipse correctly.

Using an imaginary bounding box

When Fireworks draws an ellipse, an imaginary bounding box is used, as shown in Figure 5-9. The origin point of the bounding box acts as one corner, while the end point becomes the opposite corner. As with rectangles, if Alt (Option) is pressed, the center point is used as the origin for drawing. In either case, neither the origin nor the end point is located on the path of the ellipse. It's as though you're drawing a rectangle, and Fireworks fits an ellipse inside it when you're done.

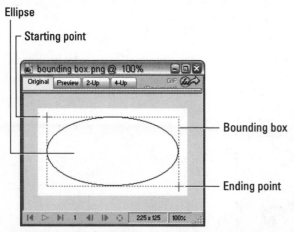

Figure 5-9: When you drag out a circle or oval using the Ellipse tool, Fireworks draws the shape using an imaginary bounding box, indicated by the dashed rectangle.

It's particularly helpful to keep the concept of the imaginary bounding box in mind when you are trying to align ellipses of different sizes. The Align commands and snapping to the grid work by using an ellipse's bounding box rather than the drawn path of the shape.

Drawing an ellipse or circle

To draw an ellipse or a circle, follow these steps:

1. Select the Ellipse tool. If the Ellipse tool is not visible, click and hold the Rectangle, Rounded Rectangle, or Polygon tool until the flyout appears, and then choose the Ellipse tool.

You can also press U until the Ellipse tool is selected. The U key shortcut cycles through the shape tools.

2. Click once to select the origin point and drag to the opposite corner to create the ellipse. As you drag your pointer, Fireworks draws a preview outline of the form.

You can refine the positioning of your ellipse or circle by temporarily holding the spacebar while you drag.

3. Release the mouse button when the ellipse is the desired size and shape. If any stroke or fill has been set, these attributes are drawn when you release the mouse button.

4. To draw a circle, press the Shift key while you are drawing the ellipse.

5. To draw an ellipse or circle that uses the center point of the shape as the origin, press the Alt (Option) key while you are drawing.

Combine the Alt (Option) key with the Shift modifier key to draw perfect circles and squares from the center.

Exploring polygons and stars

In Fireworks, the Polygon tool creates many-sided objects where all the sides — and all the angles connecting the sides — are the same. The technical term for this type of geometric shape is an *equilateral polygon*. Fireworks permits the graphic designer to specify the number of sides, from 3 to 25. You can also use the Polygon tool to create a special type of polygon, a star. Star shapes can be drawn with anywhere from 3 to 25 points (and thus, 6 to 50 sides). Moreover, Fireworks gives you the option of either specifying the angles for the star points, or having the program assign them automatically based on the number of sides.

Looking at a drag-and-draw affair

As with rectangles and ellipses, making polygons is a drag-and-draw affair. Click once to set the origin point and then drag out the shape. However, that's where the similarities end. With polygons, there's only one possible origin point: the center—there is no keyboard modifier to switch to an outside edge. You'll also immediately notice as you draw your first polygon that you can quickly set both the size and the rotation. Dragging the pointer straight out from the origin increases the dimensions of the polygon; moving the pointer side to side rotates it around its midpoint.

Drawing a polygon

To draw a polygon, follow these steps:

1. Select the Polygon tool by clicking and holding the Rectangle, Rounded Rectangle, or Ellipse tool until the flyout appears, and then choosing the Polygon button. Alternatively, press the keyboard shortcut, U, until the Polygon tool is visible.

2. To set the number of sides for a polygon:

   • Go to the Property inspector and make sure the shape type is set to Polygon (instead of Star).

   • Next, enter a value in the Sides text box, or use the Sides slider.

3. Click and hold down the mouse button where you want the center of the polygon to appear and drag out the polygon shape. Fireworks displays a preview of the polygon as you draw.

 Tip   You can use Spacebar Move to refine the positioning of your polygon by temporarily holding the spacebar while you drag.

4. Rotate the polygon to the desired position by moving your pointer from side to side.

5. Release the mouse button when you're done. Fireworks draws the polygon with the current stroke and fill settings.

Fireworks interprets the distance from the origin point to the release point as the radius to each of the points on the polygon. As you can see in Figure 5-10, just changing the number of sides results in a wide range of basic shapes.

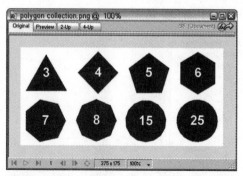

Figure 5-10: Polygons in Fireworks can have up to 25 sides — although anything above 15 tends to resemble a circle.

Pressing the Shift key while drawing a polygon constrains a side's angle to a multiple of 45 degrees. Because each shape, as it is initially drawn, is equilateral — with identical sides and angles — you only notice a couple of variations for each type of polygon. When drawing a hexagon and constraining the angle with the Shift key, you only notice three differently angled shapes, although you can actually draw eight (eight increments of 45 degrees are in a full 360-degree circle).

Tip

For most polygons, you can draw it so that the bottom of the shape is parallel to the bottom of your canvas, by either dragging straight up or straight to one side while holding down the Shift key.

Examining automatic angles

Although you can specify up to 25 sides for a polygon, polygons with more than 10 or 15 sides begin to resemble a circle. Not so with Fireworks stars, which, with the proper angle setting, can create very distinctive graphics with any number of sides. Fireworks offers both automatic and customizable angle options. When Automatic Angles is selected (the default), Fireworks draws stars so that the opposite arms are automatically aligned. With a five-pointed star, such as the one shown in the lower-left of Figure 5-11, the tops of the left and right arms are aligned.

Five-pointed star

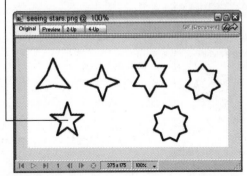

Figure 5-11: All of these stars were drawn with the Automatic Angle option enabled. Notice that the opposing points on these stars mirror each other's angles.

As is readily apparent in Figure 5-11, the automatic angles on stars with a higher number of sides tend to flatten out the sharpness of the points. These types of angles are known as *obtuse* angles. An obtuse angle is one over 90 degrees. The opposite of an obtuse angle is an *acute* angle. Acute angles create much sharper points on stars, as shown in Figure 5-12. To create an acute star in Fireworks, you need to enter a custom value in the Angle text box.

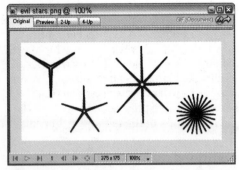

Figure 5-12: Create acute stars by lowering the Angle value in the Property inspector and drawing with Star selected for the Polygon tool type.

Creating a star

To create a star in Fireworks, follow these steps:

1. As with drawing a regular polygon, select the Polygon tool. If it is not visible, click and hold the Rectangle, Rounded Rectangle, or Ellipse tool until the flyout appears, and then choose the Polygon button. Alternatively, you can repeatedly press the keyboard shortcut, U, until the Polygon tool is visible.

2. In the Property inspector, change the shape type by selecting Star from the drop down list.

3. To change the number of points, enter a value in the Sides text box, or use the Sides slider.

4. To change the angle of the star arms, enter a value in the Angle text box, or use the Angle slider.

Tip   Use lower numbers for sharper points and higher numbers for blunter ones.

5. If you want to use the Fireworks predetermined angle for your star, choose the Automatic checkbox.

6. Click on the canvas to set the origin point for the center of the star and drag out to the desired size and rotation.

Tip   You can use Spacebar Move to refine the positioning of your star by temporarily holding the spacebar while you drag.

7. Release the mouse when you're done. As with any other shape, Fireworks applies the current stroke, fill, or effect setting, if any.

Drawing Lines and Freeform Paths

The path drawing tools in Fireworks primarily vary according to how structured they are. At one end of the spectrum is the Line tool, which only draws single straight lines; at the other end is the Vector Path tool which is completely freeform. In the middle (leaning more toward the Line tool) is the Pen tool, which draws mathematically accurate curves.

As with a geometric shape, a path is invisible unless a particular stroke or fill is applied to it. If the two endpoints that define a line are joined, the path is said to be closed. When you're drawing paths and two endpoints are about to be joined, Fireworks displays a special square cursor badge. If the two endpoints of a line are not joined, the path is said to be open. Unlike most vector drawing tools, Fireworks enables you to apply fills to open paths, as well as closed.

Precisely Adjusting a Shape's Dimensions and Position

As with any graphic design, Web graphics are a blend of visual flair and precise placement. To many artists, an image isn't right until it's aligned just so. Whereas much of Fireworks' interface enables very intuitive drawing with a mouse or graphics pad, you can also position and size objects numerically through the Property inspector or the Info panel.

Typically, I use the Info panel to get a general sense of the dimensions of an object or its X, Y coordinates. For those occasions when I need to render an exact rectangle, one that's exactly 205 pixels wide by 166 high, say, and starts at 20 pixels in from the left and 35 pixels down, I use the Property inspector. With Fireworks, you can rough out your shape and placement, and then numerically resize and reposition the object. You can enter values into each of the four text boxes on the Property inspector representing the dimensions and the position of the bounding box surrounding the object. If the object were a circle or a triangle, for example, the height and width displayed would be that of the invisible rectangle encompassing them.

To specify a new dimension or placement of an object, follow these steps:

1. Select the object you want to alter.

2. Double-click the value that you want to change in the Property inspector, or the Info panel. The four possibilities are

   - W (width)

   - H (height)

   - X (horizontal origin)

   - Y (vertical origin)

3. Enter a new value.

4. Confirm your entry by pressing Tab. Fireworks changes the selected object.

5. To change another value, repeat Steps 2–4.

Making straight lines

The Line tool is perhaps the simplest member of the Fireworks Tools panel. Click and hold to set the beginning of the line, drag in any direction, and release to set the end of the line. Two endpoints and a straight line in between; that's it and there's not a whole lot more to the tool. Straight lines are, by definition, open paths. You can only display the fill settings on a straight line if you set the stroke to none. You can also apply effects and Styles to Line-created paths, as shown in Figure 5-13.

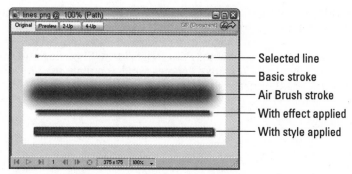

Figure 5-13: The Line tool draws straight-as-a-ruler lines that can take on a stroke setting and even an effect.

To use the Line tool, follow these steps:

1. Select the Line tool or use the keyboard shortcut, N.

2. Position the pointer where you would like the line to begin and click and hold the mouse button.

Tip

Holding down the Shift key while drawing with the Line tool draws perfectly horizontal or vertical lines only. Many drawing tools take advantage of the Shift modifier to make drawing common shapes more convenient.

3. When the line is at the desired size and angle, release the mouse button.

Drawing with the Vector Path tool

The Vector Path tool is also a drag-and-draw tool, but without any of the restraints imposed on all the other tools. Anything you can draw with a mouse or graphics tablet, you can draw with the Vector Path tool. As you move your pointer on the screen, Fireworks tracks the movements and plots points to replicate your drawing. Remember, these are vector objects not bitmap objects like the brush tool; to draw a perfectly straight line, Fireworks only needs two points to depict the line. All the points that make up a line can be edited — moved, deleted, or increased — and the line changes accordingly.

Cross-Reference

Fireworks not only tracks your pointer's movement across the screen, it also follows the speed with which you draw your lines. With certain strokes, such as Watercolor and Charcoal, the velocity is translated visually when the stroke is rendered. For more details on varying your strokes, see Chapter 8.

Freehand drawing with the mouse is particularly difficult, and many artists avoid it whenever possible. I prefer a graphics tablet and highly recommend them to others whenever I get the chance. For some images that require an unrestrained look— such as the fellow in Figure 5-14—the Vector Path tool is ideal. Choosing one of the Fireworks strokes that are pressure sensitive enables you to emulate the look of a calligraphy pen, a pencil, or other drawing implement.

Paths with
Calligraphy
Quill stroke

Selected
paths
only

Figure 5-14: Freehand drawing is best done with a graphics tablet using the Vector Path tool set to a pressure-sensitive stroke.

Applying strokes automatically

The major difference between this tool and all the other geometric shape tools (including Line), is that the Vector Path tool automatically applies a particular stroke, even if none is selected. This feature enables you to see all paths completed with the tool instantly—instead of having to wait until a stroke is selected and applied.

As noted previously, the Vector Path tool is capable of creating either open or closed paths. Remember, a closed path is one in which the beginning and final endpoints meet.

Using the Vector Path tool

To use the Vector Path tool, follow these steps:

1. Select the Vector Path tool, from the Pen tool flyout, or press the keyboard shortcut, P, to cycle through.

2. Click and drag the pointer on the canvas. Fireworks renders the drawn path with the current settings on the Stroke section of the Property inspector.

3. To draw a perpendicular line, press the Shift key while you're dragging the pointer. If your movement is primarily left to right, a horizontal line is drawn; if it is up and down, a vertical line is drawn.

Here's a rather interesting feature of the Vector Path tool: If you use the Shift key to constrain your path to a perpendicular line and then release the mouse button — but not the Shift key — a small plus sign appears next to a Paintbrush cursor. Draw another stroke (still holding down the Shift key), and Fireworks connects the final point of your previous stroke with the beginning point of your new stroke.

Constructing Bézier Curves

Remember those plastic stencils you used in school to trace different-size circles, stars, and other shapes? One of those "other shapes" was probably an asymmetrical, smoothly curving line that was referred to as a French curve. The Frenchman who invented this type of curve was a mathematician named Pierre Bézier. His theoretical work, collectively known as *Bézier curves,* forms the foundation for much of vector computer graphics, both in print through PostScript and on the screen through programs such as FreeHand, Illustrator, and, of course, Fireworks. The learning curve — pun definitely intended — for Bézier curves is a steep one, but it's one that every graphic designer using vectors must master. Bézier curves are amazingly flexible, often graceful to behold, and worth every bit of effort it takes to understand them fully. So let's get started.

Pierre Bézier's breakthrough was the realization that every line — whether it was straight or curved — could be mathematically described in the same way. Imagine a rainbow. The shape appears to start in one place, arch to the sky, and then land some distance away. The beginning and ending points of the rainbow are easily described; if we were plotting them on a piece of graph paper, we could set down their location as X and Y coordinates. But what about the arc itself? Consider an imaginary element in the sky that attracts the rainbow, almost magnetically, which causes the center of the rainbow to arch up, anchored by the beginning and ending points. Bézier postulated that every anchor point on a curve had two such magnetic elements, called *control points* — one that affects the curve going into the anchor point and one that affects it coming out of the anchor point, as shown in Figure 5-16. In the Bézier vernacular, an anchor point with curves on either side is called, naturally enough, a *curve anchor point.* An anchor point with a curve on just one side is known as a *corner anchor point.*

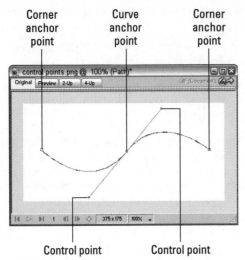

Corner anchor point   Curve anchor point   Corner anchor point

Control point   Control point

Figure 5-15: Use control points to alter the shape of a Bézier curve, as defined by the placement of the curve and corner anchor points.

Drawing lines with the Pen

Although all path objects use Bézier curves, Fireworks' primary tool for creating Bézier curves is the Pen tool. But how could a Bézier curve describe a straight line? When the control points are in the same location as the anchor points, the line is not pulled one way or the other; it remains straight. In fact, the Pen is terrific for creating connected straight lines. Unlike the Line tool, which draws a single straight line by clicking and dragging, the Pen draws a series of straight lines by plotting each point and enabling Fireworks to draw the connecting lines.

To draw a straight line with the Pen, follow these steps:

1. Select the Pen, or use its keyboard shortcut, P.

2. Click once where you want the line to start.

3. Move your pointer to where you want the line to end, and click once. Fireworks draws a path from your starting point to the second point.

To draw a continuing series of straight lines with the Pen, follow these steps:

1. Select the Pen, or use its keyboard shortcut, P.

2. Click once where you want the line to start.

3. Move your pointer to where you want the next point on the line to be, and either double-click to finish your line, or click once to add another point and continue drawing. Fireworks draws paths between the points as you work, as shown in Figure 5-16.

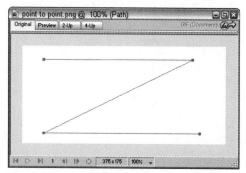

Figure 5-16: Create a Z with the Pen tool much like Zorro carves one with his sword, moving and clicking from point to point.

4. Repeat Step 3 as many times as is necessary to draw your series of lines.

As with the Brush and Pencil tools, you can close an open path created by the Pen by moving the pointer over the beginning point.

Creating smooth curves with the Pen

Laying out a series of straight lines is a fine feature, but the Pen tool really shines when it comes to drawing curves. The key difference between Pen-drawn lines and curves is that, with curves, you drag the pointer after you've set the anchor's position to drag out the control handles and start a curve, whereas with lines, there is no dragging whatsoever; you are just plotting corner points.

Follow these steps to create a smooth curve:

1. With the Pen tool, click and drag out control points where you want your curve to start. This creates an anchor point with control handles that is the start of your line.

2. Choose the location of your next anchor point, click to add it, and then drag to pull out the control handles. Fireworks joins the two points with a path. While keeping the mouse button held down, you can move your cursor to adjust the control points to set the angle of your curve. Let go of the mouse button when you're done (see Figure 5-17).

Click and
drag out handles

Click and drag out handles
or double-click to finish

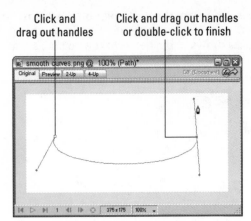

Figure 5-17: When you drag out one Bézier
curve, you begin to create this curve.

3. Select the Subselection tool and fine-tune your curve by manipulating the control points.

Tip

Hold down the Ctrl (Command) key while using the Pen tool to switch temporarily to the Subselection tool, which is suitable for manipulating control points. When you let go of the Ctrl (Command) key, the Pen tool is automatically selected again.

Mixing lines and curves

You can, of course, combine the straight and curved line techniques with the Pen by alternating just clicking with both clicking and dragging. However, because dragging a control point affects curves on either side of the curve point, placing a straight line directly next to a curve is often difficult. Fireworks uses the Alt (Option) key to constrain the control point that affects the previous curve, while permitting you to manipulate the current curve. As an example of this option, follow these steps to create a shape such as the one shown in Figure 5-18.

1. Use the straight-line capability of the Pen to draw the outer edge of the arch by clicking once for each of the outside points, starting at the inside left corner and moving in a clockwise direction. After you've drawn all the straight lines, you have the outer shell of the arch, minus the inner arc, completed.

2. Move your pointer back over the beginning point. The closed path cursor is displayed.

3. Click and hold the mouse button as if you are going to drag it. Press the Alt (Option) key while continuing to hold down the mouse button.

4. Drag the control point away from the arch. If Alt (Option) was not pressed, the connecting line (on the left side of the arch) would be affected by the control-point drag.

5. Release the mouse button when the arch is in the desired shape.

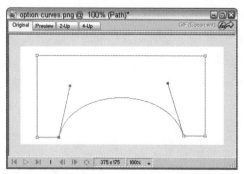

Figure 5-18: Use the Pen to manipulate Bézier curves and create objects with combinations of straight and curved lines.

You can also use this constraining property to draw uneven curves, where you drag a little bit before pressing Alt (Option) and effectively lock the previous curve.

Adjusting curves

The alternative name for the two control points in Bézier curves is *control handles*. As the name implies, you can grab and manipulate control handles. By changing the position of the control handle, you can adjust the shape of the curve. Here are a few guidelines for moving control handles:

✦ The closer the control handle is to its associated curve point, the flatter the curve.

✦ Alternatively, the further away the control handle is from its curve point, the steeper the curve.

✦ If a control handle is on top of its curve point, the curve becomes a straight line, and the curve point becomes a corner point.

✦ You can convert straight lines into curves by pulling the control handle away from the corner point.

✦ After you've drawn a curve point, you can retract one of the control handles so that the next segment can be either a curve or a straight line.

All the manipulations involving control handles can be accomplished after the fact using the Subselection tool; you can find a discussion of how to use this point adjustment device in Chapter 9. However, you can perform a few of these operations while drawing with the Pen. The two key operations involve adding and removing a control handle.

Adding a control handle to a corner point

To add a control handle to a corner point, follow these steps:

1. Use the Pen to draw a path with a curve point. Two control points are visible.

2. Move the pointer over the last curve point set.

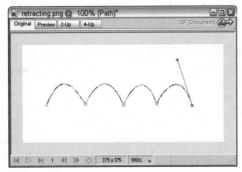

Figure 5-19: By retracting one control handle, you can continue the curve in the same direction.

3. Click once. The curve point is converted into a corner point, and one control handle is retracted.

4. To draw a straight line from the corner point, move your pointer away and click once.

5. To draw a curve, move your pointer away and click and drag out the control handles.

This technique is very handy for drawing a series of scallop or wave shapes where the curves all go in the same direction.

Extending a control handle from a corner point

The opposite of retracting a control handle is extending one. To extend a control handle from a corner point, you need to enlist the aid of a couple of keyboard modifiers: Ctrl+Alt (Command+Option) to be specific. When you extend a control handle while drawing, you are, in effect, changing your mind. Instead of proceeding with the straight line that you first indicated you wanted with the corner point, you can now draw a curve.

To extend a control handle from a corner point while drawing, follow these steps:

1. Draw a straight line segment with the Pen.

2. Move the pointer over the last point set.

3. Press Ctrl+Alt (Command+Option) and then click and drag a control handle out from the point. When you press the keyboard modifiers, the pointer changes to a white arrowhead.

4. Release the mouse button when you've positioned the control handle where desired.

5. Move the pointer to the position for the curve to end.

6. Continue drawing or double-click the final point to complete the shape.

In this technique, it's important that you press the keyboard modifiers before you drag the control handle. If you begin dragging before pressing the special keys, you move the anchor point instead of extending a control handle. This is actually a feature that enables you to move a previously set point by starting the drag and then pressing the Ctrl (Command) key; the Alt (Option) key has no effect on this sequence.

Note
Bézier curves are not easy to master and you may find yourself getting frustrated. Stick with them as, once you have them tamed, they open a whole new creative door.

Using the keyboard modifiers

Bézier curves in Fireworks use a fair number of keyboard modifiers to achieve various effects. While these special keys are explained throughout this section in context, it is useful to put them all in one place (see Table 5-1) for easy reference.

Cross-Reference

There's a lot more to manipulating Bézier curves and other Fireworks objects, as you find out in Chapter 9.

Table 5-1 Bézier Curves Keyboard Modifiers		
Windows Keys	**Macintosh Keys**	**Description**
Shift	Shift	Constrains the straight line or control handle to a 45-degree angle
Ctrl	Command	Moves a set curve or corner point or a control handle to a new position
Ctrl and double-click	Command and double-click	Completes an open path without adding another point
Ctrl+Alt	Command+Option	Extends a control handle from a corner point

Summary

I once had to indoctrinate a corporate design team into "The Fireworks Way" in a two-day training session. When it came to vector objects, I described them as being the "skeleton" of Fireworks graphics. After the vector object is completed — and the body of fills and clothing of strokes have been applied — you won't be able to see its underlying structure, but it is the basis of the image. As you begin to build vector objects, keep these points in mind:

✦ Paths are the most basic element of Fireworks' vector objects. A path must be stroked and/or filled before it becomes visible in your image.

✦ The geometric shape tools — Rectangle, Rounded Rectangle, Ellipse, and Polygon — can also create squares, circles, and stars.

✦ Spacebar Move enables you to move geometric shapes while drawing by simply holding the spacebar and repositioning your shape. Spacebar Move works while drawing Rectangles, Rounded Rectangles, Ellipses and Circles, as well as Polygons and Stars.

✦ The Line tool creates one straight line at a time.

✦ The Vector Path tool enables you to draw on the Fireworks canvas without restriction.

✦ The Pen draws Bézier curves, which use a series of corner and curve points in conjunction with control points and handles to make smooth curves and connected straight lines.

In the next chapter, you learn about the other side of Fireworks graphics: bitmap objects.

✦   ✦   ✦

Working with Bitmaps

Vector objects are the backbone of Fireworks, and are
perfectly suited for the bulk of a Web artist's work—
building navigation bars, drawing shapes and lines, and
inserting editable text. These design elements benefit from
the precision that vector drawing provides, and are the type
of things you're likely to draw right from scratch in Fireworks.

Some kinds of images couldn't possibly benefit from a vector-
based substructure, though. Photographic images that started
life in a digital camera or scanner are pure bitmap, through
and through. Think of product photographs for an online
store, or digitized paintings for an online art gallery; incorporating them into a Web page won't involve drawing. Instead
you cut and paste pixel selections and manipulate alpha
masks and blending modes.

This chapter begins with a discussion of how Fireworks
generally handles bitmaps. We delve into an exploration of the
various tools available for bitmap editing. And, finally, this
chapter covers how to change a vector object into a bitmap
object and the benefits you might realize by doing so.

Understanding Bitmaps in Fireworks

Here's a quick refresher course on bitmap images—just in
case you're coming from the world of vector graphics and
can't tell a pixel from a pig in a poke. The word *pixel* is
derived from the term *picture element* (*pix* for picture and *el*
for element). A pixel is the smallest component part of a
bitmap image. In the early days of computer graphics, the
color of each pixel was stored in 1 bit of memory, which was

either on for white or off for black. Map these bits along an *x* and *y* axis and you can create an image out of them. Editing a bitmap basically involves adding or removing pixels, or changing their colors. Even when you erase part of an image, you're just setting the color of those excess pixels to your chosen background color (or to "transparent" so that they show another image underneath) so that they appear to have been erased.

The best way to describe the difference between a bitmap image (also called a *raster graphic*) and a vector object, is to ask you to think of a line, 100-pixels long and 1-pixel wide. With vector graphics, all you need to make this line visible is two points and a stroke in between. With a bitmap, you need exactly 100 pixels. To move one end of the vector version of this line up a notch, you just need to move one of the endpoints. With pixel-based images, however, you have to erase all the pixels in the line and redraw them in another location.

Examining bitmap preferences

The two Bitmap options under the Editing category of the Preferences can prove useful.

✦ **Turn Off Hide Edges:** Turns off the View ➪ Hide Edges command when you select vector or bitmap objects. This is convenient to make your selection easy to find, but if you really think edges are a visual nuisance, uncheck this preference. Turn Off Hide Edges takes effect immediately upon exiting the Preferences.

✦ **Display Striped Border:** Tells Fireworks to draw a striped "barber-pole" border around the canvas when you're working on a bitmap object. Changes to this preference take effect immediately upon exiting the Preferences.

Opening existing bitmaps

I'm sure you've heard the expression, "Success is 1 percent inspiration and 99 percent perspiration." In the Internet graphics field, the formula is a bit different: "Web design is 20 percent creation and 80 percent modification." Of course, this is just my rough estimate—but it definitely feels as if I spend most of my day revising an image already created by me or someone else.

Fireworks offers multiple ways to open existing bitmaps—and it supports a wide range of file formats as well. Increasingly, more of your work will be stored in Fireworks' PNG-based format, which enables both vector and bitmap editing. However, many times you find yourself working with a bitmap file created in another application such as Photoshop.

As with many computer programs, Fireworks loads images and other files through the File ➪ Open command. This command displays the Open dialog box (see Figure 6-1), which previews various file types. You can select multiple files by pressing Shift or Ctrl (Command) as you click on filenames. The Open dialog box also has a very useful option, Open as Animation, which creates an animation from multiple files by distributing them across the frames of one document. Make sure you select more than one file in order to enable the Open as Animation checkbox.

Cross-Reference For detailed information on how to use the Open command to load any type of file, see Chapter 14.

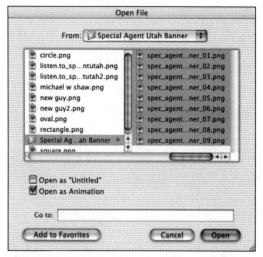

Figure 6-1: Opening an image sequence as an animation using Fireworks' Open as Animation option

Scaling bitmaps

Changing the size of a pixel-based bitmap image is something probably taken for granted, but it's actually a pretty complex task, requiring Fireworks to literally create a new image — with the newly specified dimensions — by analyzing the old image. Fireworks examines groups of pixels and basically makes a best guess about how to represent them, with either more or fewer pixels. Coming up with intermediate values based on analysis of known values is called interpolation.

Fireworks offers you four interpolation methods (see Figure 6-2):

✦ **Bicubic:** With bicubic interpolation, Fireworks averages every pixel with all eight pixels surrounding it — above, below, left, right, and all four corners. This scaling option gives the sharpest results under the most conditions and is recommended for most graphics.

✦ **Bilinear:** Bilinear interpolation is similar to bicubic, but only uses four neighboring pixels (above, below, left, and right), instead of eight.

✦ **Nearest Neighbor:** The Nearest Neighbor algorithm causes Fireworks to copy neighboring pixels whenever a new pixel must be interpolated. Consequently, the Nearest Neighbor scaling option creates very pixelated, stairstep-like images. This is the fastest interpolation method available.

✦ **Soft:** Soft interpolation offers a smoothing blur to the scaled-down images. The Soft Interpolation scaling option is a good choice if your images are producing unwanted artifacts using the other scaling options.

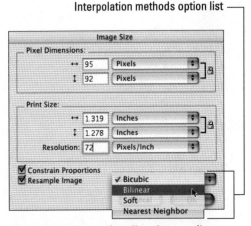

Figure 6-2: Fireworks offers four scaling options to suit different kinds of images.

Although I tend to use Bicubic Interpolation most of the time, I do turn to Bilinear and Soft Interpolation in some cases, usually when small text is involved. I haven't found much use for the blockiness produced by the Nearest Neighbor scaling option. Experimenting with the different interpolation methods is the best way to become familiar with the results.

Inserting a bitmap into a document

Collage — the mixing of various images and other graphics — is a very important design tool, on or off the Web. Whether you're overlapping bitmaps or just laying them side-by-side, Fireworks' File ⇨ Import command enables you to include an existing graphic wherever necessary in an open document.

To include a bitmap in a document, follow these steps:

1. Choose File ⇨ Import, or use the keyboard shortcut, Ctrl+R (Command+R). Fireworks displays the Import dialog box.

2. Select your image and choose Open when you're done. The cursor changes to the Import cursor: a corner bracket.

3. Position the Import cursor wherever you would like the upper-left corner of the image to be initially located, and click once. The chosen image is inserted into the document as a new bitmap object and selected.

If you need to adjust the position of the newly inserted bitmap object, select the Pointer tool, and click and drag it to a new place. For more precise placement, use the cursor keys to move the selected bitmap object any direction, one pixel at a time or the Property inspector to move the bitmap to a specific location.

Tip   When pressing Shift, the arrow keys move the selected bitmap object in 10-pixel increments.

Inserting an empty bitmap

So far you've seen how Fireworks can open a wide range of file formats for bitmap editing. But what if you want to create a bitmap image directly from within Fireworks? Whereas vectors are far more editable than bitmaps, occasionally only a bitmap will do. For those times, you can use a Fireworks feature that creates an editable bitmap area by choosing Edit ⇨ Insert ⇨ Empty Bitmap.

Tip   The Empty Bitmap command is extremely helpful when you need to paint a fairly large background with a brush, such as the Air Brush, and don't want to use the Fill tool. You can then modify the Air Brushed background with any of the pixel-based tools, such as the Eraser.

Using bitmap tools

The scoreboard shows an almost equal number of Fireworks tools dedicated to working with bitmaps and vectors at eight to six respectively. Naturally, the better you understand what a tool is intended for and how it is best used, the more fluid your workflow becomes. This section discusses the bitmap tools.

The bitmap specific tools are primarily concerned with *pixel manipulation,* and there's a very good reason for this emphasis: Selecting and manipulating pixels is much harder than selecting and manipulating vectors. The most complicated vector possible can be selected with just one click. Pixels are chosen either by their position with a tool, such as the Marquee, or by their color with the Magic Wand. Quite often you need to use a combination of tools and methods to get the desired results.

Luckily, Fireworks offers a full range of pixel manipulation tools: Pointer, Marquee, Oval Marquee, Lasso, Polygon Lasso, and Magic Wand. Each has its own way of working, as well as a variety of user-definable options.

Examining the Pointer

Although the Pointer tool is listed as one of the selection tools, capable of being used in both modes, it's included here for a simple reason. You can use the Pointer to quickly and easily reposition your bitmaps by clicking and dragging anywhere within the bitmap object, as shown in Figure 6-3. Just make sure that there are no active pixel selections.

Figure 6-3: You can use the Pointer to move whole bitmap objects around the canvas.

Tip   You can also use the Pointer to resize a bitmap object. You can drag the control handles, the solid squares in the corners of the selection indication border surrounding the image, to a new position, resizing the graphic much like the Distort tool does. You can even obtain proportional resizing by holding Shift while dragging a corner.

Using the Marquee tools

The Marquee tool is one of the most frequently used selection tools. The Marquee selection tool is quite similar to the Rectangle vector drawing tool. Both are generally used by selecting a point for one corner of the rectangular shape and dragging diagonally to the opposite corner. However, the Marquee tool doesn't draw a shape on the bitmap; it temporarily surrounds and selects an area of pixels for another operation to take place, such as a copy or a fill.

Examining the Rectangular and Oval Marquee tools

There are actually two different Marquee tools. The first is the default rectangular Marquee, which you select through its button on the toolbar, or by pressing the keyboard shortcut, M. The second parallels the Ellipse vector drawing tool: The Oval Marquee selects an oval or circular area. Pressing and holding down the Shift key while using the Marquee and Oval Marquee tools constrains the shapes you draw to perfect squares and circles, as it would when using the vector Rectangle or Ellipse drawing tools.

Tip   If you find yourself making a lot of perfect square and circle marquee selections, click the Marquee or Oval Marquee tool and choose Fixed Ratio from the Style box on the Property inspector. Set the ratio at 1 to 1, and it's easy to draw perfect square and circle selections instead of rectangles and ovals, with no need to hold the Shift key.

To use the Marquee or Oval Marquee tool, follow these steps:

1. To select a rectangular or square region, select the Marquee tool from the Tools panel or through its keyboard shortcut, M.

2. To select an elliptical or circular region, select the Oval Marquee tool from the Tools panel by clicking and holding the Marquee tool and choosing the button from the flyout menu. Alternatively, you can press the keyboard shortcut, M, twice.

3. Click where you want one corner of your selection to begin, and drag to the opposite corner. Fireworks displays a moving dashed line, called a marquee or, more familiarly, "marching ants" (see Figure 6-4).

Tip   You can refine the positioning of your marquee selection by temporarily holding the Spacebar while you drag.

Figure 6-4: The Marquee tools are used for marking rectangular, square, oval, or circular areas for selection.

Exploring the Property inspector

The two Marquee tools also share a set of options available from the Property inspector. You can display the Property inspector, as shown in Figure 6-5, by selecting Window ➪ Properties, or by pressing Ctrl+F3 (Command+F3). The Marquee properties affect two separate items: Style and Edge.

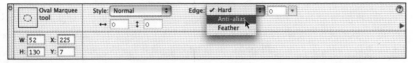

Figure 6-5: Use the Property inspector to set the Marquee to a predetermined size or ratio; you can also choose a type of edge for the selection: Hard, Anti-Alias, or Feather.

Discovering the Style portion

Generally, the Marquee tools are unrestrained, meaning the selection can be any size or shape drawn out. But sometimes it's useful to specify the needed selection dimensions. The Style section of the Marquee Property inspector has three possible settings:

✦ **Normal:** This default state enables you to drag out your rectangular or elliptical selections freely.

✦ **Fixed Ratio:** Sets the horizontal-to-vertical ratio for the Marquee selection tools. Enter horizontal values in the first text box (marked with the side-to-side double-headed arrow) and vertical values in the second (marked with the up-and-down double-headed arrow). This option is useful when you know that the selection must be a particular proportion. If, for example, the selection should be twice as wide as high, you would enter a 2 in the horizontal text box and a 1 in the vertical text box. To get a perfect square selection, specify 1 to 1. When you use either Marquee tool with a Set Ratio option enabled, the selection size varies, but not the proportion.

✦ **Fixed Size:** Sets the dimensions to a particular pixel width and height. Enter the desired pixel values in the horizontal and vertical text boxes. When either Marquee tool is selected with this option enabled, a selection outlining the specified dimensions is attached to the pointer and can be easily repositioned on the screen. After you've located the area to be selected, clicking once drops the selection outline on the bitmap. The Fixed Size option works especially well when you need to create a number of same-sized selections.

Tip

If you enter a value in one of the Fixed Size text boxes, but leave the other blank, Fireworks creates a selection outline the width or height specified that spans the entire bitmap. It's a great way to grab a slice of an image, one or two pixels wide or tall, and ensures that you get the full image without having to draw it. For this technique, using the Marquee tool rather than the Oval Marquee tool is best.

Learning the types of edges

The Marquee Property inspector also controls the type of edge that the selection uses. The default edge type is a hard-edged line — what you select is what you get. The other two types, Anti-Alias and Feather, act to soften the selection. Anti-Alias is the more subtle of the two options. When you choose the Anti-Alias option for your selection, any jagged edges caused by an elliptical or circular selection are blended into the background, much like bitmap type is antialiased to make it appear less jagged.

Tip

You can get a very smooth bitmap crescent by making a circular selection using the Oval Marquee tool on a solid color. Set the Edge type on the Marquee Property inspector to Anti-Alias, and make your selection. Then, use the arrow keys to move the selection one or two pixels vertically and the same distance horizontally. You're left with a crescent shape that blends smoothly into its points.

Feathering a selection is much more noticeable. Basically, think of feathering as blending. After selecting the Feather option, the value box becomes active with a default of 10 pixels. Any feathered selection blends equally on either side of the selection outline. If, for example, you choose a small Feather value of 2 pixels for a rectangular selection, four rows of pixels are altered — two inside the selection and two outside. If you delete a feathered selection, you're left with a hole in the image, blending smoothly into the canvas, because both the selection and the surrounding image are feathered. If you move a feather selection and the pixels it contains, the selection has a blended edge, as shown in Figure 6-6.

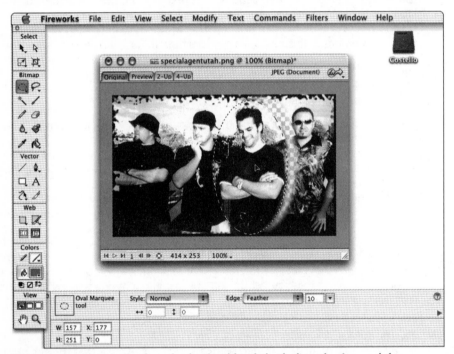

Figure 6-6: Moving a feathered selection blends both the selection and the remaining image to create a gentle transition.

Tip   Remember to hold Ctrl (Command) while you move a Marquee selection in order to move both the selection and the pixels it contains.

Using the Lasso and Polygon Lasso tools

Not all regions to be selected are rectangular or elliptical. The Lasso tools select irregularly shaped areas of an image. As the name implies, the Lasso tools surround or *lasso* the desired pixels to select them. The standard Lasso tool is a click-and-drag type instrument that enables freeform selection, in the same way the Vector

Path tool used for freeform drawing. The Polygon Lasso tool, on the other hand, is similar to the Pen tool in its straight-line mode, and makes selections through a series of connected straight lines.

All Lasso selections are by their very nature closed paths. As with the drawing tools, when you drag the pointer near the beginning of a Lasso selection, Fireworks displays a closed-path cursor with a black square, as shown in Figure 6-7. You can also close a Lasso tool selection by releasing the mouse button; Fireworks draws a line from the beginning point to the ending point, closing the shape. With the Polygon Lasso, double-click the last point to close the shape automatically in the same manner.

If you're selecting an area that has more curves than straight lines, use the Lasso. If your selection has some long straight lines, you may find the Polygon Lasso is more suitable, even if you also have some curves to deal with because the straight lines are quick and accurate. Lots of short lines with the Polygon Lasso enable you to draw around curves.

Figure 6-7: Drawing with the Polygon Lasso. The little block on the Polygon Lasso cursor means that one more click closes the path and creates the selection.

To make a freeform selection, follow these steps:

1. To use the Lasso, select it from the Tools panel, or use the keyboard shortcut, L.

2. With the Lasso, click at the starting point for your selection, and drag the mouse around the desired area, releasing the mouse when you're done.

3. To use the Polygon Lasso, select and hold the Lasso tool until the flyout appears, and then choose the Polygon Lasso, or press the keyboard shortcut, L, twice.

4. With the Polygon Lasso, click at the starting point for your selection, and then move the mouse to the next point on the outline, surrounding the desired area and click again. Fireworks connects each point that you set down with a straight line.

5. Repeat Step 4 until you've outlined the entire area, and then close the selection by moving your pointer over the starting point and clicking once or double-clicking to permit Fireworks to connect the first and final points.

As a matter of personal preference, I get a lot more use out of the Polygon Lasso than I do the regular drawing Lasso. Selecting an area of pixels is often a painstaking chore, and I find the Polygon Lasso to be far more precise. Generally, I use the Lasso to outline some stray pixels for deletion only when there's little chance that I'll select part of the main image.

You can determine the type of edge the Lasso tools use through the Property inspector. As with the Marquee tools, the three edge options are Hard, Anti-Alias, and Feather, and they work in exactly the same manner as described in the previous Marquee section.

Working with the Magic Wand

The Magic Wand is a completely different type of selection tool from those already discussed. Instead of encompassing an area of pixels, the Magic Wand selects adjacent pixels of similar color. This type of tool enables you to select single-color backgrounds or other regions quickly.

Using the Magic Wand is very straightforward. Choose the Magic Wand tool from the Tools panel, or use the keyboard shortcut, W. Now click on any pixel in the bitmap — it, and all pixels of a similar color next to it, are selected.

Tip   With both the Magic Wand and the Lasso, I find that the representational pointers sometimes get in the way. It's hard to see exactly which pixel you're pinpointing if there is a sparkly wand cursor obscuring the area. You can toggle Precise Cursors — a crosshair pointer — whenever you like, by pressing the Caps Lock key.

The key phrase in the description of the Magic Wand is "pixels of a similar color." Many bitmap images, especially photographic JPEGs, tend to use a range of colors, even when depicting a seemingly monochromatic area. You control what Fireworks defines as a "similar color" through the Tolerance setting on the Property inspector. The Tolerance scale goes from 0 to 255; lower tolerance values select fewer colors and higher values select more.

Here's how the Magic Wand and the Tolerance work. By default, the initial Tolerance is set to 32. The Tolerance value is applied to the RGB values of the selected pixel — the exact one selected by the Magic Wand. If the Tolerance value is 50 and the selected pixel's RGB values are 200, 200, and 200, Fireworks judges any adjacent pixel with an RGB from 150, 150, 150 to 250, 250, 250 as being similar enough to select. Pixels within that color range, but not in some way touching the originally selected pixel, are not chosen.

In addition to varying the Tolerance, you can also determine the type of edge for a Magic Wand selection. Edge options, as with Marquee and Lasso tools, are Hard, Anti-Alias (the default), or Feather. For a detailed explanation of how these tools work, see the "Using the Marquee tools" section earlier in this chapter.

Increasing or Reducing the Selection Area

Fireworks selection tools are very full-featured, but, for complex selections, you need more flexibility. Adding several selections together, or using one selection tool to eliminate part of an existing selection, opens up a whole range of possibilities.

The key to adding or removing pixels is to use the keyboard modifiers as you draw your selections: Press Shift to add selections and Alt (Option) to remove them. Notice that the pointer indicates the operation; a plus sign (+) appears when Shift is pressed and a minus sign (−) appears when Alt (Option) is pressed.

For example, I often use Shift in combination with the Magic Wand to select additional areas of an image, rather than alter the Tolerance. Your first Magic Wand selection may have a couple of small gaps that need filling. Holding down Shift and clicking in those gaps is usually the quickest way to fill out the selection, as shown in the accompanying figure.

Continued

Continued

Just as you can add onto selections, you can take away from them, too. Use the Alt (Option) key when applying any of the selection tools to reduce an existing selection. The basic technique is to "carve out" the undesired selection; in the following figure, the donut shape was created by first drawing a circular selection, and then pressing Alt (Option) while drawing a smaller circular selection inside. An Xtra was then applied to the donut-shaped selection to create a frame around the subject's face. Obviously, the selection reduction feature enables you to create some very unusual shapes.

Rubber Stamping

If you're looking for a unique tool, look no further than the Rubber Stamp. One of the few pixel-based drawing tools, Rubber Stamp acts like a real rubber stamp: picking up a section of your document and stamping it out somewhere else. The Rubber Stamp tool makes picking up portions of an image and blending them into other areas of the graphic easy.

The Rubber Stamp is a two-part tool, with both source and destination pointers. The source, or origin, pointer is initially placed on the area of the document that you want to duplicate. The destination pointer draws the duplicated section in a different location on the image. While you are drawing, the two pointers maintain the same relationship to each other; if you move the destination pointer to the left, the source pointer moves to the left as well. Because the "ink" that the Rubber Stamp tool uses is always changing while you move it (because the source pointer is also moving), you can achieve a smooth blend, as in Figure 6-8. Getting a handle on this tool is a little tricky, but well worth the time you spend mastering it.

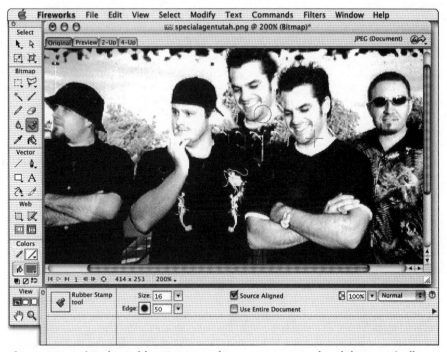

Figure 6-8: Using the Rubber Stamp tool to create an extra head that practically draws itself

To use the Rubber Stamp tool, follow these steps:

1. Select the Rubber Stamp tool from the Tools panel, or use the keyboard short-cut, S.

2. Set the source pointer by clicking once on the bitmap. If you attempt to set the source pointer on a vector object, Fireworks tells you that the Rubber Stamp tool can only be used on floating bitmap objects.

3. Move the destination pointer to where you want the copied image to appear, and draw by clicking and dragging. As the source pointer moves over the image, following the movement of the mouse, the image is copied under the destination pointer.

Understanding Source Alignment

You can use the Rubber Stamp in two basic modes, selectable from the Property inspector once you've chosen the Rubber Stamp tool. First, with Source Aligned mode (checked by default), you can always keep the relationship between the source and destination pointers constant, not just when you're drawing. This is useful if you want to copy different portions of the image to a remote area, but keep them proportionally spaced. For example, if I wanted to position two eyes as if they were floating in space above my model's head, I would copy one eye using the Rubber Stamp tool, release the mouse button, and position the source pointer over the second eye and then begin dragging and drawing again until the second eye was completed.

By unchecking the Source Aligned box, you switch to a Fixed Source mode. In Fixed Source mode, whenever the mouse button is released, the source pointer snaps back to its original starting place. This mode enables you to copy the same image in several locations. If, for example, I wanted to place a series of floating eyes around my model's head, I would use Fixed Source mode.

Tip Press Alt (Option) to reset the origin for the Rubber Stamp.

Learning about other options

There are a couple of other controls on the Property inspector that change how the Rubber Stamp tool behaves. The Edge Softness slider affects the hardness of the duplicated image's edge; the higher the slider, the softer the edge. To blend a copied image more, use a softer edge. You can also change the size of the source and destination pointers with the Stamp Size slider. The range of the Stamp Size slider is from 0 to 72, and the default is 16 pixels. The selected Stamp Size includes any feathering that may be required by the Edge Softness setting.

Exploring the Eraser

As you might suspect, the Eraser removes pixels from an image, just like the trusty gum-based version erases pencil drawings.

To use the Eraser, follow these steps:

1. Select the Eraser from the Tools panel; alternatively, you can use the keyboard shortcut, E.

2. If necessary, select the image you want to work on.

3. Click and drag over the pixels you want to remove. Fireworks deletes the pixels leaving the canvas showing through, as shown in Figure 6-9.

In addition to being able to set the Edge Softness and Size of the Eraser on the Property inspector, as you can with the Rubber Stamp tool, you can also select its basic shape. By default, the Eraser is circular, but you can change it to a square by choosing the Square Eraser button.

Figure 6-9: The Eraser tool removes pixels from your image according to the settings established on the Property inspector.

Understanding the Touchup tools

Manipulating bitmaps pixel-by-pixel is all well and good but what about the fun stuff? What do you do when you have a bitmap image that could use a little retouching? That's where the touchup tools come into play. They allow you to make sharp edges blurry so they're not as obvious, or make blurry edges sharper so you can view things more clearly. They let you lighten the dark images and darken the light ones. You can even shove your colors around to mix them into each other. Of course, you're not limited to using these tools on a one shot per image basis; you can use combinations of any, or all, of them to get your bitmaps just right.

New Feature Fireworks MX adds new tools designed to help you touchup your bitmaps. They are Blur, Sharpen, Dodge, Burn, and Smudge.

Blur and Sharpen

The Blur and Sharpen tools have opposing effects on pixels. Like their filter counterparts, the Blur and Sharpen tools are used to decrease or enhance the focus on areas of a bitmap image. Unlike the filters, the Blur and Sharpen tools allow you very fine control over what gets blurred or sharpened because you're applying them directly with the mouse cursor rather than applying the filter to a selection, or the entire document.

The options for the Blur and Sharpen tools are as follows:

✦ **Size:** This setting controls the size of the tip of the Blur and Sharpen tools. It affects how large, or how small, an area the tool touches. The size range extends from 1 to 100.

✦ **Edge:** The Edge setting determines how soft or how hard the edge of the tip is. The valid range is from 1 to 100, with 1 being a solid shape and 100 being fairly feathered around the edges.

✦ **Shape:** Determines whether the tip of the tool is round or square.

✦ **Intensity:** The intensity sets the degree of blurring or sharpening. The valid range is between 1 and 100.

What do you do when you want to remove someone's head and make it look like it's attached to someone else's body? You know that almost everyone has done this kind of thing and if you haven't, you've certainly seen it done. After all, you know that wasn't a real picture of Britney Spears that arrived in your e-mail. Once you've cut out the head, and resized it to match the body, what do you do about that line where the neck attaches or the face gets put in? That's where the Blur tool comes in. In figure 6-10, you see, from left to right, the source image, the image for the new face, and then the completed job. If it weren't for the Blur tool, the edges of the cut out face would all be totally obvious.

Figure 6-10: At 300 percent magnification, you can see the areas in the final shot (at right) where the Blur tool was used to blend the edges of the face transplant.

To use the Blur tool, follow these steps:

1. If necessary, select the image you want to work on.

2. Select the Blur tool from the Tools panel; alternatively, you can use the keyboard shortcut by pressing R.

3. Tweak the settings in the Property inspector until they're set up the way you want them.

4. Click and drag over the pixels you want to blur. Fireworks uses the settings in the Property inspector to blur the pixels in your image.

5. Repeat steps 3 and 4 for any other areas you wish to blur.

Use the sharpen tool to bring clarity to blurry or out-of-focus portions of bitmap images. It can fix up those fuzzy photos or you can add crispness to some blurry text (see Figure 6-11). With only a few swipes of the Sharpen tool, you can add new life to your images.

Figure 6-11: The text on the right is the blurry original; the text on the left has been sharpened. With a little more work, it will be restored perfectly.

To use the Sharpen tool, follow these steps:

1. If necessary, select the image you want to work on.

2. Select the Sharpen tool from the Tools panel; alternatively, you can use the keyboard shortcut by pressing R twice.

3. Tweak the settings in the Property inspector until they're set up the way you want them.

4. Click and drag over the pixels you want to sharpen. Fireworks uses the settings in the Property inspector to sharpen the pixels in your image.

5. Repeat steps 3 and 4 for any other areas you wish to sharpen.

Tip   Holding down the Alt (Option) key temporarily switches from the Blur tool to the Sharpen tool and vice versa. This allows you to blur and sharpen different areas of the same image without having to constantly switch between tools.

Dodge and Burn

Like Blur and Sharpen, Dodge and Burn go hand-in-hand as they also perform opposite functions. You can use the Dodge tool to lighten any dark or badly lit portions of a bitmap image. The burn tool, on the other hand, is used to darken areas of an image that appear too light.

The options for the Dodge and Burn tools are as follows:

✦ **Size:** This setting controls the size of the tip of the Dodge and Burn tools. It affects how large, or how small, an area the tool touches. The size range extends from 1 to 100.

✦ **Edge:** The Edge setting determines how soft or how hard the edge of the tip is The valid range is from 1 to 100, with 1 being a solid shape and 100 being fairly feathered around the edges.

✦ **Shape:** Determines whether the tip of the tool is round or square.

✦ **Range:** The Range option list has three settings:

　• **Shadows:** Causes the Dodge and Burn tools to affect the dark tones in an image.

　• **Highlights:** Causes the Dodge and Burn tools to affect the light tones in an image.

　• **Midtones:** Causes the Dodge and Burn tools to affect the middle tonal range in an image — the tones between the light and dark ranges.

✦ **Exposure:** The Exposure value can be set from 1 to 100. If you want a low level of effect to be added, choose a low number; for those areas that you really want to modify, choose a higher number.

Though its name is the least descriptive of the touchup tools, the Dodge tool is great for those occasions when you need to lighten areas of an image that turned out a little darker than expected. You can remove the shadow left by the brim of a hat or simply brighten flesh tones. In Figure 6-12, I use the Dodge tool to lighten this young scholar's face, hands, and reading material. While I could have used the Brightness/Contrast command, that would have brightened the walls and possibly made the image too washed out.

Figure 6-12: The Dodge tool can work wonders to brighten areas of a photograph that are slightly too dark.

To use the Dodge tool, follow these steps:

1. If necessary, select the image you want to work on.

2. Select the Dodge tool from the Tools panel; alternatively, you can use the keyboard shortcut by pressing R three times.

3. Tweak the settings in the Property inspector until they're set up the way you want them.

4. Click and drag over the pixels you want to lighten and release the mouse button when all of the desired pixels have been affected.

5. Repeat steps 3 and 4 for any other areas you need to lighten.

The Burn tool is one of those tools whose name says it all. If you need to darken some areas of a bitmap image, simply get out the Burn tool and apply it. Those over-exposed areas dim down in no time. Let's say you want some focaccia, with goat cheese and olive oil, and you ask to have it cooked well done so that the crust is extra crispy. You get home, only to discover that the crust isn't quite as crispy as you'd like. Rather than head all the way back to Villa Agnese, in La Habra, California, to have it cooked a little more, get out your digital camera, take a photograph, and use the Burn tool to crisp the focaccia to your exact specifications. You can see the results of the Burn tool in Figure 6-13 where I toasted my focaccia crust a little to give it that extra crunch. An undocumented advantage to using the Burn tool for this project is that you're less likely to burn the roof of your mouth — your focaccia's been cooling down while you've been burning its crust.

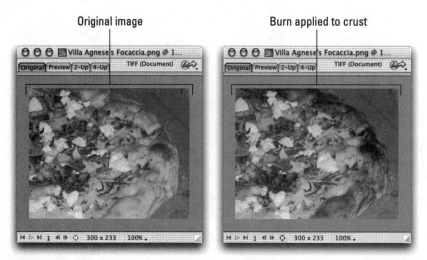

Figure 6-13: The Burn tool is a great way to darken, or shade, areas of an image that are too light — especially when you don't want to get into trouble with the chef.

To use the Burn tool, follow these steps:

1. If necessary, select the image you want to work on.

2. Select the Burn tool from the Tools panel; alternatively, you can use the keyboard shortcut by pressing R four times.

3. Tweak the settings in the Property inspector until they're set up the way you want them.

4. Click and drag over the pixels you want to darken. Fireworks uses the settings in the Property inspector to darken the pixels in your image.

5. Repeat steps 3 and 4 for any other areas you wish to darken.

Tip Holding down the Alt (Option) key temporarily switches from the Dodge tool to the Burn tool and vice versa. This allows you to dodge and burn different areas of the same image without having to constantly switch between tools.

Smudge

At some point in life, everyone's done finger-painting. Pour some paint on a piece of paper, get your hands in there, and push all the colors around, into, and through each other. In many ways, the Smudge tool does for pixels what fingers do for finger-painting. Essentially, the Smudge tool blends colors in a bitmap in whatever direction you push or pull. It's like grabbing the colors and smearing them across other pixels (see Figure 6-14).

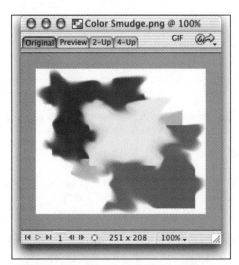

Figure 6-14: What started out as four rectangles can soon become impressionist art with some overzealous use of the Smudge tool.

The options for the Smudge tool are as follows:

✦ **Size:** This setting controls the size of the tip of the Smudge tool. It affects how large, or how small, an area the tool touches. The size range extends from 1 to 100.

✦ **Edge:** The Edge setting determines how soft or how hard the edge of the tip is. The valid range is from 1 to 100, with 1 being a solid shape and 100 being fairly feathered around the edges.

✦ **Shape:** Determines whether the tip of the tool is round or square.

✦ **Use Entire Document:** Check this option if want the Smudge tool to affect bitmaps on all of the layers in your document at the same time. With this option unchecked, only bitmaps on the selected layer are affected.

✦ **Smudge Color:** With this option checked, the color in the color well is applied to the beginning of each smudge stroke you make. If this option is unchecked, the color under the Smudge tool at the beginning of the stroke is used.

✦ **Pressure:** This controls how intense your smudge is. The valid range for this option is from 1 to 100. A lower setting smudges a small amount of color; a higher value smudges your colors deeper and further.

To use the Smudge tool, follow these steps:

1. If necessary, select the image you want to work on.

2. Select the Smudge tool from the Tools panel; alternatively, you can use the keyboard shortcut by pressing R five times.

3. Tweak the settings in the Property inspector until they're set up the way you want them.

4. Click and drag over the pixels you want to smudge. Fireworks uses the settings in the Property inspector to smudge the pixels in your image.

5. Repeat steps 3 and 4 for any other areas you wish to smudge.

You can accomplish an interesting effect with the Smudge tool by checking the Use Entire Document option and using the Edit ➪ Insert ➪ Empty Bitmap command. Follow these steps to discover a creative way to make some interesting graphics:

1. Open an existing banner or logo, or add some colorful text to a new document. Text objects, or a logo, tend to be the best candidates for this procedure.

2. For this example, you should have extra space on all sides of your bitmap. If your bitmap stretches right to the edges of the canvas, then select Modify ➪ Canvas ➪ Canvas Size to add 20 or 30 extra pixels to all four sides.

3. Select Edit ➪ Insert ➪ Empty Bitmap to insert a blank bitmap into your document.

4. Select the Smudge tool from the Tools panel; alternatively, you can use the keyboard shortcut by pressing R five times.

5. Check the Use Entire Document option in the Property inspector.

6. Click and drag all across your document window. Don't worry if you can no longer make out the details in your image. This effect looks best when you've got colors mixed up everywhere, especially off the sides of your image and out onto the extra canvas space. Once you do, release the mouse button to stop blurring.

7. Switch to the Pointer tool and click the middle of your document to ensure that the Empty Bitmap you inserted earlier is selected.

8. Choose Modify ➪ Arrange ➪ Send to Back to send the Empty Bitmap to the bottom of the stacking order.

You should now see your banner, logo, text, or image sitting on top of the Empty Bitmap that you applied the Smudge tool to. The blank border of your document should be strewn with smudges of color as in Figure 6-15.

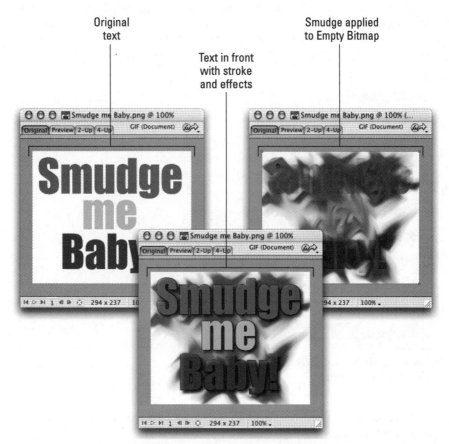

Figure 6-15: Only the colors in your document get smudged on the Empty Bitmap you inserted, leaving your original bitmap image, or text, untouched.

If you used text, you add Live Effects and/or a stroke to your text, as I did, to help it stand out from the smudged colors. Play with this technique, applying it to any number of bitmap or text objects, and you'll come up with some interesting and eye-catching combinations.

Fireworks Technique: Limiting Your Drawing Area

Not only can the selection tools modify your images after they're created, but they can also help to structure them while they're being made. When you place a selection on an image canvas — whether it's an existing image or an inserted Empty Image — any subsequent drawing is limited to that selected area. The selected area can be any shape possible, with any or all the selection tools: Marquee, Oval Marquee, Lasso, Polygon Lasso, and Magic Wand. In Figure 6-16, a feathered selection around the subjects' faces was inverted so that everything in the document, except the faces, was selected. The entire document was then painted over with the Brush tool. Note that the Brush could only paint in the selected area.

Selected, paintable area

Deselected area

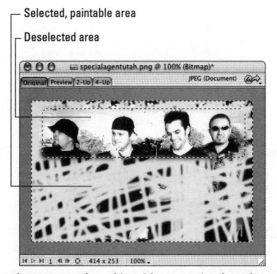

Figure 6-16: The subjects' faces aren't selected, so they don't get painted.

Tip   If you have a pixel selection in your document, a Filter will only be applied to the selected area as well.

The only prerequisite for using this technique is to make sure that the selection is active — it has a marquee border — before you begin drawing.

Making Pixel Selections

The Tools panel's selection tools are handy, but they aren't the only selection options in Fireworks. The Select menu contains a host of useful options for fine-tuning and even saving and restoring your pixel selections.

After you've made a pixel selection, the "marquee" or "marching ants" border acts almost as if it's a new object. You can drag the marquee selection around, or modify its properties, without affecting the underlying pixels of your image. When you want to move pixels along with a marquee selection, hold down the Ctrl (Command) key while you drag your marquee. Fireworks adds a small scissors icon to your cursor when Ctrl (Command) is pressed, indicating that you're about to edit the selected pixels.

Selecting all

When you need to select all the objects — both bitmap and vector — in the current document, choose Select ⇨ Select All. I often find myself using the keyboard short-cut for this command, Ctrl+A (Command+A), in combination with the Delete key when I want to erase all the work in a document and start over. Of course, any oper-ation that needs to be applied universally to every portion of a document benefits from the Select All command.

Selecting similar

The Select Similar command is an extension of the Magic Wand selection tool. Whereas the Magic Wand selects pixels within a particular color range adjacent to the one initially chosen, Select Similar selects *all* the pixels in a document within that color range, whether they are adjacent to the original pixel or not. To use this command, choose Select ⇨ Select Similar, after setting the Tolerance level on the Magic Wand tool on the Property inspector.

Select Similar is a very powerful command that you should use with care. It's often extremely difficult to predict all the areas of an image that will be affected. You may find yourself using this command in concert with Undo or the History panel, until you get a feel for what it does.

The Select menu's Superselect and Subselect commands are concerned with groups and are therefore covered in Chapter 13.

Selecting none

The opposite of Select All is Deselect. I use this command so frequently, it goes on my Top 10 Keyboard Shortcuts to Memorize list: Ctrl+D (Command+D). It's a very straightforward and extremely useful command. Choose Select ➪ Deselect to remove all selections in the current document for any bitmap, vector, or text object.

Selecting inverse

Sometimes I think I select inverse more than I select the pixels I want directly. Often, the background in an image contains fewer or flatter colors than the foreground, making it easier to select with the Magic Wand tool. After the background is selected, use the Select Inverse command to invert the selection, and select the foreground elements. On the other hand, if you want to select a background full of irregular colors and shapes, selecting the foreground elements and then inverting the selection to select the background may be easier. This command can be a time-saver over and over again.

1. First, select your foreground object through whatever tool or combination of tools is required.

2. Choose Select ➪ Select Inverse, or use the keyboard shortcut, Ctrl+Shift+I (Command+Shift+I). Fireworks inverts the marquee selection so that the background is now selected (see Figure 6-17).

Figure 6-17: Selecting the foreground element and inverting the selection quickly isolated this complex, blended background.

Feathering an existing selection

You've seen the Feather option for all the selection tools, but you may have noticed that in each case, feathering has to be established prior to the selection being made, whether through the Marquee or the Magic Wand. But what do you do when you want to feather an existing selection? Make your selection and choose Select ➪ Feather to open the Feather Selection dialog box, as shown in Figure 6-18. Whatever value you enter into the Radius text box is then applied to the current selection.

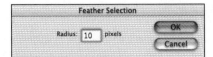

Figure 6-18: The Feather Selection dialog box permits you to feather the edges of the current selection.

Remember that the Feather command does not blur the selection's edges, but rather alters the selection's alpha channel, which controls transparency. To see the effect of a feathered selection, moving or cutting and pasting the selection is often necessary. As with all the other feathering options, both the selection and the area adjacent to the selection are affected.

Cross-Reference

If you just want to blur all or part of an image, you'll want to use one of the Blur commands found under the Filters menu. Find out more about these commands in Chapter 12.

Expanding or contracting a marquee

Sometimes a hand-drawn marquee selection is just a few pixels too large or small. Make a selection, and then choose Select ➪ Expand Marquee to open the Expand Selection dialog box and specify the number of pixels by which you want to expand the selection. Conversely, if you want to contract the selection, choose Select ➪ Contract Marquee, and enter the number of pixels to contract the selection in the Contract Selection dialog box. Click OK when you're done in either case.

Adding a border

To create an additional marquee around a current marquee, choose Select ➪ Border Marquee, enter the width of the border you want to create in the Select Border dialog box, and click OK when you're done. Instead of your previous selection, what is now selected is a border around the previous selection.

Using the Smooth command

The Smooth command smoothes the outline of a selection to turn a jagged, complicated marquee into a simpler one. This command is especially useful for the jagged marquees that are easily created with the Magic Wand tool. Create a selection, and then choose Select ➪ Smooth Marquee. Enter a sample radius in the Smooth Selection dialog box; a higher number means a greater smoothing effect. Click OK when you're done.

Saving and restoring selections

The Select menu has two final commands that you haven't yet looked at. Choose Select ➪ Save Bitmap Selection to save the current pixel selection to a sort of selection clipboard within Fireworks. This selection is stored until you choose Select ➪ Save Bitmap Selection again, and overwrite it with another selection. Choose Select ➪ Restore Bitmap Selection to restore a saved selection at any time.

Converting a Vector into a Bitmap

Keeping parts of your document in vector form for easy modification is best, but occasionally you may want to convert a vector object into a bitmap object. To accomplish this, select one or more vector or bitmap objects, and then choose Modify ➪ Flatten Selection, or use the keyboard shortcut Ctrl+Shift+Alt+Z (Command+Shift+Option+Z). Fireworks converts the vector outline to a rectangular bounding box, surrounding all the pixels from the vector object's fill, stroke, and effect settings.

If you have selected multiple objects, you can convert them all at one time with this command. However, you lose the capability to reposition them individually, as they all become part of one image; as the command's name implies, you are flattening the images.

After you've converted a vector to a bitmap, you can't go back without using the Undo command or the History panel to actually reverse your work. New bitmap objects in documents that have been saved and reloaded cannot return to their vector state under any circumstances. Fireworks throws away the vector information when you convert a vector object into a bitmap object.

Similar to Flatten Selection is the Merge Down command. Let's say you're working on a graphic where you've started out with a picture, perhaps that of a skyline, and you've added a portion of text and some vector buttons to it. Once you've got everything just right, you may want to flatten some of your vectors, text, or even another bitmap onto the original skyline bitmap. All you need to do is select the various objects and then go Modify ➪ Merge Down, or use the keyboard shortcut Ctrl+E (Command+E). Fireworks then merges the selected objects — text, vectors, or other bitmaps — with the bitmap they were on to create a new bitmap image. While you lose future editability, you can greatly reduce the number of items filling up the Layers panel.

For more about layers and the Layers panel, see Chapter 13.

Summary

Bitmap images are used throughout the Web, and Fireworks offers a robust set of tools for creating and manipulating them. Whereas bitmaps don't have the flexibility of vectors, editing them is an important part of the Web designer's job. When the time comes to begin modifying an existing image in Fireworks, keep these points in mind:

✦ Images are composed of pixels, and each pixel is assigned a particular color. At the most basic level, editing images involves changing the colors of pixels.

✦ A wide variety of photo retouching tool tools exist in Fireworks to help you manipulate images.

✦ All the pixel selection tools in Fireworks — Marquee, Oval Marquee, Lasso, Polygon Lasso, and Magic Wand — have numerous options available through the Property inspector.

✦ Marquee — or "marching ants" — selections can be moved, modified, and even saved without affecting the underlying image pixels.

✦ By selecting an area of the image prior to drawing, you can limit your drawing area.

✦ Vector and text objects can be converted into bitmaps by either flattening them, or merging them with bitmaps that they're sitting on.

In the next chapter, you find out how to handle color in Fireworks.

✦   ✦   ✦

Managing Color

For any graphic designer, the importance of color is a given. Not only can color attract the eye and convey emotions, but it's also an important commercial consideration. On the Web, as with any mass medium, color also becomes a key factor in branding. After all, if you're working on a logo for the Coca-Cola Web site, you had better make sure you're using genuine Coca-Cola red.

Fireworks outputs graphics for a screen-based medium. You won't find complex color separation, halftone, or calibration tools in Fireworks; those instruments are for the world of print. Moreover, Fireworks is not just screen-based, it's Internet-based — a distinction that signifies an important balance of freedoms and restrictions.

This chapter covers color on the Web — both its basic theory with the various standards, and its actual practice with Fireworks. If you're familiar with how computers handle color in general, feel free to skip the initial part of the chapter, and dive right into the more hands-on Fireworks sections. If, on the other hand, you think RGB is a one-hit wonder band from the '80s and hexadecimal is a library catalog system, the first section should be pixel-perfect for you.

Working with Color on the Web

Color in the natural world comes at us full force, without any impediments. Color on the Web, however, passes through many filters. At the most basic level, the computer dictates how color is generated. Rather than using a system of blending inks as with print, the computer blends light — red, green, and blue light, to be precise. Next, the color settings and capability of a viewer's specific system determine the range of colors to be used. The final filter for Web-based color is the browser, in all of its varied configurations and versions.

To get the most out of your Web graphics, you need a basic understanding of how computers create color. The smallest component of a computer screen that you can see is the pixel, which, you'll remember, is short for *picture element*. Pixels are displayed by showing three colors in combination: red, green, and blue, often referred to by the initials, RGB. The blend of red, green, and blue at full intensity creates white.

Tip If you're coming from a print background, you'll probably be more familiar with the CMYK (cyan, magenta, yellow, and black) color model than the RGB model. It's generally not too difficult to make the transition; Fireworks offers ways to convert a color in one system to its equivalent in the other, as explained in the section, "Using the Color Mixer," later in this chapter.

If RGB blended at full intensity creates white, and if a pixel that's turned off displays black, how are other colors created? The intensity of each of the key colors in a pixel — red, green, and blue — and their combinations can be varied. For example, if you have red set all the way up and both blue and green off, you get pure red; if you add a full dose of blue to the red, you create a deep purple. However, having only the capability to turn a color on or off greatly limits the number of color combinations possible. What's needed is an increase in the number of steps or levels between on and off.

Examining bit depth

The number of accessible RGB levels is called the *bit depth*. A bit is the smallest element of computer memory, and each bit is basically an on-off switch. A computer display with a bit depth of one is capable of showing two colors — one color in the on position and another in the off position. Now, if the bit depth is doubled, twice as many colors can be defined.

Each time you increase the bit depth, the number of colors increases exponentially. Table 7-1 takes a look at how bit depth affects color range.

Table 7-1 Bit Depth and Color Range		
Bit Depth	*Number of Colors*	*Description*
1	2	Black and white, corresponding to the "on" or "off" possible with one bit.
2	4	Typically, computers with two-bit color depth (usually handhelds or portables) display four shades of gray.
4	16	The minimum color depth of VGA (Video Graphics Adapter) displays, the most common computer display technology.

Bit Depth	Number of Colors	Description
8	256	Most computers manufactured after 1995 can display 8-bit color or better.
16	65,536	Often called "Thousands of Colors" or "HiColor."
24	16,777,216	Referred to as "Millions of Colors" or "True Color."
32	16,777,216	True Color with an additional 8-bit alpha mask.

In Table 7-1, I skipped some bit depths because they're not commonly used on computer displays. Note that 32-bit color has the same number of colors as 24-bit. Although with 32-bits you could potentially describe more than four billion colors, the human eye can't differentiate that many. Thirty-two-bit color is therefore a combination of 24-bit color, with its 16.7 million colors, and an 8-bit grayscale overlay (known as a *mask*), which primarily specifies transparency and how graphics should be composited. For example, a mask can be used to make a graphic appear round or have holes in it, by showing parts of the graphic beneath it. This grayscale mask is known as an alpha mask, or the *alpha channel*.

Because bit depth is directly related to computer memory (remember that a bit is a chunk of memory), the higher the color range, the more memory required. And not just any memory, but video memory. Until recently, video memory was fairly limited, and most computer systems were shipped displaying only 256 colors (8-bit). Therefore, when designing for the Web, artists have been forced to work with the lowest common denominator and create work in 256 colors.

Note Increasingly, the average computer used for surfing the Web has a greater bit depth and can display more colors. A recent poll showed that out of 7 million Web visitors, less than 10 percent were using 256 color systems. However, this doesn't mean that all graphics can now be in millions of colors. The more colors used in an image, the larger the file size, and download speed over the Internet is a major consideration in Web design.

Cross-Reference You can find examples of the appearance of various bit depths in the color insert.

Understanding hexadecimal colors

In HTML, the language of the Web, RGB color values are given in *hexadecimal* format. Hexadecimal (or *hex*, as it is more commonly called), is a base-16 number system, which means that instead of the numbers running from 0 to 9 and then repeating, there is an initial series of 16 number values:

```
0, 1, 2, 3, 4, 5, 6, 7, 8, 9, A, B, C, D, E, F
```

The single letters represent values that would normally take two digits in the decimal system: A equals 10, B equals 11, C equals 12, and so on. When you want to count beyond single hex digits — in other words, go higher than F — you place a one in front of the numbers and continue, just as you do in decimals when you want to go beyond single digits. Although this looks strange to our decimal-trained eyes, continuing the above hex series appears as follows (keep in mind that "10" is actually 16):

```
10, 11, 12, 13, 14, 15, 16, 17, 18, 19, 1A, 1B, 1C, 1D, 1E, 1F, 20
```

In the decimal number system, two digits can be used to express any number up to 99; but in the hexadecimal number system, the highest two-digit number is FF. Although they're both two-digit numbers, in hex, you have to count 255 things to fill up two digits.

Tip   Don't cheat and convert FF to 1515 and think of it as one thousand, five hundred and fifteen. When you look at the decimal number 99, you assume that the first 9 is really 90, or 9 multiplied by (base) 10. When you look at the hexadecimal number FF, remember that the first F is really 15 multiplied by (base) 16, which is equal to 240 in decimal. Add the other F, and you can see how FF is equal to 255.

RGB values are expressed in hex with a set of three two-digit numbers, with each of the three values corresponding to 256 levels of red, green, and blue, respectively. For example, white in RGB values would be represented as 255, 255, 255 — each color being its most intense. The equivalent in hex is FF, FF, FF, which in HTML is written all together, like this: FFFFFF. Black is 0, 0, 0 in RGB and 000000 in hex, whereas a pure red would be 255, 0, 0 in RGB, and FF0000 in hex.

Although it may seem completely foreign to you initially, hexadecimal colors quickly become recognizable. You'll even start to notice patterns; for example, any color where the hex triplets are all the same represents a shade of gray — 111111 is the darkest gray, and EEEEEE is the lightest.

Exploring Websafe colors

As noted previously, the generally accepted lowest-common denominator in monitor displays is 8-bit, or 256 colors. Unfortunately, yet one more restriction exists on Web colors: the browser. Each of the major browsers from Microsoft and Netscape uses a fixed palette of 256 colors to render 8-bit images on both Windows and Macintosh operating systems. After the 40 unique colors used for system displays in both Macintosh and Windows platforms are subtracted — because you generally would like your Web graphics to look the same on both Windows and Macintosh platforms — a common palette of 216 colors remains. Because any system can safely use any of these colors without dithering (faking the color with a combination of two others), they are collectively referred to as the *browser-safe* or *Websafe* palette.

Tip   Interestingly enough—and thankfully—Websafe colors are easy to spot when given in hexadecimal. Any hex color that contains some combination of 00, 33, 66, 99, CC, or FF—such as 0000FF, 336699, or FFCC00—is Websafe.

It's important to realize that the Websafe palette is for use with flat-color images, such as illustrations, logos, and headline text—the kinds of images that are drawn or created right on a computer and exported in the GIF format. Using Websafe colors in these images keeps flat areas of color flat. Photographic images are still exported with a 24-bit palette—usually in the JPEG format—and dithered by the browser if necessary.

Because of its importance in Web design, Fireworks makes extensive use of the Websafe palette, and includes a number of features for efficiently working with it:

✦ By default, the color picker that is accessible from every color well in the program is set to the Websafe palette.

✦ Holding down the Shift key when you use the Eyedropper tool causes the tool to convert any color that it samples to Websafe.

✦ The Find and Replace panel can search for colors that fall outside the Websafe palette and snap them to their nearest neighbor, in one document or a range of documents, all in one step.

Cross-Reference   For more about using the Find and Replace panel, see Chapter 18.

✦ The Fill panel has a Web Dither category that can convert any color into a pattern of Websafe colors that closely approximates the color.

As you continue to work with Fireworks and in Web design in general, you'll become more and more familiar with the Websafe palette.

Looking at platform differences

Not only does the Web designer have to contend with a limited palette and a host of issues with the wide variety of browsers in the market, but also many differences worth noting exist between the Windows and Macintosh platforms. Chief among these is the *gamma* setting.

The gamma setting, or more properly, the *gamma correction* setting, is designed to avoid having midtones onscreen appear too dark. The problem is that different gamma settings exist for different systems. The Macintosh typically defaults to a setting of 1.8, whereas Windows uses 2.2, which is also the standard for television. The lower gamma setting on the Mac works well to emulate print output, but the display seems brighter when compared to Windows. Consequently, the same graphic appears darker on a Windows machine than on a Macintosh.

Tip

Mac users who want to set their system to 2.2 for Web or television work can do so if they have ColorSync enabled. Open the Monitors or Monitors and Sound Control Panel, click the Color button, and then follow the instructions to calibrate your display. Choose 2.2 as a gamma setting. You can also choose to use the "native" gamma setting of your display, which may be 2.2.

It's also worth noting that Windows machines are typically paired with much more diverse varieties of display hardware, while most Macs typically use very similar graphics adapters and a matching, or even built-in, display. Actual testing might lead us to find that typical Windows gamma varies more than typical Mac gamma; after all, we're talking about many different manufacturers instead of one. Aiming squarely at 2.2 in your work won't necessarily guarantee that your work is viewed properly by all Windows users.

One solution to this problem — still, unfortunately, at the "coming soon" stage — is Fireworks' native format, PNG. Images saved in a PNG format have built-in gamma correction, so that they are displayed correctly, regardless of the user's system. Although displaying a PNG image in a browser is old hat these days, support for the gamma correction elements of the format is still unavailable anywhere except in Internet Explorer for Windows.

In the future, the influence of television on the Internet, and the Internet on computing, may result in a 2.2 gamma correction setting becoming standard on the Macintosh (I already run my Mac at this setting). For now, the best solution is to view your work under both settings and compromise a little when necessary, in order to achieve acceptable results on both platforms. To aid in this, Fireworks provides a shortcut for viewing the "other" gamma setting: the Macintosh Gamma and Windows Gamma commands.

Choose View ➪ Macintosh Gamma in Fireworks for Windows in order to see a representation of how your work will appear on most Macs. Similarly, choose View ➪ Windows Gamma in Fireworks for Macintosh in order to view the way your work will look on most Windows machines.

Tip

Mac users: If you're using a gamma setting of 1.8 while preparing an image for television, remember that Windows gamma is the same as TV gamma, so the Windows Gamma command doubles as a TV gamma preview.

Cross-Reference

See the effects of Fireworks' cross-platform gamma view in the color insert.

Working with color management

ColorSync (Macintosh only) and Kodak color management systems work with Photoshop and certain other applications to achieve accurate color representations across monitors, scanners, and printers. If you import an image from one of these applications into Fireworks, you may find that the color values are shifted slightly because Fireworks does not work with color management systems.

The easiest way to prevent this color shifting is to disable color management in the source application before exporting or saving an image. Alternatively, you can import the image into Fireworks and use the Hue slider on the Hue/Saturation Xtra to adjust all the colors slightly, moving them all back to Websafe values, for example.

Mixing Colors

The general color mechanism in Fireworks is the Color Mixer. With the Color Mixer, you can select your Fill and Stroke colors from the entire spectrum available to you in any of five different color models. You can also directly determine a color by entering the appropriate values through the sliders or text boxes.

Using the Color Mixer

To open the Color Mixer, choose Window ➪ Color Mixer. The Color Mixer, shown in Figure 7-1, is divided into three main areas:

✦ **Color wells:** The Stroke and Fill color wells display the active color for the selected object stroke and fill, respectively. The color defaults can also be applied and swapped through buttons in this section.

✦ **Color sliders:** Use the color sliders to choose a color by altering its components.

✦ **Color ramp:** The color ramp displays all colors of a particular color model and enables you to select them with an Eyedropper tool.

Figure 7-1: Open the Color Mixer to select your Stroke and Fill colors from the color ramp, or set them with the color sliders.

Choosing a color

The Web artist alternates between creating new graphics fresh from the mind's eye and matching or adapting existing imagery. Both methods are valid ways of working, and Fireworks enables you to select the colors you need accordingly. Should you want to create visually, selecting your colors direct from the palette, you can sample colors either from a full-spectrum color ramp, the more limited showing of the active swatches, or directly off the screen from another image. If you would prefer to work more formulaically, the color sliders enable you to enter a precise value in five different color models.

Using the color ramp

To select a color from the color ramp, follow these steps:

1. Open the Color Mixer by choosing Window ➪ Color Mixer.

2. Select either the Stroke or Fill color well. The selected color well is highlighted with a border around it.

3. Move your pointer over the color ramp. The pointer changes into one of two Eyedropper tools. The Eyedropper tool with a wavy line indicates that a Stroke color is to be selected, whereas the Eyedropper tool with the solid block indicates that you're choosing a Fill color.

Initially, the color ramp display matches the chosen color model, such as RGB, Hexadecimal, or Grayscale. You can change the color ramp, however, by Shift+ clicking it. With each Shift+click, the color ramp cycles through one of three displays: the Websafe, full-color, and grayscale spectrums.

4. Choose any desired color in the color ramp by clicking it once.

If you click and drag your pointer across the color ramp, the wells and the slider settings update dynamically. This gives you a better idea of the actual color you're selecting — the swatch in the color well is large and the color values are easy to follow. If the color chosen is unsatisfactory, select Edit ➪ Undo in order to return to your previous setting.

5. After you've selected the color by releasing the mouse button, both the color well and sliders display the new color. If an object was selected when the new color was chosen, its Fill or Stroke color changes to match the new one.

Using Color Mixer sliders

Another method of selecting a color uses the Color Mixer sliders. As with other Fireworks sliders, you can enter the values either directly in the text boxes, or by dragging the slider handle up or down. The availability of sliders depends upon the color model chosen. Sliders for RGB, CMY, and HSB all match their respective initials.

Choosing the Hexadecimal model displays the R, G, and B color sliders. Selecting Grayscale shows just one slider, K, which represents the percentage of black.

If you're not trying to match a specific RGB or other value, you can visually — as opposed to numerically — mix your colors by moving the slider and watching the selected color well. If you have an object selected, its stroke or fill settings update when you release the mouse button.

Accessing the color models

Aside from the previously described RGB and Hexadecimal models, Fireworks offers three other possible color models. The capability to switch between different color models is important in Web design. Quite often the Web artist is asked to convert graphics from another medium, be it another computer-based medium or print. You can also switch from one system to another in order to take advantage of its special features. For example, switching the HSB enables you to select a tint of a particular color by reducing the saturation.

All color models are chosen by selecting the panel's Options menu in the upper-right corner of the Color Mixer. Choose a color model from the list that appears, as shown in Figure 7-2.

Figure 7-2: Choose from five different color models in the Color Mixer's panel Options menu.

RGB

Choosing the RGB color model enables you to select any one of 16.7 million colors that are available in the 24-bit color spectrum. Whereas not all the colors are represented on the RGB color ramp (at a resolution of 72 pixels per inch, displaying all pixels would require over 19,000 square feet — that's a mighty big monitor), you can enter any required value in the color sliders shown in Figure 7-3. The color sliders use values from 0 to 255.

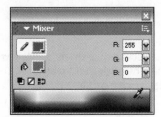

Figure 7-3: Work with the RGB color model to specify any one of 16.7 million colors.

If your computer display is not capable of showing as many colors as are viewable in the color model — for example, if your system is set on 256 colors and you choose RGB — you'll see some dithering in the color ramp. *Dithering* is the combination of two or more colors to simulate another color, and it appears as noticeable dots. Although the display may dither, the colors that the Eyedropper tool chooses are accurate RGB values.

Hexadecimal

When you select the Hexadecimal color model, two things happen. The Color Mixer sliders translate their displayed values to hexadecimal values, and the color ramp depicts a Websafe spectrum, as shown in Figure 7-4. With a Websafe color ramp (which is the default when Fireworks first starts up after installation), you'll notice what's referred to as *banding*. Banding occurs when the range of colors is not large enough to make a smooth gradation.

Figure 7-4: Although you can enter any valid hexadecimal RGB value in the color sliders with the Hexadecimal color model, only Websafe colors are selectable in the default color ramp.

Caution   All values entered manually in the slider text boxes must be in the proper hexadecimal pair format. If you try to enter a numeric value outside of hexadecimal range, such as 225, Fireworks just drops the first number without properly converting the value.

CMY

As mentioned previously in the section "Working with Color on the Web," most designers coming from a print background are used to expressing color as a mixture of cyan, magenta, yellow, and black: CMYK, also known as the four-color process. In theory, the color range should be representable with just the first three colors, but in printing practice, the fourth color, black, is necessary to produce the darker colors.

Fireworks presents CMY colors as a range of numbers from 0 to 255. In some ways, CMY can be considered the opposite of RGB. RGB is referred to as an *additive* process because you add the colors together to reach white. CMY is a *subtractive* process because you take colors away to make white. When you choose CMY from the panel Options menu, the Color Mixer panel displays a slider for C (Cyan), one for M (Magenta), and one for Y (Yellow), as shown in Figure 7-5.

Figure 7-5: Print designers new to the Web will find the CMY color model familiar.

Fireworks isn't concerned with output to a print medium, so it can express the color spectrum with just cyan, magenta, and yellow, without resorting to the addition of black. This, however, does make translating a CMYK color to a CMY color difficult. The best workaround I've found is to use a common third model, such as RGB, or a specific Pantone color. Given the broad spectrum of colors, pun intended, available in each color mode, you may notice some shifting of color as the best match is found. It's difficult to obtain a precise match when you convert colors.

HSB

HSB is short for Hue, Saturation, and Brightness. It is a color model available on numerous graphics programs, including Photoshop. Hue represents the color family, as seen on a color wheel. Because of the circular model, Hue values are presented in degrees from 0 to 360. Saturation determines the purity of the color, in terms of a percentage. Saturation of 100 percent is equal to the purest version of any hue. The Brightness value, also expressed as a percentage, is the amount of light or dark in a color — 0 percent is black, and 100 percent is the brightest that a color can appear. If the brightness is reduced to zero, the Hue and Saturation values are automatically reduced to zero, as well. After choosing HSB from the panel Options menu on the Color Mixer panel, the three sliders change to H, S, and B (see Figure 7-6).

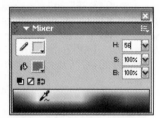

Figure 7-6: Use the HSB color model to easily lighten or darken a particular hue.

Caution

Don't attempt to directly translate HSB values from the similarly named HLS color model. HLS (Hue, Luminosity, and Saturation), a color model used in FreeHand and other drawing programs, also available in the Mac OS color picker, uses Luminosity rather than Brightness as its "light" component. The key difference between Luminosity and Brightness lies in how a color is affected at the higher end of the scale. In HSB, when full Brightness is combined with full Saturation, colors are at their most vivid. In HLS, full Luminosity, regardless of Saturation level, makes colors white.

Grayscale

Despite the richness of the realm of color — or maybe because of it — grayscale images have an undeniable power. Whether you're constructing graphics as homage to black-and-white movies, or blending black-and-white photographs in a full-color site, access to a grayscale palette is essential. The Fireworks grayscale palette is a full range of 256 tones, ranging from absolute white to absolute black.

When you select Grayscale from the Color Mixer's panel Options menu, the three sliders of the other palette are reduced to one slider and marked K, for black. As Figure 7-7 shows, the black value is expressed as a percentage, where 100 percent is black and 0 percent is white.

Figure 7-7: To access any one of 256 shades of gray, select the Grayscale color model.

Selecting Swatches of Color

Quite often the graphics for a Web site are designed with a particular palette in mind. The most common palette contains the 216 Websafe colors, which people use to keep images from shifting colors on different platforms. Palettes are also devised to match a particular color scheme—either for an entire Web site or for one particular area. Each palette can be saved as a separate swatch file.

Fireworks provides very full palette support through its Swatches panel. You can modify, store, load, or completely scrap swatches to start fresh. You can even grab the palette from a sample image.

Choosing from the color wells

The standard Fireworks color picker is quite powerful. When it's open, your cursor changes into an Eyedropper tool that enables you to select a color from any onscreen image—whether it's in the color picker, in another part of Fireworks, or even anywhere else on your computer display. You can quickly set a stroke or fill to None by using the No Color button, without opening the respective panels. Finally, the Palette button gives you instant access to your operating system's color picker(s).

To access the colors in the current swatch set, select the arrow button next to any color well. When the color picker appears, as shown in Figure 7-8, move your pointer over any of the color swatches. As you move your pointer, notice that the color chip in the upper-right corner dynamically updates to show the color underneath the pointer; the color name in hexadecimal is also displayed. Click once to choose a color.

Figure 7-8: You can open the color picker from any color well in Fireworks.

Tip   If you've selected a color for a stroke or fill where previously none existed, Fireworks automatically enables the setting, turning the Stroke type to Pencil and the Fill type to Solid for the selected color.

Even though the color picker is handy, you might want to switch between different swatch sets quite regularly. For example, if you decide to focus your work on an object that's composed entirely of grayscale colors, changing the color picker to the grayscale swatch set will simplify your work. The panel Options menu on the color picker enables you to quickly choose another swatch set (see Figure 7-9).

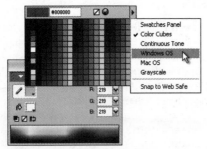

Figure 7-9: The panel Options menu on the color picker enables you to quickly choose another set of swatches.

Using the Eyedropper

The Eyedropper is a great tool for ensuring color fidelity across images. Need to match a particular shade of purple in the background graphic for the outline of the navigation bar you're building? Click once with the Eyedropper to grab that color, and the selected color well fills with the chosen color.

The Eyedropper tool is straightforward to use. Once you've displayed the color picker, the Eyedropper is already "in your hand," and your cursor changes into its namesake shape. Now you can easily select a color from anywhere within Fireworks.

Moreover, the Eyedropper tool is not limited to sampling colors from Fireworks. You can pick up a color from any application or graphic displayed on your computer. However, a slight difference exists in the way this feature works on each computing platform:

✦ With Macintosh systems, the Eyedropper works the same way outside of Fireworks as it does within Fireworks. Any color anywhere on your display is fair game, at all times.

✦ With Windows systems, click within the Fireworks window and hold down the mouse button, then drag the mouse cursor outside of the Fireworks window. Release the mouse button when the cursor is over the color you want to sample.

Tip

It's possible — even likely — that the color you sample with the Eyedropper won't be Websafe. To snap the sampled color to the closest Websafe value, press Shift when you select your color. Pressing Esc on the keyboard closes the color picker, canceling the selection of a new color, if you change your mind about using it.

Accessing the system color picker(s)

If you work with a number of graphics applications, you may find working with your operating system's color picker(s) rather than with those in Fireworks is more convenient. To open the system color picker(s), click the Palette button on the Fireworks color picker. Closing the system color picker(s) automatically assigns the last selected color to the Fireworks color well.

The Macintosh system color picker dialog box has several color pickers from which to choose. Table 7-2 details these different schemes.

	Table 7-2	
Color Models in the Macintosh Color Picker Dialog Box		
Color Model	*Description*	
CMYK	Standard model for color printing.	
Crayon	A box of crayons with names such as Banana and Cool Marble. Click a crayon to select that color.	
HLS	Hue, Luminosity, and Saturation.	
HSV	Hue, Saturation, and Value model with a color wheel.	
HTML	RGB expressed in hexadecimal numbers, with an optional Websafe snap.	
RGB	Standard model for computer displays, with an optional Websafe snap.	

Choose a color model from the left part of the Color Picker dialog box, as shown in Figure 7-10, and specify settings on the right. The color that the Fireworks color picker is set to is shown in the upper right of the window as the "original" color, for comparison with the color you're currently choosing.

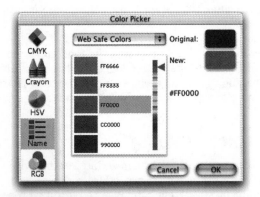

Figure 7-10: The Macintosh Color Picker dialog box offers numerous color models from which to choose.

Tip   If you hold down Option while you're in the Macintosh color picker dialog box, the cursor changes into an Eyedropper tool that works just like the one in Fireworks. Use it to sample colors from anywhere on the screen.

In addition to these default color pickers, the Macintosh color picker system is extensible, so you may have other color pickers, depending on the hardware and software you have installed. Color pickers are installed by Apple Display Software, for example, or you may have installed a third-party color picker yourself.

The Windows system color picker is split into two parts, as shown in Figure 7-11. On the left, you have 48 color chips from the Windows system palette. Located on the right is a full-color spectrum with a value bar for mixing colors. Both RGB and Hue, Saturation, and Luminance text boxes are available below the spectrum. To choose a color beyond the basic 48, you must create it by choosing a color from both the main spectrum and the value bar on the right, and then adding it to one of the 16 custom color wells on the left.

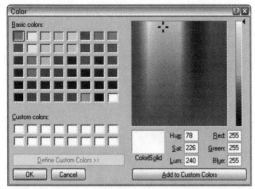

Figure 7-11: The Windows color picker offers easy access to colors from the Windows system palette, or create 16 of your own colors from the full spectrum.

 Tip

In order to avoid overwriting a previously created custom color, select an empty custom color well in the Windows color picker before creating a new custom color.

Opting for no color

When it comes to stroke and fill colors, remember that "no color" is as valid an option as any color. To disable a fill or a stroke, just choose the No Color button from the Fireworks color picker. When you select the No Color button, the color chip displays the checkerboard pattern used to depict transparency in Fireworks.

Using the Swatches panel

The Swatches panel is deceptively simple in appearance. Consisting of just colors (with the exception of the panel Options menu), the Swatches panel enables you to choose a stroke, fill, or effect color from the active palette. As with all other Fireworks floating panels, the Swatches panel can be moved and resized—the latter feature is especially important if you want to show a larger palette.

 Caution

Remember that the Swatches panel displays the current Fireworks palette, not the palette of the current document.

The most basic use of the Swatches panel is similar to that of the Color Mixer and the color picker. Select the color well you want to alter, and then choose a color by clicking any of the color chips in the Swatches panel, as shown in Figure 7-12. There's no real feedback in the Swatches panel to identify the color other than visually; you would need to have the Info panel visible to see the RGB or other components.

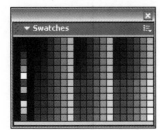

Figure 7-12: Pick a color, any color, from the Swatches panel.

As you find out in the next section, you can choose from a number of preset color palettes. However, you can also add any custom mixed color — or color selected with the Eyedropper — to a swatch. The custom color then becomes available from anywhere in the program where you can click a color well or access the Swatches panel. You can add new colors, extending an existing palette or replacing a color on the palette. You can also delete standard or custom colors from a palette.

To add, replace, or remove a color in the Swatches panel, follow these steps:

1. Mix or sample the color you want to add, so that it appears in the active color well.

2. Display the Swatches panel by choosing Window ➪ Swatches, or by clicking the Swatches tab if the panel is behind other panels in a group.

3. Position your pointer over an open area in the Swatches panel and click once to add a new color to the current palette. When over an open area, the Eyedropper pointer becomes a paint bucket.

4. Press Shift while you position your pointer over the color to be replaced, and click once to replace an existing color in the current palette. If you press Shift when the pointer is positioned over an existing color, the pointer becomes a paint bucket.

5. Hold down Ctrl (Command), position the pointer over the color to be deleted, and click once to remove a color from the current palette. When you press Ctrl (Command), the pointer becomes a pair of scissors. For best results, position the scissors so that the crossing of the blades — the middle of the X — is placed directly over the color you want to delete.

To reset any standard palette that has been modified, select that palette from the panel Options menu.

Picking preset swatches

Fireworks has four standard palettes that you can select at any time:

✦ **Web 216 Palette:** Colors common on both major browsers, Netscape Navigator and Internet Explorer, on Macintosh and Windows

✦ **Windows System:** The color palette used by Windows to display its system elements

✦ **Macintosh System:** The color palette used by the Macintosh operating system

✦ **Grayscale:** A monochrome palette ranging from white to black

All palettes, with the exception of Web 216, are composed of 256 colors.

To switch palettes, select a different one from the Swatches panel Options menu, as shown in Figure 7-13.

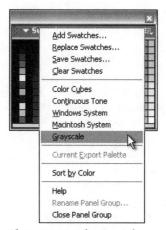

Figure 7-13: The Swatches panel Options menu enables you to select different standard palettes, or to load your own.

One additional palette is available from the panel Options menu: the Current Export palette. Choosing this option loads the current document's export palette from the Color Table panel—detailed later in this chapter—into the Swatches panel.

Managing swatches

The real power of Fireworks swatches is in the capability to load and store custom palettes. The remaining five commands on the panel Options menu are dedicated to managing swatches. Fireworks can load and save palettes in a format known as Active Color Table (ACT). Adobe Photoshop can also read and write ACT files, so loading Photoshop palettes in Fireworks is easy.

However, you don't have to save your palettes as ACT files in order to work with them in the Swatches panel. Fireworks can also glean the palette from any GIF or other 8-bit indexed color file. Moreover, you have two different ways to access a previously stored palette. You can either append the saved palette to the current swatch, or you can use just the saved palette.

To load palettes into the Swatches panel, follow these steps:

1. Click the panel Options menu button in the Swatches panel.

2. Choose Add Swatches if you want to extend the existing palette with a new palette.

3. Choose Replace Swatches if you want to use the just saved palette.

   In either case, the Open dialog box appears for you to select a palette.

4. Choose the type of palette you want to load:

   • Color table (filename typically ends in .act)

Note On the Mac, a color table file may not have (and doesn't require) the .act filename extension. Color table files have a File Type code of 8BCT. Although Fireworks doesn't provide an icon for its color table files, color table files saved by Photoshop have an icon with color wells and the description CLUT on them.

   • GIF files (filename ends in .gif)

5. Locate the file and click Open when you're ready.

If you chose Add Swatches, the new palette is appended to the end of the existing swatch. If Replace Swatches is used, the existing swatch is removed, and the new palette is displayed in its place.

Tip Although the feature is a bit hidden, you can also load Adobe Swatches in addition to Adobe Color Tables. Adobe Swatches have a file extension of .aco, rather than the Color Tables extension of .act. Fireworks for Windows does not offer the .aco file type in its Open dialog boxes; enter ***.aco** in the File Name text box, and press Return in order to force the dialog box to list files with the filename extension .aco.

In Fireworks, all palettes are saved in Active Color Table format. To save a current swatch, simply choose Save Swatches from the panel Options menu, and name the file in the standard Save As dialog box.

You can erase the entire palette from the Swatches panel by choosing Clear Swatches from the panel Options menu. This removes any palette displayed in the Swatches panel, but it doesn't affect the default palettes at all. If you issue the Clear Swatches command, the color wells revert to using the default Websafe palette in the color pickers.

The final panel Options menu command in the Swatches panel is Sort by Color. As the name implies, Sort by Color displays the active palette by color value, rather than by the default mathematical order. If new colors have been added—or a completely new palette loaded—those colors are sorted, as well. Please note that you can't undo a Sort by Color command; to restore a standard palette to its previous configuration, choose the particular palette from the panel Options menu.

Accessing the Color Table

If you've specified a reduced export palette in the Optimize panel—generally by specifying to export as a GIF—then the current document's export palette is reduced accordingly and won't match any standard palette. The Color Table, shown in the lower portion of the Optimize panel, offers easy access to the export palette.

To display the Optimize panel, shown in Figure 7-14, choose Window ➪ Optimize, or click the Optimize panel tab if the Optimize panel is docked behind another panel.

Figure 7-14: The Color Table on the Optimize panel enables you to access the current document's export palette.

If you've carefully reduced the export palette for your document to 16 or 32 colors, you probably don't need or want access to colors outside that range while you're still working with the document. Accidentally adding a new color at this point may simply undo optimization work you've already done.

If the Optimize panel displays a button entitled "(Rebuild)" at the bottom, the colors displayed are "out of date" because you've made some modification to the export palette. Click the Rebuild button to update it.

Cross-Reference   For more about working with the Color Table on the Optimize panel, see Chapter 15.

Fireworks Technique: Converting Pantone Colors to Websafe Colors

Many Web designers have clients with specific concerns regarding the use of their logos, trademarks, and other brand identifiers. Many larger companies have spent large amounts of money to develop a distinct look in their print, television, and other media advertising and marketing — and they want to ensure that their look continues over the Internet. Most designers work with a set series of colors — Pantone colors are among the most popular — that can be specified for print work. It should come as no surprise to discover that many of these colors fall outside of the Websafe palette of 216 colors.

A way exists, however, to bring the two seemingly divergent worlds together. In fact, several ways exist. Pantone makes a product called ColorWeb Pro that converts its colors so they are usable in computer graphics. ColorWeb Pro is a small utility that enables you to look up a Pantone color by number and then displays a color chip with the equivalent RGB and/or HTML color values.

ColorWeb Pro runs in two modes: the Pantone Matching System, which enables you to choose from all 1,012 Pantone colors; and the Pantone Internet Color System, which converts your choice to a Websafe color before sending it to Fireworks. If you're satisfied with a simple conversion from Pantone to Websafe, use the Internet Color System to choose a Pantone color and convert it to Websafe.

To get a more accurate representation of a Pantone color, you can combine the Pantone Matching System with Fireworks' Web Dither fill, sampling a Pantone color and enabling Fireworks to create a Web Dither equivalent. This option opens many of the Pantone colors for use on the Internet where it counts the most — in the fill areas. Though this system is not perfect — I occasionally find Pantone colors that do not have a good duplicate in the Web Dither mode — it's quite close.

In Windows, ColorWeb Pro runs as an application that is basically a floating color chip. Double-clicking this chip opens the Pantone color pickers. Right-clicking the chip displays a context menu that enables you to specify options.

On the Mac, ColorWeb Pro simply installs its color pickers into the Mac's extensible color picker dialog box. Access these new color pickers as you would access any other system-level color picker.

Caution Mac users may find that they already have Pantone color pickers because they were installed by ColorSync or the Apple Display Software. In this case, installing the ColorWeb Pro demo overwrites your Pantone color pickers, necessitating a reinstall of ColorSync or the Apple Display Software if you don't purchase ColorWeb Pro after the demo times out.

Using ColorWeb Pro for Windows

To convert a Pantone color to a Web Dither color in Fireworks for Windows, follow these steps:

1. If it isn't already running, start ColorWeb Pro.

2. Select the object you want to fill with a Pantone color.

3. Choose the Web Dither category from the Fill section of the Property inspector.

4. Select the Fill color well and then click on the color well entitled Source Color to open the Fireworks color picker.

5. Click the Palette button to display the System Color Picker. The Pantone Color Picker opens, as shown in Figure 7-15.

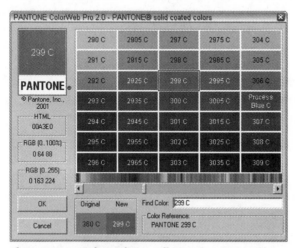

Figure 7-15: ColorWeb Pro offers you an extensive palette of Pantone colors.

6. Locate the desired color either by entering its number in the Find Color text box, or by selecting it. Click OK when you're done in order to return to your document with the selected Pantone color filling your object.

Fireworks calculates the closest match using the Web Dither technique. If the Pantone color is Websafe, both dither color wells hold the same color.

Using ColorWeb Pro for Macintosh

To convert a specific Pantone color to a Web Dither color in Fireworks for Macintosh, follow these steps:

1. Select the object you want to fill with a Pantone color.

2. Choose the Web Dither category from the Fill section of the Property inspector.

3. Select the Fill color well and then click on the color well entitled Source Color to open the Fireworks color picker.

4. Click the Palette button in order to display the Macintosh Color Picker dialog box.

5. Select the Name category from the left portion of the Color Picker dialog box and then choose PANTONE(r) solid coated from the option list at the top, as shown in Figure 7-16.

6. Choose the desired Pantone color from the list in the center and then click Done to return to your document with the selected Pantone color filling your object.

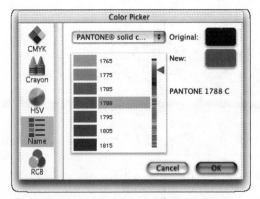

Figure 7-16: ColorWeb Pro offers you an extensive palette of Pantone colors within the Macintosh color picker dialog box.

Fireworks calculates the closest match using the Web Dither technique. If the Pantone color is Websafe, both dither color wells hold the same color.

Summary

Fireworks offers brisk color control, enabling the designer to select from the overall color model and specific palette that best serves. As you begin to delve deeper into color with your Fireworks graphics, considers these points:

✦ RGB is the language of color for the screen. Pixels depend on a mixture of red, green, and blue in order to achieve their color variations. HTML uses hexadecimal notation to designate RGB colors.

✦ Fireworks enables you to switch between several color models, such as Hexadecimal, RGB, CMY, and grayscale.

✦ To ensure that your colors appear the same regardless of which browser you use to view them, work with Websafe colors. Fireworks enables you to choose a Websafe palette to pick colors from, and it enables you to snap selected colors to their nearest Websafe equivalent.

✦ Fireworks uses three floating panels for color control: the Color Mixer, the Swatches panel, and the Optimize panel. The Color Mixer enables the designer to specify a new custom color or to modify an existing one. The Swatches panel displays a series of color chips that can come from a standard palette, such as Web 216, or from a custom palette. The Optimize panel displays a Color Table of the current document's export palette.

✦ The Eyedropper tool in the color picker can sample colors from any onscreen image, whether the image is in Fireworks or another application.

In the next chapter, you explore working with the fine lines of Fireworks graphics — strokes.

✦   ✦   ✦

Choosing Strokes

Strokes are one of the three key features of a Fireworks document. Along with fills and effects, strokes can give each element its own unique character. While the stroke is what makes a path visible, it offers far more than just "visibility." You can vary a stroke's width, color, softness, and shape, as well as control how it reacts to the speed, pressure, and direction of your drawing. Moreover, you can modify strokes already applied to any selected path and instantly see the results.

In addition to 48 built-in standard strokes in Fireworks, you can customize your strokes with an almost infinite set of variations. Numerous options, such as color, stroke width, and edge softness, exist right in the Strokes section of the Property inspector for easy experimentation. Additionally, Fireworks enables you to custom build your own stroke from the ground up. You can find explanations for all the controls in this chapter, as well as step-by-step instructions for developing special strokes, such as dotted lines.

Using the Stroke Settings

The Stroke section of the Property inspector is your control center for all stroke settings. Although you can set the stroke color in two other places, the Tools panel and the Color Mixer, the Stroke section of the Property inspector is the only place to select all the options.

Here's the typical process for setting up or modifying an existing stroke that uses all the options available for Strokes:

1. Choose Window ➪ Properties to open the Property inspector (see Figure 8-1). Alternatively, you can use the keyboard shortcut, Ctrl+F3 (Command+F3).

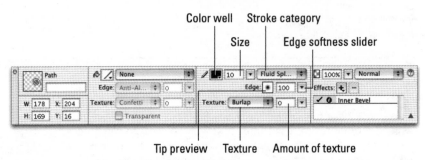

Figure 8-1: Use the controls in the Stroke section of the Property inspector to modify the stroke for an existing path or to establish a stroke before you draw.

2. Select one of the 11 categories from the Category option list. To turn off the stroke, select None from the Category option list.

3. Choose any of the available types listed for each category from the Type option list. When you choose a type, the default settings for that type's size, edge softness, and texture are also selected.

4. If desired, select a new color from the stroke color well.

5. To change how the stroke blends, use the Edge Softness slider.

6. Alter the size of the stroke by using the Size slider, or by entering a value directly in the Size text box.

7. Add a texture by choosing one from the Texture option list and setting its opacity through the Amount of texture slider.

As noted previously, you can either modify the stroke for an existing, selected path, or you can set up the stroke before you draw. To select a path, with or without a stroke already applied, move the Pointer tool over the desired path and then click the highlighted path once (assuming the Mouse Highlight preference has been left at its default setting of enabled). The path displays a red highlight if it is capable of being selected and, by default, a light-blue highlight after it has been selected.

Tip   If your work includes the same or similar color as Fireworks uses for highlighting a chosen path, you can change the color. Choose Edit ➪ Preferences, and, in the General category select the Highlight color well in order to pick a different hue or shade.

Sometimes selecting the path for stroke modification by using the selection feature of the Pointer tool is easier. If you click and drag the Pointer, a temporary rectangle is drawn out. Any paths touched by this rectangle are selected. The Pointer selection is a great way to select multiple paths if you want to simultaneously change the stroke settings for several paths. Alternatively, pressing Shift enables you to select multiple paths, one at a time, with the Pointer tool.

Tip　You can quickly switch to the Pointer tool from any other tool by pressing and holding Ctrl (Command). When you release the key, the previously selected tool returns.

When you're setting up your next stroke, be sure that no path or object is selected — otherwise, that selected object will be modified. Use the Pointer to click an empty canvas area, or choose Edit ⇨ Deselect — or its keyboard equivalent, Ctrl+D (Command+D) — to clear any previous selections.

Stroke categories and types

With the None option, Fireworks offers a dozen stroke categories. From the simplest, Pencil and Basic, to the most outrageous, Random and Unnatural, the stroke categories run the gamut, as evident in Figure 8-2. When you select a category, its types become available, with the first one in an alphabetical list chosen.

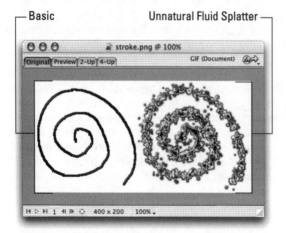

Figure 8-2: Choose any of the preset stroke types — from the Basic to the farthest out Unnatural Fluid Splatter.

The standard strokes are covered in detail later in this chapter, but two primary factors apply to all the basic strokes. First, when a particular stroke category and type are selected, the default settings for that stroke are selected — even if you just modified it seconds ago and are returning from trying out another stroke. Second, you can modify, alter, and adjust every facet of all the standard strokes.

Cross-Reference Later in this chapter, in the section "Creating New Strokes," you discover how to store and reuse a modified stroke.

Stroke edge and size

If you're reading this book in sequence, you've already discovered the concept of feathering as it relates to bitmap images in Chapter 6. As you'll remember, a feathered edge is one that blends into the background. You can "feather" strokes through the Edge Softness slider found in the Stroke panel. Moving the slider all the way to the bottom creates the hardest edge, with no blending, whereas sliding it to the top creates the softest edge, with maximum blending for the current stroke size.

As in feathering, edge softness is actually an application of the alpha channel, which controls transparency. There are 256 degrees of transparency in the alpha channel and only 100 degrees of edge softness, but the overall control is similar. Although you can select any degree of softness from the full range for any stroke, you won't see much of a difference if the stroke is thin. The thicker the stroke, the more softness variations are apparent. At the softest setting, Fireworks maintains roughly two-thirds of the stroke size. The object's opacity and the other one-third are blended into transparency equally on either side of the stroke.

You can change the thickness of a stroke either by entering a value in the Size box, or by using the Size slider to select from the range of possible values: 1 to 72 pixels wide. The Tip preview is not big enough to show the full stroke width. On both Windows and Macintosh, the Tip preview in the Property inspector stops being useful with anything much above 15 pixels and just goes black. If you need a larger, more accurate, preview you can open the Stroke Options, covered later in this chapter, where you'll notice "2x" or "4x" appears after about 50 pixels to indicate the actual width of large strokes, as shown in Figure 8-3.

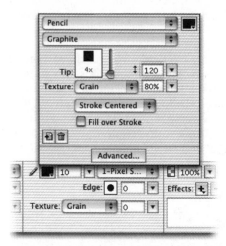

Figure 8-3: When you select a stroke size larger than the Property inspector's preview can display, the Stroke Options preview compensates numerically.

Stroke texture

Applying texture to a stroke can give a line true character and depth. Fireworks comes with a number of standard textures built in and an additional library of them on the product's CD-ROM. You can apply each of these textures to any stroke with a variable degree of intensity. Some of the preset strokes, such as the Textured Air Brush or the Basic Crayon, use a texture to create their distinctive look.

To apply a texture to a stroke, follow these steps:

1. In the Stroke section of the Property inspector, select the category and type of stroke to which you want to apply the texture.

2. If necessary, set the size, color, and edge softness for the stroke. Note: Many textures are not apparent if the stroke width is too small.

3. Choose a texture from the Texture option list.

4. Set a degree of intensity for the Texture from the Amount of texture slider. You can also enter a percentage value (with or without the percent sign) into the Amount of texture text box.

Note   You must enter a percentage value greater than 0 percent, or no texture will be visible.

Textures, in effect, are image patterns that are overlaid on top of the stroke. The amount of texture slider controls how transparent or opaque those textures become. At 0 percent, the texture is transparent and, for all intents and purposes, nonexistent. At 100 percent, the texture is as visible as possible. Figure 8-4 displays the same stroke with several variations of a single texture. As a general rule, textures containing highly contrasting elements show up better, whereas those with less contrast are more subtle and probably only useful on extremely thick strokes.

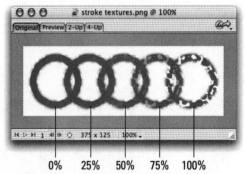

0%   25%   50%   75%   100%

Figure 8-4: The higher the amount of the texture value, the more visible the texture becomes.

On the CD-ROM   Can't get enough of those fabulous textures? You'll find another 50, courtesy of Massimo Foti, in the Extensions folder of the CD-ROM.

Working with the Built-in Strokes

One of the key advantages of Fireworks' preset strokes is speed—just pick one and go. The other main advantage is consistency. You can use the Textured Air Brush time and again to always get the same effect. Even if you prefer to work only with custom strokes, you generally begin the creation process with one of the standard ones.

This section explores each of the stroke categories and the different presets each one offers. Fireworks starts the stroke categories with two of the simplest, Pencil and Basic. After these, the list proceeds alphabetically from Air Brush to Unnatural. The overall impression, however, is that the more often used standard strokes are at the top of the list, and the more elaborate decorative strokes at the end.

Using a Graphics Tablet

Using a mouse to create objects is often derided as being like "drawing with a bar of soap," and for good reason. In the past, graphics tablets — flat panels that you draw on with a pen-like stylus — were often expensive, insensitive, and unwieldy. But, as with most technologies, graphics tablets have steadily become cheaper and better. These days, a range of sizes and specifications are available for any Macintosh or Windows computer. For beginners or casual use, Wacom's Graphire2 is a 4×5-inch tablet that hardly costs more than a mouse. Wacom's professional range of Intuos2 tablets extends from 4×5 inches to 12×18 inches with features and options to satisfy any artist. However, a 4×5-inch tablet can be quite acceptable for the typically small canvases used for Web graphics.

There's really almost no learning curve to using a graphics tablet with Fireworks. Everything works as with the mouse, except that you have far more control. The first advantage is the accuracy provided by the tablet's one-to-one relationship with areas on the screen. The classic test is a signature — try signing your name with a mouse and then with a pen and tablet — there's a world of difference because similar horizontal and vertical movements of the mouse don't correspond to similar movements of the mouse pointer.

The more obvious advantage is that you're drawing with a pen, and the pressure that you apply directly affects the appearance of the strokes that you create. Press down harder and you get a heavier line, or use a lighter touch for a softer line. This feature often leads to a slightly more imperfect or "human" look to the graphics that you create, and the imperfect appearance can be quite pleasing. Many standard Fireworks strokes are sensitive to pressure, including all the Air Brush, Calligraphy, Charcoal, Oil, and Watercolor presets. How strokes respond to pressure is also adjustable, as you discover later in this chapter when you look at how to create strokes.

Even if you're not much of an artist, selecting tools and drawing rectangles and ovals is easier with a graphics tablet. After a short while, you'll find yourself "reaching" for objects on your canvas without having to look at them or track them down with a mouse because they're always in the same place on your tablet. It's an intuitive and creative way to assemble computer graphics.

If you don't have a tablet, you can simulate increased or decreased pressure with your keyboard. Press 1 to decrease the pressure and 2 to increase it. Be aware, however, that unlike a graphics tablet, the pressure doesn't even out when you stop drawing. If you press 1 three times to decrease the pressure, the pressure continues to be light until you press 2 three times to restore it to its default state, or until you relaunch Fireworks.

Pencil

When you start to draw with the Pen tool, the path is rendered in the Pencil 1-Pixel Hard stroke, regardless of any previous stroke settings for other tools. If you use the Vector Path tool, and no stroke settings have been established, you get the same Pencil 1-Pixel Hard stroke. You might say that the Pencil is one of the real workhorses of the preset strokes.

The Pencil is a fairly generic stroke, intended to give a simple representation to any path without any embellishments. You can see the differences between its four presets, listed in Table 8-1, and depicted in Figure 8-5. The 1-Pixel Soft Pencil stroke antialiases the path to avoid the jaggies that may be apparent with the 1-Pixel Hard setting. The Colored Pencil, at four pixels, is slightly wider and is affected by pressure and speed in the same way that a real colored pencil would be affected. The final preset, Graphite, is also affected by the pressure and speed at which the paths are drawn; in addition, a high degree of texture is added to further break up the stroke.

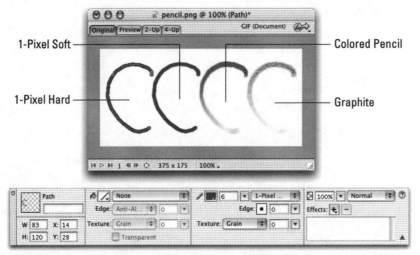

Figure 8-5: The 1-Pixel Hard and 1-Pixel Soft strokes remain constant when drawn, but the Colored Pencil and Graphite strokes are affected by pressure and speed.

Table 8-1
Pencil Type Attributes

Name	Size	Edge Softness	Texture	Amount of Texture
1-Pixel Hard	1	0 percent	None	n/a
1-Pixel Soft	1	0 percent	None	n/a
Colored Pencil	4	0 percent	None	n/a
Graphite	4	0 percent	Grain	80 percent

Basic

Another, slightly heavier variation of the simple path is the appropriately named
Basic stroke. All the Basic presets, detailed in Table 8-2, are 4-pixels wide and vary
only with the basic shape of the line (square or round) and its antialias setting.
Hard Line and Hard Line Rounded are not antialiased, whereas both Soft Line and
Soft Line Rounded are. The variations, shown in Figure 8-6, are subtle, but can make
quite a difference on some objects.

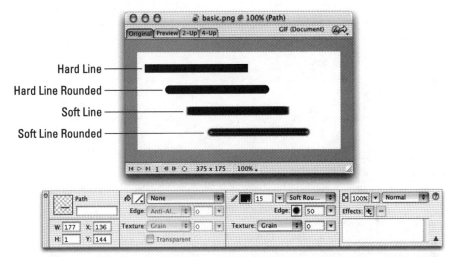

Figure 8-6: You can see the differences between the four Basic stroke types when
you look closely at them.

Table 8-2			
Basic Type Attributes			
Name	*Size*	*Edge Softness*	*Texture*	*Amount of Texture*
Hard Line	4	0 percent	None	n/a
Hard Line Rounded	4	0 percent	None	n/a
Soft Line	4	0 percent	None	n/a
Soft Line Rounded	4	0 percent	None	n/a

Air Brush

I'll 'fess up—I'm an airbrush addict. I can't get enough of the variations that the Fireworks Air Brush stroke offers. Both presets (see Table 8-3) are very sensitive to changes in speed and pressure; plus—like a real airbrush—the ink builds up if you stay in one spot, as shown in Figure 8-7. The Textured Air Brush is significantly different from the Basic Air Brush and offers a good example of what's possible when applying a texture to a stroke.

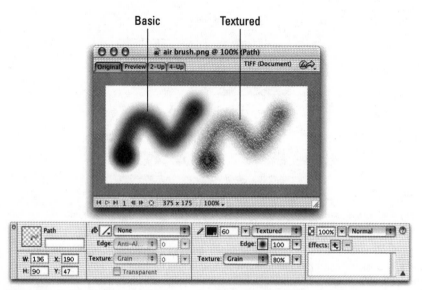

Figure 8-7: The difference between the two Air Brush presets is quite noticeable, as is the build-up on each at the end of the two strokes.

Table 8-3
Air Brush Type Attributes

Name	Size	Edge Softness	Texture	Amount of Texture
Basic	60	100 percent	None	n/a
Textured	50	100 percent	Grain	80 percent

Calligraphy

Calligraphy is an elegant handwriting art in which the thickness of a stroke varies as a line curves. The Calligraphy stroke in Fireworks offers five variations on this theme, as detailed in Table 8-4 and shown in Figure 8-8. Only the Bamboo preset does not create distinct thick-and-thin curved lines — that's because all the others use a slanted brush, whereas Bamboo's brush is circular, like a bamboo stalk. The Quill preset is pressure- and speed-sensitive and, along with the Ribbon and Wet presets, builds up ink as it rounds a curve, emphasizing the angles.

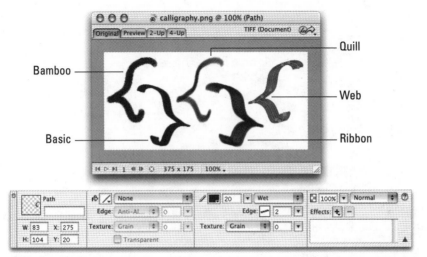

Figure 8-8: Great lettering possibilities are the hallmark of the Calligraphy stroke.

Table 8-4
Calligraphy Type Attributes

Name	Size	Edge Softness	Texture	Amount of Texture
Bamboo	20	0 percent	Grain	50 percent
Basic	14	0 percent	None	n/a
Quill	20	20 percent	Grain	25 percent
Ribbon	25	0 percent	None	n/a
Wet	20	0 percent	None	n/a

Charcoal

The Charcoal strokes are notable for their textures, both within the strokes themselves and on their edges. As you can see in Table 8-5, each preset uses some degree of Grain texture. The Creamy and Pastel presets vary according to a stroke's pressure and speed—Creamy more so than Pastel. The key difference between the Soft preset and the other preset strokes is that with the Soft preset the size of the brush changes randomly as you draw—the width fluctuates from a maximum of 20 pixels to a minimum of 5 pixels. Figure 8-9 shows a side-by-side comparison of the Charcoal presets.

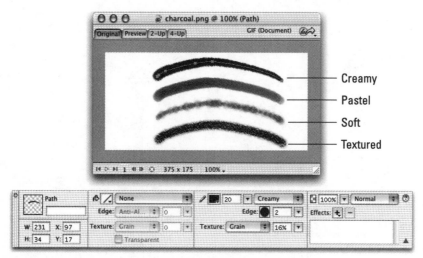

Figure 8-9: The Charcoal strokes offer a range of rough textures.

Table 8-5 Charcoal Type Attributes				
Name	**Size**	**Edge Softness**	**Texture**	**Amount of Texture**
Creamy	20	0 percent	Grain	16 percent
Pastel	20	0 percent	Grain	24 percent
Soft	20	20 percent	Grain	30 percent
Textured	20	60 percent	Grain	85 percent

Crayon

Kids can never understand why their parents like to draw with crayons as much as they do. The Crayon stroke in Fireworks captures that broken edge that gives real-world crayons character. The three Crayon presets are interesting to compare; if you look at the samples in Figure 8-10 and their details in Table 8-6, you see an obvious anomaly. The Rake preset has the smallest stroke size, but actually appears slightly thicker than both the Basic and Thick preset because the Rake preset uses four tips. It's as if you were simultaneously drawing with four crayons. With four tips, the lines overlap, and one tip can extend farther than the other three.

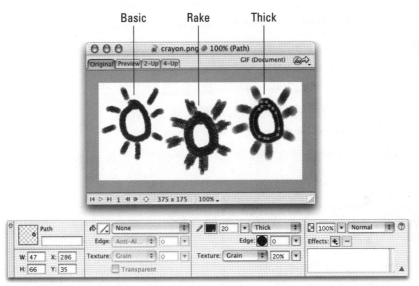

Figure 8-10: Return to your childhood — this time with scientific precision — through the Crayon strokes.

| | | Table 8-6 | | |
| | | **Crayon Type Attributes** | | |
Name	*Size*	*Edge Softness*	*Texture*	*Amount of Texture*
Basic	12	0 percent	Grain	65 percent
Rake	8	0 percent	Grain	65 percent
Thick	20	0 percent	Grain	20 percent

Felt Tip

The four presets for the Felt Tip stroke, shown in Figure 8-11, offer different degrees of transparency that mimic the real-world drawing implements they're named after. The Highlighter and the Light Marker presets are largely transparent, in fact. The Light Marker also uses a slightly softer edge than the other presets, as noted in Table 8-7.

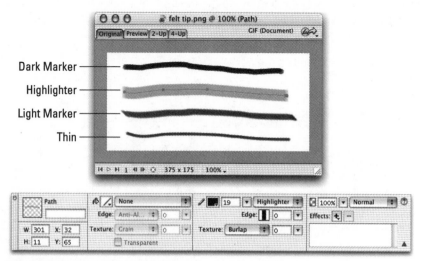

Figure 8-11: The various Felt Tip strokes achieve transparent and opaque effects when used over graphics or images.

		Table 8-7 **Felt Tip Type Attributes**		
Name	*Size*	*Edge Softness*	*Texture*	*Amount of Texture*
Dark Marker	8	0 percent	None	n/a
Highlighter	16	0 percent	None	n/a
Light Marker	12	5 percent	None	n/a
Thin	4	0 percent	None	n/a

Oil

When you look at the five Oil stroke presets in Figure 8-12, it's hard to believe that the second stroke from the left, Broad Splatter, is a single stroke. Although the size for Broad Splatter is only 10 pixels — the same as for the Bristle and Splatter presets, all shown in Table 8-8 — the larger width is because it uses two tips instead of one, and they're spaced 500 percent apart. In other words, the Broad Splatter preset can be five times the width of its pixel size. All but the Splatter preset use multiple tips, as well, but because they're set to be less than 100 percent apart, the strokes appear as single lines.

Figure 8-12: Looking for a stroke that doesn't look like a line? Try the Oil Splatter and Oil Broad Splatter presets.

Table 8-8 Oil Type Attributes				
Name	**Size**	**Edge Softness**	**Texture**	**Amount of Texture**
Bristle	10	0 percent	Grain	20 percent
Broad Splatter	10	0 percent	Grain	30 percent
Splatter	10	0 percent	Grain	30 percent
Strands	8	43 percent	None	n/a
Textured Bristles	7	0 percent	Grain	50 percent

Watercolor

As with any of the pressure- and speed-sensitive strokes, you can't get a true Watercolor feel if you draw using one of the geometric shapes; you have to use a freeform tool, such as the Brush, to achieve the more realistic look apparent in Figure 8-13. The Thin preset especially appears to run out of ink when completing a stroke. Both the Heavy and Thick presets are quite transparent and blend well when applied over an image because of their relatively soft edges (see Table 8-9).

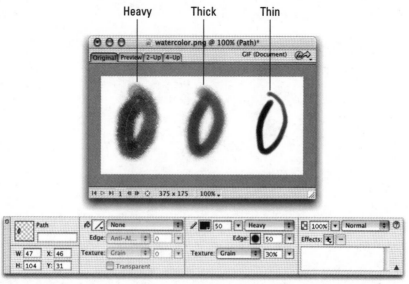

Figure 8-13: Watercolor strokes blend well and fade naturally due to their pressure and speed sensitivity.

Table 8-9
Watercolor Type Attributes

Name	Size	Edge Softness	Texture	Amount of Texture
Heavy	50	50 percent	Grain	30 percent
Thick	40	70 percent	Grain	5 percent
Thin	15	25 percent	None	n/a

Random

So much for natural media—it's time to create strokes that only a computer can create. In addition to the varying sizes, edge softness, and textures shown in Table 8-10, Random strokes also change the shape and color of the resulting stroke. The basic brush shape is evident both by the Random preset names—Dots, Fur, Squares, and Yarn—and in the sample strokes shown in Figure 8-14, but you have to turn to the color insert to really see the color variations. The Confetti preset is the most colorful and Dots the least colorful, but all the Random strokes exhibit some changing hues.

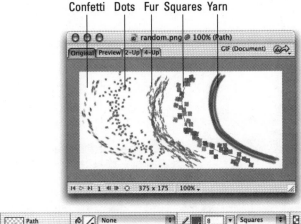

Figure 8-14: The Random strokes provide five fanciful alternatives to natural media strokes.

<table>
<tr><td colspan="5" align="center">Table 8-10
Random Type Attributes</td></tr>
<tr><td>*Name*</td><td>*Size*</td><td>*Edge Softness*</td><td>*Texture*</td><td>*Amount of Texture*</td></tr>
<tr><td>Confetti</td><td>6</td><td>25 percent</td><td>None</td><td>n/a</td></tr>
<tr><td>Dots</td><td>3</td><td>20 percent</td><td>None</td><td>n/a</td></tr>
<tr><td>Fur</td><td>10</td><td>0 percent</td><td>None</td><td>n/a</td></tr>
<tr><td>Squares</td><td>5</td><td>0 percent</td><td>Grain</td><td>20 percent</td></tr>
<tr><td>Yarn</td><td>8</td><td>0 percent</td><td>None</td><td>n/a</td></tr>
</table>

Unnatural

I think it's a pretty safe bet that the Unnatural strokes were developed in a, shall we say, party-like atmosphere. How else do you explain the messiness of Fluid Splatter, or the glow-in-the-dark feel of Toxic Waste — not to mention the otherworldliness of Viscous Alien Paint? No matter how they were developed, I find myself returning to them time and again when I need a unique and distinctive look for my graphics. Experiment by applying them to almost any object when you're up against a creative wall; the results are often surprising and useful. As you can see in Table 8-11, all the presets are roughly the same size, with the exception of Chameleon. Several of the strokes have a transparent area: 3D Glow, Fluid Splatter, Outline, Paint Splatter, and Toxic Waste. Although you can get a sense of the preset variations from Figure 8-15, you must turn to the color insert to see the Unnatural strokes in all their glory.

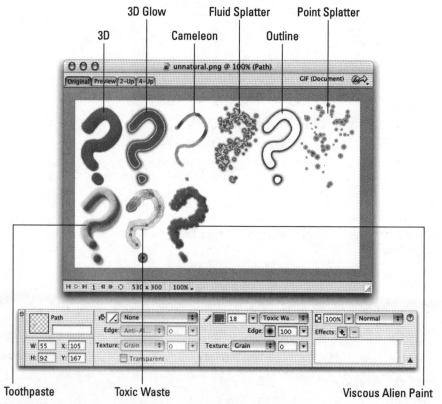

Figure 8-15: The Unnatural strokes provide an offbeat alternative to Fireworks' natural media strokes.

Table 8-11
Unnatural Type Attributes

Name	Size	Edge Softness	Texture	Amount of Texture
3D	20	12 percent	None	n/a
3D Glow	19	100 percent	None	n/a
Chameleon	6	0 percent	Grain	31 percent
Fluid Splatter	12	100 percent	None	n/a
Outline	19	100 percent	None	n/a
Paint Splatter	12	100 percent	None	n/a
Toothpaste	18	50 percent	None	n/a
Toxic Waste	18	100 percent	None	n/a
Viscous Alien Paint	12	30 percent	None	n/a

Creating New Strokes

What, the standard 48 strokes aren't enough? You need a slightly smaller Air Brush or a Calligraphy stroke with more texture? What about a dashed or dotted line instead of a solid one? Fear not; in Fireworks, custom strokes are just a click or two away. Not only can you store your minor adjustments as new strokes, but you can completely alter existing strokes and save them, either within the document or as a Fireworks Style that you can use in any document, or export and share with a colleague or workgroup.

This section is divided into two parts. The first section explains how to manage your strokes so that the ones you need are always available. The second part delves into the somewhat complex — but altogether addictive — option of editing your strokes.

Managing your strokes

Stroke management is handled by selecting Stroke Options through the Stroke category option list on the Property inspector, which is shown in Figure 8-16.

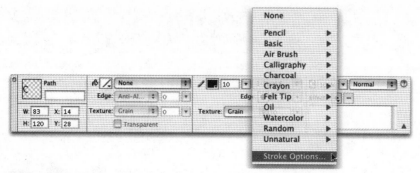

Figure 8-16: Manage your strokes through the Stroke Options menu entry in the Stroke category option list.

The Stroke Options pop-up dialog contains a number of items you should be familiar with by now — Stroke category, Stroke type, size, color, and so on — as well as a few new buttons. The new buttons, as shown in Figure 8-17, are as follows:

✦ **Save Custom Stroke:** Stores the current stroke under a new name within the active document

✦ **Delete Custom Stroke:** Removes the current stroke, custom or standard, from the Stroke category of the Property inspector

✦ **Advanced:** Displays the Edit Stroke dialog box, covered in detail later in this chapter

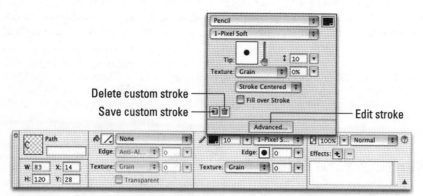

Figure 8-17: Save customized strokes, Edit existing strokes, or Delete strokes from your current document through the Stroke Options pop-up dialog.

Caution Use the Delete Stroke command carefully — although Fireworks asks for confirmation, you can't undo removing a stroke.

To store a modified stroke, follow these steps:

1. Modify any existing stroke by changing the Edge Softness, Size, Texture, and/or Amount of texture. The stroke color is not stored as part of the stroke.

2. Choose Stroke Options from the Stroke category option list. The Stroke Options pop-up dialog appears.

3. Click the Save Custom Stroke button to open the Save Stroke dialog box.

4. Enter a unique name for the stroke. If you choose a name already in use, Fireworks asks whether you want to replace the existing stroke.

5. After entering a new name, choose Save. The new stroke name is displayed alphabetically in the Type option list of the active Stroke category.

It's important to understand that any new or modified strokes are stored within the document in which they're used. The newly defined stroke is always available for use in the document in which it was stored, even if no paths currently employ it. To use the stroke in another document, follow these steps:

1. Open the document containing the stroke you want to use.

2. Select a path using the new stroke. If no path currently uses the stroke, draw a temporary one and select it.

3. Open the new document in which you want to use the new stroke.

4. Copy the selected path to the new document, either by using Edit ➪ Copy and Edit ➪ Paste, or by dragging and dropping the path from one document to the other. The new stroke setting is added to the Stroke category in the Stroke section of the Property inspector when the path containing the stroke is pasted into the document.

5. If desired, delete the copied path from the new document; the stroke is still available for later use in the document.

You can achieve the same effect of transferring strokes from one document to another in several other ways:

✦ Import a document containing one or more custom strokes. After you've clicked once to place the document, choose Undo. The graphics vanish, but all custom strokes are incorporated into the Stroke category on the Property inspector. With this technique, only custom strokes actually applied to paths in the source document are transferred.

✦ Copy the path with the custom stroke in one document, and just paste the attributes to a path in the new document by selecting that path and choosing Edit ➪ Paste Attributes.

Perhaps the best way to always be sure your custom strokes are available is to use the Styles feature. To create a new style using a custom stroke, follow these steps:

1. Select a path that uses the custom stroke.

2. If necessary, choose Window ⇨ Styles, use the keyboard shortcut Shift+F11, or click the Style tab, if visible, to display the Styles panel.

3. On the Styles panel, select the New Style button. The New Style dialog box appears, as shown in Figure 8-18.

Figure 8-18: Declaring a stroke through the New Style dialog box stores the stroke definition for easy access from all Fireworks documents.

4. In the New Style dialog box, enter a descriptive name for your stroke in the Name text box and deselect all checkboxes except Stroke Type.

5. Click OK when you're done. A new style is created in the Styles panel.

Any style added in the fashion just described is always available for any Fireworks document. To apply the stroke, just highlight any Fireworks path object and select the new style. Your custom stroke is then added to the Stroke category in the Stroke section of the Property inspector.

Cross-Reference   To discover more about the powerful Styles feature, see Chapter 16.

Editing the stroke

Whereas you can make certain modifications through the Stroke section of the Property inspector, if you really want to customize your strokes, you have to use the Edit Stroke dialog box. Although the array of choices the dialog box offers can be a bit overwhelming, after you understand how to achieve certain effects, creating new strokes becomes easy, fun, and compelling.

You can access the Edit Stroke dialog box in one of two ways:

✦ Select a path in your document and click the Stroke color well on the Tools panel. Then click the Stroke Options button, followed by the Advanced button.

✦ Select Stroke Options from the Stroke category option list in the Property inspector and then click the Advanced button.

The Edit Stroke dialog box is divided into three tabs: Options, Shape, and Sensitivity. Each of the tabs contains a preview panel that updates after every change is made. If you have selected a stroke prior to opening the Edit Stroke dialog box, you can also see the effect by using the Apply button.

Caution   In my explorations of the Edit Stroke dialog box, I uncovered one technique that worked differently than I expected — if you make a change to a stroke without selecting a path, the change does not register. Always select a path, even a temporary one, before you create a custom stroke.

The Options tab

The Options tab hosts a number of general, but important, attributes. In addition to providing controls for familiar parameters, such as a stroke's degree of texture and opacity, the Options tab, as shown in Figure 8-19, also holds the key to affecting the tightness of the stroke, how it reacts over time, and what, if any, edge effect is employed.

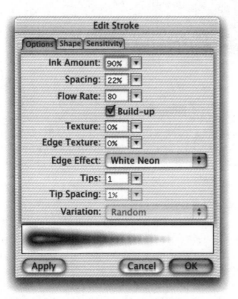

Figure 8-19: The Options tab of the Edit Stroke dialog box contains many critical controls.

Ink Amount

The first stroke attribute on the Option tab is Ink Amount. Generally, this parameter is set at 100 percent, but it's possible to lower it for any stroke. The Ink Amount value is responsible for a stroke's opacity: 100 percent is completely opaque, and 0 percent is completely transparent. The bottom of the two "CLICK" buttons in Figure 8-20 shows how a stroke is affected when the Ink Amount is reduced to 60 percent.

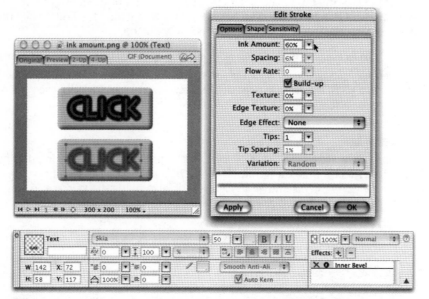

Figure 8-20: Reducing the Ink Amount of a stroke reduces its opacity.

You can also alter an object's overall opacity through the Property inspector, but changing the Ink Amount value alters just the stroke. Combine the two and the effect is additive; if, for example, you see a stroke's Ink Amount at 50 percent and you reduce the opacity of the path object to 50 percent, the stroke would appear to be 25 percent opaque (because half of 50 percent is 25 percent). The Felt Tip Highlighter preset is a good example of a stroke that uses a reduced Ink Amount in order to obtain transparency.

Spacing

Technically, each stroke consists of a long series of stroke *stamps*. A stamp is the smallest unit of a stroke; you can see it by selecting a stroke and the Vector Path tool, and then clicking the mouse once, without moving. As you draw with the Vector Path tool, or another tool, one stamp after another is laid down. The Spacing attribute determines how close those stamps are to each other. As detailed later in this chapter, you can create dotted lines by changing the Spacing value.

Note If you try to modify the Pencil 1-Pixel strokes or any of the Basic strokes, you find that no matter what you do, you won't be able to enable the Spacing or Flow Rate options. These strokes actually use a different rendering engine than all the other strokes, which sacrifices spacing and flow control to gain pinpoint pixel accuracy. To see the effects of changing either the Spacing or Flow Rate options, edit any other stroke.

The Spacing value ranges from 0 percent to 1,000 percent. If the Spacing attribute is set at 100 percent, stroke stamps in a straight line are positioned directly next to each other. If the Spacing is less than 100 percent, the stamps are overlaid on top of one another. If the Spacing is greater than 100 percent, the stamps are separated from one another. Strokes with a soft edge, such as the Air Brush, appear to be separated even when the Spacing is set to less than 100 percent, but this is only because the soft edge is incorporated into the stroke stamp. The effect in Figure 8-21 is achieved by increasing the spacing of a Felt Tip stroke to more than 200 percent.

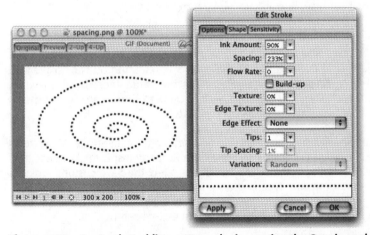

Figure 8-21: Create dotted line patterns by increasing the Spacing value.

Flow Rate and Build-up

Most stroke settings alter how a stroke changes as it's drawn across a screen. However, the Flow Rate percentage value represents how fast ink flows; the higher the number, the faster it flows. The Air Brush category is the best example of the use of Flow Rate. Both preset Air Brushes, Basic and Textured, use a fairly high value of 80 percent.

The Build-up option is another way of affecting a stroke's opacity. If Build-up is enabled, for example, as with the Air Brush preset, and the stroke crosses itself as in Figure 8-22, you'll notice a darker area at the overlap of the stroke. If you disable the Build-up option, the stroke has a much flatter, monochrome appearance.

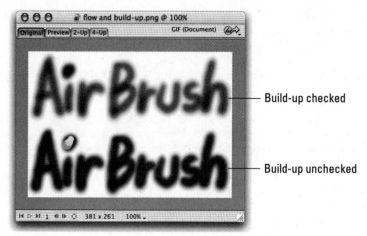

Build-up checked

Build-up unchecked

Figure 8-22: With the Build-up option enabled, the Air Brush stroke acts as if it's a real airbrush, building up where it crosses itself.

Texture, Edge Texture, and Edge Effect

The Texture setting in the Edit Stroke dialog box is reflected on the Stroke section of the Property inspector as the Amount of Texture value. Increase the Texture value to make the chosen texture more visible on the opaque portion of the stroke; a value of 0 percent effectively turns off the texture.

Caution You cannot specify the type of texture from within the Edit Stroke dialog box; you must set it through the Stroke section of the Property inspector. Whereas the texture type is saved with the stroke when you select the Save custom stroke command, if another texture type is chosen temporarily, the original texture does not reappear when you reselect the custom stroke. Reload the document with the saved stroke in order to establish the custom texture settings.

Just as the Texture value causes the chosen texture to appear over the opaque portion of the stroke, the Edge Texture setting causes the texture to appear over the transparent portion. Remember that in Fireworks, you create edge softness by affecting the stroke's alpha channels or transparency. By increasing the Edge Texture and lowering the Texture value, the soft edge of the stroke is textured more noticeably than the center.

Note Edge Texture values, no matter how high, are, in effect, invisible if the Edge Softness is at 0 percent.

In addition to altering an edge's texture, you can also create an Edge Effect. Technically speaking, the five Edge Effects are created by applying an algorithm affecting the alpha channel for both the stroke and its edge. In this case, descriptions are a poor second to a visual representation of the intriguingly named Edge

Effects, shown in Figure 8-23. Because Edge Effects rely on the transparency of the stroke's edge, you can't apply an Edge Effect to a stroke with a 0 percent Edge Softness value.

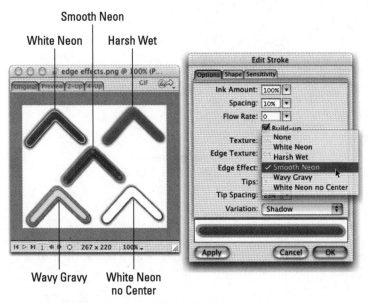

Figure 8-23: The five preset Edge Effects combine both stroke and edge transparency.

Tips, Tip Spacing, and Variations

Have you ever drawn with a fistful of colored pencils or noticed, too late, that your paintbrush has dried with the bristles separated? In each case, the result is a series of separate strokes that curve and move together. In Fireworks jargon, each pencil or separate bristle is referred to as a *tip* and is determined by the Tips attribute. Every stroke must have at least one and can have as many as ten tips.

Note   For either the Tip Spacing or Variations attribute to become active, you must have more than one tip.

Whether the number of tips is apparent or not is determined primarily by the Tip Spacing attribute. Similar to the Spacing parameter, Tip Spacing is set in a range from 0 percent (where each tip is drawn on top of one another) to 1,000 percent (where each tip is as far apart as possible). You can see the results of an extreme experiment in Figure 8-24, where the Unnatural 3D stroke is set to use one, five, and ten tips with a Tip Spacing of 1,000 percent. A single star was drawn for each graphic.

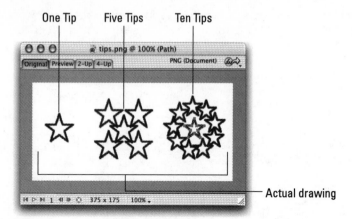

Figure 8-24: Although it appears that the stars in the two groups were cloned, only a single star was drawn in each group; multiple tips and wide Tip Spacing are the key to drawing many identical images with one stroke.

Variations are the final elements on the Options tab. When multiple tips are used, how the different tips are depicted is determined by which of the Variations are selected. Each of the Variations alters the color of the additional tips. The five Variations are as follows:

✦ **Random:** A new color is selected at random for each tip with each new stroke.

✦ **Uniform:** All tips use the base color selected in the Stroke color well.

✦ **Complementary:** If the stroke uses two tips, one tip is displayed in the complementary color (on the opposite side of an HLS (Hue, Lightness, Saturation) color wheel) of the base color. If more than two tips are specified, the additional tips are selected from evenly spaced hues that are located between the initial complementary colors.

✦ **Hue:** Multiple tips are presented in hues similar (plus or minus 5 percent on an HLS color wheel) to the stroke color.

✦ **Shadow:** Additional tips are shown in alternating lighter and darker shades of the stroke color (the Lightness).

The Shape tab

Compared to the Object tab, the Shape tab of the Edit Stroke dialog box (see Figure 8-25) is almost self-explanatory. The upper pane shows the stroke stamp, and the lower pane shows a representation of the stroke over distance.

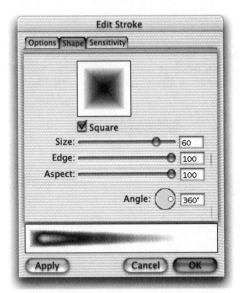

Figure 8-25: The look of the stroke stamp, and ultimately the stroke itself, is influenced by the attributes of the Shape tab.

The Shape tab offers the following five parameters:

✦ **Square:** When enabled, the Square option makes the stroke stamp square or rectangular, according to the Aspect setting. If Square is disabled, the stroke stamp is circular or elliptical.

✦ **Size:** Sets the initial stroke width, in pixels, from 1 to 100. The value is displayed in Stroke panel.

✦ **Edge:** Determines the softness of the stroke's edge. This value is also reflected in the Stroke panel.

✦ **Aspect:** Sets the height to width aspect ratio. Values 0 and 100 make circles or squares — any other value creates rectangles or ellipses.

✦ **Angle:** Determines the angle of the stroke stamp. You can enter values directly, or drag the dial in a circle.

You can achieve a wide range of different shapes by combining different parameters from the Shape tab. I've found the Aspect and Angle controls to be especially useful. For example, I used them to create a diamond dotted stroke, as detailed later in this chapter.

The Sensitivity tab

The Sensitivity tab of the Edit Stroke dialog box, shown in Figure 8-26, permits you to establish somewhat interactive controls for custom strokes. By altering your drawing pressure, speed, or direction, your strokes can assume different sizes, angles, opacities, or colors. You can even set up the stroke to alter any of its properties randomly.

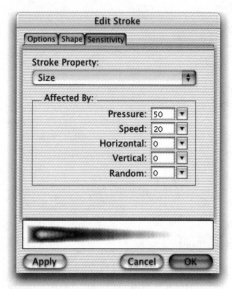

Figure 8-26: Create interactive strokes through the Sensitivity tab of the Edit Stroke dialog box.

The basic procedure for working in the Sensitivity tab is to select one of the stroke attributes from the Stroke Property option list, and then set the desired control found in the Affected By area. For example, if you want your stroke to shift colors when it is drawn across the document but not down it, you would choose Hue from the Brush Properties option list and set the Affected By Horizontal value to a high percentage value. The higher the value, the more impact the condition (Pressure, Speed, and so on) has.

The seven stroke attributes are as follows:

✦ **Size:** When the Size property is affected, the stroke always gets smaller than the initial width, never larger. If the setting is at 50 percent, the stroke loses, at most, one-half of its size.

✦ **Angle:** The angle of the stroke stamp can be affected by as much as 90 degrees if Angle property is selected and an Affected By value is set to its maximum, 100 percent.

✦ **Ink Amount:** As on the Options tab, Ink Amount refers to opacity. At the highest setting, the affecting condition can make the stroke transparent.

✦ **Scatter:** The amount of variance with which stroke stamps are drawn away from the path. Scatter is really only effective with the Random condition.

✦ **Hue:** The color of the stroke. Multicolored strokes, such as those in the Random category, make great use of this property.

✦ **Lightness:** The amount of white in a color. To make a stroke fade more as you draw faster, choose the Lightness property and increase the Speed condition.

✦ **Saturation:** The intensity of the color. The higher the value set in the condition, the more the Saturation lessens. A stroke with a high Speed setting for Saturation becomes grayer as the path is drawn faster.

The conditions that affect these properties each have a separate slider and text box for entering values directly:

✦ **Pressure:** The degree of pressure applied by a stylus used with a pressure-sensitive graphics tablet.

✦ **Speed:** The amount of speed used when a path is drawn either with a graphics tablet or a mouse.

✦ **Horizontal:** Drawing paths from left to right, or vice versa.

✦ **Vertical:** Drawing paths from top to bottom, or vice versa.

✦ **Random:** The selected property is affected without any additional input from the user.

The Affected By conditions can be used together. For example, setting Angle to be equally affected by both the Horizontal and Vertical conditions causes a stroke, such as Random Fur, to change direction as the path is drawn.

Generally, the Sensitivity tab settings tend to react more predictably with hand-drawn paths, such as those created with the Vector Path tool, than paths constructed with one of the geometric shapes, such as the Rectangle or Ellipse. However, experimentation is the key to uncovering unique effects with almost all the Edit Stroke parameters, and you have nothing to lose by trying a particular setting.

Fireworks Technique: Making Dotted Lines

All the strokes in Fireworks' standard arsenal are more or less solid lines with nothing that you can use as a dotted line. Although a few exceptions exist, such as most of the Random presets, these tend to be too unconventional to use for a basic dotted line. As discussed in the previous section, however, Fireworks offers you a tremendous degree of control in customizing your own strokes. The procedure for creating a dotted line is fairly straightforward and a good introduction to the world of custom stroke creation.

The key to creating a dotted line is in the Spacing control found on the Options tab of the Edit Stroke dialog box. When the Spacing value is 100 percent, each stroke stamp (the smallest component of a stroke) is right next to the one following it. If the value is less than 100 percent, the stroke stamps overlap and—here's the heart of the dotted line—when the value is greater than 100 percent, the stroke stamps are separated.

When creating any custom stroke, start with the built-in stroke that's closest to your goal. Although either of the Basic or Pencil 1-Pixel strokes would be ideal, the key attribute for creating a dotted line, Spacing, is not available for these strokes. As explained earlier in this chapter, these strokes are rendered with an eye toward pixel precision that is incompatible with the Spacing and Flow attributes. However, one of the other Pencil presets, Colored Pencil, works quite well as a stroke on which to build a custom dotted line, with a minimum of adjustments required.

To create a simple dotted line, follow these steps:

1. Choose Pencil from the Stroke Category option list in the Stroke section of the Property inspector.

2. Choose Colored Pencil from the Type submenu.

3. Open the Edit Stroke dialog box by choosing Stroke Options from the Stroke category option list and then clicking Advanced.

4. On the Options tab of the Edit Stroke dialog box, change the Spacing value from 15 percent to 200 percent.

   Notice in the preview pane that you now have a dotted line, as shown in Figure 8-27.

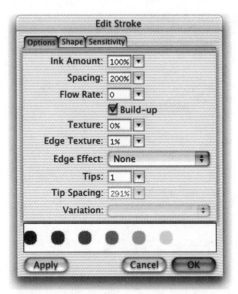

Figure 8-27: You can easily create a dotted line by modifying the Edit Stroke settings.

5. Click OK when you're done.

6. Select Stroke Options, from the Stroke category option list in the Stroke section of the Property inspector, and click Save custom stroke.

7. In the Save Stroke dialog box, enter a unique name for the custom stroke.

Test out your new dotted line by using almost any of the path drawing tools — the Rectangle, Ellipse, Polygon, Vector Path, or Pen.

Now that you've seen how easy customizing a brush stroke is, try a few variations, such as the ones shown in Figure 8-28. Each set of instructions assumes that you're working in the Edit Stroke dialog box.

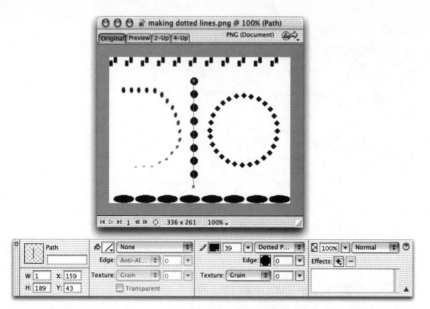

Figure 8-28: You can create a wide variety of dotted lines by modifying the Edit S troke settings.

To give the dotted line a harder, more consistent edge, make these changes:

✦ Change the Edge Texture value on the Options tab to 0 percent.

✦ On the Shape tab, change the Edge value to 0 percent.

✦ On the Sensitivity tab, change the Size Speed setting to 0, the Ink Amount Pressure and Speed settings to 0, and the Lightness Pressure and Speed settings to 0.

Make these changes in order to create a dotted line with circles instead of squares:

✦ On the Shape tab, deselect the Square option.

✦ Also on the Shape tab, change the Aspect value to 100.

To create a horizontal line with dashes, change these values:

✦ From the Shape tab, change the Aspect value to 50.

✦ Also on the Shape tab, change the Angle to 0.

To create a vertical line with dashes, change these values:

✦ From the Shape tab, change the Aspect value to 50.

✦ Also on the Shape tab, change the Angle to 270.

Change the following values in order to create a dotted line with diamonds:

✦ From the Shape tab, make sure the Square option is selected.

✦ Also on the Shape tab, change the Aspect value to 100.

✦ Change the Angle to 45.

Orienting the Stroke

Strokes are useful, whether they are intended for an open path, such as a line, or a closed path, such as a circle or rectangle. When a stroke is applied to a closed path, however, Fireworks offers an additional set of options. By default, when strokes are rendered they are centered on a path. Select any closed path object and the stroke is rendered on either side of the actual path. The orientation of a stroke to a path can be changed: The stroke can also be drawn completely inside the path or outside the path. As you can see from Figure 8-29, wildly different effects are possible with this option.

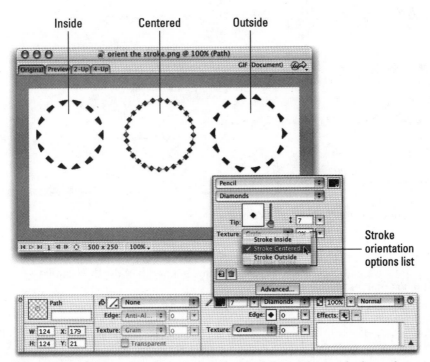

Figure 8-29: The same stroke is rendered, from left to right, inside the path, centered on the path, and outside the path.

The controls for orienting a stroke to a path are in the Stroke Options dialog box reachable via the Stroke category on the Property inspector. The three choices place the stroke inside the path, centered on the path, or outside the path. A fourth option, Fill over Stroke, is located below the stroke orientation controls. By default, the stroke always appears on top of the fill color, Pattern, or gradient. However, by enabling the Fill over Stroke option, you can reverse this preference.

 Tip   By combining the Fill over Stroke option with a stroke rendered on the center of the path and a fill with a feathered edge, the stroke appears to blend into the fill while retaining a hard outer edge.

One of my favorite applications of the stroke orientation controls is to use inside strokes as a sort of auxiliary fill, creating the effect of a more complex fill, as shown in Figure 8-30. Hard to believe Fireworks enables you to do this kind of thing completely with paths!

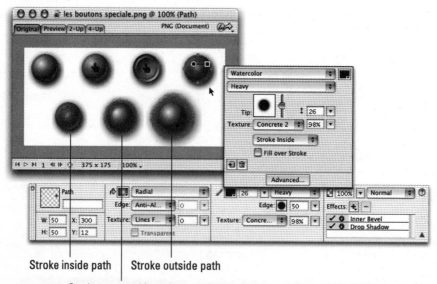

Stroke inside path   Stroke outside path

Stroke centered in path

Figure 8-30: Inside strokes figure prominently in this set of buttons. The bottom row is the selected button shown again, this time after each of the three stroke orientation options has been applied.

Summary

In many ways, the stroke is the defining surface of a graphic. Fireworks offers a superb catalog of standard strokes and even more flexibility to create your own. As you begin to work with strokes, use these guidelines:

✦ Strokes make paths visible. An unstroked line cannot be seen unless the path is closed and a fill added.

✦ The Stroke panel offers immediate control over a stroke's color, size, edge, and texture. Tip preview shows the tip of the stroke.

✦ Fireworks includes 48 different preset strokes spread over 11 categories. Many of the stroke presets are interactive and vary according to the speed and pressure with which you draw.

✦ You can customize Fireworks strokes with a great number of variations through the Edit Stroke dialog box.

✦ After you've customized your stroke, you can save it with the document by using the Stroke Options on the Stroke category option list. You can also store your custom strokes as Fireworks Styles.

✦ Although Fireworks doesn't come with a preset dotted-line pattern, creating one is easy.

✦ Fireworks works well with graphics tablets and takes great advantage of their pressure sensitivity.

In the next chapter, you find out how you can employ advanced path techniques in Fireworks.

✦   ✦   ✦

Structuring Paths

Even with the coolest stroke, the snazziest fill, and the wildest effect, you rarely get exactly the graphic you need the first time you draw an object. Maybe it needs to be a little bigger, smaller, taller, or wider, or maybe it's perfect — but it's facing the wrong way, and it's upside down. Whatever the problem, Fireworks has the tools to fix it and, because Fireworks blends pixel surfaces with vector skeletons, you get amazingly sharp results.

Fireworks has the kinds of tools you would normally expect to find in a full-fledged vector drawing application. You can combine several vector objects in any number of ways with evocatively named tools, such as Union, Intersect, Punch, and Crop. Naturally, what you have joined together you can split apart and regroup as needed. Vector objects can be simplified, expanded, or inset with Fireworks commands.

This chapter covers all the tools and techniques in Fireworks for transforming and combining objects. You'll also find a section that describes how you can use Fireworks to create perspectives in your imagery.

You really begin to appreciate the power of Fireworks' vector/ bitmap combination when you start transforming your objects. In a pure bitmap graphics application, if you increase the size of a bitmap, you have to add pixels, whereas shrinking a bitmap causes the program to throw away pixels — you rarely achieve ideal results in either situation. However, in Fireworks, when you rescale a vector object, the vector path is altered (a snap for vector graphics), and the pixels are reapplied to the new path, just as if you had drawn it that way to begin with.

Transforming Objects Visually

Fireworks includes methods for transforming objects, both visually and numerically. The visual method relies on three key tools found in the Select section of the Tools panel: Scale, Skew, and Distort.

Note   Although I primarily use vector objects as examples in this section, all the transformation tools work with bitmap objects, as well.

Using scaling

In Web design, the size of an object frequently needs adjustment. Sometimes a button is too large for the current navigation bar, or the client wants the "On Sale" notice to be much bigger. Other times a graphic just looks better at a particular size. Regardless of the reason, Fireworks gives you a quick way to resize an object — up or down — through the Scale tool.

The Scale tool is the first of three transformation tools in the Tools panel that become active when an object is selected. Choose the Scale tool (or use the keyboard shortcut, Q) and the standard selection highlight is replaced with a transforming highlight, as shown in Figure 9-1. There are eight sizing handles — one on each corner and one in the middle of each side — and a centerpoint on the transforming highlight. You can drag any of the sizing handles to a new position in order to resize the selected object. Dragging any corner handle scales the object proportionately.

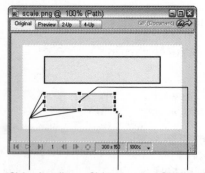

Sizing handles   Sizing cursor   Centerpoint

Figure 9-1: Choose the Scale tool and sizing handles, and a centerpoint appears on the selected object.

To resize an object using the Scale tool, follow these steps:

   1. Select the object you want to resize.

2. Choose the Scale tool from the Tools panel, or use the keyboard shortcut, Q. Alternatively, you can use the menu command, Modify ⇨ Transform ⇨ Scale. Sizing handles and a centerpoint appear on the selected object.

3. Position your pointer over any sizing handle until it changes into a two-headed arrow.

4. Click and drag the sizing handle in the direction you want the object to grow or shrink. To scale an object while maintaining the current proportions, click and drag a corner-sizing handle.

5. To cancel a resizing operation and return the object to its original dimensions, press Esc.

6. To accept a rescaled object, double-click anywhere on the document.

You can also move or rotate an object when any of the transform tools are selected. When the pointer is positioned within the selected object and it becomes a four-headed arrow, click and drag the object to a new position. If the pointer is outside of the selected object's bounding box, the pointer turns into a rotate symbol; clicking and dragging when this occurs rotates the object around its centerpoint.

The transform tools all have a Scale Attributes option available through the Info panel Options menu. By default, when you resize an object, the stroke, fill, and effect settings are resized, as well. If you disable the Scale Attributes option in the Info panel Options menu, these settings are reapplied without being recalculated. Why might you want to do this? Although the results can be unpredictable, interesting variations can occur, such as the variations in Figure 9-2.

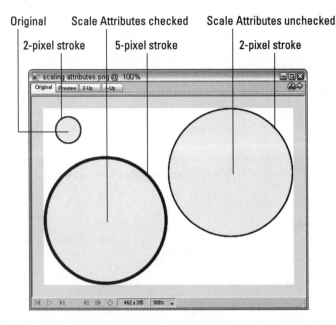

Original   Scale Attributes checked   Scale Attributes unchecked

2-pixel stroke   5-pixel stroke   2-pixel stroke

Figure 9-2: Most of the time you want your stroke, fill, and effects to rescale along with your object, but turning off the Scale Attributes option can lead to some interesting effects.

Tip In my experiments with the Scale Attributes option, the most interesting effects occurred when my object was filled with a gradient and the Scale Attributes option was turned off.

Examining skewing

The Skew tool is used to move one side of an object, while the opposing side remains stationary. Select the Skew tool by clicking and holding the Scale tool until you can choose the Skew tool from the flyout menu, or by pressing the keyboard shortcut, Q, twice. Selecting the Skew tool causes transform handles to appear on the selected object, as it does when selecting the Scale tool. The Skew handles work somewhat differently, though:

✦ Drag any middle Skew handle in order to slant that side of the object.

✦ Drag any corner Skew handle in order to slant that side and the opposing side in the opposite direction.

Skewing a corner is a useful technique for giving an object a dynamic appearance, as shown in Figure 9-3.

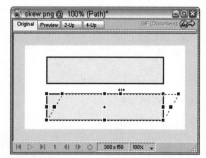

Figure 9-3: Skew an object along one side by dragging the middle handle.

Completing a Skew operation is handled the same as completing a scaling operation: Press Esc to cancel, or double-click anywhere to accept the new shape.

Discovering distorting

With both the Scale and Skew tools, entire sides move when you adjust one of the transform handles. The Distort tool (the third tool on the transform flyout) removes this restriction. When the Distort tool is selected, you can adjust the bounding box surrounding the selected object by dragging the handles in any direction. The object is then redrawn to fit within the confines of the new bounding box shape, as in Figure 9-4.

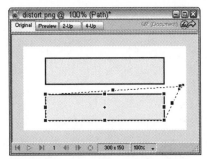

Figure 9-4: Use the Distort tool to reshape a bitmap or vector object by altering its bounding box.

The Distort tool is useful for warping flat objects — especially bitmaps — into novel shapes, or for fitting an object into the shape of another object.

Tip Use the Distort tool to flip a bitmap horizontally or vertically by dragging a middle handle across the opposite side. This technique won't automatically size the bitmap to match the original size, as do the Flip Horizontal or Flip Vertical commands, but you can control the sizing.

Understanding rotating

Rotating is available with any of the transform tools: Scale, Skew, or Distort. Moving your mouse cursor just outside of the bounding box causes the Rotate cursor to appear. As you can see in Figure 9-5, an object rotates around its centerpoint and can rotate a full 360 degrees.

Rotate cursor   Centerpoint

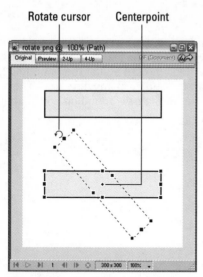

Figure 9-5: An object rotates around its centerpoint when the Rotate cursor drags the object.

To rotate any object, follow these steps:

1. Select any one of the transform tools from the Tools panel, or choose the equivalent tool from the Modify ⇨ Transform menu.

2. Move your pointer outside of the bounding box. The pointer turns into a Rotator cursor.

3. Click and drag in any direction to rotate the object.

4. To cancel the rotation and return to the original object, press Esc.

5. To accept the transformation, double-click anywhere on your document.

An object's centerpoint is placed in the middle of the transform bounding box by default. To change the rotation axis, click and drag the centerpoint to a new location—the centerpoint can remain within the object's bounding box or be placed outside of it. If the centerpoint is placed outside of the object, the radius used connects the centerpoint and the nearest corner handle, as shown in Figure 9-6.

Centerpoint   Rotation radius

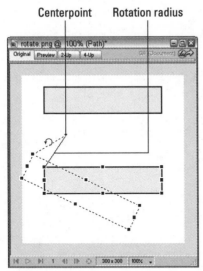

Figure 9-6: Rotate an object around a different axis by dragging the centerpoint to a new location, even outside of the object's bounding box.

Tip   Pressing Shift while you rotate an object constrains the rotation to 15-degree increments.

Transforming Objects Numerically

Transforming an object interactively by clicking and dragging works well for many situations, but sometimes specifying your new measurement or rotation precisely is preferable. For those exacting occasions, turn to Fireworks' Numeric Transform feature. With Numeric Transform, you can scale any object up or down by a percentage, set a specific pixel size, or rotate to an exact degree.

To use Numeric Transform, follow these steps:

1. Select the object you want to change.

2. Choose Modify ➪ Transform ➪ Numeric Transform, or use the keyboard shortcut, Ctrl+Shift+T (Command+Shift+T). The Numeric Transform dialog box, shown in Figure 9-7, appears.

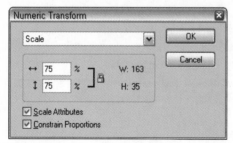

Figure 9-7: The Numeric Transform dialog box gives you exacting control when scaling or rotating an object.

3. Check Scale Attributes to reapply the object's attributes after the transformation.

4. Check Constrain Proportions to preserve the object's aspect ratio.

5. To scale an object proportionately:

  a. Choose Scale from the Option list.

  b. Enter a new percentage value in either the height or width text boxes.

Tip   If the height and width boxes are "locked" and you want to unlock them, uncheck Constrain Proportions.

6. To resize an object to a specific pixel size:

  a. Choose Resize from the Option list.

  b. Enter the pixel dimensions in either the width or height text boxes.

7. To rotate an object by a specific number of degrees:

  a. Choose Rotate from the Option list.

  b. Enter a degree value in the text box, or drag the knob to select a rotation degree.

8. Click OK when you're done.

Fireworks Technique: Creating Perspective

Although Fireworks is hardly a 3D-modeling program, you can quickly generate perspective views using several of its transform and other tools. If you've ever taken Drawing 101, you understand the basic principles of perspective: The particular view you're illustrating has a vanishing point where the imaginary lines of the drawing meet on the horizon. The vanishing-point concept is most simply applied by using a special property of the Skew tool.

To give an object the illusion of perspective, follow these steps:

1. Select the object you want to modify.

2. Choose the Skew tool from the Tools panel, or press the keyboard shortcut, Q, twice.

3. Choose the direction of perspective:

    • To make the object appear as if it is along a left wall, vertically drag the top- or bottom-left corner away from the object.

    • To make the object appear as if it is along a right wall, vertically drag the top- or bottom-right corner away from the object.

    • To make the object appear as if it is on the floor, horizontally drag the bottom-left or -right corner away from the object.

    • To make the object appear as if it is on the ceiling, horizontally drag the top-left or -right corner away from the object.

4. To intensify the perspective, repeat Step 3 with the opposite corner, dragging in the opposite direction. For example, in Figure 9-8, I dragged the bottom-right corner away from the object and the bottom-left corner into the object to exaggerate the effect.

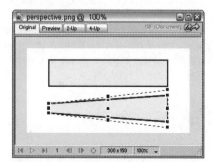

Figure 9-8: Make a flat figure appear to have perspective by using the Skew tool.

Applying textures to a rectangle fill is a good way to start building a perspective background. I've found that breaking up the textures into small rectangles, rather than use one large rectangle is better. The room depicted in Figure 9-9 uses a series of rectangles with a Wood-Light Pattern fill, which are then grouped and skewed together to gain the perspective feel. By duplicating and flipping this skewed group, I'm able to quickly build the other sides of the room.

Cross-Reference Texture fills are discussed at length in Chapter 11.

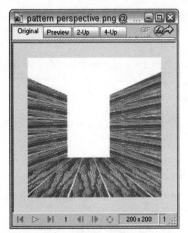

Figure 9-9: When using a pattern for perspective, try smaller rectangles of the same pattern, grouped and skewed together.

Tip   Dragging a corner with the Skew tool always moves the top opposite sides equally. This operation makes an object's vanishing point appear to be evenly spaced between the sides of an object, which is not always the case. You can also use the Distort tool to drag one corner unevenly. But use the Distort tool with caution — or perhaps with the Grid visible; there's no way to snap a dragged corner when using the Distort tool, and straight lines are often difficult to maintain.

Managing Points and Paths

Sometimes transforming an object in its entirety is more than you really want or need to do. Fireworks offers numerous options for adjusting vector paths on a point-by-point basis. You can easily move, add, or delete points. In addition, paths can be joined, either to themselves — changing an open path to a closed path — or to another path. Naturally, you can also split joined paths at any point.

Moving points with the Subselection tool

Much path work on the point level is handled through the Subselection tool. Similar to the Pointer tool in that you use it for selecting and dragging, the Subselection tool works on the components of the path, rather than on the path itself.

The Subselection tool is located directly to the right of the Pointer in the Tools panel. You can also choose it through its keyboard shortcut, A. When you select a path with the Subselection tool, all the points that create the path appear, not just the path that becomes visible when you use the Pointer. Each point on a path initially resembles a small hollow square. When you approach a point with the Subselection tool, the white pointer changes into a single white arrowhead, indicating that a point is available for selection, as shown in Figure 9-10. Clicking that point selects it and changes the hollow square to a solid square.

Points on the path   Selected point

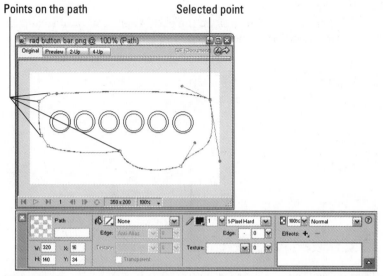

Figure 9-10: Adjust paths on the point level with the Subselection tool.

Tip   If Bézier control handles aren't visible from a point on a path, you can use the Subselection tool in combination with the Alt (Option) key in order to drag them out.

Clicking and dragging any point causes the path to move with it. You can completely reshape any path by using the Subselection tool.

Adding and removing points

Adding or deleting points on a path is easy. Why would you want to increase the number of points? Most commonly, the object you're working on has a line that you need to extend in a different direction, and the Bézier curves create too smooth a transition. The reasoning behind removing points is just the reverse: You have a sharp break where you would prefer a smooth curve. Additionally, drawing any path with a freeform tool, such as the Brush or Pencil, creates many points. Not that there is really any increased overhead, such as file size, associated with additional points; working with an object that has fewer points is just easier.

To add a point on a path, follow these steps:

1. Choose the Pen tool from the Tools panel, or use its keyboard shortcut, P.

2. Press and hold Ctrl (Command) to temporarily switch to the Subselection tool.

3. Select the path that you want to work on.

4. Release Ctrl (Command).

5. Position your pointer over the area on the path where you want to add a point. A small plus sign is added to the Pen tool pointer, as shown in Figure 9-11.

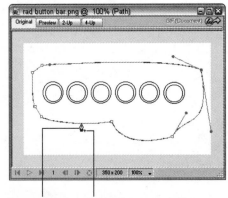

Pen tool cursor   Add Point cursor badge

Figure 9-11: Add points with the Pen tool by clicking a selected line.

6. To add a single point, click once.

7. To add a point with Bézier control handles, click and drag.

8. Continue adding points by repeating Steps 5 through 7.

9. When you're finished adding points, select another tool.

To delete points from a path, follow these steps:

1. Choose the Subselection tool from the Tools panel.

2. Select the path from which you want to delete points.

3. Move the pointer over the point you want to delete. A small X is added to the pointer when you are over a point on the path.

4. Click once to select the point.

5. Press Backspace (Delete) to remove the point.

Tip To delete multiple points, press Ctrl (Command) to temporarily use the Pointer tool and drag a selection rectangle around the points that you want to remove. Alternatively, hold down Shift while selecting points to keep adding to your selection. Press Backspace (Delete) to remove the points.

Closing an open path

Whether by accident ("Drat, I thought I closed that path") or design ("I like the simplicity of the open path"), sometimes you need to convert an open path to a closed path. The Pen tool makes this a simple operation.

Tip If your path is almost closed—the end points are right next to each other—you can also select both points with the Subselection tool and choose Modify ⇨ Combine Paths ⇨ Join, or you can use the keyboard shortcut Ctrl+J (Command+J) to close your path.

To close an open path, follow these steps:

1. Select the path you want to close.

2. Choose the Pen tool from the Tools panel.

3. Position your pointer over one endpoint of the path. An X is added to the lower right of the Pen cursor when it is over an existing endpoint.

4. Click once on the endpoint. A small square replaces the X at the lower right of the Pen cursor, as shown in Figure 9-12.

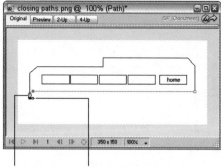

Pen tool cursor   Join Path cursor badge

Figure 9-12: Use the Pen tool to close any open path.

5. Continue the path with the Pen. With each plotted point, any stroke or effects attributes are applied to the extended path.

6. To close the path, position the Pen over the remaining endpoint. A hollow square appears on the lower right of the Pen cursor.

7. Click once to close the path.

Tip   If your stroke varies its thickness or opacity by speed or pressure, the section of the path that was completed with the Pen tool may look odd because the Pen tool recognizes neither speed nor pressure. However, you can use the Path Scrubber tools, discussed later in this chapter, to increase or reduce these types of effects.

Working with multiple paths

You can join any path with another path with a simple command. Initially, this capability may appear to fall into the "Yeah, so what?" category; but after you realize that paths don't have to overlap, touch, or even be near each other, the design possibilities expand considerably. Joining a number of simple shapes is an easy way to make one complex shape. For example, joining empty circles with an object effectively cuts holes in the object, as shown in Figure 9-13. Note that the joined object has the attributes — stroke, fill, effect, and so on — of the original object that was lowest in the stacking order (in other words, closest to the canvas).

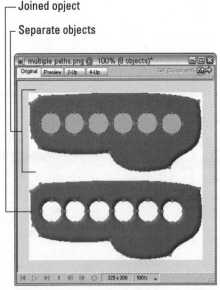

Figure 9-13: Joining paths is an easy way to create complex objects.

To join two or more paths, follow these steps:

1. Select each path you would like to join with the Pointer tool.

2. Choose Modify ➪ Combine Paths ➪ Join, or Ctrl+J (Command+J).

    Windows users can also select the Join button on the Modify toolbar.

After you've joined paths, they stay that way until you split them. To split joined paths, choose Modify ➪ Combine Paths ➪ Split, or use the keyboard shortcut, Ctrl+Shift+J (Command+Shift+J). In Windows, you can also select the Split button on the Modify toolbar.

Editing Paths

So far in this chapter, most of the path editing tools have been fairly extreme; delete, distort, rescale, rotate—these terms don't promise much degree of subtlety. Fireworks does offer several other tools, however, that can redraw portions of a path or reshape an area with a varying amount of pressure. And for those times that require a precise, almost surgical removal of path segments, Fireworks offers a Knife tool that performs as sharply as any real blade.

Redrawing a path

If you've ever drawn a shape that was perfect except for one little area of it, you'll greatly appreciate the Redraw Path tool. As the name implies, this tool enables you to redraw any portion of a completed path, in effect throwing away the portion of the original path that you're replacing.

The Redraw Path tool, found in the flyout under the Pen tool, is a freehand drawing tool. When you're redoing a segment of a path, you initially select any part of the path to start redrawing and then reconnect to the original path. Fireworks erases the portion of the original path that is between the beginning and the ending points of your redrawn section and connects your new path to the old path.

To redraw a portion of a path, follow these steps:

1. Select the path you want to redraw.

2. Choose the Redraw Path tool from the flyout under the Pen tool. Alternatively, you can press the keyboard shortcut, P, three times.

3. Move the pointer over the area of the path where you want to start redrawing. Fireworks displays a small caret (^) in the lower right of the pointer when you are in position over the path.

4. Click and drag out your new path.

5. Position your pointer over the original path in the spot where you want to connect the new and old paths, and then release the mouse button. Fireworks removes the old path segment and connects the new path segment.

The Redraw Path tool isn't just for correcting mistakes, though. Figure 9-14 shows how you can use the Redraw Path tool to make a portion of a geometric shape more organic-looking.

Modified with Redraw Path tool

Original object

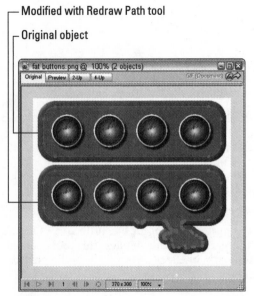

Figure 9-14: The Redraw Path tool can easily alter a standard shape into something unique.

Tip   Pressing Shift while using the Redraw Path tool constrains your replacement path to lines in increments of 45 degrees.

Examining the Freeform and Reshape Area tools

Looking for a cool tool to give your objects that unique twist? Look no further than Freeform tool and the Reshape Area tool. Rather than add or delete points as with other tools, these reshaping features enable you to sculpt a path, pulling and pushing a line like stretchable clay.

Although similar, a couple of key differences exist between the two tools:

✦ **Freeform:** Both pushes and pulls a segment of a selected path.

✦ **Reshape Area:** Only pushes a path, but controls the degree it pushes through the strength field in the Property inspector. Moreover, this tool can reshape an entire object, as well as just a segment.

Pushing a path into a new shape

To push a path into a new shape with the Freeform tool, follow these steps:

1. Select the path you want to alter.

2. Choose the Freeform tool from the Tools panel, or use its keyboard shortcut, O.

3. Position your cursor slightly off the path that you want to push. This could be to either side of an open path, or inside or outside of a closed path.

Positioning your cursor slightly off a path enables the Freeform push cursor. Positioning your cursor directly on a path enables the Freeform pull cursor, covered later in this chapter.

The cursor changes into a circle, as shown in Figure 9-15. Think of the circle as an object that you use to push against the stroke.

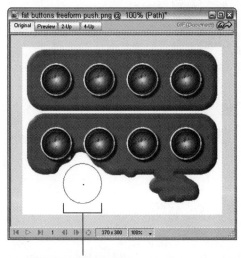

Freeform push cursor

Figure 9-15: Round out your paths with the Freeform tool's push mode.

4. Click and drag the ball cursor into the path, pushing it into a new shape.

Caution

Pushing a closed path too fast or too far results in an overlapping path line with unpredictable results.

5. Release the mouse button when you're satisfied with the shape.

Pulling a path segment into a new shape

To pull a segment of a path into a new shape, follow these steps:

1. Select the path you want to alter.

2. Choose the Freeform tool from the Tools panel, or use its keyboard shortcut, O.

3. Position your cursor directly over the segment of the path that you want to pull. An S-curve is added to the lower right of the Freeform tool's cursor, as shown in Figure 9-16.

Freeform pull cursor

Figure 9-16: The Freeform tool is used to pull out a segment of a path.

4. Click and drag in the direction that you want to pull the segment. You can pull the path away from or into the object.

5. Release the mouse button in order to complete the pull.

Fireworks adds as few pixels as possible when you are pulling with the Freeform tool. Pulling is like pinching just the one point of the path and dragging it away from the rest of the shape. By contrast, the push mode of the Freeform tool is similar to using a ball to reshape the path. The size of the ball with which you push is determined through the Property inspector when the Freeform tool is selected.

Learning about the Freeform tool's options

To alter the size of the ball used with Freeform push mode, select the Freeform tool to view its options in the Property inspector, shown in Figure 9-17, and enter a new value in the Size text box, or use the slider to choose a new pixel size. The Size option ranges from 1 to 500 pixels.

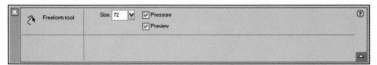

Figure 9-17: The Property inspector enables you to set the Freeform tool's options, such as the size of the push cursor.

The Property inspector offers two other options for the Freeform tool. The Preview option draws the stroke and fill, if any, while you use the Freeform tool. Although this can be a bit processor-intensive, I enable it whenever I'm using Freeform on an object with a wide stroke, such as an Airbrush, because the final effect can be so different from just the path. When the Preview option is not on, you see both the old outline and the new one while you are using the tool; when you stop drawing, the old outline vanishes.

The other option, Pressure, is generally useful only if you're using a pressure-sensitive graphics tablet. When enabled, a medium amount of pressure specifies a push cursor to the size set in the Property inspector; lighter amounts of pressure reduce the size, and greater amounts increase it.

Altering a vector object with one operation

Though the Reshape Area tool, when set to a small size, achieves similar effects to the Freeform tool, that's not what makes it special. The Reshape Area tool is best when used to warp or to reshape an entire object. Take Figure 9-18, for example. I start with a star created with the Polygon tool and then apply the Reshape Area tool, set to a size on the Property inspector that is larger than the star. By dragging the Reshape Area tool over the star, I transform the entire standard shape — not just one segment — into something unique.

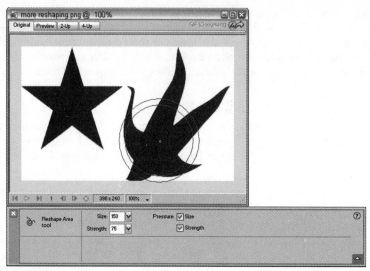

Figure 9-18: The Reshape Area tool can alter an entire vector object with one operation.

To use the Reshape Area tool, follow these steps:

1. Select the path you want to alter.

2. Choose the Reshape Area tool from the flyout underneath the Freeform tool, or press the keyboard shortcut, O, twice.

 Tip Each time you press O, you toggle between the Freeform and Reshape Area tools.

3. Position your pointer over the object that you want to reshape.

4. Click and drag in the desired direction.

5. Release the mouse button when you're satisfied with the resulting object.

As with the Freeform tool, the Size is set on the Property inspector; you'll also find a Pressure option that functions in the same manner as the Freeform tool. In addition, the Reshape Area tool has a Strength option. The Strength value determines the strength of the Reshape Area tool's gravitational-like pull. Strength is percentage based; at 100 percent, you get the maximum effect from the tool. If you're using a pressure-sensitive graphics tablet, you can alter both the size and the strength of the Reshape Area tool while drawing with your stylus.

 Tip Don't have a graphics tablet yet? To simulate a lighter stylus touch, use either 1 or the left arrow key; pressing 2 or the right arrow key simulates increasing the pressure on a graphics pad.

Discovering the Path Scrubber

The Path Scrubber tools are fairly subtle compared to the other tools covered in this chapter. If you've experimented with strokes such as Airbrush, you've noticed how the stroke can change according to how fast or, with a graphics tablet, how much pressure you use when you draw. The Path Scrubber tools alter these variables, after you've completed the path. One Path Scrubber tool increases the interactive effect, and one lessens it, as shown in Figure 9-19.

Figure 9-19: The Path Scrubber tools can turn a simple path into one that resembles one created with a pressure-sensitive pen and tablet.

To use the Path Scrubber tools, follow these steps:

1. Apply a stroke to your path that uses speed- or pressure-sensitive effects, such as Air Brush.

2. If you want to increase the pressure effect, choose the Path Scrubber Plus tool; if you want to decrease the pressure effect, choose the Path Scrubber Minus tool. Both are in the flyout underneath the Freeform tool.

3. Trace over the portion of the path where you want to adjust the speed or pressure effect.

Using the Property inspector

When Fireworks draws a path, both speed and pressure data are gathered. The Path Scrubber tools can work with either the speed or pressure information, or both; moreover, they can do it at a variable rate. The Property inspector has all the controls you need for these tools:

- ✦ **Rate:** The relative strength of the tool. Pick a value from 10 (the most effect) to 1 (the least effect).
- ✦ **Pressure:** Enabling this option directs the Path Scrubber tools to adjust the path, according to the simulated pressure of the stroke.
- ✦ **Speed:** Enabling this option directs the Path Scrubber tools to adjust the path according to the simulated speed of the stroke.

Understanding the Knife

One of my favorite — and most useful — design tools is my X-acto knife. The capability to finely trim the tightest curves has saved me many times. The computer equivalent of this excellent implement is the Knife tool. Basically, the Knife tool divides one path into two separate paths.

The Knife cuts paths by drawing a line where you want the separation to take place. You can use the Knife tool on open or closed paths, or on any path-based object. With an open path, you need only intersect the path once in order to make the cut once. With a closed path, you have to draw a line all the way across the object with the Knife, as shown in Figure 9-20.

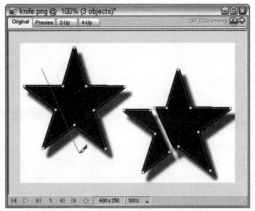

Figure 9-20: The Knife stroke on the left cut the object into two pieces, which can then be pulled apart, as shown on the right.

To use the Knife, follow these steps:

1. Select the path you plan to divide.

2. Choose the Knife tool from the Tools panel, or use the keyboard shortcut, Y.

3. Draw a line through the path with the Knife tool. Fireworks separates the path, although this is not always immediately obvious because both new paths are still selected.

4. To move one of the newly divided paths, choose the Pointer tool and click once on the canvas away from any object. The split paths are deselected.

5. Select either portion of the original path. Only one part is now selected and can be deleted, moved, or otherwise modified.

The Knife tool is also great for making specific shapes, such as arcs. Just draw a standard circle and then use the Knife to slice off a portion of it. As with many tools, pressing Shift constrains the Knife to angles with increments of 45 degrees.

Discerning path operations

The more you work in vector-based drawing programs such as Fireworks, the sooner you begin to look for new and novel shapes. Face it, no matter how many points you put on that star, it's still a star. Whereas you can warp and reshape any existing object using the various tools described elsewhere in this chapter, creating a compound shape composed of two or more basic shapes is often far easier.

You can find all the commands that merge paths — Union, Intersect, Punch, and Crop — under the Modify ➪ Combine Paths menu option. You can find the stroke commands — Simplify, Expand Stroke, and Inset Path — under Modify ➪ Alter Path menu.

When you combine multiple paths, the stroke, fill, and effects settings of the bottom object in the stacking order — the one closest to the canvas — are applied to the new combined object.

Understanding the Union command

The Union command enables you to combine two or more objects into one merged object. One technique that helps me decide whether the Union is the proper command to use is that time-honored artist's tool, squinting. After I've positioned objects with which to form my new shape, I lean back from the monitor and squint so that I can see just the outline of the new shape. That's precisely what Union does — it combines the shapes into an overall outline and removes any overlapping areas.

The technique for using Union, as with all the Combine commands, is straightforward. Just position your objects, select them all, and then choose Modify ➪ Combine Paths ➪ Union. Occasionally, you have to adjust the individual paths to get them just right. For example, when I created the martini glass in Figure 9-21, I united three objects: a triangle, a rectangle, and a custom Pen-drawn shape for the base. After my first attempt, I realized that the rectangle and the base didn't quite match, so I chose Edit ➪ Undo — okay, I actually used the shortcut, Ctrl+Z (Command+Z) — and adjusted the base. Then, after reselecting them and reissuing the command, I was ready to pour.

Figure 9-21: I combined the three objects on the left with the Union command to form the new object on the right.

Examining the Intersect command

Whereas Union throws away the overlapping parts of combined paths, Intersect keeps only the overlapping areas from all selected paths. Believe it or not, the key word in the previous sentence is *all* — if even one object doesn't overlap at least some part of all the other selected objects, the Intersect operation erases all of your objects. With that caveat out of the way, you'll find Intersect to be a useful command. I mean, how else could you create the perfect pizza slice, as I did in Figure 9-22? After the two objects on the left were selected, I chose Modify ➪ Combine Paths ➪ Intersect. Pizza's ready!

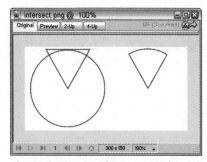

Figure 9-22: Combining a circle and
a triangle with the Intersect command
creates the perfect pizza slice.

Using the Punch command

Remember the paper punch you had in school? That little handheld device that took a round bite out of whatever you could get between its jaws? The Punch command uses the same concept, except you define the punch shape to be anything you want. When two vector objects overlap, the shape on top is punched out of the shape on the bottom. You can see the Punch command illustrated in Figure 9-23, as I continue the food metaphors with the creation of a doughnut, of sorts. After making sure that my two circles were centered on each other, I selected them both and chose Modify ➪ Combine Paths ➪ Punch.

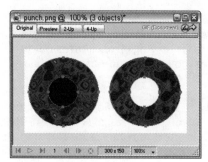

Figure 9-23: The Punch command
removes the shape of the top object
from the bottom object.

Tip

What happens when you apply the Punch command to more than two selected objects? The top object is still used as the punch pattern—and all the objects are affected, but not joined.

Exploring the Crop command

Plainly put, Crop is the opposite of Punch. With Punch, the top object is cut out of any other selected object. With Crop, the bottom object forms the clipping path for the top object. To round out our food-like illustrations of the Combine commands, Figure 9-24 disposes of all but the last bite of a cookie. I created the shapes of the remains, joined the shapes into a single object, selected that object and the cookie, and then chose Modify ➪ Combine Paths ➪ Crop. Almost completely gone in one bite.

Figure 9-24: With the Crop command, the shape of the original top object provides the shape of the resulting object.

Looking at the Simplify command

Freeform drawing tools are terrific for quickly sketching out a specific shape. But, quite often, the computer representation of your flowing strokes turns out pretty blocky. The Simplify command is designed to reduce the number of points used in a path while maintaining the overall shape of the object.

If you choose Modify ➪ Alter Path ➪ Simplify, the Simplify dialog box opens and enables you to specify the number of pixels affected. The range is from 1 to 100; a relatively low value of 12 was used to dramatic effect in Figure 9-25. The original hand-drawn fellow on the left has too many points; trimming them down by hand would be arduous. After I applied the Simplify command, a smoother, simpler object resulted. That's not necessarily the last step, though. Usually, you find yourself tweaking a simplified object's Bézier handles in order to get things just right.

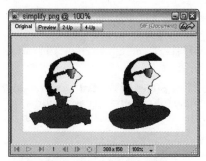

Figure 9-25: After the Simplify command is applied to the original hand-drawn paths, the result is the smoother and simpler gentleman on the right.

Applying the Expand Stroke command

Although you can accomplish much with an open path through the Stroke section of the Property inspector, sometimes you need a fill, as well. The Expand Stroke command offers an easy way to convert any path—open or closed—into a larger closed path by enclosing the existing path, and then deleting it.

When you apply this command by choosing Modify ➪ Alter Path ➪ Expand Stroke, the Expand Stroke dialog box appears, as shown in Figure 9-26. As you can see, it offers quite a few options that enable you to control exactly what kind of path to use to expand the stroke. The options include the following:

Figure 9-26: Choose your options in the Expand Stroke dialog box in order to make a wide range of Expanded strokes.

✦ **Width:** Determines the final width of the expanded stroke. The range is from 1 to 99 pixels.

✦ **Corners:** Choose from three types of corners. From left to right, the buttons represent:

  • **Miter:** With a miter corner, the outside edges of the path extend until they touch in a sharp corner. Because miter corners can become quite long, you can limit their length with the Miter Limit option, which is explained in this list.

  • **Round:** The corner is rounded equally from both sides of the path approaching the corner. Round corners and round end caps are often used together.

  • **Bevel:** The corner is cut off at the center of the meeting paths, rather than on the outside edge, as with the miter corner. This results in a truncated corner.

✦ **Miter Limit:** The number of pixels the miter corner can extend before being cut off. The Miter Limit works only with miter corners.

✦ **End Caps:** Choose among the following three End Cap types for closing off the expanded path:

  • **Butt Cap:** The Butt Cap creates a right-angle End Cap where the end is perpendicular to the last point of the stroke.

  • **Square Cap:** Similar to the Round Cap, the Square Cap attaches a square to the end of the path, extending it the same radius as half the set width.

  • **Round Cap:** A Round Cap attaches a semicircle to the end of the path, extending it the same radius as half the set width.

Figure 9-27 shows the three different End Cap types, as well as an example of what it looks like to change an object that consists of strokes and fills into an object made up entirely of fills. After you've expanded the strokes, set the stroke to None, and apply a fill to the whole object. Note that the third and fourth face use the hair from the first face.

Discovering the Inset Path command

Whereas Expand Stroke applies strokes on both sides of a selected path, Inset Path only applies strokes on one side. The Inset dialog box is identical to the Expand Stroke dialog box, except for the addition of Inside and Outside options. You get the most predictable results with Inset Path if you apply it to closed paths, but you can use it with any kind of path, except straight lines.

Often, a plain and boring object can be replaced with an interesting variation just by applying the Inset Path command, as shown in Figure 9-28.

Original object   No stroke, radial fill

Strokes expanded   No stroke, pattern fill

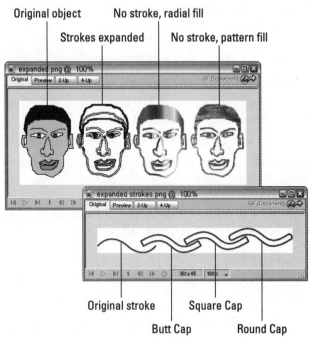

Original stroke   Square Cap

Butt Cap   Round Cap

Figure 9-27: The Expand Stroke command can change strokes to fills.

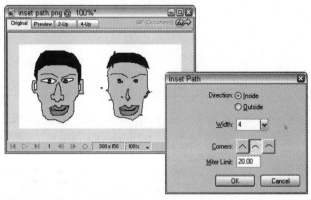

Figure 9-28: Create variations of an object with the Inset Path command.

One of my favorite applications of the Inset Path command is to create concentric shapes, each one within the next.

To use the Inset Path command to create concentric shapes, follow these steps:

1. Select the closed path to which you want to add concentric shapes.

2. Choose Edit ➪ Clone. Because Inset Path erases the original path, you must apply the command to a clone of the original path.

3. Choose Modify ➪ Alter Path ➪ Inset Path. The Inset dialog box appears.

4. Choose the Direction, Width, and Corner option. If you choose the Miter Corner, you can enter a Miter Limit. Click OK when you're done. The new path is drawn and the old path is deleted.

5. Repeat Steps 2 through 4 for as many concentric shapes as desired, keeping the same values in the Inset dialog box in order to create equidistant shapes.

After you've created your basic shapes, you can go in and vary the stroke width or other settings in order to create interesting effects.

Summary

Mastering the manipulation of paths is essential in order to achieve the most that's possible with Fireworks. You can distort, resize, rotate, and adjust vector objects in many subtle ways in order to create the basic shapes you need for unique Web graphics. When altering Fireworks objects, keep these points in mind:

✦ You can manipulate objects as a whole by using the transform tools: Scale, Skew, and Distort.

✦ You can rotate an object using any one of the transform tools.

✦ For precise sizing or rotation, use the Numeric Transform feature.

✦ The Skew tool is great for simulating perspective views — especially of bitmap objects. You can enhance the illusion by adding simulated light and shadow effects.

✦ Whereas the Pointer is used to move an entire path, the Subselection tool is used to maneuver individual points — and their Bézier control handles.

✦ After you draw a path, you can edit it in numerous ways by using tools such as Freeform, Redraw Path, Redraw Area, and Path Scrubber.

✦ The Union, Intersect, Punch, Crop, Simplify, Expand Path, and Inset Path commands are extraordinary power tools for working with paths in Fireworks.

In the next chapter, you learn about adding text to your Web graphics in Fireworks.

✦ ✦ ✦

Composing with Text

CHAPTER

10

Text has a special place in Web graphics. Although most text — paragraphs, lists, and tables of information — is a product of the HTML page viewed through a browser, graphic-based text is generally used to create logos, fancy headings, and other decorative elements that aren't possible with basic HTML. In addition, text is an integral part of a key Web element: navigation. Many navigation buttons use text, either alone or in combination with symbols, to quickly convey meaning.

Before Fireworks, a recurring nightmare for Web designers involved modifying a text graphic. Whether it was a typo or a client change-of-mind that forced the revision, the designer was stuck having to redo an entire graphic because any text, once applied, was just another bunch of pixels. Fireworks changed all that with the introduction of editable text. Now, if a client's logo changes because of a $7-billion merger, or you just forgot to put the period at the end of *Inc.*, text modifications are just a double-click away.

A few programs have since followed Macromedia's lead, but Fireworks still leads the way. In this chapter, I show you basic things such as choosing fonts and aligning text, as well as more advanced features, such as attaching text to a path. You also learn a technique that enables you to combine images with text using Fireworks Mask Groups.

Working with Text

In Fireworks, all text creation and modification can take place onscreen, right in your document window just like the other drawing tools. For those who like to compose inside the box, Fireworks includes a Text Editor, covered later in this chapter, but onscreen text, combined with the options available in the Property inspector, makes for a more robust experience.

When you click the text tool on the canvas, a bounding box appears in the current Fireworks document, with a flashing cursor waiting for your text input. The text object has many, but not all, of the properties of a path object — you can, for example, use the transform tools such as Skew, but you can't use the Reshape Area tool to warp the text as you can a path. On the other hand, text objects have features unlike any other object, such as the capability to be aligned to a path, for example, a circle. If necessary, converting a text object to a path object or an image object is possible, but you can no longer edit the text.

New Feature Onscreen text is new to Fireworks MX. No longer are you confined to the Text Editor; now you can type directly onto the canvas. Talk about thinking outside of the box! Of course, should you want to use it, the Text Editor is only a menu away.

You can use the Text tool two ways:

✦ Click once on the canvas with the Text tool to set a starting point for your text. If necessary, the text flows to the edge of the current document and expands downward toward the bottom of the document.

✦ Drag out a rectangular text region with the Text tool. The text created in the Text Editor wraps on the horizontal boundaries of the established region and, if necessary, expands downward.

The general steps for inserting text into a Fireworks document are as follows:

1. Select the Text tool from the Tools panel, or use the keyboard shortcut, T.

2. Set the text area by

   • Clicking once on the document where you want the text to start

   • Dragging out a text area for the text to fit into

   Either method creates a text object bounding box and prepares Fireworks for text entry.

3. From the Property inspector, choose the text characteristics, such as font, size, color, and alignment.

4. Type the text you want to type, and it appears directly in the document window. As you can see in Figure 10-1, when the Text tool I-beam is inside a text block, you see a small, right pointing triangle. This indicates that you can select text or move the insertion point within a text block.

Tip If you find that you need to reposition your text block as you're typing, hold down Ctrl (Command) to temporarily enable the Hand tool, and you'll be able to drag your text block around. When your text block is positioned correctly, simply release Ctrl (Command) and continue typing.

5. Click the canvas, or the workspace, once when you're done typing to cease text entry.

Figure 10-1: Text is typed directly into the document window, making it easy to position. The Text tool changes when you're over a text block.

When you've finished with a text object, you can move it as you would any other Fireworks object, by clicking and dragging with the Pointer tool. To adjust the shape of the text object, drag any of the six handles that become available when you select the object.

Note

Dragging a text object's handles doesn't resize the text itself, but instead changes the outside boundaries of the text object, after which the text reflows through its new boundaries. A text object can only be vertically resized to fit the current text it contains. If you want your text object to take up more vertical room, select it and choose a larger font size from the Text ➪ Size menu or from the Property inspector.

When you need to edit an existing text object, there are a couple of ways to accomplish the task. You can choose the Text tool and hover it over an existing text object; when the I-beam cursor gains a small, right-pointing triangle, click once to place the cursor in that position in your text object. You also can select the text object as you would any other Fireworks object, and then choose Text ➪ Editor. Finally, the most efficient method (and certainly my most often used one) is to double-click the text object with the Pointer or Subselection tool; your insertion point appears at that location within the text box.

Using the Text Editor

The Text Editor, shown in Figure 10-2, is a separate window with a full range of text controls and its own preview pane. After you click the canvas with the Text tool, a *text object* appears in the current Fireworks document, surrounded by a bounding box. The Text Editor can then be opened by either selecting an existing block of text, choosing the Text tool and clicking the canvas to create a new text block, and then choosing Text ➪ Editor. Alternatively, if you already have a text block in your document, you can select it and then choose Text ➪ Editor.

Figure 10-2: You can use the Text Editor to compose and edit text for those occasions when onscreen text use can be awkward, such as when dealing with very small font sizes.

The general steps for inserting text with the Text Editor are as follows:

1. Select the Text tool from the Tools panel, or use the keyboard shortcut, T.

2. Set the text area by

   • Clicking once on the document where you want the text to start

   • Dragging out a text area for the text to fit into

3. Choose Text ➪ Editor to open the Text Editor.

4. From the Text Editor, choose a text characteristic, such as font, size, color, or alignment.

5. Click in the Preview pane and input the text. If Auto-Apply is enabled, Fireworks updates the text object in the document after each keystroke.

6. Click OK when you're done.

Tip   Pressing Enter (Return) when your cursor is in the Preview pane adds a line break, as you might expect. Unfortunately, the OK button in the Text Editor is highlighted, which may tempt you to press Enter (Return) to dismiss the Text Editor dialog box. Instead, press the other Enter—on the numeric keypad—to dismiss the Text Editor.

After the text object is onscreen, you move it by clicking and dragging with the Pointer tool, just as with any other Fireworks object. To change the shape of the text object, drag any of the six handles that become available when you select the object.

When you want to edit an existing text object using the Text Editor, select the text object as you would any other Fireworks object, and then choose Text ⇨ Editor.

Enabling Text Editor options

The final elements found in the Text Editor are the options: two for the Text Editor itself and three for the final product. To get the closest approximation possible in the Preview pane, enable both the Show Font and Show Size & Color options. The Show Font option displays the text in the current selected typeface. When the Show Font option is turned off, the Preview pane shows text in a sans serif font, such as Arial or Helvetica. The Size & Color option—no surprises here—enables you to see your text in the current size and color. Without this option enabled, you see text at approximately 24 points and black.

The three other options, Anti-Alias, Auto Kern, and Apply, are applicable to the text object. The Anti-Alias option smoothes the text by providing an antialiased edge to the fill for the text object. Auto Kern, as discussed in the upcoming section "Adjusting text spacing," uses a font's kerning pairs. Apply enables any changes made in the Text Editor to be automatically updated and viewed in the document's text object.

In my way of working, only occasionally do these features actually become optional. If I have a large block of text in the Preview pane, I might disable the Size & Color option, but I almost never turn off the Font option. Only when trying to achieve a special effect would I even consider disabling either Anti-Alias or Auto Kern. But I've noticed that I'm totally dependent on the Apply function for constant feedback as I work.

Choosing basic font characteristics

With either the Text tool, or a text object, selected, you have full control over the look and style of your text through the Property inspector. The Property inspector offers two methods of working when it comes to setting up your text. To set your options, use either one of the following techniques:

✦ Select the Text tool and set the font attributes prior to clicking the canvas to create a text object.

✦ Use the text tool to select the text you want to modify in the document window—all or a portion—and then alter the attributes.

You can find all the core characteristics in the Property inspector, as shown in Figure 10-3.

Text size slider Color well

Font list Text size box Text styles

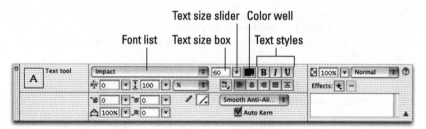

Figure 10-3: Select your font typeface, size, color, style, and so forth from the Property inspector.

The basic attributes are very straightforward to establish:

✦ **Font:** To choose a typeface, select a name from the Font list. The Font list displays all the available TrueType or Type 1 fonts on your system.

Windows users can also select the Font list itself and either use the cursor keys to move up or down the list, one font at a time, or type the first letter of a font's name to jump to that part of the list.

✦ **Size:** Choose the text size using the Text Size slider, or by entering a value directly in the Text Size box. Size is the height of a font in points. Fireworks accepts sizes from 4 to 1,000 points, although the slider only goes from 8 to 128.

You can also adjust text size by using the Scale tool on your text object, just as you would resize any other object. Although the text remains editable, its point size in the Property inspector or Text Editor doesn't change as you resize it. This can become confusing when you attempt to edit a huge text object and find that it says it's 10pt.

✦ **Color:** Initially, text is applied based on the color specified in the Fill color well. However, you can easily choose a new text fill color by clicking the color well in the Property inspector. The standard pop-up color picker is displayed with the current swatch set. Each character in your text object can have its own color.

✦ **Style:** Choose from Bold, Italic, and Underline styles for your text; each style button is a toggle, and you can apply any or all to one text object.

The Underline style is useful for mimicking hyperlinks in design mock-ups you might create for client approval, before actually making any HTML.

All the basic attributes are applicable on a letter-by-letter basis. You can—although it's inadvisable for aesthetic reasons—change every letter's font, size, color, or style. Ransom notes were never easier.

Discovering paragraph spacing

The amount of spacing that is applied to paragraphs in Fireworks is user configurable. If you don't like the default amount of space that appears between paragraphs, then you can adjust it through the Property inspector.

New Feature The paragraph spacing options are new to Fireworks MX.

The steps for adjusting paragraph spacing in text in Fireworks document are as follows:

1. Select a block of text that you have entered, ideally consisting of at least two paragraphs, or enter some new paragraphs now.

2. If you wish to adjust the space before a paragraph, enter a value in the Space preceding paragraph field on the Property inspector, or adjust the slider to the desired point.

3. If you wish to adjust the spacing following a paragraph, enter a value in the Space after paragraph field on the Property inspector, or adjust the slider to the desired point.

Adjusting text spacing

Adjustments to determine how text is situated within the text object occur in the Property inspector. Fireworks includes five text-spacing controls, as shown in Figure 10-4.

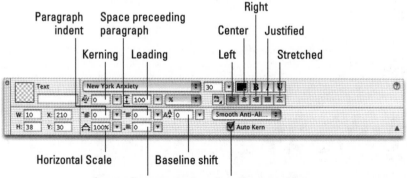

Figure 10-4: Control your text character and line positioning through the Fireworks text-spacing controls.

Kerning

Kerning determines how close letters appear to each other. The default value of 0 percent uses the standard font spacing. Increasing the Kerning slider (1 percent to 100 percent) moves letters further apart, whereas decreasing it (–1 percent to –100 percent) moves letters closer together, or overlaps them. Alter the kerning between two letters by placing the cursor between the letters in the Preview pane of the Text Editor and moving the Kerning slider, or entering a new value. To change the kerning for a range of letters, or the entire text in the Preview pane, select the letters before changing the kerning value.

Note   If you are using the Text Editor, the Preview pane does not show changes in the kerning. However, if you have the Auto-Apply option checked, you can see the effect of kerning on your text object in the document itself after each change.

Tip   In the Text Editor, you can position your cursor between characters and use Alt+Left/Right Arrow Keys and change the kerning between characters more easily and quickly. This is not possible in Text mode (typing directly on the canvas).

Auto Kern

Many fonts define the spacing for *kerning pairs,* such as the letters "WA" or "ov," which fit together, to make text more legible. Some fonts come with as many as 500 kerning pairs defined. Fireworks applies the kerning pair information whenever the Auto Kern option is enabled. The Auto Kern option affects the entire text object.

The effect of kerning pairs is most noticeable in the larger font sizes. The top text object in Figure 10-5 has Auto Kern enabled, which is the default. The bottom object is identical, except that the Auto Kern option has been unchecked. Note the differences in the overall length of the word, as well as how the first *A* fits between the *W* and the *V.* Leave Auto Kern checked unless you have a specific reason not to do so.

Figure 10-5: The Auto Kern option uses a font's built-in spacing for better kerning, as shown in the top text object.

Leading

Leading (pronounced *ledding* as in lead, the metal) is the printer's term for line spacing. In Fireworks, leading is expressed as a percentage of the font size and only affects text with multiple lines. Single-spaced lines use the default 100 percent; a value of 200 percent would give you a double-spaced paragraph. Leading values less than 90 percent or so cause lines to touch or overlap (see Figure 10-6). Unless you're creating a special effect, you probably want to keep your leading at 90 percent or higher.

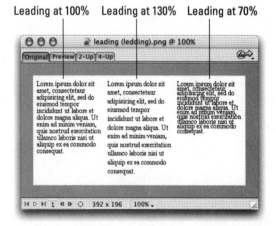

Figure 10-6: The Leading value controls the space between multiple lines of text.

Horizontal Scale

You can alter the relative width of any text through the Horizontal Scale control. The range of the Horizontal Scale slider is from 50 percent to 300 percent, but you can specify another value through the text box. You can see the effect of the Horizontal Scale in Figure 10-7, where the same text is presented at 200 percent, 100 percent, 50 percent, and 25 percent. Horizontal Scale does not display in the Preview pane of the Text Editor.

Note   Don't confuse kerning and Horizontal Scale. Kerning affects the space between individual characters while Horizontal Scale affects the characters themselves.

Baseline Shift

If you're building a Web site on which chemical formulas are a key element, you'll be happy to discover the Baseline Shift control. Normally, all text is rendered along the same baseline so that the bottoms of most letters are aligned. The Baseline Shift control enables you to place letters or words above or below the normal baseline. Fireworks specifies the Baseline Shift value in points: Negative values go below the baseline, and positive values go above. For a standard subscript letter, such as the 2 in H_2O, use a negative value about half the size of the current font (see Figure 10-8). Likewise, for a superscript, choose a positive value; again, about half the current font size.

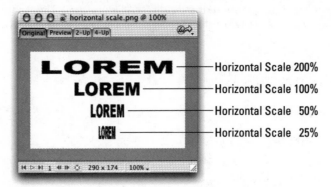

Figure 10-7: Change the width of a text object by adjusting the Horizontal Scale slider in the Text Editor.

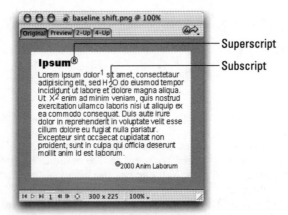

Figure 10-8: Specify a new Baseline Shift value for subscript characters such as the 2 in H_2O, and superscript characters such as the (r) and the (c).

Aligning text

All text objects, when selected in the Fireworks document, are surrounded by a bounding box. The bounding box sets the position of the text through its upper-left corner coordinates, but it also determines the limits for the text block. Most importantly, all alignment for the text is relative to the bounding box.

You can apply different alignment options to different text in the same text object, as long as each piece of text is on its own line. Figure 10-9 illustrates this capability with each of the five horizontal alignment options in one paragraph, as well as showing whole paragraphs of each option.

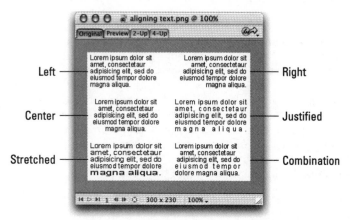

Figure 10-9: Fireworks offers many text alignment options.

The Text Editor contains controls for specifying text alignment (see Figure 10-10). Text can be Horizontal Left to Right (the default), Horizontal Right to Left, Vertical Left to Right (the default), or Vertical Right to Left, depending on what you choose from the Set text orientation pop-up.

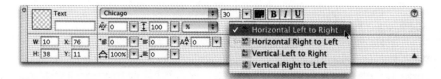

Figure 10-10: Use the Set text orientation pop-up Horizontal Alignment controls to align text left, center, right, justified, or stretched.

When Horizontal Left to Right or Horizontal Right to Left are selected, the alignment options affect your text the same way. The only thing that changes is the direction in which your text is rendered across the screen. The alignment options affect you text as follows:

✦ **Left Alignment:** Text is aligned to the left edge of the bounding box.

✦ **Right Alignment:** Text is aligned to the right edge of the bounding box.

✦ **Center Alignment:** Text is centered between the left and right edges of the bounding box.

✦ **Justified Alignment:** Text is evenly spaced so that the letters of each line touch both the left and right edges of the bounding box; the letters, however, remain the size specified in the Font size.

✦ **Stretched Alignment:** Text is expanded horizontally so that the letters of each line touch both the left and right edges of the bounding box.

Tip   The middle sizing handles on a text object's bounding box are always adjustable. This feature is very useful because you can quickly center text in a document by dragging the middle sizing handles to either edge of the canvas and choosing the Center alignment option in the Property inspector.

When Vertical Left to Right or Vertical Right to Left are chosen, the alignment options change. As with the Horizontal text choices, the only difference between the two vertical text options is the direction in which your words are rendered across the screen. The vertical text options are as follows:

✦ **Top Alignment:** Text is aligned to the top of the bounding box.

✦ **Center Alignment:** Text is centered between the top and bottom of the bounding box.

✦ **Bottom Alignment:** Text is aligned to the bottom of the bounding box.

✦ **Justified Alignment:** Text is evenly spaced so that the letters of each line touch both the top and bottom edges of the bounding box, however, the letters remain the size specified in the Font size.

✦ **Stretched Alignment:** Text is expanded vertically so that the letters of each line touch both the top and bottom edges of the bounding box.

Re-Editing Text

The Property inspector is perhaps the most commonly used method for editing text in Fireworks, but it's not the only one. To make a global change to a text object, such as altering the typeface or size, you can use a menu command. Although you do sacrifice the full range of features, menus can be much faster than using the Property inspector or the Text Editor, especially if you take advantage of the keyboard shortcuts.

In all, you can apply four menu items under the Text heading to a selected text object:

✦ **Font:** Lists the fonts available on your system, in alphabetical order.

✦ **Size:** To quickly change your selected text object to a set size, choose Text ⇨ Size, and then one of the dozen point sizes: 8, 9, 10, 12, 14, 18, 24, 36, 48, 72, and 96. Choose Other to enter a different size than those available or choose Smaller or Larger to decrease or increase the font size by one point.

✦ **Style:** In addition to the options available through the Text Editor (Bold, Italic, and Underline), the Text ⇨ Style menu enables you to remove all styles with one command, Text ⇨ Style ⇨ Plain.

✦ **Align:** The Text ➪ Align menu is broken up into two groups, one for horizontal text and one for vertical text. Choosing an alignment from one group automatically alters the orientation of the text, if necessary. For example, if you apply Text ➪ Align ➪ Bottom to a horizontal text object, the text object converts to a vertical text object and aligns the text to the bottom, simultaneously.

To be completely thorough, one other command in the Text menu could be listed in this category: Text ➪ Editor, which opens the Text Editor for the selected text object.

Preserving Look or Editing Text

Ideally, source files such as Fireworks documents would never go anywhere without the fonts that were used to create them. Of course, this is not always the case. You may archive a document, find a need for it a year later and then, upon opening it, discover that you no longer have one or more of the fonts you originally used. You might send a document to someone and forget to send the fonts, or need to open a Fireworks document on another platform where your fonts won't work without conversion. Suddenly, a careful design is thrown into disarray because the substituted fonts don't have the same spacing or characteristics.

New Feature

Fireworks MX saves a bitmap representation of your document in the source PNG and substitutes that bitmap for fonts you don't have if you choose to maintain their appearance. When the file is saved again, it can be taken to a system that has the font, and the original text remains editable and in the correct font.

Fireworks solves this problem by saving a snapshot of your document within the Fireworks PNG source file. If you open a document that contains a font that's not on your system, Fireworks warns you that the font is missing and asks whether you would like to maintain the appearance of the font or replace the font with another (see Figure 10-11).

If you choose to maintain the appearance, Fireworks displays the text block taken from the archived bitmap image, giving you an exact representation of the font even though you don't have it. You can make any changes you like to other aspects of the document, and as long as you don't edit the text, you can save the file again and the original text block remains editable, and in the original font, when opened on a system that has the font.

If this sounds like a great time and energy saver, then you'll really like the next aspect of this feature. If you choose to maintain the appearance of the font, but you need to make some font changes, you can select the text tool and alter the text. When you save the file, Fireworks keeps the original font name attached to the text you have just modified. If you send the file to someone who has the original fonts, they can grab the text tool, click within the font block, and the text immediately snaps back to its original appearance.

Figure 10-11: Fireworks warns you that you do not have the required fonts and offers the choice of maintaining the appearance of the text or replacing the fonts.

If you know that you won't be using a particular font again, or if you have no idea where to get the font in the document from, you can choose to replace the font with a font on your system. Clicking Replace Fonts, on the dialog in Figure 10-11, brings up the Missing Fonts dialog, as seen in Figure 10-12.

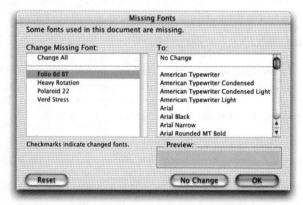

Figure 10-12: If you decide to replace fonts, you can select a different font substitute for each missing font.

You can choose fonts that have the look and feel that you want for your document without having to retype the text. When you save the file this way, Fireworks saves the font substitutions, rather than the original fonts, in your document.

Importing Text

Almost all the text that's used in Web graphics is relatively short; longer paragraphs are generally part of the HTML file rendered by the browser. There are numerous reasons why text on the Web is generally not in graphic form, although first and foremost — as with many aspects of the Web — is file size. Download time for a page of graphic text is considerably longer than for that of HTML text.

However, in the for-every-rule-there's-an-exception category, occasionally blocks of text have to be rendered as a graphic. Some clients insist on an absolute fidelity to their traditional printed material across all platforms. The only way to keep these clients happy — even at the expense of a longer download — is to render the text as a graphic. In these cases, you have the potential for taking advantage of one of Fireworks' least-known features: text import.

In addition to the numerous graphic file types supported by Fireworks, you can also open ASCII and Rich Text Format (RTF) files. ASCII (American Standard Code for Information Interchange) files are the lowest common denominator of all text files and contain no formatting whatsoever. RTF files, on the other hand, convey a good deal of basic formatting, such as typeface, size, styles (bold, italic, and underline), and alignment.

Although you can copy short passages of text from another program and paste them into a text object, for a large block of text, you're better off importing it.

To import a text file, follow these steps:

1. Be sure the file you want to import is saved in either ASCII or RTF format.

2. Choose File ➪ Import, or use the keyboard shortcut, Ctrl+R (Command+R).

   The Import dialog box appears.

3. If you're working in Windows, choose either ASCII Text (*.txt) or RTF Text (*.rtf) from the Files of Type option list.

4. Navigate to your ASCII or RTF file, select it, and click Open.

   After the Import dialog box closes, the Insert cursor appears.

5. Place the imported text in your document in one of two ways:

   • Position the cursor where you want the upper-left corner of the text object to start and click once.

   • Click and drag out the bounding box for the text file.

   The text flows into the new text object.

 The click-and-drag method for creating a text object is currently somewhat limited. Rather than have the full freedom to draw whatever shape you desire, the rectangle is constrained to a 4:1 ratio of vertical to horizontal space. In other words, the initial text object is always four times as wide as it is tall. More importantly, Fireworks renders the text to fit within this bounding box, regardless of its previous font size.

Checking Your Spelling

Have you ever created the perfect look in Fireworks, exported to your site folder, imported everything into Dreamweaver, or another web design program, just to discover that you've spelled something wrong on one of your buttons or graphics? If you're like me, doing this once is one time too many. As easy as it is, it can be a real annoyance to go back into Fireworks, fix the spelling mistake, and then export to your site again. Not to worry, Fireworks, as you may have already noticed, is an all-inclusive package that even offers spell-checking.

New Feature Spell-check is a new feature in Fireworks MX.

The spell-checking in Fireworks isn't just a plain old spell-checker. It's full featured and customizable enough for any user. The first thing to do to get ready for your spell-check is to define your language of choice from the Spelling Setup dialog box, as seen in Figure 10-13. To open the Spelling Setup dialog box, choose Text ➪ Spelling Setup.

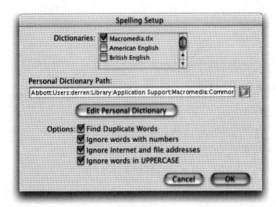

Figure 10-13: Fireworks offers you plenty of options in the Spelling Setup dialog box.

The Spelling Setup dialog box has the following options:

✦ **Dictionaries:** This is where you choose the language that you're using in your document. The entry entitled Macromedia.tlx is always selected, and placed first in the list, as this is your custom dictionary.

Note If you do not select a dictionary language to use, Fireworks prompts you for one every time you run spell-check.

✦ **Personal Dictionary Path:** The path listed here reflects the location of your custom dictionary.

✦ **Edit Personal Dictionary:** Clicking on the Edit Personal Dictionary button gives you an easy way to add, edit, or remove words in your dictionary. If spell-check doesn't recognize a word you can add it to this dictionary when you click the Add to Personal button in the Check Spelling dialog box. You can add individual words, or paste in an entire list of words, with this option.

✦ **Find Duplicate Words:** This tells Fireworks whether or not to look for duplicate instances of words directly next to each other.

✦ **Ignore words with numbers:** Very often, short form versions for software products include both the program's initials and the version number. With this option checked, Fireworks ignores words that have numbers in them, such as DW4 or FW4, in order to reduce the number of false spelling mistakes.

✦ **Ignore Internet and file addresses:** With this option checked, Fireworks skips the checking of URLs listed in your document.

✦ **Ignore words in UPPERCASE:** This tells Fireworks not to check the spelling of words that are all in uppercase. It can be useful to have this option selected so that the spell-checker doesn't continually complain about acronyms.

Spell-check in Fireworks functions much the same as spell-check in Dreamweaver, Microsoft Word, and many other programs. To check your spelling, follow these steps:

1. Open the document that you would like to perform the spell-check on. The Check Spelling dialog box opens with the first error, or unknown word displayed (see Figure 10-14).

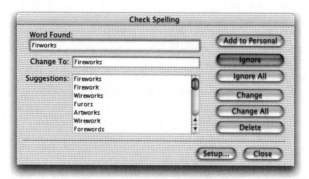

Figure 10-14: The Check Spelling dialog box resembles that of the spell-check in many other applications.

2. Fireworks offers suggestions for alternative spellings for words it doesn't know. You can select one of the suggestions, or make your correction manually in the Change To field, and click Change to accept the new word.

3. If the highlighted word is spelled correctly, but is not in Fireworks' dictionary, such as company or individual names, click the Add to Personal button to add the word to your custom dictionary.

4. If you find that you're stepping through numerous corrections of the same word, you can choose Ignore All if the word is correct, or Replace All if the word is consistently misspelled throughout the entire text.

5. When the spell-check is completed, Fireworks displays a dialog box that says Spelling check completed. Click OK or hit Enter (return) to close the dialog box and return to your document.

Transforming Text

You really start to feel the power of Fireworks after you begin adding strokes, textured gradient fills, and multiple effects to a block of text — and you're still able to edit it. You can even use any of the transform tools — Scale, Skew, or Distort — to warp the text completely, and it's still editable.

No real shortcut exists to mastering text in your images. You really can only get a sense of what's possible by working, experimenting, trying — in essence, playing. In the following sections, you'll find some avenues to begin your text explorations.

Adding strokes

When you first create a text object, only the basic fill color is applied. However, this doesn't mean you can't add a stroke to your text — any combination of stroke settings is fair game. You do have to be a bit careful, though. Some of the preset strokes, such as Basic Airbrush, are quite hefty and can completely obscure all but text in the larger font sizes. However, modifying a stroke size (or color, softness, or texture) is quite easy, and you can generally adjust the presets to find a workable setting.

One use for text with an added stroke is to create outlined text. Almost all fonts are presented with solid, filled-in letters. In Fireworks, however, you can make almost any font an outline font, with a fairly straightforward procedure:

1. Select a text object.

2. Click the Stroke color well, on the Property inspector or the Tools panel, and then click Stroke Options.

3. Change the stroke from None to any of those available in the Stroke category option list.

Tip   Try Basic or Pencil strokes for simple outlines; experiment with Airbrush or Random strokes for more unusual results.

4. Select any desired preset from the Stroke name option list, and modify its settings as needed.

5. Click the Fill color well, on the Property inspector or the Tools panel.

6. Click Fill Options and set the fill to None in the Fill category option list. The solid fill disappears, and the remaining stroke outlines the text.

The results of these steps are shown in Figure 10-15.

Figure 10-15: Fireworks' strokes can turn almost any font into an outline version.

Another technique for adjusting the look of a stroke on text is to alter the stroke's orientation. With most path objects, an applied stroke is centered on the path. With text objects, however, the default is to place the stroke on the outside of the path. Change the orientation of the stroke by selecting a text block, clicking the Stroke color well on the Property inspector, and then choosing Stroke Inside, Stroke Centered, or Stroke Outside. By altering the stroke orientation, you can get three completely different graphic looks, as shown in Figure 10-16.

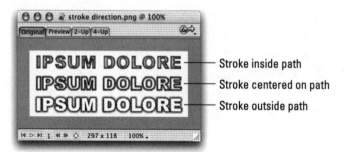

Figure 10-16: The only difference between these three variations is the orientation of the stroke.

Cross-Reference

To find out more about strokes, turn to Chapter 8.

Enhancing fills

Although the default method of displaying text already uses a colored fill, it's just the tip of what's possible with Fireworks text. Any type of fill that you can devise — solid color, Web dither, gradient, or textured — is applicable to text objects. Moreover, you can alter the edges of a fill to give either a softer or harder textual appearance.

Applying a fill to text is very straightforward. Just select the text object, and choose your fill from the Fill color well on the Property inspector. Fireworks treats the entire text object as a single unit, so gradients and Patterns flow across all the separate letters and words. You can, however, adjust the way the fill is distributed by adjusting the gradient and Pattern controls, as described in these steps:

1. Select your text object.

2. Click the Fill color well on the Property inspector, or on the Tools panel, and then select Fill Options.

3. Choose a gradient or Pattern fill.

4. Select the Gradient tool.

   The gradient editing handles appear on the filled text object, as shown in Figure 10-17.

Figure 10-17: Alter the way a gradient moves across your text by moving the Gradient Fill handles.

5. To adjust the centerpoint of the gradient, click and drag the round starting handle.

6. To adjust the direction of the gradient, click and drag the square ending handle.

   Some gradients, such as Ellipse, Rectangle, and Starburst, have a third handle, which you can move to adjust the width and skew of the gradient.

7. Click any tool, other than the Gradient tool, to cease editing the Gradient.

Cross-Reference Want to know more about fills? Turn to Chapter 11.

Using the transform tools

You can apply each of the three transform tools — Scale, Skew, and Distort — to any text object, enabling you to resize, rotate, slant, and even pull text out of shape and still edit it. In this regard, text objects act just like path objects: The same sizing handles appear, and you can even use the Flip Horizontal/Vertical or Numeric Transform commands, as in Figure 10-18.

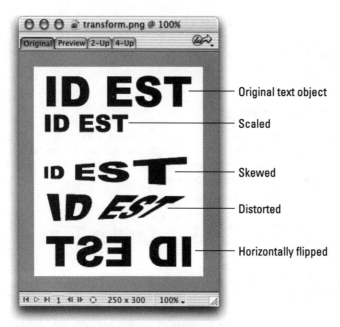

Figure 10-18: Text objects are fair game for Fireworks transform tools. Text, as always, remains editable.

Keep a couple of points in mind about transforming text:

✦ Before using the Skew tool on a text object, narrow the bounding box on either side of the text object as much as possible. Skew affects all portions of a text object, and excess area may give you an undesirable effect.

✦ As with a regular path object, both Skew and Distort are useful for providing perspective effects with text. Adding an effect to text, such as inner bevel or drop shadow, also helps the effect.

Converting text to paths

So if editability of text is such a big deal, why would you ever want to give it up? After you convert text to a path, you can combine it with other path objects by using commands on the Modify ➪ Combine Paths submenu. You might also want to alter a letter's shape, but to do that, you need to convert it to a path in order to gain access to its underlying points. You might find an interesting graphic hiding in a dingbats font and want to use it as a clipart foundation for a new drawing. In any case, select your text and choose Text ➪ Convert to Paths, or use the keyboard shortcut Ctrl+Shift+P (Command+Shift+P).

Tip   Before converting a text object to a path object, always, always, always make a copy of it and keep the copy on a hidden layer or unused frame. It's a good backup when things go wrong, and an additional design element for that unexpected creative moment, 10 or 20 steps down the line.

Converting text to an image

Not only can you convert text to paths, you can also convert it to a bitmap image. Just select the text object and choose Modify ➪ Flatten Selection, or use the keyboard shortcut Ctrl+Alt+Shift+Z (Command+Option+Shift+Z). As with the path conversion, text converted to pixels is no longer editable.

Fireworks Technique: Cookie-Cutter Text

One of my favorite things to do with text is to convert it to a path and punch it through other path objects. The resulting objects make great guinea pigs for experimentation with Filters or Live Effects. Buttons created this way are easy to turn into rollovers because the text — or rather, the hole that the text punches out — is transparent. You can make these buttons glow different colors by placing them over different backgrounds, or placing them over an image so the image shows through.

In any case, to use a former text object as a cookie cutter on other path objects, follow these steps, which are illustrated in Figure 10-19:

1. Create a text object.

2. Choose Text ➪ Convert to Paths, or use the keyboard shortcut, Ctrl+Shift+P (Command+Shift+P). Each letter in the text object is converted to a path, and then grouped.

3. Select your text path object and choose Modify ➪ Ungroup, and then Modify ➪ Combine Paths ➪ Join, or use the keyboard shortcuts Ctrl+Shift+G (Command+Shift+G) and Ctrl+J (Command+J), respectively.

   This ungroups the individual letters, and then joins them all into one composite path.

4. Create a path object — such as a rectangle — to punch your text through. Make sure that it has a fill of some sort.

5. Place the text path object on top of your path object, aligning the text path object carefully where you want it to punch through.

Tip   You may have to select your text paths and choose Modify ➪ Arrange ➪ Bring to Front to bring it higher in the stacking order than your path object. Alternatively, you could send the path object to the back.

6. Select both objects, and choose Modify ➪ Combine Paths ➪ Punch.

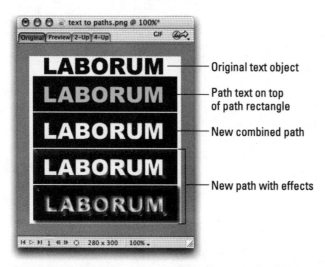

Figure 10-19: Text is converted to a path and then punched through another path object, cookie-cutter style.

Your two objects are combined into a new path object with the same fill, stroke and other properties of the bottom object. Experiment with different fills, strokes, and effects, or place your new object on top of other objects that show through.

Using the Text on a Path Command

For the most part, text is either strictly horizontal or vertical. The Text on a Path command, however, enables you to flow text in the shape of any path—whether the path is a circle, rectangle, or freeform shape.

The basic procedure is pretty simple: First, create each part—a text object and a path—and then combine them. Because paths can come in so many shapes, Fireworks offers a number of different controls and options to help you get what you want. Amazingly enough, text remains editable even after it's been attached to a path.

To align text on a path, follow these steps:

1. Draw or create any path object.

2. If necessary, create a text object.

3. Select both the path and the text object.

4. Choose Text ➪ Attach to Path, or use the keyboard shortcut, Ctrl+Shift+Y (Command+Shift+Y).

   The text flows along the path and the attributes of the path (stroke, fill, and effect) disappear, as shown in Figure 10-20.

5. To edit the text, double-click with the Pointer tool or choose the Text tool and click your text block.

6. To separate the text from the path, choose Text ➪ Detach from Path.

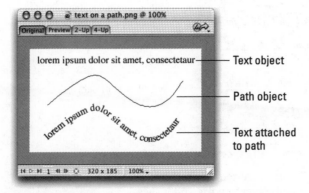

Figure 10-20: The two separate objects—text and path— are combined into one with the Attach to Path command.

Several variables affect exactly how the text flows along the path. First, the alignment of the text itself can have an effect:

✦ **Left Aligned:** The text starts at the beginning of the path.

✦ **Centered:** The text is centered between the beginning and end of the path.

✦ **Right Aligned:** The text ends at the end of the path.

✦ **Justified:** All the characters are evenly spaced along the path with additional spacing, if necessary.

✦ **Stretched:** All the characters are stretched to fit along the path with standard spacing.

It's pretty easy to guess where a linear path starts and ends, but how about a circle? If you remember the discussion on using the Ellipse tool in Chapter 5, you might recall I mentioned that circle paths generally start at about 9 o'clock and travel in a clockwise direction, around the outside of the circle. To cause the text to begin its flow in a different area, you have three options:

✦ Rotate the text attached to the path using one of the transform tools.

✦ Choose Modify ⇨ Transform ⇨ Numeric Transform, and select Rotate from the option list before choosing the angle of rotation.

✦ Enter an Offset value in the Property inspector.

The Offset value moves the text the specified number of pixels in the direction of the path. Because circle diameters vary, trial and error is the best method for using the Offset value. The Offset option also accepts negative numbers to move the text in the opposite direction of the path.

To flow the text along the inside of the circle, choose Text ⇨ Reverse Direction (see Figure 10-21). With an Offset value at 0, the text begins at 6 o'clock and flows counterclockwise.

The final aspect that you can control with regard to attaching text to a path is the text's orientation to the path. You can find the options, shown in Figure 10-22, under Text ⇨ Orientation:

✦ **Rotate Around Path:** Each letter in the text object is positioned perpendicularly to its place on the path (the default).

✦ **Vertical:** Each letter of the text object remains straight relative to the document, as the letters travel along the path.

✦ **Skew Vertical:** Rotates the letters along the path, but slants them vertically.

✦ **Skew Horizontal:** Keeps the letters straight on the path, and slants them horizontally according to the angle of the curve.

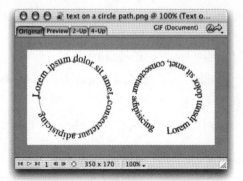

Figure 10-21: Use the Reverse Direction command in combination with Offset to properly place your text in a circle.

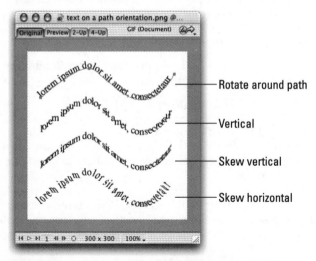

Figure 10-22: Achieve different effects by changing the orientation of the text to its attached path.

After looking at the Skew Horizontal example in Figure 10-22, you might be wondering why this option was included. One of the reasons why it looks so unappealing is that the skew changes when the underlying path changes its angles. When Skew Horizontal is applied to a path with no or fewer curves, you can achieve a more pleasing effect, as shown in Figure 10-23.

Figure 10-23: The horizontal skew orientation looks best when it's applied to a path with few or no curves.

Fireworks Technique: Masking Images with Text

What do you get when you combine images and text so that the text becomes the image? A graphic worth a thousand and one words? Actually, I think the technique of masking images is often worth far more. Moreover, its relative ease of creation in Fireworks makes it especially valuable.

A mask group is two or more objects grouped together where the bottom object is visible only through the top object. Take a look at Figure 10-24, and you'll see immediately what I mean. Because color is often so vital to a mask group's effect — and because I think it's cool — I've also included the image in the color insert.

To mask an image with text, follow these steps:

1. Create an image and a text object, or move existing image and text objects into the same document.

2. Position the text object over the image in its approximate final place.

3. Select both objects.

   4. Choose Modify ➪ Mask ➪ Group as Mask.

   The image is now only visible through the text.

   5. Use the Subselection tool to select and modify the placement of the image, if necessary.

The basic technique for masking an image with text is the same as using any other object as a mask. I've found, however, that manipulating the text into the proper shape beforehand creates a more successful mask. Try to start with a fairly wide font so that much of the image comes through, and then apply the Horizontal Scale and/or Kerning controls in the Property inspector to get the largest possible type. For example, the font used in Figure 10-20 is the very thick Arial Black, with a −12 percent Kerning value, so that the characters touch and don't break up the image.

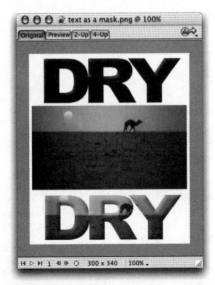

Figure 10-24: Combine imagery and text through a mask group. Note the bevel Live Effect on the text, which remains after grouping.

Summary

Text and images are codependents on the Web. It's nearly impossible to have one without the other, but the text-handling features of Fireworks make for a smooth integration. Gaining a complete understanding of creating and editing Fireworks' text objects is essential for strong Web design. Keep these considerations in mind as you work with text in Fireworks:

✦ Text is always editable for files saved in Fireworks' native format. You can apply a stroke, fill, or effect, and you can transform text repeatedly — and still be able to edit all the text, all the time.

✦ Text in Fireworks is represented in the document as a text object. You create text objects onscreen using the Text tool or import them from ASCII or RTF files.

✦ With the Text tool selected, the Property inspector contains all the controls necessary for assigning attributes, such as typeface, size, color, spacing, and alignment to text.

✦ Text alterations can be made in the Text Editor for those times when onscreen text entry is awkward.

✦ Text can accept the full range of strokes, fills, and effects available in Fireworks. The transform tools — Scale, Skew, and Distort — also work with text objects.

✦ Converting a text object into a series of paths enables you to combine those paths with other path objects for interesting effects.

✦ Fireworks has a very full-featured Align Text with Path command that enables you to flow text around a circle, down a curving slope, or tracing any path you desire. Moreover, you can adjust the spacing of the text through the Alignment and Offset features.

✦ You can easily combine text and images by using the Fireworks Group as Mask command.

In the next chapter, you get into the center of Fireworks objects, as I explain fills and textures.

✦　　✦　　✦

Achieving Effects

Fireworks graphics really begin to gain depth in Part III. The variety of fills and textures available — as well as the capability to add your own — are critical for the wide range of image production for which a Web designer is responsible. Chapter 12 explores the exciting world of Fireworks Live Effects and filters, which are exciting not just because they're easy to use and they look great, but also because of the positive impact that their always-editable nature will have on your workflow.

Most of the time, a graphic will actually contain a number of images. Chapter 13 explains the Fireworks methods for arranging and compositing multiple objects in order to achieve stunning results. The Fireworks mask-group feature, in particular, is an especially creative and powerful tool that takes the hard work out of alpha channels. Although Fireworks is a great drawing tool, it's also adept at handling bitmap imagery.

Using Fills and Textures

Fills and strokes are fairly equal partners in Fireworks graphics. A fill gives substance to the inside of an object, just as a stroke does the outside. Fills in Fireworks come in many flavors — solid colors, gradations of color, and image patterns — and, as with strokes, they are astoundingly flexible and almost infinitely variable. Moreover, fills in objects are always editable, which means changing from a flat color to a repeating pattern takes only a click or two.

After touring the standard fills included with Fireworks, this chapter begins to explore the many ways you can customize and enhance fills. In addition to the techniques for editing gradients, Patterns, and the many variations obtainable through textures, you'll see how you can add custom gradients, Patterns, and textures.

Using Built-in Fills

As with strokes and the Stroke section of the Property inspector, you generally apply and modify fills from the Fill section of the Property inspector, shown in Figure 11-1. You can display the Property inspector by choosing Window ➪ Properties, or using the keyboard shortcut, Ctrl+F3 (Command+F3).

The five primary fill categories are as follows:

- ✦ **None:** No fill.

- ✦ **Solid:** Specifies a flat color fill, selectable with the Eyedropper in the pop-up color picker.

Tip

You can switch to None from Solid, simply by clicking the no-color chip in the pop-up color picker.

✦ **Web Dither:** Extends the Web-safe color range by using a repeating pattern of two Web-safe colors that simulates an unsafe color.

✦ **Pattern:** Applies a full-color image as a repeating pattern.

✦ **Gradient:** Inserts one of eleven gradient patterns blending two or more colors. The Gradient category is not separately listed, but implied through the listing of the gradient patterns.

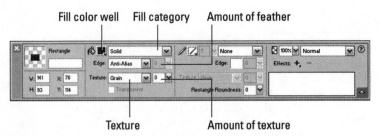

Figure 11-1: The Fill section of the Property inspector is your command center for applying and modifying any type of fill.

The Edge option works exactly the same way as the one found in the Stroke section of the Property inspector, with three choices: Hard Edge, Anti-Alias, and Feather. Choosing a Hard Edge fill uses only the fill specified with no enhancements; Anti-Alias blends the edge a bit, softening away the jaggies, if any; and Feather blends the edge the number of pixels specified through the Amount of Feather slider.

Textures work with fills in the same fashion as they do with strokes, but because they're so much more visible, you'll find a special section later in this chapter that delves deeper into their use.

Turning off an object's fill

Knowing how to remove the fill is just as important as adding a fill. In Fireworks, the easiest way to remove a fill is to choose None from the Fill category option list in the Fill section of the Property inspector. As mentioned in the previous chapter, a path with no stroke or fill assigned is invisible. Figure 11-2 shows a rectangle with no fill or stroke. As you can see, or as you can't, all that is visible are the four corners of the rectangle's bounding box. If you deselected it, you wouldn't even know it was there.

Using a Solid fill

A Solid fill is a basic, monochrome fill, sometimes called a *flat fill*. The color used in the Solid fill type is selected from the Fill color well — whether it's the one on the Property inspector, the Tools panel, or the Color Mixer. The Fill color well uses the standard Fireworks pop-up color picker, shown in Figure 11-3. The color picker displays the swatches active in the Swatches panel, which, by default, is the Web-safe, 216-color palette.

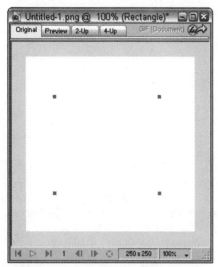

Figure 11-2: Paths are invisible until a stroke or fill is applied, as demonstrated by this rectangle with neither a stroke nor a path.

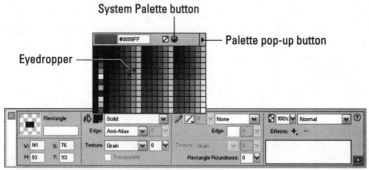

Figure 11-3: Assign a solid color fill through the Fill color well on the Property inspector.

To apply a solid color to an object, follow these steps:

1. Select the object.

2. Access the Fill color well in one of these three ways:

- Choose Window ➪ Properties to open the Property inspector, and select the color well in the Fill section.

- Select the Fill color well, as marked by the Paint Bucket, in the Tools panel.

- Choose Window ➪ Color Mixer to display the Color Mixer panel and select the Fill color well, as marked by the Paint Bucket.

Any one of these methods displays the pop-up color picker.

3. Use the Eyedropper to choose a color from the current swatch set, or select any color that's currently visible on your screen.

4. To access the operating system color picker(s), select the Palette button and select one of the colors in that dialog box.

You can adjust solid fills in several ways. You can select different edge options (Hard, Anti-Aliased, or Feather) from the Edge option list in the Fill section of the Property inspector; if you choose Feather, the Amount of Feather slider becomes available. In addition, a texture chosen from the Texture option list on the Fill panel may be applied. Remember, though, for a texture to be visible, you have to increase the Amount of texture past zero percent.

Using the Web Dither fill

Color is one of the most frustrating elements of Web design. Most Web designers use a palette of 216 Web-safe colors that the major browsers display correctly on both Macintosh and Windows computers set to 256 colors (8-bit color). The most obvious limitation is the relatively small number of colors: 216 out of a visible palette of millions of colors. Another limitation is the distance between colors; each Web-safe color is a large jump from its nearest Web-safe neighbor. These limitations become particularly acute when a client's logo contains colors that aren't available in the Web-safe palette. Luckily, Fireworks offers you a way to increase the Web-safe color variations to over 45,000: the Web Dither fill.

To understand how to use the Web Dither fill, you'll need a little more background in computer color. *Dithering* refers to the process where two or more pixels of different colors are positioned to create a pattern which, to the human eye, appears to be a third color. This technique works because a small pattern of pixels tends to blend visually; the eye can't separate the individual pixels. Dithering was originally used to overcome the 256-color restriction of early computer monitors. If you convert a photograph with millions of colors to a GIF with only 256 colors, you'll notice dithered areas where the computer graphics program is attempting to simulate the unavailable colors. For flat-color graphics, though, relying on dithering forces the designer to give up a lot of control. You don't know what you're going to get until you export.

Hybrid-Safe Colors were developed initially by Don Barnett and Bruce Heavin and later popularized by Web designer Lynda Weinman. A Hybrid-Safe color consists of two Web-safe colors in an alternating 2×2 pattern. Fireworks has adopted this technique and renamed it Web Dither. Not only does this feature now give you a total of 46,656 (216×216) Web-safe colors, but it also enables you to make any solid fill semitransparent, opening up a whole new area of graphic design.

When you choose the Web Dither category from the Fill section of the Property inspector, and then click on the Fill color well, you'll notice that the Web Dither dialog pops up, as shown in Figure 11-4. Instead of one color well, there are now three. The top color well represents the current Fill color, whereas the other two color wells are used to create the dither pattern. If the current Fill color is already Web-safe, both dither colors will be identical. If the Fill color is not Web-safe, Fireworks creates the closest match possible by dithering two Web-safe colors.

To apply a Web Dither fill, follow these steps:

1. Select your object.

2. Select Web Dither from the Fill category of the Property inspector.

3. Click the Fill color well to open the Web Dither dialog box.

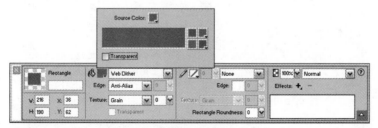

Figure 11-4: The Web Dither fill greatly expands the range of possible Web-safe colors that you can use.

4. Click on the color well in the top right of the pop-up window to open the color palette.

5. Pick a color that is not Web-safe in one of these ways:

    • To select a color from the swatch in your active palette, choose the color from the pop-up color picker. The active color must not be from the Web 216 Palette for this method.

    • To select a color from an image onscreen, sample the desired color with the Eyedropper in the pop-up color picker.

    • To select a color using your system's color picker, choose the Palette button from the pop-up color picker.

Tip   If you can't find an unsafe color, go outside of Fireworks with the Eyedropper and sample one elsewhere on your display. Windows users should hold down the mouse button while still over Fireworks, and keep the mouse button down as you hover the mouse over the color you want to sample, and release the mouse button to sample it.

Fireworks creates the closest color match possible by dithering your original color, as shown in Figure 11-5.

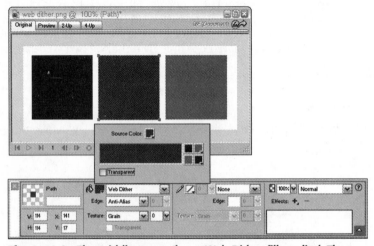

Figure 11-5: The middle square has a Web Dither fill applied. The squares on the left and right are the Web-safe colors used in the Web Dither, shown for example.

The Web Dither fill is terrific for finding absolutely must-have colors, such as those used for a logo, in a Web environment. When working from print materials, you can sample the color for the Web Dither fill.

Tip   Although the Web Dither does give you a huge range of colors to choose from, that doesn't mean all the color combinations are useful. If you choose two highly contrasting colors for the dither color wells, the dithered pattern appears to be dotted. It's usually better to select the desired color for the Fill color well by using the Eyedropper or any other method, and enable Fireworks to create the dither pattern for you.

Fireworks takes the Web Dither fill further by including a Transparent option. When you enable the Transparent option, Fireworks sets the first dither color well to None, while snapping the second dither color well to the nearest Web-safe color. The dither pattern now alternates a transparent pixel with a Web-safe colored pixel, and the resulting fill pattern is semitransparent.

Tip When you export a figure using a Transparent Web Dither fill, be sure to select either the Index or Alpha Transparency option.

Managing Gradients

A *gradient* is a blend of two or more colors. Gradients are used to add a touch of 3D or to provide a unique coloration to a graphic. A gradient is composed of two parts: a *color ramp,* which defines the colors used and their relative positioning, and a *gradient pattern,* which describes the shape of the gradient.

Fireworks includes 11 different types of gradient patterns and 13 preset color combinations. As you might have guessed, that just scratches the surface of what's possible with gradients because, as with many features in Fireworks, gradients are completely editable.

Applying a Gradient fill

A Gradient fill is applied in a slightly different manner than a Solid or Pattern fill. To apply a Gradient fill, follow these steps:

1. Select your object.

2. Select the Gradient tool from the flyout menu under the Paint Bucket tool, or by pressing the keyboard shortcut, G, twice.

3. From the Fill category option list in the Fill section of the Property inspector, choose one of the gradient options. When the selected gradient is initially applied, the current Stroke and the Fill colors are used to create the blend.

4. Click on the Fill color well in the Property inspector and the Edit Gradient pop-up dialog box appears. You can use the preset gradient colors that Fireworks offers, shown in Figure 11-6, or you can simply use one as a base and modify any colors to suit your graphic needs.

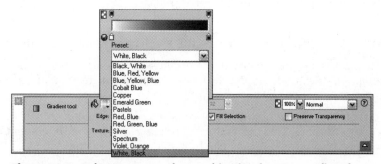

Figure 11-6: Select a preset color combination for your gradient from the Edit Gradient dialog box.

5. Change the fill edge or add a texture, if desired.

Rather than describe the standard gradients in words, grasping the differences visually is much easier, as demonstrated in Figure 11-7.

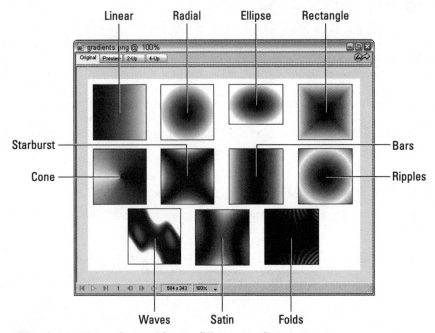

Figure 11-7: Fireworks provides 11 different gradient patterns.

Altering gradients

Fireworks' built-in gradient patterns and preset colors offer a good number of possibilities, but the real power of gradients comes in their customizability. You can modify gradients in three major ways:

✦ Every gradient pattern's center, width, and skew (if any) are all adjustable. With this facility, you can reshape the gradient's appearance with any object.

✦ The color ramp used to create the progression of colors in a gradient is completely flexible. Existing colors can be changed, deleted, or moved, and new colors can be added anywhere in the gradation.

✦ You can alter the transparency of your gradient, to enable objects beneath it to show through. This can add an interesting look to your document by only partially obscuring portions of a bitmap image for example.

 New Feature Transparent gradients are new to Fireworks MX. See later in the chapter for more information.

Modifying the gradient pattern

Each gradient object has handles. Handles are the keys to unlocking — and customizing — the gradient patterns. Selecting an object that has a Gradient or Pattern fill with the Pointer tool causes the gradient controls to appear (assuming the Show Fill Handles preference has been left at its default setting of enabled). All gradients have a starting point and an ending point, and four (Ellipse, Rectangle, Starburst, and Ripples) use two controls to adjust the size and skew of the pattern. The gradient controls are placed differently for each gradient pattern, as is evident in Figure 11-8.

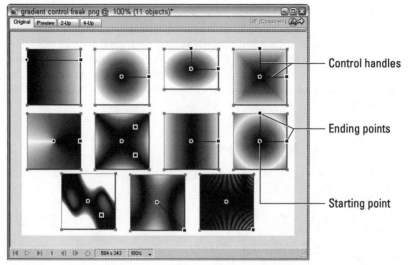

Figure 11-8: Each of the 11 standard gradients has individual control handles.

To modify a gradient pattern, follow these steps:

1. Select the object with the Gradient fill. The gradient controls appear.

2. To move the starting point for the gradient, drag the circular handle to another position.

3. To rotate the direction of the gradient, move the cursor over the length of any control handle until the Rotate cursor appears, and then drag the handles to a new location. As you rotate the gradient, Fireworks uses the gradient's starting point as a center axis.

4. To change the size of any gradient, drag the square handle straight to another position.

5. To alter the skew of an Ellipse, Rectangle, Starburst, or Ripples gradient, drag either square handle in the desired direction.

You're not limited to keeping the gradient controls within the selected object. You can move any gradient control—beginning, ending, or sizing/skewing handle—away from the object. In fact, many of my nicest gradient patterns resulted from placing the controls completely outside of the object. Experiment and think "outside the box."

Tip

If you want to copy a modified gradient pattern from one object to another, select the source gradient to be copied, choose Edit ⇨ Copy, select the destination object and choose Edit ⇨ Paste Attributes.

Editing gradient colors

If you cycle through the preset gradient color combinations, you'll notice that some presets have as few as two colors and others have as many as six. To see how the color preset is structured, select your Gradient and click on the color well in the Fill section of the Property inspector. The Edit Gradient pop-up dialog box, shown in Figure 11-9, is divided into three main areas: the color ramp, the color wells, and the preview pane. You can dismiss pop-up dialog boxes in Fireworks by clicking anywhere outside of them, or by pressing Esc.

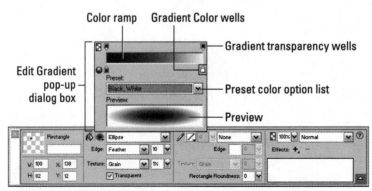

Figure 11-9: Modify the colors used in a gradient through the Edit Gradient pop-up dialog box.

The color ramp shows the current color combination as it blends from one key color to another. The key colors are displayed in the color wells, located beneath the color ramp. The preview pane shows how the color combination would be applied to the active gradient pattern. You can either modify a preset gradient, or adjust a gradient created from the Fill and Stroke colors.

To edit a gradient, follow these steps:

1. Click on the Fill color well in the Fill section of the Property inspector. The Edit Gradient pop-up dialog box appears.

2. To adjust the rate of change between colors, drag the color wells into new positions. One color well can be dragged on the far side of another color well.

3. To remove a color well completely, drag the color well and drop it outside of the Edit Gradient pop-up dialog box, or into the Gradient preview area.

4. To add a new color well, click anywhere directly below the color ramp. The added color well displays the color directly above it in the color ramp.

Tip

You'll notice a little plus sign added to your cursor where clicking adds another color well.

5. To select a new color for a color well, click the color well. The standard pop-up color picker appears. Select any of the available swatches, or use the Eyedropper tool to sample an onscreen color, including one from another color well. You can use the Palette button on the pop-up color picker to access the system color picker(s).

6. Click the Property inspector when you're done or press Escape to cancel.

Although no real limit exists as to the number of colors you can add to an edited gradient, adding more than a dozen or so is not practical. With so many colors, the color wells begin to overlap, and selecting the correct one to modify becomes increasingly difficult.

Editing gradient transparency

As previously mentioned, the color ramp shows the current color combination as it blends one key color to another. Below the color ramp are the colors in your gradient, however, you're going to focus on what's above the color ramp — the gradient settings.

New Feature

Transparent gradients are new to Fireworks MX. Gone are the days of needing to fuss with masks to obtain this functionality!

By setting certain areas of your gradient as transparent, you enable the canvas, or any vector, or bitmap object beneath your gradient, to show through in specific areas. As you can see in Figure 11-10, transparent gradients add another effect to Fireworks' widely diverse toolset.

To edit a gradient's transparency, follow these steps:

1. Select the gradient and click on the Fill color well in the Fill section of the Property inspector. The Edit Gradient pop-up dialog box appears.

2. To adjust where the transparency takes place in a particular color's ramp, drag the transparency well into a new position. One transparency well can be dragged on the far side of another transparency color well.

3. To remove a transparency well completely, drag and drop it outside of the Edit Gradient pop-up dialog box.

4. To add a new transparency well, click anywhere directly above the color ramp. The added transparency well controls the opacity of the color directly below it in the color ramp.

5. To alter the color's opacity, click on the transparency well and the opacity settings appear. Either move the opacity slider from left to right, or type a new number into the text box. A setting of 100 is opaque while 0 is completely transparent.

6. Click the Property inspector when you're done.

As with adding colors, there are no limits to the number of transparency wells you can add to a gradient. Adding numerous transparency wells can actually make for an interesting effect in your gradient. You can create waves of light and dark color across your gradient simply by adding transparency wells and then altering the opacity of every other one from high to low. Experimenting with gradients, and especially transparent gradients, is the best way to determine what's best for you.

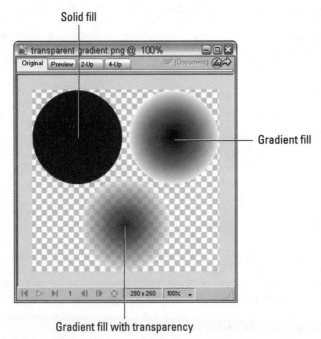

Solid fill

Gradient fill

Gradient fill with transparency

Figure 11-10: Here you see three identical objects, with one difference. One has a solid fill, one has a gradient fill, and the third has a transparent gradient fill.

Saving gradients as styles

To ensure that your custom gradients are available for use in the future, save them as styles and store them in the Styles panel. To create a new style using a custom gradient, follow these steps:

1. Select an object that uses the custom gradient.

2. If the Styles panel isn't visible, choose Window ➪ Styles, use the keyboard shortcut, Shift+F11, or click the Styles tab, if visible. The Styles panel appears.

3. On the Styles panel, select the New Style button.

4. In the New Style dialog box, enter a descriptive name for your gradient in the Name text box and deselect all checkboxes except Fill Type.

5. Click OK when you're done. A new style is entered in the Styles panel.

Any style added in the previously described fashion is always available for any Fireworks document. To apply the gradient, simply highlight any Fireworks object and select the new style. Your custom gradient is then added to the Fill category in the Fill section of the Property inspector.

To find out more about using styles, see Chapter 16.

Using Patterns

Simply put, a Pattern fill uses a repeating image to fill an object. Patterns are often used to provide a real-world surface, such as denim or water, to a computer-generated drawing. More abstract Patterns are also used to vary the look of a graphic. Fireworks includes an extensive collection of standard Patterns with even more available in the Goodies/Patterns folder of the Fireworks CD-ROM. Not surprisingly, you can also add your own images to be used as a Pattern.

Fireworks' built-in patterns are detailed in the color insert.

The Pattern fill is one of the primary categories found on the Fill section of the Property inspector. When you select the Pattern option, the Fill color well in the Property inspector and in the Tools panel becomes a preview of the currently selected Pattern. Clicking on the Fill color well opens a dialog with an option list, containing the Pattern names, and a larger preview of the currently selected Pattern. Clicking the Pattern name causes the option list to expand showing the names of all the available Patterns. As you move up and down this option list, a small preview of the Pattern is displayed next to each highlighted file, as shown in Figure 11-11.

Pattern fill images can be saved in PNG, TIFF, GIF, BMP, or JPEG format. However, not all images are well suited to making Patterns; the best Patterns are those that repeat seamlessly so that the boundaries of the original file cannot be detected. All the standard Fireworks files fill this requirement, as is clearly visible in the color insert.

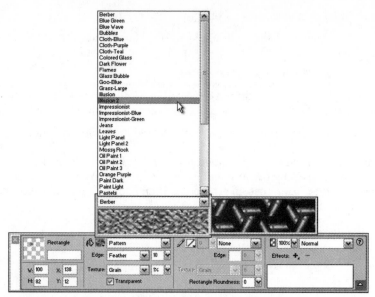

Figure 11-11: Choose your Pattern fill from the Pattern Fill Name option list in the Fill section of the Property inspector.

As with any other fill, you can apply Pattern fills to any shape object. The other fill attributes — edge and texture — are also applicable.

Adding new Patterns

The two ways to add Patterns to the Pattern Name option list so that they are available every time you use Fireworks are as follows:

✦ Save or export a file, in PNG, TIFF, GIF, BMP, or JPEG format, into the Configuration/Patterns folder within the Fireworks program folder.

Tip The Fireworks program folder is typically found at C:\Program Files\ Macromedia\Fireworks MX\ **on Windows-based computers, and at** Macintosh HD:Applications:Macromedia Fireworks MX: **on the Mac.**

✦ Through the Fireworks Preferences dialog box, assign an additional folder for Patterns.

Pattern images are usually full-color (whereas textures are displayed in grayscale), but that's not a hard-and-fast rule. Likewise, Patterns are generally 128-pixels square, but that's just a convention, not a requirement; one of the Patterns found on the Fireworks CD, Light Panel, is 12-pixels wide by 334-pixels high.

After you've saved a file in your Patterns folder and restarted Fireworks, the new Pattern is listed along with the other Patterns. As shown with my new Patterns in Figure 11-12, they even preview in the same way.

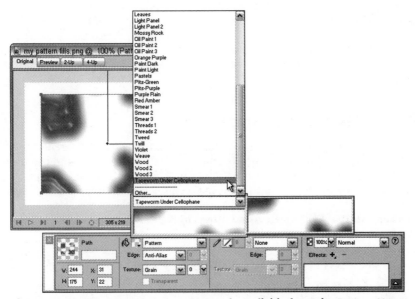

Figure 11-12: My own Tapeworm Pattern is available from the Pattern Name option list after saving it in the Configuration/Patterns folder and restarting Fireworks.

Assigning an external Patterns folder is a very easy way to add a whole group of folders at one time, as well as a good way to share resources in a networked environment. To assign an additional Patterns folder, follow these steps:

1. Choose Edit ➪ Preferences. The Preferences dialog box opens.

2. Select the Folders tab (choose Folders from the option list on the Macintosh).

3. Choose the Browse button in the Additional Materials section, next to the Patterns option. A navigation dialog box appears.

4. Locate the external folder that contains the PNG files you want to access as Patterns. Click OK when you've selected the folder. The Patterns checkbox is now enabled on the Preferences dialog box.

5. Click OK to accept the changes and close Preferences.

6. Relaunch Fireworks to make the additional Patterns available for use.

Tip   Want quick access to the Patterns on the Fireworks CD? Assign your external Patterns folder in Preferences to the Goodies/Patterns folder and restart Fireworks. When Fireworks opens, if the CD is present, the additional Patterns are integrated into the Fill panel list—and you can remove the CD after Fireworks has finished loading, and the Patterns are still available. If the CD is not available, Fireworks loads normally, but the additional Patterns are not incorporated.

Caution   The more Patterns you add, the longer Fireworks takes to start because it needs to initialize all the Patterns. For optimal performance, load only the patterns you use regularly.

Adding Patterns to a document

Adding commonly used Patterns to your default list in Fireworks is great, but what if you want to quickly grab an image file and use it as a Pattern without the hassle of moving it into the Fireworks Patterns folder first? On such an occasion, Fireworks enables you to work with Patterns on a document-by-document basis.

To access an external PNG image as a Pattern in the current document, follow these steps:

1. Select the object you would like to apply the Pattern to.

2. Choose Pattern from the Fill category option list in the Fill section of the Property inspector.

3. Click the Fill color well to display the Pattern selection pop-up dialog with the Pattern preview and the Pattern Name option list.

4. From the Pattern Name option list, choose Other to display an Open dialog box.

5. Navigate to the file you would like to use as a Pattern and select it. Click OK when you're done.

Fireworks adds your new Pattern to the Pattern Name option list and applies it to your selected object. The Pattern will be accessible from the Pattern Name option list only within the current document. When you save the document, the Pattern is saved within the document.

Tip   Patterns are saved within a document, making them portable. If you share work with someone at another location, adding your custom Patterns to your document automatically makes them available to coworkers when they receive the document.

Altering Patterns

You can adjust Patterns in the same manner as gradients. After a Pattern fill has been applied to an object, selecting it causes the control handles to appear, as shown in Figure 11-13. The same types of vector controls are available:

Tip   If you've changed the default setting for Show Fill Handles in the Editing section of the Preferences, then you have to select either the Paint Bucket tool or the Gradient tool to get the control handles to appear.

✦ Adjust the center of the Pattern fill by dragging the round starting point.

✦ Rotate the Pattern fill by moving the cursor over the length of any control handle until the Rotate cursor appears, then drag the handles to a new angle.

✦ Change the size of any Pattern by dragging either square handle straight to another position.

✦ Alter the skew of any Pattern by dragging either square handle in the desired direction.

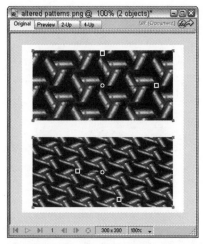

Figure 11-13: Both rectangles were filled with the standard Illusion2 Pattern and then the control handles of the bottom rectangle were rotated to change the Pattern direction.

Unlike gradients, all Patterns have two control handles in addition to the starting point of the fill. The handles are always perpendicular to one another and presented in the same ratio as the height to the width.

Fireworks Technique: Creating Seamless Patterns

The biggest problem with creating new Pattern fills is making them appear seamless. When Fireworks tries to fill an object larger than the size of the Pattern file, it repeats or tiles the image until the object is completely filled. If an image is used with even the smallest border, the repeating pattern is immediately noticeable; in most cases, this is not the desired effect. Several methods eliminate the appearance of seams.

The first, and simplest, technique is to avoid placing graphic elements near the edge of your Pattern image. This enables the canvas — or background color — to blend smoothly from one instance of a Pattern into another. For example, the image shown in Figure 11-14 could be made into a Pattern without showing any seams.

Figure 11-14: An image that has the same color all around its outside border can easily be made into a Pattern because areas of identical color appear seamless when they touch.

Many images, of course, rely on a visually full background where the canvas color is completely covered. To convert this type of graphic into a Pattern, a fair amount of image editing is necessary to make the edges disappear. Luckily, Fireworks contains enough graphic editing power to make this procedure feasible.

A tiled Pattern places images next to every side of the original image. To remove any indication of a boundary, you need to simulate a tiled Pattern and then blend the images so that no edges show. The following steps detail the procedure I use to smooth Pattern edges in Fireworks.

Note Throughout this technique, I refer to the menu syntax for the command, such as Edit ⇨ Copy. Naturally, feel free to use whatever keyboard shortcuts you're familiar with.

1. Open the image you want to convert to a Pattern.

2. Select a portion of the image to use as the basis for your Pattern.

   Using a portion of a scanned image or other graphic as a Pattern is quite common. The best technique I've found for this is to determine how large you want your Pattern to be (128×128 pixels is a good size), and then use the Fixed Size feature of the Marquee tool available through the Property inspector to set those dimensions. This enables you to work with a preset Marquee and move it into position more easily.

3. Choose Edit ⇨ Copy to copy the selected area.

4. Choose File ⇨ New to create a new document. The document should be large enough to contain your original graphic four times over. Because mine is 128 pixels square, 256×256 pixels would be my minimum size.

5. To guide placement, choose View ⇨ Grid ⇨ Edit Grid to set the size of the grid the same as your image, and enable the Show Grid and Snap to Grid options.

6. Choose Edit ⇨ Paste to paste the copied area in the upper-left corner of the document, as shown in Figure 11-15.

Figure 11-15: After setting the grid to help with alignment, the first image is pasted down.

7. Copy the image with the Alt+drag (Option+drag) method. Place the copy of the image to the right of the original.

8. Repeat Step 7 twice more, but place the two new image copies below the two already in place, as shown in Figure 11-16.

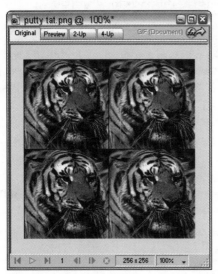

Figure 11-16: With all four copies in place, the edges are plainly visible.

9. Turn off both the grid (toggle View ➪ Grid ➪ Show Grid) and the Snap to Grid options (toggle View ➪ Grid ➪ Snap to Grid).

10. Select all four copies of the image and choose Modify ➪ Flatten Selection. This step is necessary because the core of this technique uses the Rubber Stamp tool, which only works with bitmap objects. By selecting all copies, the four separate bitmap objects have been merged into one.

11. Select the Rubber Stamp tool from the Tools panel.

   The next step is the core of this procedure and, as such, requires a bit of finesse and trial-and-error to get it right. You might want to save the document at this stage so you can restart the process without having to start completely over.

12. Working on the vertical seam between the copies on the left and the right, click the Rubber Stamp origin point down one side a few pixels to the side, near the edge. Drag over the edge in a left-to-right motion (or from right to left, depending on which side the Rubber Stamp origin is located), extending the side of one image into the side of another.

Follow this procedure down the vertical seam. Occasionally, you might need to switch directions and origin point to vary the blurring. Press Alt (Option) to reset the origin point of the Rubber Stamp tool. If necessary, set the Rubber Stamp options to the softest possible edge on the Property inspector.

13. After you've blurred the vertical seam, repeat the process for the horizontal seam, changing the direction of the Rubber Stamp as needed.

   When you're done blurring both the vertical and horizontal edges, the resulting image should appear to be a seamless Pattern, as shown in Figure 11-17. After this step, it's time to copy the portion of the image used to make the Pattern.

Figure 11-17: After the edges are blurred, it's hard to tell where one image stops and another starts.

14. Choose View ➪ Grid ➪ Edit Grid, and reset the grid to half of its former size, enabling both the view and the snap options as well. Using a half-sized grid enables you to easily grab the center of the current image. My original grid was 128×128 pixels, so my new one for this step is 64×64.

15. Choose the Marquee tool from the Tools panel. The Marquee's Options should still be set to the Fixed Size option, using your original dimensions.

16. Use the Marquee tool to select the central portion of the overall image, as shown in Figure 11-18. Notice that the selection takes a portion of all four images, previously separate.

17. Choose Edit ➪ Copy to copy the selection.

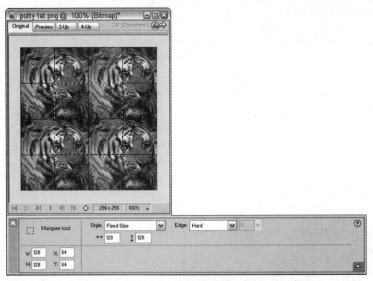

Figure 11-18: The combination of the grid and the Fixed Size marquee selection make selecting part of all four original images easy.

18. Choose File ➪ New to create a new document. Fireworks automatically sizes the new document to match the graphic on the clipboard.

19. Choose Edit ➪ Paste to paste the selection. This is your finished Pattern file (see Figure 11-19).

Figure 11-19: The final Pattern uses the center of four adjacent images so that its edges meet seamlessly when patterned.

20. Choose File ➪ Save, and store the image in the Configuration/Patterns folder, within your Fireworks program folder.

21. Restart Fireworks.

Tip

If you don't want to restart Fireworks, you don't have to, but you'll have to use the Other option from the Pattern Name option list to select your Pattern file for use.

22. Test your Pattern by drawing out a closed path and filling it with your new Pattern.

23. If necessary, open the just-saved Pattern file and edit to remove any noticeable edges.

Numerous other ways to blur the line between your edges exist, such as with the Blur or Smudge tools, but the Rubber Stamp tool works in many situations. Although it does take a bit of practice to get the hang of the tool and this technique, the results are definitely worth it.

Cross-Reference

For more information on the Blur, Smudge, and Rubber Stamp tools, as well as their options, see Chapter 6.

Adding Texture to Your Fills

A common complaint about computer graphics in general is that their appearance is too artificial. If you take a quick look around the real world, very few surfaces are a flat color — most have some degree of texture. Fireworks simulates this reality by enabling any fill (or stroke, for that matter) to combine with a texture. In Fireworks, a texture is a repeating image that you can apply on a percentage basis.

As with Fireworks patterns, textures are PNG images designed to be repeated, and are stored in a specific folder. But that's where the similarity with patterns ends. Whereas a pattern replaces any other fill, a texture is used in addition to the chosen fill. A texture is, in effect, another object, which is blended on top of the original object. As you increase the degree of a texture through the Amount of setting in the Fill section of the Property inspector, you are actually increasing the opacity of the texture. When the amount of texture is at 100 percent, the texture is totally opaque and the textured effect is at its maximum.

Another difference between pattern and texture is color: Patterns can be any range of color, whereas textures are displayed in grayscale. The reason for this is purely functional: If textures included color, the color of the original fill or stroke would be altered. One consequence of the grayscale property is that flat white fills are almost totally unaffected by textures.

Tip

Generally, textures work better with darker colors, which permit more range of contrast.

Fireworks includes a wide range of textures, and provides even more on the Fireworks CD-ROM. Each texture is chosen from an option list on the Fill section of the Property inspector and, as with patterns, a preview is displayed for each texture. Next to the Texture option list is a slider that controls the chosen texture's degree of intensity. The higher the amount of texture, the more pronounced the texture's effect on the fill, as shown in Figure 11-20.

Extending Textures to Strokes and Images

Textures aren't limited to enhancing fills. You can just as easily apply them to strokes and, with a little more work, images as well. Sometimes a stroke is used to define a filled object, and it's best not to extend the texture onto the stroke. Certain images, however, benefit from a continuation of the texture from fill to stroke.

Take, for example, the following figure. I created a very simple texture of alternating lines that is applied to the stroke (a big Air Brush) in the top example. Because the same set of textures are available from both the Fill and Stroke sections of the Property inspector, it's easy to duplicate settings from one section to the other, so in the middle example, a fill has been added and the same lines texture applied to it. The bottom example has had some Live Effects added, but the lines still show through and bring the stroke and fill together.

Applying a texture to an image requires an additional step. Strokes and fills cannot be applied directly to an image. The technique then is to create a vector object that completely covers the image and apply the texture to that vector object. Blend it into the image either by altering the opacity of the vector object, and/or its blending mode (these controls can be found in the Layers panel as well as above the Effects section of the Property inspector), or by using the vector object as a mask for the image. As is often the case with Fireworks, a little experimentation can lead to some very interesting results.

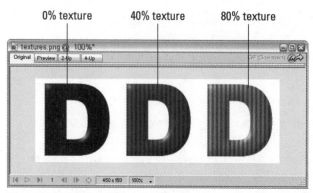

Figure 11-20: Increasing the amount of texture on the Fill panel makes the texture more visible.

An additional property of textures is transparency. If your textured object is on top of other objects, the background objects show through the light portions of the texture when the Transparent option is enabled. The higher the degree of texture, the more transparent an object becomes.

Adding new textures

New textures are added exactly the same way that new patterns are added:

✦ Save or export a file to the Configuration/Textures folder within your Fireworks program folder.

✦ Through the Preferences dialog box, assign an additional folder for textures.

Textures files work best when they enable a repeating pattern without visible edges and, as mentioned previously, all textures are shown in grayscale.

Converting a color image to grayscale

Although you don't have to convert images to grayscale before saving them as textures — Fireworks simply displays color textures as grayscale, anyway — converting them enables you to get a better sense of how the texture will ultimately look. It also gives you a chance to alter the overall brightness and contrast to achieve the best-looking texture.

To convert a color vector or bitmap object to grayscale using the Convert to Grayscale Command, follow these steps:

1. Select the object you want to convert.

2. Choose Commands ➪ Creative ➪ Convert to Grayscale. Fireworks converts your object to grayscale.

Assigning an additional textures folder

If you have an entire group of textures you want to add at one time, you can assign an additional folder for Fireworks to include in the texture list. To assign an additional Textures folder, follow these steps:

1. Choose Edit ➪ Preferences. The Preferences dialog box opens.

2. Select the Folders category (choose Folders from the option list on a Macintosh).

3. In the Additional Materials section, choose the Browse button next to the Textures option. A navigation dialog box appears.

4. Locate the external folder that contains files you want to access as textures. Click OK when you've selected the folder. The Textures checkbox is now enabled on the Preferences dialog box.

5. Click OK to accept the changes and close Preferences.

6. Restart Fireworks to make the additional textures available.

 Can't get enough textures? You'll find more in the Textures folder on the CD-ROM accompanying this book.

Adding textures to a document

As with patterns, you can open textures one at a time and use them with your current document, enabling easy access to textures stored anywhere on your computer. Textures opened in this way are saved within the current document.

To access an external PNG image as a texture in the current document, follow these steps:

1. Choose Solid, Pattern, or a gradient from the Fill category option list, in the Fill section of the Property inspector, to view the Texture Name option list.

2. From the Texture Name option list, choose Other to display an Open dialog box.

3. Navigate to and select the file you want to use as a texture. It can be a color or a grayscale image, but the result is always a grayscale texture. Click OK when you're done.

Fireworks adds your new texture to the Texture option list.

Filling with the Paint Bucket Tool

The Paint Bucket tool is used to fill a selected area with the settings that are currently in the Fill section of the Property inspector — whether those settings involve a solid color, a gradient, or a pattern. The Paint Bucket can be used to fill both vector objects and bitmap objects. The Paint Bucket fills all of a vector object completely, whereas it only fills the selected portion of a bitmap object, or a range of like, adjacent colors if there is no selection, as shown in Figure 11-21.

Path objects   Image objects

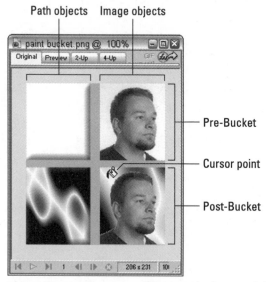

Pre-Bucket

Cursor point

Post-Bucket

Figure 11-21: The vector object on the bottom left is filled completely by the Paint Bucket. Applying the same fill to the bitmap object on the bottom right only affects pixels colored similarly to those under the cursor.

With vector objects, nothing is as simple as using the Paint Bucket. Choose the Paint Bucket tool (or use the keyboard shortcut, G), and then click the object once to apply the current Fill settings from the Property inspector.

Caution   Fireworks doesn't distinguish between open and closed paths when the Paint Bucket is used. If the Paint Bucket is used on an open path, such as an S-curve, an invisible line is drawn from the beginning to the ending point and the fill is applied.

Bitmap objects are a different story with regard to the Paint Bucket. If you click a bitmap object with the Paint Bucket without selecting an area using one of the selection tools (Marquee, Ellipse Marquee, Lasso, Polygon Lasso, or Magic Wand), one of the following three things happens:

✦ The current Fill settings are applied to the selected pixel and the neighboring pixels that fall within the Tolerance range set in the Property inspector.

✦ The entire bitmap object is filled with the current Fill settings, if the Fill Selection option is selected from the Property inspector.

✦ The entire document is filled with the current Fill settings, if the Fill Selection Only object is selected from the Property inspector.

The Property inspector, shown in Figure 11-22, becomes very important when you apply the Paint Bucket tool to bitmap objects.

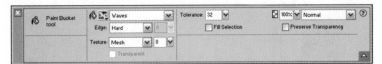

Figure 11-22: The Property inspector options for the Paint Bucket tool have a major effect on how bitmap objects are filled.

The available options are as follows:

✦ **Fill Selection:** Fills a selected area and disregards color tolerance settings, or if no area is selected, fills either the bitmap object or document according to the Expand to Fill Document setting.

✦ **Preserve Transparency:** Only colors existing pixels, so that transparent pixels stay transparent.

✦ **Tolerance:** Sets the range of colors to be filled when Fill Selection is not enabled. The Tolerance slider accepts values from 0 (where no additional colors are filled) to 255 (where all additional colors are filled).

✦ **Edge:** Determines the type of edge on the fill — Hard, Anti-Aliased, or Feather. If Feather is selected, the Amount of Feather slider becomes available, which sets the degree to which the fill is blended into surrounding pixels.

Tip   After you've made a selection in a bitmap object, you don't have to click in the selected area with the Paint Bucket to change it. Clicking anywhere in the document automatically fills the selected area.

Summary

Fills are one of Fireworks' basic building blocks. Without fills, objects would appear to have outlines only and arranging objects on top of one another would be difficult, if not impossible. As you begin to work with fills, keep these points in mind:

✦ You can apply Fills to any Fireworks object: vector or bitmap.

✦ Access all the fill settings through the Fill section of the Property inspector. You can also find the Fill color well on the Tools panel and the Mixer.

✦ The five options for fills are None, Solid, Web Dither, Pattern, and Gradient.

✦ The Web Dither fill visually blends two Web-safe colors to make a third color outside the limited Web-safe palette.

✦ You can modify a Gradient or Pattern fill by selecting the filled object with the Pointer, Paint Bucket tool, or Gradient tool and adjusting the control handles.

✦ New gradient color combinations can be saved as a Style and reused.

✦ A Pattern fill can be made from any repeating image, stored in PNG format, or can be stored within a document.

✦ Textures can bring a touch of realism to an otherwise flat graphic, and can also be stored within a document.

✦ The Paint Bucket options control whether the entire bitmap object is filled, or just a selection is filled.

In the next chapter, you find out about the razzle-dazzle side of Fireworks: Live Effects and Filters.

✦   ✦   ✦

Creating Live Effects and Filters

Many Fireworks graphics are based on three separate but interlocking features: strokes, fills, and effects. Not everyone would put effects — the capability to quickly add a drop shadow or bevel a button — on the same level as strokes and fills, but most Web designers would. Effects are pretty close to essential on the Internet. Not only is the look and feel of many Web sites dependent on various effects, but also much of their functionality, especially when techniques such as button rollovers are concerned, demands it.

Live Effects are a Fireworks innovation. For the first time, designers can edit common effects without having to rebuild the graphic from the ground up. But what makes Live Effects truly "Live" is Fireworks' capability to automatically reapply the effects to any altered graphic — whether the image is reshaped, resized, or whatever. You can even use many standard Photoshop-compatible filters as Live Effects, and apply, edit, or remove them as easily as Fireworks' own classic bevels and glows.

Later in the chapter, we look at how you can apply filters and what you can apply them to. You work with the filters that are included with Fireworks and examine some of the techniques that you can use to apply them creatively. You also see how you can add more filters to Fireworks, including ones that you may already have as part of another application. Finally, this chapter reviews some very popular third-party image filter packages, including Eye Candy 4000, Kai's Power Tools, and Auto FX's DreamSuite series.

Understanding Fireworks Effects

Although the Filters menu contains the definitive image-filters list to which Fireworks has access, many image filters are also available in "live" versions from the Effects section of the Property inspector. You can treat Photoshop-compatible filters in the Effects section of the Property inspector just like any other Live Effect: Add and remove them as you please, reorder them, or adjust their settings at any time.

New kinds of creative experimentation are made possible with many of the same image filters that you may have used for years in Photoshop. Rearranging the order that filters are applied without having to start from scratch, or easily saving favorite combinations of filters, is truly liberating. Exciting new combinations of effects are made possible because they're so easy to mix, match, and experiment with.

Using Effects in the Property inspector

The Effects section of the Property inspector, shown in Figure 12-1, is a powerful tool that centralizes almost all the effects in Fireworks, with the exception of some third-party image filters, which remain only accessible from the Filters menu. The Effects section of the Property inspector offers you access to two key sections: the Add and Delete Effects buttons, which offer you a menu containing all the Live Effects to which you have access; and the Effects list, which contains only the Live Effects that are currently applied to a selection.

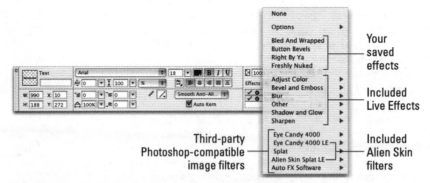

Figure 12-1: The Add Effects menu in the Effects section of the Property inspector is a central access point for almost all the effects available in Fireworks.

The Add Effects menu is divided into five distinct parts:

✦ **None:** Choosing this option removes all the effects from the selection.

✦ **Options:** The Options submenu is the place to go if you want to save your effects as Fireworks Styles, turn all effects on or off for a selected object, or choose your Photoshop-compatible plug-ins folder.

✦ **Effects combinations that you save:** This section is not visible until you save your first combination.

✦ **Included Live Effects:** Such as bevels, blurs, and glows.

✦ **Third-party Photoshop-compatible image filters:** All third-party plug-ins available in your Filters folder or through the Photoshop Plug-Ins option in the General section of the Preferences.

Not all third-party image filters can be used as Live Effects. Those that can't simply don't show up in the Add Effects menu and can only be accessed from the Filters menu.

Applying Live Effects

You can only apply Live Effects to objects selected in vector mode. If you want to apply a Live Effect to a pixel selection, you have the following two choices:

✦ Select an area with the pixel selection tools and copy it to the clipboard. Next, paste the selection as a new bitmap object. The new bitmap object is placed exactly where your pixel selection was located. Apply the Live Effect to your new bitmap object. If you like, you can then group or flatten the new bitmap object and the original bitmap object from which the pixel selection was taken.

✦ Some Live Effects are also available from the Filters menu and can be applied to a pixel selection from there, although this doesn't maintain editability.

Although each effect has its own unique settings, you apply them all in basically the same fashion:

1. Select an object or objects. Fireworks can simultaneously apply the same effect to multiple objects.

2. Click the Add Effects button (the Plus sign) in the Effects section of the Property inspector and choose the desired effect from the Add effects menu. If the effect has editable settings — most do — Fireworks displays a pop-up window, a regular dialog box (see Figure 12-2), or a plug-in package specific dialog box, depending on the effect you selected.

3. Modify the settings to achieve the desired effect. After you're done, click anywhere outside a pop-up window, click OK in a regular dialog box, or press Enter (Return) in either.

4. The effect is applied to all selected objects.

After an effect is applied, it is added to the Effects list in the Effects section of the Property inspector, and Fireworks keeps it alive throughout any other changes that the object may undergo. Fireworks actually recalculates the required pixel effects and reapplies the effect after a change is made for vector, bitmap, or text objects. In my opinion, the capability to make completely editable vector artwork (see Figure 12-3) resemble bitmaps that have undergone numerous image filter modifications is a superb addition to the Web designer's toolbox.

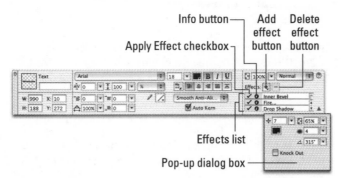

Figure 12-2: The Effects section of the Property inspector offers a high level of control over the way effects are applied, edited, and removed.

Figure 12-3: Fireworks' always-editable Live Effects make these vector objects resemble bitmaps that have been extensively modified with image filters.

To edit the parameters for an applied effect, select the object, and click the Info button next to the effect that you want to modify in the Effects list on the Property inspector. Fireworks displays the effect's dialog box. Edit the parameters and dismiss the dialog box by clicking OK, or by clicking anywhere outside it if it is a pop-up window.

As good as Fireworks effects look, sometimes objects look better with no effects. To remove all effects from an object, select the object, click the Add Effects button (plus sign) and then choose None from the Add Effects menu. To temporarily disable a single effect, deselect the checkbox next to that effect in the Effects list. To temporarily disable all effects, choose Options ⇨ All Off from the Add Effects menu in the Effects section of the Property inspector. Of course, choosing Options ⇨ All On from the Add Effects menu enables all applied effects. To remove a single effect permanently, select the effect in the Effects list and click the Delete Effect button (minus sign) in the Effects section of the Property inspector.

Examining the Filters menu

Many bitmap-editing applications offer a dedicated menu that contains Photoshop-compatible plug-in image filters. Fireworks is no exception, and the Filters menu, shown in Figure 12-4, is it. When you launch Fireworks, it populates the Filters menu with all the image filters it can access. Generally, these are installed in Fireworks' Filters folder (more on that later), or in a separate Photoshop plug-ins folder specified in your Fireworks preferences.

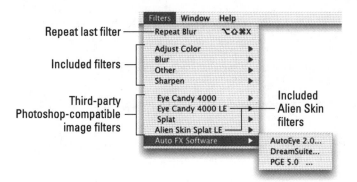

Figure 12-4: The Filters menu contains built-in Fireworks image filters, as well as any third-party, Photoshop-compatible image filters you've added.

Tip   Image filters are called "filters" because every pixel in the image is evaluated— filtered—and either modified or not according to the settings and the effect that's being applied. The terms plug-ins and filters are used interchangeably throughout this chapter.

In a nutshell, the difference between the effects contained in the Filters menu and the ones in the Effects section of the Property inspector are that the ones in the Filters menu are not live. You can only apply filters to bitmap objects; applying them to a text or vector object flattens the object into a bitmap object. After a filter is applied, there is no way to remove the effect except with the Undo command or the History panel.

The Filters menu is divided into three sections. From top to bottom, they are the following:

✦ A single menu command that identifies and repeats the last-used filter

✦ Image filters that are included with Fireworks itself

✦ Third-party, Photoshop-compatible image filters

Caution   One exception is the DitherBox filter that's included with Photoshop 5. It finds its way onto the Other menu if you make it available to Fireworks.

Plug-in image filters automatically organize themselves into submenus that are specified by the developer of the plug-in so you have no control over the arrangement.

Working with Included Live Effects

Fireworks is shipped with a range of useful Live Effects built-in, contained in the following submenus of the Add Effects menu in the Effects section of the Property inspector:

✦ **Adjust Color:** Auto Levels, Brightness/Contrast, Color Fill, Curves, Hue/Saturation, Invert, and Levels

✦ **Bevel and Emboss:** Inner Bevel, Inset Emboss, Outer Bevel, and Raised Emboss

✦ **Blur:** Including Blur, Blur More, and Gaussian Blur

✦ **Other:** The unclassifiable Convert to Alpha and Find Edges

✦ **Shadow and Glow:** Drop Shadow, Glow, Inner Glow, and Inner Shadow

✦ **Sharpen:** Including Sharpen, Sharpen More, and Unsharp Mask

Table 12-1 details the Live Effects that are included with Fireworks, and what each one does.

Table 12-1
Included Live Effects

Live Effect	Description
Auto Levels	Automatically produces an image with the maximum tonal range.
Brightness/Contrast	Adjusts the brightness and/or contrast of all the pixels in an image.
Color Fill	Colors the pixels of an object.
Curves	Enables you to adjust the level of a particular color in an image, without affecting other colors.
Hue/Saturation	Adjusts the color in an image.
Invert	Changes the color of each pixel to its mathematical inverse. Creates a photo-negative-type effect.
Levels	Enables you to adjust the tonal range of all the pixels in an image.
Inner Bevel	Adds a three-dimensional look to an object by beveling its inside edge.
Inset Emboss	Simulates an object in relief against its background.
Outer Bevel	Frames the selected object with a three-dimensional, rounded rectangle.
Raised Emboss	Simulates an object raised from its background.
Blur	Blurs pixels together to create an unfocused effect.
Blur More	Same as Blur but across a slightly larger radius, for a more pronounced blur.
Gaussian Blur	Same as Blur More but with a Gaussian bell curve and a dialog box that enables you to specify the blur radius.
Convert to Alpha	Converts an image into a grayscale image that's suitable for use as an alpha mask. White pixels are colored transparent.
Find Edges	Detects the outlines of forms and converts them to solid lines.
Drop Shadow	Shadows the object against the background to make it stand out more effectively.
Glow	Puts a halo or soft glow around an object.
Inner Glow	Puts a glow within the inner edge of an object.
Inner Shadow	Puts a shadow within the inner edge of an object.
Sharpen	Sharpens by finding edges and increasing the contrast between adjacent pixels.
Sharpen More	Same as Sharpen but across a larger radius.
Unsharp Mask	Same as Sharpen More, but with control over which pixels are sharpened (and which are left "unsharp"), according to the image's grayscale mask.

Cross-Reference   For more about mask groups, see Chapter 13.

Adjusting color

The Adjust Color submenu of the Add Effects menu contains powerful tools for adjusting the tonal range and color correcting, or for adding special effects to objects. Traditionally, these tools have only been available in a destructive form: You adjust an image's tonal range, and if you find out later you went a little too dark or light, you had to start with an earlier iteration of a document and redo your work. Introducing these tools to Fireworks users as Live Effects provides a dramatic increase in workflow flexibility.

Adjusting tonal range

Ideally, a photographic image would have a fairly even ratio of dark tones, mid-tones, and light tones. Too many dark pixels hides detail; too many light pixels and your image appears washed out. Too many midtones — darks aren't dark enough and lights aren't light enough — and your image appears bland, as in the Before image in Figure 12-5. Fireworks offers you a few different methods for adjusting the tonal range of images; which one you choose to use depends on how bad the damage is.

Before   After

Figure 12-5: Before and after increasing an image's tonal range to add contrast. Dark pixels are darkened and light pixels are lightened.

Dissecting Brightness/Contrast

For images that are only a little too dark or light, or lacking slightly in contrast, slight adjustments made with the Brightness/Contrast effect may be all you need. Fireworks can provide visual feedback by previewing your adjustments in the document window.

To use the Brightness/Contrast filter, follow these steps:

1. Select the object that you want to apply the effect to.

2. In the Effects section of the Property inspector, click the Add Effects button and choose Adjust Color ➪ Brightness/Contrast from the Add Effects menu. Fireworks displays the Brightness/Contrast dialog box, as shown in Figure 12-6.

Figure 12-6: Adjust an image's brightness or contrast with the controls in the Brightness/ Contrast dialog box.

3. Check Preview to view your changes as you make them in the document window.

4. Use the Brightness and/or Contrast sliders to adjust the settings. Values for the sliders range from –100 to 100. Click OK when you're done.

Coloring with Color Fill

The Color Fill Live Effect enables you to color the pixels of an object without permanently altering them.

To use the Color Fill Live Effect, follow these steps:

1. Select the object that you want to modify.

2. Click the Add Effects button and choose Adjust Color ➪ Color Fill from the Add Effects menu. Fireworks displays the Color Fill dialog box.

3. Select the desired fill color from the pop-up color picker.

4. Alter the opacity setting with the Opacity slider.

5. Choose a blending mode from the Blending Mode option list.

Cross-Reference

See Chapter 13 for more about opacity and blending modes.

6. Click anywhere outside the pop-up dialog box to dismiss it, or press Enter (Return).

Fireworks applies the effect to your selected object.

Getting to know Levels and Auto Levels

For images that need more adjustment than is possible with Brightness/Contrast, Fireworks offers the Levels and Auto Levels filters. Auto Levels works just like Levels, except that you skip the Levels dialog box entirely, and Fireworks maps the darkest pixels in your image to black and the lightest ones to white. For many images, you may find that Auto Levels does the trick in record time. If not, you can take matters into your own hands with Levels.

Cross-Reference   See the Auto Levels filter demonstrated in the color insert.

The Levels dialog box introduces a special set of three eyedropper tools, shown in Figure 12-7. (These are also available in the Curves dialog box, which is discussed in the next section.) The trio of eyedroppers, one for highlights, one for midtones, and one for shadows, enable you to remap the highlights, midtones, or shadows of an image to new levels by pointing to a pixel with the desired level. For example, if your image is too dark, use the Shadow eyedropper and select a pixel that is a little lighter than the darkest pixels. Fireworks substitutes the tones of the newly selected "shadow" pixels for the darkest pixels in your image, lightening the image. The highlights and midtones eyedroppers work in a similar fashion, providing target levels for highlights and midtones, respectively.

Tip   Clicking Auto in the Levels dialog box is just like using the Auto Levels filter.

Midtone eyedropper

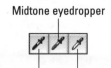

Shadow eyedroper   Highlight eyedropper

Figure 12-7: These special Eyedropper tools enable you to specify a new highlight, midtone, or shadow level by pointing to pixels.

Note   Identify the three eyedroppers by the ink they seem to contain. The highlight eyedropper has white ink, whereas the midtone eyedropper has gray ink, and the shadow eyedropper has black ink.

The Levels dialog box also includes a Histogram — essentially a chart — that reports the levels of dark, middle, and light tones in your image, giving you a quick graphical representation of what might need to be fixed. The horizontal axis is dark to light, from left to right. The vertical axis is a level from 0 to 255.

To apply the Levels filter and modify the tonal range of an image, follow these steps:

1. Select the object that you want to modify.

2. Click the Add Effects button in the Effects section of the Property inspector, and choose Adjust Color ➪ Levels from the Add Effects menu. Fireworks displays the Levels dialog box, as shown in Figure 12-8.

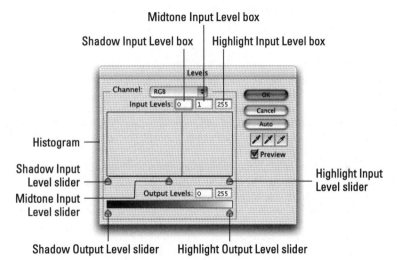

Figure 12-8: The Levels dialog box displays a Histogram of the light, midtone, and dark tones in your image.

3. Check the Preview checkbox to view your changes as you make them in the document window.

4. Select which channels you want to modify from the Channels option list: just Red, just Green, just Blue, or RGB to modify all three.

Tip

Modifying just the Red channel in an RGB image is similar to adjusting a color by increasing or decreasing the R value in the Color Mixer panel when it's set to RGB or Hexadecimal.

5. Modify the highlights and shadows in your image with the Highlight, Midtone, and Shadow Input Levels sliders, or enter new values directly in the Highlight and Shadow Input Levels boxes. Highlights and shadows are specified from 0 to 255, whereas midtones are specified with 1.0 being neutral, or 50 percent gray.

Note The Shadow value can't be higher than the Highlight value, and the Highlight value can't be lower than the shadow Value.

6. Use the Highlights and Shadows Output Levels sliders to adjust your image's overall contrast.

7. If desired, use the Highlight, Midtone, or Shadow eyedropper to sample a target color to be used as a level for highlights, midtones, or shadows, respectively, from your image.

8. Click OK when you're satisfied with the changes you've made.

The changes you've made are applied to the selected object.

Cross-Reference Turn to the color insert to see a demonstration of the Levels filter.

Evaluating Curves

The Curves filter essentially serves the same purpose as the Levels filter, but it presents the information to you in a different way. Whereas the Levels filter enables you to adjust the individual levels of light, mid, and dark tones in an image, the Curves filter focuses on the levels of individual colors. You can adjust the level of red, for example, without affecting the balance of light to dark in an image.

The Curves dialog box contains a grid. The horizontal axis is the original brightness values, which are also shown in the Input box. The vertical axis displays the new brightness values, which are also shown in the Output box. The values that are represented are 0 to 255, with 0 being complete shadow. The line plotted on the grid always starts out as a perfect diagonal, indicating that no changes have been made (the Input and Output values are the same).

As mentioned previously, the Curves dialog box also contains a trio of eyedropper tools similar to the Levels dialog box. The Curves dialog box also contains an Auto button, which yields the same result here as it does in the Levels box: The darkest pixels in your image are mapped to black and the lightest to white, as if you had used the Auto Levels filter.

To use the Curves filter, follow these steps:

1. Select the object that you want to modify.

2. Click the Add Effects button (plus sign), in the Effects section of the Property inspector, and choose Adjust Color ⇨ Curves from the Add Effects menu. Fireworks displays the Curves dialog box, as shown in Figure 12-9.

3. Check the Preview checkbox to view your changes as you make them in the document window.

New brightness axis   Original brightness axis

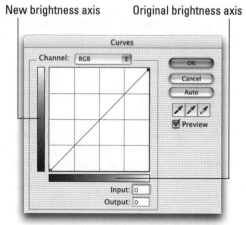

Figure 12-9: The Curves dialog box enables you to graphically alter a color curve.

4. Select which channels you would like to modify from the Channels option list: just Red, just Green, just Blue, or RGB to modify all three.

5. Click a point on the grid's diagonal line, and drag it to a new position to adjust the curve. Changing the curve changes the Input and Output values.

6. To delete a point from the curve, select it and drag it out of the grid.

You can't delete the curve's endpoints.

7. If desired, use the Highlight, Midtone, or Shadow eyedropper to sample a color to be used as a target level for highlights, midtones, or shadows, respectively, from your image.

8. Click OK when you're satisfied with the changes you've made.

Fireworks applies the changes you've made to the selected object.

See the color insert to compare the effects of the Curves filter.

Looking into Hue/Saturation

The Hue/Saturation filter is similar to specifying colors using the HSL (Hue, Saturation, and Lightness) color model. If you're familiar with the concept of a color wheel, adjusting the hue is the same as moving around the color wheel, selecting a new color. Adjusting the saturation is like moving across the radius of the color wheel, selecting a more or less pure version of the same color.

Tip   Find examples of color wheels in your operating system's color picker(s), accessed by clicking the Palette button on the Fireworks pop-up color picker. Mac users can choose to view different color methods, including an HLS picker.

To adjust the hue or saturation of an image with the Hue/Saturation filter, follow these steps:

1. Select the object that you want to modify.

2. Click the Add Effects button, in the Effects section of the Property inspector, and choose Adjust Color ➪ Hue/Saturation from the Add Effects menu. Fireworks displays the Hue/Saturation dialog box, as shown in Figure 12-10.

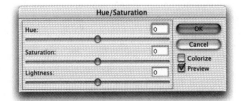

Figure 12-10: The Hue/Saturation dialog box offers Hue, Saturation, and Lightness sliders.

3. Check the Preview checkbox to view your changes in the document window as you make them.

4. Choose Colorize to add color to a grayscale image, or change an RGB image into a two-tone image.

Note   If you choose Colorize, the range of the Hue slider changes from −180 through 180, to 0 through 360; the range of the Saturation slider changes from −100 through 100, to 0 through 100.

5. Adjust the purity of the colors with the Saturation slider.

6. Adjust the color of the image with the Hue slider.

7. Adjust the lightness of the colors with the Lightness slider.

8. When you're satisfied with the changes you've made, click OK.

The changes you've made are applied to the selected object.

Cross-Reference   See the Hue/Saturation filter in action in the color insert.

Using three dimensions with Bevel and Emboss

The Bevel and Emboss effects are Fireworks' key to 3D. Both types of effects simulate light coming from a specific direction, illuminating an object that seems to be raised out of, or sunken into, the background.

Identifying Bevel effects

The Bevel effects are similar in terms of user interface, available attributes, and preset options. In fact, they only differ in the following two key areas:

✦ As the names imply, the Inner Bevel creates its edges inside the selected object, whereas the Outer Bevel makes its edges around the outside of the selected object.

✦ The Outer Bevel effect has one attribute that the Inner Bevel does not: color. The Inner Bevel uses the object's color to convert the inside of the graphic to a bevel, whereas the Outer Bevel applies the chosen color to the new outside edge.

When you select either Inner Bevel or Outer Bevel from the Add Effects menu in the Effects section of the Property inspector, Fireworks displays their pop-up windows so that you can adjust their parameters, as shown in Figure 12-11.

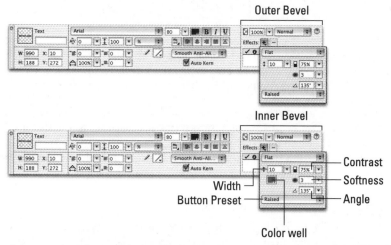

Figure 12-11: The Outer Bevel's pop-up dialog box is the same as the one for Inner Bevel, except for the addition of a color well.

Table 12-2 explains how to control aspects of bevel effects.

	Table 12-2 Bevel Effects	
Bevel effect	**Description**	
Effect name	Seven different types of bevel effects are accessible through the Effect name option list. Each type of effect alters the number, shape, or degree of the bevel.	
Width	Sets the thickness of the beveled side. The Width slider has a range from 0 to 10 pixels, although you can enter a higher number directly in the text box.	
Contrast	Determines the difference in relative brightness of the lit and shadowed sides, where 100 percent provides the greatest contrast and 0 percent provides no contrast.	
Softness	Sets the sharpness of the edges used to create the bevel, where 0 is the sharpest and 10 is the softest. Values above 10 have no effect.	
Angle	Provides the angle for the simulated light on the beveled surface. Drag the knob control to a new angle or enter it directly in the text box.	
Button Preset	Offers four preset configurations, primarily used for creating rollover buttons.	
Color	Available for Outer Bevel, this standard color well is used to determine the color of the surrounding border.	

Caution   Although you can apply the bevel effects to any object, if the object's edge is feathered too much, you won't be able to see the effect. To combine a feathered edge with a bevel, set the Amount of Feather to less than the width of the bevel.

Each of the bevel effects has the same types of edges. Compare the Inner Bevel and Outer Bevel effects in Figure 12-12, and you see the similarities among the seven types for both effects. Found under the Effect name option list, these types vary primarily in the shape of the bevel itself. Looking at each of the bevel shapes from the side makes differentiating between the possible shapes easier.

Mastering Bevel effects Button presets

Bevel effects are terrific for creating buttons for all purposes: navigation, forms, links, and so on. One of the most common applications of such buttons involves *rollovers*. Rollover is the commonly used name (another is *mouseover*) for the effect when a user moves the pointer over a button and it changes in some way. Both bevel effects provide four presets under the Button preset option list—Raised, Highlight, Inset, and Inverted—that you can employ for rollovers.

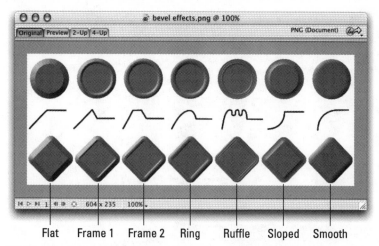

Flat   Frame 1   Frame 2   Ring   Ruffle   Sloped   Smooth

Figure 12-12: Inner Bevel effects are all contained within the original vector of the object, whereas Outer Bevel effects create edges outside the original vector. The side views, shown in the middle row, make telling the types of effects apart easier.

Unlike Stroke or Fill presets on the Property inspector, the bevel Button presets do not actually change the dialog box's attributes, but rather internally change the lighting angle and lighten the object (see Figure 12-13). The Raised and Highlight presets use the same lighting angle, derived from the Angle value, but Highlight is about 25 percent lighter. The Inset and Inverted presets, on the other hand, reverse the angle of the lighting—and, of this pair, Inverted is the lighter one.

Tip   To take the fullest advantage of the bevel effect Button presets in creating rollovers, set your lighting angle first with the Angle knob in the Effect's pop-up window. Then duplicate the object and apply the different Button presets to each copy.

Outlining embossing

If you've ever seen a company's Articles of Incorporation or other official papers, you've probably encountered embossing. An embossing seal is used to press the company name right into the paper—so that it can be both read and felt. Fireworks' emboss effects provide a similar service, with a great deal more flexibility, of course.

Both emboss effects replace an object's fill with the canvas color or the color of background objects, and then add highlights and shadows. Inset Emboss and Raised Emboss each reverse the placement of these highlights and effects in order to make the embossed object appear to be pushed into or out of the background, respectively, as shown in Figure 12-14.

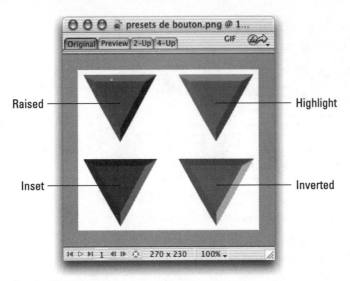

Figure 12-13: Both the bevel effects offer four Button presets: Raised, Highlight, Inset, and Inverted.

Figure 12-14: The two emboss effects make an object appear to be part of the background — either pushed into or out of it.

The Emboss effects are applied as any other Live Effect, with the options presented in a pop-up window, shown in Figure 12-15.

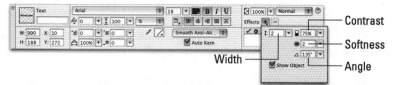

Figure 12-15: Adjust the parameters of either the Inset Emboss or Raised Emboss effects through their identical pop-up dialog boxes.

Following are the adjustable emboss parameters:

✦ **Width:** Determines the thickness of the embossed edges. As with other effects, the slider's range is from 0 to 30, but you can enter higher values directly into the associated text box.

✦ **Contrast:** Contrast controls the relative lightness of the highlights to the darkness of the shadows.

✦ **Softness:** Sets the sharpness of the embossed edges, higher numbers make the edges fuzzier.

✦ **Angle:** Establishes the direction of the embossed edges.

✦ **Show Object:** Shows or hides the embossed object. The emboss itself is always visible.

Adding depth with blurring

Sometimes, what should be the focal point of your image can get lost among other elements of the composition. This is especially true when you're compositing multiple objects, or really laying the filters on thick. Adding a little blur to the background area of an image can cause the foreground to stand out, immediately drawing the viewer's eye to it.

To add depth to the background area of an image, follow these steps:

1. Use one of the marquee selection tools to create a pixel selection around the part of your bitmap object that you want to remain in the foreground. You might create a circle to focus attention within that circle, or use the Magic Wand to create a complex selection, such as around a person's head or face.

2. Choose Select ⇨ Select Inverse to invert your selection and select the background of your image.

3. Choose Filters ⇨ Blur ⇨ Gaussian Blur. Fireworks displays the Gaussian Blur dialog box.

Note   Some Live Effects and Filters have an ellipsis after their menu command, which indicates that choosing that command opens a dialog box in which you can specify settings. Filters without the ellipsis either don't have any parameters for you to change, or display their parameters in a pop-up dialog box.

4. Adjust the Blur Radius slider to specify the intensity of the effect. The more blur you add, the more depth you add to your image. Generally, a blur radius of between 1 and 2 creates a depth effect without destroying the edges of the elements in the image. Click OK when you're done.

Tip   You may want to feather the edge of your selection before applying your blur by choosing Select ⇨ Feather, or by clicking the Edge option list on the Property inspector. This gives a smoother transition between the pixels that are blurred and those that aren't.

The area that was within your original pixel selection now seems to stand out and draws the eye at first glance (see Figure 12-16), because it is clear and sharp and appears to be closer to your eyes. In addition, the blurred background creates an overall feeling of depth because background elements seem to be a little further away.

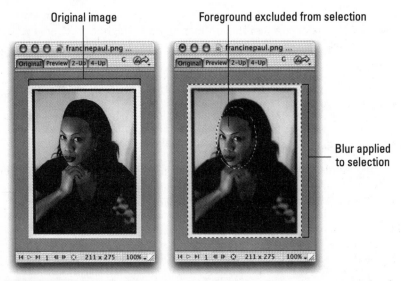

Figure 12-16: Blurring the background seems to give an image extra depth and makes the foreground stand out. Notice how your eye is immediately drawn to the subject's face.

The Blur and Blur More effects work similarly to the Gaussian Blur effect, except that they don't have parameters. Blur provides a slight blurring effect, and Blur More — well, you get the idea.

Learning holdover effects

The two effects on the Other submenu of the Add Effects menu, in the Effects section of the Property inspector, are holdovers all the way from Fireworks 1.

The Convert to Alpha filter is unnecessary now that Fireworks has mask groups, but you may find creative uses for it. Applying it converts the selection to grayscale and sets white to transparent. The Find Edges filter detects the outlines of forms and converts them to solid lines. This feature can be useful for special effects, or for creating masks.

Examining Shadow and Glow

The shadow and glow effects help to create depth and softness in your Fireworks documents.

Understanding drop and inner shadows

I remember the overwhelming sense of pride I felt after I made my first drop shadow in an early version of Photoshop. Of course, it had taken me all afternoon to follow two different sets of instructions and involved masking layers, Gaussian blurs, nudged layers, and who remembers what else. My pride was quickly deflated when I tried out my new drop-shadowed image against a color background — and found a completely undesired halo of white pixels around my graphic.

All of that effort and anxiety is out the window with Fireworks. Applying a drop shadow to an object can be a simple, two-step process: Select the object and then choose Drop Shadow from the Add Effects menu in the Effects section of the Property inspector. Best of all, you can position the drop shadow against any colored background; Fireworks adjusts the blending of shadow to background, eliminating the unwanted halo effect.

Note   I'm not trying to defame Photoshop, which is a fine application. It's only fair to acknowledge that newer versions also have a Drop Shadow effect that's easily applied and also easily imported into Fireworks, with editability intact.

A drop shadow is a monochrome copy of an image, offset so that it appears behind the image to one side. Drop shadows are usually presented in a shade of gray (although they can be any color) and can be either faded on the edge or hard edged. Drop shadows are used extensively on the Web — some would say that they're overused. However, the effect of giving flat images dimension by adding a shadow behind it is so compelling and downright useful that I think drop shadows will be around for a long time.

In addition to Drop Shadow, Fireworks also offers an Inner Shadow effect. Both effects are essentially the same — and even use the same pop-up dialog box for setting parameters — except for the location of the shadow. Inner Shadow places the shadow within your object, as though it is recessed and the shadow is being cast by the edges of whatever it's recessed into.

To apply a Drop Shadow or Inner Shadow to any object in Fireworks, follow these steps:

1. Select the object you want to apply the effect to. Drop shadows work well on most any object: open or closed vectors, geometric shapes, bitmap objects, text objects, and more.

2. Choose either Drop Shadow or Inner Shadow from the Add Effects menu, off of the Add Effects button in the Effects section of the Property inspector. The initial parameters — which are the same for both effects — are displayed in a pop-up dialog box, as shown in Figure 12-17.

Figure 12-17: The default Drop Shadow effect offers a classic soft shadow, slightly cast to the right, but you can modify it in the pop-up dialog box.

3. To make the shadow appear farther away or closer, change the Distance slider, or enter a value directly in the associated text box.

Tip   The Distance slider has a range from 0 to 100 pixels, but you can enter a higher number in the text box to make the shadow appear even farther away. The text box also accepts negative numbers, which cause the shadow to be cast in the opposite direction of the Angle setting.

4. To change the shadow color from the default black, pick a color from the color well.

5. To change the transparency of the shadow, alter the Opacity slider or text box. Opacity is given in a percentage value; 100 percent is completely opaque and 0 percent is completely transparent (and therefore invisible).

6. To make the edge of the shadow softer or harder, move the Softness slider, or enter a value in its text box. The Softness slider goes from 0 to 30, but you can enter a higher value directly in the text box.

7. To change the direction of the shadow, drag the Angle knob to a new location, or enter a degree (0 to 360) directly in the text box.

8. To display just the shadow and make the object disappear, choose the Knock Out option.

I find myself using a hard-edged shadow almost as much as I do the soft-edge versions, particularly in graphics, where file size is paramount. Any image with a blended edge is larger than the same image with a solid edge because more pixels are necessary to create the faded look — typically half as many again. When file size is key — and you like the look of a solid drop shadow — bring the Softness slider all the way down to zero.

I do find softer shadows particularly effective, however, when one shadow overlaps another. A good way to enhance the three dimensionality of your Web graphics is to place one object with a shadow over another object, also with a shadow.

Using the Knock Out option

The Knock Out option offered in the shadow effects deserves special mention. The phrase knock out is an old printer's term referring to the practice of dropping the color out of certain type to enable the background to show through. Obviously if you eliminated the color from an ordinary bit of type — without an outline or other surrounding element — the type would seem to disappear. A shadow is perfect for surrounding knocked out type because of the way the mind has of filling in the details that are missing from the actual image. Selecting the Knock Out option removes both the fill and stroke color of the object and leaves just the shadow, as shown in Figure 12-18.

Figure 12-18: Use a Drop Shadow effect with Knock Out checked to highlight text or other objects with just the shadow.

Tip

In the introduction to this section, I noted how it's easy in Fireworks to avoid the so-called halo effect that occurs when you move a drop shadow built against one background to another. In Fireworks, there are really two ways to do this. If you don't need the object or its shadow to be transparent, change the canvas color to the background color of your Web page and export the image normally. To avoid the halo effect, but maintain a transparent image, make the background color transparent during export.

Exploring Glow

Whereas a shadow is only visible on one or two sides of an object, the glow effects — Glow and Inner Glow — create a border all around the object. The glow's color is user selectable, as is its width, opacity, and softness.

To apply a glow, follow these steps:

1. Select the object you want to apply the effect to.

2. Click the Add Effects button, in the Effects section of the Property inspector, and choose either Glow or Inner Glow from the Shadow and Glow submenu on the Add Effects menu. Fireworks displays the glow parameters in a pop-up window, which is identical to the drop-shadow dialog box, shown previously in Figure 12-17, except for the lack of a Knock Out option.

3. Set the other options — Width, Color, Opacity, and Softness — as desired.

All the Glow effect parameters are the same as those found on the shadow effects.

Tip　One effect you can create with Glow that's not immediately obvious is a border. Apply the Glow effect to an object and set the Softness to 0 and the Opacity to 100 percent. *Voilà,* a border.

Sharpening to bring out detail

Sharpening an image can bring out depth that's not there by finding the edges of objects and creating more contrast between pixels on either side of that edge. It can especially help to fix a bad scan, or bring out detail after you go overboard with special effects filters.

To sharpen an image a little bit, select it and choose Sharpen ➪ Sharpen, or Sharpen ➪ Sharpen More from the Add Effects menu in the Effects section of the Property inspector.

To sharpen an image with control over individual settings, follow these steps:

1. Select an object.

2. Click the Add Effects button, in the Effects section of the Property inspector, and choose Sharpen ➪ Unsharp Mask from the Add Effects menu.

   Fireworks displays the Unsharp Mask dialog box, as shown in Figure 12-19.

Figure 12-19: Specify the parameters for Unsharp Mask in the Unsharp Mask dialog box.

3. Moving the Sharpen Amount slider specifies the intensity of the effect. You might start with this slider at about midway and increase or decrease it later, after setting other options.

4. Move the Pixel Radius slider to control how many pixels are evaluated simultaneously. A larger radius value results in a more pronounced effect, because the differences among a larger group of pixels typically are greater.

5. Move the Threshold slider to determine which pixels are affected. Only pixels that have a grayscale value higher than the threshold value are affected. A lower threshold affects more pixels. Click OK when you're done.

Your image should now have a crisper, sharper look (see Figure 12-20).

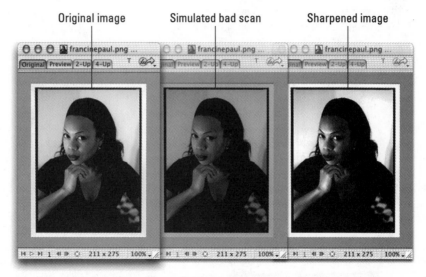

Original image   Simulated bad scan   Sharpened image

Figure 12-20: Sharpening an image may seem to bring out extra detail.

Tip

Sometimes, a sharpened image appears too harsh. Adding a touch of blur with the Blur Live Effect, or applying the Auto Levels filter may help to remedy this.

Fireworks Technique: Making Perspective Shadows

Fireworks is flexible enough to enable you to extend its Live Effects to create many of your own effects. One such possibility is perspective shadows. Unlike drop shadows, perspective shadows are not flat carbon copies of the selected object, but rather shadows that appear to exist in a three-dimensional world. In addition, perspective shadows can appear in front, behind, or to the side of the object.

Cross-Reference Alien Skin's Eye Candy 4000 filters, covered later in this chapter, include a perspective shadow effect that's worth investigating, if you have the Eye Candy 4000 package.

This perspective shadow technique takes advantage of Fireworks' facility with vector objects and its capability to adjust gradients and edges. With this technique, you can add perspective shadows to text, bitmap, or vector objects. A bitmap object that received this treatment is shown in Figure 12-21.

Figure 12-21: Create perspective shadows in Fireworks by combining gradient fills with distorted copies of an object.

To create a perspective shadow, follow these steps:

1. Duplicate the outline of the original object to create a new shadow object. Depending on the type of object, this first step is either very simple, very time-consuming, or something in-between. Here are techniques for working with the three basic types of objects:

   • **Vector objects:** By far the easiest of the three, simply choose Edit ➪ Clone to copy any vector object. Cloning is a better choice than Duplicating because aligning the shadow and its source later is easier.

- **Text objects:** Although it's not absolutely necessary, I've found it sometimes easier to work with text as a vector for my shadow object than with regular text. In my experience, distorting vector objects gets more predictable results than distorting text. Therefore, I first Clone the text and then choose Text ➪ Convert to Paths. Finally, to reduce the gradients of the separate letters to one, choose Modify ➪ Combine Paths ➪ Union.

- **Bitmap objects:** Bitmap objects can be simple rectangles, or irregular shapes. If your object is rectangular or another geometric shape, use the Rectangle, Ellipse, or Polygon to create a same-size copy of the object. Otherwise, the best tool for this particular job is the Pen. For outlining an image, I use the Pen primarily in its straight-line mode, clicking from one point to the next, although occasionally when I need to copy a curve, I use the Pen's Bézier curve feature. The outline doesn't have to be exact, although the more details you include, the more realistic your shadow.

2. If necessary, flip the shadow object. Depending on your hypothetical light source, you want to flip the shadow object vertically so that the perspective shadow falls in front of the original object.

3. If necessary, move the shadow object into position.

   You won't need to move the shadow object if the perspective shadow falls behind the original object. However, for perspective shadows in front, you do need to move the shadow object so that the bases of each object meet. Although using the mouse to drag the shadow object into position is entirely possible, I often find myself using the cursor keys to move the selected shadow object in one direction. Pressing Shift+Arrow keys moves the object in ten-pixel increments and the regular arrow keys, one pixel.

4. Send the shadow object behind the original object.

   Whether you choose Modify ➪ Arrange ➪ Send Backward, or Modify ➪ Arrange ➪ Send to Back depends on what other objects are in the document and how you want the shadow to relate to them. But even if the perspective shadow falls in front of the source object, you'll want to put it behind to mask the meeting point.

5. Distort the shadow object.

   Here's where the real artistry — and numerous attempts — enter the picture. Select the shadow object, and choose the Skew tool from the Tools panel to slant the shadow in one direction; again, the direction depends on where the apparent "light" for the shadow is coming from. Next, while the Skew tool is still active, switch to the Scale tool. (By pressing the keyboard shortcut, Q you don't have to move the mouse.) You can now easily resize the same bounding box. Choose the middle horizontal sizing handle on the edge farthest away from the original object. Now you can drag that handle to either shorten or lengthen the shadow.

6. Optionally, fill the shadow object with a gradient.

You may be satisfied with the shadow as it stands now, but adding and adjusting a gradient adds more depth and realism to the image. From the Fill section of the Property inspector, choose the Linear gradient with a Black, White preset color combination.

7. Adjust the gradient of the shadow object.

As applied, the Linear gradient just goes left to right. If you need it to flow at a different angle (and you probably do), choose the Gradient tool while the shadow object is selected to activate the gradient controls. Reposition and angle the gradient, so that the starting point is at the juncture of the source and shadow object, and the ending point is just beyond the end of the shadow. This enables the shadow to gently fade away.

8. If desired, slightly feather the edge of the shadow object.

To my eye, shadows look a bit more realistic if they're not so hard-edged. I like to set the Edge option list in the Fill section of the Property inspector to Feather and set the Amount of Feather relatively low, about three or four pixels. You may have to adjust the shadow object a bit to hide the feathered edge where it touches the original object.

You can add many enhancements to this technique. For example, you could add an object for the shadow to fall over, by bending or pulling the shadow object with the Freeform or Reshape Area tools, or the shadow itself could be not so realistic to make a point. Computer graphics make turning anyone's shadow into a horned devil or winged angel oh-so-tempting. Play with perspective—you'll be glad you did.

Managing Live Effects

As with strokes and fills, you can save custom configurations of Live Effects with each document. You can then later apply these custom effects to other objects in the same document or, if the object is copied to another document, other graphics. As with strokes and fills, management of custom effects is easily handled through the Add Effects menu.

The commands on the Options submenu of the Add Effects menu, in the Effects section of the Property inspector, are as follows:

✦ **Save As Style:** Displays the New Style dialog box to store the effects settings of the currently selected object as a new Style in the Styles panel.

✦ **All On** and **All Off:** Turns all applied effects on or off, respectively. This is the same as checking or unchecking all the checkboxes in the Effects list.

✦ **Locate Plugins:** A shortcut to specifying a folder of Photoshop-compatible plug-ins for Fireworks to use. This is the same as modifying the Photoshop Plug-Ins option in the Folders area of Fireworks preferences. Fireworks must be restarted for changes to this option to take effect.

Storing a customized effect

Creating your own effects is a tremendous time-saver and an enjoyable creative exercise, as well. You can apply even complex effects with one action. The effects shown in Figure 12-22 combine Fireworks default effects with some that are borrowed from Photoshop 5.5.

Figure 12-22: A range of effects such as these can be created and stored under sometimes goofy names for instant recall.

To store a customized effect, follow these steps:

1. Apply effects to an object until you create a combination that you would like to save.

2. Choose Save As Style from the Options submenu of the Add Effects menu in the Effects section of the Property inspector. The New Style dialog box appears.

Cross-Reference

For more information on the power of Styles, see Chapter 16.

3. Enter a unique name for the effect. If you choose a name already in use, Fireworks asks whether you want to replace the existing effect.

4. After entering a new name, check the Style properties you would like to save with the new Style and click OK. The new effect name is displayed alphabetically in the user area of the Add Effects menu and a thumbnail preview of it is added to the Styles panel.

Caution   If you export your new style, it won't work properly on another machine that doesn't have the same effects installed. If you only use Fireworks' default Live Effects, you can avoid this problem, of course.

As well as being useful for complex combinations of effects, saving simple effects can save you time. Often, I find myself choosing the same simple drop shadow, or using the same 4-pixel flat Inner Bevel on almost every standard 88×31 pixel microbutton that I create. An effects-only style saves me a small amount of time and trouble each day.

Cross-Reference   See some saved effects in greater detail in the color insert.

Grasping missing effects

As great as it is to include all kinds of third-party filters in your saved effects, the downside is that documents that use those effects depend upon them being available. If you try to open a document from a colleague, for example, who used effects that you don't have on your system, Fireworks displays the Missing Effects dialog box (see Figure 12-23), warning you that certain effects are unavailable. Obviously, the larger remedy is to install the correct effects; however, you can edit the document in the meantime.

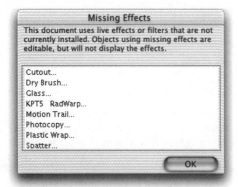

Figure 12-23: Fireworks displays the Missing Effects dialog box when you open a document that uses filters that are not available.

Reading All About Filters

Although many of the items in the Filters menu are also available in the Effects section of the Property inspector, choosing them from the Filters menu has a key difference. Unlike using Live Effects in the Effects section of the Property inspector, applying a filter from the Filters menu flattens text and vector objects into bitmaps, reducing their editability.

Before you choose a filter from the Filters menu, you have to decide what you want to modify with that filter and select it in the appropriate way. All the filters that are included with Fireworks work on any type of selection, but some third-party filters work better on pixel selections within bitmap objects, or even require such a selection to run.

Using vector objects

As mentioned previously, applying a filter to a vector object, or vector object group, flattens it into a bitmap object. The vector information is thrown away and you lose the advantages, such as smooth scalability and editability, that vector objects provide. Try using Live Effects on your vector objects to achieve the look that you want before you turn to the Filters menu. After your vector object becomes a bitmap object, there's no going back, except by using the Undo command, or the History panel.

Tip

Sometimes, though, you can get the best of both worlds. If you're using a filter that draws outside the selection (for example, the Eye Candy Fire filter, which draws flames around your image), you can apply the plug-in to a copy of your object and then place the resulting, filtered image behind your original object and group them. Later, you can still color and use Live Effects on your vector object. If you resize it, you should throw away the filtered image and reapply the saved settings of the filter to a new copy of your object. If you're applying a filter that alters within the selection, try applying the filter to a copy of your object, and then using the copy as an alpha mask for your original. You can create some interesting effects this way, without being stuck with bitmaps when you're done.

When you do apply a filter to a vector object, Fireworks warns you that doing so converts it to a bitmap object. You can disable this warning by checking the "Don't show again" checkbox. I recommend that you leave it unchecked for a little while, until you get used to this conversion. If you accidentally convert a vector object to a bitmap object and then save your file, your vector information may be gone for good.

To apply a filter to a vector object, select it with the mouse and then choose the filter's name from the Filters menu.

Examining bitmap objects

Applying a filter to a bitmap object couldn't be easier. The only thing to keep in mind is that some filters draw outside the selection to create effects such as motion trails and drop shadows. If your bitmap object is the same size as the canvas, the effect will either be invisible because it's off the canvas, or, with some filters, won't even be drawn. Before applying one of these filters, resize the canvas to give them a little room.

To apply a filter to a bitmap object, select it and then choose the desired filter from the Filters menu.

Identifying pixel selections in a bitmap object

Many filters work best when applied to a pixel selection within a bitmap object because they create a difference between the area inside the selection and the area outside the selection. Often, complex pixel selections, such as those made with the Magic Wand or the Polygon Lasso, work better than simple rectangular or circular selections. The extra complexity creates areas where some filters create things, such as bevels, shadows, or textures.

Note   Creating a pixel selection doesn't necessarily mean that you've limited a filter to drawing only inside the selection. Although most stay inside, some draw outside the selection to create their effect. Your selection marks a focal point for whatever filter you're applying.

To apply a filter to a pixel selection within a bitmap object, use one of the marquee selection tools from the Tools panel to draw your selection, and then choose a filter from the Filters menu.

Cross-Reference   For more on creating selections within bitmap objects, see Chapter 6.

Checking out false pixel selections

Some filters ignore your pixel selections and apply their effect to an entire bitmap object. If you find that a particular filter exhibits this behavior, you can work around it by creating a "false pixel selection," by copying your pixel selection to the Clipboard and pasting it as a new bitmap object.

Tip   All the filters in Kai's Power Tools, detailed later in this chapter, apply their effects to your entire bitmap object and require that you use a false pixel selection to limit them to a portion of your image.

To create a false pixel selection, follow these steps:

1. Create a selection around the area to which you want to apply the filter, by using one of the marquee selection tools from the Tools panel.

2. Copy the selection to the Clipboard by choosing either Edit ➪ Copy, or the keyboard shortcut, Ctrl+C (Command+C).

3. Paste the selection back into the document by choosing either Edit ➪ Paste, or the keyboard shortcut, Ctrl+V (Command+V).

The selection is pasted as a new bitmap object, on top of the area it was copied from. Even though it now has a square marquee selection, the bitmap object is, in fact, the same size and shape as what you originally copied to the clipboard.

4. Apply a filter to the new bitmap object by choosing the filter you want to use from the Filters menu.

The filter affects only the new bitmap object.

The original bitmap object and the new one that you created and then filtered are merged into one. The net result is that only the area of your original pixel selection is modified.

Evaluating multiple objects

In addition to individual objects, you can apply filters to a selection or group of multiple objects. If your selection or group contains any vector objects, they will be converted to bitmap objects, just as they would be if you were applying the filter to them individually. When applying filters to multiple objects, keep the following in mind:

✦ If you apply a filter to a selection of objects, the filter runs multiple times, applying to each object in turn. If you select three objects, for example, the filter runs three times in a row, once on each object. If you select Cancel in any of the filter's dialog boxes, it cancels the entire operation, and none of your objects are altered.

✦ If you apply a filter to a group of objects, the group acts as if it is one object. After you apply the filter, the objects actually are one bitmap object, and you can't separate them. To make a selection of objects into a group, select multiple objects and choose Modify ➪ Group, or use the keyboard shortcut, Ctrl+G (Command+G).

The exceptions to the preceding list are the Adjust Color, Blur, Other, and Sharpen filters that come with Fireworks (all of those above the line in the Filters menu). They act on a selection of objects as if they are already grouped.

The differences in the way groups and selections are handled by filters is actually quite handy. Imagine that you have created five objects that are going to be five buttons in a navigation interface. If you want to apply a filter with the exact same settings to all of them, group them and apply the filter. If, however, you want to apply the same filter to all of them, but tweak the settings for each—to add a slightly different texture to each one, for example—just select them and apply the filter.

Tip   Many filters start with the same settings as when you last used them. When applying a filter to a selection of objects, the second time the filter starts, it will have the same settings that you used on the first object, making it easier to apply a similar effect across a selection of objects. You can also save settings in some filters.

Using Third-Party, Photoshop-Compatible Filters

So far, you've seen what you can do with the Live Effects and filters that are included with Fireworks, but that's just the tip of the iceberg. Many third-party, Photoshop-compatible, plug-in filters are available.

Caution   Fireworks supports Photoshop-compatible filters, but some developers target their filters directly at Photoshop itself, creating filters that don't work in other applications. Check the Disabled plugins file in your Configuration subfolder, off of the Fireworks Application folder, for a list of filters that are known to be incompatible. Just because a filter is not on that list doesn't mean that it's guaranteed to work with Fireworks, though. Whenever possible, ask the software publisher about Fireworks compatibility before purchasing filters.

Installing third-party filter packages

Most filter packages come with installers that are similar to the installers provided with full applications, such as Fireworks. Before you install a package, close Fireworks. You have to restart Fireworks before you use the filters, anyway. When the installer's instructions ask you to locate your Photoshop Plug-Ins folder, specify Fireworks' Plug-Ins folder, which is inside your Fireworks program folder. If the package did not come with an installer, you have to copy the filters to your Plug-Ins folder yourself.

Tip   The Fireworks program folder is typically found at `C:\Program Files\ Macromedia\Fireworks MX` **on Windows-based computers, and at** `Macintosh HD:Applications:Macromedia Fireworks MX:` **on the Mac.**

After the installation is complete, start Fireworks. You should see a new option under the Filters menu, and — if Fireworks can use the filters as Live Effects — on the Add Effects menu in the Effects section of the Property inspector. This is a whole new submenu, which often has multiple filters available. Sometimes, new effects hide themselves on menus you already have. If you have a Distort submenu, for example (some of Photoshop 5's filters create this), and you install a filter that also wants to live in a Distort submenu, it may not be apparent that you've gained a filter until you open the Distort submenu.

Tip

Where can you get more filters? A good place to start is The Plugin Site, at `http://www.thepluginsite.com`, where you'll find lots of free filters and filter-related links. Some great individual developers: Alien Skin Software, at `http://www.alienskin.com`; Auto FX Software, at `http://www.autofx.com`, Furbo Filters, at `http://www.furbo-filters.com`; and VanDerLee at `http://www.v-d-l.com`. Of course, Adobe also sells Photoshop-compatible filters at `http://www.adobe.com`.

Using filters with multiple applications

If you use another image-editing application in addition to Fireworks, you may have a whole host of filters on your computer that you can also use in Fireworks. Sharing filters among numerous applications can instantly add many features to all of them and can also speed up your workflow because you don't have to leave an application to apply a particular effect.

Aside from Fireworks, here are some other applications that use Photoshop-compatible filters:

✦ Adobe Photoshop and Illustrator

✦ Macromedia FreeHand and Director

✦ Corel Photo-Paint and CorelDRAW

I have about six or seven applications that use filters, so I keep all of my filters in one folder, independent of all the applications, and then I have all the applications use that folder as their plug-ins folder. The alternative would be to install filters numerous times into the plug-ins folder of each and every application. If you have multiple applications that use standard filters, you might want to do the same thing.

To specify an additional filters folder, follow these steps:

1. Choose Edit ⇨ Preferences.

    Fireworks displays the Preferences dialog box.

2. Choose the Folders tab (Folders option list on Macintosh), as shown in Figure 12-24.

3. Check the Photoshop Plug-Ins checkbox.

4. Click the Browse button to the right of the Photoshop Plug-Ins checkbox.

    Fireworks displays the Browse for Folder dialog box.

5. Select the folder that contains the filters you want to use. Click OK when you're done.

6. Restart Fireworks to see the changes to the Filters menu and to use your newly available filters.

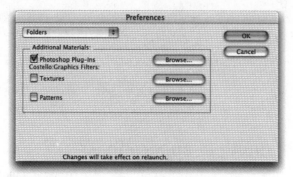

Figure 12-24: Fireworks can use filters from another folder on your computer. This means you can put all of your plug-ins into one folder and point all applications that use Photoshop-compatible plug-ins at this centralized folder.

Using shortcuts (aliases) to plug-in folders

Another method for specifying an additional plug-in folder or folders is to place shortcuts (aliases) to those folders into Fireworks' Filters folder. As well as being an intuitive way to specify where filters are located, this also has the advantage of enabling you to specify more than one additional folder (see Figure 12-25).

To create a shortcut to a folder of filters on Windows, select the folder, right-click it, and then drag it into your Fireworks Filters folder. When you drop it, choose Make Shortcut from the contextual menu that appears. On the Mac, hold down Command+Option while you drag the folder into your Fireworks Filters folder, and an alias to the plug-ins folder is created.

Exploring Alien Skin Eye Candy

Eye Candy is a popular filter collection that you can purchase and install as filters in Fireworks. Fireworks even includes three of the Eye Candy filters as Eye Candy 4000 LE. Even if you don't (yet) have the full Eye Candy 4000 package, this section introduces you to the kinds of things that are possible with filters in general, and may also help you evaluate other, similar packages for their quality and creative potential.

Tip   Alien Skin has optimized Eye Candy 4000 for use as Live Effects in Fireworks. Check out Alien Skin Software's plug-ins on the Web at http://www.alienskin.com— or go directly to the Eye Candy 4000 plug-ins at http://www.eyecandy.com.

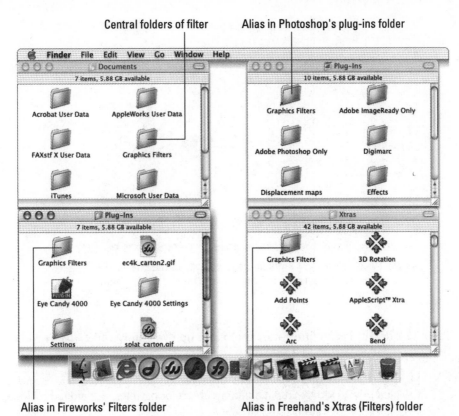

Figure 12-25: Place shortcuts (aliases) to folders that contain filters into Fireworks' Filters folder to enable Fireworks to access the filters.

The theme here is classic effects done right: beveling, drop shadows, smoke, motion trails, distortion. The Eye Candy filters are a great foundation for any filter collection because they're the kind of blue-collar, hard-working, tried-and-true effects that are used again and again in the kinds of tasks that the working Web artist does every day.

Following are some of the features you'll find in Eye Candy:

✦ Many presets for each filter enable you to start using them quickly. In addition, you can save your own settings to the preset list for later recall.

✦ A dynamic preview capability enables you to zoom in or out on your image for precise, detailed modifications.

✦ All Eye Candy filters share common interface features, which cuts down the learning curve (see Figure 12-26).

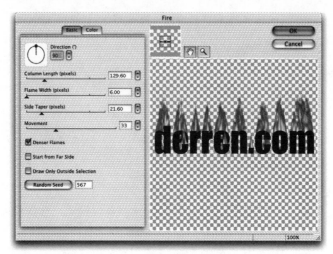

Figure 12-26: The Eye Candy filters have a dynamic interface and easy-to-use presets. This figure shows the Fire filter igniting some text.

Table 12-3 details each of the filters that make up Eye Candy and explains what they do.

Caution   Many Eye Candy filters draw outside the selection and, therefore, rely heavily on having a pixel selection within a bitmap object, or having space around a bitmap object against the canvas.

	Table 12-3
	Alien Skin Eye Candy 4000

Filter	Description
Antimatter	Inverts brightness without affecting hue and saturation values. For example, dark red becomes light red, but is still red.
Bevel Boss	Makes a pixel selection appear to be beveled or carved out of an object. Eye Candy 4000 also has a sophisticated bevel editor for advanced bevels.
Chrome	Applies a metallic effect that you can use to simulate chrome, silver, gold, and other metals.
Corona	Creates astronomical effects such as gaseous clouds and solar flares.
Cutout	Makes a pixel selection appear as a hole in the image, including a shadow, so that it appears recessed.

Filter	Description
Drip	A sophisticated version of the classic wet paint effect.
Fire	Creates a realistic flame effect rising from a pixel selection or object.
Fur	Applies randomly placed clumps of fur.
Glass	Superimposes a sheet of colored glass.
Gradient Glow	Adds a semitransparent glow around the outside edge of a pixel selection or object. Eye Candy 4000 also includes a gradient editor for more advanced glow effects.
HSB Noise	Adds noise by varying hue, saturation, brightness, and transparency.
Jiggle	Creates a bubbling, gelatinous, or shattered effect.
Marble	Creates marble textures.
Melt	Makes objects appear as if they are melting.
Motion Trail	Creates the illusion of motion by smearing a pixel selection or object outward in one direction.
Shadowlab	Adds a drop shadow or a realistic perspective shadow to a pixel selection or an object.
Smoke	Creates smoke coming from a pixel selection or object.
Squint	Unfocuses a pixel selection or object in a way similar to bad eyesight.
Star	Creates stars and other polygon shapes.
Swirl	Adds randomly placed whirlpools.
Water Drops	Adds randomly placed water drops.
Weave	Applies a woven effect.
Wood	Creates wood textures.

Using Jiggle

Jiggle produces a unique distortion based on randomly placed bubbling. The patterns that it produces are more random and organic — less computerized — than many distortion filters. A selection can seem like it's bubbling, gelatinous, or shattered. As you can see in Figure 12-27, you can create interesting effects with this filter.

To use Jiggle, select an image and follow these steps:

    1. Choose Filters ⇨ Eye Candy 4000 ⇨ Jiggle and the Jiggle dialog box appears.

Original image   Jiggled image   Jiggled image as alpha mask

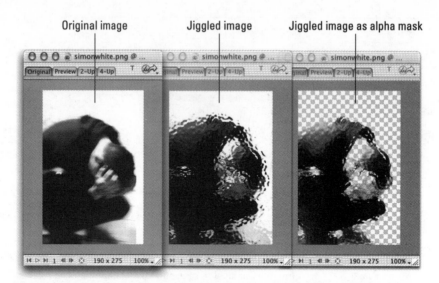

Figure 12-27: Jiggle is organic distortion in action, using the Bubbles type of movement. The third image (right) is the original image with the jiggled image as its alpha mask, and the canvas color changed to show through.

2. Adjust these controls to achieve the effect you desire:

- **Bubble Size slider:** Controls the frequency of the distortion. The lower the value, the more closely spaced the distortion.

- **Warp Amount:** Controls how much your selection is stretched.

- **Twist:** Controls the amount of twisting that occurs, measured in degrees.

- **Movement Type drop-down list:** Use to select the way you want the image jiggled. The three types of jiggling are Bubbles, which is a smooth, even distortion; Brownian Motion, which is a more ragged effect; and Turbulence, which creates sharper breaks in the image.

3. If you like, you can save your settings by using the Save Preset button. Click OK (the checkmark) when you're done.

The effect is applied to your image.

Understanding Shadowlab

The ubiquitous drop shadow has its place, but a more realistic shadow that mimics the effects of the sun can be applied with Eye Candy 4000's Shadowlab. The effect makes your selection appear to be standing up as the light comes from above and in front. The shadow is attached to the object rather than floating, which creates the three-dimensional perspective.

To use Shadowlab, select an object and follow these steps:

1. Choose Filters ➪ Eye Candy 4000 ➪ Shadowlab.

   The Shadowlab dialog box appears.

2. Select any of these preset effects and/or adjust the controls, if necessary, to achieve the effect you desire:

   • **Vanishing Point Direction:** Controls the direction in which the shadow falls behind your selection. The shadow always falls behind your selection.

   • **Vanishing Point Distance:** Controls how far the vanishing point on the horizon is from your selection. Lower values are closer.

   • **Shadow Length:** Controls the length of the shadow without affecting the tapering much. Lower values produce a shorter shadow.

   • **Blur:** Controls how blurred the edges of the shadow are. Higher values make the shadow blurrier and create the effect of a faraway light source.

   • **Opacity:** Adjusts the overall transparency of the shadow.

   • **Color:** Changes the color of the shadow.

3. If you like, you can save your settings, using the Save Preset button. Click OK (the checkmark) when you're done.

   The effect is applied to your image, as shown in Figure 12-28.

Investigating Kai's Power Tools

Kai's Power Tools (KPT) stands out from the crowd with the extremity of the modifications you can make to your images. Ending up with a completely unrecognizable image after applying just one filter is easy. In fact, making sure your image stays recognizable sometimes takes some work.

Tip   The Kai in Kai's Power Tools is Kai Krause, who became a legend among graphic artists when he introduced the original Kai's Power Tools.

Original object   Perspective Shadowed object

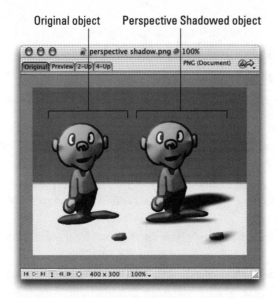

Figure 12-28: Eye Candy 4000's Shadowlab put a realistic 3D shadow at your disposal. The original is a vector object. The other is a bitmap object with the Perspective Shadow filter applied to it.

Some highlights of KPT include the following:

✦ Complex masking and transparency options

✦ Complex three-dimensional lighting and environment options

✦ Interactive Preview windows

✦ Presets with thumbnail views

✦ Common interface elements shared by the entire set of filters. Figure 12-29 shows FraxPlorer from Kai's Power Tools 5.

The color insert shows what you can do with FraxPlorer.

Table 12-4 details KPT 5 filters.

The KPT 5 package also includes Kai's Power Tools 3, with 19 completely separate and useful plug-ins, making the KPT 5 package an excellent value.

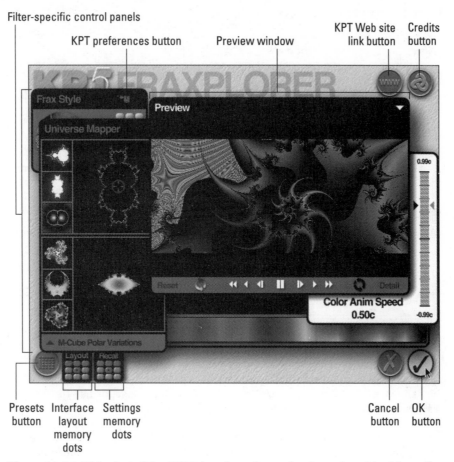

Filter-specific control panels

KPT preferences button

Preview window

KPT Web site link button

Credits button

Presets button

Interface layout memory dots

Settings memory dots

Cancel button

OK button

Figure 12-29: This shot of the KPT 5 interface shows that it can be a bit tricky at first, but it contains much functionality. This is FraxPlorer.

Table 12-4 Kai's Power Tools 5	
Filter	*Description*
Blurrrr	All the blur effects you could ever need, including spins, zooms, spirals, and motion blurs.
Noize	Typical and unusual noise effects, including transparent noise.
RadWarp	Creates or corrects a fish-eye lens effect. Sort of like a fun-house mirror on steroids.

Continued

Filter	Description
Smoothie	Multiple ways to clean up dirty, jagged edges, quickly and easily.
Frax4D	Creates 3D or "4D" fractal sculptures. The "4D" ones look like really chewed-up versions of the 3D ones.
FraxFlame	Fractal effects that resemble fire. Reminiscent of long-exposure photographs of fireworks.
FraxPlorer	An incredible Fractal Explorer with real-time fly-throughs, which are like fractal movies. Create amazing textures or backgrounds, or just have fun playing.
FiberOptix	Adds true three-dimensional fibers onto images, including masks. You can make something hairy and then composite it easily.
Orb-It	Creates very detailed three-dimensional spheres. Make bubbles, raindrops, lenses, and distortions.
ShapeShifter	Makes three-dimensional shapes from masks, including environment maps and textures.

(Table 12-4 continued — title row: Table 12-4 (Continued))

Using RadWarp

KPT RadWarp simulates a photographic effect called barrel roll. You can either add the fish-eye effect to create fantastic variations on an image, or use the filter to "unfish-eye" an image with a slight, unwanted barrel roll.

Caution All KPT 5 filters affect your entire bitmap object, even if you have created a selection. If you want to affect just a portion of a bitmap object, see the workaround in the section "Checking out false pixel selections," earlier in this chapter.

To use RadWarp, select a bitmap object and follow these steps:

1. Choose Filters ➪ KPT 5 ➪ RadWarp.

   The RadWarp dialog box appears (see Figure 12-30).

Tip By default, KPT 5 dialog boxes open up full-screen, but you can snap the dialog boxes to a number of pixel sizes, if you prefer. Hold down Ctrl (Command) and press 1 for 640×480, 2 for 800×600, 3 for 1024×768, 4 for 1152×870, 5 for 1280×1024, and 0 for full-screen. The panels are also set to Panel Auto Popup by default, which I find distracting. Click the name of the filter at the top of its dialog box to select the panel options. If your display has a low resolution, Panel Solo mode will save the day.

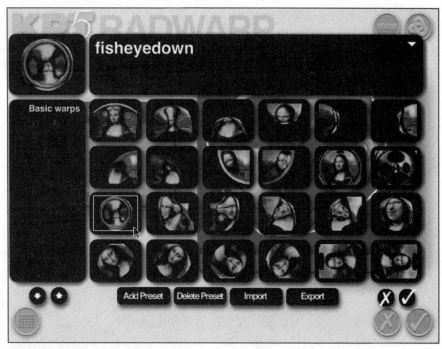

Figure 12-30: RadWarp is fun and can create extreme effects, including especially strange-looking faces.

2. Adjust these controls to achieve the effect you desire:

- **Alpha slider:** Controls how much of a rounded distortion is added

- **Beta slider:** Controls how much of another type of slightly squarer distortion is added

- **X Center:** Controls where the horizontal center of the warping effect is located

- **Y Center:** Controls where the vertical center of the warping effect is located

Tip

You can also modify *X* and *Y* Center by dragging your mouse in the real-time Preview window.

Rotation rotates the image.

3. Click OK (the checkmark) to apply the effect.

The effect is applied to your image.

Understanding ShapeShifter

When you're working with vector objects in Fireworks, you can use Live Effects to apply amazing three-dimensional effects. If you've ever tried to get the same effect with a bitmap object using Live Effects, you were probably quite disappointed. KPT 5's ShapeShifter filter enables you to make those bitmap objects compete with your vector objects.

To use ShapeShifter, select an object and follow these steps:

1. Choose Filters ➪ KPT 5 ➪ ShapeShifter.

   The ShapeShifter dialog box appears (see Figure 12-31).

Figure 12-31: Using ShapeShifter gives your bitmap objects that three-dimensional look so that they can compete with Live Effects on vector objects.

2. In the Main Shape panel, click the thumbnail preview to import a mask. The mask specifies how the three-dimensional shape is added to your image. Adjust the Bevel Scale and Height to determine how much of a three-dimensional effect you're going to create. Select from the three bevel modes.

Note   Unfortunately, Portable Network Graphics (PNG) images are not among the types that KPT 5 can use as masks. When you create a mask for KPT 5, export it from Fireworks as a Tag Image File Format (TIFF) image.

3. In the 3D Lighting panel, add light sources by clicking the plus (+) button. Drag light sources to different locations to affect the highlights and shadows on your image.

4. In the Bump Map panel, add a three-dimensional texture to your image and set the scale and height. Scale zooms in on the texture. Height specifies how three-dimensional the bump map will be.

5. In the Glow panel, add a colored glow to your image, if you desire. You can choose to offset it from the image and also vary the transparency.

Click the eye icon on the Glow panel to show or hide the glow, just like the eye icons in the Fireworks Layers panel.

6. In the Shadow panel, add a shadow to your image, if you want to. As with glow, you can offset the shadow by varying degrees, choose colors, and specify transparency.

7. In the Top Mask panel, you can import another mask to create an emboss effect on top of your three-dimensional object, as if you had stamped out a shape in the top.

8. In the Environment Map panel, load an image to be used as an environment map. This image is reflected by your three-dimensional shape as if it were the sky being reflected on a quiet lake. This adds much depth and character to your image.

You can also alter the settings by dragging your mouse across the Preview window.

9. Click OK (the checkmark) to apply the effect.

The effect is applied to your image.

Summary

Effects may be the icing on the cake, but then what's cake without icing? Seriously, effects play an important role in Web graphics, particularly when it comes to creating buttons with variations that can be used for rollovers. Fireworks makes the hardest effect easy by providing five standard effects and numerous preset looks. When you first begin applying effects to your graphics, consider these points:

✦ Filters and effects applied from the Effects section of the Property inspector remain editable. Filters applied from the Filters menu flatten text and vector objects.

✦ Fireworks applies Live Effects, which are recalculated every time a graphic is altered.

✦ All Fireworks effects are tweaked in the Effects section of the Property inspector, which changes to offer different attributes according to the effect chosen.

✦ The Inner Bevel and Outer Bevel effects are similar, but result in completely different looks. The Inner Bevel effect uses the object's color to create an edge within the object itself, whereas the Outer Bevel effect uses a separate color chosen by the designer to make a border around the outside of the object.

✦ The Drop Shadow sets off any vector, text, or bitmap object with a shadow behind the figure — large or small, subtle or bold, your choice.

✦ Emboss removes the fill and stroke from any selected object and builds edges from the underlying canvas or objects to make it appear as if the object is emerging from the background, or sinking into it.

✦ Fireworks Glow effect creates a soft glow around an object.

✦ Using a combination of other Fireworks tools and commands, any object can have a perspective shadow.

✦ In Fireworks, you can easily apply multiple effects.

✦ Custom effects combinations can be saved and quickly recalled through the use of Fireworks styles and the Styles panel.

✦ You can share filters among multiple, compatible applications, to have access to them wherever you're working.

In the next chapter, you discover how to use Fireworks to arrange and composite different objects.

✦   ✦   ✦

Arranging and Compositing Objects

Fireworks differs dramatically from other bitmap-editing applications in that the component parts of your document are independent objects — often with vector information — and are always editable. Individual objects float above the canvas and can easily be arranged and aligned with each other. One of the best aspects of this creative power is that it enables you to easily composite, layer, and blend objects and then return to them later and undo or change any aspect of your work. Even advanced operations, such as alpha masking, leave the masked image — and the mask itself — intact and editable.

Compositing is the process of combining multiple images into one image, usually by feathering, blending, masking, and altering the transparency of the images.

This chapter looks at the various ways to combine, group, arrange, align, blend, and generally lay out multiple objects within Fireworks.

Using Layers

Layers are a powerful Fireworks feature that enable you to organize your document into separate divisions that you can work with individually or hide from view when convenient. Think of an artist drawing on separate transparencies instead of one sheet of paper. He or she could take one transparency out of the stack and draw only the background elements of the drawing and then take another transparency and put related foreground elements on that. Another could have text elements, and another a signature. Restacking the transparencies produces a finished drawing.

The Layers panel (see Figure 13-1) is the central control center for using layers. To show or hide the Layers panel, choose Window ➪ Layers, or use the keyboard shortcut, F2. The Layers panel enables you to see at a glance how many layers you have in your document, which ones are locked or hidden, and even whether a selection exists on the current layer. As with most other Fireworks panels, the Layers panel also has a pop-up menu that provides easy access to commands related to the functions of the panel.

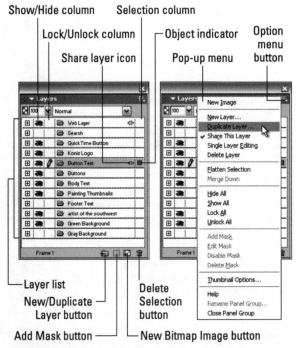

Show/Hide column   Selection column

Lock/Unlock column   Object indicator   Option menu button

Share layer icon   Pop-up menu

Layer list

New/Duplicate Layer button

Add Mask button

Delete Selection button

New Bitmap Image button

Figure 13-1: The Layers panel packs many layer-manipulation options into a small, convenient space.

You may find it helpful to refer to the Layers panel features in Figure 13-1 as you explore their functions throughout this chapter.

When you create a new document in Fireworks, it initially has two layers:

✦ **Web Layer:** A special layer just for hotspots and slices

✦ **Layer 1:** A regular layer on which all the objects you create reside until you create another layer

Adding a layer

Each new layer that you add to your document is placed above the current layer in the layers list. The stacking order in the Layers panel reflects the stacking order on the canvas, so objects on the bottom layer in the Layers panel are also the closest to the canvas.

To add a new, blank layer to your document, do one of the following:

✦ Click the New/Duplicate Layer button on the Layers panel.

Tip Hold down the Alt (Option) key while you press the New/Duplicate Layer button, and Fireworks displays the New Layer dialog box, enabling you to give your layer a custom name before creating it.

✦ Choose New Layer from the Layers panel Options menu.

✦ Choose Edit ➪ Insert ➪ Layer.

Naming a layer

To change the name of a layer, double-click its name in the layer list and type a new name in the pop-up dialog box that appears. Press Enter (Return), or click anywhere outside the pop-up dialog box to close it.

Duplicating a layer

You can also add a layer to your document by duplicating one that already exists. When you duplicate a layer, all the objects on that layer are also duplicated. Working with layers in this fashion is reminiscent of working with folders and files in Windows Explorer or the Macintosh Finder, where duplicating a file duplicates the file, and duplicating a folder duplicates the folder and all of its contents.

To duplicate an existing layer and all of its contents, do one of the following:

✦ Drag the layer from the layers list and drop it onto the New/Duplicate Layer button on the Layers panel.

✦ Hold down the Alt (Option) key, and drag and drop the layer within the layers list.

✦ Choose Duplicate Layer from the Layers panel Options menu.

Duplicating a layer and then hiding the duplicate is a quick way to make a backup of all the objects on a layer before you perform extensive edits. If the edits don't go well, you can always delete them and show the "backup" layer again, taking you back to square one. Even better, I find that making "backup" layers every once in a while builds up a library of objects that often become creatively useful at a later stage. For example, you may find yourself wrapping text around the same circle that you used earlier to mask a bitmap object. Reusing such objects automatically makes your designs more consistent.

Deleting a layer

When you delete a layer, all the objects on that layer are also deleted. If you delete a layer accidentally, choose Edit ⇨ Undo right away to get it back.

To delete a layer, do one of the following:

✦ Drag a layer from the layer list in the Layers panel to the Delete Selection button (Trash can icon) on the Layers panel.

✦ Select a layer from the layer list in the Layers panel and click the Delete Selection button.

✦ Select a layer from the layer list in the Layers panel and choose Delete Layer from the Layers panel Options menu.

Changing stacking order

After you have more than one layer in your document, you may want to change the stacking order at some point. To change the stacking order of layers in your document, simply click and drag a layer higher or lower in the layer list in the Layers panel. Layers that are higher up the layer list are higher up in the stacking order in relation to the canvas.

Editing layer by layer

By default, all objects, no matter which layer they reside on, are fair game for editing on the canvas. To protect the contents of a layer from editing, you can lock or hide the individual layer. Objects on locked or hidden layers are not editable on the canvas.

To lock or unlock a layer, click within the Lock/Unlock column of the Layers panel, next to the layer you want to lock or unlock. After a layer is locked, a padlock icon appears in the Lock/Unlock column next to the layer's name, and none of the objects on that layer can be selected or edited in the document window. When a layer is unlocked, the Lock/Unlock column next to its name is empty.

To show or hide a layer, click within the Show/Hide column of the Layers panel, next to the layer that you want to show or hide. When the eye icon is visible, the layer is visible. When the eye icon is not showing, the layer is hidden, and all the objects on that layer are invisible in the document window.

Tip   When a layer is hidden, it is also locked. When you hide a layer, you don't need to lock it as well.

The Layers panel Options menu features commands for hiding or showing all layers simultaneously, or locking or unlocking all layers simultaneously. Alternatively, you can hold down Alt (Option) and click in the Show/Hide or Lock/Unlock column to affect all layers at once.

An alternative method of layer-by-layer editing is to enter Single Layer Editing mode, by choosing Single Layer Editing from the Layers panel Options menu. When you're in Single Layer Editing mode, you can select or edit only the objects on the current layer, although you can still see objects on other layers. As you select each layer from the layers list in the Layers panel, the other layers automatically act as if they are locked. When working with a complex document, this is an easy way to limit the scope of your edits.

Giving your layers descriptive names before using Single Layer Editing really simplifies things. If your layers are named Background, Text, and so forth, you can quickly select a layer based on which objects you want to edit, without worrying about accidentally altering objects on other layers.

Tip   Two of the commands in the Command menu also enable you to quickly work on a single layer without using Single Layer Editing mode. Choose Commands ⇨ Document ⇨ Hide Other Layers to hide all but the current layer. Choose Commands ⇨ Document ⇨ Lock Other Layers to lock all but the current layer.

Using the Selection column

When you want to move objects from one layer to another, you might be inclined to cut them to the clipboard, change to another layer in the Layers panel, and then paste the objects into the new layer. That works fine, but the Layers panel provides you with another method. Whenever you select an object or objects on the canvas or in the Layers panel, a small blue box appears in the Selection column next to the layer that the selected objects are located on. Drag this box up or down and drop it next to another layer, and the objects are moved there. Hold down the Alt (Option) key as you drag and drop to copy the selection instead of moving it.

Opening layers

The Layers panel uses a folder icon for layers, and for good reason. Just as your overall document is divided into discrete layers, each layer is itself divided into objects, which appear in the Layers panel as an object sublayer, complete with thumbnail images. To open a particular layer and display its contents, click the plus/minus box (disclosure triangle on the Mac) in the Expand/Collapse column next to the layer's name, as shown in Figure 13-2. To hide the contents of the layer, click the square (disclosure triangle) again. Hold down the Alt (Option) key as you click in the Expand/Collapse column to open or close all the layers in your document at once. I often find myself Alt- (Option-) clicking to quickly close all layers when I don't want to work with individual objects.

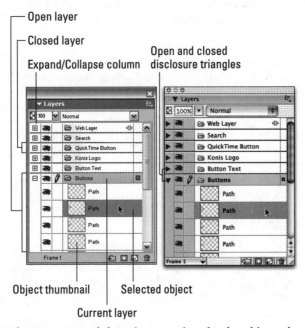

Figure 13-2: Each layer is a container for the objects that reside on it. Each object on the layer is displayed as its own sublayer.

When you drag a layer up or down in the layers list, Fireworks automatically scrolls the list of layers if you're dragging a layer below or above the ones that are currently visible within the size of the Layers panel.

Many of the same techniques you use to work with layers in the Layers panel also apply to working with object sublayers. Keep the following points in mind:

✦ **To add a new object sublayer:** Simply create a new object on the canvas with any of the usual methods, such as importing, drawing, copying and pasting, and so on. As each new object is added to your document, Fireworks adds new object sublayers to the current layer, complete with a thumbnail image. You can also click the New Bitmap Image button on the Layers panel to create a new, empty bitmap object directly above the currently selected object.

✦ **To name an object:** Double-click its generic name, such as "rectangle" in the layer list, and type a new name. Press Enter (Return) when you're done.

✦ **To change the stacking order of objects:** Drag their object sublayers up or down the layers list in the Layers panel. Note that you can move objects up or down within their layers, or further up or down into other layers (see Figure 13-3). Dragging and dropping between layers is physically easier if you open both the source and target layer, exposing the objects inside each. This also enables you to choose where your dropped object resides within the stacking order of the target layer.

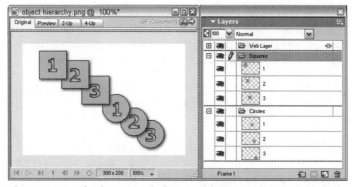

Figure 13-3: The layers and object sublayers in the Layers panel display the complete hierarchy of the stacking order in your document.

Dragging and dropping between layers is physically easier if you open both the source and target layer, exposing the objects inside each. This also enables you to choose where your dropped object resides within the stacking order of the target layer.

✦ **To duplicate an object sublayer:** Hold down the Alt (Option) key and drag and drop the object sublayer up or down the layer list. A copy is created, and your original object is unaffected. You can even drop the copy in another layer.

Use the Shift modifier key to make multiple selections of object sublayers, just as you would with objects on the canvas.

✦ **To hide an object:** Click the eye icon in the Show/Hide column next to the object's sublayer in the Layers panel. You can also hide a selection of objects by choosing View ➪ Hide Selection. To show the objects again, choose View ➪ Show All or click on the Show/Hide column again.

✦ **To delete an object:** Select it — on the canvas or in the Layers panel — and click the Delete Selection button on the Layers panel.

Tip

Old-school Fireworks users—like myself—may find it a little annoying that the Layers panel defaults to fully expanded when you initially open a Fireworks document. Derren Whiteman has created a scriptlet that sets a hidden Fireworks preference so that the Layers panel defaults to fully collapsed. Find it—and a companion script that sets the preference back to its default—on Derren's Fireworks Web site at `http://www.derren.com/geek/fireworks/`.

Examining the Web Layer

All Fireworks documents have a Web Layer on which you can draw "Web objects," such as hotspots and slice guides. You can move the Web Layer in the stacking order by dragging it up or down the layer list in the Layers panel, but you can't delete the Web Layer. The Web Layer is always shared across all frames.

Cross-Reference

For more information about using the Web Layer, see Chapters 20 and 21. For more details about sharing layers across frames, and about frames in general, see Chapter 23.

In addition to creating hotspots with one of the hotspot tools, you can create hotspots out of regular bitmap and vector objects by using the Layers panel. This is a handy way to quickly add hotspots to objects if you want the hotspots to be the same size as the objects.

To create hotspots out of objects, follow these steps:

1. Select the object or objects that you want to make into hotspots.

   Fireworks displays a selection icon (a blue box) in the Selection column of the Layers panel, next to the layer that the selected objects are located in.

2. Drag the selection icon and drop it in the same column on the Web Layer.

   If you have multiple objects selected, Fireworks asks whether you want to create one hotspot or multiple hotspots. Choosing to create one hotspot combines the shapes into one.

   The hotspots are created on the Web Layer, and your original objects are unaffected.

Aligning and Distributing Objects

One of the most basic layout techniques is aligning and distributing objects. If you've ever used any kind of drawing or publishing application, then you're familiar with the concept. When you're in vector mode in Fireworks, every object on the canvas "floats" and can be easily aligned with another.

Using a theoretical rectangle

When you're aligning a selection of objects, imagine a rectangle around your selection (see Figure 13-4) described by the objects themselves. The top of the rectangle is the topmost point on the topmost object; the left side of the rectangle is the far-left point on the farthest-left object in the selection, and so on. This theoretical rectangle is what you align objects to, and what you distribute them across. For consistent results, imagine this theoretical rectangle each time you prepare to use an Align command.

Theoretical alignment rectangle

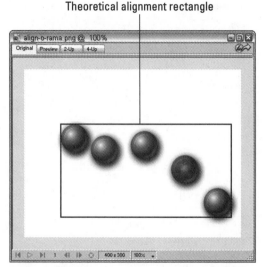

Figure 13-4: Imagine a theoretical rectangle around your selection. This is what the selected objects align to when you choose one of the commands from the Modify ⇨ Align submenu.

When you left-align a selection of objects, all the objects move left until they bump into the left border of the theoretical rectangle. Similarly, if you align to the bottom, all the objects move down until they hit the bottom border of the rectangle. It's very important to understand that alignment in Fireworks has nothing to do with a page or the canvas, as in some applications. In Fireworks, objects are aligned to other selected objects. If you try to align only one object, the alignment commands are unavailable.

Cross-Reference

I show you a workaround for aligning a single object to the canvas later in this chapter.

To align a selection of objects to the selection's left, right, top, or bottom, select the objects that you want to align and choose the appropriate alignment command:

✦ **Left alignment:** To align all objects to the far-left point of the farthest-left object (see Figure 13-5), choose either Modify ➪ Align ➪ Left, or the keyboard shortcut, Ctrl+Alt+1 (Command+Option+1).

Theoretical alignment rectangle

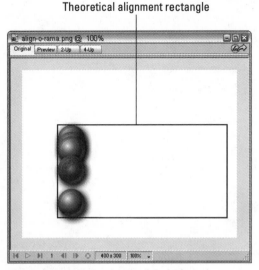

Figure 13-5: The selection of objects shown in Figure 13-4 moves to the left side of the theoretical alignment rectangle when you use the Modify ➪ Align ➪ Left command.

✦ **Right alignment:** To align all objects to the far-right point of the farthest-right object, choose either Modify ➪ Align ➪ Right, or the keyboard shortcut Ctrl+Alt+3 (Command+Option+3).

✦ **Top alignment:** To align all objects to the topmost point of the topmost object (see Figure 13-6), choose either Modify ➪ Align ➪ Top, or the keyboard short-cut, Ctrl+Alt+4 (Command+Option+4).

✦ **Bottom alignment:** To align all objects to the bottommost point of the bottommost object, choose either Modify ➪ Align ➪ Bottom, or the keyboard shortcut, Ctrl+Alt+6 (Command+Option+6).

Theoretical alignment rectangle

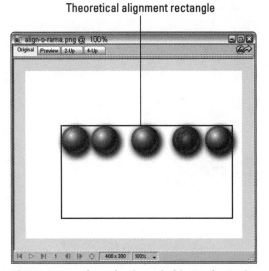

Figure 13-6: The selection of objects shown in Figure 13-4 moves to the top of the theoretical alignment rectangle when you use the Modify ⇨ Align ⇨ Top command.

Fireworks also has two alignment commands that deal with centering objects. Again, rather than centering objects on the canvas, Fireworks centers them to a theoretical horizontal or vertical line drawn through the selection. In order to understand what to expect from these commands, imagine a cross drawn over the theoretical alignment rectangle shown previously in Figure 13-4. This cross demonstrates the vertical and horizontal center lines that objects can be aligned to.

✦ **Center Vertical alignment:** To align all objects to a theoretical vertical center line, choose either Modify ⇨ Align ⇨ Center Vertical, or the keyboard shortcut, Ctrl+Alt+2 (Command+Option+2).

Remember that the center in question is not the center of the canvas, but the center of the selection.

✦ **Center Horizontal alignment:** To align all objects to a theoretical horizontal center line (see Figure 13-7), choose either Modify ⇨ Align ⇨ Center Horizontal, or the keyboard shortcut, Ctrl+Alt+5 (Command+Option+5).

Theoretical alignment rectangle

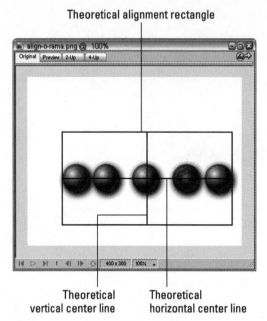

Theoretical
vertical center line

Theoretical
horizontal center line

Figure 13-7: The selection of objects from
Figure 13-4 snaps to a theoretical horizontal line
when you use the Modify ⇨ Align ⇨ Center
Horizontal command.

You can also distribute objects across a selection, which is handy when you have a
few objects, such as a row of buttons that you want to space evenly. To distribute a
selection of objects across the width of the selection, select the objects that you
want to distribute and choose the appropriate command:

✦ **Even horizontal distribution:** To space your objects evenly from left to right
(see Figure 13-8), choose either Modify ⇨ Align ⇨ Distribute Widths, or the
keyboard shortcut, Ctrl+Alt+7 (Command+Option+7).

✦ **Even vertical distribution:** To space your objects evenly from top to bottom,
choose either Modify ⇨ Align ⇨ Distribute Heights, or the keyboard shortcut,
Ctrl+Alt+9 (Command+Option+9).

Aligning to the canvas

Although Fireworks' alignment tools are very powerful, the commands in the
Modify ⇨ Align submenu have no knowledge of the canvas at all. What do you do
when you just want to snap an object to the center of the canvas, or align it to the
left edge of the canvas? Fortunately, a command and a simple technique enable you
to meet almost any kind of alignment challenge.

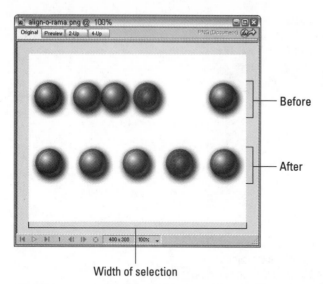

Before

After

Width of selection

Figure 13-8: A selection of objects can be distributed across the width of the selection with the Distribute Widths command. Note that the leftmost and rightmost object do not move at all. They define the width of the selection.

Note   The Align panel that ships with Fireworks MX offers much more powerful, and more user-friendly, alignment options than the standard Fireworks menu choices. The Align panel, written by Kleanthis Economou, is based on the alignment options in Flash and is available via Window ⇨ Align. With it, you are able to align to the canvas, or other objects, as you see fit. For more information on the Align panel, and the other third-party panels shipping with Fireworks MX, please see Chapter 26.

For those times when all you want to do is take a selection and center it on the canvas, choose Commands ⇨ Document ⇨ Center in Document. Your selected object or objects snap to the absolute (horizontal and vertical) center of the canvas. This handy shortcut demonstrates the power of Fireworks' built-in extensibility.

Cross-Reference   For more about Fireworks' Commands menu, see Chapter 19.

For more sophisticated canvas alignment, such as aligning a selection to the left side of the canvas, draw a rectangle the size and shape of the canvas and then align other objects to the rectangle. Visually, the effect is exactly the same as aligning to the canvas, with the added feature that you can easily create a border around your document, just by reducing the alignment rectangle in size by a small amount, as shown in Figure 13-9. You may want to keep your alignment rectangle on its own layer, so that it is very easy to hide, show, lock, or delete.

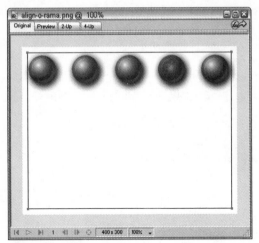

Figure 13-9: Although you can't align objects to the canvas, you can create a rectangle that's roughly the size of the canvas and align objects to the rectangle for the same effect.

Tip

Fireworks considers the edges of the canvas to be guides. Enabling View ➪ Guides ➪ Snap to Guides causes a dragged selection to snap to the edge of the canvas. Align objects to each other, and then select them all and drag them near a canvas edge to create the same effect as an alignment to the canvas.

Looking at Layout Assistance

Fireworks provides a variety of ways to precisely lay out objects on the canvas. Rulers enable you to place guides at precise locations and snap objects to those guides as you move them around. Or, you can choose to lay a grid over your document to help you align things correctly.

Using rulers

Rulers are a standard feature of nearly every drawing or graphics application. In fact, rulers (the kind that you hold in your hand) are a standard feature of traditional, paper-based layouts, as well. Rulers enable you to keep track of the size of your objects and their placement on the canvas with much more precision than the naked eye alone.

To toggle the visibility of the rulers, choose either View ➪ Rulers, or the keyboard shortcut, Ctrl+Alt+R (Command+Option+R). The rulers appear within your document, running along the top and left borders (see Figure 13-10).

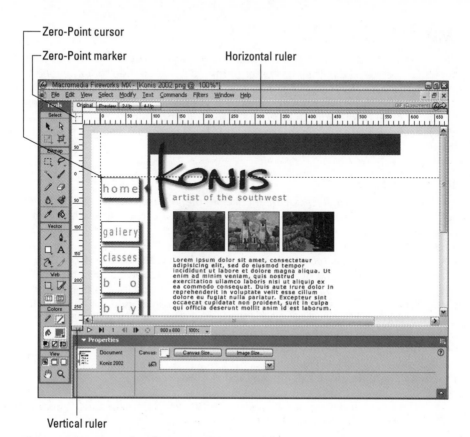

Figure 13-10: Dropping the zero-point cursor next to the top-left object you're aligning simplifies the math involved in aligning objects.

Tip   You can see your mouse pointer's position on the canvas in the rulers as they track your mouse. This is helpful when you want to draw a new object at a precise position on the canvas.

By default, the ruler's *zero-point*—the point where the horizontal and vertical rulers meet—is set to 0 pixels, but you can set it to another location in your document by dragging the zero-point marker to a new location and releasing it. The zero-point marker is in the upper-left corner of the document window when the rulers are visible. If all objects in your document are going to be at least 20 pixels from the top and 20 pixels from the left, moving the zero-point to 20×20 pixels simplifies the math that you have to do later as you align objects. To set the zero-point back to zero again, double-click the zero-point marker.

Working with guides

Guides are simply lines that you can position to mark important points in your documents, such as a margin or center point. As a design time tool intended to make laying out objects easier, guides don't print or export, and they exist above the layers of your document. For example, if your layout calls for many objects to be placed at 20 pixels from the top, then creating a horizontal guide at that position enables you easily to see where that point is located so that you can place objects there.

Creating guides

Adding a new guide to your document is a simple, mouse-only affair. Simply clicking and dragging the horizontal ruler into your document creates a new horizontal guide that you can drop anywhere.

A horizontal guide runs parallel to the horizontal ruler, so you drag from the horizontal ruler to make a horizontal guide. Sometimes, this can be a bit confusing because you tend to drop a horizontal guide after checking its position on the vertical ruler. In other words, you might place a horizontal guide at 20 pixels from the top according to the vertical ruler. If you find yourself trying to create horizontal guides by dragging from the vertical ruler, think of the guides as clones of the rulers from which you drag them—horizontal for horizontal, vertical for vertical.

To add a new guide to your document, follow these steps:

1. If the rulers aren't visible, choose either View ➪ Rulers, or the keyboard shortcut, Ctrl+Alt+R (Command+Option+R), to show them.

2. Drag from the horizontal ruler to create a new horizontal guide. Drag from the vertical ruler to create a new vertical guide (see Figure 13-11). When you reach the position where you want to place your guide, simply drop it in place by releasing the mouse button.

Locking or hiding guides

After you create quite a few guides, you may find that they get in the way. Because they aren't on a layer, you can't just lock or hide their layer to make them invisible or not editable. Carefully placing a guide in the correct spot and then dragging it somewhere else accidentally goes a long way toward negating the primary timesaving aspect of using guides.

To show or hide guides, choose either View ➪ Guides ➪ Show Guides, or use the keyboard shortcut, Ctrl+Semicolon (Command+Semicolon). Hiding guides periodically gives you a better sense of what your final image will look like.

To lock all of your guides so that they can't be moved, choose either View ➪ Guides ➪ Lock Guides, or the keyboard shortcut, Ctrl+Alt+Semicolon (Command+Option+Semicolon).

Vertical guide   Horizontal guide

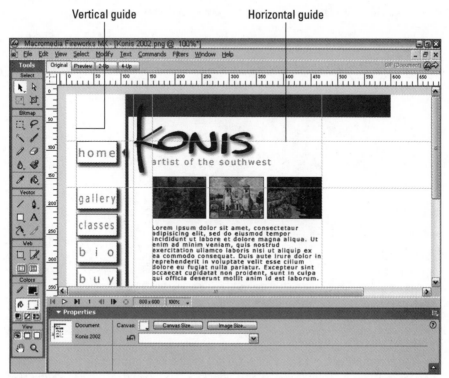

Figure 13-11: Create guides at key locations in your design to simplify object alignment.

Snapping to guides

Snapping objects to guides really uses guides to their full potential. With a little planning, you can create guides at important points in your document so that your layout comes together almost automatically as you move objects around the canvas.

To toggle whether or not objects snap to the nearest guide, choose either View ⇨ Guides ⇨ Snap to Guides, or the keyboard shortcut, Ctrl+Shift+Semicolon (Command+Shift+Semicolon).

Using guide colors

If your document contains a lot of green objects, the default green color of the guides may be hard to see. Guides can be any color. Choosing a color that contrasts sharply with the color scheme of your document makes guides easier to see and also has the effect of separating them from your document, so that you can see your layout through the guides without having to hide the guides all the time.

To change the color that guides are displayed in, follow these steps:

1. Choose View ⇨ Guides ⇨ Edit Guides.

   Fireworks displays the Guides (Grids and Guides) dialog box, as shown in Figure 13-12.

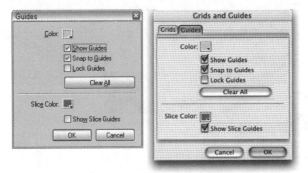

Figure 13-12: Change the color that guides are displayed in (and other options) by using the Guides (Grids and Guides) dialog box.

Note On the Macintosh, instead of a Guides dialog box and a Grids dialog box, the single Grids and Guides dialog box offers a Grids tab and a Guides tab that selects between Grids and Guides views.

2. Use the guides color picker to specify the color you want the guides to be displayed in, and then click OK.

For convenience, all the guide options have been collected into the Guides (Grids and Guides) dialog box. You can check or uncheck Show Guides to toggle the visibility of the guides; check Snap to Guides to cause objects to snap to the guides; or check Lock Guides to lock them. Options for slice guides are also available here.

Clearing guides

Removing a single guide from your document is a drag-and-drop affair, just like adding one. Simply grab the guide with your mouse and drag it out of your document. You can drag it out to the left, right, top, or bottom, and it will disappear from your document.

You can also clear all the guides out of your document simultaneously, by using the Guides (Grids and Guides) dialog box. To clear all guides, follow these steps:

1. Choose View ⇨ Guides ⇨ Edit Guides.

   Fireworks displays the Guides (Grids and Guides) dialog box (refer to Figure 13-12).

2. Click the Clear All button to remove all the guides from your document. Click OK when you're done.

Note The Clear All button removes ruler guides, but not slice guides.

Exploring the grid

The *grid* is a quick way to achieve more precise layouts. Usually, you want objects to align in a fairly regular pattern. The grid makes it easy to see the relationship between the elements of your layout by splitting the document into smaller, more manageable sections. Grid lines don't export or print, and they aren't on a layer. They're simply a visual aid at design time.

To show or hide the grid, choose either View ➪ Grid ➪ Show Grid, or the keyboard shortcut, Ctrl+Alt+G (Command+Option+G).

Snapping to the grid

You can choose to have objects snap to the grid automatically, just as you did earlier with guides. When this feature is enabled, you'll notice that objects are attracted to the grid lines like magnets. Because all of your objects are snapping to the same grid, you can get more precise layouts without any extra effort.

To make objects snap to the grid, choose either View ➪ Grid ➪ Snap to Grid, or the keyboard shortcut, Ctrl+Alt+Shift+G (Command+Option+Shift+G).

Changing grid color and frequency

Again, as with guides, you can change the color of the grid to make it stand out from your document. The default color for each new document is black.

If you're creating a navigation bar with numerous buttons that are 100-pixels wide and 50-pixels tall, set the grid so that it also is 100-pixels wide and 50-pixels tall, so that you can easily see where each button should sit. Enable Snap to Grid, and your layout comes together automatically. The default grid frequency for new documents is 36×36 pixels.

To modify the grid, follow these steps:

1. Choose View ➪ Grid ➪ Edit Grid.

   Fireworks displays the Edit Grid (Grids and Guides) dialog box, as shown in Figure 13-13.

2. Use the grid color picker to specify the color in which you want the grid to be displayed.

   For convenience, you can also toggle the visibility of the grid, or enable Snap to Grid while you're in the Edit Grid (Grids and Guides) dialog box.

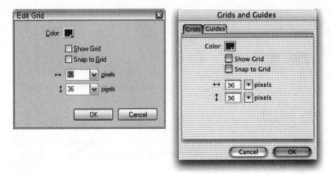

Figure 13-13: Set grid options in the Edit Grid (Grids and Guides) dialog box.

3. In the horizontal spacing box, enter the horizontal spacing that you want the grid to have. This is the space, in pixels, between vertical grid lines.

4. Enter in the vertical spacing box the vertical spacing that you want the grid to have. This is the space, in pixels, between horizontal grid lines.

5. Click Apply to see the results of your modifications without exiting the Edit Grid (Grids and Guides) dialog box. Click OK when you're done.

Grouping Objects

When you group objects, you basically create a new object that is made up entirely of other objects. You can treat a group as if it's a single object, apply Live Effects, alter blending modes, and more.

Objects in a group maintain their positions and stacking order relative to each other. They retain their effects settings until you modify the whole group. If half the objects in a group have a drop shadow, and you apply a drop shadow to the whole group, then all the objects will have a drop shadow. Fireworks is smart enough to apply that drop shadow to the whole group, as if all members were one object. You can also select and modify the component objects of a group individually, without ungrouping them.

Grouping objects is a good way to keep a complex drawing under control. For example, you might build a logo out of vector and text objects and then group those objects together so that you can easily manipulate the whole logo. Grouping together any objects that you don't need to manipulate individually essentially reduces the number of discrete objects that you have to manipulate as you work.

To group two or more objects, select them and choose either Modify ➪ Group, or the keyboard shortcut, Ctrl+G (Command+G). Your grouped objects now behave as one object. A Live Effect or opacity setting applied to a group affects the whole group, as if it were one object (see Figure 13-14).

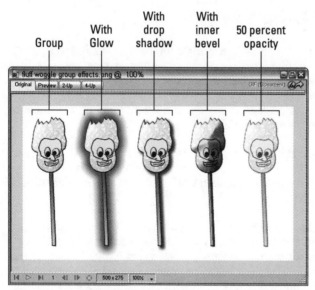

Figure 13-14: Applying a Live Effect or opacity setting to a group shows how it acts as one object.

After you make a group, you can ungroup it at any time. To ungroup a group, select it and choose either Modify ➪ Ungroup, or the keyboard shortcut, Ctrl+Shift+G (Command+Shift+G).

Caution

If you have applied Live Effects, opacity settings, or blending modes to a group, they are lost when you ungroup it.

To modify individual objects within a group, you can either ungroup them, or use the Subselection tool to subselect only the objects you want to work with. If you move a subselected object to another layer, it is removed from the group. To select all the component objects within a group, choose Select ➪ Subselect. To select the parent group of an object, choose Select ➪ Superselect.

Tip

If a text block is part of a group, you can edit the text, simply by using the Text tool and editing directly on your canvas. If you prefer to use the Text editor, you can select the text block using the SubSelection tool and then use Text ➪ Editor.

Fireworks actually has three types of groups: the plain groups discussed here; masked objects, which are discussed next; and symbols, which are covered in Chapter 24. You can use all the techniques, such as subselecting and superselecting, on any kind of group.

Working with Alpha Masks

In a nutshell, an *alpha mask* is an 8-bit grayscale image that is used to describe the transparency of another image. Areas of the alpha mask that are solid black represent areas of the resulting masked image that are completely transparent, whereas areas of solid white represent areas that are completely opaque. The 254 grays between black and white each represent a different level of translucency: Dark gray is almost transparent, and light gray is almost opaque.

New Feature   Fireworks MX handles alpha masks differently than previous versions of Fireworks. In previous versions, black was opaque and white was transparent. In Fireworks MX this relationship is now reversed, with black being transparent and white being opaque.

If you've ever created a transparent Graphics Interchange Format (GIF) with a light-colored background and then placed that GIF in a Web page with a dark background, you've seen a graphic (no pun intended) example of the challenges of compositing transparent images. The edges of your image, where they meet the transparent color, are antialiased to either a light color or a dark color. Artifacts are visible when the image is placed over the opposite-colored background.

The 8-bit alpha mask used in Fireworks and the PNG image format solves this problem, enabling you to composite transparent objects without worrying about the color of the objects on which you're placing them because transparency is specified for each and every pixel (see Figure 13-15).

Typically, your Fireworks images have three 8-bit channels — one for red, one for green, and one for blue — resulting in a 24-bit RGB image that accurately describes every color that the human eye can see. When you add one more 8-bit grayscale channel to describe the levels of transparency — the so-called "alpha channel" — you get a 32-bit image (see Table 13-1) that describes exactly the same colors as the 24-bit image, but also knows where its transparent and translucent edges are.

Table 13-1 Channels and Bit Depth		
Image	*Channels*	*Bit Depth*
Grayscale	1 grayscale	8-bit
True Color	1 red, 1 green, 1 blue	24-bit
True Color with Alpha Mask	1 red, 1 green, 1 blue, 1 grayscale (as mask)	32-bit

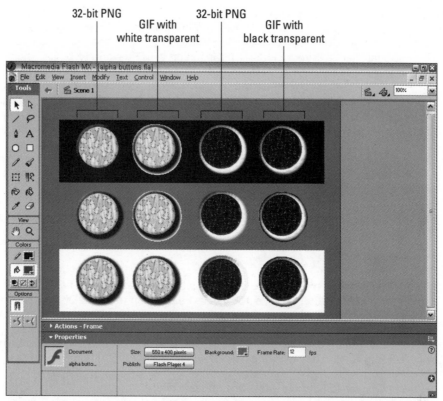

Figure 13-15: Shown here in Macromedia Flash, 32-bit PNG images created with Fireworks can be attractively placed on any background color while maintaining their transparency. GIF images, on the other hand, show artifacts when they are placed on a background color that's much darker or lighter than the one they were created for.

Each pixel of the alpha mask has a value between 0 and 255 to indicate the amount of transparency, which ranges from completely transparent (black, or 0) to completely opaque (white, or 255). The grays in between can be thought of as shades of transparency. Fireworks uses the value of each pixel of the mask to determine the transparency level for the underlying pixel of the masked object, which in turn determines how to blend that pixel with the background pixel it sits on.

If you haven't worked with 32-bit PNG images yet and are used to the limited transparency options inherent in the GIF format, the ease with which alpha transparency enables you to composite transparent objects will thrill you.

Caution

Currently, few Web browsers properly support the PNG alpha channel. Alpha transparency is still useful for working within Fireworks and exporting transparency to other applications, such as Macromedia's Director and Flash applications. Incidentally, both Director and Flash can import your Fireworks PNG files—no need to export as a regular, non-Fireworks-specific PNG.

In brief, working with masks in Fireworks is centered around the Layers panel and the Property inspector. The Layers panel contains controls and commands related to masks, and displays a thumbnail of an object's mask next to the thumbnail of the object itself. Click the thumbnail of the mask to edit it, and the Property inspector displays mask-related options. Masked vector objects have a Move Handle in their centers, which you can click and drag to reposition the masked object without moving the mask.

The various masking controls are shown in greater detail throughout this section.

Creating vector masks

Whenever possible, I try to use vector masks for the same reason I always try to use vector objects: editability. Vector masks enable you to radically alter the look of a masked object using all the standard techniques you use to edit vector objects, such as fills, strokes, and Live Effects. Vector masks can also be easily scaled, skewed, and distorted with the transformation tools. Text objects can also be used as vector masks, creating exciting text effects.

Cross-Reference

See Chapter 10 for more about text masking effects.

To create and apply a vector mask, follow these steps:

1. Choose an object to mask, as shown in Figure 13-16.

2. Create an object to act as a mask for your original object, as shown in Figure 13-17. The size of the mask specifies the size of the resulting masked object. Where the mask is white, the resulting masked object is opaque; where the mask is black, the masked object is transparent. Shades of gray in the mask vary the transparency of the group, according to how light or dark they are.

3. Position the mask in relation to the object you are masking.

4. Select the mask and choose Edit ➪ Cut, or use the keyboard shortcut, Ctrl+X (Command+X), to cut the mask to the clipboard.

5. Select the object you want to apply the mask to and choose Modify ➪ Mask ➪ Paste as Mask.

6. In the Property inspector choose Grayscale in the Mask options.

Tip

If you find that your mask is the inverse of what you wanted, the Invert Live Effect—found in the Effects section of the Property inspector—can quickly invert your mask and set things straight.

Figure 13-16: The image of the fireworks display doesn't blend into the striped background.

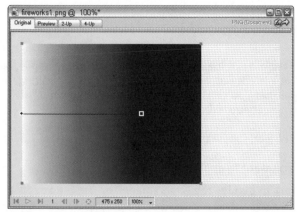

Figure 13-17: A gradient fill for the mask provides a smooth transparent fade for the masked object.

The mask is applied to the original object, as shown in Figure 13-18.

Applying bitmap masks

There are almost as many ways to create a bitmap mask in Fireworks as there are ways to create a bitmap. Whatever method you choose, however, you are ultimately creating a simple 8-bit grayscale image that masks another object. As with any alpha mask, black areas of the mask become completely transparent in the final, masked object, whereas white areas will be completely opaque, and varying shades of gray describe varying levels of transparency.

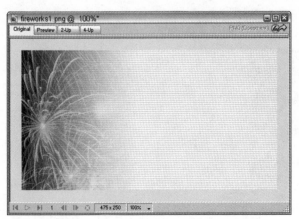

Figure 13-18: The masked object blends into the background because the mask's fade from white to black is translated into a transparency fade from transparent to opaque.

Adding a bitmap mask

The Layers panel provides a number of masking controls, including a simple Add Mask button that creates a new, empty bitmap mask and selects it for editing. If the mask you're after is so simple that you can draw it with Fireworks tools, then adding a mask is a good way to get started.

To add a bitmap mask to an object, follow these steps:

1. Select the object that you want to apply a mask to.

2. Choose Window ➪ Layers to display the Layers panel, or use the keyboard shortcut, F2.

3. If necessary, click in the Expand/Collapse column in the Layers panel to open the current layer so that you can see the currently selected object.

4. Click the Add Mask button on the Layers panel.

Fireworks creates an empty bitmap mask and applies it to the currently selected object. The mask is also selected for editing.

Cross-Reference   Find out about editing masks later in this chapter.

Using Reveal All and Hide All

Fireworks provides a quick method for getting masks started with the Reveal All and Hide All commands.

To use the Reveal All or Hide All command, follow these steps:

1. Select the object that you want to mask.

2. To apply a completely white mask to the object, choose Modify ➪ Mask ➪ Reveal All. Alternatively, you can apply a completely black mask to the object by choosing Modify ➪ Mask ➪ Hide All.

Fireworks creates the mask and selects it for editing.

Using Reveal Selection and Hide Selection

The Reveal Selection and Hide Selection commands basically change marquee selections into bitmap masks, which makes applying simple bitmap masks a breeze.

To create a bitmap mask with the Reveal Selection or Hide Selection command, follow these steps:

1. Make a pixel selection with one of the pixel selection tools, such as the Marquee.

2. To show just the pixels inside the selection, choose Modify ➪ Mask ➪ Reveal Selection. Alternatively, you can hide the pixels inside of the selection by choosing Modify ➪ Mask ➪ Hide Selection.

Fireworks creates the appropriate mask and selects it for editing.

Fireworks technique: The contrast method

One common reason for creating a bitmap mask is to remove the background from an image, isolating the foreground figure or object. Duplicating an image and then increasing the overall contrast of the duplicate can often isolate foreground and background areas, helping to create a suitable mask.

To create a mask using the contrast method, follow these steps:

1. Duplicate the bitmap object that you want to mask, as shown in Figure 13-19. The mask will be created from the duplicate.

2. Select the duplicate and choose Commands ➪ Creative ➪ Convert to Grayscale to convert it into a grayscale image.

3. From the Add Effects menu in the Effects section of the Property inspector, choose Adjust Color ➪ Brightness/Contrast.

   Fireworks displays the Brightness/Contrast dialog box.

4. Set the Contrast slider to 100%.

5. Adjust the Brightness slider until your object resembles the desired mask as much as possible, with sharply delineated foreground and background areas (see Figure 13-20). Depending on the image you use, you may need to make a large adjustment, or none at all.

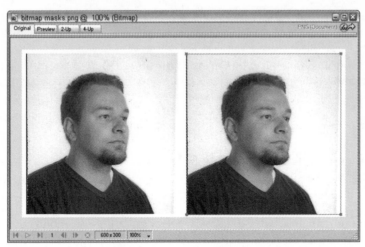

Figure 13-19: A duplicate of your original object is a good starting point for creating a mask.

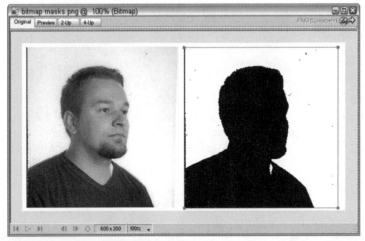

Figure 13-20: Increase the contrast to maximum, and then adjust the brightness in order to isolate foreground and background elements.

Tip

For some images, you may find that using the Levels Live Effect provides better control than the Brightness/Contrast Live Effect.

6. Choose Modify ➪ Flatten Selection to flatten your object and its Live Effects into a single bitmap object.

Caution   Your nascent bitmap mask is no longer editable after it is converted into a bitmap.

7. Use the Paint Bucket tool and/or the Eraser tool to clean up your mask, filling in and erasing pixels as required, until your mask is clear.

8. As mentioned earlier, white areas become opaque, and black areas will be transparent, so you need to invert your mask before continuing by choosing Filters ➪ Adjust Color ➪ Invert (see Figure 13-21).

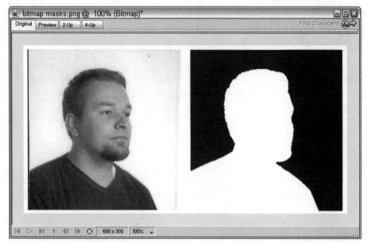

Figure 13-21: To obtain the correct mask colors, you need to invert the current selection. Now, the white will be opaque and the black will be transparent.

9. Position your mask correctly in relation to the object you are masking.

Tip   Use the commands in the Modify ➪ Align submenu, or the Align panel, to precisely align your mask and object, if required.

10. Select the mask and choose Edit ➪ Cut, or use the keyboard shortcut, Ctrl+X (Command+X), to cut the object to the clipboard.

11. Select the object that you are going to apply the mask to, and choose Edit ➪ Paste as Mask to apply the mask from the clipboard, as shown in Figure 13-22.

Figure 13-22: After the mask is applied, the background area is completely transparent.

Editing masks

After you've created a masked object — whether you used a vector or bitmap mask — the Layers panel makes it easy to select and edit it.

To edit a mask, follow these steps:

1. Choose Window ➪ Layers to display the Layers panel. It is good to keep both the Layers panel and the Property inspector in view while editing masks in order to have all the necessary controls "at your fingertips."

2. Click the mask's thumbnail in the Layers panel. Alternatively, you can select the masked object, either on the canvas or from the Layers panel, and choose Edit Mask from the Layers panel Options menu.

Tip You can also double-click the Move Handle that appears in the center of a masked object to edit its mask.

Fireworks selects the mask for editing on the canvas.

If you're editing a bitmap mask, the Property inspector says Bitmap Mask; Fireworks displays the yellow Mask Edit Border around selected masked objects, instead of the default blue outline (see Figure 13-23).

If you are editing a vector mask, the Property inspector says Vector Mask.

3. Edit the mask with any of the pixel-editing tools in the Tools panel, just as you would edit the pixels of a bitmap image. Although the mask itself is not shown on the canvas, the results of edits that you apply to the mask are shown.

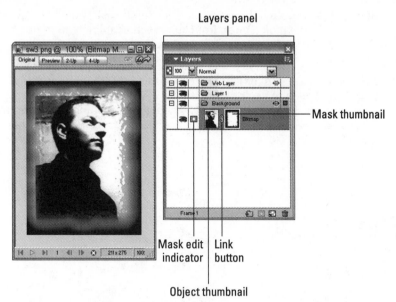

Figure 13-23: Fireworks masking controls include the Layers panel and the Property inspector.

4. Apply Live Effects or Filters to the mask, if desired.

5. If desired, convert a vector mask into a bitmap mask by choosing Modify ➪ Flatten Selection.

6. If desired, change the way the mask is applied, using the controls in the Property inspector:

- If you're editing a vector mask, choose whether to apply the mask using the Path Outline — optionally with the fill and stroke shown — or using the object's Grayscale appearance. The grayscale appearance option effectively treats the vector mask as a bitmap mask.

- For bitmap masks, choose whether to mask to the bitmap's Alpha Channel or Grayscale appearance.

7. Deselect the masked object when you're done, either by choosing Edit ➪ Deselect, or by using the keyboard shortcut, Ctrl+D (Command+D).

Tip   If you're editing a mask, you can click an empty part of the canvas to stop editing.

Your mask-editing options don't stop at directly editing the mask itself. Keep these points in mind as you edit masks:

✦ Just as you can edit a mask by selecting its thumbnail in the Layers panel, selecting the object's thumbnail enables you to edit the object independently from the mask.

✦ Click the Link button in between an object and mask thumbnail (refer to Figure 13-23) to unlink a mask from an object, enabling you to position them independently. Click again in the empty space between two unlinked thumbnails to relink them.

✦ Click and drag the Move Handle (see Figure 13-24) that appears in the center of masked objects in vector mode to position the underlying object without moving the mask. This is especially useful when cropping a bitmap with a vector mask, because it enables you to reposition the bitmap within its vector "frame."

Move handle

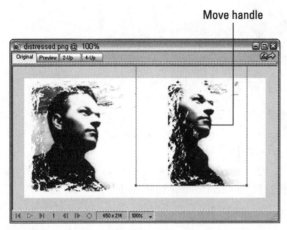

Figure 13-24: Drag the Move Handle to move the underlying image without moving the mask.

✦ To temporarily disable a mask, select the mask thumbnail or the masked object and choose Modify ➪ Mask ➪ Disable Mask, or choose Disable Mask from the Layers panel Options menu. Fireworks displays a red X through the mask's thumbnail in the Layers panel to alert you that the mask is disabled. To restore the mask, choose Modify ➪ Mask @ Enable Mask, or choose Enable Mask from the Layers panel Options menu.

✦ To remove a mask permanently — aside from the Undo command, of course — select the mask thumbnail or masked object and choose Modify ➪ Mask ➪ Delete Mask. Or, you can choose Delete Mask from the Layers panel Options menu.

Tip

A quick and easy way to delete a mask, while retaining the separate objects, is to select the mask icon in the Layers panel and drag it above or below its current position. This separates the two objects on the layer.

Masking suggestions

Masked objects are a creative and powerful tool that you can experiment with again and again. Here are some suggestions to try:

✦ Apply Live Effects or styles to vector objects, and then use them as masks.

✦ Alter the Stroke or Fill settings of a vector mask.

✦ Use a text object as a vector mask.

✦ Apply texture fills to vector masks.

✦ Apply Filters to bitmap masks.

Cross-Reference

The Fade Image command, located at Commands ➪ Creative ➪ Fade Image, allows you to apply masks to images with the click of a button. For more information on this command, see Chapter 26.

Fireworks technique: Quick photo edges

Often, when you are working with a bitmap object in Fireworks, you want to crop the image to a smaller size. Although you could use the Crop tool to crop out a section or make a pixel selection and copy out that area, those techniques are destructive. You alter the bitmap object permanently. For example, if later you want to add back 100 pixels, or add 10 pixels all around the image so that you can feather the edges, you're out of luck. That information has been thrown away.

Masked objects provide a way around this, enabling you not only to crop an image nondestructively, but also to use Live Effects and other methods to create some nice border effects. Modifying a vector object and using it as an alpha mask for an image gives you fine control over your image's shape and transparency. To create an image border, open an image in Fireworks and follow these steps:

1. Use the drawing tools to draw a rectangle on top of your image, but make the rectangle a bit smaller than the image itself (see Figure 13-25). The area outside the rectangle will be invisible after masking.

2. Color the rectangle black by selecting it and choosing black from the fill color well at the bottom of the Tools panel.

You may want to experiment at this point, giving your shape various gradient fills or textures. Remember that black areas are completely visible in your final image, whereas white areas are not. The lighter the areas in between these extremes, the more transparent they become.

Figure 13-25: Use a rectangle to block out the area of your photograph that you want to keep.

3. Select the rectangle and feather its edges by choosing Feather from the Edge option list in the Fill section of the Property inspector.

Pause at this point, if you like, and experiment with applying Live Effects, styles, Filters, or various strokes to your shape, instead of feathering it. If you have Photoshop 5.x's filters installed, the Distort, Brush Strokes, Sketch, and Stylize filters are good choices. If you use Alien Skin's Eye Candy, the Jiggle feature is a great choice, too.

4. Position the mask correctly in relation to the object you're masking.

5. Select the mask and choose Edit ➪ Cut, or use the keyboard shortcut, Ctrl+X (Command+X), to cut it to the clipboard.

6. Select the object that you're masking and choose Edit ➪ Paste as Mask to apply your mask to it.

Tip   The Paste as Mask command is also available in another menu location: Modify ➪ Mask ➪ Paste as Mask.

The masked object is now the same size and shape as the black-colored shape that you drew on top of it, as shown in Figure 13-26.

Original image   Feathered rectangle   Feathered circle
                    vector mask   vector mask

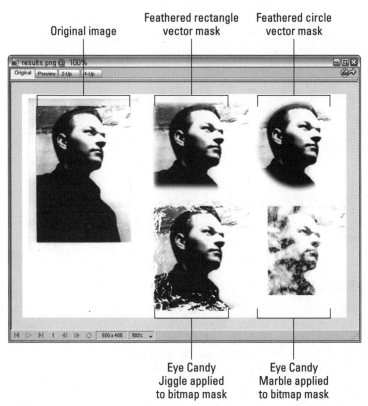

Eye Candy   Eye Candy
Jiggle applied   Marble applied
to bitmap mask   to bitmap mask

Figure 13-26: A selection of photo edge effects created by applying
Live Effects to a vector object and using it as an alpha mask for an image.

Examining Opacity and Blending

The primary tools in compositing images are opacity and blending. Altering these
properties can literally merge two images together. You can make one image show
through the other by giving the top image a lower opacity setting, or you can use a
blending mode to make them steal colors from each other. A bitmap object or pixel
selection that appears to float above a background can be seamlessly integrated in
just a few short steps.

Tip Feathering objects before compositing them often provides good results. With a
softer edge, removing the borderline between the two images is easier.
Experiment with blending Fireworks strokes, texture fills, and effects.

After you select an object in Fireworks, you can either use the Layers panel, or the
Property inspector, to control its opacity and blending (see Figure 13-27).

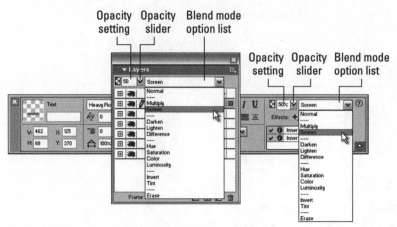

Figure 13-27: The opacity and blending controls affect the selected object(s).

Controlling opacity

As you make an object more transparent, more of the background shows through. This can go a long way toward integrating two images. While the opacity and blending options are available from both the Layers panel and the Property inspector, I'll refer to the Property inspector when describing their functionality as it's more likely that the Property inspector will always be visible in your panel layout. Keep in mind that modifying the settings on the Layers panel gives you the exact same results.

Controlling opacity in Fireworks is easy. Select an object and then slide the opacity slider. A setting of 100 equals no transparency, completely opaque. A setting of 1, with the slider all the way down, brings an object as close to invisible as possible in Fireworks (see Figure 13-28). If you do want to make an image completely invisible, you can type a zero (0) in the opacity box and press Enter (Return).

 Caution If you specify an opacity setting without an object selected, you set a default opacity for objects that you create from that point on. If you accidentally set it to 10 percent or less, you might not even be able to see some of the objects that you draw. If this happens, you know where to go to change it back. Deselect all objects with Edit ⇨ Deselect and move the opacity slider in the Layers panel back to 100.

Using blending modes

Blending modes manipulate the color of pixels in a foreground image and the color of pixels beneath them in the background image in a variety of ways to blend the two together. Before you start using blending modes, here's the terminology that you need to know:

- ✦ **Blend color:** The color of the selected object, typically a foreground object
- ✦ **Base color:** The color beneath the selected object, typically a background object
- ✦ **Result color:** The color resulting from the blend of the blend color and base color

For the sake of simplicity, this discussion primarily uses foreground, background, and result.

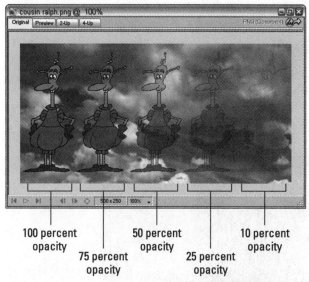

100 percent opacity   75 percent opacity   50 percent opacity   25 percent opacity   10 percent opacity

Figure 13-28: Vary the opacity level of an object with the Property inspector's opacity slider. The fellow on the left is 100 percent opaque. On the extreme right, he's 10 percent opaque.

As you've seen earlier, Fireworks enables you to alter the opacity of an object at any time with the Opacity slider in the Property inspector. The opacity of an object also effects the way it blends.

A blending mode applies to an individual object or to an entire group. If you give an object a certain blending mode and then group it, the blending mode disappears because the object is given the group's blending mode instead (although ungrouping restores the individual object's blending mode). If you're working extensively with blending modes, instead of grouping your objects, you might want to use layers to separate and organize your objects. This also enables you to stack blending modes for interesting effects, as objects on each layer blend into objects on the layer below.

Depending on what kind of object you have selected, the blending modes work in one of the following ways:

✦ **Vectors:** The blending mode affects the selected object.

✦ **Bitmaps:** If you have a marquee selection drawn, the blending mode affects the selection of pixels. If you don't have a marquee selection drawn, the blending mode affects the tools that you use from then on.

Select an object and modify its blending mode setting in the Property inspector. If an object isn't selected, modifying the blending mode creates a new default blending mode for objects that you create from that point on.

Investigating blending modes

Blending modes can be confusing and strangely mathematical. The best way to understand them is to compare their results, which is what Figure 13-29 does.

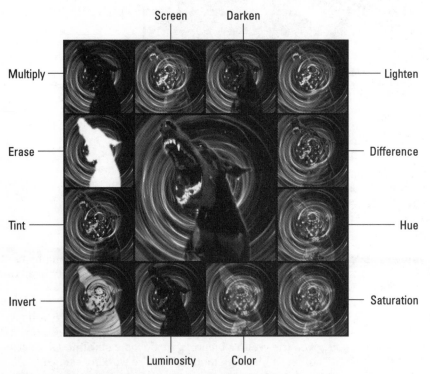

Figure 13-29: Comparing the 12 blending modes that Fireworks offers, with the unaltered image in the center

Cross-Reference You can see the dogs in Figure 13-29 in full color in the color insert.

Twelve mysterious blending modes can seem like much at first, but most modes have an opposite partner or other related modes. After you understand one mode of a group, you're well on your way to understanding them all.

References to the foreground or background color refer to the color at the pixel level, not at the object level. Individual pixels of the foreground and background objects are compared.

Multiply and Screen

Multiply mode multiplies the foreground color with the background color. It can give your blended image a deeper, richer tone. The result color is always darker. If the foreground or background color is black, the result will be black; if one of them is white, Multiply has no effect.

Screen mode is basically the opposite of Multiply. The result color is a ghostly, faded blend. It works by inverting the foreground color and then multiplying it with the background color. Whereas Multiply always results in a darker color, Screen always results in a lighter one. If either the foreground or background is white, the result color will be white. If either is black, Screen has no effect.

Darken, Lighten, and Difference

Darken compares the foreground and background colors and keeps the darkest one, whereas *Lighten* does the opposite; the foreground and background color is compared and only the lightest remains.

Difference compares the foreground color and the background color, and it subtracts the darker color from the lighter color. It can result in some surprising color choices.

Hue, Saturation, Color, and Luminosity

Hue combines the hue value of the foreground color with the luminance and saturation of the background color. Essentially, you get the foreground color, but as dark or light as the background.

Saturation combines the saturation of the foreground color with the luminance and hue of the background color.

Color combines the hue and saturation of the foreground color with the luminance of the background color. Grays are preserved, so this is a good way to add color to a black-and-white photograph, or to tint color photographs.

Luminosity combines the luminance of the foreground color with the hue and saturation of the background color.

Invert and Tint

Invert and Tint don't bother with the foreground color at all. With Invert, the foreground object's colors are replaced with inverted background colors. With Tint, gray is added to the background color to create the result.

Erase

Erase removes all background color pixels, leaving the canvas color.

Fireworks technique: Simulating a light source with blending modes

One key to creating a good three-dimensional look is providing a simulated light source. Blending an object that uses a black-and-white gradient fill into another object mimics the interplay of light and shadows. In other words, the image has a controllable light to dark range added. This enables you to adjust the "lighting" so that it looks appropriate with your particular graphic.

To use blending modes to simulate light and shadow and create objects such as those shown in Figure 13-30, follow these steps:

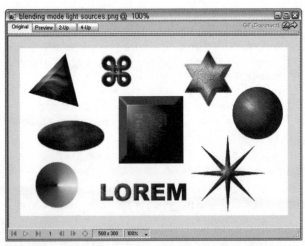

Figure 13-30: Get the lights: Blend a gradient-filled object and adjust the gradient to simulate a light source.

 The color insert provides another look at light source effects.

1. Create a new, empty layer by clicking the New Layer button on the Layers panel. Double-click the new layer in the layers list and name it **Object1**.

2. Using one of the geometric drawing tools (Rectangle, Ellipse, or Polygon), draw an object on the Object1 layer. This object is your base object (not the light source).

3. In the Fill section of the Property inspector, give your object a Solid fill and add a texture, such as Parchment, to it. Set the texture to 100 percent.

Tip Alternatively, you might also use a Pattern fill, instead of a Solid fill with a texture.

4. Choose Edit ➪ Clone to create a copy of your object directly on top of the original.

5. From the Fill section of the Property inspector, choose a Radial gradient fill for the new object with the White, Black color preset. Remove the texture (if any) by sliding the Amount of texture slider to 0 percent.

6. Change the blending mode in the Property inspector to Multiply and alter the Opacity setting to taste, depending on the color of your original object.

7. Note the Fill modification handles that appear on your object. Drag the round starting handle of the gradient fill to reposition the gradient so that the center of the white portion is located where you want the brightest "light" to fall. Slightly up and to the left is a good choice. If desired, drag the square-ending handle to adjust the angle of the gradient. In a sense, you are adjusting the light source.

Tip You may want to use the Select Behind tool to select your original object — the one with the texture or Pattern fill — and apply one of the bevel Live Effects. Adjusting the bevel height can make a big difference to how realistically 3D your object looks.

8. Select both objects and position them, if necessary. Lock the Object1 layer and don't put other objects on it. Both of the objects it contains must be moved together, but they cannot be grouped, or they will share the same blending mode and the lighting effect is lost. Keeping them on their own layer makes it easy to use Single Layer Mode to isolate them during later editing.

The Radial gradient was used in the previous example, but you can get some really great effects (such as a starburst of light) by applying different gradient types. Moreover, you can adjust the subtlety of the lighting by editing the gradient and toning down the pure white to a more muted gray. Feel free to experiment with different blending modes, as well.

Cross-Reference For more about gradients, see Chapter 11.

Fireworks Technique: Feathering Selections

A common image-editing task is to remove a subject from one image and place that subject in another document against another background. Feathering your selection can make this process much more forgiving, hiding ragged edges and stray background pixels that come along for the ride.

To copy a foreground image from one document and place it into another, follow these steps:

1. Open your source and target documents in Fireworks. The source document should have a foreground element. The target document should contain a suitable background.

2. In the source document, use the Lasso or Polygon Lasso tools to make a pixel selection (see Figure 13-31). Select your foreground element as accurately as possible.

3. Choose Select ⇨ Feather, enter **10** in the Feather Selection dialog box, and then click OK. This feathers your selection, which hides any rough edges.

4. Choose either Edit ⇨ Copy, or the keyboard shortcut, Ctrl+C (Command+C), to copy the pixel selection to the Clipboard.

5. Switch to your target document and choose either Edit ⇨ Paste, or the keyboard shortcut, Ctrl+V (Command+V), to paste the pixel selection from the clipboard into your document as a new bitmap object.

6. Move the subject around until it's placed where you want it.

Figure 13-31: Copying a feathered pixel selection into another document

Fireworks Technique: Applied Compositing

Presenting separate elements as an integrated image often means applying a few different compositing techniques. In the following example, you use masked objects, opacity, blending modes, and layering, along with texture fills and drop shadows to unify seven or eight separate objects into one final, composited image.

Cross-Reference

If you want to take a look at the final result of the techniques in this section before you start, turn to the color insert.

Starting from the bottom of the stacking order, the first step is a canvas color; in this case, it's black, as shown in Figure 13-32. Only a small portion of the canvas shows along the bottom of the final image. The background object has a mesh texture fill, which shows through other elements later and provides a feeling of depth. It also has a red drop shadow effect that softens the transition between it and the canvas. Avoiding straight lines and obvious borders — or hiding them — helps to make separate objects appear to be one.

Background object

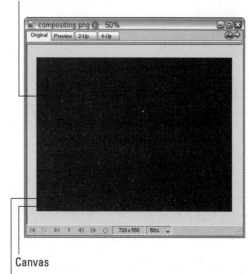

Canvas

Drop shadow

Figure 13-32: This textured background shows through translucent objects that are placed on it, whereas a drop shadow blends it into the black-colored canvas.

The next layer up contains a red and black pattern. In order to blend it with the background object, use an alpha mask to make the red and black pattern fade from opaque at the top to fully transparent at the bottom. This can be achieved by combining it into a masked object, with the mask shown in Figure 13-33. Where the mask is white, the underlying object is opaque; where it's black, the object is completely transparent. Shades of gray provide varying degrees of transparency.

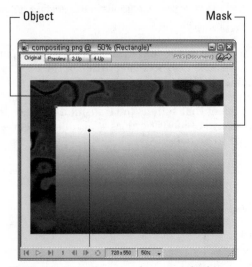

Figure 13-33: When used as a mask, this gradient-filled vector object makes the red and black pattern appear to fade away from top to bottom.

Combining the mask and object into the masked object shown in Figure 13-34 is as simple as selecting the gradient, choosing Edit ➪ Cut, and then choosing Modify ➪ Mask ➪ Paste as Mask. The background object is now showing through the mask. All the objects appear to be part of the same image, rather than distinct objects. Of course, the vector mask is still editable.

The three separate variations on the Fireworks logo in Figure 13-35 are on separate layers. The Big Crinkley Logo has holes in it where the background shows through, and its Bevel effect raises it off the canvas and provides a feeling of depth. The Real Logo — quickly purloined from the Fireworks Web site or somewhere similar — looks a little ragged, but will be mostly covered by the Hand-Drawn Logo, so that only its colors show through. The drop shadow and inner bevel applied to the Hand-Drawn Logo adds more depth and provides a nice transition between it and the Real Logo beneath it.

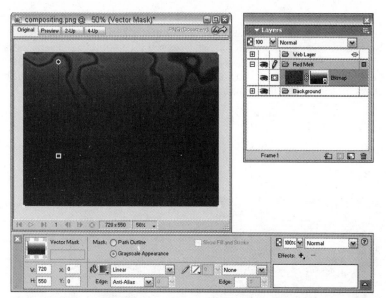

Figure 13-34: Moving the mask's gradient fill handle adjusts the opacity of the underlying object.

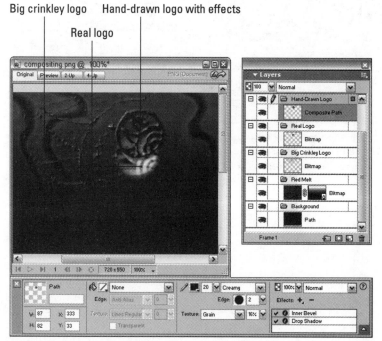

Figure 13-35: These foreground elements stack nicely because of their transparent holes and the depth provided by drop shadows and bevel effects.

The leathery look of the bottom half of the document seems as if it's a good place to put some text. In Figure 13-36, you can see that my chosen typeface—Heavy Rotation—is structured to look as if it's been pressed into something. A 50 percent opacity setting for the text object allows some of the underlying texture to show through and adds to the inset look of the text. Changing the text object's blending mode to Screen completes the illusion; inverting the foreground color and multiplying it with the background color to blend them.

50 percent opacity

100 percent opacity

Figure 13-36: The opacity setting and blending modes in the Property inspector or Layers panel help to sink the basic text object (top) into the underlying texture of the background (bottom).

The final product—completed using masked objects, opacity settings, blending modes, and layers along with texture fills and effects, such as drop shadows—is shown in Figure 13-37.

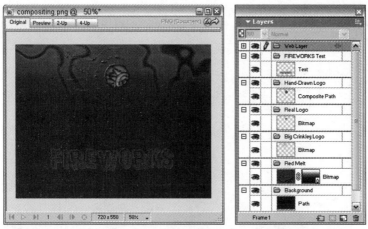

Figure 13-37: A number of compositing techniques were used to combine multiple objects into this integrated, multilayer image.

Summary

Fireworks provides lots of options for combining many types of objects to create more complex objects or special effects. When you're arranging or compositing objects in Fireworks, keep these points in mind:

✦ You can use layers to organize your document, enabling easier selection and editing of similar objects.

✦ The Layers panel is your control center for working with layers.

✦ You can choose to work with individual layers in a variety of ways, including hiding, showing, and locking layers.

✦ Layers are also containers for object sublayers. Show, hide, move, copy, and delete sublayers using the same techniques you use with layers.

✦ The ruler, grid, and guides are all available to help you precisely position objects on the canvas.

✦ Objects can be grouped, and a group behaves as if it's one object.

✦ Masks give you amazing control over alpha transparency.

✦ Blending modes enable you to blend objects quickly and easily.

✦ Multiple compositing techniques can be utilized together to integrate many objects into a seamless image.

The next chapter looks at capturing and importing images into Fireworks.

✦　　✦　　✦

Coordinating Workflow

◆ ◆ ◆ ◆

◆ ◆ ◆ ◆

Web design is an ongoing process, not a single event. Part IV is dedicated to helping you streamline your workflow, as you acquire images via scanning or importing, manipulate them in Fireworks, and then optimize them on export, either for the Web or for import into other creative tools, such as Macromedia Director or Flash.

Although it's true that Web graphic design is an art form, it's also a business — and one element of that business is applying a consistent look and feel to each element of a particular Web site. Fireworks styles enable you to save formatting instructions from one object and apply them to other objects again and again. The Library panel is a place to store *symbols,* objects you use frequently, such as logos and navigation buttons. Fireworks symbols further minimize repetitive work by linking similar objects so that changes need be made only once. Chapter 18 describes how Fireworks MX helps you update and maintain your graphics through the URL panel and the surprising Find and Replace feature. The final chapter in Part IV covers the greatly expanded Command feature set with its new Flash movie interface capability and the History panel, useful for constructing simple reusable commands from your actions.

Capturing and Importing

M oving information easily, from one application to another, has a great effect on your workflow and productivity. In addition to creating objects from scratch in Fireworks, you can also quickly and easily include elements created in a traditional drawing program, such as Macromedia FreeHand, or stock photos from a clip art collection, or photographic prints directly from a page scanner or digital camera.

From a design perspective, incorporating elements from a wide variety of sources gives your documents depth and contrast, and makes them more interesting and pleasing to the eye. You can combine and contrast simple vector shapes with detailed photographs and organic bitmap textures. After these elements are incorporated into Fireworks, they're fair game for Fireworks' unique drawing tools and comprehensive export features.

This chapter begins with a discussion of the issues involved in accessing image capture hardware, such as a scanner or digital camera within Fireworks. You look briefly at screen captures and explore how you can drag and drop, or copy and paste from other applications. You look at importing bitmap and vector art files. Finally, you examine some of the issues involved in importing animations.

Introducing Image Captures

Acquiring an image from a hardware device, such as a page scanner or digital camera, is an almost magical process — unless your hardware and software aren't talking to each other. In Fireworks, getting this conversation started involves an industry standard called *TWAIN*. TWAIN is a fully cross-platform method that enables scanners, digital cameras, and other devices to acquire images. On a Macintosh, Fireworks also supports Photoshop Acquire plug-ins. If your scanner or digital camera uses a Photoshop Acquire plug-in, see "Installing Photoshop Acquire plug-ins," later in this chapter.

Note What does TWAIN stand for? It's rumored to be an acronym for "Technology Without An Interesting Name." It might also have started as a play on bringing software and hardware together, as in "ne'er the twain shall meet." For its part, the TWAIN Working Group, which created the standard, claims that it's only a name and has no meaning at all. For more information about TWAIN, visit the TWAIN Working Group on the Web at http://www.twain.org.

Examining TWAIN-compliant devices

When you start Fireworks, if a TWAIN module or Photoshop Acquire plug-in (Mac only) is available, a Scan command will be added to the File menu, as shown in Figure 14-1. If you have multiple TWAIN-compliant devices connected to your computer, you can select any one of them from within Fireworks.

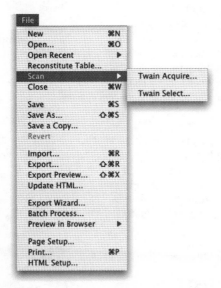

Figure 14-1: Fireworks adds a Scan submenu to the File menu if a TWAIN module or Photoshop Acquire plug-in is available.

Note If you have a scanner or digital camera and the Scan submenu is not available, verify that your capture hardware is correctly installed and that its software is current. If necessary, consult the device's documentation for details.

To select a TWAIN source in Fireworks, follow these steps:

1. Choose File ➪ Scan ➪ Twain Source.

Fireworks displays the Select a source dialog box (see Figure 14-2).

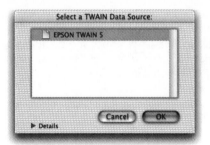

Figure 14-2: In Fireworks, select a TWAIN source from which to capture images in the Select a source dialog box.

2. Choose the TWAIN-compliant device from which you want Fireworks to acquire an image. Click OK when you're done.

If you haven't purchased a scanner or digital camera yet, but are planning to do so, visit the Fireworks Support Center by choosing Help ➪ Fireworks Support Center. Refer to the Fireworks TechNotes for a list of hardware that has been tested and found to work well with Fireworks.

Installing Photoshop Acquire plug-ins (Macintosh only)

On a Macintosh, Photoshop Acquire plug-ins provide another way to interface with a scanner or digital camera. Many devices — especially those that aren't TWAIN-compliant — generally come with a Photoshop Acquire plug-in. To use one in Fireworks, you must do one of the following:

✦ Install the Photoshop Acquire plug-in into Fireworks' Plug-Ins folder, found within the Fireworks program folder.

The Fireworks program folder is typically found at C:\Program Files\Macromedia\ Fireworks MX on Windows-based computers, and at Macintosh HD:Applications: Macromedia Fireworks MX: on the Mac.

✦ Install the Photoshop Acquire plug-in into your Photoshop Plug-Ins folder or another folder on your computer. Then, in Fireworks, choose Edit ➪ Preferences (Fireworks ➪ Preferences on OS X), select the Folders tab (option list on the Macintosh), check Photoshop Plug-Ins, and then browse to and select the folder that contains the Acquire plug-in.

You can also refer Fireworks to plug-ins that are located in an external folder by placing a shortcut (alias) to that folder into Fireworks' Plug-Ins folder.

After following either of these methods, Fireworks will add a Scan submenu to the File menu. Select your Photoshop Acquire plug-in from that menu to initiate a scan.

Some Photoshop Acquire plug-ins may not function correctly with Fireworks because they are generally marketed and tested first and foremost for use with Photoshop. If your Acquire plug-in doesn't work, check the manufacturer's Web site for an updated version that may be compatible with Fireworks, or investigate whether your hardware device is TWAIN-compliant.

Scanning Pages

A *page scanner* enables you to capture printed documents — from drawings to artwork to photographs. You can scan an image and use it in your Fireworks document unaltered, or you can transform it a little or a lot with Fireworks' drawing tools, effects, and plug-ins, and then export it for publishing on the Web.

Scanning for print publishing requires a different approach than scanning for online publishing. For the print publisher, the online image is part of the process and not an end in itself. Because Fireworks is almost exclusively a Web-publishing tool, this book looks at things from the perspective of the online publisher.

Scanning an image is the procedure of literally converting an image from a printed image to an online image (one that's viewed on a computer). Most of the confusion in scanning comes from mixing up print and online concepts, especially when it comes to resolution. *Resolution* basically means "the number of dots," which is important to scanning because print and online images fundamentally consist entirely of dots.

Resolution is measured differently for printed images than it is for online images. Printed resolution is a measure of how many dots are in an inch of the image, which is expressed as *dots per inch*, or *dpi*. An example is 300 dpi. Online resolution is a measure of how many dots are in the entire image, measured in *X* pixels by *Y* pixels. An example is 640×480 pixels. If you select an image in Fireworks and choose Modify ➪ Image Size, Fireworks displays the Image Size dialog box (see Figure 14-3), which clearly shows the relationship between online and printed resolution. If you specify 100 dpi, a 500×400 pixel image will have a print size of 5×4 inches.

The following list describes some of the resolutions that you'll encounter as you scan:

✦ **The resolution of the printed image, in dpi:** The upper limit of detail that the printed image contains.

✦ **The scan resolution, in dpi:** Before you scan an image, you must specify a scan resolution, which specifies how the scanner should translate the printed image, measured in inches, into an online image, measured in pixels. A scan resolution of 100 dpi tells the scanner to split each inch of the printed image into 100 parts, and make those 100 parts into 100 pixels of online image. You'll look more closely at scan resolution later in the chapter.

✦ **The scanner's maximum optical resolution, in dpi:** The upper limit of the scanner's ability to look at something it's scanning. A scanner with a maximum optical resolution of 300 dpi can split an inch of your printed image into 300 parts. Detail finer than that cannot be captured with that scanner.

✦ **The scanner's interpolated resolution, in dpi:** The upper limit of the scanner's ability to guess at details it can't see. A 300-dpi scanner that is asked to scan at a resolution of 600 dpi will guess at what the missing pixels should be. This is similar to resampling an online image to a higher resolution and generally should be avoided.

✦ **The online image's resolution, in pixels:** Because each pixel of an online image is represented by one screen-pixel location, an online image's resolution is the same as its size. A 640×480-pixel image has a resolution of 640×480 pixels.

✦ **The display resolution, in pixels:** A computer display might have a resolution of 800×600 pixels or 1024×768 pixels. How big the display is in inches is unknown and, therefore, unimportant.

Note   A common misconception is that computer displays have a standard resolution of 72 dpi. Early Macintosh displays did have a 72-dpi resolution, and it became a standard because Macs dominated the publishing industry, and they all had the same size and type display. Today, computer displays come in a wide variety of sizes and resolutions. A 19-inch display with a resolution of 640×480 pixels has a drastically different number of dots per inch than a 14-inch display with a resolution of 1024×768 pixels.

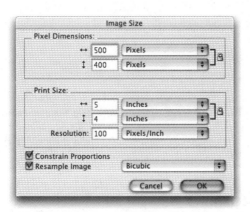

Figure 14-3: Fireworks' Image Size dialog box shows the relationship between an image's online resolution (pixel size) and print resolution.

Examining the Scanning Process

When you initiate a scan in Fireworks, a dialog box that's specific to your scanner or Acquire plug-in is displayed so that you can specify the settings that you want for the particular scan. Some scanners offer a choice of different interfaces. One interface may be a quick and simple dialog box with few options, while another interface may contain an almost bewildering array of options for the advanced user. Some scanners also offer a supplementary wizard-based interface, such as the one shown in Figure 14-4, allowing you to specify options in plain English. For example, instead of choosing a specific descreen setting — to compensate for the patterns inherent in some types of printing — you might only have to specify that your original is from a magazine or newspaper. The software then chooses the correct setting for you.

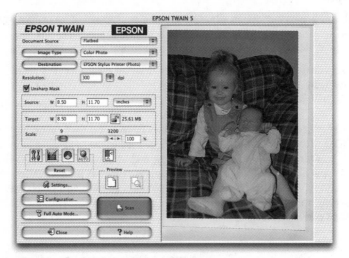

Figure 14-4: Epson's TWAIN scanner driver is tailored for beginners or advanced users and enables you to choose scanning options in plain English from option lists.

Chances are that you'll want to learn to use your scanner's advanced interface so that you can exert a greater degree of control over the settings that you use and, therefore, get the best results. The most important of these settings are the scan resolution and the color depth. We'll look at them closely, and then look briefly at some of the other options that might be presented.

Selecting a scan resolution

In simple terms, the *scan resolution* that you choose determines the size of the resulting online image — and that's all. Table 14-1 shows the relationship between the size of the original, printed image and the size of the resulting, online image at various scan resolutions.

Table 14-1
Scan Results at Various Scan Resolutions

Printed Image Size (inches)	Scan Resolution (dpi)	Online Image Size (pixels)
5×7	10 dpi	50×70
5×7	20 dpi	100×140
5×7	50 dpi	250×350
5×7	100 dpi	500×700
5×7	150 dpi	750×1,050
5×7	200 dpi	1,000×1,400
5×7	300 dpi	1,500×2,100

Note that each of the following three important pieces of information is measured in different ways:

✦ **Printed image:** Measured in inches. In print publishing, the inch is the constant. If you create an 8.5×11-inch page layout and print it at different print resolutions, it will still be an 8.5×11-inch page layout, but it will have a different number of dots on each page.

✦ **Scan resolution:** Measured in dots per inch. This is the translation of the printed image (in inches) to the online image (in dots, or pixels). How many pixels of online image do you want for each inch of printed image? Fifty? That's a scan resolution of 50 dpi.

✦ **Online image:** Measured in pixels. In online publishing, the pixel, or dot, is the constant. If you create a 640×480-pixel image and view it at different screen resolutions, it will still be a 640×480-pixel image, but it will be a different size in inches on each screen.

Determining the ideal resolution

To determine an ideal scan resolution, follow these steps:

1. Decide how wide you want your online image to be, in pixels.

2. Divide that number by the width of the printed image, in inches.

   The result is your scan resolution in dots per inch.

Tip

If you're not sure how big you want the final image to be, overestimate rather than underestimate. Making an image smaller later in the process is not as detrimental to its quality as trying to make it larger. A scan resolution of 100 dpi is a good place to start, because it makes the translation from inches to pixels easy to calculate. A 3×5-inch printed image will be 300×500 pixels after scanning. If 300×500 ends up being too big or too small, adjust the scan resolution from there.

Running out of printed resolution

When selecting a scan resolution, keep in mind the resolution of the printed image that you're scanning. At the point when the scan resolution is equal to either the resolution of the printed image, or the maximum optical resolution of your scanner, increasing the scan resolution stops capturing more detail. Consider the following examples:

✦ If your printed image was printed at 200 dpi, a scan resolution of 300 dpi will not add detail that isn't already there. Scan the image at 200 dpi and resample it to a larger size in Fireworks, if necessary.

✦ If your scanner's best optical resolution is 300 dpi, you won't be able to capture more than 300 dots for each inch of the printed image. Many scanners allow you to choose a higher scan resolution than they can really achieve, and then the scanner "interpolates," or fills in, the missing information with a best guess. This is equivalent to scanning the image at your scanner's maximum optical resolution and resampling it in Fireworks, if necessary.

Choosing a color depth

Choose a *color depth* based on the type of document you are scanning. Typically, a scanner has three main color settings for you to choose from: line art, grayscale, and color. You may also be able to specify bit depth for grayscale and color scans. Higher bit depths scan a higher number of colors and are more accurate, but also result in a larger file size.

Examining line art

Line art refers to black-and-white images that don't contain shades of gray. This might include cartoons, blueprints, or diagrams. Line art is scanned with one-bit color depth. In other words, each pixel is either on or off: black or white.

Exploring grayscale images

Grayscale images contain actual shades of gray. Typically, a grayscale setting will be 8-bit, meaning that your image will have 256 different shades of gray. This is the best setting for black-and-white photographs.

Looking at color images

The *color setting* is obviously used for scanning any sort of color image. Typically, this is 24-bit color, but some scanners have a 36-bit setting. Twenty-four-bit color means that each pixel can be any one of 16.7 million colors. A 36-bit scanner can record 68.7 billion colors. Scan at your scanner's best setting and then remove extra colors when you export your image as a Graphics Interchange Format (GIF), a Joint Photographic Experts Group (JPEG), or a Portable Network Graphics (PNG) for use on the Web.

 For more about color depth, see Chapter 7.

Setting other options

Consult the documentation that came with your scanner for specific information on other options or features that your scanner has.

Here are some of the common options you may encounter:

✦ **Preview window:** A window in which you can see a thumbnail of the original before you perform the actual scan. You can usually draw a border in this window to limit the scan to the portion of the scanner window. Some scanning interfaces will draw a best guess selection themselves, which you can adjust as required.

✦ **Brightness and Contrast:** Adjust these only if your original is exceptionally bright or dark, or lacking in contrast.

✦ **Image enhancements:** For example, dust, scratch, or moiré removal.

✦ **Orientation:** You may be able to specify that the scanner flip the image vertically or horizontally.

✦ **Settings:** For different types of original documents, such as transparencies and slides.

✦ **Gamma correction:** Most Macs are set to a gamma correction of 1.8, whereas most Windows machines use 2.2.

✦ **Descreen:** A descreen setting enables you to scan newspaper or magazine clippings with better results.

Scanning directly into Fireworks

To scan directly into Fireworks, follow these steps:

1. Place the original document onto your scanner's scanning bed.

2. If you're using a TWAIN source and have multiple TWAIN-compliant devices, choose File ⇨ Scan ⇨ Twain Source and select the appropriate device.

3. If you're using TWAIN, choose File ⇨ Scan ⇨ TWAIN Acquire. If you're using a Photoshop Acquire plug-in (Macintosh only), choose File ⇨ Scan and the name of that plug-in.

   Your scanner's options dialog box appears.

4. In the scanner's options dialog box, adjust the settings for the scan, specifying resolution, color depth, and other settings, as required. Consult your scanner's documentation for specific information about the options you're presented with. Click OK after you're done.

The device begins scanning and then sends the image to Fireworks. When the scan is completed, the image appears as a new document in Fireworks.

Looking at Digital Cameras

Increasingly, images are staying completely digital. The advantages of creating images for the Web using a digital camera are obvious: no film or printing expenses, nearly instant access to the photographs, no loss of quality as photos are printed and then scanned. Whether you consider yourself a great photographer or not, graphics professionals are increasingly called upon to get behind the camera, even if only to grab a couple of quick snapshots for the company intranet.

Some of the same considerations that apply to scanning also apply to using images from a digital camera. You use TWAIN or a Photoshop Acquire plug-in to interface with the camera, and you are presented with a dialog box full of options that help you transfer the images from the camera into Fireworks.

Cameras differ from scanners in that you don't have to worry about print resolution because no printing is involved. Resolution is specified — just like online images — in terms of width by height in pixels. Generally, you'll want to use the camera at its highest resolution in order to get the best quality image and leave yourself the most editing options in Fireworks. A larger image can be made smaller without losing quality, but the reverse is not true. For the most part, though, images on the Web tend to be smaller, rather than larger, and photos from even a basic digital camera are often 640×480 pixels or larger, plenty big enough for most Web applications.

Capturing images for use in Fireworks

To capture images from a digital camera directly into Fireworks, follow these steps:

1. Take some pictures.

Tip If your camera supports it, create pictures in a lossless file format, rather than a lossy format, such as JPEG. JPEG images should — whenever possible — be considered a final product only. They will display noticeable artifacting when exported from Fireworks.

2. Connect the camera to your computer according to the camera's documentation. Cameras that connect with a universal serial bus (USB) can be hot plugged into a Windows or Macintosh machine and accessed immediately. If your camera uses a legacy interface, you will have to shut down your computer before making connections.

3. Run the software that came with your digital camera to transfer the pictures you have taken to your computer's hard drive.

If your camera software is like most, it begins transferring the images and you see thumbnails of the images that it contains while they transfer, as shown in Figure 14-5.

Figure 14-5: Digital cameras often show thumbnails of their images as they transfer them, as seen in Apple's free iPhoto software.

When the camera's interface software has finished transferring all the images, you're ready to choose which images you want to transfer into Fireworks, as shown in Figure 14-6.

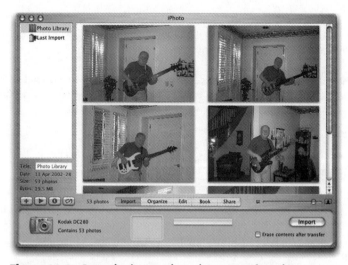

Figure 14-6: Once the images have been transferred to your computer, pick and choose which images to transfer into Fireworks through the camera's software, or in this case, Apple's iPhoto software.

Exploring digital camcorders

Many digital camcorders offer a still photo mode, making them an alternative to regular, digital still cameras. This mode captures one frame at the camera's highest resolution and typically writes this image onto seven seconds of tape, creating a much better image than a single freeze-frame of video. An advantage to using a camcorder rather than a camera is that a camcorder can typically store 500 still images on an hour-long, digital video tape with one battery charge, whereas most still cameras max out well below 100 photos and eat batteries with a vengeance.

Digital camcorders can also transfer their images to a computer or another camcorder at high speeds, using an IEEE 1394 interface, often called FireWire or i.Link. FireWire interfaces are standard on all Macintosh computers, and they are included on many Windows machines from Sony, Hewlett-Packard, and other manufacturers. FireWire interfaces can also be added to most computers with an add-in card. Connecting the camcorder simply involves hot plugging the camcorder and the computer together with the correct cable. Most camcorders have a 4-pin IEEE 1394 connector, whereas most computers offer a 6-pin connector. No special converter is required, though, just an inexpensive cable with a 4-pin connector on one end and a 6-pin connector on the other end.

Although you can't transfer images from a digital camcorder directly into Fireworks as you can with a scanner or still camera, many camcorders and FireWire interfaces include the necessary software. Typically, the output from the camera is presented in real time in an onscreen window. This preview enables you to pick and choose which images you would like to transfer from tape to an image file on disk.

After an image is stored as an image file on your hard disk—usually as a TIFF, PICT, or BMP—you can easily open it in Fireworks. Because the images are always stored digitally, they do not lose quality as they move from tape to disk.

Caution   Make sure to use still video mode when capturing still images with a digital camcorder. Still frames of a moving video are only half of an interlaced image and will make poor quality photographs.

Inserting Objects from Other Applications

So far, I've showed how you can import a document from external hardware or a screen capture, but what if the elements that you want to include are sitting right there on your computer screen, but within another application? Fireworks has two methods for directly inserting elements from other applications: copy and paste, and drag and drop.

Copying and pasting

The simplest and most widely used method for moving information from one application to another is with the system clipboard and the commands Cut, Copy, and Paste.

You can paste the following formats into Fireworks:

✦ Bitmap images

✦ Vector art from Macromedia FreeHand or Adobe Illustrator

✦ ASCII text

To copy from another application and paste into Fireworks, follow these steps:

1. In the source application, select the object(s) or pixel area that you want to copy.

2. Choose Edit ➪ Copy, or use the keyboard shortcut, Ctrl+C (Command+C).

   Your selection is copied to the clipboard.

3. In Fireworks, choose either Edit ➪ Paste, or the keyboard shortcut, Ctrl+V (Command+V).

4. If your source selection has a different print resolution than your Fireworks document, Fireworks displays a dialog box, shown in Figure 14-7, and offers to resample the pasted image to match the target document. Choose Resample to maintain the pasted object's original width and height, adding or subtracting pixels as necessary. Choose Don't Resample to keep all the original pixels, which may make the relative size of the pasted image larger or smaller than expected.

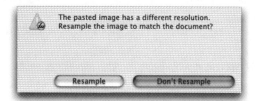

Figure 14-7: If your source selection has a different print resolution than your target document, Fireworks offers to resample the selection for you.

Your selection is inserted into the active document, centered on the canvas.

Tip   If you're pasting into Fireworks and you want to fill a new, empty canvas, copy from the source application and then create a new Fireworks document. Fireworks will offer to make the new document the same dimensions as the clipboard.

Dragging and dropping

You can drag and drop objects into Fireworks from any application that supports OLE (object linking and embedding) drag and drop on Windows, or Macintosh drag and drop on a Macintosh. Dropped objects are rendered as images, unless they're vector art from Macromedia FreeHand or Adobe Illustrator. Following are a few other applications that support drag and drop:

✦ Macromedia Flash

✦ Adobe Photoshop

✦ Microsoft Word

If you're not sure whether a specific application supports drag and drop, try it to find out. As you drag and drop, you can tell whether it's working in Windows if your mouse cursor changes when you hover above a target application. Similarly, on the Mac, sounds provide feedback when things become "droppable." The target application on the Macintosh may also provide some visual indication.

To drag and drop an object into Fireworks from another application, follow these steps:

1. Make sure that you have a Fireworks document open to drop objects into.

2. Position the source application and Fireworks side by side so that you have a clear path to drag between them (see Figure 14-8).

3. In the source application, select the object(s) that you want to drag and drop into Fireworks.

4. Click the selected object(s) and hold down the mouse button in order to "pick up" the object(s).

5. While keeping the mouse button down, position the mouse cursor over the target Fireworks document.

6. Release the mouse button to drop the object(s) into Fireworks.

The object(s) appear centered on your Fireworks canvas and are now part of your Fireworks document.

Tip   You can also drag and drop between two open Fireworks documents.

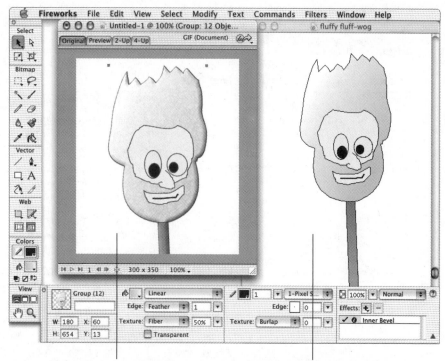

Fireworks document window   Freehand document window

Figure 14-8: This FreeHand vector object instantly became a Fireworks vector object after being dragged and dropped, and then it quickly fell victim to the Inner Bevel Live Effect and a Fiber texture fill.

Importing External Files

Sharing objects between applications on your computer is fine, but sometimes you'll want to import whole files into Fireworks. This is as easy as opening Fireworks' own PNG files. The process is slightly different depending upon whether you're importing bitmap image files or vector art.

Tip

In addition to using File ➪ Import, you can quickly import entire files into Fireworks by dragging them from Explorer on Windows or the Finder on Macintosh, and then dropping them into a Fireworks document window.

Grasping bitmap image files

Imported bitmap image files appear as bitmap objects in Fireworks. Table 14-2 details the bitmap image file formats that Fireworks understands.

Table 14-2
Bitmap Image Files Fireworks Can Import

Format	Filename Extension	Macintosh Type Code	Notes
Fireworks File Format	.png	PNGf	A PNG file with Fireworks-only information, such as vectors, added. This is the default file format for Fireworks 3 and 4.
Fireworks 4.0	.png	PNGf	Updated automatically when opened. Can be saved and opened again in Fireworks 4.0.
Fireworks 3.0	.png	PNGf	Updated automatically when opened. Can be saved and opened again in Fireworks 3.0.
Fireworks 2.0	.png	PNGf	Updated automatically when opened. Cannot be saved and then opened again in Fireworks 2.0.
Fireworks 1.0	.png	PNGf	Updated automatically when opened. Cannot be saved and then opened again in Fireworks 1.0. The Background is placed on its own layer.
Portable Network Graphic	.png	PNGf	Standard PNG documents that don't have extra Fireworks information.
Photoshop Document	.psd	8BPS	Version 3.0 or later only. Layers, Layer Effects, and editable text are preserved, except for editable text layers from Photoshop 6.
GIF	.gif	GIFf	Graphics Interchange File Format. Static or animated. Each frame of an animated GIF is placed on its own frame in Fireworks.
JPEG	.jpg, .jpeg, .jpe, .jfif	JPEG	Avoid importing JPEG images due to their lossy compression scheme and low quality.
Targa	.tga	TPIC	Common UNIX image format.
WBMP	.wbm	WBMP	Wireless bitmap format. Used in wireless devices.

Format	Filename Extension	Macintosh Type Code	Notes
TIFF	.tif or .tiff	TIFF	Tag Image File Format. High-quality lossless compression similar to PNG.
Microsoft Bitmap	.bmp	BMP	Default image format for Windows 3.0 and later.
PICT (Macintosh only)	.pict, .pic, .pct, .p	PICT	Default image Combination vector-bitmap format. Fireworks renders any vector as a bitmap.

Importing a bitmap image into an existing document

To import a bitmap image into an existing Fireworks document, follow these steps:

1. Choose File ⇨ Import, or use the keyboard shortcut, Ctrl+R (Command+R). Alternatively, you can use the command Insert ⇨ Image.

   Fireworks displays the Import File dialog box (see Figure 14-9).

Figure 14-9: The Import File dialog box shows previews as you navigate and then choose a file to import into Fireworks.

2. In the Import File dialog box, select your file and click Import after you finish.

3. Hover your mouse cursor over the Fireworks document window into which you would like to import.

   The cursor changes to the import cursor, which resembles a right angle.

4. Position the import cursor where you want the upper-left corner of the imported image to be located, and then do one of the following:

   • If you want to insert the image at its original size, click once.

   • If you want to insert the image so that it fits a specific area in your document, click and drag a box that delineates that specific area. Fireworks resizes the image to fit that area while maintaining the image's aspect ratio.

The chosen image is inserted into the document as a new bitmap object.

Bringing in Photoshop files

Most of the bitmap files that Fireworks can import are fairly interchangeable; importing a PNG or TIFF image results in a single bitmap object inside Fireworks. Photoshop documents are a bit different, though, because they contain layer information. Therefore, they can contain the equivalent of multiple Fireworks bitmap objects. Photoshop files also contain unique attributes, such as editable text and layer effects, which have corresponding features in Fireworks.

If your Photoshop file contains layers, they are changed into Fireworks objects upon import, instead of into Fireworks layers. Although the nomenclature is different, Photoshop layers and Fireworks objects perform a similar function within each application. Importing multiple Photoshop files into a Fireworks document results in each document being placed into its own Fireworks layer, while still maintaining the individual elements of each document as Fireworks objects.

Layer Effects are similar to many of Fireworks Live Effects, creating editable bevels, drop shadows, and glows. In fact, when you import a Photoshop document into Fireworks, all Layer Effects are converted directly into their corresponding Live Effects and remain editable, as shown in Figure 14-10. Also note that the four layers of the Photoshop document have been translated into four separate Fireworks objects within one Fireworks layer.

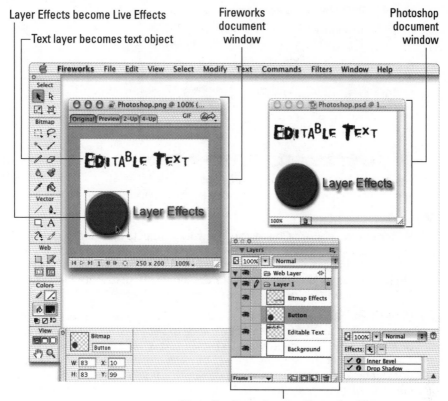

Layer Effects become Live Effects

Text layer becomes text object

Fireworks document window

Photoshop document window

Photoshop layers become Fireworks objects

Figure 14-10: Importing Photoshop files maintains layers, layer effects — converted to Live Effects — and editable text.

Although the translation of a Photoshop document into a Fireworks document can be remarkably accurate, you can fine-tune the process to suit your workflow in the Import panel of Fireworks Preferences. To modify the way that Fireworks imports a Photoshop document, follow these steps:

1. Choose Edit ⇨ Preferences, or use the keyboard shortcut, Ctrl+U (Command+U).

   Fireworks displays the Preferences dialog box.

2. In the Preferences dialog box, select the Import tab (Windows), or the Import option (Macintosh).

   Fireworks displays the Import preference options (see Figure 14-11).

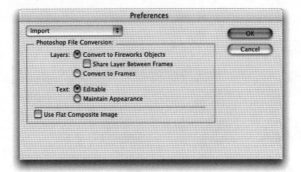

Figure 14-11: The Import preference options enable you to choose how Fireworks imports a Photoshop file.

3. Under Layers, choose Convert to Fireworks Objects in order to change the layers of the Photoshop document to Fireworks objects; check Share Layer Between Frames in order to share the Fireworks layer that contains your new objects across all the frames of your document. To distribute Photoshop layers to Fireworks frames instead, choose Convert to Frames.

4. Under Text, choose Editable to convert Photoshop editable text to Fireworks text objects. Choose Maintain Appearance to flatten editable text into Fireworks bitmap objects. You might want to flatten text when you know you won't need to edit it so that the appearance will be even closer to the original Photoshop document. You might also choose this option if you know you don't have the correct typefaces installed.

5. Check Use Flat Composite Image to ignore all the special attributes of the Photoshop document and import it as a single flat image, as though it were a TIFF. This provides the maximum similarity to the original Photoshop image, and is a good choice if you're only using Fireworks to optimize and export your Photoshop document.

6. Click OK when you're done.

After your Import preferences are set, you're ready to import a Photoshop document, confident that it will be imported in the way that's most useful to you.

To import a Photoshop document into a Fireworks document, follow these steps:

1. Choose File ➪ Import, or use the keyboard shortcut, Ctrl+R (Command+R).

   Fireworks displays the Import File dialog box.

2. Navigate to and select the Photoshop file that you want to import. Click Open when you're done.

3. Hover your mouse cursor over the Fireworks document window into which you would like to import.

   The cursor changes to the import cursor, which looks like a right angle.

4. Position the import cursor where you want the upper-left corner of the imported image to be located, and then do one of the following:

   • If you want to insert the image at its original size, click once.

   • If you want to insert the image so that it fits a specific area in your document, click and drag a box that delineates that specific area. Fireworks resizes the image to fit that area while maintaining the image's aspect ratio.

The Photoshop document is inserted into your Fireworks document.

Fireworks can import Photoshop file formats from version 3 through version 7. Photoshop was a Macintosh-only application before version 3, and the file format was also different. Photoshop 2.5 or earlier documents have a Macintosh Type of "8BIM," rather than the newer format's "8BPS," and they typically don't have a file-name extension. Open them in Photoshop 3, or higher, and then save them in the newer format before attempting to import them into Fireworks.

Although Fireworks can't directly import the native file formats of applications other than Photoshop, many other bitmap-editing applications, such as Painter, can export as Photoshop documents. You can then import them into Fireworks with layers intact.

Corel Photo-Paint is a popular Photoshop alternative that can save images as Photoshop documents and retain layer information. Unfortunately, Fireworks imports Photo-Paint-created Photoshop documents as flat images.

Discovering vector art files

If you prefer to do your drawing in a traditional vector graphics drawing program, Fireworks is the ideal place to finish up your work and prepare it for the Web. Under most circumstances, vector objects remain vector objects, just as if you had created them in Fireworks itself.

Table 14-3 details the vector file types that Fireworks can import.

These file types cover the most common vector drawing tools. One vector art file format that is notable for its absence is Macromedia's own open vector standard, Shockwave Flash (.swf). Moving objects between Flash and Fireworks involves exporting from Flash as an Illustrator document and then importing into Fireworks. Another fairly common format that Fireworks can't import is a Windows Meta File (.wmf), which is commonly used for vector graphics clip art collections for Windows users. To open these files, first open them in another application and export them as one of the file types in Table 14-3.

Table 14-3
Vector Graphics File Types Fireworks Can Import

Format	Filename Extension	Macintosh Type Code	Notes
FreeHand Document	fh7, .fh8, .fh9, or fh10	AGD3	The vector-based format of FreeHand 7 through 10.
Illustrator 7 Document	.ai	uMsk	Adobe Illustrator 7's vector-based default format.
CorelDRAW 8 Document	.cdr	CDR8	CorelDRAW's vector-based format must have been saved without CorelDRAW's built-in bitmap or object compression in order to be openable in Fireworks.
Encapsulated PostScript	.eps	EPSF	A format that most desktop publishing applications can export. Fireworks opens and imports EPS files as bitmap objects only, and does not retain vector information.

Importing a vector art file

To import a vector art file from Macromedia FreeHand, Adobe Illustrator, or
CorelDRAW into an existing Fireworks document, follow these steps:

1. Choose either File ⇨ Import, or use the keyboard shortcut, Ctrl+R
   (Command+R).

   Fireworks displays the standard Import File dialog box.

2. In the Import File dialog box, select your vector art document and click
   Open after you're done.

   Fireworks displays the Vector File Options dialog box (see Figure 14-12),
   with suggested settings appropriate to the document you are importing.

3. In the Vector File Options dialog box, change the dimensions or resolution of
   the vector art, if necessary. Change the dimensions with the Scale, Width, or
   Height boxes. Change the print resolution with the Resolution box, if you have
   a reason to do so.

4. Choose whether Fireworks should antialias paths and/or text, and the type
   of antialiasing you desire, using the Anti-Alias checkboxes and the Anti-Alias
   Type option list.

5. Under File Conversion, select what to do with pages from the Page Import
   option list. You can choose to open a single page by choosing Open a Page
   and putting the page number in the Page box. You can also choose Open
   Pages as Frames to distribute all the pages in the file to frames in Fireworks.

Layers import option list

Page import options list

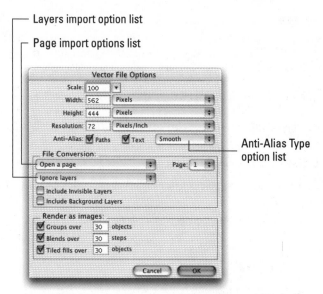

Anti-Alias Type
option list

Figure 14-12: The Vector File Options dialog box allows
you to specify how your vector file is imported.

6. Under File Conversion, select what to do with layers from the Layers Import option list. Choose Ignore Layers to flatten the layers. Choose Remember Layers to keep them as they are. Choose Open Layers as Frames in order to distribute all the layers in the file to frames in Fireworks.

7. To include invisible and background layers, select the appropriate checkboxes.

8. Under Render as Images, select how you want to handle complex vector objects. Deselect all the boxes to maintain vector information under all circumstances.

9. Hover your mouse cursor over the Fireworks document window into which you would like to import.

   The cursor changes to the import cursor, which looks like a right angle.

10. Position the import cursor where you want the upper-left corner of the imported vector art to be located, and then do one of the following:

    • If you want to insert the vector art at its original size, click once.

    • If you want to insert the vector art so that it fits a specific area in your document, click and drag a box describing that specific area. Fireworks resizes the image to fit that area while maintaining the image's aspect ratio.

The vector information is inserted into the document as a new vector object.

Importing an EPS file

Most desktop publishing applications can export to an Encapsulated PostScript (EPS) file. Although an EPS file technically contains vector information, opening EPS files in Fireworks flattens the entire file into one bitmap object.

To import an EPS file into an existing Fireworks document, follow these steps:

1. Choose either File ➪ Import, or use the keyboard shortcut, Ctrl+R (Command+R).

   Fireworks displays the standard Import File dialog box.

2. In the Import File dialog box, select your EPS file, and click Open when you're done.

   Fireworks displays the EPS File Options dialog box (see Figure 14-13).

Figure 14-13: The EPS File Options dialog box enables you to fine tune how your EPS document is imported.

3. In the EPS File Options dialog box, change the dimensions or resolution of the incoming image information, if necessary. Change the dimensions with the Width, or Height boxes. Change the print resolution with the Resolution box, if you have a reason to do so. Check Constrain Proportions to keep from distorting the height to width ratio of your image.

4. Choose whether Fireworks should antialias the image using the Anti-Alias checkbox. Click OK when you're done.

5. Hover your mouse cursor over the Fireworks document window into which you would like to import.

   The cursor changes to the import cursor, which resembles a right angle.

6. Position the import cursor where you want the upper-left corner of the imported vector art to be located, and then do one of the following:

- If you want to insert the vector art at its original size, click once.

- If you want to insert the vector art so that it fits a specific area in your document, click and drag a box describing that specific area. Fireworks resizes the image to fit that area, while maintaining the image's aspect ratio.

The EPS file's information is inserted into the document as a new bitmap object.

Working with clip art

In a commercial or production environment, the constraints of deadlines often preclude creating documents completely from scratch. Besides, there's no need to keep reinventing the wheel. Often, things such as icons and buttons can be quickly based on existing clip art images, which are easily modified in Fireworks to suit a particular project.

Fireworks includes an extensive collection of clip art on its CD-ROM; almost 2,000 separate Fireworks documents. Thankfully, these documents are also referenced by an Extensis Portfolio database file called "Fireworks MX Clipart.fdb." This document opens in the free Extensis Portfolio browser — also included on the CD-ROM — displaying thumbnails for each and every clip art document. Use the Portfolio Browser to search or browse for a particular document. Double-click a thumbnail in order to view it at full size; right-click (Control-click) a thumbnail, and choose Edit Original from the context menu in order to open it in Fireworks for editing. After you open the thumbnail in Fireworks, you can drag and drop elements into other Fireworks documents.

Tip   Look in the Goodies folder on your Fireworks CD-ROM and find the Fireworks clip art in the Clipart folder and the Extensis Portfolio Browser inside the Portfolio Browser folder.

Clip art collections are also commonly included with vector drawing tools, such as FreeHand and CorelDRAW. In fact, Corel is famous for including extensive collections of clip art with its products, often 10,000 items or more. Clip art in FreeHand, CorelDRAW, and Illustrator formats is easily imported into Fireworks.

Many stand-alone clip art collections are also available, either on CD-ROM, or on the Web. Be careful to choose collections in formats that Fireworks can import and favor collections of vector images because they provide maximum flexibility in Fireworks.

Tip

Extensis also offers a full version of Portfolio that enables you to organize your own files into Portfolio databases (available for both Macintosh and Windows at `http://www.extensis.com`). On a Macintosh, iView Multimedia from Script Software—find it at `http://www.scriptsoftware.com`—is an excellent shareware alternative, providing similar functionality at one-eighth the price.

Digging into text files

Obviously, Fireworks can work with a multitude of image formats, but Fireworks is also adept at handling text and can import two types of text files: Rich Text Format (RTF) and ASCII. Either kind of text file is imported by choosing File ➪ Import and navigating to and selecting the file.

RTF is native to Microsoft Word; therefore, RTF files contain formatting, such as typefaces, and italicized or bold text. Many word-processing applications other than Word can also save RTF files. If you need to preserve text formatting, use an RTF file.

ASCII text files are plain text without formatting, but they can be read with few or no translation problems by any application that handles text. If you want to move blocks of text from another application into Fireworks and you're not worried about preserving formatting, ASCII text files are a good choice.

Cross-Reference

For more about importing and using text in Fireworks, see Chapter 10.

Looking at common problems

The fact that Fireworks can import a particular document doesn't mean that the transition from the original file to the Fireworks document will be seamless. Converting data between different applications may involve some compromises along the way.

Examining missing fonts

Ideally, documents would never leave home without their font suitcases (or font files on Windows). Unfortunately, this is not always the case. When you open or import a document that relies on a typeface that's not available on your system, Fireworks warns you by displaying the Missing Fonts dialog box (see Figure 14-14).

To replace a missing font, select its name from the Change Missing Font box and select a font to replace it from the To box. Repeat this process for every font listed in the Missing Font box. Click Reset to restore the original state of the Missing Fonts dialog box at anytime. Click No Change to open your document without making any substitutions. Click OK after you're done.

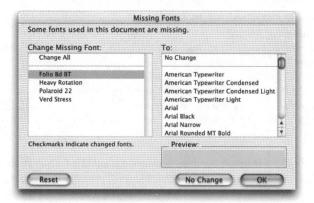

Figure 14-14: The Missing Fonts dialog box enables you to substitute a font that *is* present on your computer for one that isn't, when the document that you're opening requires it.

If you choose No Change, you can edit and even save the document while leaving the font information intact for a future time when the document can be opened with the correct fonts available.

Tip   If your document uses Type 1 (PostScript) fonts, make sure to install or enable Adobe Type Manager before opening the document.

Discerning font spacing

In general, you can expect many of the print-related features of your vector documents to be unsatisfactorily translated. These include the following:

✦ PostScript strokes, fills, and effects

✦ Fine letter spacing, leading, and kerning

Rendering text as paths before saving a vector document for Fireworks import generally leads to better results, although the text will not be editable in Fireworks. If you want to keep text editable throughout your workflow, leave any fine text positioning or even text creation until you're in Fireworks.

Sharing files across platforms

Almost all the documents that Fireworks can open or import are cross-platform. On the surface, this would seem to suggest that you can ignore any cross-platform issues, but what it really means is that you're likely to be working with files from the "other" platform at some point. Although there are no insurmountable issues, keeping a few points in mind can quickly save the day — and your deadline.

Importing Macintosh files into Fireworks for Windows

Files don't need to have filename extensions on a Macintosh, but they do on Windows. Although most Mac users understand this and add the correct filename extensions before "shipping out" a document, occasionally you may find yourself trying to import a file into Fireworks for Windows that does not have an extension. If you know what kind of file it is, add the correct filename extension; if you don't, you'll probably have to ask the Mac user who sent you the file, or take a few best guesses. Without the correct filename extension, Fireworks for Windows will not import a file.

You may also receive a file with a four-character filename extension rather than the three-character extension that Windows favors. For example, you receive a file with .jpeg as its filename extension rather than .jpg. Windows sometimes treats these as the same file type and sometimes it doesn't. Fireworks for Windows will import JPEGs with the extensions .jpg, .jpeg, or .jpe; but not with the less-common extension .jfif.

Fireworks for Windows cannot import Macintosh PICT files (.pict, .pct, .pic, or .p), although they can be imported and exported by Fireworks for Macintosh.

Importing Windows files into Fireworks for Macintosh

When you move documents to a Macintosh system from a Windows system, the Mac OS typically adds the correct Macintosh Creator and File Type codes based on filename extensions. Even if a particular file type is not listed in your File Exchange preferences — in which case it appears with a blank icon — after you have chosen File ➪ Import, Fireworks for Macintosh goes the extra mile and imports it on faith, as long as it has the correct filename extension.

You can also manually "bless" files with Creator and File Type codes by using certain utilities, such as File Buddy, FinderPop, or Snitch. Adding the Fireworks Creator code MKBY to a file causes it to open in Fireworks after it is double-clicked.

Tip   If you're using OS X, and your document is set to open in an application other than Fireworks, select it and choose File ➪ Show Info (Command+I) from the Finder, select Open with application from the option list, and select Fireworks MX from the application list.

Rebuilding Imported Web Pages

A fairly common occurrence is the need to modify a navigation menu or a Web site header that someone worked on before you. It's perfectly normal for a client, or a company, to want to have their existing site redone because the design is outdated or a corporate merger has caused a name change. What's not quite so common is for the client, or even a large corporation, to have the original source files for the site. Without the original PNG file, if the site was created using Fireworks, you're confronted with the much larger task of redoing the whole site, or going through the painstaking process of trying to reconstruct the navigation or the header like a digital jigsaw puzzle. Fireworks' Reconstitute Table feature makes this reassembly a snap.

New Feature The Reconstitute Table feature is new to Fireworks MX. Now you can rebuild Web sites in seconds, keeping all behaviors and JavaScript intact.

Not only does Fireworks rebuild a Web page's graphical elements, it also rebuilds all text areas within the file as text slices within Fireworks. The Reconstitute Table command works on standard HTML and XHTML files. As if this functionality weren't enough to make your redesign job much simpler, Fireworks, as always, goes that extra mile. If you open the Behaviors panel, by choosing Window ➪ Behavior or by using the keyboard shortcut Shift+F3, you'll notice that all of the Behaviors that were applied to the original site, such as Pop-up menus and JavaScript rollovers, are preserved and properly applied in the new Fireworks document.

The Reconstitute Table feature has three methods of importing Web pages. You can open all of the tables within an HTML or XHTML file, you can open the first table only, or you can import the first table into a Fireworks document that you already have open.

To use the Reconstitute Table command to open all of the tables in a Web page, follow these steps:

1. Choose File ➪ Reconstitute Table.

2. Select the HTML or XHTML file you want to rebuild from the Open File dialog box and click Open or press Enter (Return) on your keyboard.

3. Fireworks opens the HTML or XHTML file and rebuilds the table, the graphics, and the behaviors. It leaves the file ready for you to save as a source PNG and then edit, as needed, for your site redesign.

To open just the first table in a Web page, follow these steps:

1. Choose File ➪ Open.

2. Select the HTML or XHTML file you want to rebuild from the Open File dialog box and click Open or press Enter (Return) on your keyboard.

3. Fireworks opens the HTML or XHTML file and rebuilds the first table and its graphics and behaviors. It leaves the file ready for you to save as a source PNG and then edit, as needed, for your site redesign.

To import the first table in a Web page into an open document, follow these steps:

1. Choose File ➪ Import.

2. Select the HTML or XHTML file you want to rebuild from the Import dialog box and click Open or press Enter (Return) on your keyboard.

3. Position the Import cursor where you want the first table of the Web page to be imported and click the left mouse button.

4. Fireworks imports the HTML or XHTML file and rebuilds the graphics and the behaviors in the first table. It leaves the file ready for you save as a source PNG and then edit, as needed, for your site redesign.

Making Screen Captures

Capturing all or part of your computer screen to the clipboard or to a file has applications above and beyond creating illustrations for computer books. There are sometimes workflow advantages to screen captures at design time. Two applications may refuse to maintain the proper formatting if you copy and paste between them, but a capture of one will paste or import easily into the other. If you are presented with an esoteric file format — a specialty of Web design clients — you may find that you can open the file in a viewer, but not convert it to a file format that Fireworks can use. A quick screen capture will have you pasting or importing that image into Fireworks in no time.

In addition, a screen capture of a browser window dropped into an e-mail is a good way to send a client quick design proofs of a site that is not yet live, or to build a portfolio page of your Web-design work. Screen captures of a browser window might also make good link icons for a Web page, if appropriately resized.

Exploring built-in screenshot tools

Screen-capture tools are built right into Windows and Mac OS. Windows provides just enough functionality to get the job done, whereas Mac OS provides a few extra features over and above the call of duty.

Examining Windows

What Windows lacks in screen-capture functionality it probably makes up for in utility: Everything is centered around the easy-to-remember PrintScreen key, which is sometimes marked Prt Scrn, or similarly marked. Pressing PrintScreen copies an image of the entire screen to the clipboard. Pressing Alt+PrintScreen copies only the active window or dialog box to the clipboard. From there, paste the contents of the clipboard into Fireworks.

Tip   When you choose File ⇨ New, Fireworks offers to create a document with the same dimensions as the clipboard. Take your screen capture before you create a new document in order to automatically size the canvas correctly.

Examining Mac OS

On a Macintosh, you can capture the whole screen, a single window or dialog box, or a selected portion of the screen to either a picture file (PICT), or the clipboard.

To make a screen capture on the Macintosh and save it as a picture file in the root folder of your startup disk, press and hold Shift+Command and then do one of the following:

✦ Press 3 to capture the entire screen.

✦ Press 4 and then draw a selection with the mouse to capture only the contents of that selection.

✦ Enable Caps Lock, press 4, and then click on a window or dialog box in order to capture only that window or dialog box.

To place a screen capture on the clipboard instead of saving it to a file, follow the preceding instructions, but hold down Control in addition to Shift+Command.

If you captured to the clipboard, paste your capture into Fireworks. If you captured to a file, open your startup disk and then drag the picture file(s) onto the Fireworks icon. Alternatively, you can choose File ➪ Open or File ➪ Import in Fireworks, navigate to the picture file(s), and then open them.

 Tip
If you're using OS X, you can use the included Grab utility to graphically capture screen elements.

Delving into specialized applications

Numerous third-party applications provide additional screen-capture features, such as on-the-fly palette changes, individual menu captures or individual "child" windows in Windows, or a choice of file formats, sometimes including movie files. One such application for the Macintosh is Ambrosia Software's Snapz Pro X, shown in Figure 14-15. Snapz Pro X was used to create all the screen captures in this book. Many screen-capture applications are also available for Windows. Most screen-capture tools fit perfectly into the Shareware or Freeware application categories, you can find them on Web sites that feature those listings.

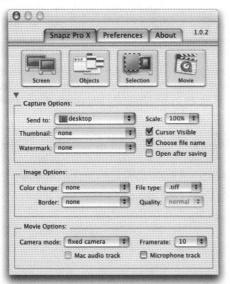

Figure 14-15: Snapz Pro X for Macintosh offers many different screen-capture options and a variety of file formats, including QuickTime movies.

Opening Animations

Opening an animated GIF by choosing File ➪ Open works just as you might expect; the animated GIF is opened and the individual frames are available on — what else — Fireworks frames. You can then modify the GIF, if you like, and optimize and export it for the Web.

For more information about animation in Fireworks, see Chapter 23. For more information on exporting, see Chapter 15.

However, if you import an animated GIF into an existing animation, you may be in for a surprise. Only the first frame of the animated GIF will be imported. If you want to import one animation into another, the workaround is to open both animations in Fireworks and then copy and paste objects from one to the other until you have the combined animation that you require.

Importing multiple files as a new animation

Most animation programs can export their animations as a series of individual documents, one frame of animation to one document. If your animation is ten frames long, you export ten files, each with a similar filename and numbered 1–10. You can open these files as an animation in Fireworks by checking Open as Animation in the Open dialog box. Each document becomes a frame within a single new Fireworks document, and you have an animation again.

Imagine that you've created an exciting, full-color animation with your favorite 3D animation program, and you want to change it into an animated GIF for use on the Web. Unfortunately, this 3D animation program is not very Web-savvy, and the GIFs it creates are always dithered and contain a full 256-color palette. You could create a much more optimized GIF if you could only create it in Fireworks. The way to achieve this is to export your animation as a series of high-quality PNG or TIFF bitmaps, and then import that series into Fireworks.

Importing a group of files as a new animation renders them as images, even if they are vector art documents or Fireworks PNG files with vector information. For a workaround using Macromedia Flash as an example, see "Importing Flash animations," later in this chapter.

To open a group of independent documents as one animation, follow these steps:

1. Choose File ➪ Open, or use the keyboard shortcut, Ctrl+O (Command+O).

   Fireworks displays the Open dialog box (see Figure 14-16).

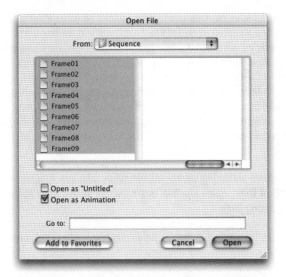

Figure 14-16: Files become frames when you import an animation series with the Open dialog box's Open as Animation checkbox enabled.

2. Navigate to the folder that contains your animation series.

Caution If the files you are importing are similarly named and include numbers — movie01.png, movie02.png, for example — Fireworks will distribute them to frames in the correct order. If the files are not numbered, they are imported in alphabetical order.

3. Select the files that you want to open. To select all the files in the folder, press Ctrl+A (Command+A). To add or remove an individual file to or from your selection, hold down Ctrl (Shift) and click the individual file.

4. Make sure the Open as Animation checkbox is checked. Click Open when you're done.

A new Fireworks document is created, and your files are now frames in that document.

Tip Test your animation by playing it with the VCR-style controls on the bottom of the document window. Adjust each frame's timing in the Frames panel.

Importing Flash animations

Macromedia Flash has more sophisticated animation tools than Fireworks, but its animated GIF export features pale in comparison to Fireworks.

If you want to use Fireworks tools on the vector elements of your Flash animation, you have to go a little further to import your Flash animation as vectors. Ideally, you would export from Flash as an Adobe Illustrator Sequence, and bring those files into Fireworks, using the File ➪ Open command, with the Open as Animation check-box enabled. Unfortunately, Open as Animation always renders vectors as image objects. A workaround is to turn your Flash movie into a multilayer Adobe Illustrator document, in which each layer is actually a frame of your movie, and then convert the layers to frames while importing into Fireworks. Although this example uses Flash, if you use another vector animation application the principles might still apply.

Tip

If you're not worried about retaining vector information, you can export from Flash as a PNG sequence, and then open the file in Fireworks with Open as Animation checked in the Open dialog box.

To import a Flash animation into Fireworks while retaining vector information, follow these steps:

1. Export your movie from Flash as a Flash SWF movie.

2. Create a new Flash document and import the SWF movie into it.

   You have effectively flattened the layers of your Flash movie, leaving you with a single-layer, frame-by-frame animation.

3. Export your movie from Flash as an Adobe Illustrator Sequence.

4. Create a new Flash document and import the Adobe Illustrator Sequence into it. Select all the files in the sequence by individually Ctrl-clicking (Command-clicking) each file until they are all selected. Click OK when you're done.

   You have effectively converted the frames of your Flash movie to layers. Frame 1 is now Layer 1, Frame 2 is Layer 2, and so on.

5. Export your movie from Flash as an Adobe Illustrator file.

   This is the file you will import into Fireworks. Flash can export seven vector file types, and Fireworks can import three vector file types (plus EPS as a bitmap object), but Adobe Illustrator is the only vector file type that they have in common.

Caution

Choose Adobe Illustrator, not Adobe Illustrator Sequence.

6. In Fireworks, choose either File ➪ Open, or the keyboard shortcut, Ctrl+O (Command+O).

   Fireworks displays the Open dialog box.

7. Choose the Adobe Illustrator file that you created in Step 5. Click OK when you're done.

   Fireworks displays the Vector File Options dialog box.

8. Under File Conversion, select Convert Layers to Frames in the Layers Import option list, so that each layer of your Adobe Illustrator file is placed in a Fireworks frame.

9. Under Render as Images, deselect Groups Over and Tiled Fills Over. Click OK when you're done.

Fireworks imports the file, and your Flash animation is now a Fireworks animation, complete with vector information. Objects are editable and are ready to be manipulated with Fireworks' tools and exported as an animated GIF.

Summary

You can incorporate elements into Fireworks documents from external sources. When you're importing elements into Fireworks, keep these points in mind:

✦ You can acquire images directly into Fireworks from TWAIN-compliant hardware devices, such as page scanners and digital cameras. On a Macintosh, you can also use Photoshop Acquire plug-ins.

✦ Resolution — the number of dots — is the most important thing to understand about scanning.

✦ You can copy and paste, or drag and drop elements from other applications into Fireworks.

✦ You can import a long list of bitmap and vector file types into Fireworks.

✦ Fireworks imports Photoshop files with layer information, editable text, and layer effects intact. Fireworks can also export to the Photoshop file format.

✦ Fireworks includes an extensive collection of clip art, as well as the Portfolio Browser for accessing it.

✦ Screen captures are a simple, but effective tool.

✦ You should open animated GIFs instead of import them. Opening them gets you an animated GIF, whereas importing them gets you only the first frame of an animation.

✦ You can import a series of files as an animation. Extra steps are necessary to maintain vector information.

In the next chapter, you find how to export your images from Fireworks.

✦   ✦   ✦

Exporting and Optimizing

The cross-platform, almost universal access of the Web is achieved with limitations. Although many different image file formats exist, browsers are currently limited to displaying only three of them: GIF, JPEG, and PNG. What's more, only GIF and JPEG enjoy truly wide acceptance. Bandwidth is severely limited for the mass market. Although an increasing number of Web surfers enjoy the speed of a DSL or cable modem, the vast majority still view the Internet through a 56K dial-up modem.

These limitations make optimizing and exporting graphics a necessity, not just a nicety. Your work in Fireworks has to be exported in the correct format and with the smallest file size possible. Macromedia realized the importance of export features when it created Fireworks; much of the program centers around making the best looking graphic, with the smallest file size, in an accepted format. The features covered in this chapter rank among the best available with advanced controls, such as lossy GIF, selective JPEG, and color locking. Fireworks takes the limitations imposed by the Web and turns them into an art form.

Cross-Reference This chapter covers the fundamentals of exporting and optimizing your graphics. For more specific information on exporting graphics with hotspots and slices, see Part V. You can find details on exporting animations in Chapter 23.

Exploring Optimization Features

Although using a graphic stored in Fireworks' native format, PNG, in a Web page is possible, it really isn't practical, nor is it the intention of the program for you to do so. The PNG images that you create with the Save command in Fireworks contain extra Fireworks-specific information beyond the simple PNG bitmap image. Although this makes them great for opening and editing in Fireworks, the file size is too heavy to place in a Web page. Publishing your work requires the use of the Export command, which enables you to create a number of image file types in both bitmap and vector formats. Although some of these formats, such as GIF and JPEG, are suitable for publishing on the Web, others, such as BMP and Photoshop, are more suited to moving your work between different graphics applications, or sharing your work with colleagues (see Figure 15-1).

Figure 15-1: Create a Fireworks PNG document (center) with the Save command, and the entire surrounding family of image file formats can be created from it with the Export command. The "private" formats enable you to move your work to other applications, whereas the "public" formats are ready to publish as is on the Web — or wireless Web in the case of WBMP (Wireless BitMaP).

Working hand-in-hand with selecting an appropriate file type is the other main goal of exporting, referred to as *optimization*. Optimization is the process of producing the best looking, smallest possible file. An optimized image loads faster, without sacrificing perceived quality. Because data is thrown away in the optimization process, avoid opening and editing the so-called public file types, shown in Figure 15-1, whenever possible. Store your work and move it between applications using the private file types. Think of the private file types as originals, and the public file types as photocopies made for sharing.

Optimizing and exporting in Fireworks is focused around the preview tabs of the document window, the Optimize panel, and the Frames panel for animations. Adjusting settings in these panels is a necessary precursor to choosing File ➪ Export to create your exported image file. After you've made these settings, they are saved with your Fireworks PNG file for next time. Export settings are as much a part of a document as the kinds of fills or strokes you used.

The hardest part of optimizing is finding a balance between image quality and file size. Fireworks takes a lot of the guesswork out of this task by providing up to four comparison views of different formats at various color resolutions or compressions.

Optimizing every image that goes out on your Web page is important because the smaller your files, the shorter the loading time of your Web pages — and the quicker visitors can view your work.

You'll explore individual export features in much greater depth throughout this chapter, but for now, here's an overview of the typical procedure to use when optimizing a file.

1. Create your image with optimization in the back of your mind at all times; scale and crop images as small as possible, and create large areas of flat color or horizontal stripes of color to make the smallest GIFs.

2. Select a file format in the Optimize panel, based on the type of image you're working on. Choose an indexed color format, such as GIF, for illustrations and flat-color artwork, or a continuous-tone, True Color format, such as JPEG for photographic images.

3. For indexed color images, reduce the number of colors as much as possible, using the Color Table in the Optimize panel. Reducing the number of colors is the primary method of reducing the file size of indexed color images. The fewer colors used, the smaller the file.

4. For the JPEG format, use the Quality slider in the Optimize panel to choose the lowest acceptable quality in order to achieve the smallest file size.

5. Select any additional format-specific options in the Optimize panel, such as Interlaced GIF or JPEG Smoothing.

6. Choose File ⇨ Export to export your document and create the optimized file.

Optimize panel

The Optimize panel is the main control center for your image optimization efforts in Fireworks, containing nearly all the controls you use to set export options. Choose an export file format and modify settings unique to that format. The Optimize panel's settings affect your entire Fireworks document, except when you have an individual slice object selected, in which case the settings are for that slice only.

If the Optimize panel (see Figure 15-2) is not visible, choose Window ⇨ Optimize to view it. Many factors contribute to image optimization, but the format of an image plays perhaps the most important role. In Fireworks, all format selections are made in the Optimize panel's Export File Format option list. Selecting a particular format displays the available options, such as Bit Depth or Quality, for that format. Choosing GIF, for example, makes the transparency controls available, whereas choosing JPEG removes the transparency controls and displays the Quality slider.

The Optimize panel also allows you to save its settings as a preset at any time. Your preset is added to the default presets on the Saved Settings option list. Choosing a preset and then adjusting any setting (except Matte) creates a custom setting. To save a custom export setting, click the Save Settings button (the disk icon) on the bottom of the Optimize panel. A simple Preset Name dialog box appears for you to enter a unique name for the setting. After you enter the name and click OK, the setting is added to the preset list and is always available. To delete the current saved setting, click the Delete Current Saved Settings button (the Trash icon).

Note We look more closely at the features of the Optimize panel as we work with specific export formats later in this chapter.

Export File Format option list

Saved Settings option list

Save Settings button

Delete Current Saved Settings button

Optimize panel Options menu

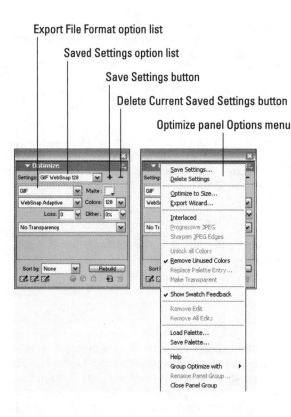

Figure 15-2: Virtually all export options are set in the Optimize panel.

Optimize panel's Color Table

The Color Table on the Optimize panel (see Figure 15-3) comes alive when you optimize an indexed color image, such as a GIF or 8-bit PNG. These formats carry their own limited palette of colors with them, and limiting the size of this palette is the primary way to limit the file size of indexed color images. The Color Table portion of the Optimize panel provides easy access to this palette, and enables you to add, remove, and lock specific colors and more. Clicking the Rebuild button from the bottom of the Optimize panel displays swatches of the current document's export palette. The number of colors in your document replaces the Rebuild button when the palette is up to date.

Optimize panel Options menu

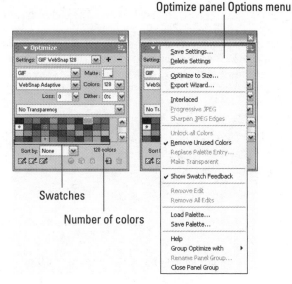

Figure 15-3: The Optimize panel's Color Table displays the export palette for 8-bit indexed color images.

Swatches

Number of colors

Workspace preview

The Preview tab of the document window, shown in Figure 15-4, offers you an optimized view of your document according to the settings in the Optimize panel. The Preview tab provides a view so similar to the working Original view that I sometimes find myself grabbing a tool and trying to get back to work without switching away from Preview first.

Figure 15-4: An optimized preview of your work is never more than a click away, thanks to the document window's in-place previews.

Previewing Cross-Platform Gamma

As well as seeing what your work will look like after it's exported, Fireworks can also give you an idea of what your work will look like on both the Windows and Macintosh platforms. Windows machines use a gamma correction setting of 2.2, whereas most Macs use 1.8 by default. The difference in gamma correction settings — which regulate how dark or light the display looks — means that the same image will look brighter on a Mac than on Windows.

At any time during a Fireworks session — not just when you're looking at one of the preview tabs of the document window — a Windows user can choose View ➪ Macintosh Gamma, or a Mac user can choose View ➪ Windows Gamma, to toggle the document window to simulate the other platform. Viewing your images at both gamma settings enables you to avoid a surprise when seeing your work on the opposite platform.

Multiple previews

Fireworks' capability to offer side-by-side comparisons of the effects of different export settings on an image is often crucial to optimizing a graphic. This chapter has noted several times that an optimized graphic is one that strikes a balance between the best appearance and the smallest file size. That balance can be directly judged through Fireworks' multiple previews.

The 2-Up and 4-Up tabs show you both sides of the export equation: how the image looks, and the file size. The file size is given in both kilobytes and its approximate download time with a 56 Kbps modem. Although the visual representation of your document is an obvious benefit, the file size information that accompanies a preview is just as important. Every adjustment you make in the Optimize panel is reflected in a recalculated and updated file size estimate. The file size is shown in both kilobytes and the approximate length of time the exported image will take to download.

Note   If your image contains multiple frames, the file size shown is for the current frame only, unless the chosen format is Animated GIF. Images with rollovers, for example, use multiple frames, and each frame is exported as a separate image. To find the total "weight" of a multiple-framed image, you must add all the frames together.

Each of the document window's three preview tabs offers its own kind of multiple preview.

Preview tab

You can access a somewhat hidden multiple preview by choosing Window ➪ New Window to create a second document window for your current document. Then select the Preview tab in the new window, as shown in Figure 15-5. With one document window set to Original and one set to Preview, your work in the Original window is immediately reflected in the Preview window.

Set to Original tab   Set to Preview tab

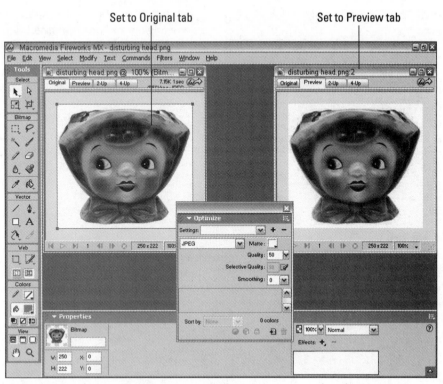

Figure 15-5: Choose Window ➪ New Window to create another document window and set one to Original and one to Preview.

2-Up tab

The 2-Up tab splits the document window vertically and provides two views of your image (see Figure 15-6). By default, the left pane displays your original image, while the right displays the optimized version, according to the settings in the Optimize panel. An option list at the bottom of each pane enables you to choose whether to display an original view (your work as it looks in Fireworks), or an export preview. Setting a second preview in the left pane enables you to closely compare two sets of export settings without looking at the original image. When you select a pane with the mouse, Fireworks draws a border around it. The Optimize panel affects only the settings for the selected pane.

Tip   When viewing the 2-Up preview, you can stretch the document window to get a complete side-by-side view.

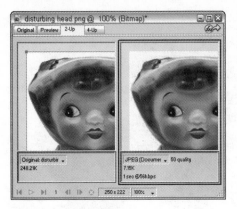

Figure 15-6: The 2-Up preview shows you one original and one optimized view of your document by default.

4-Up tab

The 4-Up tab (see Figure 15-7) offers four views, each approximately one-quarter of the document window, arranged in a square. The upper-left view is initially your original document, while the other three panes display optimized views. 4-Up works just like 2-Up in other respects.

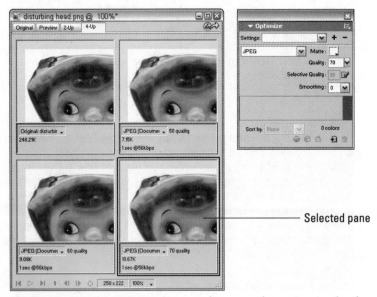

Selected pane

Figure 15-7: In the 4-Up preview, you have to select a pane to be the focus of your work in the Optimize panel. Here, the lower-right pane is selected.

I find that the 4-Up view is especially useful when optimizing an image for JPEG export. The JPEG format is finicky; reducing the quality to 70 percent might make one image look terrible, whereas another might still look great with the quality dropped all the way down to 50 percent. Achieving the perfect JPEG quality setting for a particular image is often best accomplished by viewing it at three different settings at once.

Tip　　You may have to resize the document window to get a good look at your document, especially if your document is small. A portion of each preview pane is given over to the file size report, which can be most of the window for a 200×200 or smaller document.

Panning

If the image is too big to view all at once in the preview area, you can use the Hand tool to pan the image. When you select an image in a preview area with the Hand tool, the cursor becomes a hand, and you can drag the other parts of the image into view. The panning capability of the Hand tool is especially valuable when viewing multiple settings. Panning one of the multiple views causes all the other views to pan as well, as shown in Figure 15-8. This feature makes direct comparison very straightforward.

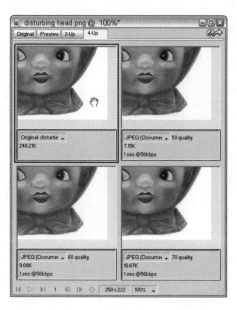

Figure 15-8: With multiple views, if you pan in one view, all views pan.

Zooming

One of the export features in Fireworks is *color locking;* you can lock the color of any pixel in the preview by selecting it and then clicking the Lock Color button in the Color Table section of the Optimize panel. How do you identify just the right pixel? You zoom in, naturally. The Zoom tool and the document window view controls work exactly the same way in the preview views as they do in the original view of the document window. To magnify a view, either select the Zoom tool and click the image, or choose a magnification from the magnification option list on the bottom of the document window. To reduce the magnification of the view, press Alt (Option) while clicking with the Zoom tool — or choose a lower magnification.

Tip   Keep in mind that your Web graphics will almost *always* be viewed at 100 percent. Although you might be tempted to make a decision on which file format to use based on a magnified view, the magnified view is largely irrelevant to how the graphics are ultimately viewed.

If you have two or four multiple views enabled, changing the magnification of one view changes the magnification for all of them, as shown in Figure 15-9.

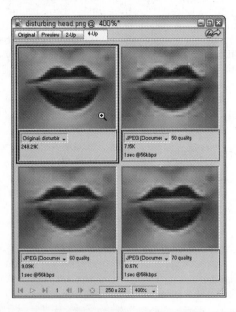

Figure 15-9: When you zoom in on one view, the accompanying views also zoom in.

Tip   To pan around a close-up view without having to switch away from the Zoom tool, press and hold down the spacebar to temporarily switch to the Hand tool.

Frame controls

You can use the VCR-like animation controls on the document window no matter which document window Original/Preview tab you are currently viewing. When optimizing in one of the preview tabs, you can use the frame controls to quickly call up a specific frame for optimization, or to play the frames in sequence.

The controls, from left to right, are as follows:

- ✦ **First Frame:** Displays the first frame of the image.
- ✦ **Play/Stop:** Plays all the frames in sequence. When the frames are playing, the button image changes to a square and, if pressed, stops the playback.
- ✦ **Last Frame:** Displays the last frame of the image.
- ✦ **Current Frame:** Displays the current frame number of the image.
- ✦ **Previous Frame:** Displays the frame before the current one.
- ✦ **Next Frame:** Displays the frame after the current one.

In addition to being useful for viewing the separate frames of an animation, I often use the VCR controls to step through the frames of a rollover. Remember that each frame in your document is exported as a separate file, and thus can be optimized individually.

Cross-Reference In addition to the VCR controls, the Frames panel also contains frame-timing controls. Explore these animation and export features in Part VI.

Exporting Indexed Color

Images that have large areas of flat color (typically illustrations, as opposed to photographic images) and that can get by with only a limited number of colors are exported in an indexed color format. Indexed color formats have a maximum of 256 different colors, also known as 8-bit color. A particular image file contains information about which 256, of all available colors, the file uses. The information is maintained in a color index inside the file, hence the name *indexed color*.

A key feature of indexed color files is that their index can be reduced to only the specific colors actually used in the image. Reducing the number of colors has a major impact on file size. In fact, this method is the primary one for optimizing indexed color files. The Color Table section of the Optimize panel provides a comprehensive access point to this index.

When an indexed color graphic needs to create the impression of more than 256 colors, you can use dithering. A dithered color is made from a pattern of two or more colored pixels that, because the eye cannot differentiate the individual pixels, blend into the new color.

The indexed color formats that Fireworks exports are detailed in Table 15-1.

Of all the indexed color formats, only GIF and PNG 8 can be used on the Web. GIF is the most popular and the most suitable on today's Web because an overwhelming number of browsers support it. Although PNG is a superior format in many ways, its transparency features have yet to find support in a wide range of browsers.

	Table 15-1
	Indexed Color Export Formats
Format	*Description*
GIF	Graphics Interchange Format. The overwhelmingly most popular indexed color format for the Web. Excellent Web browser support; small file sizes; 1-bit transparency.
Animated GIF	Same as GIF, except that it contains multiple images that are shown one after the other, usually rapidly, as in a film or flipbook.
PNG 8	Portable Network Graphic. Offers similar features to GIF, but transparency is not supported by most Web browsers.
WBMP	A 1-bit (black/white) file format specifically for Wireless Application Protocol (WAP) pages, which are displayed on mobile devices with small screens and limited color depth.
TIFF 8	Tag Image File Format. Not suitable for the Web, but common for print work.
BMP 8	Microsoft Bitmap image. The native graphics format of Microsoft Windows. Not suitable for the Web, but a good way to share images between Windows applications.
PICT 8 (Macintosh only)	Macintosh Picture. The native graphics format of Mac OS. Vectors are not supported by Fireworks. Not suitable for the Web, but a good way to share image files between Mac applications.

Both GIF and PNG support transparency, but again, PNG suffers from lack of browser support. Transparency is extremely valuable on the Web because it enables you to create graphics that appear nonrectangular, or create the illusion that one image is in front of another. Both GIF and PNG files can be optionally interlaced. An interlaced image appears to be developing on the page as it downloads.

The WBMP format is notable for its color support, or lack thereof. This 1-bit format stores each pixel as either on or off, yielding a color palette that's essentially one dark gray and one light gray, once the WBMP image is ultimately viewed on the limited gray display of a mobile device. The process of exporting any indexed color image is very similar, no matter which format you choose. The GIF format has more options, and is the most popular, so I'll focus mainly on the GIF format throughout this section. After you can export a GIF, applying that knowledge to exporting any of the other indexed color formats is easy because when you switch from GIF to another format in the Optimize panel, Fireworks removes the controls that are no longer applicable, while those that are left function in the same way.

Color palette

A *palette* is the group of colors actually used in the image. Fireworks offers nine pre-set palettes in the Optimize panel's Indexed Palette option list, plus the Custom setting that refers to a deviation from one of the preset palettes. After you customize a palette, you can store it as a preset and add it to the Indexed Palette option list.

Each of the nine different palettes (available to all indexed formats, not only GIF) accesses a different group of colors. The WebSnap Adaptive and Web 216 palettes are the choices generally made for Internet graphics, although other palettes are appropriate in some situations. The following are the preset palettes:

✦ **Adaptive:** Examines all the colors in the image and finds a maximum of the most suitable 256 colors; it's called an *adaptive* palette because the best 256 colors are adapted to the image, instead of a fixed set of colors. If possible, Fireworks assigns Websafe colors initially and then assigns any remaining non-Websafe colors. The Adaptive palette can contain a mixture of Websafe and non-Websafe colors.

✦ **WebSnap Adaptive:** This palette is similar to the Adaptive palette insofar as both are custom palettes in which colors are chosen to match the originals as closely as possible. After selecting the initial matching Websafe colors, all remaining colors are examined according to their hexadecimal values. Any colors close to a Websafe color (plus or minus seven values from a Websafe color) are "snapped to" that color. Although this palette does not ensure that all colors are Websafe, a greater percentage of colors will be Websafe.

Note Exactly how does Fireworks decide which colors are within range for the use of WebSnap Adaptive? The plus or minus seven value range is calculated by using the RGB model. For example, suppose that one of the colors is R-100, G-100, B-105 — a medium gray. With the WebSnap Adaptive palette, that color snaps to R-102, G-102, B-102, because the difference between the two colors is seven or less (R-2, G-2, B-3 = 7). If, however, the color were slightly different, say R-99, G-100, B-105, the difference would be outside the snap range and the actual color would be used.

✦ **Web 216:** All colors in the image are converted to their nearest equivalent in the Websafe range.

✦ **Exact:** Uses colors that match the exact original RGB values. Useful only for images with less than 256 colors; for images with more colors, Fireworks alerts you to use the Adaptive palette.

✦ **Macintosh:** Matches the system palette used by the Macintosh operating system when the display is set to 256 colors.

✦ **Windows:** Matches the system palette used by the Windows operating system when the display is set to 256 colors.

✦ **Grayscale:** Converts the image to a grayscale graphic with a maximum of 256 shades of gray.

✦ **Black & White:** Reduces the image to a two-tone image; the Dither option is automatically set to 100 percent when you choose this palette, but you can modify this setting.

✦ **Uniform:** A mathematical progression of colors across the spectrum is chosen. This palette has little application on the Web, although I have been able to get the occasional posterization effect out of it by severely reducing the number of colors and by reducing the 100 percent Dither setting that is automatically applied.

✦ **Custom:** Whenever a stored palette is loaded or a modification is made to one of the standard palettes, Fireworks labels the palette Custom. Such changes are made through the Export File Format option list on the Optimize panel.

Given these options, what's the recommended path to take? Probably the best course is to build your graphic in Fireworks by using the Websafe palette, and then export them by using the WebSnap Adaptive palette. This approach ensures that your image remains the truest to its original colors, while looking the best for Web viewers whose color depth is set to 24-bit or higher, and still looking good on lower-end systems that are capable of showing only 256 colors.

Keep in mind that even if you use all Websafe colors in your graphic, the final result won't necessarily be within that complete palette. Fireworks generates other colors to antialias, to create drop shadows, and to produce glows, and the colors generated may not be Websafe. For this reason, either the Adaptive palette or WebSnap Adaptive palette often offers the truest representation of your image across browsers.

Number of colors

One of the quickest ways to decrease an image's file size is to reduce the number of colors. Recall that GIF is referred to as an *8-bit format;* this means that the maximum number of available colors is 256, or 8-bit planes of information — math aficionados will remember that 256 is equal to 2^8 (two raised to the eighth power). Each bit plane used permits exponentially more colors and reserves a certain amount of memory (but also increases the file size). For this reason, the Number of Colors option list contains powers of 2, 4, 8, 16, 32, 64, 128, and 256.

The Color Table section

For complete control of individual colors, the controls in the Color Table section of the Optimize panel enable you to add, edit, and delete individual colors, as well as store and load palettes. Fireworks enables you to select a color from the swatches and then lock it, snap it to its closest Websafe neighbor, or convert it to transparent by clicking one of the Color Table's buttons, or choosing a command from the Optimize panel Options menu.

Locking one or more colors in your graphic ensures that the most important colors—whether they're important for branding, a visual design, or both—can be maintained. After a color is locked, it does not change, regardless of the palette chosen. For example, you could preview your image by using the Web 216 palette, lock all the colors, and then switch to an Adaptive palette to broaden the color range, but keep the basic colors Websafe. Websafe colors are displayed in the swatches with a diamond symbol in them, and locked colors are identified by a square in the lower-right corner of the swatch, as shown in Figure 15-10.

Sort color option list

Websafe color   Locked color

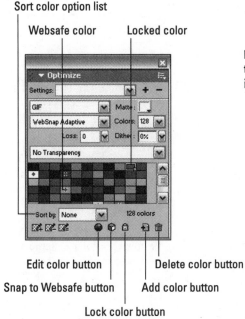

Figure 15-10: The Color Table section of the Optimize panel is your window into an image's color index.

Edit color button   Delete color button

Snap to Websafe button   Add color button

Lock color button

 Tip   Clicking a pixel in the preview with the Pointer tool selects its color in the Color Table section of the Optimize panel.

The Optimize panel's Color Table specific commands are detailed in Table 15-2, along with information detailing whether they are represented by a button or an option list, or if they're on the Optimize panel Options menu.

Tip   All of these commands are also available from the shortcut menu that appears when you right-click (Control+click) an individual swatch.

Table 15-2
Optimize panel's Color Table Commands

Command	Location	Description
Rebuild Color Table	Button	Rebuilds the color table swatches according to the settings in the Optimize panel.
Add Color	Button	Allows you to insert an additional color into the current palette by choosing it from the system color picker(s).
Edit Color	Button	Opens the system color picker(s) to permit a new color to be chosen to replace the selected color.
Delete Color	Button	Removes the selected color(s).
Replace Palette Entry	Options menu	Swaps the selected color for the color chosen through the system color picker(s).
Snap to Websafe	Button	Converts the selected color(s) to the closest color in the Websafe palette.
Add color to transparency	Button	Makes the selected color(s) transparent.
Remove color from transparency	Button	Restores the color(s), removing it from the list of transparent colors
Select transparent color	Button	Makes a single color you select transparent.
Lock Color	Button	Maintains the current color during any overall palette transformations, such as bit-depth reduction or palette changes. The color, however, can still be edited directly.
Unlock All Colors	Options menu	Allows all colors to be changed.
Sort by Luminance	Option list	Sorts the current palette swatch set from brightest to darkest.
Sort by Popularity	Option list	Sorts the current palette swatch set from most pixels used to least pixels used.

Command	Location	Description
Sort by None	Option list	Restores the default swatch arrangement.
Remove Edit	Options menu	Reverts the swatch to its original color.
Remove All Edits	Options menu	Restores the current palette to its original state.
Load Palette	Options menu	Allows a palette to be loaded from Adobe Color Table (ACT) files or from GIF.
Save Palette	Options menu	Stores the current palette as a Color Table file.

Sort by popularity

The Sort by Popularity command is available from the Sort by option list, and is very helpful when it's time to trim file size down by cutting colors. By default, the swatches are displayed in an unsorted order. After you choose Sort by Popularity from the Sort by option list, the most-used color is displayed first, in the upper-left corner, and the least-used color is shown last, in the lower-right corner. This makes it easy to select and delete the colors that are least likely to be missed. You can Shift+click two colors to select them and the range between them, or Ctrl+click (Command+click) to select multiple swatches that are not adjacent to each other.

Matte

When a photograph is framed, the framer often mounts the image on a matte, which provides a different, contrasting background to make the photograph stand out. Fireworks uses the matte idea to allow the Web designer to export images with varying canvas colors — without changing the canvas. One of the biggest problems with GIF transparency is the unwanted "halos" that result from creating a drop shadow or other gradation against a different background. The traditional method of handling this problem is to change your canvas color in the graphics program to match the background color on the Web page. This solution works well for graphics you're only going to use once, but many Web designers find that they need to use the same graphic in many different situations, against many different backgrounds. The Matte feature enables you to keep one master graphic and export as many specific instances — against as many different mattes or canvases — as necessary, as shown in Figure 15-11.

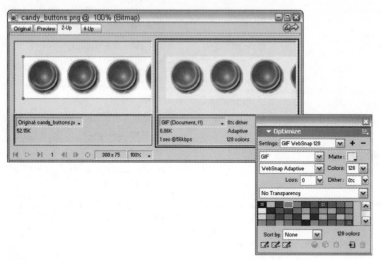

Figure 15-11: The Matte feature enables you to export your image against different canvas colors, without having to modify the original image.

Choosing a matte color is very straightforward: Simply click the Matte arrow button to display the standard pop-up color picker. From there, choose one of the swatches or a color from elsewhere onscreen using the Eyedropper tool. To return a matte color to transparent, click the No Color button in the pop-up color picker.

Lossy GIF compression

Recall that the GIF format uses lossless compression; so what's this Loss option in the Optimize panel all about? The so-called Lossy GIF is not a separate format at all, but rather a method for optimizing an image so that when it's actually saved as a GIF it will have a smaller file size. When it comes to determining the ideal Loss setting, Fireworks multiple previews are invaluable, as shown in Figure 15-12. I usually start with an extreme setting, such as 60 or 70 percent, and then gradually reduce it until the image looks acceptable.

I find that the Loss option works for some images and not for others. Sometimes it will actually increase the resulting file size until you really get into a high Loss setting. For those times when it trims a particular image down to a much lower weight, you'll be happy to have this tool in your export toolkit.

Figure 15-12: In the lower-left pane, the lossy compression at 30 percent is starting to become visible. In the lower-right pane, at 60 percent, it's unacceptably so.

Dither

One way — although not necessarily the best way — to break up areas of flat color caused by the lower color capabilities of GIF is to use the Dither option. When the Dither option is enabled, Fireworks simulates new colors by using a pattern of existing colors — exactly how the Web Dither fill is created. However, because dithering is not restricted to a single area, but instead is spread throughout the graphic, the dithering can be significantly more noticeable — dithering makes the image appear "dotty," as shown in Figure 15-13, and usually increases your file size. The degree of dithering is set by changing the Dither Amount slider, or by entering the amount directly in the text box.

Transparency

One of the main reasons GIF is often selected as a format over JPEG is GIF's capability to specify any one color — and thus certain apparent areas — of the graphic transparent. As mentioned previously, transparency is the key to making nonrectangular-shaped graphics, and the Fireworks transparency controls (see Figure 15-14) are the key to making transparency.

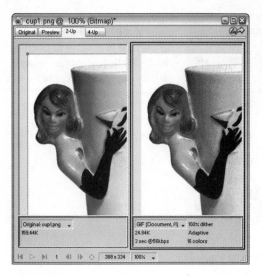

Figure 15-13: The image on the right was produced with dithering at 100 percent, which caused the solid color to be heavily dotted.

Type of transparency option list

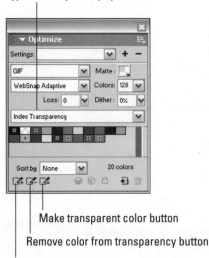

Figure 15-14: The Optimize panel contains transparency controls for file formats that support it, such as GIF.

Make transparent color button

Remove color from transparency button

Add color to transparency button

The transparency controls in detail are as follows:

✦ **Type of Transparency option list:** Choose No Transparency, Index Transparency, or Alpha Transparency to specify the transparency type. By default, the canvas color is initially made transparent.

✦ **Add Color to Index Transparency button:** Enables you to choose additional colors to make transparent, either from the swatch set or sampled directly from the previewed image.

✦ **Remove Color from Index Transparency button:** Converts transparent colors to their original color, either from the swatch set, or sampled directly from the previewed image.

✦ **Set Transparent Index Color button:** Select to choose a single color to be transparent, either from the swatch set, or sampled directly from the previewed image.

When a color is made transparent, its swatch and pixels in the Preview image are replaced with a gray-and-white checkerboard pattern, as shown in Figure 15-15. You can choose as many colors as you would like to make transparent.

Figure 15-15: Part of the power of the GIF format is the ability to make any color transparent, so that the GIF image can be seamlessly composited into a Web page.

To make portions of your GIF image transparent, follow these steps:

1. Select a document window preview tab to view a preview of your document.

2. If the Optimize panel is not visible, choose Window ➪ Optimize to view it.

3. If necessary, select GIF from the Optimize panel's Export Format option list.

4. To make the canvas color transparent, select Index Transparency from the Type of Transparency option list.

5. To make a color other than the canvas transparent, click the Set Transparent Index Color button and sample a color either from a swatch or from the preview image.

Tip   If you want to select a small area in your image for transparency, use the Zoom tool to magnify that selection before choosing the color.

6. To make more colors transparent, click the Add Color to Index Transparency button and sample the colors, either from the swatch or from the Preview image.

7. To restore a transparent color to its original color, click the Remove Color from Index Transparency button and select the color either from a swatch or from the Preview image.

8. For even greater control, select a color or colors from the Color Table panel and click the Transparent button.

As noted in the Transparency option list description, two different types are available: Index and Alpha Transparency. Index Transparency enables you to make any color totally transparent—think of it as an On/Off switch; the color is either transparent or it isn't. Alpha Transparency, on the other hand, enables you to create degrees of transparency, such as tints and shades of a color. You can discover more details about Alpha Transparency in the PNG section, later in this chapter.

Index Transparency is generally used for the GIF format, because, technically, only the PNG format truly supports Alpha Transparency. However, the Fireworks engineers have left Alpha Transparency enabled for GIFs, to achieve a slightly different effect. When Alpha Transparency is chosen, a new color register is created for the canvas and then made transparent. How is this different from converting the canvas color to transparent, as occurs with Index Transparency? If you've ever created an image where part of the graphic is the same color as the background—the white of a person's eyes is also the white of a canvas—you'll quickly understand and appreciate this feature. Basically, Alpha Transparency, as applied in Fireworks' GIF format, leaves your palette alone and only makes the canvas transparent, as shown in Figure 15-16.

Note   If you don't notice a new color register being added when you select Alpha Transparency, check to see whether the Optimized option is enabled. If it is, Fireworks may combine other colors to keep the same number of colors.

Figure 15-16: The Alpha Transparency feature enabled me to make the white background of this image transparent without also making the white areas within the subject transparent.

Remove unused colors

The Remove Unused Colors option — which is enabled by default — is a Fireworks-only feature that causes the program to discard duplicate and unused colors from a palette. This can seriously reduce your file size, particularly when choosing one of the fixed palettes, such as Web 216, or either of the operating system palettes. Find the Remove Unused Colors option on the Optimize panel Options menu.

Interlaced

The Interlaced option on the Optimize panel Options menu enables a GIF property that displays a file as it downloads. The file is shown in progressively finer detail as more information is transferred from the server to the browser. Although a graphic exported with the Interlaced option won't download any faster, it provides a visual cue to Web page visitors that something is happening. Interlacing graphics is a matter of taste; some Web designers would never design a page without them; others are vehemently opposed to their use.

Saved settings

Four of the six presets in the Saved Settings option list in the Optimize panel relate to the GIF format:

✦ **GIF Web 216:** Sets the GIF format using the Web 216 palette.

✦ **GIF WebSnap 256:** Sets the GIF format using the WebSnap Adaptive palette and a maximum of 256 colors.

✦ **GIF WebSnap 128:** Sets the GIF format using the WebSnap Adaptive palette and a maximum of 128 colors.

✦ **GIF Adaptive 256:** Sets the GIF format using the Adaptive palette and a maximum of 256 colors.

Use these presettings when exporting GIFs, or use them as a starting point for your own optimizations.

Fireworks technique: Creating GIF-friendly images

Before you even get to the Optimize panel, you can make an image more GIF-friendly by paying attention to the patterns of pixels that make up the image, and understanding how the GIF format compresses pixels. Taking a little time to create more GIF-friendly images can be an even more effective means of reducing export file size than the obvious methods offered by Fireworks' export tools.

The easiest way to create a GIF-friendly document is to include large areas of flat color. Any changes from pixel to pixel are less compressible than large similar areas. A small experiment shows just how much the GIF format loves flat color. Create a new document, 400×400 pixels, and choose a canvas color. Click the Preview tab of the document window and note the tiny export file size of about 600 bytes, or 0.6K (you may have to stretch the document window to see the file size). Switch back to the Original tab and use the Pencil tool to draw a large *X* through your document, touching each corner. Go back to Preview and note that your file size has increased to about 1.74K—or almost triple—all for that skinny, penciled X.

The next best thing to large areas of flat color in the GIF format is horizontal lines. GIF compresses pixels from left to right, so a horizontal line of identically colored pixels is very compressible. Without compression, a line of red pixels might be expressed as "red pixel, red pixel, red pixel, red pixel, red pixel." You can see that expressing only five pixels takes a lot of explaining. With GIF compression, that same line might be "red pixel×5." That's an enormous savings in and of itself, but "red pixel×300" is an even more dramatic savings when compared to spelling out each pixel in turn. It's obvious that paying a little attention to using horizontal lines in your designs can minimize GIF file size.

The simplest way to put more horizontal lines into your images is to replace complex, chaotic texture fills such as Fiber with a simpler, horizontal lines texture, as shown in Figure 15-17. The two documents are identical except that the one on the left uses a 50 percent Fiber texture fill in the circle, and the one on the right uses a 50 percent Line-Horiz texture fill. Other export settings are the same, but the one with the horizontal lines texture is one third of the weight.

Figure 15-17: Replacing a Fiber fill with an alternating lines texture reduced the export file size from 19K to less than 6K because of the compressibility of long horizontal lines of similar pixels in the GIF format.

Another way to make an image more GIF-friendly is to reduce areas of stray pixels. Sometimes an area of otherwise flat color will have some randomly placed pixels of colors one or two shades away. When viewed at 100 percent, these pixels may not be obvious, but their random nature is reducing the GIF-compressibility of your image. Zooming in and cleaning up those stray pixels is optimization-time well spent.

Tip   One way to end up with lots of stray pixels is to work from a JPEG original. Sometimes an image goes through a few hands before it ends up in yours. I've had clients submit flat-color artwork such as illustrations or logos — obvious candidates for GIF export — as JPEGs, in spite of my protestations. What's worse, they've lost the original PNG or TIFF files. As good as the JPEG format can be for photographic images, it mangles areas of flat color, creating lots of unsightly and uncompressible stray pixels. Use the following technique to reduce or eliminate stray pixels and reclaim the image for the GIF format.

You can use the Pencil tool to clean up areas of stray pixels, as shown in Figure 15-18. Drawing the predominant flat color over the strays creates more areas of flat horizontal lines, often dramatically reducing export file size.

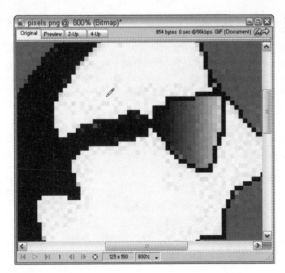

Figure 15-18: Zoom in on an image and eliminate stray pixels to create bigger areas of flat color that compress better upon GIF export.

To zap stray pixels, follow these steps:

1. Choose the Pencil tool from the Tools panel.

2. Use the Stroke color well on the Tools panel, or in the Stroke section of the Property inspector, to sample a predominant flat color from your image.

3. Use the Pencil tool to color over stray pixels that are adjacent to that flat color, converting them to the flat color.

4. Repeat Steps 2 and 3 until you have flattened as many stray pixel areas as possible.

Tip   While you're zoomed in on your image, Choose Window ➪ New Window to create a new, 100% window to monitor how your changes are affecting your image at its true size.

Exporting Photographic Images

Photographic images are most often displayed in 24-bit True Color, in a format such as JPEG, rather than the limited palette of an indexed color image, such as a GIF. Photographic images contain subtle gradations that are not easily reproduced in fewer colors, and yet are dithered quite serviceably by the browser if the client machine is running in a 256-color video mode.

What's more, the JPEG format excels at compressing the smooth tones of photographic images down to unbelievably small file sizes, without an appreciable loss of quality. The fact that the JPEG format is so good at the things the GIF format fails miserably at is part of the reason for their enduring, successful partnership as the king and queen of Web graphics formats.

The True Color formats that Fireworks exports are detailed in Table 15-3.

Table 15-3 True Color Export Formats	
Format	**Description**
JPEG	Joint Photographic Experts Group image file format. Used for almost all the true color images on the Web. Uses lossy compression to achieve maximum reduction in file size.
PNG 24, PNG 32	Portable Network Graphic. Offers lossless compression that results in larger file sizes than JPEG — often much larger — but maintains pristine quality.
TIFF 24, TIFF 32	Tag Image File Format. Print artists commonly use 24- and 32-bit TIFFs, although they are not suitable for the Web.
BMP 24	Microsoft Bitmap image. The native graphics format of Microsoft Windows. Not suitable for the Web, but a good way to share images between Windows applications.
PICT 24 (Macintosh only)	Macintosh Picture. The native graphics format of Mac OS. Vectors are not supported by Fireworks. Not suitable for the Web, but a good way to share image files between Mac applications.

Cross-Reference

The Photoshop file format can also contain photographic images, as well as layers and other extended attributes. Exporting a Photoshop document from Fireworks is covered later in this chapter.

Of all the formats in Table 15-3, only JPEG and PNG 24 can be used on the Web. PNG 32's alpha mask is ignored by most browsers, rendering it the same as PNG 24. If you want to display an image with the highest quality, regardless of file size, then PNG 24 is a good choice. If bandwidth is an issue at all — and it's very rare that it isn't — then JPEG is the better choice, providing excellent quality photographic images in a much smaller file size than PNG.

To alter the bit depth for an exported image, choose a lower bit-depth export format from the Optimize panel's Export Format option list. Instead of PNG 32, for example, choose PNG 24. Although a change from 24-bit to 8-bit means lowering the maximum number of colors supported, a change from 32-bit to 24-bit supports the same colors, but removes the alpha mask. The upper 8 bits of a 32-bit image are always an alpha channel — an 8-bit grayscale image that defines the image's transparency.

Cross-Reference

For more about alpha masks, see Chapter 13.

JPEG

Whereas GIFs generally are made smaller by lowering the number of colors used, JPEGs use a sliding scale that creates smaller file sizes by eliminating pixels. This sliding scale is built on a *lossy* algorithm, so-called because the lower the scale, the more pixels are lost. The JPEG algorithm is a very good one, and you can significantly reduce the file size by lowering the JPEG Quality setting.

Other characteristics of the JPEG format include the following:

✦ JPEG images are capable of displaying over 16 million colors. This wide color range, also referred to as *24-bit,* enables the subtle shades of a photograph to be depicted easily.

✦ Although JPEG images can display almost any color, none of the colors can be made transparent. Consequently, any image that requires transparency in a Web browser must be stored as a GIF.

✦ For JPEG images to be viewed as they are downloaded, they must be stored as Progressive JPEGs, which appear to develop onscreen, like an interlaced GIF. Progressive JPEGs have a slightly better compression engine and can produce smaller file sizes.

Note   Internet Explorer doesn't fully support Progressive JPEGs. They are displayed just as if they were not Progressive, though, so there's no harm in using them.

Quality

The major method used to alter a JPEG's file size is to change the Quality value. In Fireworks, the Quality value is gauged as a percentage, and the slider goes from 0 percent to 100 percent. Higher values mean less compression, and lower values mean that more pixels are discarded. Trying to reduce a JPEG's file size by lowering the Quality slider is always worthwhile; you can also enter a value directly in the text box. The JPEG compression algorithm is so good that almost every continuous-tone image can be reduced in file size without significant loss of quality, as shown in Figure 15-19. On the other hand, increasing a JPEG's Quality value from its initial setting is never helpful. Whereas JPEG is very good at losing pixels to reduce file size, adding pixels to increase quality never works — you'll only increase the file's size and download time.

Tip   With the JPEG image-compression algorithm, the initial elements of an image that are "compressed away" are least noticeable. Subtle variations in brightness and hue are the first to disappear. With additional compression, the image grows darker and less varied in its color range.

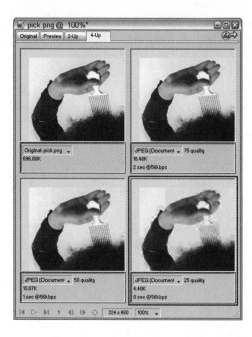

Figure 15-19: Each of these four previews uses a different JPEG quality value; only when the quality is lowered significantly (bottom right) does the image become unacceptable.

A good technique for comparing JPEG images in Fireworks is to use the 4-Up preview option. The upper-left pane shows your original document, so that you always have an image on which to base your comparisons. In another view, reduce the Quality to about 75 percent or so. If that image is acceptable, reduce the Quality setting to 50 percent in another view. By then, you'll probably start to get some unwanted artifacts, so use the fourth window to try a setting midway between the last acceptable and the unacceptable Quality settings, such as 65 percent. Be sure to view your images at 100 percent magnification. That's how your Web audience will see them, so you should, too.

Tip Don't forget that you can stretch the document window to a larger size to increase the size of the multiple preview panes.

Selective Quality

The Selective Quality setting works just like the Quality setting, except that its value only applies to areas of your document that are covered by a JPEG mask. This enables you to isolate foreground areas and apply a high Selective Quality setting to them while applying a very low quality setting to the rest of your image. Basically, you trade some of the quality of the least important areas of an image for better quality where it matters most.

You can create JPEG masks from Marquee selections by choosing Modify ⇨ Selective JPEG ⇨ Save Selection as JPEG Mask. Fireworks displays JPEG masks as a translucent pink overlay by default, as shown in Figure 15-20.

Figure 15-20: Convert a marquee selection into a JPEG mask and Fireworks colors it pink.

If you've ever created a JPEG image that contains text or flat color graphics such as buttons, you know that the JPEG compression process is murder on GIF-like images. Text and flat color areas turn into an unsightly, blocky patchwork. You can choose to have your Selective Quality setting also apply to the text objects and Button Symbols in your document, without having to cover each element individually with a JPEG mask. To do so, choose Modify ⇨ Selective JPEG ⇨ Settings to display the Selective JPEG Settings dialog box (see Figure 15-21), and check the Preserve Text Quality and/or Preserve Button Quality checkboxes. You can also enable or disable the Selective Quality setting in the same dialog box.

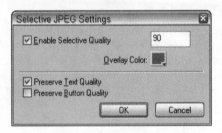

Figure 15-21: Choose whether the Selective Quality setting also applies to text and buttons in the Selective JPEG Settings dialog box.

Tip You can also click the Edit Selective Quality Options button that appears on the Optimize panel when it's set to JPEG to display the Selective JPEG Settings dialog box.

Figure 15-22 shows the Quality and Selective Quality settings in action, using the image and JPEG mask from Figure 15-20.

Figure 15-22: The text and the area under the JPEG mask are clear and sharp because they have a high Selective Quality setting of 90. The rest of the image, however, is all but obscured by JPEG artifacting, due to its low Quality setting of 25.

Sharpening edges

Graphics on the Web are often a montage of photographs, illustrations, and text. Although JPEG is the right choice for a continuous tone image, such as a photograph, it can make text that overlays a photograph appear fuzzy because JPEG is far better at compressing gradations than it is at compressing images with hard edges and abrupt color changes. To overcome these obstacles, use Fireworks' Sharpen JPEG Edges option, which is on the Optimize panel Options menu.

As the name implies, Sharpen JPEG Edges restores some of the hard-edge transitions that are lost during JPEG compression. This is especially noticeable on text and simple graphics, such as rectangles superimposed on photographs (see Figure 15-23). Keep an eye on the balance between image quality and file size, though, because Sharpen JPEG Edges can sometimes increase file size to the point where you may be better off simply increasing the Quality setting for your whole image.

Figure 15-23: When a photographic image includes sharp edges such as text, keep them from getting too blurry by enabling the Sharpen JPEG Edges option in the Optimize panel Options menu.

Smoothing

The more that a JPEG file is compressed, the "blockier" it becomes. As the compression increases, the JPEG algorithm throws out more and more similar pixels — after a certain point, the transitions and gradations are lost and areas become flat color blocks.

Fireworks' Smoothing feature slightly blurs the overall image so that stray pixels resulting from the compression are less noticeable. The Smoothing scale in the Optimize panel runs from zero to eight. Smoothing offers two benefits: It reduces the blockiness that is sometimes evident with JPEG compression, and it also slightly decreases file size.

Just as images with lots of straight lines or text benefit from the Sharpen JPEG Edges setting, Smoothing works best for images with lots of curves and generally smooth shapes.

Progressive

To most, Progressive JPEG is seen only as an incremental display option for JPEGs, similar to Interlaced for the GIF format. The Progressive JPEG option on the Optimize panel Options menu is more than that, however: It actually enables a different compression algorithm — a second generation one — that often offers lower file sizes at the equivalent quality of the original JPEG compression. The Progressive JPEG format was developed by Netscape, but has won the support of recent browser versions from Microsoft, as well.

Note   Although Internet Explorer displays Progressive JPEG images, it displays them without the progressive look of developing as they download. They appear to the user to be regular JPEG images.

In practice, I find that enabling the Progressive JPEG option often (but not always) gives me a smaller file size. For me, choosing this option generally depends on whether the client prefers to see the images slowly develop as they download or prefers them to download completely and appear as a finished image.

PNG 32 and 24

As a Web format, PNG is still in its infancy — well, maybe early childhood — as far as general browser acceptance is concerned. The PNG format holds great promise for Web graphics. Combining the best of both worlds, PNG has lossless compression, like GIF, and is capable of millions of colors, like JPEG. Moreover, PNG offers an interlace scheme that appears much more quickly than either GIF or JPEG, as well as transparency support that is far superior to both other formats.

One valuable aspect of the PNG format is that it makes the display of images stored as PNG files appear more uniform across various computer platforms. Generally, graphics made on a PC look brighter on a Macintosh, and Mac-made images seem darker on a PC. PNG includes *gamma correction* capabilities that alter the image, depending on the computer used by the viewer.

Until recently, the various browsers supported PNG only through plug-ins. After PNG was endorsed as a new Web graphic format by the World Wide Web Consortium (W3C), both Netscape and Microsoft 4.0 browser versions added native, inline support of the new format. Perhaps most importantly, however, Macromedia's Dreamweaver was among the first Web-authoring tools to offer native PNG support. Inserted PNG images preview in the document window as GIFs and JPEGs do. Then, Fireworks was introduced, which not only allows you to export PNG images, but uses PNG as its own format.

Although support for PNG is growing steadily, browser support currently is not widespread enough to warrant a total switchover to the PNG format. PNG is capable of many more features, such as Alpha Transparency, that are not fully in use by any major browser. Interestingly enough, Fireworks is way ahead of most other graphic programs in its support of PNG. Greg Roelofs, one of the developers of the PNG format, calls Fireworks, "the best PNG-supporting image editor available."

Unlike an Index Transparency color, which is either completely transparent or completely opaque, an Alpha Transparent color can be partially transparent — in fact, the transparency can use as many as 256 gradations. This allows a 32-bit image to be easily composited with other images, meaning that although PNG is not yet the best choice for the browser, it is an excellent choice for creating graphics for use in multimedia presentations, such as Shockwave or Flash movies, where animated objects are often stacked on top of each other, or composited with different backgrounds. Director and Flash are also both happy to import your actual Fireworks PNG files, Fireworks header and all.

Caution   The Fireworks native PNG format is considered an extended PNG format because of the additional effects, text, and other data included in the header of each file. Other programs capable of generally displaying PNG files may show the basic Fireworks image, but won't be able to edit it in the same way. To display a file in PNG format on a Web page, specifying PNG as the format when you export is best, so that your PNG image lacks extra Fireworks information and is as small as possible.

Other formats

The issues that are involved in exporting a PNG 24 or PNG 32 image are the same as those for exporting a TIFF, BMP, or PICT (Macintosh only) image from Fireworks. Generally, this export is straightforward, involving only the Matte setting.

Sending Images to Other Programs

Fireworks offers a number of different methods for you to export files so that they're ready to use in other applications. You can choose File ⇨ Export if you know your settings are correct; you can choose File ⇨ Export Preview if you wish to tweak any settings on the way out; or you can take advantage of the Quick Export pop-up menu to send your file out to another application via the standard export settings for that program. If you were working on a document that was destined for FrontPage, you could click on the Quick Export pop-up menu, select the Other category, and then choose Export to FrontPage (see Figure 15-24). This would export your image, with the settings in the Optimize panel, and create the FrontPage style HTML/XHTML file, if necessary.

Figure 15-24: The Quick Export pop-up menu enables you to export your file to Macromedia's main applications as well as others, such as Microsoft's FrontPage.

Another feature of the Quick Export pop-up menu is something that's available only for the Macromedia products listed in the menu (refer to Figure 15-24). One of the options on the submenus for the Macromedia applications allows you to launch any of those programs that you have on your system without having to go to the Start Menu, your Applications folder, or the Dock. This can be a real time saver since your mouse is most likely to be close to the Fireworks document window, thus, the Quick Export pop-up menu.

Integrating Fireworks with FrontPage

Fireworks has a long history of working well with Dreamweaver. The integration between the two applications makes it a breeze to take images, and even whole Web site designs, back and forth between the two applications. But what happens if you're not using Dreamweaver for your Web page designs? Don't worry, Fireworks still has you covered.

New Feature

Fireworks MX allows you to jump easily between using Microsoft FrontPage for your layout work and Fireworks for your graphic editing, all with the click of a button.

When you install Fireworks, the installation program detects the presence of Microsoft FrontPage and offers to install the files required to enable Fireworks integration with FrontPage, as shown in Figure 15-25.

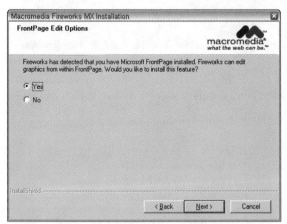

Figure 15-25: The Fireworks installer detects that FrontPage is installed and asks whether or not you wish to install the FrontPage integration.

If you aren't interested in installing Fireworks integration into FrontPage then it's a simple matter of clicking the No radio button and then clicking the Next button to continue the installation. If you decide you want to enable the integration, clicking

Next causes the Fireworks installer to continue the installation, giving FrontPage a powerful new feature. When everything is installed, you can open FrontPage and see a new button among those in its toolbars. Now, when you open a webpage with an image in it, you can select the image and click the Launch and Edit Selected Graphic in Fireworks button, as seen in Figure 15-26, to open Fireworks and begin the editing session.

Figure 15-26: With FrontPage integration installed, you are able to launch and edit your graphics in Fireworks with the click of a button.

Fireworks opens the Find Source dialog box asking if you'd like to continue editing the file you're working with, or if you'd like to open the Fireworks PNG file that originally created it. To look for, and then edit, the Fireworks PNG, click Yes. If you would like to continue with the current image, click No, and Fireworks finishes loading with your image in the current document window. You can make the changes you need to make, and then click Done at the top of the document window to return to FrontPage. Once you are back in FrontPage, the newly edited image is in your document window.

Cross-Reference For more on integration between Dreamweaver and Fireworks, see Chapter 22.

Working in the Export Preview

As convenient as optimizing and previewing images in Fireworks' workspace is, you may sometimes find that you want to access all the export features in one centralized location. Fireworks' Export Preview dialog box (see Figure 15-27) is just the place, and offers some extra export options that are unavailable in the workspace, to boot.

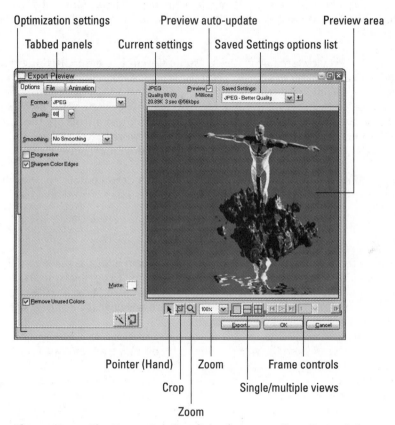

Optimization settings   Preview auto-update   Preview area

Tabbed panels   Current settings   Saved Settings options list

Pointer (Hand)   Zoom   Frame controls

Crop   Single/multiple views

Zoom

Figure 15-27: The Export Preview dialog box centralizes Fireworks' export features, and offers a few special features of its own.

The three tabbed panels in the Export Preview dialog box are as follows:

✦ **Options:** The primary panel for optimizing your image. The file format, bit-depth, compression, transparency, and other preferences are selected here. All color control—such as locking, editing, and deleting colors—is handled here, as well. The controls here are analogous to those found in the Optimize panel.

✦ **File:** Controls two aspects of an exported file — scale and numeric cropping. The exported image can be resized either by a percentage or to a precise pixel measurement. The image can be cropped by entering X and Y coordinates for the upper-left corner, and width and height dimensions of the new area. In Fireworks, the exported image can also be cropped visually in the Preview area.

✦ **Animation:** Contains all the settings for running an animated GIF, including the frame delay, disposal method, and looping preferences. Many of these options are also available in the Frames panel when you're optimizing in the workspace.

The always-visible Preview area provides a visual reference to compare different settings, and also allows you to visually crop the image. Also included are a panning tool (the Pointer), a Zoom tool (the magnifying glass), and a VCR-like control for playing an animation or other multiframe file. You may experience some *déjà vu* as you look around the Export Preview dialog box. Many of the controls are the same or very similar to those you use when optimizing in the workspace, and with good reason. There's no need to learn the Export Preview dialog box from scratch.

As previously mentioned, the Export Preview dialog box does contain some additional, unique export features, such as cropping and scaling exported images.

Cropping

The Export Area tool found on the Tools panel might seem a logical place to define an export area within the document window, but using the Export Area tool is only a first step to exporting an image with the Export Preview dialog box. In other words, although the Export Area tool is used in the document window, it's not part of the document window's in-place preview or export.

You can export a cropped version of a document by outlining an area with the Export Area tool and double-clicking that area to open the Export Preview dialog box, or you can simply open the Export Preview dialog box directly and then crop your image in its preview. When you initiate a cropping session in the Export Preview dialog box by clicking the Export Area button in the Preview area, the familiar dashed cropping outline surrounds the image, as shown in Figure 15-28. The eight handles are used to narrow the exported area. The original image is not permanently cropped or altered in any way.

Note   Unlike the regular Crop tool in the document window, you can't use the Export Area tool to expand the boundaries of the canvas.

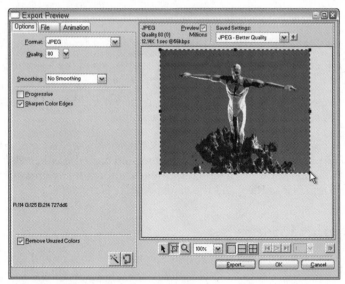

Figure 15-28: In Fireworks, you can crop visually right in the Export Preview dialog box.

If the File tab is displayed in the Export Preview while you're cropping, the X and Y coordinates of the upper-left corner of your exported area, as well as the width and height dimensions, are visible. The numeric cropping information is updated each time after a cropping handle is dragged to a new position. Alternatively, you can adjust the visual cropping precisely by entering values in the appropriate Export Area text boxes.

Tip

> You can also crop an image by selecting an area in the document window with the Export Area tool (the camera on the flyout under the Pointer tool) and double-clicking the area. The Export Preview opens, and you can export your cropped image without affecting the original.

To crop an image visually, follow these steps:

1. Choose either the Export Area tool beneath the Preview window(s), or the Export Area option on the File tab. An outline with cropping handles appears around the image.

2. Drag the handles to a new position so that only the area you want to export is displayed.

3. Choose any other tool (Pointer or Zoom), or click either the Set Defaults or the Next button to accept the newly cropped area.

To crop an image numerically, follow these steps:

1. From the File tab, select the Export Area option.

2. Select a new upper-left coordinate by entering new values in the X and/or Y text boxes, and press Tab to accept the changed value.

3. Select a new image size by entering new values in the W (Width) and H (Height) text boxes, and press Tab to accept the changed value.

Both cropping methods — visual and numeric — work together as well as separately. While viewing the File panel, select the Export Area tool and crop the image visually. When you release the mouse button, the numeric values automatically update. Similarly, change the numeric values, and the visual display is redrawn.

Scaling exported images

It might seem redundant to note that "Web graphics come in all shapes and sizes" — except it's also true to say that the *same* Web graphic often comes in different shapes and sizes. Reusing graphic elements is a very key design strategy in product branding in most media, and the technique is especially useful on the Web. Fireworks makes it very easy to export resized or cropped graphics from a master file, through the Export Preview dialog box.

Scaling controls are under the File tab in the Export Preview dialog box. You can resize a graphic by specifying either a percentage or an exact pixel size. By default, all rescaling is constrained to the original height-to-width ratio — however, you can disable the Constrain option to alter one dimension separately from the other.

To resize an image, follow these steps:

1. From the Export Preview dialog box, select the File tab.

2. To rescale an image by percentage, use the % slider, or enter a value directly into the % text box.

   The % slider's range is from 1 percent to 200 percent, but you can enter any value in the text box.

3. To resize an image to an exact dimension, enter a figure in the W (Width) and/or H (Height) text box.

   If the Constrain option is selected, enter a value in only one of the dimension text boxes and press Tab. The other dimension will be calculated for you according to the image's original height-to-width ratio.

4. To alter the height-to-width ratio, deselect Constrain and perform Step 3.

Tip

One of my favorite image optimization techniques is to scale an image to 50 percent of its size upon export and then place it in an HTML page at double size; doubling the width and height attributes of the `img` tag. The effects of this are usually noticeable, but often not objectionable, especially for flat color images. One thing's for sure: no faster way exists to halve the weight of an exported document. Experiment with this technique and see whether it works for you.

Using the Export Wizards

Fireworks' export options are very full-featured and can certainly be overwhelming if you're new to Web graphics. If you're not even sure how best to begin optimizing your image, let one of Fireworks' Export Wizards guide you. In addition to the original Export Wizard, which is very helpful for selecting the appropriate file format, Fireworks introduces the Export to Size Wizard to meet those absolute file-size limits.

If you are ready to export, but don't know where to start, bring up Fireworks' Export Wizard, which not only helps you to determine the correct file format best suited to the graphic's purpose, but it also provides you with an alternative in certain cases. For this reason, seasoned Web designers can also use the Export Wizard to get quickly to a jumping-off place for further optimization.

Regardless of the selection that the Export Wizard makes for you, it always presents you with a visual display through the Export Preview dialog box, covered extensively earlier in this chapter. Feel free to either accept the recommendations of the Export Wizard as is — and click the Next button to complete the operation — or tweak the settings first before you proceed.

The Export Wizard has three primary uses:

✦ To help you select an export format

✦ To offer suggestions to optimize your image after you select an export format

✦ To recommend export modes that will reduce a graphic to a specified file size

To use the Export Wizard to select an export format, follow these steps:

1. Choose File ➪ Export Wizard.

The initial screen of the Export Wizard appears, as shown in Figure 15-29.

2. With the "Select an export format" option selected, click Continue.

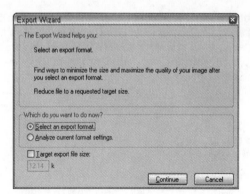

Figure 15-29: The Export Wizard provides a good launch pad for export selections.

3. The next screen of the Export Wizard appears and offers four choices for the graphic's ultimate destination:

   • **The Web:** Restricts the export options to the most popular Web formats, GIF and JPEG.

   • **An image-editing application:** Selects the best format for continuing to edit the image in another program, such as Photoshop. Generally, Fireworks selects the TIFF format.

   • **Desktop publishing application:** Selects the best print format, typically TIFF.

   • **Dreamweaver:** The same as The Web option, restricts the export options to the most popular Web formats — GIF and JPEG.

Note If your graphic uses frames, the Export Wizard asks instead whether your file is to be exported as an Animated GIF, a JavaScript button rollover, or a single image file.

4. Click Continue after you make your choice.

   Fireworks presents its analysis of your image, with suggestions on how to narrow the selection further if more than one export choice is recommended.

Caution If you select Animated GIF as your destination for your multiframe image, you must select the resulting Preview window to display the details in the Options panel.

5. Click Exit to open the Export Preview dialog box and complete the export operation.

If you choose either The Web or Dreamweaver for your graphic's export destination, Fireworks presents you with two options for comparison: a GIF and a JPEG. The file in the upper Preview window is the smallest file size. Fireworks is fairly conservative in this aspect of the Export Wizard and does not attempt to seriously reduce the file size at the cost of image quality.

If you would like to limit the file size while selecting an export format, select the "Target export file size" option on the Export Wizard's first screen. After you enable this option, you need to enter a file size value in the adjacent text box. File size is always measured in kilobytes. After you enter a file size, click Continue for Fireworks to calculate the results.

When Fireworks attempts to fit a graphic into a particular file size, it exports the image up to 12 times to find the best size with the least compression. Although it's usually very fast, this process can take several minutes to complete with a large graphic. Again, for graphics intended for the Web, Fireworks presents two choices — both at, or under, your specified target size.

In addition to specifying a file size through the Export Wizard, you can choose the Optimize to Size Wizard by clicking the button on the Options tab of the Export Preview dialog box. The Optimize to Size Wizard opens a simple dialog box that asks for the specified file size. The major difference between this wizard and the Target export file size option on the Export Wizard is that the Optimize to Size Wizard works only with the current format — no alternative choices are offered. Consequently, the Optimize to Size Wizard is faster, but it's intended more for the intermediate-to-advanced user who understands the differences between file formats.

Examining Additional Export Options

The vast majority of the time, graphics are exported from Fireworks as single images, or as an HTML document with separate image slices, or as a Dreamweaver Library item. However, Fireworks also offers several other export options. You can export the following:

✦ Fireworks layers, frames, or slices as Cascading Style Sheet (CSS) layers in an HTML document for use in Dynamic-HTML-capable Web browsers

✦ Fireworks layers or slices as an HTML document for easy import into Macromedia Director

✦ The layers of a Fireworks document as separate image files

✦ Fireworks frames as separate image files

✦ The four frames of a rollover button as an Image Well format image used by Lotus Domino Designer

✦ Vector artwork as a Flash movie

✦ Vector artwork in Adobe Illustrator format

✦ Your complete Fireworks document as a multi-layer Photoshop document, suitable for further editing in Photoshop

All of these additional export methods are grouped in the Save as type (Save As on the Mac) option list in the Export dialog box, as shown in Figure 15-30. To display the Export dialog box, choose File ➪ Export.

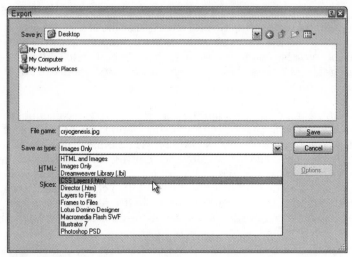

Figure 15-30: The Save as type (Save As) option list in the Export dialog box handles a variety of individual export situations.

Tip   Regardless of which type of export operation you undertake, the current settings in the Optimize panel determine the image file format and other settings where applicable.

Cross-Reference   Chapter 21 covers the two items on the Export dialog box's Save as type (Save As) option list: HTML and Images, and Dreamweaver Library.

Exporting as CSS layers

The term *layers* is used quite often in the Web graphics field. To the Photoshop user, a "layer" is a division capable of holding a single graphic element. In Fireworks, a "layer" is a useful organizational tool that can hold any number of objects. In Dynamic HTML and in Web-authoring tools such as Dreamweaver, a "layer" is a type of container that can be precisely positioned, hidden, or displayed — or flown across the screen with JavaScript-driven animation. You can create these layers by using a standard known as Cascading Style Sheets (CSS). Fireworks enables you to save the contents of Fireworks layers, frames, or slices along with the CSS-based HTML. This facility enables you to achieve effects, such as the "flying" buttons in Figure 15-31.

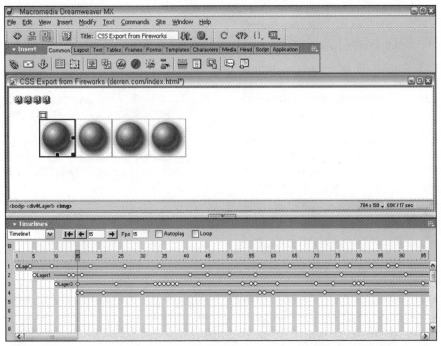

Figure 15-31: These buttons, exported from Fireworks as separate CSS layers and then animated in Dreamweaver, fly into place.

To export Fireworks components as CSS layers, follow these steps:

1. Specify format and optimization settings in the Optimize panel.

2. Choose File ➪ Export.

   The Export dialog box appears.

3. Choose CSS Layers from the Save as type (Save As) option list.

   Fireworks displays further options relating to exporting CSS Layers.

4. From the Source option list, select the Fireworks component to export as CSS Layers. The options are Fireworks Layers, Fireworks Frames, or Fireworks Slices.

5. Check the Trim Images checkbox to export the individual components on the smallest-sized canvas necessary.

   If Trim Images is not selected, each exported file will be the same dimensions as the original image.

6. If you're exporting from Fireworks Frames, check the Current Frame Only checkbox to limit the export to the current frame only.

7. Check the Put Images in Subfolder checkbox to have Fireworks place the image files in their own folder.

Click the Browse button to select a particular folder.

8. Click Save when you're done.

After you complete the export process, you'll have both the separate images and the HTML necessary to place each image in its own CSS layer. To use the layers on your Web page, you need to incorporate the generated code into your own Web page. You can accomplish this with any Web-authoring tool that allows you to access the HTML directly. Initially, the code appears overwhelming, but only the plain-English phrases that bracket it are important. In your favorite HTML or text editor, select the code from the line

```
<! --------- BEGIN COPYING THE CODE HERE ---------->
```

and end your selection with the line

```
<! --------- STOP COPYING THE CODE HERE ---------->
```

After you select the code, copy it to the clipboard and then open your working HTML page and paste the clipboard contents anywhere in the `<body>` section. Now, you can continue to manipulate the layers in any manner that you prefer in your Web-authoring program.

Note Dreamweaver users don't have to use the HTML Source window or any other text tool to copy and paste the Fireworks code. In Dreamweaver, simply find the Invisible Element symbols that enclose the layer code — you'll see a Dreamweaver HTML comment symbol on either side of the layer symbols. Select all of these symbols and then copy and paste them into your working document. You must have Invisible Elements enabled for this technique to work.

Exporting for Director

Fireworks is a key component of Macromedia's Director Shockwave Internet Studio, and as such, has developed some extra features that simplify creating and editing bitmaps for use in Director. Buttons and rollovers that you've created in Fireworks can be exported as images and HTML that can then be imported into Macromedia Director. Director does its part by converting the JavaScript-based Fireworks Behaviors into Director Behaviors. In addition, each object or layer from Fireworks becomes a Director cast member, with antialiasing and correct alpha transparency.

To export a Fireworks document for use in Director, follow these steps:

1. Choose File ➪ Export.

The Export dialog box appears.

2. Select Director (.htm) from the Save as type (Save As) option list.

3. Select either Fireworks Frames or Fireworks Layers from the Source option list.

4. Select the Trim images option to export the individual components on the smallest canvas necessary.

5. Click Save when you're ready.

Caution Director 7 or above is required in order to import the Fireworks-generated HTML. A Director Xtra may also be required to enable this feature. Consult your Director documentation and/or Macromedia's Web site.

Exporting files

Occasionally, you may want to break up the component layers or frames of your Fireworks document into separate files. Perhaps you need to reuse some of these elements in another part of the Web site, or maybe you want to process the files in another application before reintegrating them in Fireworks. Whatever the reason, Fireworks provides a fairly straightforward method for generating separate graphic files for almost any situation.

Cross-Reference Chapter 20 discusses exporting a single slice as an image file.

To export a Fireworks element as a separate file, follow these steps:

1. Specify format and optimization settings in the Optimize panel.

2. Choose File ⇨ Export.

   The Export dialog box appears.

3. To export frames as files, select Frames to Files from the Save as type (Save As) option list. Alternatively, to export layers as files, select Layers to Files.

4. Select the Trim images option to export the individual components on the smallest-sized canvas necessary.

   If Trim images is not selected, each exported file will be the same dimensions as the original image.

5. Click Save when you're ready.

Tip You can control which frames or layers are exported by turning off their visibility in their respective panels. The visibility is controlled by the Eye symbol next to each item name. The frame or layer will not be exported if it is not visible when you choose the Export command.

Exporting as Image Wells

Image Wells are used by Lotus Domino Designer to create rollover effects. Just as Fireworks uses frames to separate the different rollover states — up, over, down, and overdown — Domino Designer uses Image Wells. An Image Well is a single graphic with each rollover state side by side, separated by a single-pixel vertical line, as the example in Figure 15-32 shows.

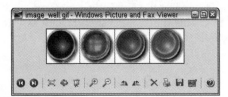

Figure 15-32: The final output of an Image Well export is used by Lotus Domino Designer to create rollover button effects.

> **Note** Image Wells are similar to the four state rollovers in Fireworks, but not exactly the same. The last two states — over and overdown — are reversed. Fireworks, however, understands this difference and exports your Image Well so that it will work correctly in Lotus Domino Designer.

This feature is best used to convert your existing multiframe images to Image Wells for use as rollovers. To export a graphic as an Image Well, follow these steps:

1. Specify format and optimization settings in the Optimize panel.

2. Choose File ➪ Export.

   The Export dialog box appears.

3. Select Lotus Domino Designer from the Save as type (Save As) option list.

4. Select Fireworks Frames, Fireworks Layers, or Fireworks slices from the Source option list to create an Image Well from frames, layers, or slices, respectively.

5. Select the Trim images option to export the individual components on the smallest-sized canvas necessary.

   If Trim images is not selected, each exported file will be the same dimensions as the original image.

6. Click Save when you're ready.

Fireworks saves your document as an Image Well, in the image format specified in the Optimize panel.

Exporting vectors

You can choose to export the vector shapes in your document as either a Flash SWF movie or an Adobe Illustrator document. The Flash format can be viewed in the majority of Web browsers as-is, and the Illustrator format can be imported into the majority of vector drawing applications, such as Adobe Illustrator and Macromedia FreeHand.

It's important to keep in mind that although Fireworks works with vector lines, it uses vector lines only as a substructure or "skeleton" for bitmaps and bitmap-based effects, such as bevels and drop shadows. Exporting this vector skeleton is a useful feature, but keep in mind that the exported objects will often bear only a passing resemblance to their Fireworks-native counterparts, as shown in Figure 15-33.

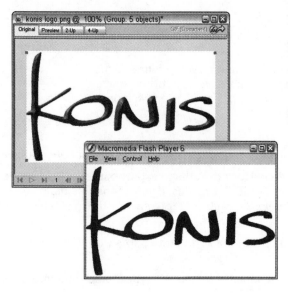

Figure 15-33: The object in Fireworks (top left) is a vector shape, but much of its look comes from Fireworks' stroke settings and Live Effects. After exporting as a Flash movie, shown bottom right, the object is expressed only in vector lines and its appearance changes dramatically.

To export vector shapes from Fireworks, follow these steps:

1. Choose File ⇨ Export.

   Fireworks displays the Export dialog box.

2. To export as Flash, choose Macromedia Flash SWF from the Save as type (Save As) option list. Alternatively, to export in Illustrator format, choose Illustrator 7.

Caution Fireworks Illustrator export is Adobe Illustrator 7 compatible, and may not import correctly into applications that expect a previous or later version of the Illustrator format.

3. Click the Options button to specify format-specific options.

Fireworks displays the options dialog box for the vector type you are exporting, as shown in Figure 15-34.

Figure 15-34: Specify export options for a vector format in the Macromedia Flash SWF Export Options dialog box (left), or the Illustrator Export Options dialog box, depending on which vector export format you choose.

4. If you are exporting as Macromedia Flash SWF, set the appropriate options:

- Set the Objects radio buttons to Paths to export paths, or to Maintain Appearance to export as JPEG bitmaps. If you choose Maintain Appearance, set the JPEG Quality slider to specify the quality of the JPEGs.

- Choose to maintain text, or convert text to paths with the Text radio buttons.

- Export all frames, or a range of frames with the Frames option.

- If necessary, change the target frame rate in the Frame Rate box. Otherwise, leave it at its default of 15.

Click OK when you're done.

5. If you are exporting Illustrator 7, set the appropriate options:

- Choose to export the current frame only, or to export Fireworks frames as Illustrator layers.

- If you are going to import your file into Macromedia FreeHand, make sure the FreeHand 8 Compatible checkbox is checked.

Click OK when you're done.

6. Click Save in the Export dialog box when you're done.

Your document's vector shapes are exported.

If you have the standalone Flash Player, double-clicking your Flash SWF file opens it for viewing. If not, you can also view Flash movies in a Web browser that's equipped with the Flash Player plug-in, or in the QuickTime Player.

If you exported as an Illustrator 7 document, open this document with Illustrator, FreeHand, Flash, or another vector art application.

Exporting Photoshop documents

Exporting your Fireworks document in the Photoshop format enables you to open and edit your Fireworks work in Photoshop, while maintaining the editability of individual objects, text objects, and Live Effects. You can later import the Photoshop document into Fireworks again for further editing and optimization. This feature is invaluable if you use both applications, or if your workgroup is made up of a mix of Fireworks and Photoshop users.

To export a Fireworks document as a Photoshop document, follow these steps:

1. Choose File ➪ Export.

   The Export dialog box appears.

2. Select Photoshop PSD from the Save as type (Save As) option list.

 Tip PSD refers to PhotoShop Document, and also to the typical filename extension for Photoshop documents: .psd.

3. From the Settings option list, choose one of the following:

   • Maintain Editability over Appearance strictly converts Fireworks elements to their corresponding Photoshop elements, but may result in your work looking slightly different after it's opened in Photoshop. This option is the default, and the best one for most situations.

 Caution Keeping at least a backup of your original Fireworks document is always a good idea, even after exporting to Photoshop format. If you choose any option other than Maintain Editability over Appearance, though, be absolutely certain to keep your original Fireworks document. The other export options all result in editable information being flattened or thrown away.

   • Maintain Fireworks Appearance keeps your Fireworks objects as Photoshop layers, but renders Live Effects and text objects as bitmap images, sacrificing editability for the cause of strictly maintaining the look of your work.

   • Smaller Photoshop File converts Fireworks layers to Photoshop layers, flattening all the objects on each Fireworks layer.

   • Custom enables you to choose specifically whether to maintain or flatten layers, and whether to maintain or render text and effects.

4. Click Save when you're ready.

Fireworks exports a Photoshop document, ready to be opened in Photoshop.

Caution   Importing files with more than 100 layers requires Photoshop 6 or above. Flatten or remove some objects or layers from your Fireworks document before export if you are using Photoshop 5.5 or earlier.

Summary

Every graphic created or edited in Fireworks is eventually exported for use on the Web or in another application. Reducing file size is a key facet of making Web graphics, so Fireworks offers a wide variety of export options. Keep the following points in mind as you optimize and export images:

✦ Maintaining at least two versions of any file is considered the best practice: one version in the Fireworks PNG format as a master copy, and a second version in whatever format you've exported for use on the Web.

✦ The primary goal of an export operation for the Web is to create the best-looking image with the smallest file size. This is called optimizing a graphic.

✦ Fireworks provides access to optimization and export options directly in the workspace, through the Optimize and Frames panels, and with the multiple tabs of the document window. Alternatively, you can choose to use the Export Preview dialog box, which you open by choosing File ➪ Export Preview.

✦ Fireworks offers up to four comparison views of an image being exported, so that you can quickly judge appearance alongside the displayed file size and approximate download time.

✦ The two major formats for the Web — GIF and JPEG — are each best used for different types of images. The GIF format is good for graphics with flat color, for which transparency is important, such as logos. The JPEG format works best with continuous-tone images, such as photographs.

✦ Another format, PNG, is considered the heir apparent to GIF, but still doesn't have enough support to warrant widespread usage. The PNG format has many advantages, such as full alpha transparency and gamma correction, which ameliorate image differences on different platforms. These are currently poorly supported by common Web browsers, however.

✦ Images can be easily — and precisely — scaled and cropped during the export operation, by using the Export Preview dialog box.

✦ Fireworks' advanced color control enables you to lock or replace any color in an indexed palette.

✦ Fireworks offers expert export guidance in the form of the Export Wizard.

✦ In addition to the standard image export, Fireworks can also export components of an image, such as layers, frames, or slice objects, in several different ways. Fireworks can even export just the vector shapes of your Fireworks objects as Macromedia Flash SWF or Illustrator documents.

✦ Fireworks can export to the Adobe Photoshop format, while maintaining the editability of individual elements.

In the next chapter, you find out how to maintain a consistent look and feel for your Web graphics through Fireworks Styles.

✦   ✦   ✦

Working with Fireworks Styles

Although not obvious to the beginning designer, Web graphics is as much about repetition as it is creation. After you establish a particular look and feel, that theme — the palette, fonts, effects, and more — is often carried through Web page after Web page. Several reasons exist for this repetition:

✦ Consistency of approach is one of the fundamental tenets of design work.

✦ For commercial sites, a consistent look and feel often ties in with the particular marketing message or branding that is being pursued.

✦ On the Internet, repetition of graphic elements aids visitors in the navigation of a Web site: If navigation buttons look the same from page to page, users can quickly learn how to move around the site — even on their first visit.

However, no matter how many reasons there are to use repetition, it can also be mind-numbing drudgery. Fireworks rescues Web designers from repetitive drudgery by offering a marvelous time- and work-saver known as *styles*. By using styles, you can easily apply the overall look and feel to any selected object. A single style can contain a variety of user-definable settings, and styles are always available as you move from document to document. Moreover, Macromedia designed styles to be very portable — you can import and export them as a group. This facility enables you, as a working Web designer, to keep different style files for different clients. Styles are, without a doubt, a major boost in Web productivity.

Understanding Styles

A Fireworks object is potentially composed of several separate formatting choices: a path, a stroke, a fill, and one or more Live Effects. Each of these elements can be broken down further; for example, a stroke consists of a particular stroke type set to a specific color. Duplicating all the individual settings, one by one, that are necessary to establish a custom look would be extremely time-intensive and error-prone. Although you can copy an object to the Clipboard and then paste its formatting onto another object, this requires that you first have a suitable object available to copy. Rather than keep example objects around just in case you want to re-create their look, Fireworks allows you to separate the appearance of an object from the object itself, and save that appearance as a style.

New Feature   Fireworks MX now saves even more text attributes than before. By checking Text Other in the New Style dialog box, you instruct Fireworks to also save the text alignment, antialiasing, auto-kerning, horizontal scale, range kerning, and leading right in your style.

Fireworks provides a very novel, graphical method of maintaining and presenting styles: the Styles panel, shown in Figure 16-1. Acting as a formatting library, the Styles panel enables you to create, import, export, delete, and otherwise manage styles.

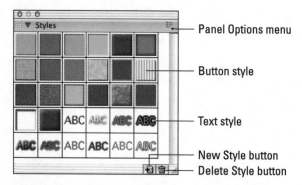

Figure 16-1: Fireworks includes a default palette of styles, available through the Styles panel.

Styles are visually divided in the Styles panel with two different types of icons: button styles and text styles. The only difference between the two is that a text style contains additional information: a typeface, size, and style, or any combination of the three. Button styles are depicted as squares and text styles are displayed as the letters ABC, but both preview the appearance that their style contains. Fireworks comes with 20 button styles and 10 text styles in its built-in default collection (which can be restored at any time) and over 300 more styles are available on the

Fireworks CD-ROM, or on the Web at http://www.macromedia.com/software/fireworks/download/styles. If you think the default styles are a little bland for your taste, be sure to check out the wide variety of additional styles.

On the CD-ROM

Find even more styles to add to your collection.

Caution

The more styles you add, the longer Fireworks will take to start because it needs to initialize all the styles.

Even though the Styles panel is divided between the button and text style types, you can apply both to any Fireworks object. In other words, you can apply button styles to text objects, and text styles to path objects. Any unusable style information (such as font color for a path object) is disregarded. You might think of button styles as styles, and text styles as "styles-plus"; the extra information they contain doesn't stop them from being a perfectly good choice for a button or other graphic.

Caution

The term *styles* is commonly used in computer programs. Unlike the styles you typically find in word processing, Fireworks styles do not maintain a link between the original style and the applied objects. If you edit a style, any objects that the style was previously applied to remain unaffected.

Applying Styles

To apply a style, you must first access the Styles panel, which you can open in a number of ways:

✦ Choose Window ➪ Styles.

✦ Use the keyboard shortcut, Shift+F11.

✦ Click the Styles tab, if the Styles panel is docked behind another, visible panel.

After the Styles panel is available, actually applying the style is very straightforward: Simply select the object you want to apply the style to and then click a style from the Styles panel. If you don't like the results, you can select another style. You can even duplicate the object and apply several styles to select the best option, as shown in Figure 16-2.

Caution

Applying one style overrides another style but only if both styles affect the same settings. Styles that contain every possible setting can be mixed and matched freely because they will always override the previously applied style. However, applying multiple styles that contain only a few of the possible settings—just a fill and stroke color, or just an effect, for example—will lead to your object having a mix of those styles. Suppose that you apply a style that only contains a green fill and then apply another style that only contains a drop shadow effect. Your object will now have a green fill and a drop shadow.

Original path object   Modified with styles

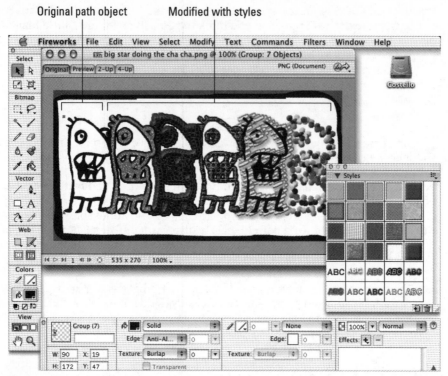

Figure 16-2: Applying different styles to the same object gives you a wide range of choices.

After you apply a style, the object remains completely independent of the style, and you can adjust all the settings on the various panels — Stroke, Fill, Effects, and Text — to customize the object. Regardless of what changes you make to a styled object, the style itself is unaltered.

Creating New Styles

Although using the standard styles — or any of those included on the Fireworks CD-ROM — is a quick way to establish a consistent look and feel, you may not be able to find the exact style that you want. The real power in Fireworks styles comes from the capability to create, save, and use your own styles. The look of any object — the stroke, fill, effect, or text settings — can be converted to a style and easily used over and over again by you or a colleague.

Imagine you've created an object — a button, say — with a finely tuned stroke setting, a perfect fill color, and five complex effects modifications with a mix of Fireworks' built-in drop shadows and bevels and third-party Photoshop plug-ins such as Kai Power Tools or Alien Skin's Eye Candy. The entire process might take five minutes to re-create, but instead of doing so, select your object and create a style from it. Image or path objects can look incredibly textured and fussed-over in the time it takes to apply a style. It's worth noting again that these effects remain completely editable on each new object they're applied to.

For more about Live Effects and Xtras, see Chapter 12.

To create a new style, follow these steps:

1. Select the object upon which you want to base the style.

If you want to base your new style on a style you already have, apply the style to your object, modify the object's formatting accordingly, and then continue with Step 2.

2. If the Styles panel is hidden, choose Window ⇨ Styles to view it, or use the keyboard shortcut Shift+F11, or click the Styles panel's tab if it is docked behind another, visible window.

3. Click the New Styles button at the bottom of the Styles panel. The New Style dialog box appears, as shown in Figure 16-3.

Figure 16-3: Create a new style by selecting available options in the New Style dialog box.

4. Enter a unique name for your new style in the Name text box.

Fireworks automatically names new styles Style 1, Style 2, Style 3, and so on, which it considers to be different from the Style 01, Style 02, Style 03, and so on with which its built-in styles are named. You can rename your new style by deleting the suggested name and entering your own choice. Be aware, however, that Fireworks does not check for conflicting names, so you can easily end up with two or more styles with the same name. I find it's best to make very descriptive names for the styles I create, so that they're easy to recall later, and harder to duplicate accidentally. If you hover your cursor over a style's icon in the Styles panel, Fireworks shows you the style's name at the bottom of the panel.

5. Select which of the available style settings you want to save with your style. Available settings are the following:

- **Fill Type:** Stores the Fill category (Solid, Gradient, Web Dither, or Pattern), the name of the gradient or Pattern, the edge settings (including the Amount of Feather, if applicable), and all the texture settings (name, degree, and transparency).

- **Fill Color:** Stores the Fill colors for Solid fills. For Gradient, Web Dither, and Pattern fills, the colors are stored with the Fill Type option.

- **Stroke Type:** Stores the category, name of stroke, all stroke stamp information (even if customized through the Edit Stroke command), the edge softness, the stroke size, and the texture settings (name and amount of texture).

- **Stroke Color:** Stores the selection in the current object's Stroke color well.

- **Effect:** Stores all the settings for an object's Live Effect, whether single (Inner Bevel, Outer Bevel, Drop Shadow, Glow, or Emboss) or multiple.

- **Text Font:** Stores the name of the current font for a text object.

- **Text Size:** Stores the size of the current font for a text object.

- **Text Style:** Stores the style (bold, italic, and/or underline) for a text object.

- **Text Other:** Stores the extra formatting (alignment, antialiasing, auto-kerning, horizontal scale, range kerning, or leading) for a text object.

6. Click OK when you're done.

For all the information that styles are capable of retaining, you should note that although a style remembers gradients, Fireworks styles do not retain any gradient settings pertaining to modified Gradient Control handles, accessed through the Gradient tool.

You should remember two points when you are creating and applying new styles. First, if a style does not affect a particular setting, that setting is left as is on the selected object. Second, a Stroke, Fill, or Effect set to None is as valid a setting as any other. For example, if the object on which you base your new style does not include a fill, but you've selected Fill Type in the Edit Style dialog box, any object to which this style is applied — whether it has a fill or not — will have the fill removed.

Managing Styles

Every time you add a style, it stays available for every document opened in Fireworks. If you really become adept at using styles, you'll quickly begin to have a massive collection of styles — truly too much of a good thing. Fireworks offers several commands, mostly grouped under the Styles panel's Options menu, for managing your styles.

Tip   Before you start selecting styles in order to delete or modify them, make sure that you don't have any objects in your document selected, or selecting a style will apply that style to the object. Click the mouse in an empty area of the canvas, or choose Select ➪ Deselect, or use the keyboard shortcut Ctrl+D (Command+D).

You've seen how you can create a style by selecting the New Style button from the bottom of the Styles panel. Its obvious companion is the Delete Style button (the trash can) right next to it. To remove any unwanted style, select its icon in the Styles panel and choose the Delete Style button.

Tip   You can select multiple styles at the same time. Hold down Ctrl (Command) while you select styles to add one at a time. Hold down Shift to select a range of adjacent styles; Fireworks will select the two styles you click on and every style along the shortest route between them. This selection method is more similar to a spreadsheet than a word processor. To select a row of styles, hold down Shift and click the first and last in the row. To add another row to your selection, keep holding Shift and click the last style in the second row. To add part of a row to your selection, switch to holding down Ctrl (Command) and add the final styles one by one. The same technique applies to selecting columns.

A total of seven commands are available in the Styles panel's Options menu, shown in Figure 16-4:

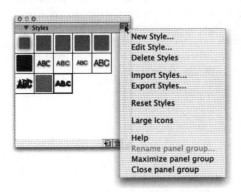

Figure 16-4: Manage your styles through the commands in the Styles panel's Options menu.

✦ **New Style:** Creates a new style based on the selected object. This command is identical to the New Style button.

✦ **Edit Style:** Opens the Edit Style dialog box, enabling you to select or deselect the setting options.

Tip   You can also access the Edit Style dialog box by double-clicking a style's icon in the Styles panel.

✦ **Delete Styles:** Removes a selected style or styles.

✦ **Import Styles:** Loads a new set of styles after the currently selected one. You must store styles in the Fireworks Styles format, and you can't import them from a Fireworks document, for example.

✦ **Export Styles:** Stores the currently selected style or styles in the Fireworks Styles format.

✦ **Resets Styles:** Removes any styles you have added to the Styles panel and reloads the default configuration of styles.

✦ **Large Icons:** Toggles between regular and large-sized icons. When checked, icons are displayed twice their normal size.

Earlier in this chapter, I showed you how to create and delete styles; the New Style and Delete Styles commands work in the same way as their respective buttons. Editing an existing style is also a familiar process. Choose Edit Style, and you are presented with the same options in the Edit Styles dialog box as when you create a new one. Just make any changes, click OK, and your revised style is ready to use.

Tip
The Edit Style command is also a good way to check what formatting options a particular style affects before applying it. Double-click the style or select it and choose Edit Style from the Options menu to see which formatting options are checked.

The Export Styles command opens a dialog box, shown in Figure 16-5. Fireworks offers to save your new file in its Styles folder under the name Custom Styles.stl, ("Custom Styles" on the Macintosh) but you can change the name to anything else and store the file wherever you want (as long as you can find it later). If you use a Macintosh, the .stl filename extension is not necessary, but leaving it on keeps your style files cross-platform-ready, and will enable you to share your styles with Windows users or use them yourself on a Windows machine.

Figure 16-5: Export a collection of styles and save them as a Fireworks style file with the filename extension .stl.

The Import Styles command opens a standard Open dialog box. Choose a style file and click Open to import it.

Tip   Mac users: If you receive a Fireworks style file from a Windows-using friend or download it unarchived from the Internet, it may not have a Mac OS Creator or Type and will appear with a blank icon. As long as it still has its .stl filename extension, though, Fireworks will recognize it and allow you to import and use it. If you want, you can use the File Exchange Control Panel or a utility such as File Buddy or FinderPop to give the file the proper creator of *MKBY* (Fireworks, of course) and type of *STYf*, which restores its icon.

As noted previously, when you import a set of Fireworks styles, all styles are inserted after the currently selected style. For this reason, I typically find it best to select the last currently loaded style before importing. You also can create a spacer or two — create a style from a plain object with no fill, stroke, or effects. The style icon will appear blank and acts to separate your imported styles from the standard ones.

On the CD-ROM   You'll find a style file called No Style.stl in the Configuration/Styles folder that contains only one style that applies a Fill, Stroke, and Effect of None. This makes a handy spacer and a quick, easy way to unformat an object before applying another style. You could also save this as the first or last style in your exported style files to provide an easy-to-see start or finish.

The final two Styles panel commands, Reset Styles and Large Icons, are fairly self-explanatory. Reset Styles removes all styles currently in the Styles panel and reloads the standard set of styles in their place. Because this measure is fairly drastic, Fireworks asks for confirmation before proceeding. Selecting Large Icons displays the style icons at twice their standard size — they enlarge from 36 pixels square to 72. This feature is sometimes useful when trying to differentiate between two similar styles.

Fireworks Technique: Isolating Patterns and Textures from Styles

A close look at some of the styles that come with Fireworks — both the defaults and the extras found on the Fireworks CD-ROM — reveals several exciting Patterns and textures. On the CD you'll find a style — quite innocently named Style 37, and contained within text1-201.stl — that has an intriguing spotted Pattern, shown in Figure 16-6. A quick check of the Fill panel reveals that a texture, called (appropriately) cow, is in use as part of the style. However, no such file exists in the Textures folder; so, where did it come from? The texture is actually embedded in the style.

Tip   Find text1-201.stl on the Fireworks CD-ROM at Goodies/Styles/Styles/text/text1-201.stl.

Figure 16-6: Examine the cow texture from Style 37. It works fine on a plain circle and also specifies 170pt Arial Black when applied to text.

Donna Casey, a Web designer whose work you can see at www.n8vision.com, uncovered a technique for extracting the embedded textures and Patterns that you may find in a style. Why would you do this? You might find that the Pattern and/or texture is, to your eye, better when combined with a different stroke or effects setting — or you might want to incorporate only the Pattern or texture in an image. This problem has two approaches. First, you could edit the style, removing all the options except for Fill Type. This is, at best, a partial solution. The Pattern/texture is still encased in the other pertinent settings; textures, for example, could be part of a Solid, Pattern, or Gradient Fill. To completely separate the texture or Pattern and then save it, follow these steps:

1. Draw a fairly large rectangle or square, approximately 500×500 pixels.

   The goal is to make the object large enough so that the pattern clearly repeats.

2. From the Styles panel, select the style whose texture or fill you want to isolate.

   The style is applied to the object.

3. From the Property inspector, choose None in the Stroke section.

4. Select any Effects in the Property inspector and click on the minus to delete them.

5. To retrieve a texture, make the following changes to the Fill section of the Property inspector:

   • Set the Fill category to Solid.

   • Set the Fill color to black.

   • Set the Amount of texture to 100%.

6. To retrieve a Pattern, set the Amount of texture to 0%.

7. Choose the Crop tool from the Tools panel.

8. Crop the object to encompass the repeating pattern.

   This is, by far, the hardest part; it might take several attempts to get it just right. It is a good idea is to save the file before you begin to crop the object. With most textures, the repeating pattern will actually be smaller than it might first appear.

9. When you finish cropping, save the file in either the Patterns or Textures folders in the Configuration folder within your Fireworks program folder.

10. Restart Fireworks to refresh the Pattern and texture lists.

Tip   You can also use your new Pattern or texture without restarting Fireworks by choosing Other, from the Pattern or texture list in the Fill section of the Property inspector, and selecting your newly saved file.

Your new extricated Pattern or texture should now be available to you in the Stroke and Fill sections of the Property inspector.

Summary

Styles are a major production boost, enabling you to easily build up a library of formatting choices and add a consistent look and feel to all of your graphics on a client-by-client or site-by-site basis. Styles are also a significant work-saver — rather than having to add individually all the characteristics that compose a particular look, you can add them all with one click of the Styles panel. The main points with regard to styles are:

✦ Styles are accessible through the Styles panel.

✦ A style may contain almost all the information for reproducing a graphic's stroke, fill, effect, and text settings.

✦ Unlike some other programs, such as Macromedia FreeHand, Fireworks styles do not retain a link to objects that use them.

✦ Any newly created style is available to all documents until the style is removed from the Styles panel.

✦ Styles can be edited, imported, exported, and otherwise managed through the commands found in the Styles panel's Options menu.

✦ A style can be "reverse engineered" to isolate the Pattern or texture that it contains.

In the next chapter, you find out how to use Symbols and Libraries to cut down on even more repetitive work.

✦   ✦   ✦

Using Symbols and Libraries

Many Fireworks features are specifically designed to prevent duplication of effort on the part of the busy Web artist. Perhaps none more so than the symbols. In a nutshell, a *symbol* is an object that's been designated as a master copy and stored in a Symbol Library. Copies of a symbol, called *Instances*, retain a link to their symbol so that they can be modified as a group. Editing the symbol causes its Instances to inherit the changes.

This chapter begins with a discussion of the basics of using symbols, Instances, and Libraries in Fireworks. Later, you discover how to make, modify, and manage symbols, Instances, and Libraries.

Understanding Symbols and Instances

Symbols in Fireworks are like templates for single objects. The symbol itself is like a rubber stamp that you dip in ink. You can "stamp out" virtually unlimited copies of any symbol, called *Instances*. Instances are copies of symbols that retain a link to their parent symbol. Editing the symbol causes its Instances to inherit many of the changes, such as fill and stroke settings. On the other hand, Instances have some independent properties of their own: You can apply the Transform tools to them, add Live Effects, or alter opacity settings on an individual basis, as shown in Figure 17-1. From a design perspective, symbols and Instances enable you to maintain a common look without losing a feeling of variety.

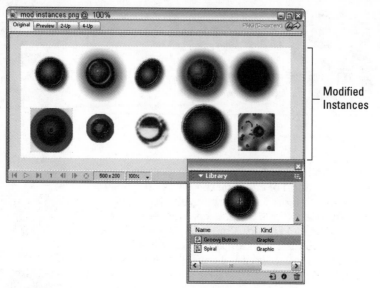

Modified
Instances

Figure 17-1: These are all Instances of the same symbol, with modifications made to scale, skew, opacity, and with Live Effects. The Instance at top left is unmodified and looks exactly like the parent symbol.

When you edit a symbol in the Symbol Editor, the link that its Instances have with the parent symbol causes them to inherit the changes, as shown in Figure 17-2. Fireworks automatically updates Instances to match their parent symbol as soon as you close the Symbol Editor. Note that any modifications that were made to the individual Instances — such as applying a Live Effect, Photoshop filter, or Transform tool — are unaffected.

Symbols themselves are always stored in a *Library*, accessible through the Library panel, shown in Figure 17-3. Converting an object to a symbol places it in the Library and leaves a copy behind — an Instance — in the document window. The Library panel provides a range of functions for managing and modifying symbols and Libraries, but its most basic function is as a way to make Instances. Dragging a symbol from the Library and dropping it in the document window makes a new Instance, much like making a shortcut to a file in Windows, or a file alias on the Mac. In fact, Instances even have the little arrow badge that Windows shortcuts and Mac aliases share.

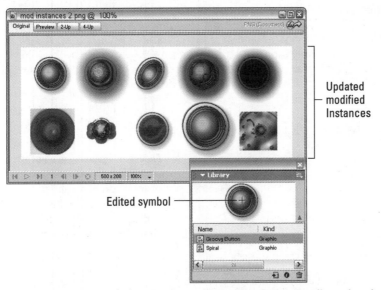

Updated modified Instances

Edited symbol

Figure 17-2: The Instances from Figure 17-1 are automatically updated by Fireworks after their parent symbol is modified. Even though most of the Instances have been heavily modified themselves, the change to the basic Instance (top left) shows through.

Figure 17-3: Symbols are stored in the Library panel. Dragging them into a document creates an Instance, identified by the arrow badge in its bounding box.

One advantage of using Instances is that they are simplified renderings of their parent symbol. Where a symbol might be a complex vector object with an intricate stroke and gradient fill, an Instance of it is just a simple bitmap object. Using many Instances rather than using independent objects, as shown in Figure 17-4, improves your computer's performance because Fireworks draws bitmap objects instead of the more complex vector objects over and over again.

Original vector drawing

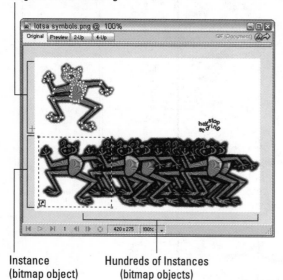

Instance
(bitmap object)

Hundreds of Instances
(bitmap objects)

Figure 17-4: Instances are simplified, bitmap versions of their parent symbols. You can use numerous Instances without adversely affecting Fireworks' performance.

Although this chapter only deals with two Symbol types, three types of symbols are available to you:

✦ **Graphic Symbols:** You might think of a Graphic Symbol as a basic, vanilla symbol. Generally, when you refer to a symbol, you're talking about a Graphic Symbol. An Instance of a Graphic Symbol acts much the same way as any Fireworks object. You can place it anywhere on the canvas, move it to another layer, and modify many of its properties.

✦ **Animation Symbols:** What separates an Animation Symbol from a regular Graphic Symbol is that an Animation symbol has multiple frames, usually with slightly differing versions of a Graphic Symbol on each frame. When the frames are shown in succession, the different frames animate to make your Symbol into a mini-movie.

✦ **Button Symbols:** Button Symbols are *Symbols-Plus*. A Button Symbol has multiple frames that contain the different states of the button, such as Up, Over, and Down. Instances of Button Symbols carry their own slice object with them, which can have a URL or Behavior attached. In a sense, a Button Symbol is a combination of all the separate Fireworks objects you would need to use to make a button, wrapped up into a tidy package that's easy to edit and reuse.

Animation Symbols are covered in Chapter 23.

The steps you take to create and modify the two types of symbols are slightly different, as each type of symbol has its own editor, but they are also similar in many ways. Button Instances share the same properties with their parent symbols as Graphic Instances.

Instances also enable advanced animation building because Fireworks can tween two or more of them and automatically create intermediate steps, simplifying and speeding up the animation process. Tweening a scaled-down Instance with a scaled-up one, for example, causes Fireworks to connect them with stair steps of new Instances, which are then easily distributed to frames to create an animation of a single object growing or shrinking.

Find out more about tweening Instances in Chapter 23.

Introducing the Library Panel

The *Library panel*, shown in Figure 17-5, is a central place to access and manage a Symbol Library. Every symbol in the current document is displayed in the symbol list in the Library panel, and they are identified as either a Graphic Symbol or Button Symbol by a distinctive icon. Like most other Fireworks panels, the Library panel has an Options menu and can be grouped with other panels. To display the Library panel, choose Window ➪ Library, or use the keyboard shortcut, F11.

Following are the main features of the Library panel:

✦ **Symbol list:** As you create or import symbols, they are added to the symbol list automatically. Initially, when you create a new document, the Library panel is completely empty. The symbol list is divided into columns that detail different properties of the symbols it contains, similar to the columns you see in a Windows or Macintosh folder that is set to List view. Double-clicking a symbol's entry in the symbol list opens the Symbol Properties dialog box for that symbol, enabling you to rename the symbol, or convert it from a Button to a Graphic Symbol, or vice versa.

✦ **Symbol preview:** Selecting a symbol from the symbol list displays a preview of the symbol. Dragging the symbol's preview into a document creates an Instance of the symbol in the document. Double-clicking the symbol preview opens the symbol for editing.

✦ **Options menu:** The Options menu contains commands for creating and managing symbols.

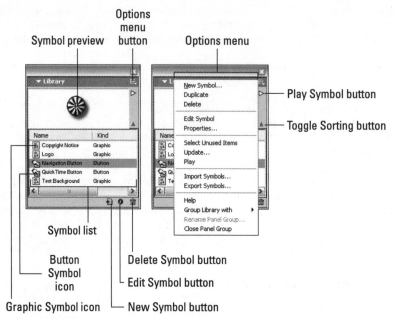

Figure 17-5: The Library panel is a central place to store and manage Symbol Libraries.

You'll look more closely at the Library panel as you use it throughout this chapter to create, edit, and manage symbols.

Making and Modifying Symbols

Most of the time, you create and manage symbols using the commands in the Edit ⇨ Insert menu, although similar commands are also available through the Options menu on the Library panel, which you look at in detail later in this chapter.

Creating a symbol

Obviously, the first step in using symbols is to actually make one. Fireworks provides three routes to a new symbol: convert an existing object into a symbol, create a symbol from scratch, or duplicate an existing symbol. Converting an existing object is probably the most common method of creating a new symbol. Fireworks even betrays this bias for converting existing objects in the keyboard shortcuts it uses: plain F8 to convert an object into a symbol, and the slightly less convenient Ctrl+F8 (Command+F8) to create a symbol from scratch.

Caution Mac OS 9 users: If you have mapped the keyboard's function keys in the Mac OS Keyboard Control Panel to start programs or perform other tasks, function key shortcuts in Fireworks are superceded by those mappings. Use the menu commands in Fireworks instead, or disable the mappings in the Keyboard Control Panel.

Converting an object

You can convert almost any object into a symbol, whether it is a vector object or a bitmap object, or even a group.

Note Although you can convert an Instance into a symbol, doing so breaks the link to its original parent symbol.

To convert an object into a symbol, follow these steps:

1. Select the object you want to convert to a symbol.

2. Choose Modify ➪ Symbol ➪ Convert to Symbol, or use the keyboard shortcut, F8. Fireworks displays the Symbol Properties dialog box (see Figure 17-6).

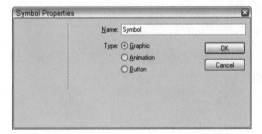

Figure 17-6: Give a symbol a name in the Symbol Properties dialog box and decide whether it will be a Graphic or a Button Symbol.

3. In the Name box, change "Symbol" to a unique name for your symbol.

4. By default, Fireworks offers to create a Graphic Symbol. Leave the Type radio buttons set to Graphic. Click OK when you're done.

Cross-Reference I cover Button Symbols later in this chapter, and Animation Symbols in Chapter 23.

Fireworks places your original object into the Library panel and leaves an Instance behind in its place in the document. You can identify the Instance by its arrow badge.

Creating a symbol from scratch

When you have the presence of mind to know that an object should be a symbol right from the start, you can make one entirely from scratch. You may also want to create a symbol that's a combination of different objects. In this case, you can create a new symbol and then copy and paste different elements from the document window into your new symbol.

To create a brand-new symbol, follow these steps:

1. Choose Edit ⇨ Insert ⇨ New Symbol, or use the keyboard shortcut, Ctrl+F8 (Command+F8). Alternatively, you can choose New Symbol from the Library panel Options menu. Fireworks displays the Symbol Properties dialog box.

2. Change the generic "Symbol" name in the Name box to a unique name for your symbol.

3. Leave the Type radio buttons set to Graphic to create a Graphic Symbol. Click OK when you're done.

4. Fireworks displays the Symbol Editor (see Figure 17-7).

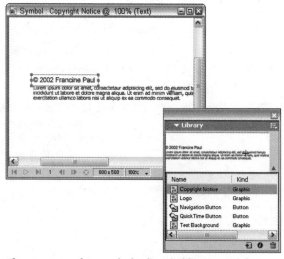

Figure 17-7: The Symbol Editor is like a special document window for creating or editing Graphic Symbols.

5. Create your new symbol in the Symbol Editor, just as you would in the document window, using any combination of Fireworks tools, panels, or the Property inspector. You can copy and paste between the Symbol Editor and the document window, as well.

Tip   You can easily edit and modify your new symbol later, so don't worry about making it absolutely perfect.

6. Close the Symbol Editor when you're done by clicking its Close box, located in the upper-right corner of the dialog box in Windows and in the upper-left corner on a Mac.

   Your new symbol appears in the Library panel, and an Instance is placed in the document window.

Caution A bug in Fireworks MX disables the Save command when the Symbol Editor is open. Pressing Ctrl+S (Command+S) while in the Symbol Editor does not save your current document. The workaround is to save your document before opening the Symbol Editor.

Duplicating an existing symbol

The final way to create a new symbol is to duplicate an existing one.

To duplicate a symbol, follow these steps:

1. Choose Window ⇨ Library, or use the keyboard shortcut, F11, to view the Library panel, if it is not already visible.
2. Select a symbol to duplicate from the symbol list.
3. Choose Duplicate from the Library panel Options menu.

Fireworks duplicates the selected symbol, adding a number after its name to distinguish it from the original.

Tip To rename a symbol, double-click its name in the symbol list and change its name in the Symbol Properties dialog box.

Modifying symbols

You can easily edit symbols in the Symbol Editor. When you're done editing a symbol and have closed the Symbol Editor, the changes that you've made are applied to the symbol and to all of its Instances. Editing a symbol, then, is also editing all of its Instances.

To modify an existing symbol, follow these steps:

1. Choose Window ⇨ Library, or use the keyboard shortcut, F11, to view the Library panel, if it isn't already visible.
2. Select the symbol you want to edit from the symbol list.
3. Double-click the symbol preview to open the symbol in the Symbol Editor. Alternatively, you can choose Edit Symbol from the Library panel Options menu.
4. Modify the symbol in the Symbol Editor. When you're done, close the Symbol Editor by clicking its Close box, located in the upper-right corner in Windows and in the upper-left corner on a Mac.

   Your edits are applied to the symbol and to all of its Instances.

Using symbol-editing shortcuts

Fireworks also provides these two shortcuts for editing symbols:

✦ If you have an Instance selected in the document window and you just want to edit its parent symbol, choose Modify ➪ Symbol ➪ Edit Symbol to view the Instance's parent symbol in the Symbol Editor.

✦ If you are editing a symbol's properties in the Symbol Properties dialog box (detailed in the next section), you can click the Edit button to open the symbol in the Symbol Editor.

When using either of these shortcuts, closing the Symbol Editor applies your changes to all the symbol's Instances.

Tip

If you take a wrong turn with your edits in the Symbol Editor, you can close the Symbol Editor — which applies your changes — and then choose Edit ➪ Undo to undo those changes.

Modifying symbol properties

In addition to modifying the symbol itself, you can also modify a symbol's properties, changing its name, or converting it from a Graphic Symbol to a Button Symbol, or vice versa.

To edit a symbol's properties, follow these steps:

1. Choose Window ➪ Library, or use the keyboard shortcut, F11, to view the Library panel, if it isn't already visible.

2. Open the Symbol Properties dialog box by doing one of the following:

• Double-click a symbol's name in the symbol list.

• Select the symbol in the symbol list and choose Properties from the Options menu.

• Click the symbol's name in the symbol list and then click the Symbol properties button on the Library panel.

Fireworks displays the Symbol Properties dialog box, shown in Figure 17-8.

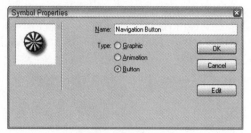

Figure 17-8: The Symbol Properties dialog box displays a thumbnail of an existing symbol and enables you to rename a symbol, or convert its Type.

3. Modify the symbol's properties in the Symbol Properties dialog box and click OK when you're done.

Fireworks applies your changes to the symbol. If you converted the symbol's Type, all of its Instances also take on that change. For example, if you converted a symbol from a Graphic Symbol to a Button Symbol, all of its Instances become buttons.

Deleting a symbol

Deleting a symbol is an easy affair, but keep in mind that if the symbol has Instances, they will be deleted, too.

To delete a symbol, follow these steps:

1. If the Library panel is not visible, choose Window ➪ Library, or use the keyboard shortcut, F11, to display it.

2. Select the symbol you want to delete in the symbol list.

3. Choose Delete from the Library panel Options menu. If the symbol doesn't have any Instances, it is deleted immediately without confirmation. If the symbol does have Instances, Fireworks displays the Delete Symbol dialog box, shown in Figure 17-9.

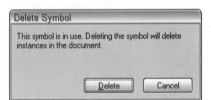

Figure 17-9: The Delete Symbol dialog box confirms that you really want to delete a symbol.

4. Click the Delete button in the Delete Symbol dialog box to delete the symbol.

The symbol and its Instances are removed from your document.

Creating Instances

Creating an Instance is a common task that you can accomplish with one of two simple methods:

✦ Drag and drop a symbol from the Library panel onto the canvas. You can drag it from either the symbol preview, or from the symbol list.

Tip

You can create Instances of multiple symbols in one step by selecting a group of symbols from the symbol list and dragging them all onto the canvas.

✦ Duplicate an Instance in the document window. A copy of an Instance is also an Instance. Any of the methods that you're used to using to duplicate objects in Fireworks also work to duplicate Instances:

• Choose the Instance and then choose Edit ⇨ Duplicate or Edit ⇨ Clone.

• Copy the Instance to the clipboard and paste back a copy.

• Hold down the Alt (Option) key, and drag an Instance to create a copy.

You can identify the new Instance as another Instance by the arrow icon in the lower-left corner of its bounding box.

Modifying Instances

Although modifying a symbol passes changes on to all of its Instances, you can also make modifications to individual Instances. Fireworks treats Instances like groups, enabling you to apply similar transformations. The relationship between transformations applied to a symbol and transformations applied to an Instance is the same as making transformations to individual objects, and then grouping them and applying a transformation to the group. In fact, you can observe the group-like behavior of an Instance by breaking the link with its symbol. What you're left with is a group.

Although you can apply a filter to an Instance, doing so breaks the link and turns it into a bitmap object.

Applying modifications to an Instance has no effect on any other Instance, or on the parent symbol. Scale one Instance, for example, and its parent symbol and other Instances of that symbol are unaffected. In other words, the link goes one way, only from symbol to Instance.

You can apply these transformations to Instances:

✦ **Shape transformations:** Adjust the width, height, skew, distortion, and rotation, or flip the Instance vertically or horizontally. Anything on the Modify ⇨ Transform submenu is fair game.

✦ **Opacity:** Alter the opacity settings on the Property inspector.

✦ **Blending mode:** Alter the blending mode on the Property inspector.

For more about opacity and blending modes, see Chapter 13.

✦ **Live Effects:** Apply Live Effects from the Add Effects menu, in the Effects section of the Property inspector. The effects that are applied to the symbol are flattened in the Instance, so even though an Instance may appear to have Live Effects, there are actually no Live Effects applied until you add them to an individual Instance.

For more about Live Effects, see Chapter 12.

Breaking links

If you want to break the link between an Instance and its parent symbol, select the Instance and choose Modify ⇨ Symbol ⇨ Break Apart. The link is broken and your Instance is now a regular group, even if the symbol only contained one object. To separate the group, choose Modify ⇨ Ungroup.

Deleting Instances

Deleting an Instance works just like deleting any Fireworks object and has no effect on the parent symbol or any other Instance. To delete an Instance, select it and press Delete.

Working with Buttons

Button Symbols enable you to encapsulate up to four button states, such as Up, Over, and Down, along with a slice object containing a URL or a Behavior into a single object that you can think of as a button.

You can place button Instances onto the canvas again and again, and change the link and Button Text independently for each one. In addition, Behaviors are applied to the Button Symbol itself, meaning that you only have to build one rollover for an entire Web site of rollover buttons. Button Instances do not appear on shared layers. Instead, they appear on their own layer on Frame 1 of the document.

Fireworks MX adds Instance-level button properties. In previous versions of Fireworks, changing the text on a button meant creating a new symbol. Now, you can alter button text and much more.

I cover Behaviors in Chapter 21.

Making and modifying Button Symbols

The Fireworks Button Editor is a special Symbol Editor window with tabs for each state of a button that makes it easy to make or modify a Button Symbol.

To create a Button Symbol, follow these steps:

1. Choose Edit ⇨ Insert ⇨ New Button.

   Fireworks displays the Button Editor, as shown in Figure 17-10.

Figure 17-10: The Button Editor has individual tabs for each state of a button.

2. Create the Up state of your button in the Up tab of the Button Editor.

3. Select the Button Editor's Over tab and create the Over state of your button. To start with the Up state and modify it to be an Over state, click Copy Up Graphic. Fireworks copies the Up state to the Over tab, ready for whatever modification you desire.

4. If you want to include a Down state in your button, select the Down tab and create the Down state of your button. Fireworks automatically checks Include Nav Bar Down State when you start building a down button. Again, you can click Copy Over Graphic to copy the previous state to this tab for modification.

5. To add an Over While Down state to your button, switch to the Over While Down tab and either create a new state, or copy the previous one — click Copy Down Graphic — and modify it to create the Over While Down state.

6. Switch to the Active Area tab. Fireworks automatically creates a slice in the Active Area tab that encompasses the area of your button. Adjust the size of the slice if necessary.

Tip

If your button has a drop shadow, or other effect, the slice that Fireworks creates encompasses the space your effects take up as well. To avoid having your button change when you viewer's mouse is over a drop shadow, for example, you can uncheck Set Active Area Automatically and resize the slice to include only the button itself. This can lead to buttons that feel more realistic because they do not change until the mouse is really over the button.

7. Close the Button Editor when you're done.

Your new Button Symbol is added to the Library panel, and an Instance is placed in the document window.

To modify a Button Symbol, double-click its name or its symbol preview in the Library panel, or select it in the symbol list and choose Edit Symbol from the Library panel Options menu.

Converting existing objects into Button Symbols

Converting an existing object into a Button Symbol is a quick way to get a button started. Because each state of a multistate button is usually a variation on the first state, converting an existing object into a Button Symbol, and then modifying it slightly in the Button Editor to create Over, Down, and Over While Down states is an excellent strategy.

To convert an object into a button, select it and choose Modify ⇨ Symbol ⇨ Convert to Symbol, or use the keyboard shortcut, F8. Choose Button from the Type setting in the Symbol Properties dialog box, give your button a unique name in the Name box, and click OK. Fireworks converts your object into a Button Symbol, creating a slice object on top of it in the document window, as shown in Figure 17-11.

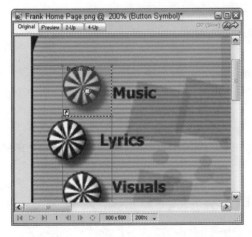

Figure 17-11: Converting an object into a Button Symbol also covers it with a slice object.

Add more states to your button by editing it in the Library panel.

Converting Button Symbols into Graphic Symbols

If you convert a Button Symbol into a Graphic Symbol by editing its properties in the Symbol Properties dialog box, the slice object that makes up the Active Area of the button remains with the symbol. To remove it, edit your symbol in the Symbol Editor and manually delete the slice object.

Using Button Instances

In addition to the standard, modifiable Instance properties, such as opacity, X and Y coordinates, width, height, and Live Effects, Button Instances have two additional editable properties: their Button Text and the links that are applied to their slice objects (see Figure 17-12). Selecting the Button Instance and viewing the Property inspector allows you to modify both of these, enabling you to assign each Button Instance a separate URL and some unique text.

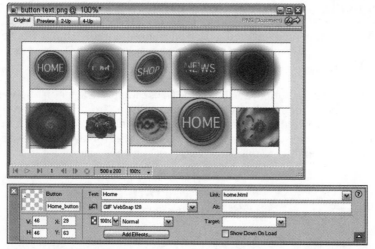

Figure 17-12: Modify the Button Text and the URL for each Button Instance in the Property inspector to truly turn each Instance into a separate button.

To modify the Button Text, type new text into the Button Text box in the Property Inspector and press Enter (Return).

Note   You can only modify Button Text if your Button Symbol contains a text object. If it doesn't, the Button Text area of the Property inspector is grayed out.

To modify a button's link, simply click the Link field in the Property inspector and add the URL for your Instance.

Instance Level Button Properties

Fireworks MX takes individual control over buttons a step further. For most people, the amount of control over Instances and buttons in Fireworks 4 was enough. While the level of control over Instances mentioned so far allows for a great deal of flexibility and ease of use, Fireworks always seems to be able to go that extra mile if you need it to. In Fireworks MX, whenever you have an Instance selected, you can edit all of the Instance Level Button Properties from the Property inspector (see Figure 17-13).

New Feature Fireworks MX lets you take the control over Buttons to the next level by enabling you to change the export settings, add Behaviors, and so much more—all at the Instance level.

Instance Level Button Properties give you control over the following:

✦ **Export Settings:** Export settings for the Instance, such as GIF WebSnap 128.

✦ **Behaviors:** You can use the Behaviors panel to apply additional Behaviors to just one Instance.

✦ **Link:** A URL, as well as ALT text, for the button.

✦ **Target:** A target window or frame for the hyperlink to open in.

✦ **Filename:** A filename for the button's Instance, or Auto-Name Slices can be left on to have Fireworks name the slice on its own.

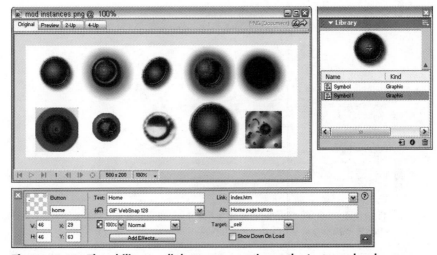

Figure 17-13: The ability to edit button properties at the Instance level means that a group of Instances can be significantly changed without altering the original symbol.

Managing Libraries

Making and managing buttons is a common task for the Web artist, and having a central place to store buttons and an easy way to reuse them—drag and drop from the Library panel to a document—saves time and work, again and again.

Libraries exist in one of two places: within a document by default, or as a standalone PNG file that you create by exporting a Library.

Importing a Library

You can import Libraries from other Fireworks documents, or from Library-only PNG files that are created by exporting a Library from Fireworks.

To import a Library into the current document, follow these steps:

1. Choose Window ➪ Library, or use the keyboard shortcut, F11, to view the Library panel, if it's not visible.

2. From the Library panel Options menu, choose Import Symbols.

Fireworks displays an Open File dialog box.

3. Navigate to the Fireworks PNG file that contains the Library you want to import, and choose Open when you're done.

Fireworks displays the Import Symbols dialog box, as shown in Figure 17-14.

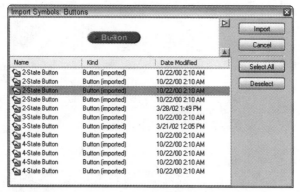

Figure 17-14: Fireworks displays the Import Symbols dialog box when you import a Library.

4. Choose symbols to import in one of the following ways:

- To import all the symbols, click the Select All button.

- To import a contiguous list of symbols, hold down Shift and click the first and last symbol in the contiguous list.

- To pick and choose symbols from the list, hold down Ctrl (Command) and, in turn, click each symbol you want to import.

Tip   To quickly import a single symbol, double-click its name in the Import Symbols dialog box.

5. After you make your selection, click Import to import the symbols into the current document.

Fireworks imports the symbols and makes them available in the Symbol list.

Accessing often-used Libraries

Choose a Library from the Edit ➪ Libraries submenu to begin importing it. This submenu reflects the contents of Fireworks' Libraries folder, shown in Figure 17-15. The Libraries folder is located inside the Configuration folder, inside your Fireworks program folder. Placing a Fireworks PNG file into this folder and restarting Fireworks makes it available as a Library on the Insert ➪ Libraries submenu. If you frequently access the same sets of Libraries, this can be a real timesaver.

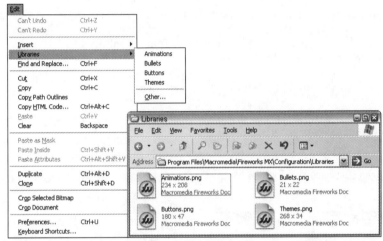

Figure 17-15: Place often-used Libraries into Fireworks' Libraries folder for easy import.

Tip The Fireworks program folder is typically found at C:\Program Files\Macromedia\ Fireworks MX on Windows-based computers, and at Macintosh HD:Applications: Macromedia Fireworks MX on the Mac.

You can also import a Library from the Edit ➪ Libraries submenu without restarting Fireworks by choosing Edit ➪ Libraries ➪ Other and navigating to the Library PNG file anywhere on your computer. Fireworks imports the Library into the current document.

Updating imported Libraries

Fireworks remembers where it originally acquired an imported symbol and can update imported symbols from that original source. This enables you, for example, to maintain a single Library of buttons for a Web site and to import that Library into multiple documents. If you need to modify a button later, modify it in the Library, and then click Update in each of the documents that uses that Library. In one step for each document, any number of documents can be updated from a single edit of the master Library.

To update imported symbols from their original sources, choose Update from the Library panel Options menu.

Caution   If you try to edit an imported symbol, Fireworks notifies you that doing so breaks the link to the original symbol. In effect, you are creating a new symbol based on that symbol by editing it.

Exporting and sharing Libraries

Although you can import Libraries directly from any Fireworks document that contains symbols, exporting a group of symbols as a standalone Library—which is still a standard Fireworks PNG file—is a good way to share symbols with colleagues or to create archives of symbols for later use.

To export symbols as a standalone Library, follow these steps:

1. Choose Window ⇨ Library, or use the keyboard shortcut, F11, to view the Library panel, if it is not visible.

2. Choose Export Symbols from the Library panel Options menu.

   Fireworks displays the Export Symbols dialog box, as shown in Figure 17-16.

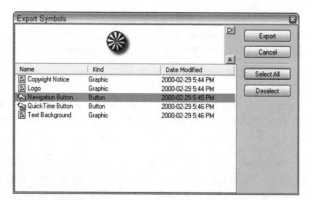

Figure 17-16: Fireworks displays the Export Symbols dialog box, enabling you to choose which symbols you'd like to export.

3. Choose symbols to export in one of the following ways:

   • To export all the symbols in your document, click Select All.

   • To export a contiguous list of symbols, hold down Shift and click the first and last symbol in the contiguous list.

   • To pick and choose symbols from the list, hold down Ctrl (Command) and click each symbol you want to export.

4. After you make your selection, click Export.

Fireworks displays the Export Symbols As dialog box.

5. Navigate to a folder where you want to save your symbols file and provide a filename. Click Save when you're done.

The exported file contains your exported symbols, and you can import it into another document or share it with others.

Summary

Symbols and Libraries can greatly simplify many of the most common tasks of the Web artist. Keep the following points in mind:

✦ Fireworks has three kinds of symbols: Graphic, Animation, and Button.

✦ Symbols are kept in the Library panel. Dragging a symbol from the Library panel onto the canvas creates an Instance of the symbol.

✦ Symbols can contain any object, except Instances.

✦ Every copy that you make of an Instance is another Instance.

✦ Some properties of Instances, such as Live Effects, and some transformations, such as scale and skew, can be modified independently of the parent symbol or other Instances. Some properties, such as fill and stroke, can be modified only on the symbol and are then inherited by its Instances.

✦ Symbols are stored in Libraries, which you can export from and import into the current document using the Library panel.

In the next chapter, you look at how to update and maintain your graphics in Fireworks.

✦　　✦　　✦

Updating and Maintaining Web Graphics

I'm sure you've heard the expression, "One percent inspiration and 99 percent perspiration." In my experience, Web graphics is more balanced—half the time you're creating a new work, and the other half you're revising something that you've already done. Updating Web pages is a continual, seemingly never-ending process, and although some of the work involves importing new text, quite often you need to alter the graphics, as well. No product can completely turn such a chore into a joyful, creative pleasure, but at least Fireworks helps you to get the job done in the most efficient manner possible.

Web-graphic maintenance is at the core of Fireworks' "everything-editable, all-the-time" philosophy. When Fireworks first arrived, Web designers everywhere were thrilled with the ease with which changes to images could be made. Fireworks has since extended that ease-of-use philosophy to include production tasks, such as updating URLs and replacing colors. This chapter explores all the production enhancement techniques—from previewing your graphics directly in a browser to optimizing entire folders of images at one time.

Using Preview in Browser

It's amazing to me how many so-called Web-graphics programs don't enable you to easily see your work through its intended medium: the Web browser. Fireworks enables you to preview in not one, but two browsers at the press of a keyboard shortcut. Not only do you quickly get to see how the browsers are interpreting your graphics, but you can also test any rollovers or other Behaviors you may have included in Fireworks.

Web designers, as with most Internet users, tend to work with a particular version of Navigator or Internet Explorer most of the time. But, unlike ordinary Web surfers, Web designers must be able to view work under various conditions in order to ensure consistency across platforms and browser versions. As of this writing, Microsoft has the lion's share of the browser market, with Netscape in second. Although Internet Explorer 6 and Netscape 6 are in many ways more compatible than the corresponding 4 and 5 versions, you still must test early and often in multiple browsers to guarantee a professional quality of work.

Tip You can even use the Preview in Browser feature to display different versions of the same graphic side by side, without having to make additional copies in Fireworks. Just make a new Web browser window after previewing the first time (File ➪ New Window in your browser), and — at least on Windows — the second preview opens in the second window.

Before you can use the Preview in Browser feature, you have to tell Fireworks which two browsers you want to use. Although you don't have to define both a primary and a secondary browser, it's a good idea (if you have two browsers on your system). To set the browsers, follow these steps:

Tip Fireworks automatically sets the primary browser from what is configured in your operating system. You need to follow this step only if you wish to alter the primary browser that Fireworks selects.

1. Choose File ➪ Preview in Browser ➪ Set Primary Browser.

   The Locate Primary Browser dialog box appears, as shown in Figure 18-1.

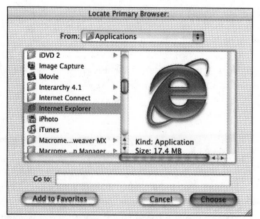

Figure 18-1: Declare your primary browser through the Locate Primary Browser dialog box.

2. In the Locate Browser dialog box, navigate to the browser directory to locate the application itself. Table 18-1 shows typical locations for browser application files, although you may have chosen a different location if you installed the browser yourself. If you're using a Macintosh, you may also have moved it after installation, or if the browser doesn't have an installation program (Internet Explorer 5, for example), then it remains wherever you left it.

Table 18-1
Typical Browser Locations

Browser	Windows Location	Macintosh Location
Microsoft Internet Explorer 4.*x*	C:\Program Files\Internet Explorer\ Iexplore.exe	Macintosh HD: Internet: Microsoft Internet Applications:Internet Explorer 4.01 Folder: Internet Explorer
Microsoft Internet Explorer 5.*x*	C:\Program Files\Internet Explorer\ IEXPLORE.exe	Macintosh HD: Applications: Internet Explorer 5: Internet Explorer / Macintosh HD:Applications: Internet Explorer (OS X)
Microsoft Internet Explorer 6.*x*	C:\Program Files\Internet Explorer\ IEXPLORE.exe	n/a
Netscape Navigator 4.*x*	C:\Program Files\Netscape\ Navigator\netscape.exe	Macintosh HD: Internet: Netscape Navigator: Netscape Navigator
Netscape Communicator 4.*x*	C:\Program Files\Netscape\ Programs\netscape.exe	Macintosh HD: Applications: Netscape Communicator: Netscape Communicator / Macintosh HD:Applications: Netscape Communicator: Netscape (OS X)
Netscape 6.*x*	C:\Program Files\Netscape 6\ netscp6.exe	Macintosh HD: Applications: Netscape 6.*x*:Netscape
Opera	C:\Program Files\Opera\Opera.exe	Macintosh HD: Applications:Opera:Opera

Tip Although the Web TV Viewer for Macintosh or Windows is a great way to get an idea of what your work looks like on the MSN TV service, formerly Web TV, the application itself can't receive a URL from another application. So it can't be used as a primary or secondary browser in Fireworks. Preview in a regular browser instead and then copy and paste the file:\\ URL from there to the Web TV Viewer. If you don't have the Web TV Viewer, it's free at http://developer.msntv.com/.

3. Click Open after you locate the browser.

4. To define the secondary browser, choose File ➪ Preview in Browser ➪ Set Secondary Browser and repeat Steps 2 and 3.

After you define your browsers, they're immediately available for use. If you selected Netscape Navigator as one of your browsers, you can preview your work in it by choosing File ➪ Preview in Browser ➪ Preview in Netscape Navigator. I heartily recommend memorizing the keyboard shortcuts for this command: to preview in your primary browser, press F12; to preview in your secondary browser, press Shift+F12.

Caution Depending on the version of Windows and Internet Explorer that you are using, an entirely new instance of Internet Explorer may be launched each time you preview in IE. This can heavily tax your system's resources. A workaround is to close Internet Explorer for Windows before previewing again.

Working with a client who depends on a different browser, or a different browser version than the one you normally use, isn't an unusual circumstance. It's a good idea to install as many different browsers — and different browser versions — as possible.

Caution Internet Explorer (IE) for Windows only enables you to have one version installed at a time. The (sort of) exception to this is if you install IE 5 over IE 4 and select the "Compatibility Mode" custom install option. You can continue to launch IE 4 as before, and you'll get an IE 4/5 hybrid that mimics most — but not all — of IE 4's unique quirks and formatting. Installing IE 4 on a version of Windows that comes with IE 5 preinstalled is not possible. If possible, keep multiple Windows systems or multiple Windows partitions with a different version of IE on each.

Previewing early and often in multiple browsers helps to avoid surprises caused by browser incompatibilities or bugs.

Tip Macintosh users might want to investigate an IBM PC-compatible emulator, such as Connectix Virtual PC. Because you can create multiple "hard drives" with multiple and varied installations of the different flavors of Windows and Internet Explorer, maintaining every Windows and Macintosh Web browser on one machine is possible. It's even possible to install Linux and OS/2 into Virtual PC and run browsers there, too.

Managing Links with the URL Panel

To me, links are the lifeblood of the Web. Without the ability to jump from one section, page, or site to another, the Internet would be a very linear medium — and nowhere near as popular. Before Fireworks, the normal course of Web graphics production kept the images and the links completely separate until the final Web page was assembled. However, because Fireworks extends its graphic capabilities into HTML and JavaScript code through Behaviors and hotspots, links can actually be incorporated during the creation phase.

A link is more technically known as a *URL* (generally pronounced as if it were spelled out, U-R-L). URL is short for Uniform Resource Locator and is best thought of as the Web's address system. Every Web page on the Internet has a URL. Web design deals with two kinds of URLs: absolute and relative. An *absolute URL* is the exact address that enables a Web page to be accessed from anywhere on the Internet, such as `http://www.idest.com/fireworks/index.htm#book`.

In the preceding example, the URL is divided into five main parts:

✦ **Method:** The method specifies the protocol used to address the server. Web servers use *HTTP* (HyperText Transfer Protocol). Other methods include *FTP* (File Transfer Protocol), for transmitting files; News, for accessing newsgroup servers; and Mailto, for sending e-mail.

✦ **Domain:** The domain name (in this example, `www.idest.com`) is registered with an Internet authority, such as Network Solutions, so that the server to which the domain name refers can be found. The *IP* (Internet Protocol) address (for example, 199.227.52.143) can be used in place of a domain name.

✦ **Path:** Depending on exactly where on the server the Web page is located, the path can be a single folder, as it is in this example (`fireworks`), or many folders, in which case each folder is separated by a forward slash (/).

✦ **Page:** The name of the Web page itself is the name under which it is stored — in the example the name is `index.htm`. The file extension used depends on the type of server and the authoring system. Most typically, Web pages end in either .html or .htm; however, you'll also see extensions such as .shtml, .asp, .cfm, and .taf, just to mention a few.

✦ **Named anchor:** A portion of the page marked with an HTML tag, called an anchor (in the URL example it is `#book`). With named anchors, you can quickly move from one section of a long document to another, all on a single page.

All but the target portion is mandatory for an absolute URL. The other type of URL, a *relative URL*, however, can use as little as just the page, or even just the named anchor. Whatever the link is, its location is relative to the current page. For example, if you need to link to another Web page in the same folder as the current one, the link would look something like this example:

```
contact.html
```

On the other hand, if you need to link to a page that is stored in a subfolder of the current page, the relative link would resemble the following:

```
old_news/pr2001.htm
```

The more that your site structure is developed — blank Web pages and empty folders created — before working in Fireworks, the more you can take advantage of the program's URL tools.

Accessing the URL History list

In Fireworks, links are attached to either of the two types of Web object: a hotspot or a slice. You can assign a link to a selected Web object either through the URL panel or the Property inspector. The URL panel, shown in Figure 18-2, enables you to assign a link in one of two ways:

✦ Enter the URL directly into the Link text box.

Caution   If you choose to type your new URL into the Link text box, double-check your text to avoid any mistakes. Computers are literal when it comes to URLs, and thus every element — names, punctuation, and even case (uppercase or lowercase) on some servers — must match.

✦ Select the URL from the Current URL option list.

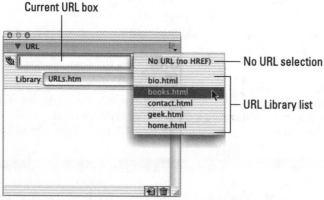

Figure 18-2: Enter a new URL or select one from the Current URL option list on the URL panel.

The Current URL option list is divided into two parts: the No URL selection and the URL History list. Choose the No URL (no HREF) selection when you want to specify that a slice or hotspot does not have a link assigned; this is the default selection for

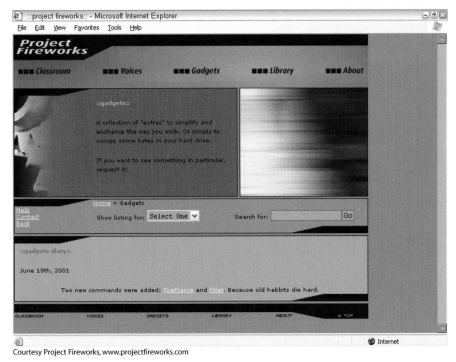

Courtesy Project Fireworks, www.projectfireworks.com

Fireworks is capable of graphics ranging from simple, clear navigation systems to wildly layered and sophisticated graphics. Web sites don't need to light up and flash; they can be straightforward and easy to navigate, as shown here in a site design by Kleanthis Economou.

Courtesy N8Vision, www.n8vision.com

Fireworks handles object-oriented shapes, photorealistic graphics, and straightforward text with equal ease, as illustrated in this Web page by Donna Casey for N8Vision. Each of the navigation elements swaps a monochromatic image with a full-color image when a mouse passes over it, while the blurred text becomes crystal clear.

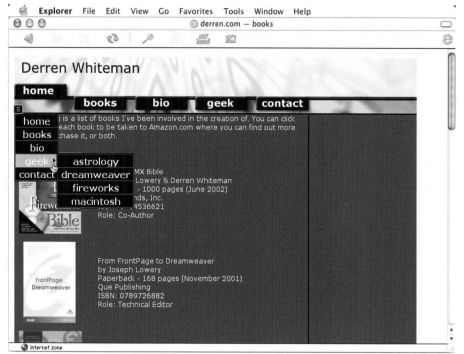

The Set Pop-up Menu behavior provides an easy way to create advanced navigational interfaces that work in a variety of Web browsers.

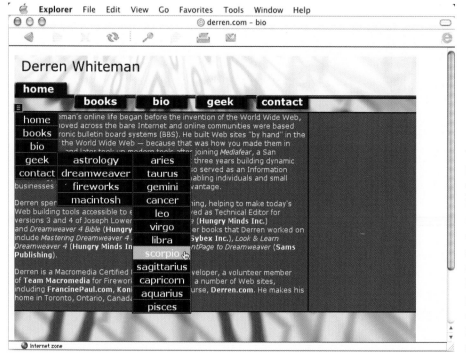

You can work on individual images in Fireworks, just as you might in a traditional image editor, such as Photoshop. In addition, you can design complete Web sites within one Fireworks document, as shown here. Building in one document means you can export everything with one command and share elements and effects easily.

In 32-bit color, an image contains four channels: eight bits of red, eight bits of green, and eight bits of blue, which together cover the range of colors that the eye can see, as well as an 8-bit grayscale alpha channel that describes a transparency mask. Here, an image with a feathered edge is placed on a white background. The alpha mask ensures that the feathered edges have a variable transparency, with more of the white background showing through at the extreme edges of the image. This image could be placed against a black background, or any other color, and the transparency of the feathered edges would remain apparent.

The preceding image loses its alpha channel — and its transparency — when reduced to 24-bit color.

The image from the previous color plate suffers when it is reduced to 8-bit color, which doesn't allow for the fine gradations necessary to represent a photographic image accurately. The obvious lines in the color changes in the sky are called *banding*.

Reducing the number of colors further — in this case to four — sometimes produces an attractive effect, but it doesn't portray the original landscape accurately.

Windows gamma —

— Macintosh gamma

This image was created in Windows and looks good at Windows' standard gamma correction setting of 2.2.

Macintosh gamma —

— Windows gamma

Choosing View ⇨ Macintosh Gamma in Windows reveals what this image would look like on a Mac, with the standard Mac gamma correction setting of 1.8.

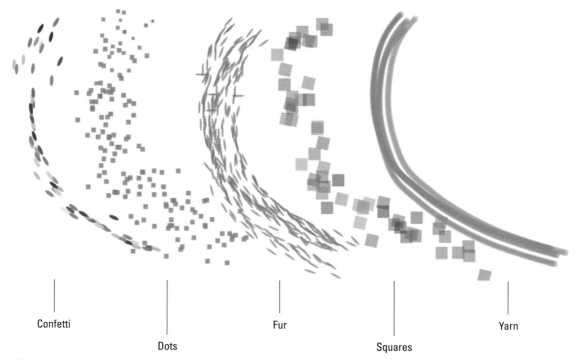

Confetti

Dots

Fur

Squares

Yarn

The Random Strokes category takes advantage of Fireworks' stroke capability by randomizing the size, opacity, hue, and other characteristics.

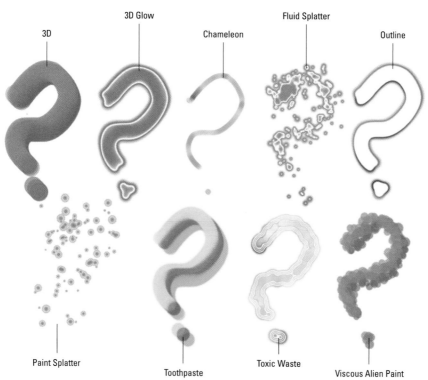

3D

3D Glow

Chameleon

Fluid Splatter

Outline

Paint Splatter

Toothpaste

Toxic Waste

Viscous Alien Paint

Wild color and style variations are the norm with the distinctive Unnatural category of Fireworks Strokes.

The desert vignette was manipulated to place the camel on the horizon and combined into a mask group with a text object. Note the bevel effect on the text, which remains for the mask group.

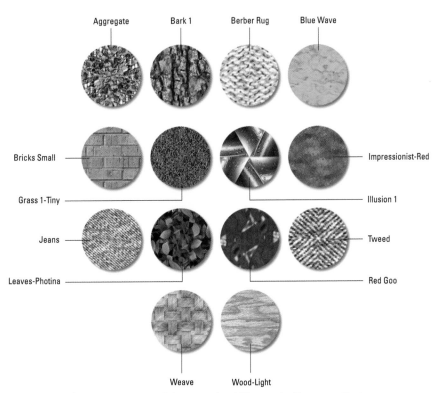

These are some of the standard Fireworks Patterns that are always available for Pattern fills. You can add your own, too.

Choose subtle variations on a button graphic in order to make all four states: up, over, over down, and down. Here, the buttons in the top row show four states that rely on fake mouse cursor shadows to create the over and over down states, while the down state appears to be corroded. The bottom row relies on color changes to create different states.

"Bath Time"

Courtesy Simon White, www.simonwhite.com

Using a graphics tablet with some of the pressure sensitive strokes in Fireworks enables you to create images that look remarkably like paintings done on a real canvas.

The sunset in this unaltered image looks fine, but the farmhouse near the bottom is too dark. Applying the Auto Levels filter to the farmhouse and nearby details will bring them out by removing some shadow.

Here, the Lasso tool is used to select the pixels that need to be adjusted. A feather of 2 pixels is applied to the selection with Select ⇨ Feather. The feathered selection helps to hide the border between altered and unaltered pixels.

After you apply the Auto Levels filter to the pixel selection by choosing Filters ⇨ Adjust Color ⇨ Auto Levels, the selected area has its own complete tonal range and is not so shadow-heavy.

Adjusting the Midtone Input Level Slider in the Levels dialog box (Filters ⇨ Adjust Color ⇨ Levels) enables you to brighten the whole image. Compare this color plate to the unaltered image at the top of the previous page.

This image is flat-looking because the shadows and highlights are too close together in value.

The Curves filter (Filters ➪ Adjust Color ➪ Curves) enables you to make fine adjustments to an image's tonal range until the image has dark shadows and bright highlights. You often can achieve good results by moving a single point on the Curves filter's graph.

This unaltered image contains very little color variation. To use it in a page design that includes a very different range of colors, use the Hue/Saturation filter to modify the overall color of the image and match the page design, as shown in the following color plates.

Change the overall color of an image by using the Hue slider in the Hue/Saturation dialog box. Here, the overall green cast of the image in the preceding color plate has been changed to purple.

Increasing the Saturation value increases the amount of color in the image.

Moving too far from the original settings with the Hue/Saturation filter can result in a posterization effect. Areas of color become flat, edges stand out, and the overall tonal range is adversely affected.

original
RightByYa
BledAndWrappedInPlastic
LowToner
Flipped
NouveauLawnFurniture

Using third-party filters as always-editable Live Effects provides a wonderful degree of creative freedom. Once you find that perfect effect, it's easy to save it under your own made-up name (like the ones in this image) and apply it to all kinds of objects. These are vector objects.

Kai Power Tools is an example of a third-party Photoshop-compatible filter set that doesn't limit you to making slight changes to your images. FraxPlorer enables you to turn pretty much any image into a remarkable fractal study.

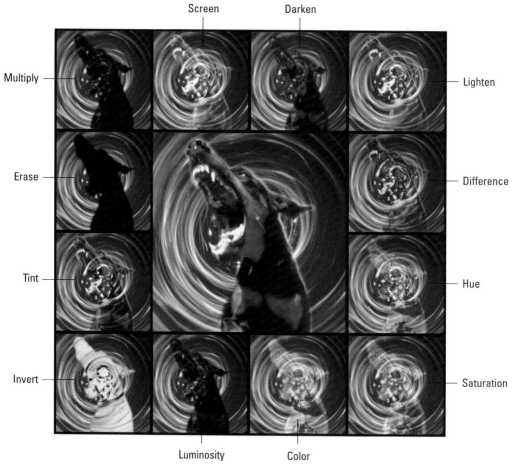

The blend modes are best understood by comparing the various effects. Here, the dog is blended against the whirlpool pattern. The center image shows the Normal blend mode.

Each of these objects is actually two objects: the obvious one, and a not-so-obvious, gradient-filled one blended on top to provide the "lighting" across the fills. This effect is especially obvious in the center object, where the pattern fill has a "light" shining across it. Fireworks provides some 3D lighting on the edges of objects with its bevel effects; continuing the lighting effect across the fill enhances the realism of these simple, vector-based objects. Of course, all of these remain completely editable.

Compositing multiple objects — and multiple types of objects — is easy in Fireworks, where everything is editable all the time. The black, textured background shows through the gooey red layer (a bitmap image) thanks to a mask group. The Fireworks logo is a combination of a bitmap image and a hand-drawn vector path that hover above the other objects because of a Drop Shadow Live Effect. Blending modes and opacity settings allows the texture to shows through the editable text object, making it seem to be stamped out of the underlying layers.

Courtesy Konis, www.konis.com

The buttons in this figure are Symbols. They had to be made only once, stored in the Library, and inserted into a document from there. Each Button Symbol has unique text and URL properties.

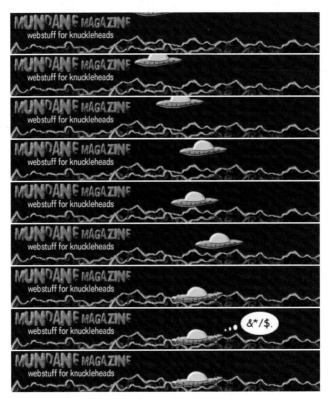

A simple story line is easiest to convey within the limited space and time you are given with a banner ad. Confining the motion to a small region, using a highly-compressible flat color background, and limiting the number of colors contributed to keeping this banner ad under 12K. This ad is built standard-size: 468 x 60.

The Eye Candy 4000 LE Motion Trail image filter that is included with Fireworks MX is great for creating the appearance of fast motion without adding extra frames and increasing bandwidth. Here, the flying saucer travels more than half the width of the ad in just three frames, and very obviously "stops."

Web objects. The URL panel shows a history of the links that have been added to the current document. Every time that you manually enter a new link in the Current URL text box, it is stored as part of the URL panel's history.

If your URL panel's history list is filled with links that are no longer used, a command that is available through the URL panel Options menu, Clear Unused URLs, can remove all but the links actually used in the document. Another command, Add Used URLs to Library, can save your document links so that they can be retrieved independently of the current document.

Adding URLs to the URL Library

The URL Library represents a more permanent list of links than those found in the URL History. URL Libraries can be stored, edited, and reloaded to work with any document. This facility makes building all the graphics involving rollovers and image maps — anything that needs a URL — far easier on the site level. From a Web graphics production perspective, a different URL Library can be maintained for each site or client, which further simplifies your workflow.

Tip   Once a URL has been entered into the URL Library, it's accessible from the Property inspector, the URL panel, and even the Pop-up Menu Editor. Entering your URLs once, and then selecting them from any of these locations, makes URL Libraries real time savers.

Although you can access what's in the URL Library from the Property inspector for a selected Web object, all management of the Library is handled through the URL panel, shown in Figure 18-3. To open the URL panel, choose Window ⇨ URL, or press the keyboard shortcut, Alt+Shift+F10 (Option+Shift+F10). Alternatively, if the URL panel is docked with another panel, click the URL panel's tab to bring it to the front of the panel group.

Figure 18-3: Use the URL panel to build, access, and store URL Libraries.

The URL Library is stored in an HTML file format used for browser bookmark files; the default Library is called URLs.htm. However, you can add URLs to the Library in several ways, almost all of which are commands available in the URL panel's Options menu. The commands are shown in Figure 18-4 and in the following list:

✦ **Add Used URLs to Library:** Enables you to save the current document's URL History as part of the URL Library.

✦ **Add URL:** Adds a single URL directly to the Library.

✦ **Import URLs:** Inserts URLs found within any HTML file, including Bookmark pages.

✦ **Add to Library button:** Adds the URL in the History text box of the URL to the Library.

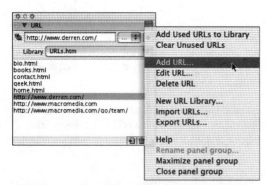

Figure 18-4: Most URL Library commands are accessible through the URL panel Options menu.

Combining the document's URL History with the current URL Library is a one-step process — just choose the Add Used URLs to Library command from the panel Options menu. Fireworks automatically integrates the two lists of links, alphabetically. If any links appear in both lists, Fireworks eliminates the duplicates.

To add a single URL to the Library, choose the Add URL command from the panel Options menu. The New URL dialog box appears. Enter the new link directly in the large text area, and click OK when you're done. The new link is added to the Library list.

 Tip   You can also click the New URL button located at the bottom of the URL panel to add a new link.

The Import URLs command is a wonderful work-saver and is extremely flexible. Because you can import the links from any HTML file, you can quickly bring in all the links from a site just by importing a Web site's home page.

To import links from an HTML page, follow these steps:

1. From the URL panel Options menu, choose Import URLs.

   The standard Open dialog box appears.

2. Locate the HTML page containing the links you want to incorporate into a Library. Click Open after you find the HTML page.

   Any link, relative or absolute, found on the selected HTML page is integrated with the current URL Library.

As you find out in the next section, you can also create, edit, delete, store, and load URL Libraries through the URL panel.

Managing URL Libraries

URL Libraries are extremely flexible in Fireworks. You can create new Libraries with a single command, and you can edit, delete, load, or store existing Libraries.

From time to time, a Web page moves to a new location on the Web. If you have the page's URL in your URL Library, you have to change it. To do so, follow these steps:

1. Select the URL you want to change from the URL panel list.

2. From the URL panel Options menu, choose Edit URL.

   The Edit URL dialog box, shown in Figure 18-5, appears.

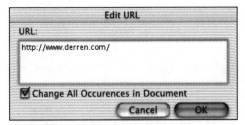

Figure 18-5: Update your URL Library links with the Edit URL command and the Edit URL dialog box.

3. Enter the new URL in the text area. To also update any existing links in the current document, select the Change All Occurrences in Document checkbox. Click OK when you're done.

   The URL is modified in the Library.

Following are the two ways to remove a URL from the Library:

✦ Select the unwanted URL, and then click the Delete URL button in the lower-right corner of the URL panel.

✦ Select the URL, and then select Delete URL from the URL panel Options menu.

By default, Fireworks starts with one URL Library, URLs.htm. You can add others by following these steps:

1. Choose the New URL Library command from the URL panel Options menu.

The New URL Library dialog box, shown in Figure 18-6, appears.

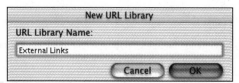

Figure 18-6: Organize a new Library for each client through the New URL Library command.

2. Enter a unique name for the new library.

If you don't include a .htm or .html file extension, Fireworks automatically appends one.

Fireworks creates a new file in the URL Libraries folder, inside the Configuration folder. This file is updated when Fireworks closes; you don't need to save your URL Library in a separate operation.

Cross-Reference   For more information regarding the Configuration folder and its location for your operating system, see Chapter 25.

Although Fireworks makes creating a new Library a breeze, removing an unwanted Library is a little more hands-on. No command is available to delete a Library, so you have to open the URL Libraries folder located inside your Fireworks Configuration folder, and delete the HTML file using Windows Explorer or the Macintosh Finder. The deleted Library disappears from the URLs list when Fireworks is restarted.

If Fireworks automatically stores the URL Libraries that you create, why would you need an Export command? The Export URLs command, found in the URL panel Options menu, enables you to save the URL Library as an HTML file in another directory. The HTML file, as shown in Figure 18-7, is a straightforward list of links. If your URL Library is complete, you could use the exported Library file as the basis for a text-only home page to go along with the graphical one you're making in Fireworks.

Tip If you create popup menus, and you've already created your links in the URL panel, all those links are available in the Popup Menu wizard at a click of button.

Figure 18-7: Exporting a URL Library results in a list of links in HTML format.

Caution On the Macintosh, even if you name your exported file with an .html filename extension, Fireworks still saves it with an .htm filename extension.

Updating Graphics with Find and Replace

Fireworks has always been great about enabling you to alter any aspect of your graphic at any time; before Fireworks, you had to make every change by hand. Graphics for a Web site often have a great deal of overlap — a consistent color scheme, the same typeface, even the same URLs embedded in image maps and buttons. Replacing a misspelled client name in one graphic is one thing, replacing them in all the graphics, sitewide, is another.

Fireworks offers a robust Find and Replace feature that automates the onerous chore of modifying text, fonts, colors, and URLs. Through the Find and Replace dialog box, you can direct your updates to the current selection, frame, document, or to a selection of documents. The Find and Replace options for text and URLs include a powerful wildcard capability, known as Regular Expressions. You can also track your changes through Fireworks' Project Log.

Outside of batch processing and scriptlets, all automated modifications in Fireworks are handled through the Find and Replace dialog box, shown in Figure 18-8, which displays different options depending on which attribute is being altered. The five attributes and their options are as follows:

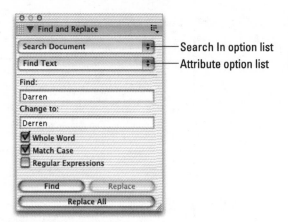

Search In option list
Attribute option list

Figure 18-8: Use the Find and Replace dialog box to automate changes to text, fonts, URLs, and even color.

✦ **Text:** Any text object in a Fireworks file can be modified under Find and Replace. The text search can include anything from a single character to full sentences. Options include Whole Word, which ensures that the text to be found is not within another word; Match Case, which seeks out the exact text entered and replaces it verbatim; and Regular Expressions, a system of wild-card matching discussed in detail later in this chapter.

✦ **Font:** Every text object must use a particular font with a set style (or lack of one), in a particular size. The Find and Replace feature of Fireworks enables you to update all of these characteristics, either separately or combined. You can even search for a font in a range of sizes and convert all occurrences to one size.

✦ **Color:** In a Fireworks object, color is just another attribute that you can search for and replace, if necessary. You can alter color in strokes, fills, effects, strokes and fills, or all properties.

✦ **URL:** The URL Find and Replace option is similar to the Find and Replace option for text. Any link can be altered in any way; you can even use the Find and Replace feature to remove all links. The Whole Word, Match Case, and Regular Expressions options are available for the URL attribute, just as they are for the Text attribute of Find and Replace.

✦ **Find Non-Web 216:** This option searches for non-Websafe colors and changes them to their nearest Websafe color. You can apply it to fills and/or strokes, effects, or every object.

Regardless of the specific attribute, with each Find and Replace operation, you have the option of making changes on a case-by-case basis, or all at once. Click Find Next to locate the next item fulfilling the search criteria, and then click either Replace, to make a change to the selected item, or Find Next, to locate the next item without making a change. You can also click Replace All at any time to make the alterations within your search scope to all matches in the document(s).

Tip What if you're running a Find and Replace operation and you make a mistake, such as clicking Replace All instead of Replace? If you're working within a single document, you can use Edit ⇨ Undo or the History panel to reverse all the changes and start over. This method has no effect on Find and Replace actions applied to multiple files.

With all attributes, the scope of the search is defined by the value set in the Search In option list, which includes the following possible options:

- ✦ **Selection:** You can modify only the currently selected object or objects.
- ✦ **Frame:** Limits the search to the current selected frame of the active document.
- ✦ **Document:** Enables the search to be applied to the entire active document.
- ✦ **Project Log:** Limits the search to files listed in the Project Log. Use of the Project Log is covered in detail later in this chapter.
- ✦ **Files:** Carries out the Find and Replace operation on any accessible file or files. Selecting the Files option displays the Open Multiple dialog box, in which files are added to the selection list, either individually or by the folder.

Tip If you need to adjust the selected files for a Multi-File Find and Replace operation, reopening the Open Multiple dialog box involves a small trick. Temporarily choose a different Search In option, such as Document or Frame, and then select Files again. The Open Multiple dialog box reopens.

Although the Search In options have their place, Fireworks' Multi-File capability really gives the Find and Replace feature its power. Naturally, such increased power also brings increased risk for making a mistake. To offset that risk, Fireworks offers two backup options. To set the backup options, choose Replace Options from the Find and Replace panel's Options menu. The Replace Options dialog box (see Figure 18-9) appears. If the first option, Save and Close Files, is selected, Fireworks closes each file after it makes a replacement; if the option is not selected, the files are left open. The Backup Original Files drop-down list box includes three choices:

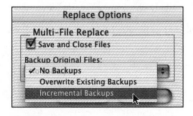

Figure 18-9: Choose your backup options from the Replace Options dialog box.

✦ **No Backups:** The target files are overwritten and no backups are saved.

✦ **Overwrite Existing Backups:** The target files are copied to a subfolder called Original Files, and the Find and Replace operation is performed on the files in their original location. Each time you perform another Find and Replace operation, the existing backup in the Original Files folder is overwritten with a newer backup. In a sense, this is similar to having an Undo feature with only one Undo. The Original Files folder always contains files that are one step older than the last Find and Replace operation.

✦ **Incremental Backups:** If you don't want to risk losing any changes, choose this option. Each time you perform a Find and Replace, the target files are copied to the Original Files folder, but rather than overwriting the other files, they are renamed incrementally. For example, the first time a file named Star.png is changed, the source file is saved in the Original File subfolder as Star.png. The next time you use Find and Replace, the copy of Star.png in the Original Files folder is renamed Star-1.png and the target file is copied there as Star.png. The most recent version always retains the original name, and the oldest version ends with the highest number. This essentially gives you an unlimited Undo for Find and Replace (except for running out of hard drive space).

You could use the Incremental Backups option as a type of version control, but the downside is that this choice stores *all* the files. Your choice may depend on how much free hard drive space you have and/or how big your target files are. If you have 10GB of hard drive space, go ahead and use Incremental Backups. After you've finished your work session, you can easily go into the original file's folder and delete (Trash) anything with a number higher than three, so that you're saving only the last few versions.

Searching and replacing text

I recently had a client come to me with every Web designer's major nightmare — a name change. Not only did every logo need to be altered, but also the name was incorporated on much of the Web site as a graphic background. I was faced with days upon days of pure drudgery — until I realized that I could use Find and Replace to automate the process. I was able to make the revisions in a few short hours, spending much of the time quite amazed at how quickly the job was getting done.

To find and replace text, follow these steps:

1. If the Find and Replace panel is not visible, choose Edit ⇨ Find and Replace or, if it is behind another tabbed panel, click its tab to bring the panel forward.

2. Choose the scope of the search operation, by selecting one of the choices from the Search In option list.

3. Make sure that the Attribute selection is set to Text.

4. Enter in the Find text box the text that you want to find.

5. If you intend to change the text, enter its replacement in the Change To text box.

6. Select any options desired: Whole Word, Match Case, or Regular Expressions.

7. To make changes on a case-by-case basis, first click Find Next and then click either Replace, to change the text, or Find Next again, to move to the next matched text.

8. To change all the text at once, click Replace All.

   If no changes are made, Fireworks reports that the search is complete. Otherwise, Fireworks informs you of how many occurrences it changed.

Although the Find and Replace Text operation may be the most straightforward of all the attributes, you still need to be aware of some issues, as follows:

✦ Text objects expand to make room for new words, but if you add a lot of text, you may find objects hanging off canvas. Left-aligned text expands to the right, right-aligned text expands to the left, and centered text expands in both directions.

✦ During Multi-File Find and Replace operations, if one of the selected documents is open in Fireworks, the document must be activated before any changes can be made.

Searching with Regular Expressions

The serious power in the Find and Replace feature is the Regular Expressions option. I've referred to Regular Expressions as being similar to wildcards in other programs, but the Fireworks capabilities are really far, far more extensive.

Regular Expressions are best described as a text pattern-matching system. If you can identify any pattern in your text, you can manipulate it with Regular Expressions. For example, suppose that you're building a navigation bar in which the buttons are all contact names that are listed in a Lastname, Firstname format. With Regular Expressions, you could match the pattern and reformat the entire list, placing the Firstname before the Lastname, without the comma—all in one Find and Replace operation.

You can apply Regular Expressions to either the text or URL attributes by selecting the Regular Expressions option. When you enable this option, Fireworks processes the text entered in both the Find and Change To text boxes differently, looking for special key characters, such as backslash and asterisk.

The most basic Regular Expression is the text itself. If you enable the Regular Expressions option and then enter "th" in the Find What text box, Fireworks locates every example of "th" in the text and/or source. Although this capability by itself has little use, it's important to remember this functionality as you begin to build your patterns.

Using wildcard characters

Initially, it's helpful to be able to use what traditionally are known as *wildcards*: characters that match different types of characters. The wildcards in Regular Expressions all represent single characters only, as described in Table 18-2. In other words, no single Regular Expression represents all the characters, in the same way the asterisk does when used in DOS file searches. However, such a condition can be represented with a slightly more complex Regular Expression (described later in this section).

Table 18-2
Regular Expressions Wildcard Characters

Character	Matches	Example
.	Any single character.	**w.d** matches **wide** but not world.
\w	Any alphanumeric character, including the underscore.	**w\wd** matches **wide** and **world**.
\W	Any nonalphanumeric character.	**jboy\Widest.com** matches **jboy@ idest.com** and **jboy$idest.com**.
\d	Any numeric character 0-9.	**y\dk** matches **Y2K**.
\D	Any nonnumeric character.	**\D2\D** matches **Y2K** and **H2O**.
\s	Any white-space character, including space, tab, form feed, or line feed.	**\smedia** matches **media** but not Macromedia.
\S	Any nonwhite-space character.	**\Smedia** matches Macro**media** but not media.

Caution Be careful with the \S wildcard. In Fireworks, it actually matches one more character than it should; for instance **\Sworks** actually matches Fir**eworks**, instead of just Fire**works**.

The backslash character (\) is used to escape special characters so that they can be included in a search. For example, if you want to look for an asterisk, you need to specify it as *. Likewise, when trying to find the backslash character, precede it with another backslash character: \\.

Matching character positions and repeating characters

With Regular Expressions, you not only can match the type of character, but also match its position in the text. This feature enables you to perform operations on characters at the beginning, end, or middle of the word or line. Using Regular

Expressions also enables you to find instances in which a character is repeated either an unspecified or specified number of times. Combined, these features broaden the scope of the patterns that you can find.

Table 18-3 details the options available for matching by text placement and character repetition.

<table>
<tr><td colspan="3">Table 18-3
Regular Expressions Character Positions</td></tr>
<tr><td>Character</td><td>Matches</td><td>Example</td></tr>
<tr><td>^</td><td>Beginning of a line.</td><td>^c matches "Call me Ishmael."</td></tr>
<tr><td>$</td><td>End of a line.</td><td>d$ matches the final d in "Be afraid. Be very afraid."</td></tr>
<tr><td>\b</td><td>A word boundary, such as a space or carriage return.</td><td>\btext matches textbook but not SimpleText.</td></tr>
<tr><td>\B</td><td>A nonword boundary inside a word.</td><td>\Btext matches SimpleText but not textbook.</td></tr>
<tr><td>*</td><td>The preceding character zero or more times.</td><td>b*c matches BBC and cold.</td></tr>
<tr><td>+</td><td>The preceding character one or more times.</td><td>b+c matches BBC but not cold.</td></tr>
<tr><td>?</td><td>The preceding character zero or one time.</td><td>st?un matches stun and sun but not strung.</td></tr>
<tr><td>{n}</td><td>Exactly n instances of the preceding character.</td><td>e{2} matches reed and each pair of two e's in Aieeeeeee!, but nothing in the word red.</td></tr>
<tr><td>{n,m}</td><td>At least n and at most m.</td><td>C{2,4} matches #CC00FF and #CCCC00, but not the full string #CCCCCC.</td></tr>
</table>

Matching character ranges

Beyond single characters or repetitions of single characters, Regular Expressions incorporates the capability to find or exclude ranges of characters. This feature is particularly useful when you're working with groups of names or titles. Ranges are specified in *set brackets*. A match is made when any one of the characters within the set brackets is found, not necessarily all the characters.

Table 18-4 describes how to match character ranges with Regular Expressions.

	Table 18-4	
	Regular Expressions Character Ranges	
Character	*Matches*	*Example*
[abc]	Any one of the characters a, b, or c.	[lmrt] matches the *l* and *m*'s in **l**e**mm**ings and the *r*'s and *t* in **r**oad**t**rip.
[^abc]	Any character except a, b, or c.	[^etc] matches each of the letters in **GIFs**, but not **etc** in the phrase "GIFs etc."
[a-z]	Any character in the range from a to z.	[l-p] matches *l* and *o* in **lo**wery and *m*, *n*, *o*, and *p* in **p**oi**n**t**m**a**n**.
x|y	Either x or y.	**boy|girl** matches both **boy** and **girl**.

Using grouping with Regular Expressions

Grouping is perhaps the single most powerful concept in Regular Expressions. With it, you can easily manipulate any matched text pattern—for example, a list of names such as this:

```
Schmidt, John Jacob Jingleheimer
Kirk, James T.
Fishman, Cara
```

could be rearranged so that the last name comes last and the comma is removed, such as this:

```
John Jacob Jingleheimer Schmidt
James T. Kirk
Cara Fishman
```

Grouping is handled primarily with parentheses. To indicate a group, enclose it in parentheses in the Find text field. Regular Expressions can manage up to nine grouped patterns. Each grouped pattern is designated by a dollar sign ($) in front of a number, (1 to 9) in the Change To text field, such as this: **$3**.

To switch the series of names as previously described, enter the following in the Find text box:

```
(/w+),/s(.+)
```

In Regular Expressions speak, this translates into "(Pattern 1 matches any alphanumeric character, one or more times) followed by a comma, a space, and (Pattern

2 matches any character—including white spaces—one or more times)." In the Change To text field, enter

    $2 $1

This configuration places the second matching pattern before the first, with just a space in between.

Caution Remember that the dollar sign is also used after a character or pattern to indicate the last character in a line.

Table 18-5 shows how Regular Expressions uses grouping.

<table>
<tr><td colspan="3" align="center">Table 18-5
Regular Expressions Grouping</td></tr>
<tr><td>*Character*</td><td>*Matches*</td><td>*Example*</td></tr>
<tr><td>(p)</td><td>Any pattern p.</td><td>(/d).(/d) matches two patterns, the first before a period and the second after a period, such as in a filename with an extension.</td></tr>
<tr><td>$1, $2...$9</td><td>The nth pattern noted with parentheses.</td><td>The replacement pattern **$1's extension is .$2** would manipulate the pattern described in the preceding example so that Chapter07.txt and Image12.gif would become **Chapter07's extension is .txt** and **Image12's extension is .gif**.</td></tr>
</table>

Altering font characteristics

Choosing the Font attribute in the Find and Replace panel enables you to search based on any or all of three different font characteristics:

✦ **Font:** Choose Any Font or select from a list of installed fonts.

✦ **Style:** Choose Any Style or choose standard options, such as Plain, Bold, Italic, or Underline. You can also choose combinations, such as BoldItalic or ItalicUnderline.

✦ **Size:** Use the Min and Max boxes to target a range of font sizes, or set them both to the same value to find only one size.

The real power of the Font Find and Replace is that you can search on one criteria, such as Size, and if a match exists, you can change another criteria, such as Font.

This flexibility enables you to, for example, search all graphics in a site and, if the font size is between 8 and 12, change the font from Times to Helvetica, without changing the original size (leave the Change to size box empty). This feature might cover all the "body text" in your document in one shot.

To change the font characteristic with Find and Replace, follow these steps:

Note   Start at the top of the Find and Replace box and work down as you go.

1. If the Find and Replace panel is not showing, choose Edit ➪ Find and Replace or, if it is behind another tabbed panel, click its tab to bring the panel forward.

2. Choose the scope of the search operation by selecting Search Document, Search Selection, and so on, from the Search In option list.

3. Select Font from the Attribute option list to specify a Font Find and Replace.

   The Find and Replace panel displays the Font options, as shown in Figure 18-10.

Figure 18-10: Change font size, typeface, or style when the Font attribute is selected from the Find and Replace panel.

4. To search for a specific typeface, change Any Font to an installed font by choosing the font from the list.

5. To search for a specific font style, change Any Style to one of the other options on the list, such as Plain or Bold.

6. To search for a specific range of font sizes, set the minimum point size in the Min box and the maximum point size in the Max box; to search for a single point size, set the Min and Max text boxes to the same value.

Tip   The Min and Max boxes also have pop-up sliders to adjust their values.

7. To change target objects to a specific font, change Same Font to another installed font by choosing a font from the list.

8. To change target objects to a specific style, change Same Style to another option, such as Italic.

9. To change target objects to a specific size, enter a value in the Size text box, or use the slider to select a value.

10. Click the Find button to find the first target object, and then click Replace to replace it, or click the Replace All button to make all the changes in one step.

Changing colors throughout a site

A color can be as important to a brand as a logo—for example, IBM blue. Web graphics often use a specific color scheme to make a marketing point or to assist with navigation. Manually updating graphics to incorporate a color change could be an extraordinarily tedious chore. In Fireworks, you can search for and replace colors just as easily as you can text—and, in some cases, even more easily.

Fireworks applies color to objects via three primary elements: strokes, fills, and effects. When the Color attribute is selected in the Find and Replace panel, you can change colors associated with any single one of these components, associated with both strokes and fills, or associated with all properties. To search and replace a color, follow these steps:

1. If the Find and Replace panel is not showing, choose Edit ➪ Find and Replace or, if it is behind another tabbed panel, click its tab to bring the panel forward.

2. Choose the scope of the search operation by selecting one of the choices from the Search In option list.

3. From the Attribute option list, select Color.

   The Find and Replace panel displays the Color options, as shown in Figure 18-11.

Figure 18-11: Update all the colors across a site with the Find and Replace panel's Color attribute.

4. In the Find color picker, select the color to search for.

   You can select one of the available swatches, or any other onscreen color using the Eyedropper tool, or select the Palette icon to open the system color picker(s).

5. From the Apply To option list, set which component of Fireworks the search should be limited to.

6. In the Change To color picker, select the color to replace the color being searched for.

7. Click the Find and Replace buttons to make changes on a case-by-case basis, or click the Replace All button to make global changes.

Snapping colors to Websafe

Replacing colors with their nearest Websafe equivalent is unfortunately a reality of today's Web. Until the vast majority of computer users have 32-bit color hardware (and know how to enable it), sticking to Websafe colors gives you the best chance of your work looking similar for the majority of your audience.

Find Non-Web 216 is similar to the Color Find and Replace. The same caveats apply, but in this case, Fireworks chooses the colors. To search for non-Websafe colors and replace them with Websafe colors, follow these steps:

1. If the Find and Replace panel is not showing, choose Edit ➪ Find and Replace or click its tab to bring the panel to the front of a panel group.

2. Choose the scope of the search by selecting one of the choices from the Search In option list.

3. From the Attribute option list, select Find Non-Web 216.

   The Find and Replace panel displays the Find Non-Web 216 options, as shown in Figure 18-12.

Figure 18-12: Search for non-Websafe colors in a selection, a document, or across multiple files and snap them to their nearest Websafe color.

4. From the Apply To option list, set which component of Fireworks the search should be limited to.

5. Click the Find and Replace buttons to make changes on a case-by-case basis, or click the Replace All button to make global changes.

Updating URLs

After you spend any amount of time designing for the Web, you learn to appreciate how active the Web is. Sites are constantly in motion, with new pages being added and old ones deleted or moved. Because Fireworks graphics are tied so directly to the Web through the URLs embedded in hotspots and slices that Fireworks creates, you need a way to modify the links quickly, if necessary. The URL attribute of the Find and Replace panel fulfills that need.

The URL attribute works much the same way that the Text attribute does — in fact, the interfaces for the two are identical, as you can see in Figure 18-13. A link to be searched for is entered in the Find text box and the new link is entered in the Change To text box. The same three options (Whole Word, Match Case, and Regular Expressions) apply. With URLs, however, a whole word is not designated by a space, but rather by a separator — either a period, a forward slash, or a colon.

Figure 18-13: Update your links with the URL attribute of the Find and Replace panel.

To search and replace links embedded in Fireworks graphics, follow these steps:

1. If the Find and Replace panel is not showing, choose Edit ➪ Find and Replace or, if it is visible, click its tab to bring the panel to the front of a panel group.

2. Choose the scope of the search operation by selecting one of the choices from the Search In option list.

3. From the Attribute option list, select URL.

   The Find and Replace panel displays the URL options.

4. Enter the link to be found in the Find text box.

5. If you intend to change the link, enter its replacement in the Change To text box.

6. Select any options desired: Whole Word, Match Case, or Regular Expressions.

7. To make changes on a case-by-case basis, first click Find Next and then click either Replace, to change the link, or Find Next again, to move to the next matched URL.

8. To change all the URLs at once, click Replace All.

As noted earlier in the chapter, the URL attribute can take advantage of Fireworks' Regular Expressions features when the Regular Expressions option is selected. The pattern-matching features of Regular Expressions go far beyond any simple wildcard character. For example, suppose that you have to convert from absolute to relative an entire site's worth of links inside of graphics, where all the links are within the same folder. This would require changing files from `http://www.idest.com/fireworks/main.htm` to just `main.htm`. Moreover, suppose that you have links to files from both Windows and Macintosh designers, so that some files end in .htm and others in .html. With Fireworks' Regular Expressions option enabled, here's what you would enter in the Find text box:

```
(.+)/(/b.*/.html?)
```

Translated from Regular Expressions language, this means "(Pattern 1 contains all characters) before a forward slash and (Pattern 2, which can be any single word followed by a period, and then either htm or html)."

To change these patterns to just the filename, enter **$2** by itself into the Change To text box. This returns just the results of pattern 2, without any other characters.

Working with the Project Log

One of the dangers of working with a find-and-replace feature as powerful as Fireworks' Find and Replace is that you can inadvertently make unwanted changes. This is especially true when you use the Multi-File Search & Replace option — Fireworks can open, modify, and close a file so quickly that you won't know what happened. You won't know, that is, unless you enable the Project Log option to track all changes.

With the Project Log option turned on, all Multi-File changes are noted. The Project Log, shown in Figure 18-14, lists the filename, the frame in which the change was made, and the date and time that the modification took place. Moreover, you can immediately check the alteration by double-clicking the filename in the Project Log in order to open the file in Fireworks.

Figure 18-14: Keep track of all your Multi-File Find and Replace operations through the Project Log.

You enable the Project Log to note search-and-replace changes by selecting the Add Files to Project Log command found in the panel Options menu on the Find and Replace panel. Once selected, any file altered when the search scope is set to Files is listed by name, frame number, date, and time. To verify a change — or to reverse it — open the file from the Project Log by double-clicking its name or selecting it, and then clicking the Open button.

The Project Log panel Options menu offers some additional functionality with the following four commands:

✦ **Export Again:** Because all Find and Replace operations are conducted only on source files, after you alter a file, you usually need to re-export it. The Export Again command repeats the last export and overwrites the previously exported file.

✦ **Add Files to Log:** You don't have to run a Find and Replace procedure on a file to include it in the Project Log. By selecting the Add Files to Log command, you can select which additional files are listed in the Project Log. This is a handy way of having your working files close at hand, but not opened until they're necessary.

✦ **Clear Selection:** Removes the currently selected listing from the Project Log.

✦ **Clear All:** Removes all entries from the Project Log.

The Project Log has yet another use: All files or selected files in the Project Log can be processed together with Fireworks Batch Processing feature, discussed in the next section.

Tip
To get a separate hard copy of the Project Log, detailing all the changes in a session, open the `Project_Log.htm` file found in the Fireworks Configuration folder and then print the page from your browser. The `Project_Log.htm` file is updated with every change.

Batch Processing Graphics Files

The unfortunate truth is that producing graphics for the Web involves about as much mindless repetition as it does creative expression. The more automated the processes, the more time you have to experiment and create, rather than resize and convert. The Batch Process dialog box, shown in Figure 18-15, is the automation control center.

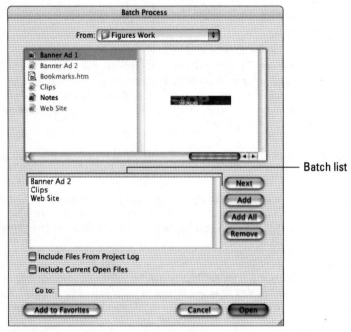

Figure 18-15: Select your automation options — and the files you want to process — in the Batch Process dialog box.

Grasping the basic procedure

Following is the basic procedure for running an automated session:

1. Choose File ⇨ Batch Process to open the Batch Process dialog box.

2. Specify which files are to be affected by the batch process, by using one or all of the following techniques:

    • Add a file to the batch list by navigating to it, selecting it, and clicking the Add button. Repeat as required.

- Add multiple files from the same folder to the batch list by navigating to the folder, holding Ctrl (Shift) as you select each file, then clicking the Add button. Repeat as required.

- Add all the files from one folder to the batch list by navigating to the folder and clicking the Add All button. Repeat as required.

Tip   Select a file from the batch list and click the Remove button to remove it from the batch list. The file itself is unaffected.

- Include all the files listed in the Project Log panel, whether open or not, by checking the Include Files from Project Log checkbox.

- Include all the files that are currently open in Fireworks by checking the Include Current Open Files checkbox.

3. When you are satisfied that you have compiled a complete list of target files for your batch job, click the Next button. The Batch Process dialog box changes to enable you to specify the operations to be performed upon your files (see Figure 18-16).

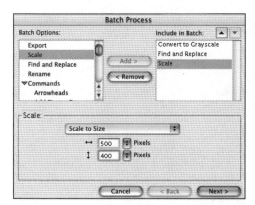

Figure 18-16: When you press the Next button, the Batch Process dialog box changes so that you can specify which operations will be part of your batch.

4. Under Batch Options, select an operation to apply to your batch and click the Add button to add it to the Include in Batch list. The newly added operation is selected by default, and options for that operation (if any) appear in the lower portion of the Batch Process dialog box. Of course, you can click the Remove button to remove an operation from the Include in Batch list, as well.

5. Specify options for newly added operation. For example, if you add a Scale operation (as shown in Figure 18-16), you can choose No Scaling, Scale to Size, Scale to Fit Area, or Scale to Percentage, and specify the appropriate height, width, or percentage, as required.

Tip Some batch operations require you to click an Edit button in the lower portion of the Batch Process dialog box in order to display another dialog box with the appropriate options.

6. Repeat Steps 4 and 5 as many times as necessary in order to create the desired batch operation. Use the up and down arrow buttons in the Batch Process dialog box in order to move operations up and down in the Include to Batch list. Operations are executed in the order they appear.

7. When you're satisfied that your batch operations are completely specified, click the Next button. The Batch Process dialog box changes again, to a final form that enables you to finalize and execute your batch operation (see Figure 18-17).

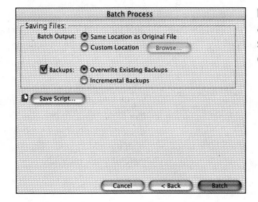

Figure 18-17: Finalize your batch and execute it and/or save it as a scriptlet in the final configuration of the Batch Process dialog box.

8. Choose whether you want your batch output to be saved in the Same Location as Original File, or in a Custom Location. If you choose Custom Location, use the Browse button to navigate to and select a folder.

9. Check the Backups checkbox to make one of two kinds of backups. Select Overwrite Existing Backups to maintain only one set of backups, which is equivalent to having one Undo. Select Incremental Backups to maintain a backup of each batch operation, as described earlier in the "Updating Graphics with Find and Replace" section.

10. After setting all other criteria, you can optionally choose to save your batch operation as a scriptlet (discussed in the next section) by clicking the Save Script button. The scriptlet enables you to run the whole batch operation again without re-entering any options.

11. Click the Batch button to execute your batch operation.

A Batch Progress dialog box reports how many files have been processed and how many are remaining. When finished, the total number of affected files is displayed.

Running scriptlets

Scriptlets are Fireworks script files, written in JavaScript. You can generate scriptlets by using the Batch Process dialog box, by hand-coding them, or by using a combination of both options. The simple, yet powerful, idea behind scriptlets is that they are reusable.

After you save a scriptlet, with an identifying .jsf filename extension, you can run it in any of these ways from the Batch Process dialog box:

✦ Double-click the Scriptlet icon.

✦ Choose File ➪ Run Script and select the scriptlet.

✦ Drag the Scriptlet icon onto the Fireworks application, onto a shortcut, or onto an alias of it.

✦ Drag the Scriptlet icon into the Fireworks window (Windows only).

All scriptlets run immediately. Fireworks includes many custom JavaScript "hooks" so that you can take advantage of the functions that are accessible through scriptlets.

Cross-Reference   For more detailed information on scriptlets, see Part VII.

Summary

The term production can't be overemphasized in Web graphics production. Much of a Web designer's job is devoted to updating and editing existing graphics. Fireworks offers a number of workflow solutions to reduce the workload:

✦ You can preview graphics immediately — with or without rollovers — and directly in the primary and secondary browsers of your choice.

✦ Links used in Fireworks Web objects, such as rollovers and hotspots, are coordinated through the URL panel, which maintains both the current document's links (URL History) and an independently stored set of links (URL Library).

✦ You can import the links from any HTML file into a separate URL Library.

✦ The Find and Replace panel enables you to update text, font attributes, colors, and URLs, and it even snaps colors to Websafe in the current document, frame, selection, or a series of selected documents.

✦ Export operations — including optimization and scaling of images — can be automated through the Batch Process features of Fireworks, saving you from lots of tedious, repetitive work.

✦ A batch processing session can be saved as a special JavaScript file, known as a scriptlet. Scriptlets can be customized or run, as is, any time they are needed.

In the next chapter, you work with Fireworks' Commands menu and History panel.

✦   ✦   ✦

Automating Workflow

How long does it take to design the graphics for a site? In an ideal world, it takes as long as necessary — but few designers get to live in that world. Most designers are faced with stringent production deadlines and hefty workloads. Fireworks provides some relief for those of us living in the real world with the productivity-saving features of the History panel and the default commands.

In a nutshell, the *History panel* is a combination super-Undo tool and macro recorder. Actions you take while working in Fireworks are recorded in the History panel automatically. Although the obvious side effect of this is the capability to step back through those actions as though rolling back time, the truly exciting consequence is that you can save those steps as commands and replay them again and again. Constantly resizing buttons to 40×40 pixels to satisfy corporate guidelines? Do it once, save it as a command, and make it a one-step process forever after. In this chapter, you learn about the History panel's other *raison d'être:* Undo central.

Next, this chapter covers the built-in default commands of the Commands menu, as well as how to add to the menu's contents with the History panel. The commands in Fireworks MX have gotten a major face-lift and productivity boost with their ability to incorporate a Flash user interface. Fireworks commands can do virtually anything from add an arrowhead to a line to generate a series of graphics based on an XML data file.

Finally, we'll touch on the kind of housekeeping you can do to keep the Commands menu from scrolling off your screen as you fill it with workflow shortcuts. Fireworks includes two tools to help you manage your automation workhorses, one for saved History panel commands and one for full-blown extensions.

Running Built-in Commands

Fireworks arrives from the factory with a group of standard commands that enable you to take its underlying extensibility for a serious test drive. The built-in commands, some of which are shown in Figure 19-1 and detailed throughout this section, are extraordinarily useful additions to the Fireworks toolkit. Let's look at the Creative category of commands first.

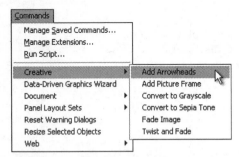

Figure 19-1: The Commands menu contains a range of commands — organized into submenus like the Creative category — that demonstrate Fireworks' extensibility.

Examining the Creative commands

Looking for a new spark of inspiration? Or maybe just a more efficient way to handle a complex graphic embellishment? The commands grouped under the Creative category are both artistic and functional. There are six commands in all:

✦ **Add Arrowheads:** Inserts one of 17 different arrowheads on one or both ends of a path.

✦ **Add Picture Frame:** Creates a patterned border around the current document.

✦ **Convert to Grayscale:** Changes the current selection to a grayscale image.

✦ **Convert to Sepia Tone:** Alters the current selection to a sepia color scheme.

✦ **Fade Image:** Applies a transparency gradient to an image in one of eight styles.

✦ **Twist and Fade:** Replicates the selected graphic as many times as desired, while optionally changing the scale, rotation, and opacity of the replications.

While two of the commands — Convert to Grayscale and Convert to Sepia Tone — have no interface at all, the rest are all products of Fireworks MX's capability to incorporate Flash movies as a user interface. You'll notice a wide range of interface approaches as a result.

Add Arrowheads

As you might expect, the Add Arrowheads command adds arrowheads to a selected path. What you probably do not expect is the sheer number of options and the flexibility available in this feature. Created by Kleanthis Economou, the technical editor for this book, the Add Arrowheads command enables you to apply any one of 17 differently shaped arrowheads to either end of any open path.

 New Feature With its classy Flash-built interface, shown in Figure 19-2, Add Arrowheads provides both a practical and elegant solution to a very specific production problem. Paths with arrowheads are essential for explanatory diagrams and they're a key graphical symbol. The Add Arrowheads command works with any open selected path by appending a designated shape on either or both ends and then grouping all the elements. The arrowhead drawn uses the characteristics of the current stroke. You have the option of scaling the arrowheads to any chosen size; additionally you can specify whether you want to apply just the stroke, just the fill, or both to the new arrowhead shape.

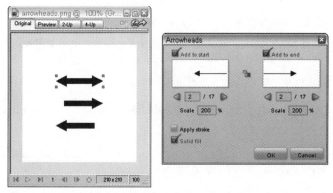

Figure 19-2: Add the arrowhead of your choice to either end of an open path — or both — with the Add Arrowheads command.

To use the Add Arrowheads command, follow these steps:

1. Select any single open path.

   Although you can use any path tool available in Fireworks, I find that the Add Arrowheads command works best with those created with the Line and Pen tools.

2. Choose Commands ➪ Creative ➪ Add Arrowheads.

   The Add Arrowheads dialog box is displayed.

Caution   If you choose a closed path, such as a rectangle, or multiple paths, you'll still be able to choose the command, but when you attempt to apply your choices in the Add Arrowheads dialog box, an alert informs you that you've made an invalid selection and you're returned to the document without any changes being made.

3. Choose which ends of the path you want the arrowheads to appear on by selecting Add to Start and/or Add to End.

4. If you want both ends to use the same arrowhead and be scaled the same, make sure the padlock symbol is shown as locked.

   The padlock toggles between locked and unlocked positions.

5. Choose the desired arrowhead shape for the end(s). Use the left and right triangles to preview each of the available shapes or enter the number of the shape in the text field.

6. Set the size of the arrowhead by entering a percentage value in the Scale text fields.

   Enter 100% to use the default size of the arrowhead.

7. Select the desired drawing options: Apply Stroke and/or Solid Fill.

   It's possible to leave both options unselected; the arrowhead(s) will still be drawn but will not be visible until either a stroke or fill is applied.

8. Click OK when you're done.

Fireworks creates the arrowhead(s) as specified and then groups the path and the new elements.

Tip   Add Arrowheads remembers your settings from one use to the next, so you don't have to start from the default settings each time.

Add Picture Frame

The next command in the Creative category, Add Picture Frame, affects the whole document rather than a selection. When executed, this command extends the canvas area to accommodate a border around the document, as you can see in Figure 19-3. The border is beveled and filled with a user-selected pattern; the figure shown uses a wood pattern.

Figure 19-3: Place an instant picture frame around a document with the Create Picture Frame command.

To create a picture frame around your document, follow these steps:

1. Choose Commands ➪ Creative ➪ Add Picture Frame.

   Fireworks displays the Add Picture Frame dialog box.

2. Choose a pattern for the picture from the drop-down list.

3. Enter a width for the picture frame in pixels.

4. Click OK when you're done.

Fireworks creates a new layer, entitled Frame, for the created border and locks the layer. The canvas is automatically expanded to accommodate the additional graphic. Technically, the frame consists of two rectangles, one set inside the other, which are combined with a Punch command. To achieve a three-dimensional look, an Inner Bevel effect is applied to the composite path.

You can modify the appearance of the frame in numerous ways. Before any modifications can be made, however, you must unlock the Frame layer. Once it's available, you can select the composite path object. Once selected, the fill handles become available and can be rotated or manipulated in other ways. To alter the pattern, choose Pattern ➪ Fill Options from the Property inspector and then select another fill pattern.

Tip
The available patterns are taken from those found in the standard Fireworks Configuration\Patterns folder. If you add your own file to the folder, the next time you launch Fireworks your pattern will be available from the drop-down list in the Add Picture Frame dialog box; the list, however, is not sorted and you may have to scroll to the bottom to see your custom pattern.

Convert to Grayscale and Convert to Sepia Tone

Two of the three commands in the Creative submenu convert the palette of selected objects:

✦ Commands ⇨ Creative ⇨ Convert to Grayscale simply converts any object to a grayscale palette, which is 256 shades of gray.

✦ Commands ⇨ Creative ⇨ Convert to Sepia Tone is similar to Convert to Grayscale, but the resulting image has a sepia tint.

No dialog box is used for either of these commands — just select your object(s), choose the command, and you're done. Essentially, these commands apply the Hue/Saturation effect at preset values. Once the command has been executed, choose the Edit button next to the Hue/Saturation effect to alter the values, if desired.

Tip
If you have to export a photographic image as a Graphics Interchange Format (GIF) (in order to create a transparent portion, or to include it in an animated GIF, for example) converting it to grayscale or sepia first often leads to much better results than dithering the True Color image. Grayscale and sepia both contain 256 shades or less, just like the GIF format.

Fade Image

One of the most common questions on the Fireworks newsgroup is "How do I make an image fade in?" The standard Fireworks technique is as follows:

1. Draw a rectangle or other shape over the existing image.

2. Fill the new shape with a black to white gradient.

3. Select both the shape and your original image.

4. Choose Modify ⇨ Mask ⇨ Group as Mask.

While not overly difficult, the method often proves difficult to grasp for designers new to Fireworks. To eliminate this confusion and provide an easy path for a commonly used technique, the Fade Image command was created.

New Feature The Fade Image command fades any selected image in one of eight different styles. Conceived by Sandee Cohen, author of the *Fireworks Visual QuickStart Guide* series, and programmed by the author of this book, Fade Image automates the masking technique just described. To keep this effect at its most flexible, the fill handle of the gradient mask is made available immediately after the command is completed. Moving the fill handle adjusts the fade.

Fade Image uses a visual interface, completely designed in Flash, as shown in Figure 19-4. The eight fade possibilities are (listed in left-to-right, top-to-bottom order):

✦ Rectangular fade in from left

✦ Rectangular fade in from right

✦ Rectangular fade in from top

✦ Rectangular fade in from bottom

✦ Circular fade in from all sides

✦ Elliptical fade in from all sides

✦ Rectangular fade in from all sides

✦ Wave-shaped fade

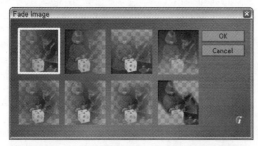

Figure 19-4: The Fade Image command fades any single or grouped image in any of eight directions.

To use the Fade Image command, follow these steps:

1. Select an object or object group.

Fade Image works with bitmap or vector objects. To fade more than one object at a time, group the objects first.

2. Choose Commands ⇨ Creative ⇨ Fade Image.

The Fade Image dialog box is displayed.

3. Select the type of fade desired from the eight possibilities.

As you move your mouse over each of the fade styles, a red outline shows the basic shape of the fade. A white outline notes a selected style.

4. Click OK when you're done.

Once the fade is applied, adjust the angle and the degree of transparency by dragging the gradient fill handles of the mask.

Tip

Fade Image uses the variations on the standard gradient fills—such as Linear, Radial, and Elliptical—to achieve its effects. Once the command is applied, you can alter the type of transparency mask by selecting a different gradient fill type from the Property inspector.

Twist and Fade

For pure creative pleasure, it's hard to beat the Twist and Fade command. Repetition of an image is a key principle of graphic design—a principle that you can explore wildly with Twist and Fade.

New Feature

The Twist and Fade command duplicates any selected object any number of times, automatically scaling down each duplicate and placing the new images however far apart you like at whatever degree of rotation desired. You can even control the opacity of the objects. Developed by Steven Grosvenor and Stephen Voisey of www.phireworx.com, Twist and Fade takes full advantage of the Flash user interface structure, as shown in Figure 19-5. Control elements within the interface are moveable and some, like the Preview pane, can be hidden.

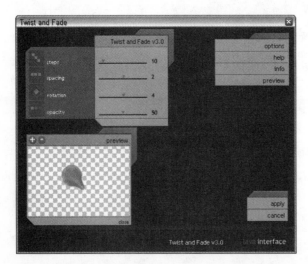

Figure 19-5: With Twist and Fade, you can create novel transfigurations, automatically.

To use Twist and Fade, follow these steps:

1. Select one or more objects in your Fireworks document.

2. Choose Commands ⇨ Creative ⇨ Twist and Fade.

   The Twist and Fade interface appears.

3. Set the basic parameters by dragging their respective sliders:

   - **Steps:** Determines how many times the object(s) will be duplicated.

   - **Spacing:** Sets how far apart the images will be placed. The spacing value is applied both horizontally and vertically so that the duplicates appear below and to the right of the original. Negative spacing values move the image above and to the right of the original.

   - **Rotation:** Determines the angle of rotation for each duplicate.

   - **Opacity:** Sets the overall opacity for both the original and each duplicate.

4. To set any of the additional parameters, select Options from the menu and choose one or more of the following:

   - **Random Effect:** Randomly resets the four basic parameters.

   - **Convert to Symbol:** Creates a new symbol for the original and the duplicates.

   - **Fade Opacity:** Reduces the opacity of each duplicate.

 Caution Twist and Fade uses a single name for all of the symbols it creates: Twist and Fade Symbol. Because the same name is used multiple times, each succeeding symbol incorporates the symbol previously created with Twist and Fade. To avoid this occurrence, give your Twist and Fade symbols unique names.

5. To see an example of the results of your settings, make sure the Preview pane is visible by choosing Preview from the menu.

   You can zoom into or out of the Preview pane by clicking the plus and minus buttons, respectively. You can also drag the preview symbol within the pane itself.

6. When all of your settings are selected, choose Apply.

If you don't like the results, undo the action and re-run the command. The standard settings are remembered from one session to the next, although the options (Random Effect, Convert to Symbol, and Fade Opacity) are not.

Resize Selected Objects

While it's not under the Creative category, the Resize Selected Objects command is a great tool for fine-tuning your creative masterpieces. Although Fireworks scaling facilities work well for general adjustments, it's often difficult to rescale an element in small increments in a single direction. With the Resize Selected Objects command, you can increase or decrease any side of an object by as little as one pixel.

New Feature

The Resize Selected Objects command was created by John Dunning. Its snazzy Flash interface makes scalar adjustments a point-and-click affair; you can rescale any selected objects smaller or larger—in any of four directions—by single or 10 pixel increments. The Resize Selected Objects command works extremely well with multiple objects, rescaling each independently.

To rescale page elements with the Resize Selected Objects command, follow these steps:

1. Select the desired elements.

2. Choose Commands ⇨ Resize Selected Objects.

   The Resize Selected Objects dialog box is displayed, as shown in Figure 19-6.

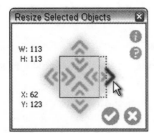

Figure 19-6: The Resize Selected Objects command works extremely well with rounded rectangles.

3. Select the small arrows to resize your elements by 1 pixel and the larger arrows to resize your elements by 10 pixels. The arrows outside the rectangle make the object larger and the arrows inside rectangle, smaller.

   Hold down the mouse button after you've selected an arrow to continue incrementing or decrementing the size.

4. Click the checkmark when you're done.

Data-Driven Graphics Wizard

One of the most innovative new features in Macromedia Fireworks MX is the Data-Driven Graphics Wizard. With this new command—created by the author of this book—you can produce multiple graphics from a single data source and automate your Web graphics production process.

New Feature The Data-Driven Graphics Wizard combines data from XML files with variables embedded in a Fireworks template to generate new graphics based on the original template. If you ever had the chore of churning out a slew of images where only a few key phrases and maybe a central graphic were different, you're going to love the Data-Driven Graphics Wizard.

The Data-Driven Graphics Wizard works with standard-format XML files, which can be exported by a database program such as Access 2002 or created by hand in Dreamweaver MX or any text editor. The XML file should follow a format like this:

```
<?xml version="1.0" encoding="iso-8859-1"?>
<records>
    <record>
        <varModel>ZX2002</varModel>
        <image>luxury.png</image>
        <url>http://www.triomotors.com/zx2002</url>
    </record>
    <record>
        <varModel>M210</varModel>
        <image>power.png</image>
        <url>http://www.triomotors.com/zr2002</url>
    </record>
</records>
```

You'll notice that within each of the two `<record>` tags shown here, there are three separate fields. The field names, `varModel`, `image`, and `url`, form the tags enclosing the data for that particular field. In an XML file, you can have as many records and fields as you need.

The graphics template itself is created in Fireworks. To turn any Fireworks file into a template, simply add variables. The Data-Driven Graphics Wizard recognizes any text enclosed by curly braces — like {varModel} — as a variable. You can use as many variables as you like and you can repeat the same variable multiple times.

In addition to text variables, the Data-Driven Graphics Wizard works with two other variable types: images and URLs. To turn any image into a variable, select it and, in the name field of the Property inspector, enter a unique name in curly braces, like {varImage}. Effects applied to the template image are applied to the replacement images. For URLs, the process is similar. Select any slice or hotspot and enter a variable — such as {url} — in the Link field.

While you can use any name you want for a variable, it's best to choose the same name used in the data file for the corresponding field. If, for example, there was a field in the data file called "`lastName`", use the variable {`lastName`} wherever you'd like the data from that field to appear. Naming your variables in this manner will save you a step in the process as the Data-Driven Graphics Wizard automatically maps template variables to data fields with the same name.

Be sure to save all the changes to your template graphic before beginning to run the Data-Driven Graphics Wizard.

Let's work through a typical Data-Driven Graphics Wizard session by following these steps. The Data-Driven Graphics Wizard is a six-step wizard; contextual help is available on every screen by selecting the question mark icon.

If you want to try out the Data-Driven Graphics Wizard, you'll find sample files—including a Fireworks template and XML data files—on the CD-ROM in the Examples folder.

Choosing your data sources

In this first step, you point to the proper XML data file and, if necessary, the folder containing the replacement images for any image variables.

The replacement images are usually the same height and width as the image variable. The replacement images can be any image format capable of being imported into Fireworks.

1. With your template graphic selected as the current document, choose Commands ➪ Data-Driven Graphics Wizard.

   On the opening screen, the Data-Driven Graphics Wizard identifies all the variables in your template.

2. Locate the XML data file by selecting the folder icon next to the first field.

3. If you have any image variables, you need to select the folder holding the replacement images.

4. Choose Next when you're ready.

Looking at the data records

The next step of the Data-Driven Graphics Wizard displays the records found in your data file. You can page through the various records with the VCR-like controls. There are four record controls:

✦ First Record

✦ Previous Record

✦ Next Record

✦ Last Record

This screen is especially helpful in identifying the fields as well as any specific records you'd like to process. When you're through reviewing your records, click Next to continue.

Selecting the proper records

In the third step, you choose which records you'd like to process. The choices are as follows:

✦ **All:** Processes all the records in the data file.

✦ **First Record Only:** Uses the data from the first record to process a single record.

✦ **Specific:** Processes specific records, designated by comma-separated numbers, like "1,3,5" or "2,4".

First Record Only is often chosen to run a test of the Data-Driven Graphics Wizard and make sure the results are what you expect. After the First Record Only is processed, the PNG source file remains open.

Linking variables to data

Step 4, shown in Figure 19-7, is the heart of the Data-Driven Graphics Wizard. Here, you map variables found in your document to fields in the data file. As noted earlier, variables and fields with the same name are automatically mapped to one another. To map unlinked variables to data, follow these steps:

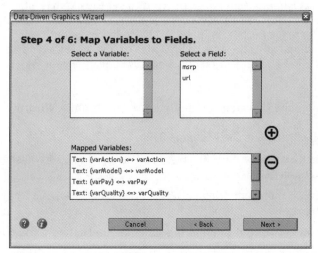

Figure 19-7: The Data-Driven Graphics Wizard automatically matches variables and data fields with the same names; this matching capability is not case-sensitive so a variable named {varName} will match a data field named VARNAME.

1. Choose a variable found in your Fireworks template from the Variable list.

   The type of variable is displayed first, like `Image: {varImage}`.

2. Select a data field from the Field list.

   Your selection appears next to the Add Link and Remove Link buttons.

3. Confirm your selection by choosing the Add Link button.

   The variable and field are moved into the Mapped Variables list.

4. To unlink a variable and field combination, select it from the Mapped Variables list and choose the Remove Link button.

5. When you've mapped all your variables, click Next.

Managing files

We're almost done! Step 5 is mostly devoted to housekeeping: naming files, choosing folders for export, and so on. First you need to choose a naming scheme for the generated files. The naming scheme combines a base name with an automatically generated number. By default, the base name picks up the name of the template; you can substitute any valid filename, without the extension. You have three different types of autonumbering to choose from.

After you've decided upon a naming scheme, you need to set the export options. You can choose any of the standard settings available within Fireworks or use the export option currently in place for the template. You also have the option to just export graphics or export and save the source PNG files or just save the source files. All you need to do is select the desired checkbox(es) and specify a folder for storing the files.

Follow these steps to complete this stage of the Data-Driven Graphics Wizard:

1. Enter the desired base name in the Filename field.

   The base name will be used for both exported and source files, so you should enter a name without an extension.

2. Select one of the three autonumbering patterns: no leading zero, one leading zero, or two leading zeros.

3. Enter a starting value for the autonumbering scheme. Alternatively you could just leave the default.

4. If you want to export the files, select the type of export from the drop-down list.

   The default option in the drop-down list, Template Export Settings, picks up whatever settings your template is using.

5. If exporting, choose the folder icon to open a Select Folder dialog box and pick a folder to store the generated images in.

If you select the folder icon, the Export Images option is automatically checked.

6. If you want to generate PNG source files, choose a folder for them as well.

7. Click Next to move to the final step.

Generating the files

Use the final step to review your choices. To change any choices, select Previous to return the desired step. If everything looks good, select Done to generate the graphics. Fireworks immediately begins processing. All generated files will be saved in the selected folder(s).

Once the command has finished, open up the generated files and you'll note that all the variables have been replaced with data. If your variable image had one or more effects applied to it, those effects have been transferred to the replacement images. Furthermore, all the slices with variable URLs are linked to new addresses.

Examining the Document submenu

The Commands ⇨ Document submenu contains four commands that operate on the canvas, layers, or frames of your document.

Distributing to layers

Selecting multiple objects and choosing Commands ⇨ Document ⇨ Distribute to Layers places each object on its own layer. If there are not enough layers, Fireworks creates new ones. Objects are distributed according to their stacking order, so that the closest object to the canvas stays in the current layer, and the farthest object from the canvas ends up in the highest-numbered layer.

Tip

When you import a Photoshop document, Fireworks converts Photoshop layers into Fireworks objects and places them all within one Fireworks layer. The Distribute to Layers command enables you to quickly place each object on its own Fireworks layer.

Toggling layers

Two commands provide straightforward shortcuts to focusing in on only the current layer:

✦ Commands ⇨ Document ⇨ Hide Other Layers hides all layers except the current layer.

✦ Commands ⇨ Document ⇨ Lock Other Layers locks all layers except the current layer.

Reversing frames

Occasionally, you may find that you've imported a rollover button upside down so that the initial state is not in Frame 1 in Fireworks. This often occurs when FreeHand layers are converted into Fireworks frames. Reversing frames is also a common way to save time and work while creating animations. The Reverse Frames dialog box provides two options to reverse the order of frames in a document.

✦ Reverse All Frames simply reverses the order of all the frames in your document. The first frame becomes the last frame; the last frame becomes the first frame.

✦ Reverse Frame Range works in the same way as Reverse All Frames, except you can set the starting and ending frame in their respective drop-down lists. When executed just the frame range specified is reversed.

Fireworks technique: Completing an animation

When working on an animation, it's common to build one-half of an animation sequence, such as a sun rising, and then reverse the already built frames to create the other half of the animation, such as the sun setting. Fireworks' Reverse Frames command provides an easy way to accomplish this task in record time:

1. Create the first half of your animation, such as the previously mentioned sunrise, or an animated object flying onto the canvas.

2. Choose File ➪ Save a Copy to save a copy of your document.

3. Choose Commands ➪ Document ➪ Reverse Frames to reverse the frames of your animation, essentially running it backward.

   Choose Reverse All Frames, or choose Range of Frames and select a starting and ending frame.

4. Choose Add Frames from the Frames panel pop-up menu.

   Fireworks displays the Add Frames dialog box.

5. In the Number box, type in the same number of frames as your document currently contains. For example, if your document has 10 frames, enter **10** to create 10 new frames so that you end up with 20 frames.

6. Under Insert New Frames, select At the Beginning, and click OK when you're done.

   Fireworks creates the new frames at the beginning of your document and selects Frame 1.

7. Choose File ➪ Import. Navigate to and select the copy of your document that you created in Step 2. Click Import to import it.

8. Place the L-shaped import cursor at the top left of the canvas in order to line up the imported document with the current document. Click once to complete the import operation.

Your original animation—running forward—fills up the empty frames and provides the beginning of the animation. The reversed frames provide the end of the cycle so that the animation completes itself.

Cross-Reference Find out more about animation in Fireworks in Chapters 23 and 24.

Using Panel Layout Sets

Panel Layout Sets are saved configurations of Fireworks' floating panels. Saved sets are automatically added to the Commands ⇨ Panel Layout Sets submenu for easy recall of any particular organization of floating panels.

Fireworks provides three built-in Panel Layout Sets, each specifically optimized for a different screen resolution:

✦ Commands ⇨ Panel Layout Sets ⇨ 1024×768

✦ Commands ⇨ Panel Layout Sets ⇨ 1280×1024

✦ Commands ⇨ Panel Layout Sets ⇨ 800×600 (see Figure 19-8)

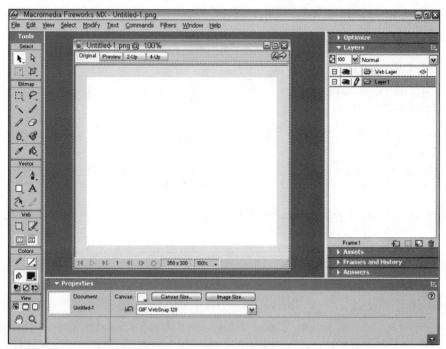

Figure 19-8: The 800×600 Panel Layout Set organizes panels into tight configurations in order to fit them on an 800×600 display.

Tip

Panel Layout Sets are a welcome solution when you change to a lower display resolution and all of your floating panels are out of the visible area. Recalling a saved set restores Fireworks to working order.

Storing Custom Panel Layouts

The Save Panel Layout command enables you to easily save your own Panel Layout. Aside from saving your One True Favorite panel setup for posterity, you might save configurations that are optimized for certain tasks, such as a drawing layout that places the Object, Info, Fill, and Stroke panels front and center, or an optimization layout that pops up the Optimize, Color Table, and Frames panels.

Tip

Although Fireworks offers some built-in Panel Layout Sets, the initial, default configuration of panels is not saved. If you're still using the initial configuration, create a Panel Layout Set and store it. If not, you can restore the initial configuration by trashing your Fireworks MX Preferences file on the Mac (in the Preferences folder inside your System Folder), or deleting the file Fireworks MX.ini on Windows (inside your Fireworks 4 folder). When you start Fireworks again, all the preferences will be at their default values, including the location of the floating panels.

To create your own Panel Layout Set, follow these steps:

1. Create a panel layout worth saving by toggling the visibility of particular panels and/or adjusting their positions. You can also create new panel groups by choosing Group `Panelname` with from a particular panel's Options menu.

2. Choose Commands ➪ Panel Layout Sets ➪ Save Panel Layout.

   Fireworks displays a JavaScript dialog box asking for a name for your new Panel Layout.

3. Enter a name for your Panel Layout in the dialog box. Click OK when you're done.

Fireworks saves your panel configuration as a new Panel Layout and adds it to the Panel Layout Sets submenu in the Commands menu.

Caution

Creating a new Panel Layout with the same name as an existing one overwrites the original without asking for confirmation. It's possible to have both entries briefly coexist on the Panel Layout Sets submenu, but your original command file will still be lost.

Using the Reset Warning dialog boxes

Many of Fireworks' warning dialog boxes have a "Don't ask again" checkbox that enables you to disable the warning in the future. Choose Commands ➪ Reset Warning Dialogs to enable all of Fireworks' warnings.

Examining the Web submenu

The Web submenu of the Commands menu has three entries that enhance
Fireworks' export features: Create Shared Palette, Set Blank ALT Tags, and Set
ALT Tags.

Creating Shared Palette

The Create Shared Palette command looks at a folder full of images and creates a
common color table file (.act) from them.

To create a shared palette from a folder of images, follow these steps:

1. Choose Commands ➪ Web ➪ Create Shared Palette.

   Fireworks displays the command's dialog box, as shown in Figure 19-9.

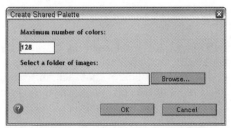

Figure 19-9: The Create Shared Palette
command lets you specify the number
of colors to include.

2. Enter the maximum number of colors in the appropriate text field.

3. Locate a folder containing the images by selecting the Browse button.

   Fireworks displays the Select Folder dialog box.

4. Click OK when you're done.

   Fireworks displays a Save File dialog box when it's done.

5. Navigate to a folder and specify a filename for the palette file. Click Save when
   you're done.

Fireworks saves the shared palette as a color table file, with the filename extension
.act. You can open this file with the Fireworks Color Table panel, or import it into
Photoshop.

Tip   Mac users: Fireworks saves the palette file with a Fireworks Creator code (MKBY), but Fireworks doesn't provide an icon for a color table file type (8BCT). If you also have Photoshop, applying a Photoshop Creator code (8BIM) to the file with AppleScript or a utility, such as File Buddy, applies an icon (from Photoshop) to it as well.

Selecting blank ALT tags

The HTML `<img>` tag (used for inserting images into Web pages) can have an `alt` attribute containing text that is displayed to users who have images turned off in their browser or are using a text-only browser. Alt text is particularly important to visually impaired Web surfers, who may have a browser that simply reads text and alt text aloud to them. You can set alt text in the Object panel while single or multiple hotspot or slice objects are selected. Choosing Commands ➪ Web ➪ Select Blank ALT Tags selects all the hotspots or slices in your document that don't have alt text, enabling you to add text to them with one step. You might set all buttons to say "button," for example.

Setting ALT tags

When you choose Commands ➪ Web ➪ Set Alt Tags, Fireworks displays a dialog box, as shown in Figure 19-10. Enter alt text and click OK, and Fireworks applies the alt text to all the hotspots and slices in your document that lack alt text. Leaving the text field empty and clicking OK is the same as clicking Cancel, and does not set the alt text to an empty string (which would effectively hide an image — such as a spacer — from text-only browsers).

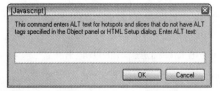

Figure 19-10: Provide `alt` text for all the Web objects in your document that lack alt text in one step.

Enhancing Productivity with the History Panel

The History panel not only enables you to undo actions, but it also enables you to save steps as commands, which you can then repeat. This productivity enhancement can be quite remarkable. If you're used to a History panel from Photoshop, you know that it's hard to do without it once you're hooked.

Tip   Macromedia's Dreamweaver also gained a History panel in version 3.

Using Undo and Redo

Fireworks has long had multiple Undo, enabling busy Web artists to Edit ⇨ Undo or
Ctrl+Z (Command+Z) their way step-by-step back through their previous actions.
With the History panel, Fireworks' Undo feature gains a friendly front-end that
makes jumping back one or ten steps a simple, intuitive affair.

The History panel contains a special slider, called an Undo Marker, that enables you
to point to any of your previous steps in order to return your document to the state
it was in right before that step. Figure 19-11 shows the History panel with the Undo
Marker.

Figure 19-11: The History
panel is empty when you
create a new document,
but from that point on, it
records your every move.

To undo steps in the History panel, try one of the following methods:

✦ Drag the Undo Marker up the History panel until it is next to the last step that
you want to undo.

✦ Click the Undo Marker track next to the last step that you want to undo. The
Undo Marker slides directly to that point.

Undone steps are grayed out in the History panel, and your document changes to
reflect the steps that have been undone.

The logical companion to Undo is, of course, Redo. After you have undone a step or steps, reversing the procedure applies those actions again.

To redo undone steps with the History panel, try one of the following methods:

✦ Drag the Undo Marker down the History panel until it is next to the last step that you want to redo.

✦ Click the Undo Marker track next to the last step that you want to redo. The Undo Marker slides directly to that point.

By default, Fireworks records 20 unique steps in the History panel, after which, the oldest step is discarded to make room for the newest step.

To change the number of unique steps the History panel can record, follow these steps:

1. Choose Edit ➪ Preferences.

   Fireworks displays the Preferences dialog box.

2. If necessary, click the General tab in Windows or choose the General option from the option list on a Mac.

3. Change the number of steps in the Undo Steps box to the number of steps that you want the History panel to record.

The number of Undo steps has a theoretical maximum ceiling of 1,009 steps, but in practice, this number is limited by the amount of RAM Fireworks has access to.

Clearing steps from the History panel can free memory and disk space, although you lose the ability to work with the steps you are deleting. For example, you will be unable to perform Undo or Redo on deleted steps. To clear all steps from the History panel, choose Clear History from the History panel pop-up menu.

Building commands without coding

Building commands with the History panel is a tremendous timesaver, and a lot of fun, to boot. Creating commands with the History panel emphasizes the minimalist, easy-to-use interface of the History panel.

The simplest way to create a command is just to replay a step or a series of steps from the History panel by using the Replay button. Select a step in the History panel by clicking it, and then click the Replay button to reapply that step to whatever is currently selected on the canvas.

For example, imagine that you colored an object a certain blue and then later decided that a few other objects should also share that same blue color. Click the Fill Color step in the History panel that represents the application of that blue fill (see Figure 19-12), and the Replay button is now a Fill With Blue button. Select objects on the canvas and hit Replay to color them blue. You can select multiple contiguous steps in the History panel by holding down Shift while clicking the first and last steps in a series. You can select multiple noncontiguous steps by Ctrl+clicking (Command+clicking).

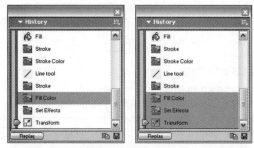

Figure 19-12: With the Fill Color step selected (left), the Replay button becomes a command that applies a fill to selected objects on the canvas. Hold down Shift to select multiple steps and apply them to selected objects with the Replay button.

But what if you decide that blue fill is so useful that you'll need it again and again? The Fill Color step moves further up the History panel as you continue your work and will eventually be removed to make space for newer steps. To keep your Fill With Blue command for later use, simply press the History panel's Save Steps as Command button, which looks like a floppy disk. Saving a step or steps as a command adds the command to the Commands menu for later use.

To save History panel steps as a command, follow these steps:

1. Perform an action or a consecutive series of actions that you would like to save as a command. Following are examples of steps you could perform before saving them:

   • Create a standard copyright/legal footer for your Web site, with associated text formatting and precise canvas placement.

   • Create a circle object, duplicate it five times, select all six objects, align them horizontally, and distribute them to widths, creating a basic button bar that can be easily built upon or modified.

2. If you want to save just one step as a command, click that step in the History panel to select it. To save multiple steps, hold down Shift and click the first and the last step in the series that you want to save. Ctrl+click (Command+click) noncontiguous steps to select them.

3. Click the Save Steps as Command button in the History panel.

   Fireworks displays the Save Command dialog box.

4. Enter a name for your new command. Click OK when you're done.

Your steps are saved as a command and added to the Commands menu in alphabetical order. To apply your command, choose the name of your new command from the Commands menu.

Limitations to saving steps as commands

The two caveats to saving steps as commands are:

✦ Some actions, such as drawing a shape with the Brush tool, are nonrepeatable. Fireworks marks these steps with a red *X*, as shown in Figure 19-13.

Figure 19-13: Items with a red *X* next to them are nonrepeatable. A separator line indicates a change in selection, which can lead to unpredictable results.

✦ Fireworks places a separator in the History panel (also shown in Figure 19-13) when you change your selection. Replaying steps across a separator can have unpredictable results because some objects can't be modified in the same way as other objects.

When you attempt to save steps that include either of these potential problems, Fireworks notifies you with a dialog box, indicating that there may be a problem and providing you with the opportunity to continue or cancel.

Fireworks technique: Quick menu command shortcuts

Fireworks offers the user a lot of editing choices and power with many menu commands that have numerous options. This creative flexibility is, of course, a wonderful feature, but there have been times I wished for a few simpler commands, such as Modify ⇨ Reduce Image to 25%. After you've opened up the Image Size dialog box and almost laboriously chosen Percentage and entered **25%** for the 20th time in a particular session, you start to think there must be a better way. And with the History panel, there is.

The History panel not only enables you to create a complex series of steps and make intricate commands, but it's also useful as a way to make one-step commands that simply use common settings. If you find yourself scaling buttons to 30×30 pixels all the time, or changing the canvas size to 300×200 pixels constantly, create new scaling and canvas-changing commands with those settings built right in.

To save a Fireworks menu command as a modified command with your own built-in settings, follow these steps:

1. Open a Fireworks document. As long as you don't save the document after creating your command, you can experiment with almost any document. Simply use it as a guinea pig in your command-building session.

2. Perform a simple, one-step transformation on your document. Here are some possibilities:

   • Choose Modify ⇨ Image Size and reduce the image's size to 50%, or another percentage (or a pixel size) that you commonly change images to.

   • Import a commonly used file, such as a logo.

3. Select the single step in the History panel that represents the command you just gave Fireworks.

4. Click the Save Steps as Command button in the History panel.

   Fireworks displays the Save Command dialog box.

5. Enter a name for your new command. Click OK after you're done.

Your step is saved as a command and added to the Commands menu in alphabetical order.

Copying steps to the clipboard

Fireworks has achieved a new level of productivity with the new capability to turn steps in the History panel into commands on the clipboard without writing a line of code. In previous versions, users had to perform tasks again and again manually. However, the History panel also has a trick or two for those of us who don't mind getting into a little JavaScript once in a while.

The Copy Steps to Clipboard button copies the History panel's selected steps to the clipboard as plain text JavaScript statements, ready for pasting into any text editor. Copy Steps to Clipboard provides a way for even the experienced JavaScript coder to get a command or scriptlet roughed out in record time.

After the steps are pasted into a text editor, they can be modified and added to until you have created a complex command. The Fireworks application programming interface (API) contains a host of entries that make it possible to build complex commands or scriptlets that access almost any feature of Fireworks.

Chapter 26 covers the Fireworks API.

To use Copy Steps to Clipboard to start building a command or scriptlet visually, follow these steps:

1. Create a series of steps that you would like to save.

2. Select the steps in the History panel.

3. Click the Copy Steps to Clipboard button to copy your steps to the system clipboard as JavaScript statements.

4. Launch or switch to your favorite text editor, such as Notepad in Windows or SimpleText on a Mac. Create a new document or open an existing one, if necessary.

5. Choose Edit ⇨ Paste within the text editor to paste your JavaScript code.

Feel free to modify the pasted JavaScript, or even to repeat the preceding steps to add more code to your project.

Chapter 26 has all the details on the Fireworks JavaScript API.

Using Commands in Commands

After you've applied a command, the action is recorded in the History panel as a step called Command Script. It might not be immediately obvious, but steps that apply commands can themselves be selected and saved as part of a command (see the figure), thus, creating *meta-commands:* commands that combine a number of commands into one.

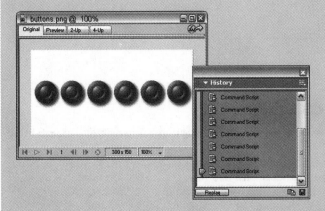

The button bar in the accompanying figure was built almost entirely by running commands that I had previously saved. One command applied a drop shadow and inner bevel, while still another command applied a radial gradient fill and offset the fill to provide a lighting effect. Selecting the steps that applied the commands and saving them creates a complex sequence of actions that can be applied in the future with just one step. There is one small caveat, though: To use the new command, the original commands must be installed and available.

Managing Commands

The extensibility of the Fireworks' Commands menu is its most useful feature. Items can be easily created and added to it. In addition to the default commands included with Fireworks, Macromedia and other extension authors are creating new extensions on an on-going basis.

Fireworks recognizes two different types of extensions:

✦ **JavaScript commands:** Stored with the extension .jsf, the Fireworks JavaScript files may be hand-coded or saved from the History panel.

✦ **Flash commands:** Saved as a .swf file from Flash, these extensions typically have a more complete interface allowing a wider variety of user interaction.

Let's look at ways of managing the JavaScript commands first.

On the CD-ROM Find even more JavaScript commands to enhance your productivity in Fireworks.

Managing saved commands

The Commands menu is all about enhancing productivity, and as such, maintaining a neat and tidy Commands menu is an important part of the process. It doesn't take too much experimentation with the Copy Steps as Command button to realize that you can fill up your Commands menu with useful — okay, and sometimes not so useful — new Fireworks commands. The Manage Saved Commands command provides a visual interface for renaming or deleting installed commands.

Working with the Manage Saved Commands dialog box

To edit your Commands menu with the Manage Saved Commands command, follow these steps:

1. Choose Commands ➪ Manage Saved Commands.

   Fireworks displays the Manage Saved Commands dialog box, as shown in Figure 19-14.

Figure 19-14: Rename or remove commands in the Manage Saved Commands dialog box.

2. Select a command to modify and apply one of the following:

   • Click Delete to delete the command from the Command menu.

Caution

Deleting a command in the Manage Saved Commands dialog box removes the command's scriptlet from your computer and cannot be undone. What's more, Fireworks offers no confirmation or warning dialog box after you press Delete.

- Click Rename. Fireworks displays the Save Command dialog box. Enter a new name for the command, and click OK to rename it.

3. Click OK in the Manage Saved Commands dialog box after you're done.

Modifying the Commands folder

In addition to removing or renaming commands in the workspace, you can get under the hood and organize or add commands in Fireworks' Commands folder.

New Feature

To accommodate multiuser systems, Fireworks MX uses different configuration files for each user as well as a master configuration folder. The master configuration folder is stored by default with the other programs on your system. On a Windows system, this would be in the Program Files\Macromedia\Fireworks MX folder while for a Macintosh user it would be in the Applications/Macromedia/ Fireworks MX folder. The location of the user's configuration files depends on the operating system. For example, Macintosh OS X users would find the configuration folder at HD\Users*User ID*\Library\Application Support\Macromedia\Fireworks MX whereas Windows 2000 and XP users would find it at C:\Documents and Settings*User ID*\Application Data\Macromedia\Fireworks MX. The Commands folder is inside the Configuration folder in your Fireworks program folder.

The hierarchy of your Fireworks Commands folder determines the hierarchy of your Commands menu. In other words, a folder inside the Commands folder becomes a submenu in the Commands menu, so that the Creative folder is shown as a Creative submenu (see Figure 19-15).

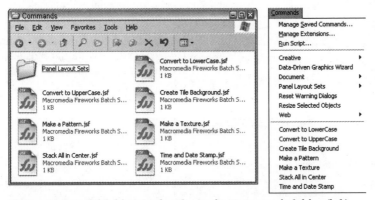

Figure 19-15: Subfolders in the Fireworks Commands folder (left) become submenus in the Fireworks Commands menu.

Create new subfolders in the Commands folder in order to better organize your commands. Placing folders within those subfolders has no effect; the hierarchy can be only one deep. Changes take effect immediately in Fireworks, without relaunching, making it easy to experiment with new arrangements.

At 1,024×768-pixel display resolution, Fireworks for Macintosh allows you about 45 Command menu entries (commands and submenus) before it begins scrolling the menu. When it's maximized, Fireworks for Windows can contain about 30 Command menu items at a 1,024×768-pixel display resolution before the menu scrolls. I find scrolling menus to be a real productivity hit. Aside from the fact that you can't see all the entries, they are sometimes hard to navigate, especially on Windows, where the menu itself does not stay fixed to the menu bar when it gets too long, and it interferes with the taskbar at the bottom of the display. Keeping your Commands menu organized with subfolders is worth the effort.

Managing Flash commands

Flash commands may be installed either as *modal* or *modeless*. If a command interrupts the general use of the program; the Add Arrowheads and Data-Driven Graphics Wizard are both examples of modal commands. Modal commands are typically found in the Commands menu. A modeless extension is one that co-exists with the program; the Align panel is an excellent example of a modeless extension.

To facilitate the process of adding new extensions, Macromedia developed the aptly named Extension Manager. The Extension Manager is a cross-product utility for use with Dreamweaver, Flash, and, now, Fireworks. The Extension Manager works with extensions created in a special format, Macromedia Exchange Package or MXP. MXP files contain the necessary files for the extension, all the required information on where the files should be installed, how to access the extension, who the author is, and more, as shown in Figure 19-16.

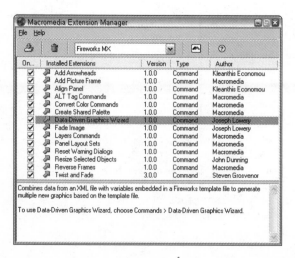

Figure 19-16: The Extension Manager can temporarily disable commands without uninstalling them.

The primary source for Macromedia Extension Package files is the Macromedia Exchange (www.macromedia.com/exchange/), but you can also retrieve these files from other sources such as developers' sites or this book's CD-ROM.

Note At the time of this writing, Fireworks extensions were only available through the Dreamweaver Exchange and could be found by choosing the Fireworks category. However, there are plans for a Fireworks Exchange; from the Extension Manager, choose File ➪ Go to Macromedia Exchange to see the latest exchanges available.

If you've located the MXP file from the Internet, your browser may offer you alternative methods to start the installation:

✦ Download the file to your system and complete the installation after that process is complete.

✦ Install the file directly from the Internet.

Tip It's a matter of personal preference, but I prefer to store all the extensions locally. The vast majority of them tend to be fairly small and if I need to install them again or on a different machine, I don't have to go through the download process again.

To complete the installation, follow these steps:

1. If you chose to open the extension from the Internet, the Extension Manager is automatically launched. If you downloaded the extension, double-click the .mxp file to launch the Extension Manager. In either case, the Macromedia Exchange legal disclaimer is presented.

2. Select the Accept button to continue with the installation or Decline to cancel it.

After you accept the disclaimer, the Extension Manager informs you whether the installation is successful or alerts you to any errors it encounters, such as existing files with the same name.

If the installation succeeds, the extension is added to your list. The list displays the name of the installed extensions, their version number, the type, and the author. Selecting the extension will give you a description of the extension, how to access the extension in the Fireworks interface, and usually a bit of help on how to use it or how to find help.

Tip If you have a great number of extensions, you can sort the list in the Extension Manager by selecting the column heading. To change the display order from ascending to descending (to show, for example, the highest version numbers first) click the heading again under Windows; on Macintosh systems, select the sort-order button on top of the scroll bar.

You can also install an extension from within Fireworks by following these steps:

1. Choose Commands ⇨ Manage Extensions to open the Extension Manager.

2. Select File ⇨ Install Extension or use the keyboard shortcut, Ctrl+I (Command+O). Alternatively, Windows users can also select the Install New Extension button.

   The Select Extension to Install dialog box opens.

3. In the Select Extension to Install dialog box, locate the desired .mxp file on your system and choose Install.

   The legal disclaimer is presented.

4. Select the Accept button to continue with the installation or Decline to cancel it.

5. After the installation is complete, choose File ⇨ Exit (File ⇨ Quit) to close the Extension Manager or click the Close button.

Caution   Some extensions may require Fireworks to be relaunched in order to take effect.

Once an extension is installed you can disable it temporarily by clearing the checkbox in the On/Off column. This removes the command from the Fireworks menu until you enable the checkbox again. To permanently remove an extension, select the entry and choose File ⇨ Remove Extension; Windows users may also select the Remove Extension button. In multiuser environments, extensions installed by the administrator — such as the standard commands and command panels — can be removed only by someone with administer privileges.

Summary

The Commands menu and the History panel are powerful productivity features and welcome additions to Fireworks. Keep the following points about them in mind:

✦ Fireworks' extensible Commands menu already contains useful commands right out of the box.

✦ The History panel offers precise control over multiple Undo and Redo.

✦ Steps in the History panel can be replayed, saved as a command, or copied to the clipboard as JavaScript code for later editing.

✦ You can add new commands to Fireworks by dropping them in the Commands folder, the structure of which represents the Commands menu.

In the next chapter, you explore image maps and slices in Fireworks.

✦   ✦   ✦

Entering the Web

Fireworks broke new ground as the first image editor to output HTML and JavaScript code. With its full-featured hotspots, image maps, and sliced images embedded in HTML tables, Fireworks is incredibly Web-savvy. Part V explains the basics of Web interactivity for those designers unfamiliar with the territory and also offers specific step-by-step instructions for linking JavaScript behaviors to graphics.

If you work with Dreamweaver (or work with someone who does), you'll want to check out Chapter 22 in order to get the most out of the integration possibilities between Fireworks and Dreamweaver.

Mastering Image Maps and Slices

Have you ever encountered a Web page in which all the image links are broken? All you see amidst the text is a bunch of rectangles with the browser's icon for "No graphic found." That's what a Web page really is to a browser: text and rectangles. You can use GIF transparency to disguise the box-like shape of an image file, but that won't limit the image link to just the visible area. For that, you need to use image maps or slices, which also enable you to create the effect of inter-twined, irregularly shaped image links, such as a yin yang symbol.

Fireworks excels in its support of image maps and slices. Collectively known as *Web objects* in Fireworks, both slices and image maps (or their individual parts, referred to as *hotspots*), serve several functions. In addition to helping designers break out of the rectangularity of the Web, Web objects add interactivity through links and a bit of flair through rollovers and other Behaviors. Although you could design a site full of Web graphics without ever coming near hotspots or slices, fully understanding their uses and limitations significantly increases your Web design repertoire.

Cross-Reference This chapter covers the basics of setting up hotspots and slices, and includes some techniques for incorporating them into your Web pages. For detailed information on building rollovers and using other Fireworks Behaviors, see Chapter 21.

Understanding Image Maps and Hotspots

To understand how an image map works, you needn't look any further than an actual map of almost any country in the world. Divisions between regions, territories, or states are usually geographic and rarely rectangular. To best translate any such map to the Web, you would make each region (territory or state) a separate clickable area (see Figure 20-1). This is exactly the type of job for which an image map is intended.

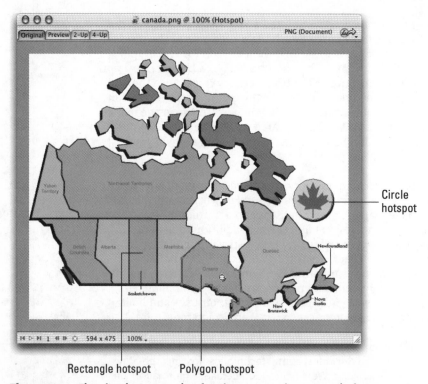

Figure 20-1: The simplest example of an image map is one made from a real map.

Each separately defined area of an image map is referred to as a *hotspot*. Hotspots come in three basic shapes: rectangles, circles, and polygons. Rectangles can be rectangles or squares, and circles can be circles or ovals; every other shape is a polygon. After you define an area of an image map, you can name it and assign a URL to it. Hotspots can also be used to trigger other events, such as rollovers or the display of messages. Hotspots are not visible on the graphic when viewed through the browser. Hotspots themselves are not actually part of the final image; to be used, the hotspot information is translated into HTML code, which is embedded in the Web page.

Because image maps and hotspots are HTML constructs and not data embedded in your graphics file, you need to export both the image and the code from Fireworks — and insert them both in your Web page. As you find out later in this chapter, Fireworks handles this dual export quite effortlessly and gives you many options for incorporating graphics and code however you like.

Using the Hotspot Tools

In Fireworks, the Hotspot tools are immediately accessible in the bottom-left area of the Tools panel. The following are the three basic Hotspot tools, corresponding to the three basic hotspot shapes:

✦ **Rectangle:** Use to draw rectangular or square hotspots. You can't round the corner of a rectangle, as you can with the standard Rectangle tool, although the keyboard modifiers work the same.

✦ **Circle:** Use to draw elliptical or circular hotspots. Again, the keyboard modifiers, Shift and Alt (Option), function the same as they do with the regular Ellipse tool.

✦ **Polygon:** Use to draw irregularly shaped hotspots. It functions similarly to the Polygon Lasso and uses a series of points, plotted one at a time, to make the hotspot shape.

When drawn, the hotspot appears as a shape overlaying the other graphics, as shown in Figure 20-2. Fireworks keeps all hotspots — and slices, for that matter — on the *Web Layer*, which is always shared across all frames and can be both hidden and locked and moved up or down in the stacking order in the same way other layers are. Hotspots are displayed initially with the same color, but you can assign each hotspot its own color, if desired, through the Property inspector.

Circle hotspot   Polygon hotspot   Rectangle hotspot

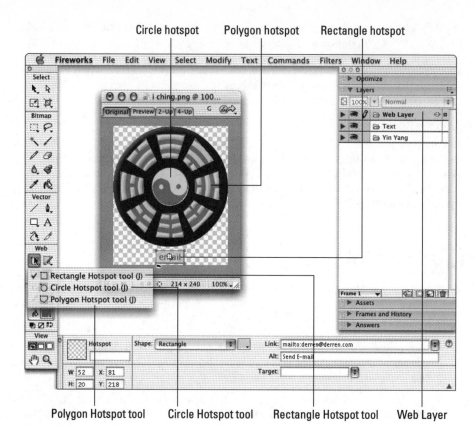

Polygon Hotspot tool   Circle Hotspot tool   Rectangle Hotspot tool   Web Layer

Figure 20-2: Use the three Hotspot tools to draw hotspots on the Web Layer.

Examining the rectangle hotspot

As noted previously, all the Hotspot tools work in a similar fashion to corresponding standard tools. However, a few key differences exist. To create a rectangle hotspot, follow these steps:

1. Select the Rectangle Hotspot tool from the Tools panel.

2. Click once to select your originating corner and drag to the opposite corner to form the rectangle. As you drag your pointer, Fireworks draws a preview outline of the hotspot.

Tip

To create a square hotspot, press Shift while you drag out your shape. To draw your hotspot from the center instead of from the corner, press Alt (Option) when dragging out the shape. You can also combine the two modifier keys to create a square drawn from the center.

3. Release the mouse button when the rectangle is the desired size and shape.

Fireworks creates the hotspot with a colored fill, as shown in Figure 20-3.

Figure 20-3: Use the Rectangle Hotspot tool to create square or rectangular hotspots.

Examining the circle hotspot

To draw an elliptical or circular hotspot, follow these steps:

1. Select the Circle Hotspot tool from the Tools panel. If it's not visible, click and hold the visible Hotspot tool until the flyout appears, and then click the Circle Hotspot button.

2. Click once to select the origin point, and then drag to the opposite corner to create the circle or ellipse. As you drag your pointer, Fireworks draws a preview outline of the form.

Hold down Shift while drawing to create a perfect circle, and/or hold down Alt (Option) to draw from the center.

3. Release the mouse button when the circle or ellipse is the desired size and shape.

Fireworks creates the hotspot, as shown in Figure 20-4.

Figure 20-4: Use the Circle Hotspot tool to create circular and elliptical hotspots.

Tip

Precisely matching the size and shape of an elliptical object with a corresponding hotspot is fairly difficult. After you create hotspot objects, however, you can move them with the pointer, resize them with the transform tools, or adjust them numerically through the Info panel or Property inspector. If the oval you're creating a hotspot for is a separate object — as opposed to a region of a larger object — the easiest method by far is to select the object and choose Edit ⇨ Insert ⇨ Hotspot, which tells Fireworks to make the hotspot for you.

Examining the polygon hotspot

To draw a polygon hotspot, follow these steps:

1. Select the Polygon Hotspot tool from the Tools panel. If it's not visible, click and hold whichever Hotspot tool is visible until the flyout appears, and then click the Polygon Hotspot button.

2. Click the starting point for your hotspot and move the mouse to the next point on the outline surrounding the desired area, and then click again.

   Fireworks connects each point that you set down with a straight line, as shown in Figure 20-5.

3. Repeat Step 2 until you've outlined the entire area.

   As you create more points, Fireworks fills in the polygon with the default hotspot color.

4. To finish creating the hotspot, click your original starting point to close the polygon.

   Fireworks creates the hotspot with a colored fill.

Figure 20-5: Fireworks fills in the polygon hotspot as you select each point.

Assigning links to hotspots

The Property inspector does much more for hotspots than choose their color. In fact, the Property inspector (see Figure 20-6) could easily be regarded as the fourth Hotspot tool. To be truly useful, you must assign hotspots a link and other HTML options — all of which you handle in Fireworks through the Property inspector.

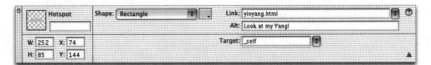

Figure 20-6: Use the Property inspector, once you've selected a hotspot, to enter essential Web data, such as the linked URL and ALT text.

The Property inspector options for a hotspot include:

✦ **Link:** Use this text box to both assign and display the link associated with the selected hotspot. You can either enter a new link by typing directly into the text field, or choose an existing link by selecting one from the option list. The option list displays URLs from the URL History for the current document as well as the current URL Library.

For more information on using the URL History and URL Library to manage your links, as well as links in general, see Chapter 18.

✦ **Alt:** Alternate image text entered here is shown when the server can't find the image, if the user has image loading turned off in their browser, or if the user's mouse is hovering over the image. In the latter case, the text appears in a tooltip attached to the pointer. Fireworks includes both the standard alt attribute and the title attribute required by Internet Explorer in the generated HTML.

✦ **Target:** The target defines where the Web page requested by a link appears. Targets are commonly used with HTML framesets. You can enter a named frame directly in the Target text box, or choose one of the following target keywords from the option list:

- **_blank** opens the link into a new browser window and keeps the current window available.

- **_parent** opens the link into the parent frameset of the current frame, if any.

- **_self** opens the link into the current frame, replacing its contents (this action is the default if nothing is specified).

- **_top** opens the link into the outermost frameset of the current Web page, replacing all frames.

✦ **Color:** When created, all hotspots are filled with the same semitransparent color. You can, however, alter an individual hotspot's color by selecting a new one from the pop-up color picker.

✦ **Shape:** Displays the current hotspot shape. This shape is initially derived from the tool used to create the hotspot, and is used to determine a portion of the HTML code. You can change the shape by selecting a different one from the option drop-down list, although doing so can radically alter your hotspot.

If you're entering links directly into the Current URL text box, be careful of your spelling. Web servers are very sensitive to typos — even whether you use uppercase or lowercase letters in some instances. You can save yourself a great deal of painstaking typing by using Fireworks' Import URL feature, located in the URL panel and covered in Chapter 18, to import links from any HTML file.

Covering an object with a hotspot

As one who has played connect-the-dots too many times while trying to create a star-shaped hotspot, I heartily embrace Fireworks' object matching hotspot creation. Instead of attempting to outline an object with any of the hotspot drawing tools, select the object and choose Edit ⇨ Insert ⇨ Hotspot. A hotspot precisely matching the shape of the object is created on the Web Layer, ready for linking. This command works for rectangular, elliptical, and irregular shapes, whether they are vector, bitmap, or text objects.

> **Note**   If you select multiple objects before using the Edit ⇨ Insert ⇨ Hotspot command, Fireworks asks whether you want to create one hotspot or multiple hotspots. Choosing to create one hotspot combines the Web Layer shapes into one rectangular hotspot encompassing all the selections.

Exporting Image Map Code

When an image map is translated into HTML, it appears in two key parts. The first part is the image tag, `<img>`, which holds the information for the overall graphic. The `<img>` attributes include `src` (the filename of the graphic), the dimensions of the image, and a connection to the map data, `usemap`. The `usemap` attribute is set to the name of the second image map element, the `<map>` tag. For every hotspot in the image map, a corresponding `<area>` tag exists within the `<map>` ... `</map>` tag pair. The following code is for an image map with five hotspots:

```
<img name="sloth" src="sloth.gif" width="300" height="125"ù
 border="0" usemap="#m_sloth">
<map name="m_sloth">
<area shape="rect" coords="14,18,68,46" href="sloth.html">
<area shape="rect" coords="68,18,122,46" href="envy.html">
<area shape="rect" coords="122,18,176,46" href="greed.html">
<area shape="rect" coords="176,18,230,46" href="lust.html">
<area shape="rect" coords="230,18,284,46" href="ties.html">
</map>
```

Fireworks handles outputting all of this code for you — and in several different styles for various authoring tools, as well. All that you're responsible for is incorporating the code in your Web page.

Choosing an HTML style

Fireworks generates the HTML or XHTML code for an image map when you export your image. The style of the code that Fireworks exports depends on the HTML Style setting in the HTML Setup dialog box, as shown in Figure 20-7. Choosing an HTML or XHTML style that matches your Web-authoring program makes incorporating the Fireworks-generated code easier.

Figure 20-7: Select an HTML/XHTML style and more through the HTML Setup dialog box.

The standard HTML and XHTML styles included in Fireworks are as follows:

✦ **Dreamweaver HTML/XHTML:** Code styled for Macromedia Dreamweaver. For image maps, no real difference exists between the Generic and the Dreamweaver code.

Cross-Reference

Fireworks can also export HTML code as a Dreamweaver Library Item. Details later in this chapter.

✦ **Generic HTML/XHTML:** The basic code, useful in hand-coded Web pages and the majority of Web-authoring tools that work with standard HTML.

✦ **FrontPage:** FrontPage uses a series of *webbots* to format its code; Fireworks includes the code necessary for an image map webbot, as well as instructional code that displays when the document is opened in FrontPage.

✦ **GoLive HTML/XHTML:** Code optimized for use with Adobe's GoLive HTML editor.

On the CD-ROM

You can find additional HTML templates in the HTML Templates folder on the CD-ROM accompanying this book. To use, just copy the desired folder with its files to the Fireworks/Settings/HTML Settings directory—you don't need to relaunch Fireworks.

To export an image map, follow these steps:

1. Optimize your image as needed in the Optimize panel.

2. Choose File ⇨ Export to begin the exporting process.

The Export dialog box, shown in Figure 20-8 appears.

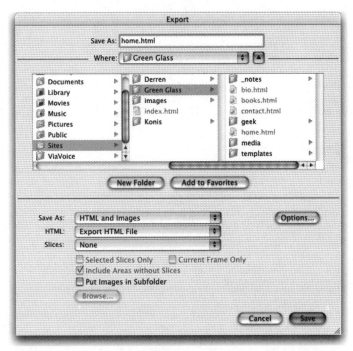

Figure 20-8: The Export dialog box enables access to export settings.

3. Choose a folder and provide a filename to save your exported file under.

4. Select HTML and Images from the Save as type (Save As) option list.

5. From the HTML option list, select whether you want to export the HTML file, or copy the code to the clipboard.

6. Select None from the Slices option list.

7. If desired, check the Put Images in Subfolder checkbox, and click Browse to choose the desired location for the image files only.

8. To alter any of the settings in the HTML Setup dialog box, click the Options button to open the HTML Setup dialog box and adjust your settings.

9. After you make your selections, click Save to complete the export.

10. If you copied the HTML code to the clipboard, paste it into an HTML editor.

Inserting image map code in a Web page

After you create the graphic, link the hotspots, and generate the code, how do you integrate all of that material within an existing Web page? Although the thought of touching code may be just this side of horrifying for many graphic designers, for most situations it's really not that bad — and for some, it's an absolute breeze. Bottom line? If you can cut and paste in a word processor, you can insert an image map in your Web page.

Although the process is much the same for most of the different style outputs, some variations exist in the procedure. The following sections detail how to integrate the Fireworks-generated code for each of the standard HTML styles.

Examining Generic code style

The Generic HTML code style is, as the name implies, used in most general situations. If you're building Web pages by hand — using a text editor, such as Notepad in Windows or SimpleText on the Macintosh — the Generic HTML style is for you. Likewise, if you're using a Web-authoring program, but not one for which Fireworks has a specific template, such as Dreamweaver, FrontPage, or GoLive, you should use Generic HTML.

The general procedure for incorporating a Generic image map is fairly straightforward:

1. Open the Generic code in a text editor or in the text editor portion of your Web-authoring tool.

2. Select and copy to the clipboard the section in the <body> tag that starts with

   ```
   <!---------- BEGIN COPYING THE HTML ---------->
   ```

   and ends with

   ```
   <!---------- STOP COPYING THE HTML HERE ---------->
   ```

3. Open your existing Web page in a text editor or in the text editor portion of your Web-authoring tool.

4. In the <body> section of your Web page, insert the code where you want the image to appear.

Caution   Be sure that you insert the code between the <body> and </body> tags, and not between the <head> and </head> tags.

5. Preview the page in a browser and adjust the placement of the <img> tag, if necessary.

It's not essential that the <img> part of the image map code and the <map> section appear side by side, as long as they are in the same document.

Note If the image map is to form the basis of your document—and you don't have another existing page to use—you don't have to delete or move any code whatsoever. Just add HTML elements around the image map as you build your new page. If you want, you can remove the HTML comments, but, frankly, they don't add much weight to a page, so removing them really isn't necessary.

Incorporating Dreamweaver code

You can incorporate the standard Dreamweaver HTML code into a Web page in two ways. The first is similar to the procedure used for including Generic code: Cut the code from the Fireworks-generated page and paste it into the Dreamweaver page in Dreamweaver's Code inspector, or in Dreamweaver's Code View. As long as you make sure to insert the code in the <body> section of the document, and not the <head> section, you won't have any problems.

The other method takes advantage of Dreamweaver's Invisible Elements to completely avoid opening the Code Inspector or switching to Code View. To incorporate Dreamweaver-style HTML visually, follow these steps:

1. In Dreamweaver, open the Fireworks-generated HTML/XHTML page, which was created with the Dreamweaver HTML/XHTML style option.

2. Make sure that View ➪ Visual Aids ➪ Invisible Elements is enabled.

   Notice an HTML Comment symbol beside your image, followed by a Map symbol, shown selected in Figure 20-9.

3. Select the image, press Shift, and click the Map symbol on the right of the image.

Note If you want to transfer all the comments as well, click the first Comment symbol, press Shift, and then click the last Comment symbol.

4. Choose either Edit ➪ Copy, or use the keyboard shortcut, Ctrl+C (Command+C).

5. Open the existing Web page to which you want to add the image map.

6. Place the cursor where you want the image map to appear.

7. Choose either Edit ➪ Paste, or use the keyboard shortcut, Ctrl+V (Command+V).

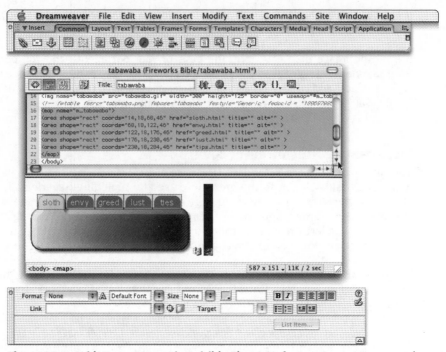

Figure 20-9: With Dreamweaver's Invisible Elements feature, you can copy and paste or drag and drop visual icons in the document window instead of moving blocks of code in the Code inspector or in Code View.

The image map — and its code — is inserted into the Dreamweaver document.

Note   If for some reason you don't see either the Comment symbols or the Map symbol in Dreamweaver's document window, choose Edit ➪ Preferences (Dreamweaver ➪ Preferences in OS X) in Dreamweaver and, from the Invisible Elements category, make sure that the Comments and Client-side Image Map options are selected. If you still don't see the Comment or Map symbols, choose File ➪ HTML Setup in Fireworks and make sure that Include HTML Comments is checked.

Tip   The easiest way to insert Fireworks HTML or XHTML in Dreamweaver is to use the Insert Fireworks HTML object in the Common category of the Insert bar. It automatically places the code in the correct areas of your page.

Using GoLive

You can easily select and then copy and paste HTML code in GoLive's HTML Source Editor, or drag and drop it between HTML Outline windows (see Figure 20-10). The HTML Outline windows make it easy to move individual tags between documents because the `<img>` or `<map>` tag can be easily collapsed to a single line. As well as the `<img>` and `<map>` tags, code exported with the GoLive style contains a `cssscriptdict` tag that tells GoLive how to edit the image map. Make sure to copy all three tags to the new document, placing the `<img>` and `<map>` tags into the body tag and the `cssscriptdict` tag into the head tag. HTML code exported with the GoLive option is very plain, with just a single "exported by Fireworks" comment.

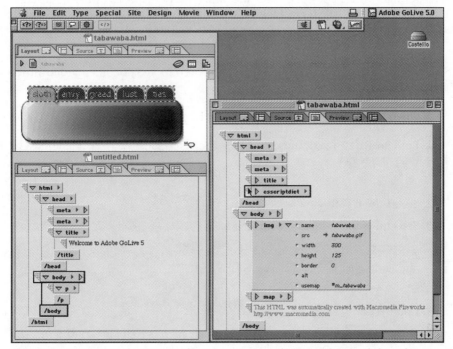

Figure 20-10: GoLive's HTML Outline view is a good way to drag and drop the `<img>`, `<map>`, and `cssscriptdict` tags from your exported code to another document.

To insert an image map from Fireworks into a GoLive document, follow these steps:

1. In GoLive, open the Fireworks-generated HTML page, which was created with the GoLive style option.

2. Switch to the HTML Outline view for both your source and target documents.

3. Select the `<img>` tag in the exported Fireworks code and drag it into place in your target document. Do the same for the `<map>` tag, placing both tags within the body tag in your target document.

4. Select the `cssscriptdict` tag from the head of your source document and drag it into the head of your target document.

Note   If you want to transfer the "created by Fireworks" comments as well, select it in the source document and drag it to the target document.

Using FrontPage

Microsoft's FrontPage is an introductory Web-authoring tool that uses proprietary code for many of its special effects, including image maps. Fireworks outputs code to match the FrontPage format when you select FrontPage from the HTML Style option list during export. The exported image map is inserted into an HTML page that instructs the FrontPage user how to incorporate the code.

To insert an image map from Fireworks into a FrontPage document, follow these steps:

1. Open the Fireworks-generated page in FrontPage.

Caution   Both the FrontPage document and the Fireworks-generated document must be in the same folder.

2. Select the HTML View.

3. Select the code starting with

   ```
   <!---------- BEGIN COPYING THE HTML ---------->
   ```

   and ending with

   ```
   <!---------- STOP COPYING THE HTML HERE ---------->
   ```

4. Choose Edit ⇨ Copy.

5. Open the document into which the image map is to be inserted.

6. While still in HTML View, choose Edit ⇨ Paste to insert the code into the document.

Understanding Slices

If image maps enable you to target areas of a graphic for links, why not use them for everything? The primary drawback to an image map is also one of its key character-istics: An image map is a single file. As such, image maps of any size — and they tend to be sizable, to take advantage of multiple hotspots — take a long time to download and can be frustrating for the Web page visitor. Moreover, with one file you're locked into one graphic format with a single panel. What if your image map contains a photographic image in one color with lots of flat color in the rest of the graphic? You would be forced to export the entire file as a JPEG to make the photo look good, and the file size would be much higher than if you exported the image as a GIF. And forget about including animations or special effects, such as rollovers — duplicating frames of a large graphic would make the file huge.

An alternative approach to image maps is a technique known as slicing. Slicing takes a large image and literally carves it into multiple smaller graphics, which are reassembled in an HTML table for viewing. Each separate image is referred to as a slice and the whole process is often just called *slices*. Here are some of the key features of slices:

✦ **Incremental download:** On most browsers, each slice appears as it's downloaded, which makes the whole image appear to be loading faster.

✦ **Linking without image maps:** Each slice can have its own link, although all such links are rectangular.

✦ **Mixed file formats:** Each slice can be optimized separately, reducing the overall file size of the image while enhancing the quality. This technique means that you not only can have a JPEG and GIF side by side, but can also export one slice as a JPEG at 100 percent and another slice as a JPEG at 30 percent.

✦ **Update image areas:** If your graphic includes an area that must be updated frequently, such as a headline or a date, you can simply alter the single image in the slice and leave the rest of the image untouched.

✦ **Embedded rollovers:** One of the chief uses of slices, especially in Fireworks, is to create rollovers (also known as *mouseovers*). With slices, you can have a series of rollovers, as with a navigation bar, all tied together in one graphic. You can also use one slice to trigger a rollover in another part of the image.

✦ **Embedded animation:** With a GIF animation in one slice, you can achieve special effects, such as a flashing neon sign in a large graphic, without doubling or tripling your file size.

The key, fact-of-life, limitation to slices is their shape: All slices are rectangular. Not only are images that make up each individual slice always rectangular, but the table cells into which the slices must fit are, too. To create any illusion of nonrectangular shapes, you must use GIF or PNG files with transparency. An additional restriction is that slices cannot overlap.

When deciding whether or not to slice an image, keep in mind that slices depend on HTML tables to hold them together in the browser. Tables, in turn, have some of their own limitations. For example, you can't place two tables side by side on a Web page; the code won't allow it. However, you can nest one table inside another to achieve a similar effect.

Because slices are tied to HTML tables, you must take special care to ensure that all browsers treat the tables identically. Under some situations, tables viewed in some browsers can "collapse" and lose all their width and height information that is necessary to appear as a single graphic. The workaround for this problem is to use very small (one pixel) transparent images called *spacer images*. Fireworks automatically generates the spacer images if you'd like, or outputs the code for the sliced image without them. Spacer images are covered in detail later in this chapter.

Cross-Reference This chapter covers the basics of creating slices. For information on how to use slices to build rollovers, see Chapter 21.

Slicing Images in Fireworks

Slices and hotspots are created in a similar manner — generally, you draw a slice area on top of an image. Although hotspots can be any shape, including circular, slices are ultimately rectangular. However, Fireworks aids in creating complex slices by enabling you to use the Polygon Slice tool to draw complex polygon-shaped slices, which Fireworks then converts into multiple rectangular slices upon export.

The two Slice tools are located in the Web section of the Tools panel, on the lower right, on a flyout similar to the one used for the Hotspot tools.

As you draw slices with the Slice tools, Fireworks creates *slice guides*, which help you to keep the number of files exported to a minimum, by aligning the slices. The fewer images you ultimately use, the faster your work displays in a browser and the less taxing the page is for the browser to display. When slices overlap, Fireworks considers slices that are higher in the stacking order to be more important.

Looking at rectangle slices

To slice an image with the Slice tool in Fireworks, follow these steps:

1. Select the Slice tool from the Tools panel.

2. Click the image and draw out a rectangle the size and shape of the desired slice, as shown in Figure 20-11.

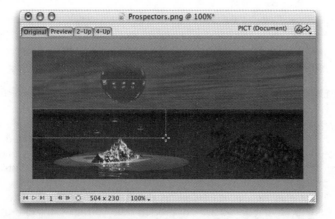

Figure 20-11: The Slice tool divides a Fireworks document into straightforward rectangular slices that are exported as individual image files.

Tip

As with the regular Rectangle tool, the Alt (Option) key causes the Slice tool to draw from the center rather than from a corner, and the Shift key constrains the slice to a square.

3. Release the mouse when you're satisfied with the shape.

Fireworks creates the slice object and fills in the rectangle with the default, semi-transparent slice color. If enabled, the slice guides appear.

After you draw the slice object, you can manipulate it as with any other object in Fireworks. You can use the four handles on the slice object to resize it — just drag one corner in the desired direction. Rectangular slices are constrained to rectangles, so moving just one point moves the entire side. In fact, you don't have to select the corner; it's just as effective to click and drag a slice object's side.

You can also use the transform tools, such as Scale, although any resulting nonrectangular shape is converted back into an encompassing rectangle. To move the slice object one pixel at a time, use the arrow keys.

An alternative to the Slice tool is to use the standard guides. In this technique, guides are dragged from the horizontal and vertical rulers to form the slicing grid. Then, during export, choose the Slice Along Guides option. This technique works well when your goal in slicing an image is to enable smaller portions of the image to appear quicker than a single large image could load. If you want to add a URL or a Behavior to a slice, you have to create slice objects.

Looking at polygon slices

As previously mentioned, polygon slices exist only within Fireworks. When you export your document, Fireworks uses your polygon slices as a guide in creating more complex rectangular slices. Polygon slices can be any shape — just like Polygon hotspots — as shown in Figure 20-12.

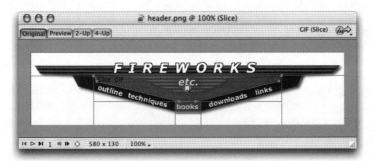

Figure 20-12: Outline nonrectangular areas with the Polygon Slice tool.

A side effect of this conversion is that polygon slices can often result in a large number of individual image files. This adds to the overhead of displaying the page in a browser. Each image file must be requested by the browser and sent by the server, and each image must be rendered by the browser separately. When you incorporate 10 or 15 images, the user may start to notice the difference in the perceived speed of the download.

To draw a polygon slice, follow these steps:

1. Select the Polygon Slice tool from the Tools panel. If it's not visible, click and hold the Slice tool until the flyout appears, and then click the Polygon Slice button.

2. Click at the starting point for your slice and move the mouse to the next point on the outline surrounding the desired area, and then click again.

   Fireworks connects each point that you set down with a straight line.

3. Repeat Step 2 until you've outlined the entire area.

   As you create more points, Fireworks fills in the polygon with the default slice color.

4. To finish creating the slice, click your original starting point to close the polygon.

   Fireworks creates the slice with a colored fill.

Working with slice guides

Before Fireworks, creating a sliced image by hand was very meticulous, eye-straining work. Each slice had to be measured and cut precisely to the pixel — if you were one pixel off, the resulting image would either have gaps or over-lapping areas. You can approximate this level of frustration by disabling the slice guide features in Fireworks.

Unlike regular guides, you don't position slice guides by hand; they are automatically created as you draw out your slices. The slice guides effectively show you the table layout that would result from the existing slices. More importantly, the slice guides take advantage of the Snap to Guide feature, enabling you to avoid overlapping slices or sliced images with gaps.

Personally speaking, I find the slice guides very useful, and I highly recommend using them. Choose View ➪ Show Guides to show or hide slice guides. Slices automatically snap to the edge of a document, but to snap to the guides themselves, choose View ➪ Guides ➪ Snap to Guides.

The standard guides and the slice guides are drawn in two different colors. Occasionally, the slice guide color is too similar to that of the current image and you can't see the guides' location. To change the color of the slice guides, select

View ➪ Guides ➪ Edit Guides to see the Guides (Grids and Guides) dialog box, shown in Figure 20-13. Select a new color from the Slice Color pop-up menu.

Figure 20-13: Choose a new slice guide color from the Guides (Grids and Guides) dialog box.

 Note On Windows, the grid and guide options are displayed in separate Grids and Guides dialog boxes. On the Mac, a single Grids and Guides dialog box contains both sets of options, separated by tabs.

You can also enable the slice guide feature from the Guides (Grids and Guides) dialog box by choosing Show Slice Guides, or turn on the Snap feature by selecting Snap to Guides.

 Note Unlike the regular guides, the slice guides can't be dragged to a new location; their position is controlled by the slices themselves. Therefore, the Lock Guides option on the Guides (Grids and Guides) dialog box applies only to standard guides.

Taming your slice guides

What happens when you inherit a Web site update and the original designer was a little overzealous in the use of slices? This designer read the same chapter you read in which I suggest that slicing up a large image makes it appear to load faster. However, the original designer decided to try to get it to appear to load really fast. As you can see in Figure 20-14, this site hasn't been sliced, it's been put through the blender. So what's the problem? With so many slices, and so many file pieces, it actually takes longer to load because the server has to keep receiving requests for image segments before it actually sends the portion that you want. Because the original designer took the advice too literally, you now have a mess to clean up.

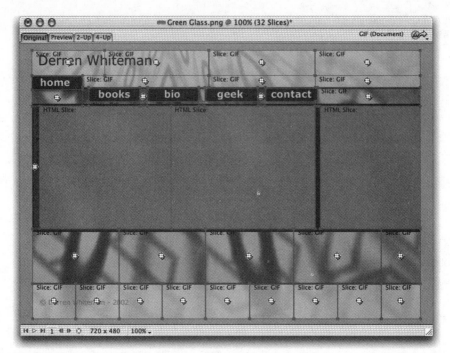

Figure 20-14: Slicing larger graphics into chunks can make things load faster, or at least appear to, but dicing them actually slows things down.

So you've got a couple of choices to make. Do you delete most of the slices, and then resize the rest, or do you delete them all and start over? Either choice can be a real nuisance but the good news is that Fireworks, as always, can assist. You can easily fix this problem using Dragable Slice Guides.

New Feature   The Dragable Slice Guides feature is new to Fireworks MX and enables you to select a slice guide, hold Shift, and drag it across other slice guides. As you cross other guides, they are picked up and a single, combined, slice is left behind.

Rather than selecting separate slices to delete, or dragging individual slice guides off the canvas, you can select a slice guide, hold Shift, and Fireworks scoops up all of the slice guides you cross. When you have dragged them off the canvas, or simply combined enough slice guides to make you happy, you can release the mouse button and you're left with one larger slice. To combine a group of slices, follow these steps:

1. Select the Pointer tool and position the arrow close to the slice you wish to drag.

2. The standard Pointer icon changes to the guide movement pointer, similar to the double-headed resize pointer, indicating that you're close enough to grab and drag a slice guide.

3. Press and hold Shift and a small solid square appears in the upper-left corner of the guide movement pointer, indicating that slice guides you cross are picked up and combined.

4. Drag your mouse across a group of slice guides to pick them up. As you approach a guide that is going to be picked up, it changes color from the default red, to a light purple. This gives you a visual cue as to exactly what you're changing.

5. When you reach the point that you want your slice guide positioned, release the mouse button and your new, simpler, slice appears.

6. Repeat this as necessary for areas in your document where you'd like to combine slice guides.

If you change your mind about removing multiple guides, simply release the Shift key before releasing the mouse button and the guides you scooped up are all snapped back to where they were. Figure 20-15 shows the previous image after dragging the right edge of the bottom-left slice all the way to the right side of the document. Presto chango!

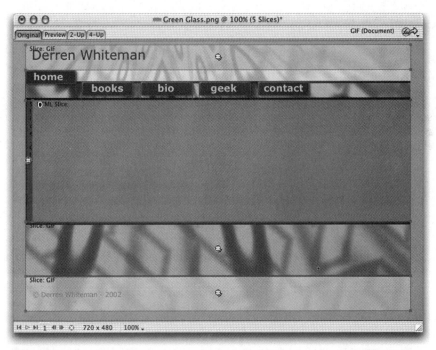

Figure 20-15: Removing a large number of extra slice guides is a simple task for Fireworks.

Copying an image to a slice

Sometimes, ensuring that you have all of a particular object can be very tricky —
especially if that object has a drop shadow or glow effect. Incorrect placement of
a slice could cut off part of the image. To avoid these problems, you can have
Fireworks do all the work for you. Just as Fireworks can convert any object to
a hotspot, any object can also be made into a slice.

To create a slice with the same dimensions as your object, select the object and
choose Edit ⇨ Insert ⇨ Slice. Fireworks draws the slice completely encompassing the
selected object — special effects and all. If you select multiple objects, Fireworks
asks whether you want to create slices for all the items together or separately.

Setting URLs in slices

To use a slice as a link, the slice must be assigned a URL. You can assign URLs to
slices in two different locations: the Property inspector or the URL panel. Slices
have the same options on both panels as those covered earlier in this chapter for
hotspots.

To assign a link to a slice by using the Property inspector, follow these steps:

1. Select the slice to which you want to assign a link.

2. Choose Window ⇨ Properties, or use the keyboard shortcut, Ctrl+F3
   (Command+F3), to display the Property inspector, as shown in Figure 20-16.

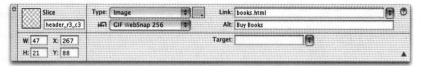

Figure 20-16: The Property inspector enables you to assign a link and
alternative text to a slice.

3. Enter a link directly in the Link text box, or select one from the option list. The
   option list shows both the URL History and the URL Library.

4. Enter the appropriate alternative text in the Alt text field.

5. To set the target for the linked page to load into, choose one of the presets
   from the Target option list, or enter a frame name.

6. To change the color of the selected slice object, click the color well and
   choose a new one from the color picker.

7. To assign a custom name for the slice, enter a new name in the text box on the
   left of the Property inspector.

You can also set a different pattern for the naming scheme in the HTML Setup dialog box, as described later in this chapter.

Using Text slices

One little known, but useful feature of slices is the ability to create a Text Slice. A Text Slice displays HTML text in your image instead of part of the image, as shown in Figure 20-17.

Figure 20-17: Setting a slice's type to Text enables you to incorporate HTML text inside a sliced graphic.

To make a Text Slice, follow these steps:

1. Select the slice and display the Property inspector.

2. From the Type option list, choose HTML.

   The Property inspector displays an Edit button next to a new HTML option.

3. Click Edit and enter the desired text and/or HTML into the Edit HTML Slice dialog box.

4. Click OK when you're done.

   Fireworks displays your entered text within its slice's overlay.

5. To edit the text, select the slice object, click Edit in the Property inspector again, and make your changes.

Tip

HTML tables used for slices typically have no borders or additional cell spacing or padding, so that all the images fit snugly next to each other. However, if you are using a Text Slice, this can be a problem because the text fits too snugly to the image, with no surrounding margin. You can work around this problem by creating a slightly larger, but empty, Text Slice in front of the Text Slice with the content.

Using slice options

Even with only two slices explicitly defined — depending on their placement — you can generate many slices for an image. For the slices to be inserted into a table, each slice has to have a unique filename. To save you the work of entering in name after name each time you export a sliced image, Fireworks enables you to create a slice-naming policy in the HTML Setup dialog box (File ⇨ HTML Setup). If desired, you can override the automatic naming on a slice-by-slice basis by entering a new, unique name in the text box directly to the right of the Slice's preview on the Property inspector. Although I like to name slices individually in a navigation bar so that I can easily find the image reference in the HTML code, I tend to allow Fireworks to automatically name most of my slices.

Fireworks can create some extremely complex tables as a result of slicing; multiple column and row spans are quite normal. In some ways, such complex tables are like a house of cards — and certain browsers are a big wind, ready to knock them down. In some circumstances, the table cells appear to lose their carefully calculated widths and heights, and the table literally breaks apart to display the separate images.

To support such tables, Fireworks uses a series of *spacer images*. A spacer image is a very small (one pixel by one pixel) transparent GIF image placed in cells along the top and right of the HTML table. Fireworks takes advantage of how HTML works, to use just one image, spacer.gif, which weighs just 43 bytes — or, in other words, .04K. The same image is used in all the spacer cells and sized appropriately in the code. HTML enables you to specify a different height and width for an image, and then enables the browsers to handle the scale. Although this is generally a bad idea for most images — browsers don't use very sophisticated scaling algorithms — it works well for spacer images. The spacer images are almost invisible: Those along the top row remain one pixel in height, and those on the side remain one pixel in width. But, most importantly, spacer images do the job for which they were intended — a sliced table with spacer images maintains its shape and integrity, regardless of the browser.

Despite all their intended good, transparent spacer images are not for every situation. Therefore, Fireworks offers a degree of user control over spacer image creation, through the Table tab of the HTML Setup dialog box. You can choose to space with a 1-Pixel Transparent Spacer, Single Table-No Spacers, or Nested Table-No Spacers. If you select Single Table-No Spacers, be sure to test the results in a variety of browsers to make sure your spacing is acceptable in each one.

Exporting Slices

When exporting an image map, you end up with an image and a snippet of HTML code. When exporting slices, you could get a whole lot of images and a bit more HTML. You need to realize that each sliced image ultimately means numerous files that must all be stored together. Fireworks offers two different slicing techniques and a variety of HTML styles from which to choose. The options you select are determined by how your slices were created and which Web-authoring tool you are using.

Exporting slices as different image types

Another advantage of slices over hotspots is that each slice can be a different image format because each slice is an individual image file. This enables you to export one slice as a JPEG, one as a GIF, and another as a PNG, if you so desire.

Specifying the export format for a slice is easy and, as with many things in Fireworks, can be done in more than one way. First, simply select the slice object in the document window and choose Window ➪ Optimize to view the Optimize panel. When a slice object is selected, the Optimize panel displays its individual export settings. Alternatively, you can select a slice and choose the export format from the Slice export settings option list on the Property inspector. In either case, choose a format and optimization options. Then select another slice and modify its options, or deselect all slices to modify the export options for the whole document.

Setting the Export options

After deciding on a path and filename for your images, you must select which slicing technique to use. In the Export dialog box, the following options are under Slicing:

✦ **None:** When this option is chosen, the image is exported in one piece, regardless of the number of slice objects.

✦ **Export Slices:** The exported slices are created from the slice objects on the image.

✦ **Slice Along Guides:** The standard guides are used to determine the slices.

For most situations, Export Slices is the best choice. Slice objects are required for rollovers or any other Behavior, and they are very easy to create. The only reason to choose Slice Along Guides is to carve a large image into numerous smaller ones, without any attached Behaviors. To use Slice Along Guides, you must have set the standard guides into place, as detailed earlier in this chapter.

To export an image in slices, follow these steps:

1. Choose File ⇨ Export.

   The Export dialog box appears.

2. Set the filename and path of the Export in the upper part of the dialog box.

3. Select HTML and Images from the Save as type (Save As) option list.

4. Choose Export HTML File, or Copy to Clipboard from the HTML option list.

5. Choose either Export Slices, or Slice Along Guides from the Slicing option list.

6. To save the image files in a different folder, check the Put Images in Subfolder checkbox, click Browse, and choose the desired folder for your images.

7. To alter any of the slice settings previously set, click Options to open the HTML Setup dialog box and adjust your settings.

8. After you make your selections, click Save to complete the export.

9. If you copied the code to the clipboard, paste it into a document in your HTML editor.

Inserting slices in a Web page

As with image maps, four HTML styles — Generic, Dreamweaver, GoLive, and FrontPage — dictate some aspects of the HTML code that Fireworks generates. Inserting code from a simple sliced image is straightforward. From an HTML perspective, all the code is contained within one tag, `<table>`. Remember, in HTML, tags containing data use both a starting and ending tag; in the case of the tags for an HTML table, the starting tag is `<table>`, and the ending tag is `</table>`. So, all the necessary code is between `<table>` and `</table>`, inclusive. Fireworks plainly marks this code with HTML comments, showing where to begin copying and where to stop.

In this chapter, the techniques for integrating slices in your Web pages are for simple sliced images, without rollovers or other Behaviors. To learn how to export slices with Behaviors, see Chapter 21.

Using the Generic template

Use the Generic template when you are hand-coding your pages in a text editor or using a Web-authoring tool without a specific template.

Follow these steps to incorporate a Generic sliced image:

1. Open the Generic code in a text editor, or in the text editor portion of your Web-authoring tool.

2. Select and copy to the clipboard the section in the `<body>` tag that starts with

   ```
   <!---------- BEGIN COPYING THE HTML ---------->
   ```

   and ends with

   ```
   <!---------- STOP COPYING THE HTML HERE ---------->
   ```

3. Open your existing Web page in a text editor, or in the text editor portion of your Web-authoring tool.

4. In the `<body>` section of your Web page, insert the code where you want the image to appear.

5. Preview the page in a browser and adjust the placement of the `<img>` tag, if necessary.

Using Dreamweaver

Although you can use Dreamweaver's Code inspector or Code View to integrate the Fireworks-generated code, you can also stay in Design View and do it visually, thanks to Dreamweaver's Tag Selector.

To insert Fireworks-generated code for a sliced image into Dreamweaver, follow these steps:

1. In Dreamweaver, open the HTML or XHTML page generated in Fireworks.

2. Click the exported image once.

   Because the image is now sliced into different sections, the entire image is not selected, just one slice.

3. On the bottom left of the document window, select the `<table>` tag from the Tag Selector, as shown in Figure 20-18.

   The entire sliced image and all the code is selected.

Figure 20-18: Use Dreamweaver's Tag Selector to easily select the entire sliced image for cutting and pasting.

4. Choose either Edit ⇨ Copy, or the keyboard shortcut, Ctrl+C (Command+C).

5. Open the existing Web page to which you want to add the sliced image.

6. Place the cursor where you want the sliced image to appear.

7. Choose either Edit ⇨ Paste, or the keyboard shortcut, Ctrl+V (Command+V).

The sliced image and corresponding code are inserted into the document.

Using GoLive

GoLive's HTML Outline view is an easy way to drag and drop HTML code between two documents. Code exported with the GoLive style also contains a `cssscriptdict` tag that tells GoLive how to edit the code. Make sure to copy the `cssscriptdict` tag, as well as your plain HTML code.

To insert Fireworks-generated code for a sliced image into GoLive, follow these steps:

1. In GoLive, open the HTML or XHTML page generated in Fireworks.

2. Switch to the HTML Outline view for both your source and target documents.

3. In the source document, select the `<table>` tag. This table contains all of your sliced images.

4. Drag and drop the table tag into place in your target document.

5. Select the `cssscriptdict` tag from the head of your source document and drag it into the head of your target document.

Using FrontPage

Microsoft's FrontPage stores external code — including any JavaScript — in a structure (or webbot in FrontPage jargon) called HTML markup. Fireworks produces the proper structure through the FrontPage template, so that the code can be seamlessly integrated.

To insert an image map from Fireworks into a FrontPage document, follow these steps:

1. Open the Fireworks-generated page in FrontPage.

Caution   Both the FrontPage document and the Fireworks-generated document must be in the same folder.

2. Select the HTML View.

3. Select the code that starts with

```
<!---------- BEGIN COPYING THE HTML ---------->
```

and ends with

```
<!---------- STOP COPYING THE HTML HERE ---------->
```

4. Choose Edit ➪ Copy.

5. Open the document in which the sliced image is to be inserted.

6. While still in HTML View, choose Edit ➪ Paste to insert the code into the document.

Exporting single slices

Sometimes I find myself wanting to quickly export a small area of the Fireworks canvas as a single image file. Rather than copying a section of the overall image and placing it into a new document and then exporting that, a quick way to define the area for an exported image file is to place a slice object on top of it, and then export that single slice. You can even separately optimize that single slice before export.

To export a single slice, follow these steps:

1. Select the slice that you want to export.

2. Choose Window ➪ Optimize to view the Optimize panel if it is not already visible.

3. Specify export settings in the Optimize panel.

   These settings affect only the selected slice.

4. Choose File ➪ Export.

   The Export dialog box appears.

5. Navigate to a folder to export your slice into, and specify a filename.

6. Choose Images Only from the Save as type (Save As) option list.

7. Choose Export Slices from the Slices option list.

8. Check the Selected Slices Only checkbox.

9. Click Save when you're done.

Your selected slice is exported as an individual image file.

 Tip
You can skip the Export preview dialog box completely if you right click (Ctrl+click on a Mac) and choose Export Selected Slice from the contextual menu.

Fireworks Technique: Exporting Dreamweaver Library Items

Library items are a powerful Dreamweaver feature that enable a section of a Web page to be updated once, after which Dreamweaver automatically updates all pages on which the section appears. Originally intended to replace page elements that are often repeated, such as a copyright line or logo, Dreamweaver Library items also enable you to regard a section of code as a single, easy-to-manage unit. If, as a designer, you're familiar with Encapsulated PostScript, think of Dreamweaver Libraries as Encapsulated HTML.

For a Library item to be recognized as such, it must be stored in a special folder for each local site. When you choose the Dreamweaver Library (.lbi) option from the Save as type (Save As) option list in the Export dialog box, Fireworks prompts you to locate your site's Library folder. If you've never created a Library item for the current site before, you need to make a new folder. You must place the folder in the local site root and name it, appropriately enough, Library. For example, if your local site root is located in a folder called Web Pages, you must create the Library folder at Web Pages/Library.

Tip   Most Web sites use a lowercase-only naming convention. You can name your Library folder "library" if that suits you, and Dreamweaver will use it without complaint.

The Dreamweaver Library (.lbi) export option exports your image map or slices within the same table as the Dreamweaver HTML style template, but it also marks the table as a Dreamweaver Library item that can be inserted over and over again. You can export using the Dreamweaver Library (.lbi) option at any time, no matter what your HTML style setting in the HTML Setup dialog box.

To export HTML and images from Fireworks as a Dreamweaver Library item, follow these steps:

1. Choose File ➪ Export.

   Fireworks displays the Export dialog box.

2. Navigate to your Dreamweaver site root folder, and then into the site's Library subfolder. If your site does not yet have a Library folder, create one and then navigate into it.

3. Specify a filename for your library item, if necessary.

4. Select Dreamweaver Library (.lbi) from the Save as type (Save As) option list.

Note   If you have not previously navigated to a Library folder, Fireworks warns you at this point that a Library folder is required. Then, Fireworks asks you to choose one. Navigating to the Library folder before selecting the Dreamweaver Library (.lbi) option avoids this warning—as you did in Step 2, earlier—enabling you to choose the Library folder in a larger dialog box, and having Fireworks return to that folder the next time you export from the same document.

5. Check the Put Images in Subfolder checkbox, and click Browse to choose your site's images folder.

6. Click Save when you're done.

Now that you've exported your Library item from Fireworks, follow these steps to incorporate the Library item into your work in Dreamweaver:

1. In Dreamweaver, choose Window ⇨ Assets, or use the keyboard shortcut, F11, to display the Assets panel.

   The current site's Assets panel appears.

Caution   Mac OS 9 users: If you have mapped the keyboard's function keys in the Keyboard Control Panel to start programs or perform other tasks, function key shortcuts in Fireworks are superceded by those mappings. Use the menu commands instead, or disable the mappings in the Keyboard Control Panel.

2. Select the Library category of the Assets panel, as shown in Figure 20-19.

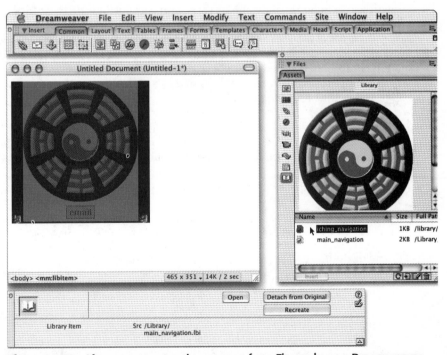

Figure 20-19: After you export an image map from Fireworks as a Dreamweaver Library item, it is available from the Library category of Dreamweaver's Assets panel.

3. Place your cursor in the document window where you want the image map to appear.

4. In the Assets panel, select your exported image map from the list window.

   The preview pane of the Assets panel displays the selected Library item.

5. Click the Insert button or, alternatively, drag the item from either the preview pane or the list window and drop it in the document window.

The image map and all the necessary code are inserted into the Dreamweaver page.

If you ever need to edit the image map, select it and then click Open from Dreamweaver's Property inspector. A document window appears with the Library item in it. From there, you can choose the image and select either Edit from the Property inspector, or Optimize Image in Fireworks from the Commands menu. After you edit the image, closing the Library document window prompts Dreamweaver to ask whether you would like to update the Library. Click Yes to update the Library items; click No to postpone the update.

Fireworks Technique: Animating a Slice

Fireworks can build terrific animations — and with just a little technique, you can integrate any animation into a larger image through slices. Animations can be fairly heavy in terms of file size. If only a small section of an overall image is moving — such as a radar screen on a control panel — converting the entire image to an animation is prohibitive, due to the file size that would result. However, with slices, you can animate just the area that you need to animate, and keep the rest of the image static, thus dropping the size of the file dramatically.

To include an animation in Fireworks, follow these steps:

1. Build your animation in Fireworks as you would normally.

 Explore Fireworks' animation features in Part VI.

2. If the animation is not already part of a larger image, go to Frame 1 in the Frame panel, choose Modify ⇨ Canvas ⇨ Canvas Size, and enlarge the canvas as desired.

3. Complete the graphics surrounding the animation.

4. Make a slice object from the animation either by choosing the animation and selecting Edit ⇨ Insert ⇨ Slice, or by using the Slice tool to draw a rectangle around the entire animation.

5. If it's not already visible, display the Property inspector.

6. In the Property inspector, set the link and any other desired options.

7. If it's not already visible, display the Optimize panel.

8. From the Export File Format option list, choose Animated GIF.

9. Specify other image optimization options as necessary.

 Chapter 15 details Fireworks' image optimization options.

10. Repeat Steps 4–9 for the static slices in your document, but choose formats other than animated GIF in the Optimize panel. Alternatively, deselect all slices and set an overall document export format in the Optimize panel. This format is used for any slices that are not explicitly set to another format.

11. When your document is ready for export, choose File ⇨ Export.

    The Export dialog box opens.

12. Set your path and filename in the upper portion of the dialog box.

13. Choose HTML and Images from the Save as type (Save As) option list.

14. Choose whether to export an HTML file, or copy the code to the clipboard from the HTML option list.

15. Select Export Slices from the Slices option list.

16. To modify HTML Setup options, click the Options button to display the HTML Setup dialog box.

17. Click Save when you're ready to complete the export.

Your animation is exported as part of the overall image, as shown in the example in Figure 20-20.

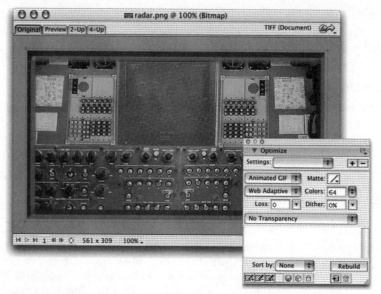

Figure 20-20: In this image, the radar screen is animated, and the rest of the graphic is static.

Summary

Fireworks Web objects — hotspots and slices — provide a gateway from graphic imagery to the Internet. By integrating Web objects with other graphic elements, the Web designer can seamlessly migrate from one medium to another, all the while maintaining editability. When working with Web objects, keep these points in mind:

✦ Fireworks supports two types of Web objects: hotspots and slices. A hotspot marks part of a larger graphic through code, whereas slices actually divide the larger image into smaller files.

✦ Hotspots come in three basic shapes: rectangle, circle, and polygon. Fireworks has a different tool for each type of hotspot. The term *hotspot* denotes an area of the overall image, called an image map.

✦ You can easily convert any Fireworks object into a hotspot by selecting the image and choosing Edit ➪ Insert ➪ Hotspot.

✦ When exporting image maps, be sure to work with both parts of the code: the `<img>` tag containing the link to the source image, and the `<map>` tag that contains the hotspot data.

✦ Fireworks makes slices in three ways: with the Rectangle or Polygon Slice tool, with the Edit ⇨ Insert ⇨ Slice command, and with the standard guides.

✦ Enabling the View ⇨ Slice Guides option enables you to reduce the number of slices to a minimum.

✦ Holding Shift while dragging a slice causes Fireworks to pick up any slice guides you cross, easily cleaning up files with too many slices.

✦ You can export individual slices as different image types, even as animated GIFs, enabling you to mix animated and static slices.

In the next chapter, you learn how to assign Behaviors for interactive effects.

✦   ✦   ✦

Activating Fireworks with Behaviors

From a user's perspective, the Web includes two types of images: graphics that you look at and graphics that you interact with. You can create the "look, but don't touch" variety of graphics with most any graphics program — Fireworks is among the few graphics programs that can output interactive graphics.

Although the result may be a complex combination of images and code, Fireworks uses *Behaviors* to simplify the process. With Fireworks Behaviors, you can create everything from simple rollovers — exchanging one image for another — to more complicated interactions, in which selecting a hotspot in one area may trigger a rollover in another, while simultaneously displaying a message in the status bar. And you can do it all in Fireworks without writing a line of code.

This chapter covers all the intricacies of using Behaviors and demonstrates some techniques that combine several Behaviors. You may never use each and every one of the Fireworks Behaviors, but after you start to use them, your Web pages will never be the same.

Understanding Behaviors

Before Fireworks, making your Web pages responsive to Web page visitors required in-depth programming skills or a Web-authoring program (such as Macromedia's Dreamweaver) that automated the process for you. The basic Web page, scripted in HTML, is fairly static; only forms enable any degree of user interaction. To activate your page, you have to use a more advanced language. Because of its integration into both major browsers, JavaScript is the language of choice for this task for most Web programmers. Although JavaScript is not as difficult to use as, say, C++, the majority of Web designers don't have the time or the inclination to master it. Because Fireworks permits Behaviors to be integrated into graphics, Web designers don't have to master a programming language.

A Behavior consists of two parts: an *event* and an *action*. An event is a trigger that starts an action—the way pushing Play on a VCR starts a videotape. Events on the Web are either user driven, such as moving a pointer over an image; or automatic, such as when a page finishes loading. Generally speaking, actions range from displaying a message to launching a whole new browser window.

Behaviors are said to be "attached" to a specific element on the Web page, such as a text or image link; Behaviors in Fireworks are always attached to slices or hotspots. Several other products in the Macromedia family, including Dreamweaver and Director, use Behaviors in much the same way as Fireworks.

In one sense, you can think of Behaviors as Encapsulated JavaScript. As a designer, you need only make a few key decisions, such as which two images to swap, and Fireworks handles the rest. Then, the code is written for you, in the HTML style of your choice. With Fireworks, you can output code that's tweaked for various Web-authoring programs, including Dreamweaver. Before you can export your images and associated Behavior code, however, you must assign the Behavior through the Behaviors panel.

Using the Behaviors Panel

The Behaviors panel is used to add and remove Behaviors. Although each Behavior has its own dialog box for selecting options and entering parameters, the Behaviors panel lists basic information for every Behavior assigned. You can assign multiple Behaviors—either the same Behavior or different ones—to any slice or hotspot; the number of Behaviors that you can attach to a single Web object has no practical limit.

Fireworks includes five main groups of Behaviors:

✦ **Simple Rollover:** Automatically swaps the image on Frame 1 with the image from Frame 2 when the user's mouse cursor rolls over the image.

✦ **Swap Image (Swap Image Restore):** Displays one image in place of another. The swapped image can be located on a different frame, in a different slice, or both. An external image can also be exchanged for the current or any other slice in the document. The Swap Image Restore Behavior is automatically applied to restore the swap to its original state.

✦ **Set Nav Bar Image (Nav Bar Over, Nav Bar Down, Nav Bar Restore):** This group of Behaviors specifies in which state of a navigation bar the selected slice should be.

✦ **Set Pop-up Menu:** This Behavior creates a pop-up menu in a Web page.

✦ **Set Text of Status Bar:** This Behavior shows a message in the browser's status bar.

The Behaviors panel (see Figure 21-1) is the central control center for Behaviors. To show or hide the Behaviors panel, choose Window ➪ Behaviors, use the keyboard shortcut Shift+F3, or click the Behaviors tab, if it is visible. The Behaviors panel enables you to select a hotspot or slice object and to add or to remove Behaviors. It also shows Behaviors that have been previously added to the selected object. After you add a Behavior to a hotspot or slice object, selecting it again enables you to remove the Behavior or change its settings.

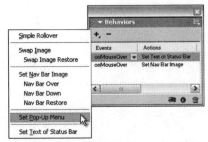

Figure 21-1: The Behaviors panel is the command center for attaching and removing Behaviors from hotspots and slices.

Attaching Behaviors

As noted previously, Behaviors are attached to Fireworks Web objects, either hotspots or slices. It's important to understand that hotspots are only capable of triggering events and are incapable of performing actions. Slices, on the other hand, can both trigger and receive events.

Practically, this means that hotspots by themselves can be used only in conjunction with the Set Text of Status Bar Behavior; all other Behaviors require slices in order to work. However, you can use hotspots to trigger an action that occurs in a slice, as explained later in the section "Working with hotspot rollovers."

Following is the general procedure for adding a Behavior to a Web object:

1. Select the hotspot or slice that you want to attach the Behavior to.

2. Choose either Window ➪ Behaviors, or use the keyboard shortcut, Shift+F3 to open the Behaviors panel. Alternatively, if it is docked behind another panel, click the Behaviors panel's tab to bring it forward.

If you have anything other than a Web object selected, Fireworks alerts you to this fact and gives you the option to create a Web object from the selected object. If nothing is selected when you try to add a Behavior, Fireworks asks you to choose a hotspot or slice first.

3. Click the Add Action button (the plus sign), and choose a Behavior from the drop-down list.

    A dialog box, which is specific to the chosen Behavior, opens.

4. Enter the desired options for the Behavior, and click OK when you're done.

    The Behaviors panel displays the newly attached Behavior in the list window.

Modifying a Behavior

To modify a Behavior that you've already added to a hotspot or slice object, select a hotspot or slice object and double-click the Behavior's entry on the Behaviors list in the Behaviors panel. Fireworks displays the Behavior's dialog box, in which you can adjust the settings that you made when you added the Behavior.

In addition to modifying the Behavior's settings, you can select another event to trigger the Behavior. By default, Fireworks initially assigns the onMouseOver event for all events. Following is a list of available events:

✦ **onMouseOver:** A user's mouse cursor hovers over an image and triggers the Behavior.

✦ **onMouseOut:** When a user's mouse cursor moves away from an image, the Behavior is triggered.

✦ **onClick:** A user clicks an image and the Behavior is triggered.

✦ **onLoad:** When the Web page has finished loading, the Behavior is triggered.

When a Behavior is selected in the Behaviors list, the Event pop-up menu button (a down-pointing arrow) appears just to the right of the event. Click this button to choose a new event from the Event pop-up menu, as shown in Figure 21-2.

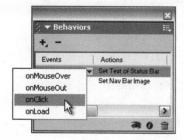

Figure 21-2: Click the Event pop-up button to choose another trigger for any selected Behavior.

Deleting a Behavior

When you delete a Behavior, all the settings that you have created are lost.

To delete a Behavior, follow these steps:

1. Select the hotspot or slice object from which you want to remove the Behavior.

2. Choose the Behavior that you want to remove from the Behaviors list in the Behaviors panel.

   The Behavior's event, action, and information are highlighted.

3. Click the Remove Action button (the minus sign) on the Behaviors panel.

The Behavior is removed from your hotspot or slice object, and its entry disappears from the Behaviors list.

Creating Rollovers

Perhaps the most common use of JavaScript on the Web is the rollover. *Rollovers* are images in a Web page that change appearance when a user rolls a mouse cursor over them.

Rollovers are popular because they're fairly simple to implement, are supported by many browsers, and are an effective way to heighten the feeling of interaction for Web site visitors.

Examining how rollovers work

To understand how a rollover works, you need to grasp a fundamental HTML concept. Web pages do not contain images in themselves — they only contain links to images. With an image, the link is referred to its source and is specified in the `<img>` tag in HTML as the src attribute. When a user's mouse pointer hovers over an image — or in some cases, clicks an image — the src attribute is changed to another image file. Because this happens quickly, it appears as if the image itself is changing.

Before the rollover effect, a typical `<img>` tag might read as follows:

```
<a href="home.html"><img src="button_regular.gif" height="100"
width="50" alt="home"></a>
```

After the rollover effect is applied, the effect is as if the code was the following code:

```
<a href="home.html"><img src="button_over.gif" height="100"
width="50" alt="home"></a>
```

As this code shows, the height, width, and alt text for the image don't change, nor does the link that the hyperlink is pointing to (in this example, `home.html`), as specified in the `<a>` tag. All that changes — and this can't be overemphasized — is the actual GIF (Graphics Interchange Format), JPEG (Joint Photographic Experts Group), or PNG (Portable Network Graphics) image file that's being used — the file referenced by the `src` attribute.

Caution   Because only the `src` attribute changes with a rollover, the original image and any swapped images must have the same dimensions. You can't swap a smaller image with a larger one, or vice versa. If you do, the browser applies the height and width dimensions of the original image, leading to a distorted image.

Note that any `<img>` tag can be modified, not just the `<img>` tag that is rolled over. This is the foundation for disjointed rollovers, as discussed later in this chapter.

Learning rollover states

Although a rollover actually switches one image for another, the illusion that most Web designers want is of a button changing into different states. Before the user triggers the rollover effect, the image is in the Up state. When the rollover is triggered, the image changes to an Over state, because the cursor of the user's mouse is over the image. In Fireworks, the easiest and most typical method of creating the different states for a rollover is with frames.

A basic rollover uses just two states (and, thus, two Fireworks frames): Up and Over. Rollovers, though, can have up to four states, in which case they would be built across four Fireworks frames. Table 21-1 details the rollover states and their typical associated frames.

Table 21-1
Rollover States

Frame	State	Description
1	Up	The way the button looks when the user is not interacting with it; how it looks when the page first loads into the browser.
2	Over	The button's appearance when the user's mouse cursor is hovering over it.
3	Down	The button's appearance after it's pressed. The Down state of a rollover button depicts the button's state on the destination Web page. For example, the Down state is commonly used to show which button was clicked to view the current Web page.
4	Over Down	The way a button that's in its Down state looks when the user's mouse cursor hovers over it.

Creating rollover images

The first step in building a rollover is to create the separate rollover images that reside on the separate frames of a Fireworks document. I use either of two basic techniques to create images, depending upon whether the rollovers are to be independently used, each in their own unique Fireworks document, or if they're part of a complete design in a larger document. Both techniques involve creating an initial button object, which is then duplicated and modified.

If your rollover buttons exist independently, use the following technique to create images:

1. Create the initial button in Frame 1, as it should appear before being clicked by the user.

2. Click the button and choose Edit ➪ Clone to create a duplicate directly on top of the button.

3. If you are going to create a Down state for this button, repeat Step 2. If you are also going to create an Over Down state, repeat Step 2, so that you have a total of four objects stacked on top of each other in Frame 1.

4. Select all of your button states by drawing a selection around them with the mouse. Click the Distribute to Frames button (which resembles the small movie strip) in the Layers panel.

   Your objects are distributed to separate frames, so that each button state is now in its own frame.

5. Frame 1 already contains a suitable Up state for your button. Go to Frame 2 and modify your button object slightly in order to create an interesting Over state for the button. You might add a Glow Live Effect to the Over state, or change the Fill or Stroke settings.

6. If you have Down and Over Down states, as well, modify them slightly on Frame 3 and Frame 4 so that each frame now contains a unique — but similar — button.

Tip

If the Over state of your button has a Live Effect bevel on it for a three-dimensional appearance, a good way to modify subsequent states is to click the button object and then modify the Button Preset settings of the bevel Live Effect (the bottom option list on the pop-up edit window). This creates the impression of a three-dimensional button moving up and down. For example, the Up state could be set to Raised, the Over state to Highlighted, the Down state to Inset, and the Over Down state to Inverted.

If your rollovers are part of a larger document that contains many buttons or objects that you want to create rollovers for, use the following technique to create the images:

1. Create all the initial objects in Frame 1 of your document.

2. From the Options menu on the Frames panel, select Duplicate Frames.

The Duplicate Frames dialog box appears.

3. In the Duplicate Frames dialog box, enter the number of frames that you want to add. In the Number text box, add one frame for each additional state used.

For a simple rollover with just an Up and Over state, add one frame. For a rollover that also uses the Down and Over Down states, add three frames.

4. Make sure that the Insert New Frame After the Current Frame option is selected and click OK when you're done.

The duplicate frames are inserted.

Tip   Another way to duplicate a frame is to drag its name to the New/Duplicate Frame button in the Frames panel. Each time you do this, another duplicate frame is added after the one you dragged. Layers can also be duplicated in this fashion in the Layers panel.

5. In each new frame, modify the rollover objects slightly in order to create a different look in each frame.

Tip   You can modify many objects simultaneously — to make them all glow, for example — by selecting all of them at once and applying the changes through the Stroke, Fill, or Effects sections of the Property inspector.

No matter which technique you use to create the separate rollover images, the best effect usually results from applying a degree of subtlety. If one button is too drastically different from another of its states, the underlying image swap becomes overt and the illusion of a single button being clicked or highlighted is lost. Instead, the user sees one image simply change into another. Small shifts in position, or an incremental change in an effect seem to work best, as shown by the examples in Figure 21-3.

Figure 21-3: Subtle modifications to your original button image create convincing state changes. Here, three buttons are exploded in order to view (from left to right) their Up, Over, Over Down, and Down states.

Tip You can preview your soon-to-be rollover by clicking Play on the animation controls; the frames of your image are then shown one after the other.

After you create your separate button images, they are ready to have Behaviors applied to them and can be used as true buttons.

Applying the Simple Rollover Behavior

Fireworks takes the *simple* in simple rollover very seriously: The Behavior creates a classic Up-and-Over rollover effect, while offering exactly zero user settings. When you just want a classic rollover, Fireworks makes creating one a snap.

The only difference between the simple rollover and Swap Image Behaviors is the interface and the number of options. The code you generate is the same compatible JavaScript you always expect from Fireworks.

To apply the Simple Rollover Behavior, follow these steps:

1. Select a slice on the Web Layer of your document.

2. From the Behaviors panel, choose Simple Rollover from the Add Action pop-up menu in the Behaviors panel.

To preview your rollover, select the document window's Preview tab and roll the mouse over your button. You can also preview your rollover in your primary browser by pressing F12.

The Simple Rollover Behavior doesn't have any options that need to be specified. In fact, if you double-click the Behavior in the Behaviors list, Fireworks just explains the Behavior, as shown in Figure 21-4.

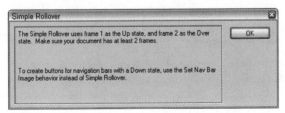

Figure 21-4: The "options dialog" for a simple rollover simply explains what a simple rollover is without offering any options; it's that simple.

Of course — as with any Behavior — you can still choose a different kind of event, such as onClick or onLoad, from the Behaviors panel Event list.

If you plan to use the rollover as a link, you need to assign it a URL. For detailed information on how to add a link to a Web object, see Chapter 20.

Exporting Rollovers for the Web

Obviously, you can export images from Fireworks. When you create rollovers, the JavaScript code that controls the behavior of your images is exported within an HTML or XHTML file. The JavaScript itself is compatible with Netscape Navigator 3 and above, and Microsoft Internet Explorer 4 and above. The Macintosh version of Internet Explorer 3 also displays your rollover effects, but in Internet Explorer 3 for Windows, your rollover effects are not visible, although hyperlinks still work. If you're exporting your rollovers in XHTML, use Netscape Navigator 4, and above, or Internet Explorer 4, and above.

 XHTML support is new to Fireworks MX.

Macromedia has continually improved the HTML editor compatibility of Fireworks' exported JavaScript. In the first version of Fireworks, only one type of rollover code was generated; it worked in browsers, sure, but you had to edit it by hand if you opened it in a visual editor. As Fireworks matured, the capability to pick the style of code that's best for your workflow, or even create templates of your own to fine-tune the settings even further, became available.

Before exporting your first rollovers, it pays to make a quick stop in the HTML Setup dialog box, if only to choose an HTML or XHTML style that suits your work-flow. For the most part, this choice is governed by the Web-authoring tool that you are using to lay out the Web page onto which the rollover is to be placed. The stan-dard HTML styles included in Fireworks are the following:

✦ **Dreamweaver HTML:** Code styled for Dreamweaver. Dreamweaver-style rollover code generated by Fireworks appears as native Dreamweaver Behaviors when opened in Dreamweaver.

✦ **FrontPage HTML:** FrontPage uses a series of *webbots* — FrontPage-only code snippets — to create Web elements; Fireworks includes the code necessary for an image map webbot, so that it displays correctly and can be further manipu-lated when the document is opened in FrontPage.

✦ **Generic HTML:** The basic functional code, useful in hand-coded Web pages and the majority of Web-authoring tools that work with standard HTML. If you're not sure which HTML style to choose, go with this one.

✦ **GoLive HTML:** Code styled for Adobe's GoLive, including special tags that make editing the code in GoLive easier.

You can also tell Fireworks to export XHTML, if that's what you'll be using in your site. The XHTML styles included with Fireworks are:

✦ **Dreamweaver XHTML:** Code styled for Dreamweaver. Dreamweaver-style rollover code generated by Fireworks appears as native Dreamweaver Behaviors when opened in Dreamweaver.

✦ **Generic XHTML:** The basic functional code, useful in hand-coded Web pages and the majority of Web-authoring tools that work with standard XHTML. If you're not sure which XHTML style to choose, or you don't plan to edit the page further using one of the supported authoring tools, go with this one.

✦ **GoLive XHTML:** Code styled for Adobe's GoLive, including special tags that make editing the code in GoLive easier.

While you're in the HTML Setup dialog box, you may also want to change the default filename extension for HTML files from the nonstandard .htm, to the standard .html. You can also choose whether Fireworks inserts its own comments in your HTML output and force Fireworks to lowercase the exported filenames for better compatibility with different kinds of servers. Mac users can also choose the Creator code that exported HTML and XHTML files should have, so that double-clicking opens them in the code editor of your choice.

Cross-Reference I cover the HTML Setup dialog box in Chapter 3.

Integrating a Fireworks-generated rollover into your Web page is a three-stage process.

✦ **Stage 1:** Create and test your rollover in Fireworks.

✦ **Stage 2:** Export the images and code from Fireworks. You can export code as an HTML file, or copy it to the clipboard.

✦ **Stage 3:** Insert the code into your Web page, using whatever Web page editor you prefer (even a plain text editor, such as NotePad or SimpleText, works). Either open the HTML or XHTML file in your editor, or if you copied the code to the clipboard, simply paste it into your editor.

Exporting the code from Fireworks

To export a rollover — and its code — from Fireworks, follow these steps:

1. Specify your image export settings in the Optimize panel.

2. Choose File ➪ Export.

   The Export dialog box, shown in Figure 21-5, appears.

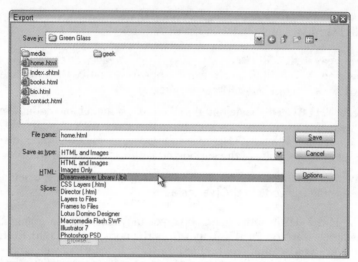

Figure 21-5: You can choose an alternative to HTML and Images from the Save as Type (Save As) option list in the Export dialog box.

3. Choose a target folder for your exported image file(s) and specify a filename for the HTML file.

4. From the Save as Type (Save As) option list, select HTML and Images to export HTML, or choose Dreamweaver Library (.lbi) to export the HTML as a Dreamweaver Library.

   If you chose the Dreamweaver Library HTML style, the Locate Site Library Directory opens so that you can identify your site's Library folder.

5. Choose either Export HTML File, or Copy to Clipboard from the HTML option list.

6. Choose from among the following options in the Slices option list:

   • **None:** Disables slicing altogether.

   • **Export Slices:** Causes your image to be sliced according to the placement of Slice objects.

   • **Slice Along Guides:** Slices your image along guides (not slice guides).

Tip   Export Slices is the option you'll probably use most of the time.

7. Check Selected Slices Only to export the selected slice(s) only.

8. Check Current Frame Only to export images from just the frame you were on when you began exporting.

9. Check Include Areas without Slices to export images that don't have a slice specified.

10. To save the image files in a different folder, check the Put Images in Subfolder checkbox, click Browse, and choose the desired folder for your images.

11. To alter any of the slice settings previously set, click Options to reopen the HTML Setup dialog box and adjust your settings accordingly.

To review the possible slice settings, see Chapter 20.

12. When you're ready to complete the export, click Save.

Inserting rollover code in your Web page

After you select your HTML style, Fireworks automatically outputs the requested type of code, either to an HTML related file or to the clipboard, according to which option you selected. If you chose to output the HTML code to the clipboard, open your target HTML file in your HTML editor and paste the code into place. If you chose to output to a file, open that file and your target HTML file in a text or HTML editor and then copy and paste between them.

The process for transferring rollover code to a Web page is essentially the same as that for transferring image maps or sliced images, with one important exception; the code generated for rollovers — and all Behaviors — generally comes in these two parts:

✦ The event portion of a code, which contains the `<img>` tags and their triggers, is stored in the `<body>` section of a Web page.

✦ The action portion of a code — with all the JavaScript functions — is kept in the `<head>` section.

You must transfer both parts of the code in order for the rollover to function properly.

With Dreamweaver, Generic, and GoLive code, the process is similar. Cut or copy the code from both the `<body>` and the `<head>` sections of the Fireworks-generated document and paste it into your existing Web page. FrontPage does not separate the `<head>` and the `<body>` sections for rollovers in its code, so simply copy the one section of code from the source to the target page. When you export as a Dreamweaver Library, the process is even simpler: Include the Library item and its code in your Web page, using the Library category of the Assets panel, just as you would any Library item.

For Dreamweaver, FrontPage, Generic, and GoLive styles of code, follow these steps to insert Fireworks code into your Web page:

1. Open the Fireworks-generated source HTML file in a text or HTML editor.

> **Tip**
>
> If you are using Dreamweaver, I recommend that you use the Fireworks HTML object, located on the Common category of the Insert bar, to import your Fireworks HTML page. It converts a series of copy and paste routines into a simple matter of locating the HTML document exported from Fireworks and letting Dreamweaver take care of the rest.

2. Select and copy to the clipboard the section in the ⟨body⟩ tag that starts with

```
<!---------- BEGIN COPYING THE HTML HERE ---------->
```

and ends with

```
<!---------- STOP COPYING THE HTML HERE ---------->
```

> **Tip**
>
> If you're using Dreamweaver, you don't have to open the HTML Source window or an external text editor in order to copy the code. Just make sure that View ➪ Visual Aids ➪ Invisible Elements is enabled and copy the icons that represent the code.

3. Open your existing target Web page in a text or HTML editor.

4. In the ⟨body⟩ section of your Web page, insert the code where you want the image to appear.

If you're using the FrontPage template, your code transfer is complete; skip the rest of the steps. You can now view your rollover.

5. Return to the source HTML file and locate the ⟨head⟩ section.

6. Select and copy to the clipboard the section in the ⟨body⟩ tag that starts with

```
<!------ BEGIN COPYING THE JAVASCRIPT SECTION HERE ------>
```

and ends with

```
<!------ STOP COPYING THE JAVASCRIPT HERE ------>
```

7. Switch to your existing Web page.

8. Paste the copied code in the ⟨head⟩ section of the document.

> **Tip**
>
> Placing the JavaScript code after the ⟨title⟩ and any ⟨meta⟩ tags makes your page friendlier to the spider programs, also referred to as *bots*, that add pages to Web search engines.

After you insert both sections of the rollover code, you can view your rollovers in any supported browser.

Preloading Rollover Images

When the HTML document that contains your rollovers is first displayed, the Up state of your rollovers is visible, along with the other image files on the Web page. Ideally, as the user interacts with your document, the other states of the rollovers become instantly available from the browser cache, instead of slowly available from the Web. Instantaneous reactions reinforce the illusion that an object is being modified — a button pushed, for example — instead of one image being replaced with another. To make sure that the other states are available from the browser cache, Fireworks includes JavaScript with its HTML output that "preloads" the Over, Over Down, and Down image files.

Dreamweaver's Library feature enables a single repeating element to be inserted in multiple Web pages, which can then all be updated simultaneously, after you modify the original item. The only stipulation is that the rollover code must be stored in a special folder, called Library, within each local site, during export. If you've never created a Library item for the current site, you need to make a new folder named "Library" in the local site folder.

After you export the HTML file as a Dreamweaver Library item, follow these steps to incorporate the rollover images and code:

1. In Dreamweaver, choose Window ⇨ Assets.

   Dreamweaver displays the Assets panel.

2. Select the Library category of the Assets panel.

   The Assets panel displays the site's current Library items.

3. Place your cursor in the document window where you want the rollover to appear.

4. Select your exported rollover's Library item from the list in the Assets panel.

   A preview of the Library item appears in the Assets panel.

5. Click the Insert button to insert your Library item in the page. Alternatively, you can drag the item from either the preview pane or the list window of the Assets panel, and drop it in your page.

The sliced image, and all the necessary code, is inserted into your Dreamweaver page.

Looking at Nav Bar Behavior

A *Nav Bar* is a way to turn a series of rollover buttons into a set of radio buttons. Each button is linked to the others, so that clicking one button and setting it to a Down state sets the other buttons to an Up state. Fireworks creates Nav Bars by using JavaScript cookies. In JavaScript, a *cookie* is a small bit of information written to the user's computer. Cookies generally are used by Web sites to record visitors' selections as they travel from one Web page to another, as with a shopping cart on an e-commerce site. Fireworks uses this same technology to keep track of which button in a group has been selected.

Nav Bars and cookies might seem like advanced topics, but if you've implemented a three- or four-frame Simple Rollover Behavior, you've already used them. Fireworks automatically creates a Nav Bar (named FwNavBar) for each simple rollover that uses a Down and/or Over Down state. You don't need to do anything else to get the toggle effect. However, if you use Swap Image to create your rollover, or want to toggle just the two Up and Over states of a simple rollover, you need to apply the Nav Bar Behavior explicitly.

Creating a Nav Bar

To create a Nav Bar, follow these steps:

1. Create your rollover buttons, with appropriate states (Up, Over, Down, and Over Down) on the appropriate frames, 1 through 4.

2. In Frame 1, draw a slice object over each rollover button.

3. Select each slice object, in turn, and turn it into a rollover by choosing Simple Rollover from the Add Action pop-up menu in the Behaviors panel.

   Your rollovers are now ready to be turned into a Nav Bar.

4. Select all the slice objects to be included in the Nav Bar.

5. Choose Set Nav Bar Image from the Add Action pop-up menu in the Behaviors panel.

   Fireworks displays the Set Nav Bar Image dialog box (see Figure 21-6).

6. If you have included the Over Down state in your rollovers, check the Include Over While Down State box. Click OK when you're done.

7. If you want one of the buttons to appear in its Down state by default, first deselect all the slices and then select the individual slice. Next, double-click the Set Nav Bar Image Behavior in the Behaviors panel, and then check Show Down Image Upon Load. Click OK when you're done.

When you view your Nav Bar on the Preview tab of the document window or in a Web browser (see Figure 21-7), the buttons change depending upon which one is clicked.

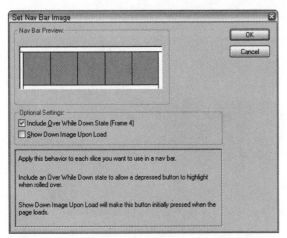

Figure 21-6: The Nav Bar Behavior makes any set of rollovers mutually exclusive; therefore, only one button can be selected at any time.

Figure 21-7: The second button in this Nav Bar is in the Down state. Only one button in a Nav Bar can be down at a time, creating the impression of a group of radio buttons.

Tip   The term *radio buttons* comes from tuning buttons on old AM/FM radios. Only one station can be tuned in at a time, so only one button can be down at a time. Clicking a button causes all other buttons to pop up.

Building buttons in the Button Editor

The Fireworks Button Editor enables you to create or assemble a button Symbol that includes a two-, three-, or four-state rollover. A special tabbed window — similar to the document window — walks you step by step through the process.

To create a rollover button with the Button Editor, follow these steps:

1. Choose Insert ➪ New Button.

   Fireworks displays the Button Editor (see Figure 21-8).

Figure 21-8: The Button Editor can display four button states — four Fireworks frames — plus a slice object on its five tabbed canvases.

2. Create the Up state of your button in the initial Up tab of the Button Editor.

3. Select the Button Editor's Over tab and create the Over state of your button. Alternatively, to start with the Up state and modify it to be an Over state, click Copy Up Graphic. Fireworks copies the Up state to the Over tab, ready for editing.

Tip   At any time, you can check the Onion Skinning box to simultaneously view all the tabs in the Button Editor, helping you to align your buttons correctly. You can also use the view controls to zoom in or out on your button, and you can choose a display option to view the buttons in Full or Draft display. Click the Play button at the bottom left of the Button Editor to cycle through the states of your button.

4. If you want to include a Down state in your button, select the Down tab and create the Down state of your button. Again, you have the option to click a button and copy the previous state to this tab for modification. Click Copy Over Graphic to do this.

5. If your button is exported as a Nav Bar, check Show Down State Upon Load to display the Down state when a page loads.

6. To add an Over While Down state to your button, switch to the Over While Down tab and either create a new state or copy the previous one — click Copy Down Graphic — and modify it to create the Over While Down state.

7. Switch to the Active Area tab. Fireworks automatically creates a slice in the Active Area tab that encompasses the area of your button, but you can adjust its size if necessary.

Tip   The slice on the Active Area tab is similar to the Hit area in Flash buttons.

8. To have Fireworks help with the process of adding a link to your button, click the Link Wizard button and move from tab to tab in the Link Wizard dialog box.

9. Close the Button Editor when you're done.

Your new Button Symbol is added to the Library panel, and a copy of it — an Instance — is placed in the document window, as shown in Figure 21-9. Switch to the Preview tab of the document window to preview your new button's rollover actions in the document window.

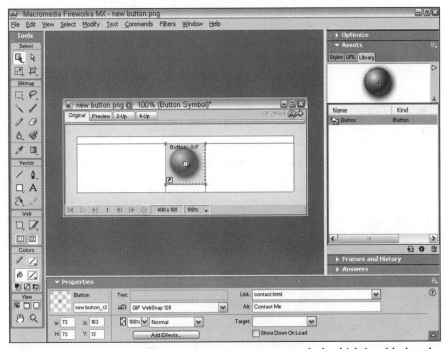

Figure 21-9: The Button Editor creates a new Button Symbol, which is added to the Library. An Instance of that symbol is placed on the canvas.

For more about symbols and Libraries, see Chapter 17.

Examining Advanced Rollover Techniques

The simple rollover is quick and easy, and I use it quite often. But sometimes a Web page needs more than just a simple rollover. You can extend traditional rollovers with advanced techniques in order to create interesting effects, or provide even more navigation help for your users. The underlying engine for the simple rollover, the Swap Image Behavior, is key to these advanced techniques.

Making disjointed rollovers

A *disjointed rollover* is one in which the user hovers his or her mouse cursor over one part of an image (the event area), and another part of the image (the target area) does the actual rollover. A typical use for a disjointed rollover is to display details of each button in a navigation bar in a common area. Creating a disjointed rollover generally involves outlining the event and target areas with slice objects, although it is possible to trigger a disjointed rollover from a hotspot.

To create a disjointed rollover, follow these steps:

1. Create a slice object over the event area (the part of your image that the mouse cursor needs to hover over in order to trigger the rollover).

2. Create a slice object over the target area (the part of the image that will seem to change).

3. Select the event area slice and choose Swap Image from the Add Action pop-up menu in the Behaviors panel.

   Fireworks displays the Swap Image dialog box (see Figure 21-10).

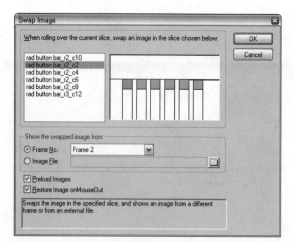

Figure 21-10: The Swap Image dialog box contains options that enable you to swap any slice in your document after any other slice is selected by the user.

4. Choose the slice for the target area by choosing it from either the Target list of slice names or the Slice preview to the right of the Target list. Whichever you choose, the other is updated to reflect your choice.

5. Choose the Source for the swap by selecting a frame number from the Frame list.

   The area below the target slice on that frame is used as the source for the image swap.

6. Check Restore Image onMouseOut to undo the swap again when the user moves his mouse cursor away from the event area. Click OK when you're done.

7. Repeat this process until all of your slices have been assigned the Swap Image Behavior.

To swap more than one slice simultaneously, repeat the preceding steps to apply multiple Swap Image Behaviors to the same Web Layer object. Through this technique, your navigation button can roll over itself and display a disjointed rollover at the same time.

Creating external rollovers

Instead of using an object in another frame as the Over state for a rollover, Fireworks can also use external GIF images (regular or animated), JPEG images, or PNG images. When the rollover is viewed in a Web browser, the external file is used as the source file for a rollover, instead of using an area of a frame within your Fireworks document. External rollovers enable you to easily include animated GIF images into an existing image.

Caution You can't swap one image file format for another because of Web browser limitations. If you're going to export a slice as a GIF, make sure to use an external GIF or animated GIF only as the Over state. Similarly, if you're exporting a slice as a JPEG or a PNG, include only external JPEG images and PNG images, respectively, as the Over state.

Keep in mind that only the image source is changed (the `src` attribute of the `img` tag), so the browser resizes your external image to fit the size of the initial slice object it's being swapped for.

Tip If you need to make a slice object the same size as an external image so that you can swap that sliced area of your image for an external file, select the slice object; choose either Modify ➪ Transform ➪ Numeric Transform, or the keyboard shortcut, Ctrl+Shift+T (Command+Shift+T); choose Resize from the list in the Numeric Transform dialog box; and then enter the desired width and height. Alternatively, you can select the slice object and enter the desired width and height on the Property inspector.

To create an external rollover, follow these steps:

1. Select the slice to trigger the external rollover.

2. Choose Swap Image from the Add Action pop-up menu in the Behaviors panel.

   Fireworks displays the Swap Image dialog box.

3. Select the slice that the external image will be swapped into.

4. To locate the external file through the standard Open dialog box, choose the Source for the swap by clicking the Folder icon.

5. Check Restore Image onMouseOut to undo the swap again when the user moves his mouse cursor away from the event area.

6. Click OK when you're done.

Working with hotspot rollovers

Hotspot rollovers enable you to create the effect of irregularly shaped rollovers. All images are rectangular boxes, so all image swaps involve swapping a rectangular area or slice. However, the image triggering the rollover does not have to be rectangular — you can use any hotspot. The key to the illusion of the hotspot rollover is Fireworks' ability to swap entire slices from different frames.

Figure 21-11 shows an image with slices that are far from rectangular, but the design requires that each area highlight independently when rolled over and link to different pages on the Web site. Hotspot rollovers swap the entire image, though, so each highlight can be any shape.

One limitation applies, though: Because each hotspot swaps the entire image, the hotspots can't overlap, or the illusion of separate highlighted areas is lost. It's also a good idea to keep the overall image small because each added hotspot requires another copy of the whole image. A larger image could lead to a significant download time for the user.

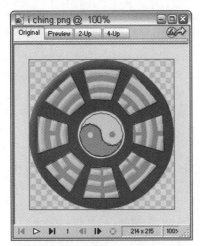

Figure 21-11: This navigation system uses hotspots to trigger a rollover of the whole image in order to create the impression of irregularly shaped rollover buttons.

To create hotspot rollovers, follow these steps:

1. Create a hotspot for each active area with the Rectangle, Circle, or Polygon Hotspot tool.

2. Create a single slice that covers your whole image.

3. Select the slice and choose Modify ➪ Arrange ➪ Send to Back to send it behind your hotspots so that you can easily access the individual hotspots in order to apply Behaviors to them.

4. Duplicate your current frame until you have a separate frame for each active area. If you have made ten hotspots, make ten frames.

5. In each frame, modify a different active area so that it appears highlighted in some way. This is the "Over" state for that area. The other areas in each frame are left in their default state.

Tip

Hiding the Web Layer—and your hotspots—makes it easier to see what you're doing when modifying your active areas. Hide the Web Layer by clicking the eye icon next to its name in the Layers panel.

6. Select a hotspot and fill in a URL for the hotspot in the Property inspector.

7. With your hotspot still selected, open the Behaviors panel and apply a Swap Image Behavior to it. In the Swap Image dialog box, make sure you follow these steps:

   • Select the lone slice in the slice list.

   • Under "Show the swapped image from," set the Frame number to the corresponding highlighted frame for the selected hotspot. If the highlight for a hotspot is in Frame 3, set the hotspot to swap to Frame 3.

8. Repeat Steps 6 and 7 for each hotspot until all of your hotspots have a URL and a Behavior attached.

9. Export your image along with the HTML code. In the Export dialog box, choose Export Slices from the Slices option list.

Fireworks exports an HTML document along with an image file for each frame of your document. When displayed in a browser, the overall impression that's created is that of a single image with eccentrically shaped, individual rollovers.

Displaying a status bar message

You can provide the user with additional navigational assistance by supplying a message in the status bar. Status bar messages are often used with hotspots and image maps. They are limited by the width of the status bar area in the viewer's browser, which in the case of Internet Explorer 4 for Windows (but not 5) is very, very small. Even in other browsers, because browser window sizes can vary tremendously, lengthy messages are not recommended.

To add a status bar message to your document, follow these steps:

1. Select a slice object or hotspot, and choose Set Text of Status Bar from the Add Action pop-up menu in the Behaviors panel.

   Fireworks displays the Set Text of Status Bar dialog box (see Figure 21-12).

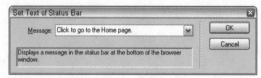

Figure 21-12: The Set Text of Status Bar dialog box enables you to add a status bar message to a slice or hotspot, which assists your users in navigating your site.

2. Type in the Message box the message that you want to display when the user activates this slice. Click OK when you're done.

3. Change the event from onMouseOver to onMouseOut, onClick or onLoad, if desired, by choosing that event from the event list.

Working with Pop-up Menus

Web sites are becoming increasingly complex and now routinely offer their visitors a choice of hundreds, or even thousands of pages of information. The traditional Web button bar with a handful of options can be strained to the seams by the bulk of topics and subtopics such complex sites contain. Luckily, the Set Pop-up Menu Behavior aids in the quick creation of powerful hierarchical navigation systems that are easy for the Web user to grasp at first glance (see Figure 21-13).

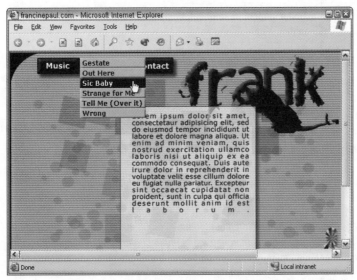

Figure 21-13: Pop-up menus are easy to create in Fireworks, and easy for the Web user to navigate when viewed in the browser.

New Feature   Pop-up menus in Fireworks MX are almost an entirely new creation. They're feature-packed, and positioning problems are a thing of the past.

The Content tab of the Pop-up Menu Editor

To add pop-up menus to your Fireworks document, follow these steps:

1. Select a slice or hotspot, and choose Set Pop-up Menu from the Add Action pop-up menu in the Behaviors panel, or choose Modify ⇨ Pop-up Menu ⇨ Add Pop-up Menu.

   Fireworks displays the Set Pop-up Menu dialog box (see Figure 21-14).

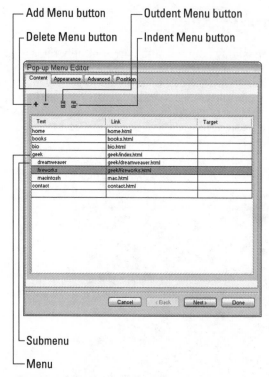

Figure 21-14: The Pop-up Menu Editor asks for the specifications for your pop-up menu in fairly plain terms.

2. To create a new menu item, click the Add Menu button or double-click in the first editable position so that your cursor becomes an insertion point. Specify a name in the Text box, a URL in the Link box, and a URL target in the Target box (if desired), and then press Tab to move to the next field, or press Enter (Return) to move to the next line.

3. To change the properties of a menu item, select the menu item and change the contents of the Text, Link, or Target boxes. The Link box is also an option list, enabling access to all the URLs in your document.

4. To convert a menu item into a submenu, select the menu item, and click the Indent Menu button. To covert a submenu into a menu, click the Outdent Menu button.

5. To move a menu item up or down the list, select it and drag it up or down.

6. To insert a menu item, select the item above where the new item should be and click the plus sign. If you want to remove a menu item, select it and click the minus sign.

7. Click Next when you're done with the available options and ready to progress to the Appearance tab.

Tip

After clicking Next, you can click Back at any time to return to the previous state of the Set Pop-up Menu dialog box.

The Appearance tab of the Pop-up Menu Editor

The Appearance tab allows you to control many of the different ways that Fireworks can arrange your pop-up menus on the screen. To get the most out of these options, follow the steps below:

1. On the Appearance tab, specify a menu style, either HTML (see Figure 21-15) or Image (see Figure 21-16).

   HTML menus are composed of plain HTML text and tables after export. Image menus use images formatted with Fireworks styles.

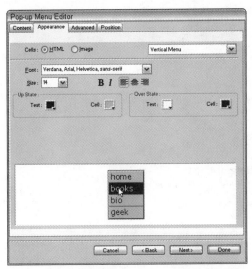

Figure 21-15: HTML pop-up menu formatting options include text and table cell colors. A preview of the look of your eventual pop-up menu system is always available.

2. Choose either Vertical Menu or Horizontal Menu from the option list to determine the orientation of your pop-up menu.

3. Specify a font, font size, bold and/or italic style, as well as justification for the text in your menu system.

4. Select Text and Cell colors for the Up State of your menu.

   This is how the menu appears initially.

5. Select Text and Cell colors for the Over State of your menu.

   This is the way the menu looks under the user's mouse cursor.

Tip   As you adjust settings, keep an eye on the preview of the finished product that Fireworks provides.

6. If you are creating an Image Pop-up Menu (see Figure 21-16), choose an Up Style and an Over Style for the images that make up the menu.

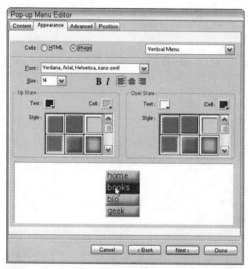

Figure 21-16: The formatting options for Image pop-up menus use Fireworks Styles to dress up otherwise drab menus.

7. Click Done if you're finished, or click Next to move on to the Advanced settings.

The Advanced tab of the Pop-up Menu Editor

The Advanced tab, shown in Figure 21-17, covers a number of standard table settings that can be applied to your pop-up menu. Follow these steps to learn more:

1. If you would like to specify specific cell widths for your pop-up menu, choose Pixels from the Cell Width or Cell Height option lists, then enter a specific value in the text box.

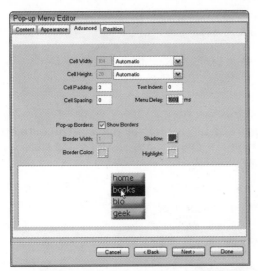

Figure 21-17: Do you want your pop-up menu to fit exactly within a column on your page? That's just one of the many cell-level modifications you can make on the Advanced tab in the Pop-up Menu Editor.

2. If you wish to change the Cell padding or Cell Spacing, enter new values in these fields.

3. Unless you alter the text's justification on the Appearance tab, the text on your pop-up menus has no extra spacing between it and the left edge of the cell. You can change this by modifying the number in the Text indent field. Numbers entered are in pixels.

4. Changing the timing, in milliseconds, in the Menu Delay field enables you to adjust the length of time that it takes your menu to disappear after the user has moved their mouse. The default is 1000 milliseconds, or one second, but Fireworks enables you to make that longer or shorter.

5. In Fireworks, the controls on the Advanced tab set the final adjustments to show borders on your pop-up menus and the colors used for those borders. The Shadow option controls the drop shadow color to be used, whereas border width adjusts how wide the border on your menu appears.

6. Altering the Border Color and Highlight settings changes the outside appearance of your pop-up menu. The Border Color option sets the thin color that surrounds your entire menu, whereas the Highlight color only appears across the top and down the left side.

> **Tip**
>
> The Border Width, Border Color, and Highlight settings only work with HTML style pop-up menus, not with image-based ones.

7. Press Done if you're finished or press Next to move to the settings on the Position tab.

The Position tab of the Pop-up Menu Editor

The Position tab, shown in Figure 21-18, enables you to precisely control the positioning of your pop-up menus and their submenus. The following steps walk you through the options on the Position tab:

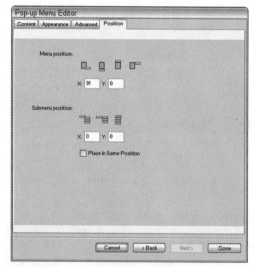

Figure 21-18: Want your pop-up menus to appear in a specific position relative to your button? It's a snap with Fireworks.

1. Selecting the Pop-up Menu position from the first section here enables you to specify the position of your pop-up menu relative to the slice, or button, it's attached to. The following are the available options:

- **Set menu position to the bottom-right of slice:** This sets your pop-up menu to line up with the bottom right-hand corner of the slice that it's attached to.

- **Set menu position to bottom of slice:** This causes your pop-up Menu to appear directly below the slice, or hotspot, that you attached the behavior to.

- **Set menu position to top of slice:** This causes your pop-up menu to appear directly above your hotspot or slice.

- **Set menu position to the top-right of slice:** This option sets your pop-up menu to appear directly to the right of your slice or hotspot.

2. Next you need to decide how your submenus should look relative to your main menu. You have the following choices:

- **Set submenu position to bottom-right of menu:** This causes the sub-menus of your pop-up menu to appear in the lower-right corner of the parent menu's cell.

- **Set submenu position to top-right of menu:** This puts your submenu directly to the right of the parent menu's cell — probably the most commonly expected appearance for a set of menus — which is a behavior akin to the way menus and submenus appear in software programs.

- **Set submenu position to bottom of menu:** This causes the submenus of your pop-up Menu to appear directly below the parent menu's cell.

Caution   If you have several menu items with submenus, be careful with this last option. When your submenu appears, it shows up higher on the z-axis than its parent menu and may obscure other menu items, frustrating your viewers by forcing them to rush past items with submenus to get where they want to go.

3. When Place in Same Position is checked, Fireworks places your submenus relative to the parent menu's cell. Without this option selected, the submenu is positioned relative to the trigger point for the entire pop-up menu.

After you add a Pop-up Menu Behavior to your document, you can edit its settings at any time by double-clicking its name in the Behaviors panel, or by double-clicking the pop-up menu outline in your document.

Note   You can't preview Pop-up Menus in the workspace. Press F12 to preview your work in your primary browser and see your pop-up menus in action.

Pop-up menu styles are stored in a folder called Nav Menu, in the Configuration folder in your Fireworks application folder. These styles are the same styles that we know and love from the Styles panel. So adding your own styles to the Set Pop-up Menu dialog box and making them available for use in a pop-up menu is as simple as exporting the styles from the Styles panel to the Nav Menu folder.

Tip   The Fireworks program folder is typically found at `C:\Program Files\ Macromedia\Fireworks MX` **on Windows-based computers, and at** `Macintosh HD:Applications:Macromedia Fireworks MX:` **on the Mac.**

To add your own styles to the Set Pop-up Menu Behavior, follow these steps:

1. Create an object with the fill, stroke, and effect properties that you would like your pop-up menu to have.

2. Choose Window ➪ Styles to display the Styles panel.

3. Select your object and click the New Style button on the Styles panel.

   The properties of your object are saved as a new style.

4. Select the new style in the Styles panel and choose Export Styles from the Styles panel's pop-up menu.

   Fireworks displays a Save dialog box.

5. Navigate to your Fireworks application folder, then into the Configuration folder, and then the Nav Bar folder. Click Save to export your selected style as a Fireworks .stl file.

Next time you use the Set Pop-up Menu Behavior, your added styles will be available for use.

Using Drag-and-Drop Behaviors

Drag-and-drop Behaviors enable you to quickly create rollovers using simple drag-and-drop methods. Instead of selecting a slice or hotspot and then interacting with the Behaviors panel, drag-and-drop Behaviors enable you to directly interact with the trigger Web object — over the area where the user hovers or clicks to trigger the Behavior — and the target Web object — where the rollover itself happens. Join the two areas with a drag-and-drop, and you have created a rollover.

When selected, each hotspot and slice object displays a drag-and-drop handle, as shown in Figure 21-19. Drag the drag-and-drop Behavior handle from a triggering slice or hotspot onto a target slice to create a rollover. You can create a simple rollover by dragging the drag-and-drop Behavior handle and dropping it on the same slice, whereas you can create a disjoint rollover by dragging the drag-and-drop Behavior handle and dropping the Behavior handle on a different slice.

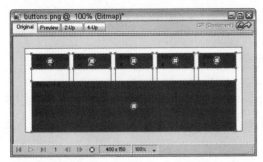

Figure 21-19: Each hotspot or slice has a drag-and-drop handle that displays when the hotspot or slice is selected.

It's important to realize that you must prepare the slices and frames before dragging and dropping. Fireworks won't add frames to your document just because you attach a rollover Behavior to a slice.

Creating a simple rollover with drag and drop

To create a simple rollover where the trigger and target areas are the same, follow these steps:

1. Make sure that you have created a second frame in your document, which contains the image that's to be shown when the user rolls his mouse over the trigger area.

2. Select the trigger slice, which covers the area of the image that triggers the Behavior.

3. Click and hold on the drag-and-drop Behavior handle in the center of the slice.

   The mouse cursor changes into a fist.

4. Drag the cursor slightly and drop over the same slice.

   A blue drag-and-drop Behavior line displays from the center to the top-left corner of the hotspot or slice (see Figure 21-20).

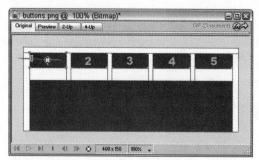

Figure 21-20: When you drag and drop within
one hotspot or slice, a drag-and-drop Behavior
line displays from the center to the top-left corner
of the hotspot or slice.

Fireworks displays the Swap Image dialog box (see Figure 21-21).

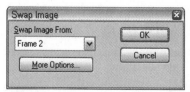

Figure 21-21: A special Swap Image
dialog box displays after you drag
and drop.

5. Choose a frame to swap for the current frame, from the Swap Image From option list.

6. To access the full Swap Image Behavior dialog box, click More Options.

The full Swap Image dialog box is covered earlier in this chapter.

7. Click OK when you're done.

Fireworks attaches the Behavior to the slice.

Creating disjoint rollovers with drag and drop

To create a disjoint rollover—where the trigger and target Web objects are not the same—join the trigger and target Web objects with a drag-and-drop Behavior line.

To create a disjoint rollover with drag and drop, follow these steps:

1. Make sure that you have created a second frame in your document, which contains the image to be shown when the user rolls his mouse over the trigger area.

2. Make sure that you have both a trigger and target hotspot or slice.

3. Select the Web object over the trigger area.

4. Click and hold on the drag-and-drop Behavior handle in the center of the hotspot or slice.

   The mouse cursor changes into a fist.

5. Drag the cursor and drop it on the target slice.

   The blue drag-and-drop Behavior line is displayed from the center of the trigger Web object to the top-left corner of the target slice, as shown in Figure 21-22.

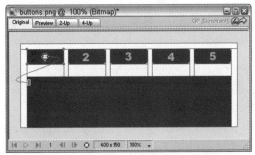

Figure 21-22: A blue drag-and-drop Behavior line shows the relationship between the trigger and target slice after a drag and drop. Here, a click on the button by the user swaps the larger slice at the bottom.

   Fireworks displays the Swap Image dialog box.

6. Select the frame to swap from in the Swap Image From option list.

7. To access the full Swap Image Behavior dialog box, click More Options.

8. Click OK when you're done.

Fireworks attaches the Behavior to the selected Web object.

Removing drag-and-drop Behaviors

To remove a drag-and-drop Behavior attached to a hotspot or slice, follow these steps:

1. Select the hotspot or slice.

   The drag-and-drop Behavior relationships for the Web object are shown as blue lines.

2. Click on the blue line you want to delete.

   Fireworks displays a dialog box, confirming that you want to remove the Behavior.

3. Click OK to remove the Behavior.

Summary

Fireworks enables you to add dynamic JavaScript effects to your images, even if you don't know JavaScript, through the use of Fireworks Behaviors. When using Behaviors, keep these points in mind:

✦ The Behaviors panel is your control center for working with Behaviors.

✦ Behaviors are attached only to Web Layer objects (either hotspots or slices) and not to regular vector or bitmap objects on other layers.

✦ Rollovers can be rollover buttons, or they can be disjointed rollovers, in which the image that changes is not the same as the one that triggered the event.

✦ Fireworks includes a Button Editor that simplifies the process of building a Button Symbol.

✦ You can preview rollovers in the document window by selecting the Preview tab.

✦ Fireworks can also show text in the browser's status bar through Set Text of Status Bar Behavior.

✦ The Set Pop-up Menu Behavior option enables you to create powerful, complex navigation systems with a minimum of time and effort.

✦ Drag-and-drop Behaviors provide a quick and easy method for creating rollover Behaviors.

In the next chapter, you look at integrating Fireworks with Dreamweaver.

✦   ✦   ✦

Integrating with Dreamweaver

Not all Web designers have the luxury—or the hardship—of just working on Web graphics. Many graphic artists create both the graphics and the layout for the Web pages on which they work. And those designers who only create imagery for the Internet must work closely with layout artists in order to incorporate their designs. No matter how you look at it, Fireworks is not—and was never intended to be—a stand-alone product. All graphics generated by Fireworks must be published on the Web by some other means.

Dreamweaver, the premier Web-authoring program from Macromedia, is the perfect partner for Fireworks. Not only do they both feature the Macromedia Common User Interface, both also speak JavaScript commands, and Dreamweaver understands Fireworks' Behaviors, as well as its own. Dreamweaver even recognizes images—whether whole or sliced—as coming from Fireworks and displays a special Property inspector, so you can seamlessly optimize images with standard Fireworks controls from within Dreamweaver— without even opening Fireworks. This chapter delves into this and many other features, including Fireworks commands that can be automatically issued from Dreamweaver.

On the CD-ROM If you don't have a copy of Dreamweaver, use the trial version included on the CD-ROM accompanying this book.

Introducing Integration

As noted elsewhere in this book, Web graphics is as much about production and maintenance as it is about creation. The more efficiently you—or someone who works with you—can insert and update images into Web page layouts, the better the workflow. Because a Web page typically has numerous graphics, as well as text and other media, such as a Shockwave or QuickTime movie, a Web designer must be concerned with how all the elements work together. Not only must the overall design function well aesthetically, but the Web page as a whole must also be practical — that is, the download time must be kept to a minimum. All of these concerns require a constant back-and-forth between graphics and layout programs. Macromedia has taken steps to reduce these problems by integrating Dreamweaver and Fireworks into a complete Web production environment.

Optimizing Images from Dreamweaver

What's the most common modification needed for graphics being added to a layout? I don't know about everybody else, but I sure do an awful lot of resizing of images to get the right fit. To me, the term *resizing* encompasses rescaling an image, cropping it, *and* getting it to the smallest possible file size — all while maintaining the original image quality. The Optimize Image in Fireworks command does just that, as well as enabling complete color and animation control. Best of all, you can do everything right from Dreamweaver in a standard Fireworks interface.

If you've never tried the Optimize Image command, that last statement might give you pause. How can you optimize an image ". . . from Dreamweaver in a standard Fireworks interface"? Aren't we talking about two different programs? Well, yes, and — most excitedly — no. You definitely need both programs for the command to work, but the full version of Fireworks does not have to be running. Instead, a special "light" version of Fireworks is launched, one that displays only the Export Preview dialog box, as shown in Figure 22-1.

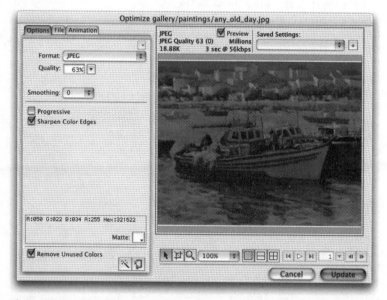

Figure 22-1: Choosing the Optimize Image in Fireworks command opens a dialog box equivalent to the Export Preview dialog box, and does so without running Fireworks.

The Optimize dialog box has all the features of Export Preview with one small change: An Update button sits in place of the Next button. In Fireworks, clicking Next from Export Preview opens the Export dialog box, in which you can select Slicing and HTML template options. The command relies on your last settings saved from within Fireworks for these options.

To optimize your image in Fireworks from within Dreamweaver, follow these steps:

1. In Dreamweaver, select the image you need to modify.

Caution You must save the current page at least once before running the Optimize Image in Fireworks command. The current state of the page doesn't need to have been saved, but a valid file must exist for the command to work properly. If you haven't saved the file, Dreamweaver alerts you to this fact when you call the Optimize Image command.

2. Choose Commands ➪ Optimize Image in Fireworks.

Tip You can also invoke the Optimize Image in Fireworks command from the context menu — just right-click (Control-click) on the image in Dreamweaver.

3. If the selected image is not in PNG (Portable Network Graphics) format, you're given the opportunity to select whether you want to use a Fireworks source file instead of the lower-quality GIF (Graphics Interchange Format) or JPEG (Joint Photographic Experts Group), as shown in Figure 22-2.

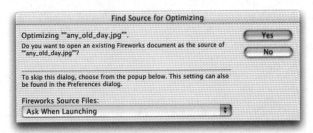

Figure 22-2: Choose whether to use a Fireworks PNG file as a source for the image, if one exists.

4. Click No in the Find Source for Optimizing dialog box to continue, and then optimize the GIF or JPEG image. Click Yes to have Dreamweaver automatically find the Fireworks source file, if possible. If not possible, you are prompted with a standard Open dialog box. Select the PNG format source file and click Open to continue.

After the selected file is located, if appropriate, the Optimize dialog box appears.

5. Make whatever modifications you want from the Options, File, and Animation tabs of the Optimize dialog box.

6. When you're finished, click the Update button.

If you're working with a Fireworks source file, the changes are saved to both the source file and the exported file; otherwise, only the exported file is altered.

If you changed the scale, size, or cropping of the image during optimization, you need to adjust the height and width values in the Dreamweaver Property inspector. To do this, click the Refresh button.

Caution   If the image to be optimized is in PNG format—whether it be in the enhanced PNG format that Fireworks uses to store all of its additional editing information, or in the bitmap PNG export—the Optimize Image in Fireworks command saves it as a bitmap file. In other words, Fireworks native files lose their editability. As always, it's best to store your Fireworks source files in one directory and use your exported Web page files—in GIF, JPEG, or PNG format—from another.

Editing Images from Dreamweaver

For many purposes, optimizing an image is all you need to do—whether it's to crop one side slightly or to reduce the file size. Often, though, you need to go further, such as when the client has decided to change a department name on a navigation button. Without Fireworks-Dreamweaver integration, in a situation such as this, you would need to start your graphics program, load in the image, make the change, save the image, switch back to your Web-authoring tool, and reload the graphic. With Dreamweaver MX and Fireworks MX, the process is greatly simplified. You need to follow these steps only:

1. Select an image in Dreamweaver, and choose Edit from Dreamweaver's Property inspector.

The image automatically loads into Fireworks, which starts, if necessary (see Figure 22-3).

Figure 22-3: Images from Dreamweaver aren't shy about it in Fireworks—note the "from Dreamweaver to Fireworks" symbols next to the Done button.

2. Modify the image in Fireworks and click Done.

The revised image is saved and automatically updated in Dreamweaver.

Setting Fireworks as the graphics editor in Dreamweaver

To take advantage of this enhanced connectivity, you first have to set Fireworks as your graphics editor in Dreamweaver's Preferences by following these steps:

1. In Dreamweaver, choose Edit ⇨ Preferences.

The Preferences dialog box appears.

2. Select the File Types / Editors category from the list on the left.

3. In the File Types / Editors pane, shown in Figure 22-4, click the image type from the Extensions section, on the left, and then click the plus sign (+) above the Editors section, on the right, to browse to the location of the main Fireworks program.

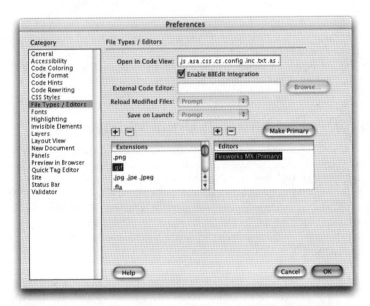

Figure 22-4: To quickly edit a graphic on a Dreamweaver page, make sure Fireworks is your default editor for common graphics files, such as GIF.

Tip   The default location for Fireworks for Windows is `C:\Program Files\Macromedia\Fireworks MX\Fireworks.exe` (the `.exe` filename extension may or may not be visible). On a Macintosh, Fireworks is usually found at `Macintosh HD:Applications:Macromedia Fireworks MX:Fireworks MX`.

Now, whenever you want to edit a graphic, select the image and click the Edit button in the Property inspector. Fireworks starts up, if it's not already open. As with the Optimize Image in Fireworks command, if the inserted image is a GIF or a JPEG, and not a PNG format, Fireworks asks whether you want to work with a separate source file. If you click Yes, you're given an opportunity to locate the file.

Note   Fireworks always follows your Dreamweaver Launch and Edit preferences, with one exception. If the image chosen is a sliced image, Fireworks always optimizes the exported file rather than the source, regardless of your settings.

After you make your alterations to your file in Fireworks, click the Done button in the title bar of the window, or choose either File ⇨ Update, or the keyboard shortcut, Ctrl+S (Command+S). If you're working with a Fireworks source file, both the source file and the exported file are updated and saved.

Caution   If you choose File ⇨ Update, make sure that your source file and exported file are the same dimensions. If your exported file is a cropped version of the source file, the complete source file is used as the basis for the export file, and any cropping information is discarded. To maintain the cropping, choose File ⇨ Export to re-export the file, instead of saving it with File ⇨ Update.

Recognizing Design Notes in Dreamweaver

Both Dreamweaver and Fireworks are capable of saving Design Notes, an innovative method for sharing information between graphic designers who use Fireworks and Web designers using Dreamweaver. A *Design Note* is basically an external file that contains editable information about any element in Dreamweaver, such as HTML pages or graphics. Fireworks adds Design Notes to images that are exported into a Dreamweaver site, storing the location of the source file. This enables Dreamweaver to optimize or edit the source file of an included image without asking the user to locate the file.

From within Dreamweaver, you can read Fireworks Design Notes — or add your own information. However, you have to make sure that Design Notes are enabled for the current site. To enable Design Notes, follow these steps:

1. In Dreamweaver, choose Site ⇨ Edit Sites.

   Dreamweaver displays the Define Sites dialog box.

2. Select your current site, and then click Edit.

   Dreamweaver displays the Edit Sites dialog box.

3. Select the Design Notes category to view the Design Notes panel.

4. Enable the Maintain Design Notes option.

5. If you want other team members to be able to view the Design Notes, select Upload Design Notes for Sharing.

6. Click OK to close the Edit Sites dialog box, and then click Done in order to close the Define Sites dialog box.

To view or add Design Notes to a Fireworks (or any other) image, follow these steps:

1. Select the image file and right-click (Control-click) to display the context menu and choose Design Notes.

   The Design Notes dialog box appears.

2. Select the All Info tab to see the path to the source file. The source file information is contained in a Design Note key called `fw_source`. It looks like this:

   `fw_source=file:///D|/DW4 Bible/images/house.png`

3. To add additional information to the Design Note, click the Add button and fill in the Name and Value fields.

Tip Rather than pressing Enter (Return), tab out of the Value field to confirm your entry.

Modifying sliced images

Placing sliced images on your Dreamweaver Web page couldn't be simpler thanks to the Insert Fireworks HTML command. But, like standard non-sliced graphics, sliced images often need to be modified. One technique that many designers use is to create a framing graphic that encompasses HTML text; in Fireworks, a sliced area designated as a text slice can hold any HTML content. Text is often modified and — if it's in a framing graphic — that could mean that the images need to be changed, or the table will separate, making the separate slices apparent.

In Dreamweaver, sliced images from Fireworks are recognized as a Fireworks table and may be modified through a dedicated Property inspector, as shown in Figure 22-5. The Fireworks Table Property inspector displays the PNG source file and an Edit button for sending the entire table back to Fireworks for alterations. As with non-sliced graphics, select Done from the document title bar in Fireworks when your modifications are complete to update the source and exported files. The newly exported images are then reloaded into Dreamweaver.

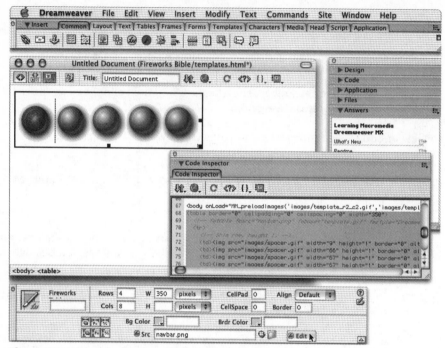

Figure 22-5: Modify sliced graphics by first selecting the surrounding table, and then choosing Edit from the Fireworks Table Property inspector in Dreamweaver.

Caution   Although Fireworks attempts to honor any changes you may have made to the HTML table, certain alterations may result in Fireworks overwriting your table. If, for example, you add or remove one or more cells from the table in Dreamweaver, Fireworks recognizes that the tables no longer match. An alert appears, indicating that Fireworks will replace the table in Dreamweaver. To keep your table the same in Dreamweaver, make no changes in Fireworks and click Done.

Exporting Dreamweaver Code

Besides outputting highly optimized graphics, Fireworks speaks fluent Dreamweaver. For all export operations involving HTML output, including hotspots, slices, and Behaviors, Fireworks is capable of writing code, either as Dreamweaver, or Dreamweaver Library. The Fireworks and Dreamweaver engineers worked closely together to ensure that the code would match across the two programs.

The type of HTML output you use for standard HTML and Images export operations is set in the HTML Setup dialog box. Choose File ➪ HTML Setup and select Dreamweaver from the HTML Style option list on the General tab. Now, when you export HTML and Images from the Export dialog box, you are exporting Dreamweaver code.

Dreamweaver's Insert Fireworks HTML

Dreamweaver features a Fireworks logo in its Insert bar, representing the Fireworks HTML object, which enables you to browse to an HTML file that you exported from Fireworks and include it in your current Dreamweaver document. Once activated, the Fireworks HTML object asks for the location of a Fireworks-generated HTML file, as shown in the following figure.

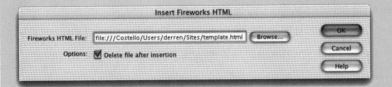

I find the Fireworks HTML object handy for times when I'm exporting a lot of code from Fireworks. Rather than worry about where the code is going, I just export it all to one folder and, later, insert it into the right places within Dreamweaver.

Cross-Reference For precise details on how to export Dreamweaver-style code from Fireworks and insert it into your Dreamweaver pages, see Chapters 20 and 21.

Working with Dreamweaver Libraries

The export of Dreamweaver Library code from Fireworks is a real time-saver. One of the most difficult tasks for graphic designers moving to the Web is handling code. With the plain HTML and Images export setting, all code must be cut and pasted from the Fireworks-generated page to the working Dreamweaver document. Although this is fairly straightforward in Dreamweaver (and Fireworks makes it as clear as possible with concise HTML comments marking the code to move), it still involves working in an environment in which many designers aren't comfortable: code.

Dreamweaver Libraries eliminate the need for designers to handle code when inserting any Fireworks output, including even the most complex Behaviors. What's a *Dreamweaver Library*? I like the explanation given to me by a Dreamweaver engineer: "Think of it as Encapsulated HTML." Designers routinely work with Encapsulated PostScript (EPS) files, and the metaphor fits. Like EPS files, a Dreamweaver Library item is capable of containing hundreds of lines of code, but the designer need only be concerned with one element — and a visual one, at that.

To export a Fireworks document as a Dreamweaver Library, follow these steps:

1. In Fireworks, choose File ➪ Export.

   Fireworks displays the Export dialog box.

2. Choose Dreamweaver Library (.lbi) from the Save as type (Save As) option list.

   Fireworks warns that it needs to know the location of your Dreamweaver site's Library folder. Click OK to dismiss the warning.

   Fireworks displays a Choose a Folder dialog box.

3. Navigate to and choose your Dreamweaver site's Library folder. Click Select (Choose) when you're done.

   Fireworks displays the Export dialog box again.

4. Click Save in the Export dialog box to save your Dreamweaver Library code.

5. In Dreamweaver, open the document into which you want to insert the exported Fireworks code.

6. Choose Window ➪ Assets, or click the Assets icon from the Dreamweaver Launcher, if visible.

   The Assets panel opens.

7. Select the Library category of the Assets panel, as shown in Figure 22-6.

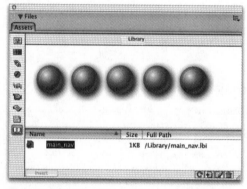

Figure 22-6: The Library category of Dreamweaver's Assets panel is where you'll find your exported Dreamweaver Library item.

8. Select the exported item from the list pane.

9. Insert the Library item on the page, either by choosing Add to Page, or by dragging and dropping the item from the list or preview pane.

   The Library item is added to your page and initially selected.

Feel free to move the Fireworks-generated Library item anywhere on the page; if necessary, the code will move as well.

A key feature of Dreamweaver Library items is their ability to be updated. Edit a single Library item, and Dreamweaver automatically updates all the Web pages using that item. This capability is a major time-saver. Unlike regular graphics, which you can modify at the click of the Edit button from Dreamweaver's Property inspector, Library item graphics first must be unlocked.

To edit a Library item, follow these steps:

1. In Dreamweaver, choose Window ⇨ Assets to open the Assets panel.

2. Choose the Library category of the Assets panel.

3. Select the Library item embedded in the page, either from the Web page or the Assets panel.

4. Click the Open button on the Library Item Property inspector, as shown in Figure 22-7.

   The Library item opens in its own Dreamweaver window.

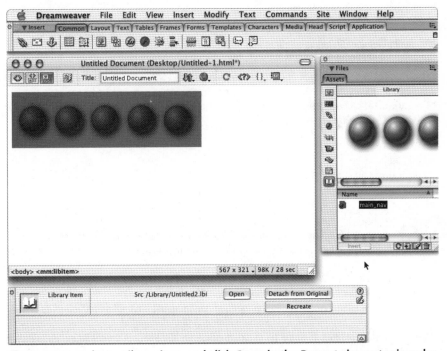

Figure 22-7: Select a Library item and click Open in the Property inspector in order to edit the item.

5. Select the graphic and choose Edit from the Property inspector.

   If the file is not in PNG format, Fireworks asks whether you prefer to edit an original source file and gives you the chance to locate it. The selected PNG file is opened in Fireworks.

6. Modify the file, as needed.

7. When you're done, choose File ⇨ Update.

   The altered file is automatically updated in the Dreamweaver Library file.

8. In Dreamweaver, choose File ⇨ Save.

   Dreamweaver notes that your Library item has been modified and asks whether you want to update all the Web pages in your site that contain the item. Click Yes to update all Library items (including the one just modified), or No to postpone the updates.

9. Close the editing window by choosing File ⇨ Close.

If you opt to postpone the Library item update, you can do it at any time by choosing Modify ⇨ Library ⇨ Update Pages.

XHTML Support

The latest version of HTML is known as XHTML, short for Extensible HTML. XHTML is based on XML and, as such, has a more rigid syntax than HTML. For example, tags that do not enclose content — the so-called *empty tags* — are written differently. In HTML, a line-break tag is:

```
<br>
```

while in XHTML, the line-break tag adds a closing slash, like this:

```
<br />
```

Note   Note the additional space before the closing slash. While the space is not required for XHTML, it is needed to be properly recognized in Netscape 4.x browsers.

Aside from the line-break tag, the other notable empty tag is the image tag, <img> — or, as it is written in XHTML, <img />. You can see why if your Web authoring program is writing out XHTML pages, your graphics program should be, too.

Fireworks makes it easy to output code in XHTML. All you need do is switch your export options by following these steps:

1. When you're ready to export your page, choose File ⇨ Export.

   The Export dialog box opens.

2. From the Save as Type list, make sure HTML and Images or Dreamweaver Library is chosen.

If Images Only or some of the other settings are selected, the Options button is not available.

3. Select Options to open the HTML Setup dialog box.

4. From the HTML Style drop-down list, choose Dreamweaver XHTML.

5. Click OK to close the HTML Setup dialog box and export your file as you would normally.

There are also options for Generic XHTML and GoLive XHTML.

Quick Export

For a more direct route to outputting files to Dreamweaver, try Fireworks' new Quick Export feature.

 Situated on the top right of every document window, the Quick Export option gives you access to the following submenu:

    ✦ Dreamweaver ⇨ Export HTML

    ✦ Dreamweaver ⇨ Update HTML

    ✦ Dreamweaver ⇨ Copy HTML to Clipboard

    ✦ Dreamweaver ⇨ Launch Dreamweaver

As the name implies, the Quick Export option offers faster access to the most commonly used Dreamweaver (and other program) export features. They all function exactly the same as if you went through the usual menus or keyboard shortcut methods—they're just a little more available.

 When choosing Dreamweaver ⇨ Export HTML from the Quick Export option, the HTML type is set as either Dreamweaver HTML or Dreamweaver XHTML, depending on the last type of code chosen. For example, if you previously output Generic XHTML, the HTML type will be Dreamweaver XHTML.

Fireworks technique: Adding CSS layers to Dreamweaver

Fireworks features another type of export that—although not strictly a Dreamweaver feature—fits so well in the Dreamweaver-Fireworks workflow that it's worth including in this chapter. Fireworks is capable of exporting images directly into Cascading Style Sheet (CSS) layers. A CSS layer is a free-floating structure that can be viewed in any version 4 or higher browser. CSS layers have several notable properties, including the following:

    ✦ **Position:** Layers—and, thus, the content they hold—can be precisely positioned. This makes layout far easier than with traditional HTML methods.

✦ **Depth:** You can stack layers one upon another, and change their depth dynamically.

✦ **Visibility:** You can hide or reveal layers at will.

✦ **Movement:** You can dynamically position layers and thus move them across the screen over time to create animation.

I've exported CSS layers to use in Dreamweaver with two different methods: exporting Fireworks layers and exporting Fireworks frames. Using Fireworks layers is useful for determining a precise layout of images against a background. For one project, eight separate artworks needed to be placed in the proper position against a background. To ease the workflow, I used the following technique:

1. In Fireworks, open the background graphic and lock it on the Layers panel.

2. Click the New Layer button on the Layers panel.

   A new layer is created.

Tip

If desired, give the layer a unique name; the layer names in Fireworks are used as the CSS layer names.

3. Choose Insert ⇨ Image to open a foreground image.

   Alternatively, you can cut and paste an object or image from an open file.

4. Position the image against the background.

5. Repeat Steps 2–4, creating a new layer for each object.

   Although each object is placed in its own layer, they appear as if side by side.

6. When all the images are properly placed, hide the layer the background is on by deselecting the appropriate eye symbol in the Layers panel.

7. Choose File ⇨ Export.

   The Export dialog box appears.

8. Choose CSS Layers from the Save as type (Save As) option list.

   Fireworks displays further options related to exporting CSS Layers.

9. From the Source option list, select the Fireworks component to export as CSS Layers. The options are Fireworks Layers, Fireworks Frames, or Fireworks Slices.

10. Make sure the Trim Images option is not selected.

11. If you're exporting from Fireworks Frames, check the Current Frame Only checkbox to limit the export to the current frame only.

12. Check the Put Images in Subfolder checkbox to have Fireworks place the image files in their own folder.

    Click the Browse button to select a particular folder.

13. Click Save when you're ready.

    Each Fireworks layer is saved as a separate image, and the CSS layer information is written out in HTML.

14. In Dreamweaver, open the Fireworks-generated HTML page.

15. Select all the CSS layers on the page by using one of the following methods:

    • From the Dreamweaver Layers panel, press Shift and select each layer.

    • In the Dreamweaver document window, press Shift and select each of the CSS layer symbols.

16. Choose Edit ➪ Copy to copy the selected layers.

17. Choose File ➪ Open and navigate to and open the target Web page for the layers. Alternatively, you can open the target Web page in the Site window.

18. Choose Edit ➪ Paste to insert the layers.

The depth of the CSS layers is determined by the order of layers in Fireworks. In CSS layers, higher numbered layers are on top of lower numbered layers, just as a layer that is higher in the Layers panel's layer list is on top of those below it.

The other method of using the CSS layer export feature of Fireworks, exporting Fireworks frames, comes in handy when you need to build complex Show-Hide layer Behaviors in Dreamweaver. Often, the layers that are alternately shown and hidden are in front of one another. You can take advantage of this positioning by setting up the separate objects as frames in Fireworks. Then, choose File ➪ Export and choose CSS Layers and Fireworks Frames from the Save as type (Save As) and Source option lists, respectively. Deselect the Trim Images option if you want each image to maintain its relative place in the frames; enable the option if you want the upper-left corner of each image to match.

 Tip
If you are displaying separately saved images, you can use the Open command and check the Open as Animation option in the Open dialog box in order to place each image automatically into its own frame. Then, export as CSS Layers, choosing to output the frames as layers.

Working with Image Placeholders from Dreamweaver

During the Web design process, the final images may not be initially available. Sometimes, the designer inserts a graphic element to act as a placeholder so that the rest of the page can proceed while the graphic is being created. Dreamweaver MX has added a new feature to facilitate this methodology. When you insert an image placeholder in Dreamweaver, you specify the width and height, a name, a color and, optionally, the alt text. The placeholder appears as a single color block with the name and dimensions prominently displayed.

New Feature

When you select an image placeholder in Dreamweaver, instead of an Edit button in the Property inspector, you find a Create button. Selecting Create opens up a new blank document in Fireworks—with the same dimensions as the placeholder. Use any and all of the Fireworks tools to make whatever image is needed to replace the placeholder. When you're finished, select Done to send the completed image back to Dreamweaver.

Fireworks prompts you for both a PNG source filename and an exported image file-name—and then conveys that information to Dreamweaver. Should the image need to be modified, you can easily modify the PNG source and Fireworks re-exports the file as previously specified.

Using Fireworks Behaviors in Dreamweaver

Fireworks writes in Dreamweaver standard code so that its Behaviors are recognized in Dreamweaver. What's the big deal about being recognized in Dreamweaver? If Dreamweaver can identify a Behavior as the same as its own, you can edit parameters in Dreamweaver that were defined in Fireworks. If you apply a Set Text of Status Bar Behavior in Fireworks and want to change the message in Dreamweaver, you can.

Fireworks exports code for five categories of Behaviors: Simple Rollover, Swap Image, Set Nav Bar Image, Show Pop-Up Menu, and Set Text of Status Bar.

Note

Another Behavior is automatically inserted for all Fireworks Behaviors: Preload Images. As the name implies, the Preload Images Behavior makes sure that the browser has all images ready for smooth rollovers.

To modify a Fireworks-applied Behavior in Dreamweaver, you must first open the Dreamweaver Behaviors panel, shown in Figure 22-8, which looks quite similar to the Behaviors panel in Fireworks. Select an object or tag in Dreamweaver, and any applied Behaviors are listed in the Behaviors panel.

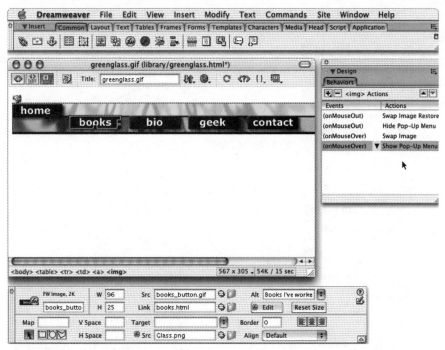

Figure 22-8: The Behaviors panel in Dreamweaver uses events and actions, just like the Behaviors panel in Fireworks.

Each of the Behaviors uses a different dialog box in Dreamweaver for modifications; however, the overall procedure is the same. To modify any of the Fireworks-generated Behaviors in Dreamweaver, follow these steps:

1. In Dreamweaver, open the file incorporating your Fireworks-generated HTML code.

2. Choose Window ➪ Behaviors to open the Behaviors panel.

   Alternatively, you can click the Behavior button from the Launcher.

3. Select the image, object, or tag that the Behavior is assigned to.

   The Behavior's event(s) and action(s) appear in the Behaviors panel.

4. To change to a different triggering event, click the desired Behavior option arrow and choose another option from the drop-down list.

Tip   The list of available events changes, depending upon the associated tag.

5. To cause one action to be triggered before another action with the same event (for example, two onClick events), click the action and use the Up and Down buttons in the Behaviors panel to move the Behavior.

6. Double-click the Behavior that you want to modify.

The appropriate dialog box appears, such as the one for the Show Pop-up Menu Behavior, shown in Figure 22-9.

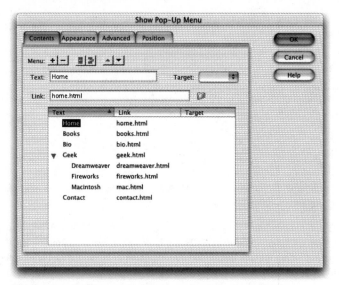

Figure 22-9: Make any necessary changes through the Dreamweaver-specific user interfaces for each Behavior.

7. Make any desired changes on the invoked dialog box.

8. Click OK when you're done.

The Set Nav Bar Image Behavior in Fireworks is translated into the following three separate Behaviors in Dreamweaver, each of which you can individually adjust in Dreamweaver:

✦ **Set Nav Bar Image:** Controls the Down and highlighted Down state (typically, Frames 3 and 4 in a Fireworks rollover).

✦ **Swap Image:** Controls rollovers for Nav Bars.

✦ **Swap Image Restore:** Restores rollovers to their Up position when the user's mouse cursor leaves the image.

Fireworks Technique: Creating a Web Photo Album

Online catalogs and other sites often depend on images to help sell their products. Full-scale product shots can be large and time-consuming to download, so it's common for Web designers to display a thumbnail of the images instead. If the viewer wants to see more detail, a click on the thumbnail loads the full-size image. Although it's not difficult to save a scaled-down version of an image in a graphics program and link the two in a Web layout program, creating page after page of such images is an overwhelming chore. An excellent example of the Dreamweaver-Fireworks interoperability comes to the rescue: the Create Web Photo Album command, which is included with Dreamweaver.

As long as you have both Dreamweaver MX and Fireworks MX, you can use the Web Photo Album command to create a presentation that enables Web users to browse thumbnail images that they can click to access the full-size version. Although the Create Web Photo Album command is a Dreamweaver command, it uses Fireworks to do the image processing, such as scaling thumbnails and converting all full-size images to a common format.

To create a Web photo album with Dreamweaver and Fireworks, follow these steps:

1. Place all the images that you intend to use into a single folder, anywhere on your computer.

   When run, the Web Photo command asks you to choose a single folder of images.

2. In Dreamweaver, choose Commands ➪ Create Web Photo Album.

   Dreamweaver displays the Web Photo Album dialog box, as shown in Figure 22-10.

3. Enter a title for your photo album in the Photo Album Title box.

   The title will be displayed at the top of the page of thumbnails.

4. If desired, enter a subheading in the Subheading Info box.

   This appears directly below the title on the page of thumbnails.

5. If desired, enter a sub-subheading in the Other Info box.

   This appears below the Title and Subheading on the page of thumbnails.

6. Click the Source Images Folder Browse button and select a folder containing the images to include in the photo album.

   Image files from the folder will be included in the photo album if they have the following filename extensions:

   - .gif
   - .jpg or .jpeg

Create Web Photo Album

Photo Album Title:	Konis Gallery
Subheading Info:	Artist of the Southwest
Other Info:	
Source Images Folder:	file:///Abbott/Users/derren/Sites/Konis/gallery/p Browse...
Destination Folder:	file:///Costello/Users/derren/Sites/Konis/gallery/ Browse...
Thumbnail Size:	100 x 100 ⬦ ☑ Show Filenames
Columns:	5
Thumbnail Format:	JPEG – Better Quality ⬦
Photo Format:	JPEG – Better Quality ⬦ Scale: 100 %
	☑ Create Navigation Page for Each Photo

OK
Cancel
Help

Figure 22-10: Choose from numerous options when building a Web photo album.

Caution   Using JPEG images as source files is never recommended. JPEG compression makes files that are suitable for viewing, but not for importing and re-exporting.

- .png
- .tif or .tiff
- .psd

Caution   Mac users: Image files that don't have filename extensions are ignored by Fireworks and are not included in the photo album. Add appropriate filename extensions to any images that don't have them.

7. Click the Destination Folder Browse button and select or create a folder for all the exported images and HTML.

8. Select a size for the thumbnail images from the Thumbnail Size option list.

   Fireworks scales images proportionally to create thumbnails that fit within the specified pixel dimensions.

9. Check the Show Filenames checkbox to display the filenames of the original images below their thumbnails.

10. Enter the number of columns of thumbnails.

11. Select a format for the exported thumbnail images from the Format option list.

12. Select a format for the exported photo album images from the Photo Format option list.

13. If desired, enter a Scale percentage for the photo album images. A setting of 100% creates full-size images the same size as the original images.

The scale setting is used for all the photo album images.

14. If desired, check Create Navigation Page for Each Photo to create an individual Web page for each image in the photo album.

If you don't select Create Navigation Page for Each Photo, the thumbnail images are linked directly to the full-size images. This is a common way to create a Web photo album.

15. Click OK when you're done.

Fireworks launches (if it's not already running). It creates a thumbnail and a full-size image for each of the imported image files in your photo album. After the images are created, Dreamweaver creates the necessary HTML.

16. Dreamweaver displays an Album Complete dialog box. Click OK to end your photo album creation session.

Open your Web photo album in a browser, or integrate it into your Dreamweaver Web site.

Making Hybrid Commands

The scripting capability of Dreamweaver and Fireworks enables the Web artist to control either application with custom commands. An exciting side effect of the enhanced control is that Dreamweaver can actually do the Fireworks scripting, making Fireworks a willing partner in executing Dreamweaver commands.

Here's how Dreamweaver is typically used to communicate with Fireworks:

1. The user runs a command in Dreamweaver.

2. Dreamweaver opens a dialog box, as with other extensions.

3. After the user has filled in the dialog box and clicked OK, the command executes.

4. All user-supplied parameters are read and used to create a JavaScript scriptlet or function, which serves as instructions for Fireworks.

5. If used, the scriptlet is stored on the disk.

6. Fireworks launches and is instructed to run the Dreamweaver-created scriptlet or function.

7. Fireworks processes the scriptlet or function, while Dreamweaver tracks its progress via a cookie on the user's machine.

8. When Fireworks is finished, a positive result is returned.

   The Fireworks application programming interface (API) includes several error codes if problems, such as a full disk, are encountered.

9. While tracking Fireworks' progress, Dreamweaver sees the positive result and integrates the graphics by rewriting the DOM (Document Object Model) of the current page.

10. The dialog box is closed and the current page refreshed to correctly present the finished product.

To successfully control Fireworks, you need a complete understanding of the Fireworks DOM and its extension capabilities. Macromedia provides documentation called Extending Fireworks, which is available on your Fireworks MX CD-ROM, or from the Fireworks Support Center at www.macromedia.com/support/fireworks.

Cross-Reference   The Fireworks API is detailed in Chapter 26. Also, See Chapter 19 for details on the History panel, which allows you to create commands—or at least get them started—without coding.

On the Dreamweaver side of the API fence, you'll find seven useful methods in the FWLaunch JSExtension, detailed in Table 22-1.

Table 22-1
FWLaunch Methods

Method	Returns	Use
`BringDWToFront()`	nothing	Brings the Dreamweaver window in front of any other running application.
`BringFWToFront()`	nothing	Brings the Fireworks window in front of any other running application.
`ExecJsInFireworks (javascriptOrFileURL)`	Result from the running of the scriptlet in Fireworks. If the operation fails, returns an error code.*	Executes the supplied JavaScript function or scriptlet.
`GetJsResponse (progressTrackerCookie)`	Result from the running of the scriptlet in Fireworks: provides information as to whether it completed successfully, returns null if it is still running, or returns an error code.*	Determines whether Fireworks has finished unning JavaScript passed to it, whether it ran successfully, or whether it returned an error.

Method	Returns	Use
MayLaunchFireworks()	Boolean	Determines whether Fireworks may be launched.
OptimizeInFireworks (fileURL, docURL, {targetWidth}, {targetHeight})	Result from the running of the scriptlet in Fireworks. of the scriptlet in Fireworks. returns an error code.*	Performs an Optimize in Fireworks operation, Fireworks operation, Export Preview dialog box.
ValidateFireworks (versionNumber)	Boolean	Determines whether the user has a specific version of Fireworks

*Error codes: 1) The argument proves invalid; 2) File I/O error; 3) Improper version of Dreamweaver; 4) Improper version of Fireworks; 5) User-cancelled operation

Don't be afraid to experiment with Dreamweaver-Fireworks integration and with extensibility in general. Exciting possibilities await.

Summary

Fireworks and Dreamweaver integration is definitely a case of the whole being greater than the individual parts. Taken on their own merits, each program is a powerful Web tool, but together, they become a total Web graphics solution. As you begin to work with Fireworks and Dreamweaver together, consider these points:

✦ Dreamweaver MX gains features when Fireworks MX is installed.

✦ With the Optimize Image in Fireworks command, you don't even have to leave Dreamweaver to rescale, crop, or store your graphics in another format.

✦ After designating Fireworks as your graphics editor in Dreamweaver, selected images can be edited and updated automatically.

✦ Fireworks outputs Dreamweaver-compliant code, making modifications within Dreamweaver seamless.

✦ Fireworks images exported as a Dreamweaver Library item can be inserted in a Web page without additional cutting and pasting.

✦ You can retain positioning set in Fireworks by exporting Fireworks layers as CSS layers.

✦ Hybrid Dreamweaver-Fireworks commands offer exciting possibilities for workflow automation.

In the next chapter, you find out about Fireworks' animation capabilities.

✦   ✦   ✦

Animation

Animations have become important to the Web. Not only do they offer an alternative to static displays, but GIF animations are used extensively in the creation of banner ads. Animation in Fireworks MX is surprisingly full-featured and easy-to-use. In Part VI, we walk step by step through the creation of a banner ad and discover tweening, onion skinning, and other basic animation techniques.

Applying Animation Techniques

Animation has become a prominent feature of the Web, and very few Web sites get by without at least a little of it. Animated GIF banner ads have proliferated from common to ubiquitous. Animated logos and buttons are an easy way to add spice to a site. Short, animated cartoons are increasingly popular as Web bandwidth increases.

This chapter looks briefly at some animation basics and then focuses on the Fireworks features that enable you to create animations. You'll work with Fireworks frames and animated GIF export features, such as timing and looping. Next, specific issues are discussed that you might confront when making animated banner ads, and then you go through the process from start to finish.

Cross-Reference You can find information on importing animations and importing multiple files as animations in Chapter 14.

Understanding Web Animation

Animation is a trick. Show a rapid succession of similar images with slight changes in an element's location or properties, and you think that you see something moving. This movement can be very complex or very simple. The 24 frames per second of a motion picture aren't even required; in as little as three frames, an object can actually appear to be moving (loop two frames and an object just appears to flash).

Because Fireworks creates animated GIF images, this chapter focuses on that format. However, many of the ideas that go into creating good animated GIF images also apply when creating images in other Web animation formats.

Getting a handle on bandwidth

Remember first and foremost that bandwidth is always an issue. Then, remember again that bandwidth is always an issue. I'll end up harping on that again and again, because bandwidth affects everything. You must analyze each and every bold, creative move for its eventual effect on the overall *weight* of the resulting animated GIF file (the total file size). Throughout the entire process of creating an animation for display on the Web, you need to balance variables carefully, such as the number of colors used, the number of frames, the timing of those frames, and how much area of your image is actually animated. If you want more colors, you may have to take out a few frames and settle for a less fluid animation. If you're animating complex shapes that don't compress well, you may have to get by with fewer colors.

The dial-up connection is the great equalizer. The Web is slow and generally static, and almost everybody knows it. If you can give your audience a quick, dynamic presentation, you'll score two times. Keep in mind the nature of GIF compression as you create your designs. Big blocks of cartoonish color and horizontal stripes compress much better than photographic images, vertical stripes, or gradients and dithers.

Making a statement

So, maybe you're not going to win an Oscar with your animation; that doesn't mean you shouldn't give it a reason for existing. Every part of your animation needs to be focused and necessary, because each little added movement also purchases a corresponding amount of bandwidth. A short, tight, and concise animation is much more popular with your audience. This applies whether you're creating a complex cartoon with an intricate story line, a flashy, abstract design, or even an animated logo. If you decide before you start what you want to accomplish creatively, you increase your chances of ending up with a tight, presentable result.

Animated GIF images are good at some things, but not so good at others. Consider those limitations carefully, and focus on creating a good animated GIF — not just a good animation that happens to be forced into the framework of an animated GIF. Logos, buttons, and simple frame-by-frame animations work best. You might find that thinking of an animated GIF image as a slideshow rather than a movie is helpful. Typically, you work with fewer frames than a movie uses, and with slow, simple, animated elements. I find that thinking of animated GIFs as little PowerPoint-style presentations reminds me of the limitations of the format. You can make a little movement go a long way. You can show that something's moving either by smoothly animating it frame by frame across the entire width of the image, or you can place it once on the left side of the canvas, followed by a blurred version in the center, and then display it again at the right side.

Tip   Don't forget everything that you learned by watching Saturday morning cartoons or reading comic books. Techniques such as word balloons and lines that illustrate movement or action in still comics can help you get your message across without adding significantly to the frame count (and the file size). Instead of moving an element off the canvas in ten smooth frames, replace it with a puff of smoke and some lines that point to which way the element went. Study animations for such tricks and make lean, mean animations that really make an impression and get your message across.

As usual on the Web, you're at the mercy of your users' browsers — and you don't even know which browsers they'll be using. However, generally, animated GIF images play back a little faster in Internet Explorer than in Navigator (and, naturally, play back faster on faster computers). Don't try to be too precise, attempting to measure the time between frames and worrying about it. Instead, embrace a little of the Web's anarchy and just try to find a good middle ground. Trust the timing settings in Fireworks and hope for the best.

Examining why to animate a GIF

Fireworks is the perfect place to create animated GIF images. Creating the illusion of animation means changing the objects on the canvas over time, and an always-editable object in Fireworks is easy to move, scale, or modify with effects. And when your animation is complete, Fireworks' unmatched image optimization enables you to create the lightest-weight animated GIF possible. (There's that bandwidth issue again.)

Tip   Although you usually create GIF animations directly in Fireworks, you also can export an animation as a series of files by choosing File ➪ Export and then selecting either Frames to Files or Layers to Files from the Save As option list. These files — which can be other image formats, such as PNG or JPEG — can then be modified in another application, or used in another animation format, such as an SMIL presentation in RealPlayer, or an interactive Dynamic HTML (DHTML) slideshow. If you're a Flash fan, you can easily export an animated GIF slice as a Flash SWF file by changing the Save As option on the Export dialog box from HTML and Images to Macromedia Flash SWF.

The animated GIF has its share of limitations and gets its share of disrespect, especially when sized up feature for feature against some of the more "serious" animation formats used on the Web. Table 23-1 makes just such a comparison.

Table 23-1
Comparing Web Animation Formats

Format	Sound	Interactivity	Streaming	Transparency	Colors
Animated GIF	No	No	No	Yes	256
Dynamic HTML	No	Yes	Yes	Yes	Millions
Java	Yes	Yes	Yes	No	Millions
Flash	Yes	Yes	Yes	Sometimes	Millions
Shockwave	Yes	Yes	Yes	No	Millions
QuickTime	Yes	Yes	Yes	No	Millions
RealPlayer	Yes	Yes	Yes	No	Millions

Note   *Transparency* refers to a transparent background when the animation is placed in a browser, not support within the editing environment or the animation format itself.

Based on this table, the animated GIF seems as if it's a fairly poor choice. Other formats feature high levels of interactivity and automatically stream or simulate streaming with multiple component files. Some have video and many have sound. What's more, Flash gets a lot more done in a much smaller file size.

So, why is the animated GIF used so often? Why haven't designers dropped it in favor of one or more of these other, seemingly superior methods? Find the answers to these questions and more in Table 23-2, which details browser support for each format.

Table 23-2
Browser Support for Web Animation Formats

Format	Navigator 2/3 and IE 3	Navigator 4 and 6 and IE 4, 5 and 6	Most Other Browsers
Animated GIF	Yes	Yes	Yes
Dynamic HTML	No	Yes	No
Java	Yes; user can disable	Yes; user can disable	No
Flash	With plug-in	With plug-in	No
Shockwave	With plug-in	With plug-in	No
QuickTime	With plug-in	With plug-in	No
RealPlayer	With plug-in	With plug-in	No

When you consider who can actually view your animation, the animated GIF doesn't look so bad after all. Other formats may be flashier, but the animated GIF is "old reliable." No matter which platform or browser, the animated GIF is always available.

Using the Fireworks Animation Toolkit

Animation in Fireworks focuses on these major tools:

✦ **Frames panel:** The heart of Fireworks' animation features, where you manipulate individual frames — such as a director editing the frames of a film — adding, removing, reordering, and specifying timing for individual frames.

 Tip The Export Preview dialog box also duplicates some of the Frames panel controls, such as animation timing.

✦ **Layers panel:** Where you manage each frame's layers. Organize your animation by keeping objects on the same layer from frame to frame, or share a layer across every frame, so that backgrounds or static objects can be created once for the entire animation.

✦ **VCR-style controls:** Where you flip through frames, or play your entire animation right in the document window.

✦ **Graphic symbols:** Fireworks can create intermediate steps between two instances of the same symbol, quickly generating a complete animation.

✦ **Animation symbols:** A multi-frame symbol that is a self-contained animation.

Managing frames

What separates an animation from a regular Fireworks document is that the animation has multiple frames. The relationship between layers and frames can be hard to understand when you first start animating in Fireworks. However, understanding how they work — and work together — is essential.

Frames resemble the frames of a traditional filmstrip (see Figure 23-1) that you might run through a movie projector. When you play your animation, only one frame is visible at a time. Frame 1 is shown first, and then Frame 2, Frame 3, and so on. When you add a frame to your document, you're extending the length of the filmstrip and making a longer movie. When you change the order of frames in the Frames panel, it's as if you're cutting a frame out of your filmstrip and splicing it back in at another point on the strip. If you move Frame 5 to the beginning of your movie, before Frame 1, all the frames are renumbered, so that what used to be Frame 5 is now Frame 1, what used to be Frame 1 becomes Frame 2, and so on.

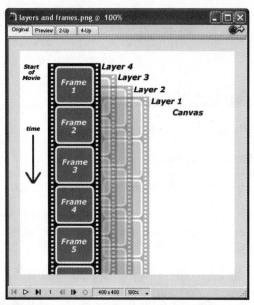

Figure 23-1: Think of frames as the frames of a filmstrip, and layers as a stack of filmstrips stuck together.

The layers in an animation are similar to separate filmstrips stacked together. When you play your animation, all the layers of Frame 1 are shown together, and then all the layers of Frame 2 are shown, and then Frame 3, and so on. Just as how you use layers in a static Fireworks document, layers provide a way to organize the order of objects and keep dissimilar objects separate from each other, for easier editing. When you add a layer to your document, you add a whole new filmstrip to the stack. Changing the order of layers in the Layers panel is analogous to changing the order of that filmstrip in the stack of filmstrips.

Note When you add a frame to your movie, it automatically has the same layers as all the other frames. To continue the filmstrip metaphor, adding a frame to one filmstrip in the stack adds it to all the filmstrips. When you add a layer to your movie, it is added to every frame. Adding a layer adds a whole new filmstrip the same length as the others.

One very useful interaction between layers and frames is the ability to share a layer. When a layer is shared, its content is the same on every frame, and no matter which frame you are viewing when you edit the objects in that layer, the changes appear on every frame. This is handy for static elements, such as backgrounds. You take a closer look at this later in the chapter.

You do the bulk of your animation work in the Frames panel (see Figure 23-2), so you need to have it open all the time while creating an animation. From there, you can add, delete, reorder, or duplicate frames. You can view and edit a single frame, a group of frames, or all of your frames simultaneously. You can copy or move objects from frame to frame. You can specify the timing each frame has in your animated GIF. As with the Layers panel, when a Frame contains a selection item, the selection indicator appears next to its name in the Frames panel.

Frame names   Frame timing   Selection icon

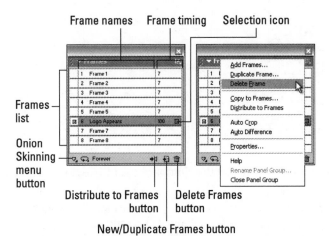

Frames list

Onion Skinning menu button

Distribute to Frames button

Delete Frames button

New/Duplicate Frames button

Figure 23-2: Manage frames with the Frames panel and its handy Options menu.

Tip

When working on animation, you might want to dock your Layers panel with your Frames panel, if it isn't already, so that you can easily move between the panels. If you're not short on screen real estate, you could even keep them side by side. Location doesn't matter, as long as they're both close at hand.

Adding frames

When you start creating an animation in Fireworks, your document has exactly one frame. Obviously, this has to change before you can simulate any kind of movement. At first, you might make a rough guess at how many frames your animation should contain, and then add that number of frames to your document. Later, you can add or remove frames as the need arises. Another approach is to start with just two frames: the first and the last. After you establish where your animation starts and finishes, filling in the intervening frames is often easier.

To add a frame to the end of the Frame list, click the Add Frames button (blank sheet of paper with a plus sign on it) at the bottom of the Frames panel, or choose Insert ➪ Frame.

To add one or more frames at a specific point in the Frame list, follow these steps:

1. Choose Add Frames from the Frames panel's Options menu.

Fireworks displays the Add Frames dialog box (see Figure 23-3).

Figure 23-3: The Add Frames
dialog box gives you careful
control over how many frames
you add and where you add them.

2. Enter the number of frames to add in the Number box, or use the slider to add
   up to ten frames.

3. Choose where to insert the new frames. The options are At the beginning,
   Before current frame, After current frame, and At the end. Click OK when
   you're done.

The new frames are created and added to the Frame list at the point you specified.

Naming frames

By default, Fireworks names each frame with a very generic "Frame 1" or "Frame 2."
When you're animating, moving objects back and forth from frame to frame, these
generic names can be very confusing. To name a frame with a descriptive name,
double-click its name in the Frames panel. Fireworks displays a small raised dialog
box that enables you to type any name you please, as shown in Figure 23-4. After
you've entered a new name, dismiss the raised dialog box by clicking anywhere
outside it, or by pressing Enter (Return).

Figure 23-4: Name your frames just as you please,
by double-clicking them in the Frames panel.

Deleting a frame

The most important thing to remember when you delete a frame is that you also delete all the objects that it contains, except for those that are on a shared layer. Take care to identify and delete the correct frame.

Tip If you delete a frame accidentally and want to restore it to the Frame list, choose either Edit ⇨ Undo, or the keyboard shortcut, Ctrl+Z (Command+Z).

To delete a frame, select it on the Frame list and do one of the following:

✦ Click the Delete Frames button (a Trash icon) at the bottom of the Frames panel.

✦ Drag the frame to the Delete Frames button at the bottom of the Frames panel.

✦ Choose Delete Frame from the Frames panel's Options menu.

Reordering frames

As you continue to work on your animation, you might want to change the order of your frames, by moving them earlier or later in the animation.

To reorder a frame, click and drag it up or down the Frame list in the Frames panel.

Note From working with layers in the Layers panel, you may be accustomed to seeing the layer retain its name as you change its stacking order by dragging it up or down the layers list. When you reorder a frame, though, all frames are renumbered to reflect their new positions. The first frame in your animation is always Frame 1.

Tip As with Layers, you may wish to give your Frames custom names. If you custom name your frames and move Frame 9, putting it between Frame 2 and Frame 3, it will still be called Frame 9 and will appear to be out of order.

Duplicating frames

One way to save a significant amount of time and effort is to copy a sequence of frames that you've already created and then modify the copies further. If you have created an animation sequence of a sunrise, you can copy those frames and then reverse their order to get an automatic sunset. This not only saves you the time and effort of creating the sunset animation from scratch, but also has the added advantage that the sun sets in the same place from which it rose.

To duplicate a single frame, drag it from the Frame list onto the Add Frames button at the bottom of the Frames panel. Fireworks inserts the copy into the Frame list, right after the original.

To duplicate one or more frames and place the copies in a specific place in the Frame list, follow these steps:

1. Choose Duplicate Frame from the Frames panel's Options menu.

   Fireworks displays the Duplicate Frames dialog box.

Note   The Duplicate Frames dialog box is very similar to the Add Frames dialog box, shown previously in Figure 23-3.

2. Enter the number of frames to duplicate in the Number box, or use the slider to duplicate up to ten frames.

3. Choose where to insert the copies. The options are At the beginning, Before current frame, After current frame, and At the end. Click OK when you're done.

The frames are duplicated and the copies are added to the Frame list at the point you specified.

Animating objects

A significant part of creating animation is managing how objects in your document change over time. If you are creating a simple, animated sunrise, the sun starts out at a low point on the canvas and, over time (through later frames), moves to a higher point on the canvas. At the same time, a cloud might move from left to right, while the ground and sky stay the same.

You certainly don't want to draw each of these objects numerous times. Aside from being a lot of extra effort, you would probably end up with objects that are not exactly the same dimensions or properties from frame to frame. If the sun were to change size slightly in each frame, it would detract from the illusion that the animation contains just one moving sun.

Instead, when you create an animation, draw objects once and then copy or distribute them from frame to frame, where the copies can be moved or modified slightly to give the appearance of the same object moving or changing over time.

Keeping similar objects on their own layers makes working with just those objects easier as you copy objects to frames. In the animated sunrise example, you might keep the sun on its own layer, the clouds on another layer, and the unchanging background objects on another.

Copying objects to frames

Most of the time, you add objects to other frames by copying them. To copy an object or objects to another frame, follow these steps:

1. Select the object(s).

2. Choose Copy to Frames from the Frames panel's Options menu.

   Fireworks displays the Copy to Frames dialog box (see Figure 23-5).

3. Choose where to copy the selection. The available options are All frames, Previous frame, Next frame, or Range, which is used to specify a specific range of frames. Click OK when you're done.

Figure 23-5: Use the Copy to Frames dialog box to copy objects to all of your frames, or just a specific range of frames.

Distributing objects to frames

When you choose to distribute a group of objects to frames, the objects are distributed after the current frame, according to their stacking order. The bottom object in the group stays on the current frame, the next one up goes to the next frame, the next one above that goes to the frame after that, and so forth. If you start with a blank canvas and create three objects, such as a square, circle, and star, the star will be on top, because it was created last. If you select those objects and distribute them to frames, the star — which was created last — will now be in the last frame of your animation. New frames are added to contain all the objects, if necessary. For example, if you distribute ten objects to five frames, five more frames are added to contain all the objects.

You can quickly turn a static document into an animation in this way. Objects that were created first on the canvas end up first in the animation.

To distribute a selection of objects across multiple frames, select the objects and then do one of the following:

✦ Click the Distribute to Frames button (a filmstrip icon) at the bottom of the Frames panel.

✦ Choose Distribute to Frames from the Frames panel's Options menu.

✦ Drag the blue selection knob on the object's bounding box to the Distribute to Frames button.

Managing static objects

Fireworks simplifies management of the objects in your animation that aren't animated because any layer can be shared across every frame of your animation. For example, if you create a background in Frame 1, you can share the layer that contains the background, and that background will appear in every frame. After the layer is shared, you can modify the objects it contains in any frame, and the modifications show up everywhere. Any static element in your animation needs to be created or edited only once.

To share a layer across all the frames of your animation, follow these steps:

1. In the Layers panel, double-click the layer that you want to share.

   Fireworks displays the Layer Options dialog box.

2. Check Share Across Frames, and then press Enter (return) or click outside of the dialog box.

   Fireworks warns you that any objects on this layer in other frames will be deleted. Click OK to delete those objects and share the layer.

Tip   When a layer is shared across frames, you see a filmstrip icon next to that layer in the Layers panel. You can see this icon next to the Web Layer as it is always shared.

To stop sharing a layer across all frames of your animation, follow these steps:

1. In the Layers panel, double-click the layer that you want to stop sharing.

   Fireworks displays the Layer Options dialog box.

2. Uncheck Share Across Frames, and then press Enter (return) or click outside of the dialog box.

   Fireworks asks whether you want to leave the contents of the layer in all frames, or just in the current frame. Choose Current to leave the contents of the layer just in the current frame. Choose All to leave the contents of the layer in all frames.

Note   Another way to modify whether or not a layer is shared is to select the layer in the Layers panel and check or uncheck Share Layer on the Layers panel's Options menu.

Using the VCR controls

As you build your animations in Fireworks, you'll no doubt want to play them to get a feel for the motion between frames. Fireworks offers VCR-style controls, available along the bottom of each document window, so that you can preview your animations (see Figure 23-6).

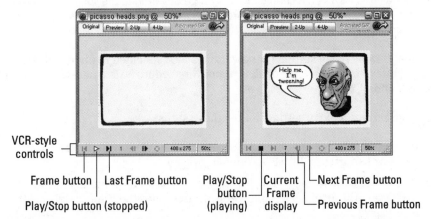

Figure 23-6: The VCR controls on the Fireworks document window enable you to control your multiframe Fireworks document like a movie.

When you click the Play button, Fireworks plays your animation, using the timing that is specified in the Frames panel or on the Animation tab of the Export Preview dialog box. If you don't set the timing yourself, your animation plays at the default of $\frac{7}{100}$ of a second between frames. Frame delay is discussed in the next section.

While the animation is playing, the Play button turns into a Stop button. Fireworks also displays the current frame, and has buttons available to jump quickly to the previous or next frame, or to the first or last frame of your animation.

Tip   You can also stop a running animation by clicking your mouse inside the document window.

When you play your animation in the document window, it always loops, whether you have looping enabled in the Frames panel or not. The setting in the Frames panel controls looping only in the animated GIF file your animation eventually becomes.

Setting frame delay timing

The first thing to remember about controlling animation speed is that the settings you specify are ultimately approximate. Although Fireworks is perfectly happy to follow your directions, after your animation becomes an animated GIF, timing is in the virtual hands of the playback software, usually a browser. Internet Explorer tends to play animations faster than Navigator, and both browsers play animated GIFs faster on faster computers.

Tip   As if approximated GIF timing isn't enough, an animation that is currently being downloaded staggers along with no attention to timing, because each frame is displayed as it arrives. A couple of tricks for getting around the staggering playback of a downloading animated GIF are detailed later in this chapter, under "Web Design with Animated GIF Images."

The default frame delay setting for new frames is 7, specified in hundredths of a second. For example, a setting of 25 is a quarter-second, 50 is a half-second, and 200 is two seconds.

To change a frame's delay setting, follow these steps:

1. If the Frames panel is not already open, choose Window ➪ Frames, or use the keyboard shortcut, Shift+F2to open it.

2. Double-click the frame timing for the frame you want to modify in the frame list. Fireworks displays a pop-up edit window with the frame's delay settings (see Figure 23-7).

Figure 23-7: Double-click the frame timing for a particular frame in the Frames panel to view a pop-up edit window with the frame's delay settings.

3. Type a new setting in the Frame Delay field.

4. Uncheck Include when Exporting if you want this frame delay setting to affect the way the animation is viewed in Fireworks, without being included in the animated GIF you export.

5. Click anywhere outside the pop-up edit window, or press Enter (Return) to dismiss it.

Alternatively, if you're using the Export Preview dialog box to export your animated GIF, you can alter frame delay by choosing the frame from the list on the Animation tab and changing the value in the Frame Delay field.

Using Onion Skinning

Most of the time, your document window displays the contents of a single frame. By flipping back and forth from frame to frame, you can get a feel for how the animation is flowing, but this is just a rough guide. To get a more precise view of the changes from one frame to the next, turn on Onion Skinning to view, and even edit, multiple frames simultaneously.

Note   *Onion skinning* is the traditional animation technique of drawing on translucent tracing paper—such as an onion skin—to view a series of drawings simultaneously.

The Onion Skinning button in the lower-left corner of the Frames panel enables you to access the Onion Skinning menu (see Figure 23-8) and select which frames you want to view. You can choose to view any range of frames within your animation, or all of them.

Onion Skinning range selector

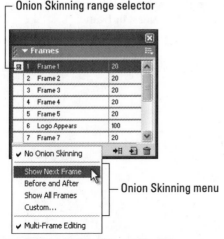

Onion Skinning menu

Figure 23-8: The Onion Skinning menu on the Frames panel provides various ways to select which frames you want to view, and even edit, simultaneously.

When Onion Skinning is turned on, objects on the current frame are displayed normally, while objects on other frames are shown slightly dimmed. When playing an animation by using the Frame controls at the bottom of the document window, Onion Skinning is switched off temporarily.

Setting the range of frames to onion skin

You can turn on Onion Skinning and choose a range of frames to display in any one of three ways:

✦ Specify a range of frames by using the Onion Skinning range selector, located in the Frame list's left margin in the Frames panel (refer to Figure 23-2). This is the quickest way to specify a range of frames, especially for shorter animations. To expand the range to include earlier frames, click inside an empty box above the selector. To expand the range to include later frames, click inside an empty box below the selector. To contract the range, click inside the selector itself. To turn off Onion Skinning, click the bottom end of the selector.

✦ Choose predefined ranges from the Onion Skinning menu on the Frames panel. To show the current frame and the next frame, choose Show Next Frame. To show the previous frame, the current frame, and the next frame, choose Before and After. To show all frames, choose Show All.

✦ Choose Custom from the Onion Skinning menu to display the Onion Skinning dialog box (see Figure 23-9), which gives you precise control over the frames that you view, all the way down to the opacity of other frames. Fill in the number of frames Before Current Frame and After Current Frame that you want to view, and specify an Opacity setting for those frames. A setting of 0 makes frame contents invisible, whereas a setting of 100 makes objects on other frames appear as though they're on the current frame.

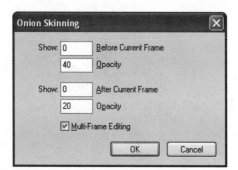

Figure 23-9: Select a specific range of frames to onion skin, and control the opacity of the onion-skinned frames with the Onion Skinning dialog box.

Exploring Multi-Frame Editing

When Multi-Frame Editing is enabled, you can select and edit objects in the document window that are on different frames. Whether an object is on the current frame and displayed regularly or on another frame and dimmed makes no difference. You can easily select all versions of a particular object across multiple frames and move or scale them as one.

To enable multi-frame editing, check Multi-Frame Editing on the Onion Skinning dialog box or the Onion Skinning menu. To switch off multi-frame editing, uncheck Multi-Frame Editing. on the Onion Skinning dialog box.

Examining export settings and options

The animated GIF format contains support for frame delay timing, looping, and various frame disposal methods. These options are built right into the Frame panel itself, or the Animation tab of the Export Preview dialog box.

The first export setting that you must specify is the animated GIF format itself. Choose Window ➪ Optimize to view the Optimize panel, if it isn't already visible, and choose Animated GIF from the format option list, as shown in Figure 23-10.

Figure 23-10: Choose Animated GIF as your export format in the Optimize panel.

As usual, the last step before publishing Web media is to put that media on a "diet." All the same rules for exporting a regular, static GIF also apply to animated GIFs. Limiting the number of colors reduces file size, and specifying a transparent background makes for easier compositing with the browser's background when your animated GIF becomes part of a Web page.

Cross-Reference For more on specifying GIF export options, such as number of colors and transparency, see Chapter 15.

Using frame disposal

In addition to regular GIF options, the animated GIF format has a special trick up its sleeve for reducing file size: frame disposal. For the most part, you can use Fireworks' default frame disposal settings to produce very lightweight animated GIF images. Learning to tweak the Export settings might save you some valuable kilobytes here and there, though, depending on the type of animation you've created.

The frame disposal options are only available from the Frame Disposal menu on the Animation tab of the Export Preview dialog box. Access the Export Preview dialog box by choosing File ➪ Export Preview. Choose from one of these options:

✦ **Unspecified:** Fireworks automatically selects the disposal method for each frame. This option is the default and generally creates the lightest animated GIF images.

✦ **None:** Overlays each frame on top of the previous frame. The first frame is shown, and then the next frame is added on top of it, and the following frame is added on top of that, and so forth. This option is suitable for adding a small object to a larger background, if the object doesn't move throughout the animation. For example, this technique works well with an animation that features parts of a logo that steadily appear until the animation is complete.

✦ **Restore to Background:** Shows the contents of each new frame over the background color. For example, to move an object in a transparent animated GIF.

✦ **Restore to Previous:** Shows the contents of each new frame over the contents of the previous frame; for example, to move an object across a background image.

In addition to the Frame Disposal menu, two related options greatly affect the export file size:

✦ **Auto Crop:** Causes Fireworks to compare each frame of the animation with the previous frame, and then crop to the area that changes. This reduces file sizes by saving information in each animated GIF only once, and avoids a situation in which, for example, a patch of blue in a certain position is saved repeatedly in each frame.

Tip

If you are exporting your animated GIF for editing in another application, turning off Auto Crop is recommended. Some applications don't handle this type of optimization very well, and you may end up with artifacts. Macromedia's Director 7 is one such application.

✦ **Auto Difference:** Converts unchanged pixels within the Auto Crop area to transparent, which sometimes reduces file size further.

Auto Crop and Auto Difference can be checked or unchecked on the Frames panel's Options menu, or from the Animation tab of the Export Preview dialog box.

Looping

Looping is fairly straightforward. An animated GIF can loop any number of times, or it can be set to loop "forever," which means it never stops. If the last frame of your animation is a final resting point that looks good all on its own, setting your animation to loop a finite number of times is a good option.

If you're creating an animated rollover button, set looping to Forever for best results. Roll over to an animated GIF that plays once, and you may find that it doesn't play at all, or you may catch it in mid-play. Different browsers treat preloaded animated GIF images in different ways.

To change the looping setting for your animated GIF, do one of the following:

✦ Choose No Looping, a specific number, or Forever from the Looping menu in the Frames panel (shown in Figure 23-11).

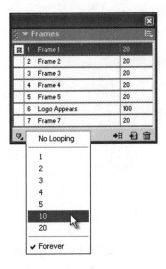

Figure 23-11: Choose your looping option from the Frames panel's Looping menu.

✦ Select the Play Once button or the Loop button from the Animation tab of the Export Preview dialog box, while exporting your animation. If you choose the Loop button, choose Forever, or a number from the Number of Loops option list, or type your own number directly into the box.

Exporting with the Export Preview dialog box

Although you can specify most of the options for your exported animated GIF within the Optimize and Frames panel, the Export Preview dialog box centralizes animation options and also provides a more realistic preview than Fireworks provides in the document window.

To export your animation with the Export Preview dialog box, follow these steps:

1. Choose File ➪ Export Preview.

   Fireworks displays the Export Preview dialog box, as shown in Figure 23-12.

2. On the Options tab, choose Animated GIF from the format option list.

3. On the Options and File tabs, specify settings, such as Bit Depth and Transparency, just as you would for a regular, static GIF image.

4. On the Animation tab, choose each frame from the list, in turn, and enter a number (in hundredths of a second) in the Frame Delay field. Set the Frame Delay to 0 to make frames display as quickly as possible. Preview the results of your timing settings by using the VCR controls, located below the Preview window in the bottom-right area of the Export Preview dialog box.

Animation tab   Frame Delay field

Frame
Disposal
menu
button

Frame
View/Hide
buttons

Play
Once
button

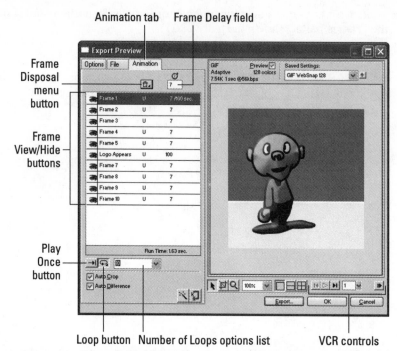

Loop button   Number of Loops options list   VCR controls

Figure 23-12: The Export Preview dialog box's Animation tab centralizes animation export settings.

For more about optimizing GIF Export settings, see Chapter 15.

5. If necessary, click the Frame View/Hide buttons (the eye icons) at the left of each frame on the list to show or hide a frame. If a frame is hidden, it isn't exported, and thus, isn't shown when the animation is played in Fireworks.

The Frame Delay settings are saved with your file after you export. Fireworks continues to use these settings when you play your animation in the document window using the VCR controls.

6. Specify a method for frame disposal by clicking the Frame Disposal menu button (the Trash icon next to the Frame Delay field) and choosing an option.

7. Choose whether or not your animation loops by clicking either the Play Once or the Loop button. If you click the Loop button, specify the number of times to loop in the Number of Loops option list. You can either choose a number from the list, type another number, or choose Forever to loop continuously. Click the Next button when you're done.

Fireworks displays the Export dialog box.

8. Choose the target folder and filename for your animated GIF, and then click Save.

Your animation is exported as an animated GIF image.

Examining Web Design with Animated GIF Images

One of the nicest things about animated GIF images is that you can place them in a Web page just as easily as you can place regular GIF images. This section describes some ways you can incorporate animated GIF images into your Web pages to create a complete presentation.

Animating background images

Version 4 and up browsers can display an animated GIF as a background image. A small-animated GIF is tiled across the whole page, creating a very dynamic presentation with a very low weight.

Reusing animations

A viewer has to download your animated GIF only once. If you use it again on the same page or on another page, it plays from their browser's cache. This is especially useful for an animated logo, or for animated buttons.

Scaling an animation

Use the `height` and `width` attributes of the `img` tag to present an animation at a larger size without increasing its weight. The slight reduction in quality that comes from scaling a bitmap image to double its size — in effect, you're halving its resolution — is a very small price to pay for the impact of a large animation. For example, if you create an animation that is 200×200 pixels, you can put it in a page at 400×400 pixels with the following `img` tag:

```
<img src="example.gif" width="400" height="400">
```

You can also use a percentage width or height to make an animation fit a page. This works better for some animations than others, but again, it can create quite an impact. Set the `width` and `height` to 100% and fill the entire browser window. The `img` tag would resemble this:

```
<img src="example.gif" width="100%" height="100%">
```

Using the browser's background image

One of the limitations of animated GIF images is the small number of colors that the GIF format can contain—and the high price you pay in weight for each extra color. However, you can give your animation a colorful background by making it transparent, and then placing it in a Web page with a JPEG background. The weight of the whole presentation remains low because you combine the strengths of the GIF format—animation and transparency—with the strengths of the JPEG format—lots of colors with a low weight.

Preloading an animation

Preloading an animated GIF in one of the following ways avoids the staggering playback that you see when an animation plays while it's downloading:

✦ **Use the** `lowsrc` **attribute of the** `img` **tag.** The browser shows the `lowsrc` image until the regular image finishes downloading. The following line of code tells the browser "Show `spacer.gif` until `animated.gif` has downloaded, and then replace `spacer.gif` with `animated.gif`":

```
<img src="animated.gif" lowsrc="spacer.gif" width="200" ù
height="200">
```

The file `spacer.gif` is the transparent 1×1-inch image that Fireworks uses to space tables. You've seen it and have a few copies of it on your hard drive if you've ever exported a sliced image from Fireworks. If you haven't, you can make your own by creating a 1×1-inch image with a transparent canvas and exporting it. Because it's lightweight, it doesn't affect the weight of your page too much. Because it's transparent, the background color shows through until the animation starts.

Note   Internet Explorer does not support the `img` tag's `lowsrc` attribute.

✦ **Use a Fireworks Swap Image behavior to swap a static image or** `spacer.gif` **with your animated image.** Modify the Event that triggers the Swap Image behavior to `onLoad`. When the entire page's content has loaded, the `onLoad` event fires and the static image is replaced with your fully downloaded animated GIF.

Cross-Reference   For more about using Fireworks Behaviors, see Chapter 21.

Using animated rollovers

Replacing the Over state of a rollover button with an animation of the same size can create an exciting effect. When the viewer's mouse hovers over your button, the animation begins. When it stops hovering over your button, the animation stops.

Caution Some browsers have problems with complex animated GIF images in rollovers. A small, simple animation that loops forever is likely to work best.

To create a simple animated rollover, follow these steps:

1. Create a rollover button with at least three states (Up, Over, and Down), and export it as a GIF in the usual way. (A rollover with two states appears to flash rather than move.) Note the filename that Fireworks gives the Over state of your button; it will be something such as button_r2_c2_f2, where f2 stands for frame 2, where you created the Over state.

Cross-Reference For detailed instructions about creating rollover buttons, see Chapter 21.

After you've exported your file once as a rollover, you need to export it again as an animated GIF. The individual frames that served as each state of the rollover button will now serve as the frames of an animation.

2. To export your file again as an animated GIF, choose File ➪ Export Preview.

   Fireworks displays the Export Preview dialog box.

3. On the Options tab, choose Animated GIF from the format option list.

4. On the Animation tab, click the Loop button, choose Forever, and then click Next.

   Fireworks displays the Export dialog box.

5. Under Slices, select None.

6. Under HTML, select None.

7. Choose the filename of the Over state of your rollover button, and click Save to save your animated GIF with that name.

   Fireworks asks whether you want to replace the original file. Click Yes.

When you open the HTML file that Fireworks created, you find that hovering your mouse over the button makes the button start cycling through its Up, Over, and Down states.

Tip You can also make an animated rollover button that stops animating when the user places his mouse over it. Instead of replacing the f2 image with an animation, as before, replace the f1 image. The animation plays as the page loads, but stops with a hover of the mouse over the button.

Slicing animations

Don't be afraid to unleash Fireworks' formidable slicing tools on your animations.

Some ideas for things you might do with slicing and animation:

✦ **Add extra colors:** Slice colorful, static areas and set the slice to export as a JPEG or PNG, and your animation appears to have sections of 24-bit color.

✦ **Add interactivity:** Replace a blank slice of your animated GIF with an HTML form element, such as an option list, or a set of radio buttons.

For more information about slicing images in Fireworks, see Chapter 20.

Tweening Graphic Symbols

You can really unleash your animations in Fireworks by incorporating graphic symbols. Symbols are reusable objects that have been placed in a Fireworks Library. Copies of symbols placed onto the canvas are called Instances. Instances maintain a link to their symbols, so that changing certain properties of a symbol also updates all of its Instances.

A basic knowledge of symbols serves you well for the rest of this chapter. Read more about graphic symbols in Chapter 17.

Two or more Instances of the same symbol can be "tweened" automatically by Fireworks. *Tweening* is a traditional animation term that refers to generating intermediate frames be*tween* two images to create the effect of the first image changing smoothly into the second image. In Fireworks, you provide the starting point for an animation with one Instance, and the ending point of the animation with another, and Fireworks creates the intermediate steps between them. Each new Instance is slightly changed from the one before it, so that the first Instance seems to evolve into the last. You can also tween more than two Instances (Figure 23-13), in which case it might be helpful to think of each Instance as a resting point, or a keyframe.

You can obviously use tweening to simulate motion, but by tweening object properties, you can also make an object appear to change over time. If you scale an Instance to a larger size and then tween it with another that's not scaled, the tweened Instances will be sized to create a smooth transition, as was the case in Figure 23-12. Any property of an Instance that can be independently modified can be tweened. These include the following:

✦ Transformations such as width, height, and skew made with the Transform tool, or with the Modify ➪ Transform submenu.

Note Fireworks always tweens two or more Instances of the same symbol, and as such, can't tween shapes (morphing) because the shapes of the Instances are always the same. If you want to tween shapes, you can do a blend in Macromedia FreeHand and then import the file into Fireworks and distribute the shapes to frames. You can also do a shape tween in Macromedia Flash, save the result as an Adobe Illustrator document, and then import that document into Fireworks in order to retain the vector information.

✦ Opacity and/or Blending modes adjusted in the Property inspector.

✦ Live Effects. As long as all the Instances have the same Live Effect applied, you can tween the properties of that Live Effect. If you want to make an object appear to go from not having an effect to having one, set the effect's settings to 0 on one of the Instances and a higher value on another.

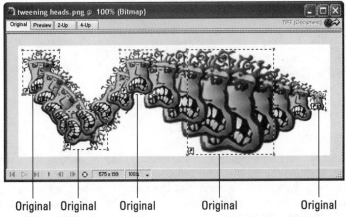

Original   Original   Original   Original   Original

Figure 23-13: Each Instance is a resting point, or a keyframe. Fireworks automatically creates the rest of the objects with tweening.

Fireworks always tweens from the canvas up; the lowest object in the stacking order is first, and the highest object last, as shown in Figure 23-14. If you're tweening more than two objects, adjust their stacking order to make sure that they tween in the order that you want them to.

Tip Don't be confused into thinking that objects tween from left to right across the canvas. The stacking order is always the guideline for tweening order.

After you set the stacking order to determine the order that objects get tweened, you also have to decide how many steps Fireworks should fill in between each object. Refer again to Figure 23-13. The number of steps in that tween was three, so Fireworks filled in three objects between each of the original Instances.

Original   Original

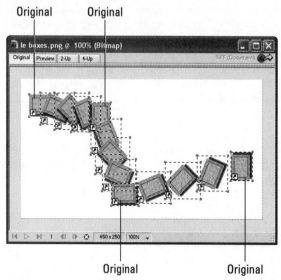

Original   Original

Figure 23-14: Four Instances become an entire animation after tweening. Note that Fireworks tweened according to the stacking order. The start of the tween is the object closest to the canvas, and the highest object in the stacking order is the end.

So far, we've tweened objects and created an interesting display across the canvas. Usually, though, you want to distribute your tweened objects to frames to create a real animation. You have the option to do this at the same time as the tweening, or you can select your tweened objects and click the Distribute to Frames button on the Frames panel at any time. Fireworks distributes objects to frames from bottom to top, the same way that it tweens, so that your objects stay in the correct order.

To tween Instances, follow these steps:

1. Create an object or a group of objects, and convert it to a symbol. Select the object and choose Modify ➪ Symbol ➪ Convert to Symbol. Name your symbol in the Symbol Properties dialog box, and click OK when you're done. Your object is converted into a symbol and stored in the Library. An Instance is left in its place on the canvas.

2. Choose Edit ➪ Duplicate, or use the keyboard shortcut, Ctrl+Alt+D (Command+Option+D) to create a copy of the Instance. Alternatively, you can create a duplicate Instance of your symbol by dragging it from the Library panel and dropping it onto the canvas. A copy of an Instance is also an Instance. Keep in mind that the duplicate is placed one higher in the stacking order.

3. Position the duplicate Instance to a spot on the canvas where you want the tween to stop.

4. Select both Instances either by dragging a selection box around them with your mouse, or by holding down the Shift key and clicking each one in turn.

5. Choose Modify ➪ Symbol ➪ Tween Instances.

Fireworks displays the Tween Instances dialog box (see Figure 23-15).

Figure 23-15: Set the number of steps to tween, and choose whether or not you want to distribute the objects to frames in the Tween Instances dialog box.

6. Enter the number of steps to tween. A setting of 3 makes Fireworks create three new objects between each of your original Instances.

7. Check Distribute to Frames to distribute the tweened objects to frames and make them into an animation. Click OK when you're done.

Fireworks creates the new objects, and you have an instant animation.

Fireworks technique: Tweening Filters

Unlike Live Effects, you can't really tween Filters, because they're applied directly to bitmap objects only. Applying them to linked objects also breaks the link and leaves you with regular bitmap objects. You can use tweening, though, to create an animation quickly, in which the only changes are the settings of the Filter as it's applied to each frame.

Cross-Reference

This example uses a Filter called Fire, which is part of a third-party package called Eye Candy, from Alien Skin Software. Fire is available in both Eye Candy 3.1 and Eye Candy 4000. If you don't have the full version of Eye Candy, use one of the Eye Candy 4000 LE filters included with Fireworks MX, or another third-party Filter — many are available free on the Web. For more information about Filters and about Eye Candy 4000, see Chapter 12.

To animate Filters in Fireworks, follow these steps:

1. Create the basic object or group to which you're going to apply the Filter, and then make the group or object into a symbol using Modify ➪ Symbol ➪ Convert to Symbol. Name your symbol in the Symbol Properties dialog and click OK when you're done. The symbol is placed in the Library and an Instance is left in its place.

2. Select your Instance and create another Instance directly on top of it by choosing either Edit ⇨ Clone, or by using the keyboard shortcut, Ctrl+Shift+D (Command+Shift+D).

3. Select both Instances by dragging a selection box around them. Alternatively, if they are the only objects in your document, you can select them both by choosing either Edit ⇨ Select All, or Ctrl+A (Command+A).

4. Create tweened Instances between your two Instances by choosing Modify ⇨ Symbol ⇨ Tween Instances.

   Fireworks displays the Tween Instances dialog box.

5. Set the number of steps to a small number, such as 5.

6. Uncheck the Distribute to Frames checkbox, and then click OK.

   Now we have a stack of identical objects, to which we're going to apply a Filter, changing the settings slightly each time so that each object looks slightly different.

7. Select all the Instances by dragging a selection around them with the mouse.

8. Choose Filters ⇨ Eye Candy 4000 ⇨ Fire.

   Fireworks displays the Fire dialog box for the first Instance.

9. Specify the settings that you want, and then click OK.

   Fireworks displays the Fire dialog box for the second Instance.

10. The controls are set the same way you left them after the first Instance. Modify the controls slightly to create a difference between this Instance and the previous one. Click OK when you're done.

    Fireworks displays the Fire dialog box for the third Instance.

11. Continue to change control settings slightly in each box as it appears, until you have modified all the Instances.

Tip   Clicking Cancel at any time in the Filter's dialog box cancels the operation for all the Instances.

12. With your Instances still selected, click the Distribute to Frames button (the filmstrip icon) on the Frames panel.

All Instances are distributed over frames to create an animation, such as the one in Figure 23-16. Preview your animation with the VCR controls on the bottom of the document window. Alternatively, you can choose File ⇨ Export Preview and preview your animation in the Export Preview dialog box, or choose a browser from the File ⇨ Preview in Browser submenu to see your work in a browser.

Fireworks technique: Tweening depth

A quick and useful effect that you can create with tweened Instances is 3D depth, wherein your object appears to fly out from the canvas.

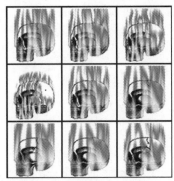

Figure 23-16: This animation depends entirely on the slight changes in the Fire effect applied to each Instance to make our subject's skull appear to be vigorously aflame.

To create a depth effect with tweened Instances, follow these steps:

1. Create the basic object or group that you're going to work with, and then convert it into a symbol using Modify ➪ Symbol ➪ Convert to Symbol. Name your symbol in the Symbol Properties dialog box, and click OK when you're done. The symbol is placed in the Library and an Instance is left in its place.

2. Move the Instance near the top of the canvas.

3. Choose Edit ➪ Clone, or use the keyboard shortcut, Ctrl+Shift+D (Command+Shift+D), to create another Instance directly on top of the first.

4. Hold down the Shift key and, at the same time, use the arrow down key to move the new Instance down the canvas, without moving it left or right. A few hundred pixels is usually all you can get away with while still keeping the depth effect resembling depth.

5. With the Instance still selected, choose Modify ➪ Transform ➪ Numeric Transform.

   Fireworks displays the Numeric Transform dialog box.

6. Scale the Instance to 30 percent of its size, by selecting Scale from the option list, checking Scale Attributes, checking Constrain Proportions, and entering 30 in one of the fields. Click OK when you're done.

7. Set the Instance's opacity to 10 percent by double-clicking it and entering 10 in the Opacity field on the Property inspector or on the Frames panel.

8. With the Instance still selected, choose Modify ➪ Arrange ➪ Send to Back, or press Ctrl+Shift+down arrow (Command+Shift+down arrow).

9. Hold down Shift and click each Instance to select all of them. If they are the only objects in your document, you can choose Edit ➪ Select All, or press Ctrl+A (Command+A).

10. Choose Modify ➪ Symbol ➪ Tween Instances.

   Fireworks displays the Tween Instances dialog box.

11. Set the number of steps you want in between the two Instances, uncheck Distribute to Frames, and then click OK.

   Fireworks tweens the Instances.

Tip   You can choose Edit ➪ Undo and then do Steps 10 and 11 again if you find that you want to change the number of steps.

12. If you prefer, you can select the original Instance and make it stand out by adding a Live Effect such as glow or inner bevel to it.

Your object now appears to fly out from the canvas (see Figure 23-17).

Figure 23-17: Fireworks created the steps between the front and back Instances with tweening. A little of the Glow Live Effect was then added to the front object to make it stand out.

Tip   To change this depth effect into an animation, select all the Instances by drawing a selection around them with the mouse (or, if they are the only objects in your document, choose Edit ➪ Select All), and then click the Distribute to Frames button on the Frames panel. Your object animates its way toward you.

Fireworks technique: Fading in and out

Fading an object in and out is a common effect that's easy to create in Fireworks. Tweening two Instances that are positioned in the same place on the canvas, one with an Opacity setting of 0 percent, and one with an opacity of 100 percent, produces a fade. The Instance that is highest in the stacking order determines whether it's a fade-in or a fade-out. In this section, we create an animation in which the object fades in, then fades back out, and then loops, so that it seems to fade in and out continuously.

To fade an object in and out, follow these steps:

1. Create the basic object or group to which you're going to apply the fade, and then convert the object or group into a symbol. Select it and choose Modify ➪ Symbol ➪ Convert to Symbol. Name your symbol in the Symbol Properties dialog box, and click OK when you're done. Your new symbol is stored in the Library and an Instance is left in its place.

2. Select the Instance and choose Edit ➪ Clone, or press Ctrl+Shift+D (Command+Shift+D), to create another Instance directly on top of it.

3. Open the Property inspector and set the Opacity of the new Instance to 0 percent.

> **Note** The Opacity setting might not seem to have any effect, because you're able to see the original Instance through the newer Instance, which is now transparent.

4. Choose Modify ➪ Arrange ➪ Send to Back to send the transparent Instance directly behind the original Instance.

5. Select both Instances by dragging a selection box around them. If they are the only objects in your document, you can select them by choosing either Edit ➪ Select All, or by using the keyboard shortcut, Ctrl+A (Command+A).

6. Choose Modify ➪ Symbol ➪ Tween Instances.

   Fireworks displays the Tween Instances dialog box.

7. Set the number of steps to 5.

> **Note** You can choose a different number of steps, if you prefer, but during this example, I count steps and frames as if you've chosen 5.

8. Check the Distribute to Frames checkbox, and then click OK.

   Play your animation. Your object should appear to fade in. You should have seven frames. In the first frame, the Instance is completely transparent (opacity of 0); in the second frame, the Instance is slightly more opaque, making it appear to fade in; and so on until the seventh frame, in which the Instance is fully opaque.

Note   At this point, you can choose to either leave your animation as is, or continue and make your animation appear to fade out as well.

9. Open the Frames panel and select the final frame in your animation to display it in the document window. This frame contains your fully opaque Instance.

10. Select the Instance and choose either Edit ⇨ Clone, or use the keyboard shortcut, Ctrl+Shift+D (Command+Shift+D), to create another Instance directly on top of the first.

11. Open the Property inspector and set the Opacity of the Instance to 0 percent.

12. Select both Instances by dragging a selection box around them. If they are the only objects in this frame, you can select them by choosing either Edit ⇨ Select All, or by using the keyboard shortcut, Ctrl+A (Command+A).

13. Choose Modify ⇨ Symbol ⇨ Tween Instances.

    Fireworks displays the Tween Instances dialog box.

14. Set the number of steps to the same number you used when fading the object in (in this case, 5).

15. Check the Distribute to Frames checkbox, and then click OK.

16. Select the final frame of your animation in the Frames panel and remove it by clicking the Delete Frame button (the Trash icon). This final frame is redundant, because the first frame is also a fully transparent object. Your animation loops more smoothly without it.

Click Play to preview your animation. The object appears to fade in and then fade out (see Figure 23-18). If you prefer, you can double-click the fully opaque frame in the middle of your animation (Frame 7 in the example), and specify a longer frame delay so that the pause between the fade-in and fade-out is longer. Choose File ⇨ Export Preview to preview your animation in the Export Preview dialog box, where it often runs more smoothly than in the document window.

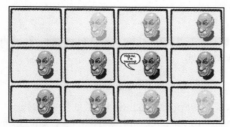

Figure 23-18: Fading an object in and out is easy with tweening.

Using Animation Symbols

Animation symbols are self-contained, multi-frame symbols with their own animation properties, such as number of frames, rotation, and scaling. You can create an animation symbol from any object, and it can even contain other symbols. As with graphic and button symbols, animation symbols are stored in the Library and can be reused.

You can graphically edit an animation symbol in the Symbol Editor, and its properties in the Object panel, or with the Modify ➪ Animate ➪ Settings command. You can edit its motion path directly in the document window.

Creating animation symbols

You can create a new animation symbol from scratch, or convert an existing object into an animation symbol.

To create an animation symbol, follow these steps:

1. Choose Edit ➪ Insert ➪ New Symbol.

   Fireworks displays the Symbol Properties dialog box, as shown in Figure 23-19.

Figure 23-19: Name your new symbol and specify animation in the Symbol Properties dialog box.

2. Enter a name for the new symbol.

3. Select the Animation radio button under Type. Click OK when you're done.

   Fireworks displays the Symbol Editor.

4. Use the drawing tools to create a new graphic.

5. Close the Symbol Editor window when you're done.

   Fireworks places the new animation symbol in the Library, and places a copy of it in your document.

6. To add new frames to the new animation symbol, select it on the canvas and adjust the Frames slider in the Property inspector.

7. To edit the symbol's animation properties, select it and choose Modify ➪ Animation ➪ Settings to display the Animate dialog box.

To convert an existing object into an animation symbol, follow these steps:

1. Select the object that you want to convert into an animation symbol.

2. Choose Modify ➪ Animation ➪ Animate Selection, or use the keyboard shortcut, Alt+Shift+F8 (Option+Shift+F8).

Fireworks displays the Animate dialog box, as shown in Figure 23-20.

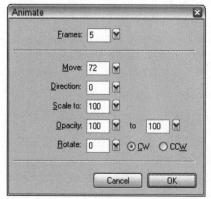

Figure 23-20: Modify animation settings in the Animate dialog box.

3. Modify the following settings in the Animate dialog box:

- **Frames:** The number of frames you want to include in the animation.

 The Frames slider only goes to 250, but you can type a higher number in the text field. Fireworks automatically adds the required number of frames to your document.

- **Movement:** The distance that you want each object to move. Possible values range from 0 to 250 pixels. The default is 72.

- **Direction:** The direction in which you want the object to move. Possible values range from 0 to 360 degrees.

- **Scaling:** The percent change in size from start to finish. The default is 100 percent. You can specify a number from 0 to 250.

- **Opacity:** Specifies how much to fade in or out from start to finish. Possible values range from 0, which is completely transparent, to 100 (the default), which is completely opaque.

- **Rotation:** The amount that the symbol rotates from start to finish, specified in degrees. The default is 0 degrees, which is no rotation. Specify 90 degrees for a quarter-turn, 180 for a half-turn, and 360 for a complete rotation. Enter a number higher than 360 to start a second rotation.

- **CW and CCW:** Clockwise and counterclockwise, respectively; determine the object's rotation direction.

4. Click OK when you're done.

Your new symbol is added to the Library, and a copy is placed on the canvas.

Editing an animation symbol

There may be a handful of skilled animators who can create the perfect animation symbol the first time through, but for most of us, the settings of our animation symbols require careful adjustment in order to achieve the desired effect.

You can use a number of methods to alter the settings of an animation symbol. Let's explore each of them.

Adjusting animation settings

Select an animation symbol and choose Modify ➪ Animation ➪ Settings to display the Animate dialog box. Alter any of the settings as desired.

 A discussion of the settings in the Animate dialog box is included earlier in this chapter, in the section "Creating animation symbols."

Using the Property inspector

When an animation symbol is selected, the Property inspector changes to display animation symbol options that are similar to the Animate dialog box, as shown in Figure 23-21. Modify any of these options to adjust the corresponding setting.

Figure 23-21: Use the Property inspector to modify animation symbol options.

Adjusting the motion path

When selected, Animation symbols display a motion path that describes their frame-by-frame movement across the canvas, as shown in Figure 23-22. The green dot on the motion path indicates the start of the animation's path, and the red dot shows the end point. The blue points on the path represent each frame of the animation. The object itself is shown on the current frame.

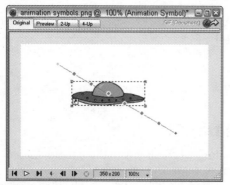

Figure 23-22: The motion path describes the movement of the animation symbol. The visible object is on the current frame, frame 4.

You can change the direction of the animation symbol's motion by changing the angle of the motion path. Drag one of the animation handles to a new location, as follows:

Tip   Hold down the Shift key while dragging to constrain the movement to perfectly horizontal or vertical.

✦ Move the green point to move the starting point of the animation.

✦ Move the red point to move the ending point of the animation.

✦ Move any blue point to move the object on the corresponding frame. Click a blue point to switch to that frame.

Converting into a graphic symbol

Choose Modify ➪ Animation ➪ Remove Animation to convert the animation symbol into a graphic symbol. Although your symbol is no longer animated, Fireworks retains the animation settings, in case you convert the symbol back into an animation symbol.

Removing the symbol

To remove an animation symbol from the Library, follow these steps:

1. Choose Window ➪ Library to display the Library panel.

2. In the Library panel, select the animation symbol you want to remove.

3. Click the Delete Symbol button (the trash can) on the Library panel.

4. Click Delete to remove the symbol.

Editing symbol graphics

Just as with button and graphic symbols, animation symbols are based on a graphic that you can edit in the Symbol Editor. When you modify the graphic that your animation symbol is based on, all of its instances — the copies on the canvas — inherit those changes, as well.

To edit the graphic in an animation symbol, follow these steps:

1. Select the animation symbol you want to edit.

2. Choose Modify ➪ Symbol @ Edit Symbol to open the Symbol Editor. Alternatively, you can choose Window ➪ Library and double-click your symbol in the Library panel.

3. Perform your graphical edits in the Symbol Editor.

4. Close the Symbol Editor window when you're done.

Cross-Reference

See Chapter 17 for more on the Symbol Editor.

Summary

Fireworks enables you to create and edit animation by using a variety of techniques, most of which revolve around the Frames panel. When working with animation in Fireworks, keep these points in mind:

✦ The overall weight of your animated GIF is always a consideration. Every creative decision must be examined for its effect on file size.

✦ The Frames panel is the heart of Fireworks' animation tools, but the Layers panel is also important.

✦ Each frame in your Fireworks document resembles a frame of a filmstrip. Copy objects to other frames by using the Frames panel, and then change the objects' locations on the canvas or their properties to create animation.

✦ Layers can be shared across multiple frames, to manage static objects better in an animation.

✦ Onion Skinning enables you to view and edit multiple frames simultaneously.

✦ The Web design opportunities for animated GIF images are numerous, such as animated rollover buttons, sliced animations, and animated browser backgrounds.

✦ Tweening is a great time- and work-saver because Fireworks fills in the middle elements of an animation automatically. Any selection of two or more instances of the same symbol can be tweened.

✦ Fireworks tweens objects starting at the bottom of the stacking order, nearest the canvas, and moving up.

✦ Distribute a tweened sequence to frames to create an instant animation.

✦ You can use tweening to create advanced effects, such as objects fading in and out, or flying out from the canvas.

✦ Animation symbols provide an intuitive way to work with animations.

In the next chapter, you look at how you can apply animation techniques to create that most common species of animated GIF: the banner ad.

✦   ✦   ✦

Animating Banner Ads

Banner ads are nearly ubiquitous on today's Web, and have contributed enormously to the rapid growth of the World Wide Web. After you have a sponsored banner ad on a page, the page begins to pay for itself, and you crave hits — requests for files made to your server — rather than worrying about the bandwidth costs of a page that grows too popular.

Understanding Banner Ad Basics

Banner ads are where animated GIF images really shine. You want a Web advertisement to be eye-catching and universally viewable, and animated GIF images are really the only choice. When does an animated GIF stop being an animated GIF and start being a banner ad? Four elements are involved:

  ♦ It is a certain size in width and height.

  ♦ It is below a certain weight in kilobytes.

  ♦ It is placed on a Web page.

  ♦ It advertises something.

Let's take a closer look at each of these points in the following sections.

Examining size — IAB/CASIE standards

When banner ads started to proliferate on the Web, it became apparent that some sort of standard sizing scheme would benefit both the advertisers and the sites displaying the advertising. If you have a Web site on which you leave a 450×50-pixel space in your design for a banner ad, and I then send you one that's 460×60, we have a problem. If ten other people send you ten other ads, all slightly different in size, then the problem becomes a big problem.

To solve this problem, the Standards and Practices committee of the Internet Advertising Bureau (IAB) and the Coalition for Advertising Supported Information and Entertainment (CASIE) got together, looked at the sizes everybody was using, and came up with a list of standard sizes. They offered this list as a recommendation to the ad buyers and sellers, who overwhelmingly accepted the list. Almost all ads on the Web now follow the IAB/CASIE standards.

Note For more about the IAB/CASIE standards, visit the IAB at `http://www.iab.net` or CASIE at `http://www.casie.com`.

Table 24-1 details the standard banner ad sizes and their names. Full Banner is by far the most common type of ad, with Micro Button probably in second place, but other sizes are gaining popularity as Web sites display advertising in newer and smaller spaces, such as margins and even inline with content. If you don't know which size to choose, choose Full Banner, 468×60.

On the CD-ROM The companion CD-ROM includes a set of Fireworks PNG format files, one for each banner ad size, that you can use as templates when creating banner ads in Fireworks.

Table 24-1
IAB/CASIE Advertising Banner Sizes

Pixel Dimensions	Name
468×60	Full Banner
392×72	Full Banner with Vertical Navigation Bar
234×60	Half Banner
125×125	Square Button
88×31	Micro Button
120×90	Button 1
120×60	Button 2
120×240	Vertical Banner

Tip These days, most people surf the Web with a display that's capable of 800×600 or greater resolution, and many Web sites are now constructed to take up the extra horizontal real estate. Advertisers have responded with the occasional 600×60 ad banner. Although this size is not in the IAB/CASIE specification, you might consider using these wide banners under some circumstances. Make sure that the site(s) you plan to advertise on will accept this banner size.

Looking at weight

In addition to making sure your banner ads are the correct dimensions, you need to consider their weight (file size). No "one true standard" exists for banner ad file sizes. Many Webmasters set an upper limit on weight, beyond which they won't accept your ad. If you're designing an ad for a specific site, check with its Webmaster first to see what the limit is, or at least check the weight of some of the ads that are already on that site. If you're not designing for a specific site, a general rule is to aim for less than 10K, and certainly to keep it under 12K. If you can produce an exciting ad in 8K, so much the better. Your ad downloads quickly, and more viewers see your entire message.

Putting it in the page

Obviously, a banner ad is as much an image as any other GIF, and the most basic way to place a banner ad in a page is with an ordinary `<img>` tag. When you export HTML from Fireworks, this is exactly the way you find your banner ad displayed.

Typically, though, most Web sites that depend on advertising have some sort of dynamic scheme for rotating through a series of banner ads, so that ads are added to pages on-the-fly by the server. Visitors who return to a page get an entirely new ad instead of seeing the same one again. The server also keeps track of how many times it displays each ad because the sponsor pays for the ad to be displayed a certain number of times.

Implementing a banner ad rotation system is not nearly as hard as it might sound. The Web has many low-cost and even free CGI (Common Gateway Interface) scripts. A few hours of work and even the smallest site can start serving ads like the big guys.

Tip

A good place to start looking for the appropriate CGI script for your needs is the CGI Resource Index at `www.cgi-resources.com`.

Advertising it

Although a complete course in Madison Avenue advertising methods is well beyond the scope of this book, it doesn't hurt to at least know the lingo:

✦ A *page view* or *page impression* is one Web page served with your ad on it.

✦ A *hit* is one request by a browser for one file — an HTML document, or an image or multimedia file — from your server. Many people use "hits" and "page views" interchangeably, but one Web page might be made up of 20 individual files, while another page is only 10 files. As a result, it's best to define your terms, and seek common ground when discussing "hits."

✦ *CPM* is the cost per one thousand (Roman numeral M) page views. This is the standard way that ad space is bought and sold on the Web. A site with excellent demographics could demand a higher cost-per-one-thousand ads served.

✦ A *click-through* is one specific time when a viewer is interested enough in a banner ad to click it and go to the advertiser's site. The Web average for click-throughs might be less than 1 percent.

✦ The *click rate* is the percentage of people who click-through a particular ad.

✦ *Mindshare* is basically brand recognition. Even though Web users don't click-through banner ads the way advertisers once hoped they would, studies have shown that people do look at banner ads and take the brand away with them.

Fireworks Technique: Creating a Banner Ad

Although banner ads are often created by a chain gang of ad people, copywriters, producers, Web artists, and others, a good way to work on the techniques involved is to just dive in and start creating ad campaigns for fictional companies of your own creation. This is exactly what we do as we go step-by-step through the process of creating a banner ad in Fireworks.

On the CD-ROM

The *Mundane Magazine* example banner ad created for this section is in both the original Fireworks PNG format and the exported animated GIF.

Step I: Set the stage

The very first step in creating a banner ad is to make sure you know what size it should be. Although you may sometimes come up with a creative idea that would dictate using a certain size, most of the time when you sit down to make a banner ad, the space has already been allotted. I follow the IAB/CASIE standards with my banner ad, and make a 468×60 Full Banner, which can be displayed on almost any Web site that accepts advertising.

Step II: Write the script

Now that you have a suitable "blank page" of the right size and shape, you are ready to sit and stare at it while you come up with an idea. All the same things that apply to regular animations apply to banner ads with regard to making a concise statement, planning ahead, and watching file size.

Let's face it: A 10K or 12K banner ad is not going to get into serious character development, or include a lot of scene changes or scenery. If you can't express your idea in a few lines, it probably won't fit into the banner. Think "bumper sticker" and you'll probably be more successful.

My ad is for a fictional magazine called *Mundane Magazine*. It's a hip, youth-oriented magazine about the Web. I want to make something that attracts the attention of the target audience of young, hip Web surfers. Here's the pitch for my ad: "A UFO crash lands on a barren alien landscape. The pilot thinks, '&*/$.'" Not much of a plot line, but again, what do you want from 12K?

Step III: Create the cast of characters

Our little movie has a stage and a script. Now it needs a cast.

Banner ads are deliberately sized as small as can be, and I find the dimensions a bit of a constraint when I'm drawing. Objects in banner ads are often cropped, scaled down, or halfway off the canvas. So I like to draw and build objects in a second, larger document window (see Figure 24-1); sort of a scratchpad — or, to keep the showbiz analogy going, a backstage area where objects wait to be placed in their scenes. Because Fireworks objects always remain editable and can be easily dragged and dropped between documents, this backstage area is a convenient way to work.

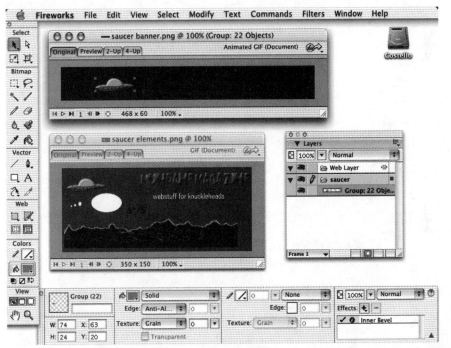

Figure 24-1: Use a second document as a scratchpad or backstage area when building objects for use in a banner ad to avoid working entirely within the puny confines of the ad itself.

Complex effects, such as drop shadows and glows, increase the weight of the final animated GIF quite a bit because flat colors compress better in the GIF format. Concentrate on drawing good-looking objects, and leave the effects for later. If your final animation is underweight (yeah, right), then you can easily go back and add some effects to objects.

These elements make up the "cast" in my ad:

✦ Some rugged, otherworldly mountains to serve as a setting

✦ Some text of the magazine's name and catchphrase

✦ A flying saucer to do the crash-landing

✦ A thought bubble with the word "&*/$." in it

Reusing Design Elements

The tiny face that banner ads present to the world can be very limiting creatively, but there is one major advantage: Design elements and even bitmap images that were originally created for a Web site or print media are easily scaled down and reused without losing quality. Creating a banner ad for a Web site often means you have no end of big logos and artwork readily available for repurposing in a banner ad, as shown in the following figure.

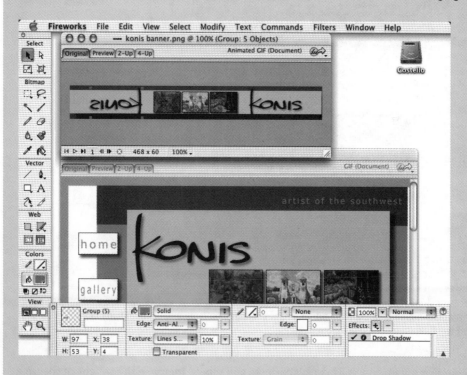

Although this strategy is efficient from a production standpoint, it's also valid from a design perspective to maintain a consistent look between a Web site and a banner ad that advertises it.

Each of these elements can be thought of as a cast member, an independent entity that we need to tell what to do as we make our ad.

Step IV: Direct the action

Now you're ready to start putting the objects where they go. Create a layer for each of your cast members. I have four cast members, and I have a pretty good idea of the order in which they should be stacked: The background should be on the bottom and the text should be on the top, so I made four layers:

✦ Text

✦ Bubble

✦ Saucer

✦ Background

Figure 24-2 shows these layers and shows that the mountains are placed into the layer called background, which is then shared so that it appears in every frame. I can lock the background layer now and forget about it.

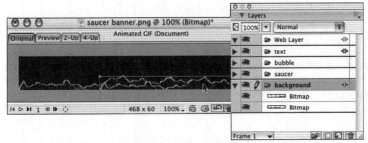

Figure 24-2: The background is going to stay the same throughout the animation, so the background layer is shared. This layer is now the same in every frame.

Tip　To share a layer, double-click its name in the Layers panel to view the Layer Options dialog box and check the Shared Across Frames box.

Splitting up objects onto their own layers enables you to share a layer at any time, if you decide that a cast member should be static. I'm not sure yet whether the text with the name of the magazine and the catch phrase is going to be static. It probably will be, but I might get to change that after I see my animated GIF's weight. For now, I place the text in the banner and share its layer, too.

At this point, the first frame is basically done. The mountains and logo are in place, and the UFO hasn't appeared yet. I like to build the last frame next, which is where the animation rests before looping. I want to make sure that the UFO and the thought bubble are the right size, so that they hang together nicely in that frame, before I animate them through a bunch of middle frames (see Figure 24-3). Creating the first and last frames before the others often makes filling in the middle frames a lot easier. Naming your first and last frame with descriptive names helps ensure that you always keep them first and last. Double-click the frame's name in the Frames panel to open a dialog box in which you can provide a name.

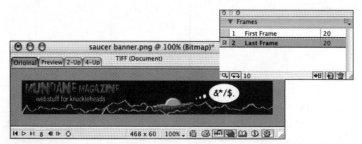

Figure 24-3: After you finish the first frame, create a new frame in which to build the last frame. Your two-frame animation now has a start and finish — named First Frame and Last Frame, here — which makes building the middle much easier.

Finally, I'm ready to start some serious animating. In the first frame, the UFO hasn't appeared yet; in the last frame, it has landed. I'm going to copy the UFO from the last frame, paste it into the first frame, and then move it to the top of the canvas, so that it's just peeking in.

So, in Frame 1, the saucer is just appearing. I want the next frame to be almost identical, except that the saucer should move a little bit closer to its landing site. The saucer doesn't have far to travel, and I would like it to do so in seven or eight frames, so that the whole animation is nine or ten frames long. Keeping the animation in a small area and on a small number of frames limits its file size.

You can distribute objects to their own frames at any time with the Distribute to Frames button on the Frames panel, so it's often easiest to build an animation entirely within Frame 1. In my case, I just keep duplicating and arranging copies of the saucer in the correct positions on the canvas. Eventually, Frame 1 contains a bunch of saucers in the correct positions on the canvas, but in the wrong frames, as shown in Figure 24-4.

Tip

The quickest way to duplicate objects is to drag them while holding down the Alt (Option) key.

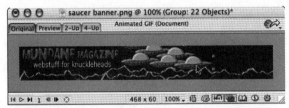

Figure 24-4: Duplicating the saucer and moving the copies into the correct positions on the canvas gets them ready to be distributed to their own frames.

Cross-Reference

If your animation features an object that moves in a straight line, use tweening to generate the intermediate steps. Tweening is covered in Chapter 23.

Because the last frame is already done, I want to manually create frames before clicking the Distribute to Frames button, so that Fireworks doesn't have to create any frames and overlap my final frame. I have seven saucers in Frame 1, so I need six new frames after Frame 1.

After distributing the saucers to frames, I can preview my animation by using the VCR controls. If necessary, I tweak the saucer's descent by moving it a bit to the left or right in certain frames, until I get the effect that I want, which is a bit of a rough landing.

When you get to the point where your animation is actually playing, the inevitable rewrites begin. In my case, I decided that I didn't want the thought bubble to be the last frame. Instead, the last three frames should go: Saucer lands, thought bubble appears, and then thought bubble disappears. I also realized that the "landed" saucer needs a little chewing up to emphasize that it has "crashed."

Chewing up the saucer is pretty easy, but it appears in Frame 7 and Frame 8. After modifying it in Frame 7, I selected it on the canvas and Alt-dragged (Option-dragged) its selection icon in the Frames panel (see Figure 24-5) from Frame 7 to Frame 8. This copies the selection from Frame 7 to Frame 8.

The quickest way to get that extra frame on the end is simply to duplicate the last frame, and then delete the thought bubble out of it. I lose very little in bandwidth this way, because the last two frames are almost identical, and the only addition to the final frame is more flat color where the thought bubble was. Duplicating the last frame is as simple as dragging it in the Frame panel to the New Frame button.

The only thing that's left now is to set the frame timing, so that the last three frames are a little slower. The frame timing, looping, and such are set either in the Frames panel, or on the Animation tab of the Export Preview dialog box. Working in the Export Preview dialog box, shown in Figure 24-6, sometimes provides smoother animation playback than the document window, and a centralized access point for animation controls. You can see that the last three frames are set to one second, two seconds, and one second, specified in hundredths of a second. I tested a few combinations of speeds by using the VCR controls in the Export Preview dialog box. Looping is set to 10 times, which is long enough that it loops for about a minute because my banner takes a little over five seconds to play. At that point, it becomes a static banner that still invites the viewer to visit *Mundane Magazine*, without annoying them by continuing to flash away.

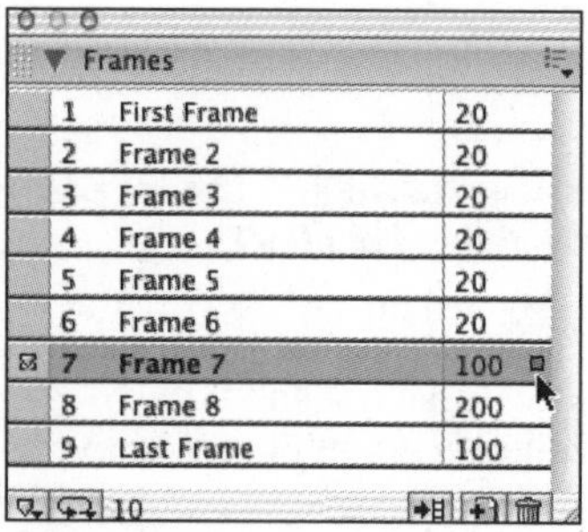

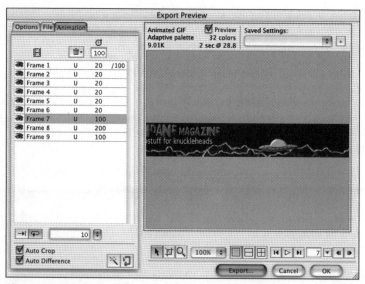

Figure 24-5: Dragging the selection icon in the Frames panel from frame to frame moves a selection. Alt-dragging (Option-dragging) copies the selection.

Figure 24-6: Set the timing of individual frames, and set the looping for the whole animation.

Tip If you don't set looping to forever, make sure the last frame of your animation has all the pertinent details, so that it provides enough information to get your message across on its own.

Step V: Leave the excess on the cutting-room floor

Don't be afraid to be brutal when exporting your animation and creating the animated GIF image itself. Remember that your focus is to get a message across quickly—not to win awards for the most colors, or the most profound use of animation. My banner came in just under 12K, but if it were any bigger, I would definitely have to consider one of the following options:

✦ Cut some frames, which might make the animation less smooth.

✦ Move the saucers closer together from frame to frame, so that the area that's animated is smaller.

✦ Flatten some areas, such as the bumpy, textured mountains. Areas of solid, flat color compress better.

✦ Take out some colors by cutting the palette further.

✦ Remove effects, such as the inner bevel on the text and the saucer, again to gain more areas of flat color.

✦ Make some objects smaller, such as the text, so that more of the flat, blue background is showing, resulting in better compression.

Sometimes, swallowing your creative pride can lead to a better overall presentation and a fast-loading, attention-attracting banner ad that's ready to take a message to the Web.

The final *Mundane Magazine* banner is exploded in Figure 24-7.

Cross-Reference Turn to the color insert for another look at the example banner ads from this chapter.

Fireworks Technique: Using Blur to Save Frames

Generally, you want your ads to be dynamic and fast-moving, but as with everything on the Web, bandwidth is always an issue. Every frame that you add to your banner increases the file size.

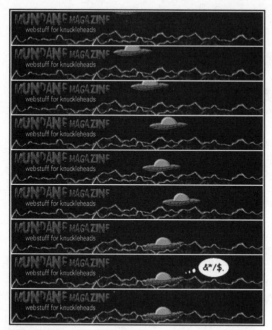

Figure 24-7: The finished banner ad keeps the animation in a small area and in a small number of frames. The flat color background compresses well. The banner weighs under 12K.

A common technique for creating a feeling of action and speed in a banner ad, without increasing the frame count and file size drastically, is to use a motion blur filter (such as the Eye Candy 4000 LE Motion Trail filter included with Fireworks) to get an object from point A to point B, as shown in Figure 24-8. Instead of moving across the banner in five or six frames, the saucer takes three steps from when it first appears to when it stops moving, but still seems to fill the intervening space. Without the Motion Trail filter, spacing the saucer so far apart would give it the appearance of disappearing and reappearing instead of moving.

Tip   This second *Mundane Magazine* banner reuses elements from the banner created earlier in this chapter. Creating banner ad "sequels" is a pretty common practice, building on the recognition of an earlier ad.

You can also make objects seem to be moving more quickly by altering their opacity settings. The motion-blurred saucers in Figure 24-7 have an opacity setting of 70 percent. Experimenting with the opacity setting and the controls in the Eye Candy 4000 LE Motion Trail filter can lead to impressive results.

Figure 24-8: The saucer seems to quickly fly across the banner, at the meager expense of just three frames.

On the CD-ROM Find the animated GIF banner ad detailed in this section, as well as the Fireworks PNG file, on the accompanying CD-ROM.

Summary

Banner ads are a practical and popular application of the animated GIF. When creating banner ads in Fireworks, keep these things in mind:

✦ Standard sizes exist for banner ads. Before you create a banner ad, make sure that you've selected the correct size so that your banner ad can be used on the widest variety of Web sites.

✦ Many Web sites have upper limits on the file sizes accepted. Generally, banner ads should be under 12K.

✦ Use motion blur to cut out frames without slowing down the action.

In the next chapter, you look at customizing Fireworks.

✦   ✦   ✦

Programming with Fireworks

One of the most amazing things about Fireworks MX is the way it can be controlled by scripts written in JavaScript, the most common scripting language for Web authoring. Fireworks offers many ways to customize the way you work with the program. In Part VII we look at each of them and discover the extensive Fireworks JavaScript API (Application Programming Interface). The final chapter explores the brave new world of Fireworks extensions and describes how you can use Flash to create user interfaces for such commands.

Customizing Fireworks

Web development has become an incredibly diverse field. It spans the range from the person building a personal home page, all the way to incredibly complex Web applications that generate pages on the fly and provide functionality that has traditionally only been found in stand-alone applications. With the variety of technologies in use on the Web today, imagining a Web development tool that could be all things to all people, without demonstrating an amazing degree of flexibility, is hard.

Macromedia has certainly demonstrated with Fireworks that it believes an extensible Web tool is a good Web tool. Almost every feature can be accessed through the extensive JavaScript API, and many features are executed in easy-to-modify HTML and JavaScript. Preferences are easily exposed in a simple text file. Extensions are added by dropping them in the appropriate subfolder of the Configuration folder, inside the Fireworks program folder.

In this chapter, I show you some of the ways that you can customize Fireworks and create your own ultimate Web graphics editor.

Using the HTML and JavaScript Engine

Part of the explosive growth of the Web is due to the relative accessibility of the underlying code. HTML is — as programming languages go — extremely easy to learn and abundantly available. Whereas JavaScript is more difficult, it is far more open than any compiled programming language, such as C or C++. The Fireworks engineers applied this accessibility to a novel approach: Portions of Fireworks itself are written in HTML and JavaScript, stored as simple text files in subfolders of Fireworks' Configuration folder.

Fireworks uses JavaScript and HTML templates to output JavaScript and HTML code; scripts that automate tasks in Fireworks are written in JavaScript. This open approach makes it easy for Web designers to customize many aspects of their Fireworks workflow completely.

Scriptlets are stand-alone JavaScript files that run on Fireworks itself. They can be placed in Fireworks' Commands folder and run from the Commands menu, run with the Commands ➪ Run Script command, or opened like any Fireworks document — with a double-click. Scriptlets have their own icon, as shown in Figure 25-1. Double-clicking a scriptlet, or dropping it onto the Fireworks icon, launches Fireworks and executes the scriptlet.

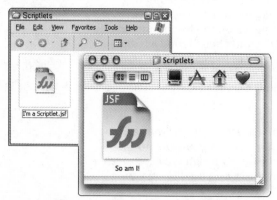

Figure 25-1: Fireworks scriptlets — JSF files — are stand-alone JavaScripts that run on Fireworks.

On Windows machines, scriptlets are their own file type, with the .jsf filename extension. Create or edit a scriptlet as a regular text file, and then change the filename extension from .txt to .jsf when you're ready to run it.

On the Mac, a scriptlet is a text file with a Fireworks Creator code, just as a Fireworks document is a PNG image with a Fireworks Creator code. Compile the following AppleScript as an application in Script Editor, and drop files on it to convert them to Fireworks' Creator code. Dropping a text file marks the text file as a scriptlet; dropping a PNG image marks it as a Fireworks PNG document. Alternatively, use a utility, such as File Buddy or FinderPop, to change Mac Creator and/or File Type codes.

```
on open
   tell application "Finder"
     set creator type of every file of selection to "MKBY"
   end tell
end open
```

You can use scriptlets to do an amazing range of tasks. Anything that the Fireworks API can access is fair game, and that's a fair number of things. Scriptlets can change preference settings, automate tasks, batch process files, and more.

Scriptlets are also commands. Placing scriptlets in the Commands folder and choosing their name from the Commands menu runs them from within Fireworks. Alternatively, you can run a scriptlet from within Fireworks by choosing Commands ⇨ Run Script and navigating to a scriptlet within the Open dialog box that follows.

Cross-Reference To make your own scriptlets, study the JavaScript API in Chapter 26.

Examining the Configuration Folder

Starting with the MX version, Dreamweaver is compatible with multiple-user operating systems including Windows NT, 2000, and XP as well as Mac OS 9 and Mac OS X. This compatibility means that multiple users can work with a single installation of the program but maintain their own preferences and configuration.

To achieve such flexibility, Dreamweaver maintains customized files in a special folder for each user. These folders are stored in different locations according to the operating system. Under multiple-user systems, the folders are within the specified user folder, designated by the user's ID or login name as shown in Table 25-1 and Table 25-2. You may wish to refer to these tables are you proceed through the chapter.

Table 25-1		
Default Windows User File Locations		
Operating System	*Multiple Users*	*Default Location*
Windows 98	No	C:\Windows\Application Data\Macromedia\Fireworks MX
Windows 98	Yes	C:\Windows\Profiles\<username>\Application Data\Macromedia\Fireworks MX
Windows ME	No	C:\Windows\Application Data\Macromedia\Fireworks MX
Windows ME	Yes	C:\Windows\Profiles\<username>\Application Data\Macromedia\Fireworks MX
Windows NT	—	C:\WinNT\Profiles\<username>\Application Data\Macromedia\Fireworks MX
Windows 2000	—	C:\Documents and Settings\<username>\Application Data\Macromedia\Fireworks MX
Windows XP	—	C:\Documents and Settings\<username>\Application Data\Macromedia\Fireworks MX

Table 25-2
Default Macintosh User File Locations

Operating System	Multiple Users	User Type	Default Location
Mac OS 9	No	—	Macintosh HD/System Folder/Application Support/Macromedia/Fireworks MX
Mac OS 9	Yes	Admin	Macintosh HD/System Folder/Preferences/Macromedia/Fireworks MX
Mac OS 9	Yes	User	Macintosh HD/Users/<username>/Preferences/Macromedia/Fireworks MX
Mac OS X	—	—	Macintosh HD/Users/<username>/Library/Application Support/Macromedia/Fireworks MX

The geographic heart of Fireworks' extensibility and customization is the Configuration folder, shown in Figure 25-2. You can find the Configuration folder within your Fireworks program folder as well as in the Configuration folder within your user folder on a multiple-user OS. Subfolders of the Configuration folder contain files that relate in a certain way to extending a particular feature of Fireworks. Placing additional files in these folders can add new textures to your texture list, more commands to your Commands menu, additional Flash panels to your Window menu, or more plug-ins to your Filters menu. Many of these files are text files containing HTML and JavaScript that you can easily customize.

Figure 25-2: The Configuration folder is the place to add custom files.

Dreamweaver users have long been making and trading Dreamweaver objects, Behaviors, and commands on the Web. Some of the same sources for Dreamweaver extensions are good for Fireworks commands, templates, and other files. There are some Fireworks-only spots, as well. Some good sources include the following:

✦ Macromedia's Fireworks Exchange at `http://www.macromedia.com/ exchange/` (click on Fireworks)

✦ Joseph Lowery's Fireworks, etc. at `http://www.idest.com/fireworks/`

✦ Derren Whiteman's Fireworks page at `http://www.derren.com/geek/ fireworks/`

✦ Kleanthis Economou's `http://www.projectfireworks.com/`

✦ Massimo Foti's excellent site at `http://www.massimocorner.com/`

As well as using extensions created by others, you can, of course, create your own. Modifying existing code is the easiest way to get quick results and better understand Fireworks capabilities. Always work on a copy of the file you are customizing, so that the original is still available, though.

Batch Code

Located only in the Configuration folder within the Fireworks program folder, the Batch code templates are placed in the Batch Code folder. By default, the Batch Code folder contains just two files: BatchGen.jst and BatchTemplate.jst.

Command Panels

This folder can be found in both the Fireworks Configuration folder as well as within the user folder if you're running a multiple-user OS. Third-party Flash panel commands are stored in the Command panels folder. The ones in the Fireworks Configuration folder show up for all users while files in the specific user's Command Panels folder are only available to that particular user.

Commands

Available in the Fireworks Configuration folder as well as your user folder, the Commands folder contains scriptlets. Each scriptlet in the Commands folder appears as a menu command in Fireworks' Commands menu.

Open a Command scriptlet in a text editor, or in Dreamweaver's Code view, and you'll see that it contains simple JavaScript code. Almost every feature of Fireworks is accessible through the Fireworks JavaScript API. Custom Functions such as `dom.applyEffects()` and `dom.setDocumentCanvasSize()` give commands the capability to automate otherwise repetitive tasks, extending the native Fireworks feature set. Even with all that, my favorite thing about commands is that you don't even have to write code to make them, thanks to the History panel.

By default, Fireworks includes 24 commands organized into 4 folders, with 6 individual commands in the Commands folder itself. New commands are added by dropping files into the Commands folder or by installing extensions using the Extension Manager. Any scriptlet within the Commands folder itself, or within subfolders one level down, are displayed in the Commands menu in Fireworks, so that you can run them by choosing a menu item. New additions are immediately available without restarting Fireworks.

Cross-Reference   Find out more about commands in Chapter 19, and study the Fireworks API in Chapter 26.

Extensions

This folder contains files used by the Extension Manager to install third-party commands. You should not touch the files within this folder because the Extension Manager needs them to remove or disable any installed commands.

jsextensions

Most computer programs are written in the C or C++ languages, and compiled into impenetrable object form before release. Fireworks leaves many functions accessible by JavaScript. More JavaScript functionality can be added through the use of C Libraries, added to Fireworks by dropping them into the jsextensions folder. By default, this folder contains the MMNotes extension.

Export Settings

The Export Settings folder, located in your user folder for multiple-user operating systems, is empty by default. When you save export settings as a preset in the Optimize panel — using the Save Settings command on the Options menu — Fireworks creates a similarly named text file in the Export Settings folder. The file contains a description of the saved setting that you can copy to another machine in order to standardize export settings across a workgroup, for example.

HTML code

Fireworks HTML output templates are stored in the HTML Code folder in the Configuration subfolder within the Fireworks application folder. HTML output templates are HyperText templates (.htt) that tell Fireworks how to create a particular "flavor" of HTML. For example, outputting HTML from Fireworks using the Dreamweaver template creates a file that fools Dreamweaver into thinking that it's a home-cooked Dreamweaver page.

Templates are stored within a subfolder of the HTML Code folder, with the folder name specifying the name of the template. By default, Fireworks offers Dreamweaver, GoLive, FrontPage, and Generic output (see Figure 25-3).

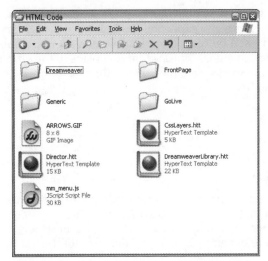

Figure 25-3: The subfolders of the HTML Code folder specify your HTML output options within Fireworks.

Because HTML Code templates are standard HTML and JavaScript, modifying a default template, or creating your own from scratch, is possible.

To enable a new template, follow these steps:

1. Using Windows Explorer or the Macintosh Finder, create a new folder within the HTML Code folder. The new folder should have a unique name to identify the template easily.

2. Name your new or modified template slices.css and place it into your new folder.

3. In Fireworks, choose File ➪ HTML Setup to display the HTML Setup dialog box.

4. On the General tab, choose your new template from the HTML Style option list. Click OK when you're done.

Restarting Fireworks to use the newly installed template is not necessary.

Cross-Reference

For more about the HTML Setup dialog box, see Chapter 3.

Libraries

The Libraries folder, located in the Configuration subfolder within the Fireworks application folder, contains Fireworks PNG images that typically contain Symbol Libraries. The Libraries folder contains just four files, initially, containing example animations, bullets, buttons, and themes. Symbol Libraries are regular Fireworks documents that contain symbols, created by exporting symbols from the Library panel. You can convert commonly used buttons, graphics, and clip art into symbols and store them in Symbol Libraries. Symbol Libraries that you place in the Libraries folder are easily accessed within Fireworks from the Edit ⇨ Libraries submenu, which displays each file as a menu item.

Explore Libraries in Chapter 17.

Nav Menu

Styles stored in the Nav Menu folder, in the user folder on multiple-user operating systems, are available to the Set Pop-Up Menu Behavior, for use when creating pop-up menus. Copy style files from the Configuration/Styles folder, or export individual styles from the Styles panel and save them in Configuration/Nav Menu.

See Chapter 21 for more about the Set Pop-up Menu behavior.

Patterns

Patterns are full-color images saved in standard Fireworks PNG format. Initially, the Patterns folder contains 46 Patterns, featuring things such as bricks, jeans, and wood. You can create any image in Fireworks and save it in the Patterns folder. After a Fireworks restart, it's available for use as a Pattern from the Patterns option list in the Fill panel. The Patterns folder is located in the Configuration subfolder within the Fireworks Application folder.

I detail Patterns in Chapter 11.

Styles

Fireworks Style files are given the filename extension .stl and, on the Mac, have the file type STYf.

Although the Styles panel contains numerous default Styles, you can easily store many Styles in one Fireworks Style file. Although Style files are typically stored in the Styles folder, within the user folder on multi-user systems, that doesn't make them immediately accessible within Fireworks. To use the Styles from a particular Style file, import the file using the Styles panel.

When you first install Fireworks, the Styles folder contains one file called Style Defaults.stl. As the name implies, this file contains the default Styles that you can reload into the Styles panel by choosing Reset Styles from the Styles panel Options menu. Copy the Style Defaults.stl file to another name, and replace it with your own favorite to make those favorites quickly accessible with the Reset Styles command.

 I cover Styles in Chapter 16.

Textures

The Textures folder, within the Fireworks application's Configuration folder, contains Fireworks PNG images that are used as textures in Fireworks. Files in the Textures folder show up as textures on the Textures option list in the Fill and Stroke panels.

Textures are images that are overlaid on objects in Fireworks, using the Fill section of the Property inspector to give the appearance of a textured surface. Although the images themselves can be full color, a texture is always converted to grayscale when it's applied in Fireworks. PNG images you add to the Textures folder are available for use after a Fireworks restart. Fireworks includes 49 textures by default, including things like sand, grass, and smoke.

 Learn to create your own textures in Chapter 11.

URL Libraries

When you first install Fireworks, the URL Libraries folder (in the user folder for systems supporting multiple users) contains the single, completely empty file called URLs.htm.

An important part of any Web development is obviously the creation and management of hyperlinks. Rather than laboriously typing URL after URL into Fireworks whenever they're needed, you can list them in an HTML document and drop the document into the URL Libraries folder. Access the file from the URL Panel and easily apply URLs to Web objects by pointing and clicking.

 Find out more about URL Libraries in Chapter 18.

Plug-Ins

The Plug-Ins folder contains Fireworks Filters and Photoshop-compatible effects plug-ins. Adding Photoshop plug-ins to Fireworks is as simple as dropping them — or shortcuts (aliases) to them somewhere else on your computer — into the Filters folder. Typically, they live in their own subfolders. Where they sit on the Filters menu is determined by settings contained within the plug-ins themselves. Restart Fireworks after adding plug-ins, and access them from the Filters menu or the Effects section of the Property inspector.

Initially, the Plug-Ins folder contains the Eye Candy 4000 LE and Splat! Photoshop-compatible filters. While this folder is in the Fireworks application folder, and not within its Configuration folder, it is covered here as it behaves in a similar manner to those previously mentioned.

Cross-Reference   I cover Filters in Chapter 12.

Looking at the Fireworks MX Preferences File

Fireworks offers you a graphical look into its preference settings with the Preferences dialog box, accessed within Fireworks by choosing Edit ⇨ Preferences. Although the choices it offers are extensive, they are just a subset of the complete preference settings contained in the Fireworks Preferences file.

Cross-Reference   Chapter 3 details the Preferences dialog box.

The Fireworks Preferences file is found in different locations depending on your operating system. To determine the location of your Preference file, please see Table 25-1 and Table 25-2 earlier in this chapter.

Note   In Windows, the Fireworks MX Preferences file is called Fireworks MX Preferences.txt in the Fireworks MX user folder. Also note that some versions of Windows are set to hide the last four characters of filenames by default, so the file may appear to be called simply Fireworks MX Preferences.

Caution   Be sure to make backup copies of the preceding files before altering them in any way, in order to avoid losing your personal preference settings in Fireworks.

The Preference file itself is a standard XML file that one could create in Dreamweaver. As such, it's best to view, and edit, it using Dreamweaver, or another Web editor that understands XML. This way you're certain that the file is saved properly once you've made your changes. To change a particular preference setting, find its keyword and alter the value next to it. Make sure not to add line breaks or otherwise alter the formatting of the file. Save the file when you're done and restart Fireworks.

Caution   As you can imagine, changing preference values haphazardly can prove very disruptive to the program. Many of the preferences are not intended to be altered by the user, such as the DragTab positions. If you ever mistakenly damage your preferences, you can restore the defaults by deleting (trashing) the Fireworks Preferences file and restarting Fireworks. Fireworks creates a new default preferences file.

The other approach to altering the Fireworks Preferences file is to attack it with the Fireworks API. The `getPref()` and `setPref()` methods of the Fireworks object (`fw` or `fireworks`) enable you to read or alter any preference setting. For example, the following code pops up a dialog box with the path to the Primary Browser:

```
alert(fw.getPref('PrimaryBrowser'));
```

Note that the specific preference setting is passed as a string. Just as you can get a preference with `fw.getPref()`, you can set a preference with `fw.setPref()`. The following code uses `setPref()` to tell Fireworks not to ever ask the user to register:

```
fw.setPref('NeverBugForRegistration', 'true');
```

You could use the preceding techniques to create a scriptlet that offers the user a list of browsers and asks them to choose a primary and secondary, or to create a command that simply changes the primary and secondary browsers from two version 5 browsers to two version 4 browsers, depending on the browser generation you're targeting. Of course, another similar command could change them back.

Summary

For me, the true power of any tool is demonstrated when it adapts to my own way of working. You can greatly extend Fireworks with custom commands, scriptlets, and more. When customizing Fireworks, keep these points in mind:

✦ You can extensively customize Fireworks just by including files in subfolders of the Configuration folder — adding commands, Filters, and more.

✦ Scriptlets are stand-alone JavaScript files that run on Fireworks. In Windows, all scriptlets must have the filename extension .jsf. On Macintosh, scriptlets should have the Fireworks Creator code of MKBY and the File Type code of TEXT.

✦ Fireworks stores your preferences in a standard XML file that you can modify in Dreamweaver, edit with another XML-compatible editor, or alter through the use of scriptlets and commands.

In the next chapter, you look closely at the Fireworks JavaScript API.

✦   ✦   ✦

Building Fireworks Extensions

How is a graphics engine like Fireworks able to process JavaScript code? Fireworks has a JavaScript 1.4 interpreter built in. JavaScript is the Web scripting lingua franca, and as such, is an excellent choice for a scripting language for controlling Web development tools. The Fireworks JavaScript API (application programming interface) includes an amazing array of special objects with properties and methods for accessing, controlling, and modifying a Fireworks document.

But all that power under the hood doesn't really do any good if you don't have a way to control it. Until Fireworks MX, user interface possibilities were severely limited — a single-line text field prompt was the only method of gathering user input. However, Fireworks MX introduced the capability to incorporate a Flash movie interface and now, the possibilities are endless.

Keep these points in mind as you work through this chapter:

- ✦ This chapter deals with advanced HTML and JavaScript concepts. If you're just getting started with JavaScript, you might want to keep a good resource nearby as you look over this chapter. I like and use *JavaScript Bible, 4th Edition*, by Danny Goodman, published by Wiley Publishing.

- ✦ Throughout this chapter, I followed certain conventions in the descriptions of each Fireworks API item. Arguments for methods are italicized; optional arguments are in square brackets.

✦ Because of the great number of objects and methods that the Fireworks API now includes, you are occasionally referred to Macromedia's Extending Fireworks documentation, which is available in PDF on your Fireworks installation CD-ROM, or on the Fireworks Web site at `www.macromedia.com/software/fireworks/extensibility.html`; a hard-copy version of Extending Fireworks is also available for ordering.

Building a User Interface in Flash

Fireworks MX includes a special version of the Flash player, which allows communication between a Flash movie and Fireworks — and thus forms the foundation of a Flash user interface. All of the flexibility of Flash MX now becomes available to the Fireworks extension developer: components, enhanced XML handling, and even video.

The new Flash command capability is evident throughout Fireworks MX. Most of the commands in the shipping version of the program are Flash commands. Flash really lends itself to interface design and almost anything is possible. Take a look at the different interfaces in some of the commands: Add Arrowheads, Add Picture Frame, Twist and Fade, and the Data-Driven Graphics Wizard to name a few.

Here's a very general overview of the process for developing Flash commands for Fireworks:

✦ Create the interface in Flash, as shown in Figure 26-1, and save as an .fla file.

✦ Code ActionScript to gather the various user input values.

✦ Add Fireworks-specific functions to the ActionScript.

✦ Publish the Flash movie as an .swf file.

✦ Store the .swf file in either the Fireworks Commands or Command Panels folder.

Of course, there's an awful lot of experimentation, debugging, and testing that goes on during the development process. But the most important aspects of Fireworks-Flash communication are handled by just two functions as you'll see in the following sections.

Executing Fireworks functions

The key to this cross-application connectivity is a single API function only available in the special Flash player embedded in Fireworks: MMExecute(). The MMExecute() function, written in ActionScript, performs the Fireworks function passed as an argument and returns the resulting value as a string. This functionality effectively opens up the entire scope of Fireworks extensibility to the Flash user interface.

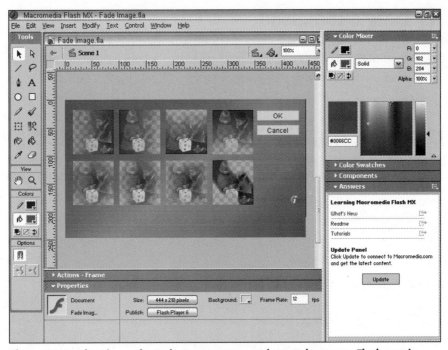

Figure 26-1: The Fireworks Fade Image command started out as a Flash movie.

Let's take a look at how it works. Here's the standard Fireworks JavaScript for placing an oval on the page:

```
fw.getDocumentDOM().addNewOval({left:309, top:74, right:424, bottom:189});
```

Now here's how you would do the same thing as a Flash command, in ActionScript:

```
MMExecute("fw.getDocumentDOM().addNewOval({left:309, top:74, right:424,
bottom:189});")
```

Note that the entire JavaScript function is quoted and passed as an argument to the `MMExecute()` function.

Tip   If the Fireworks JavaScript includes quotes, surround the argument with single quotes instead, as in this example:

```
MMExecute('fw.getDocumentDOM().setHotspotColor("hotspots
","#ff00ff");');
```

If necessary, quotes may also be escaped using the backslash character.

Finishing a command

Other than `MMExecute()`, one other key API function is used by Flash commands: `MMEndCommand()`. The `MMEndCommand()` takes two arguments, `endStatus` and `notifyString` like this:

```
MMEnd(endStatus, notifyString);
```

where `endStatus` is either *true* or *false*; *true* if the command should be executed, *false* if the command should be canceled. The `notifyString` argument is only used if `endStatus` is false and you want to alert the user to an error. So, a complete ActionScript function to place the oval in our earlier example might look like this:

```
function doCommand() {
    MMExecute("fw.getDocumentDOM().addNewOval({left:309, top:74, right:424,
bottom:189});")
    MMEndCommand(true,"");
}
```

Here's an example of a function linked to a Cancel button:

```
function cancelCommand() {
    MMEndCommand(false,"");
}
```

Integrating Flash input

Of course, the whole point of having a Flash user interface is to gather input from the user. To pass values from Flash to Fireworks using the `MMExecute()` function, you need to concatenate the Flash variables — which contain the user-supplied values — with the JavaScript function. In this example, the Flash movie has two text input fields, one for the left value (`leftField`) and one for the top (`topField`). After converting the entered text values to numbers via the `parseInt()` function, the user values are passed to Fireworks:

```
theLeft = parseInt(leftField.text);
theTop = parseInt(topField.text);
MMExecute("fw.getDocumentDOM().addNewOval({left:" + theLeft + ", top:" +
theTop + ", right:424, bottom:189});");
```

For certain Fireworks functions, a far simpler, more direct approach is available by installing the API wrapper extension for use in Flash. See the sidebar, "Rapid Fireworks Coding in Flash" for more details.

Debugging Flash commands

No one writes perfect code the first time through when working with just one application — and cross-application coding can be doubly difficult. This difficulty is even more pronounced when there is little or no feedback while the command is running. One technique that many developers use in this situation is the judicious placement of the `alert()` function. While this is effective for revealing single variables, it can be time-consuming to write `alert()` statements for large sections of code.

Rapid Fireworks Coding in Flash

While the `MMExecute()` function syntax is workable, it's not the most elegant. Quoting and concatenating values can become quite a chore. The Fireworks Commands Wrapper has been developed to integrate better with ActionScript and is available as an extension on the Fireworks CD-ROM from Macromedia as well as online at the Macromedia Exchange. To install the Fireworks Commands Wrapper in Flash, choose Help ➪ Manage Extensions to open the Extension Manager. In the Extension Manager, choose File ➪ Install Extension and locate the Fireworks Commands Wrapper.mxp file.

Once installed, you'll notice a new category in the Components panel: FW Command Components. Many of these components—such as the Checkbox and Pushbutton—are duplicates of the standard Flash elements but with a Fireworks look-and-feel. One component, however, is not intended to be seen when included in a Flash movie. When you drag the Fireworks API Wrapper component into the first frame of the Flash movie—it doesn't even have be on the stage—ActionScript is extended to include the `fwapi` object. The `fwapi` object is used in place of `MMExecute()` and with much less fuss.

To create a new oval using fwapi, the code would look like this:

```
fwapi.addNewOval({left:309,top:74,right:400,bottom:150});
```

While this may not seem like much savings over the `MMExecute()` method, consider what happens when you parameterize the same function:

```
fwapi.addNewOval({left:theLeft,top:theTop,right:400,bottom:150});
```

Note the complete lack of complex quoting and concatenation; it's all handled by the `fwapi` object.

There are over 200 functions available in the `fwapi` object. The easiest way to see if the desired function is available is to enter in ActionScript the term `fwapi` and then press period to begin the dot notation coding. A complete list of the available functions is then displayed in a pop-up window in ActionScript. As you begin typing the name of the desired function, the list automatically scrolls to the closest match. If you find the function you're looking for, press Enter (Return) to complete the code. Entering the opening parentheses displays any available code hints for the function's arguments.

The `fwapi` object and `MMExecute` functions can be used in the same movie and even in the same function without penalty.

Fireworks offers a handy way to see all the commands as they are being sent from Flash in a system alert. Place the `fw.enableFlashDebugging()` function before the code you need to debug and `fw.disableFlashDebugging()` after it and every Fireworks statement received for processing is revealed. These commands save you the extra steps involved in having to specify each of the statements in a separate `alert()`.

The debugging commands must be passed within an `MMExecute()` function, as follows:

```
MMExecute("fw.enableFlashDebugging();");
[ActionScript and Fireworks code goes here...]
MMExecute("fw.disenableFlashDebugging();");
```

Use these Flash debugging commands judiciously as each and every Fireworks statement appears in a JavaScript alert, which must be dismissed before continuing.

For a different debugging approach, try John Dunning's Fireworks Log extension, available on the CD-ROM under Additional Extensions. The Fireworks Log appears as a Commands panel and remains visible while the command is processing. Once the fwlog.as file is included in the ActionScript source, any variable or information passed with the `fwlog` function appears in the Commands panel in a scrolling text field. With this technique, you don't have to dismiss alert dialog boxes and the information is always available—until you choose to clear the Fireworks Log, of course.

Storing Commands and Commands panels

Two different types of Flash commands are possible in Fireworks, *modal commands* such as Add Arrowheads, or *modeless commands* such as the Align panel. A command is said to be modal when the dialog box must be dismissed— either by executing or canceling the command—before program execution can resume. Modeless panels, on the other hand, may remain open during the normal running of the program.

Modal commands—also just called commands—are different from modeless command panels in their coding. Commands typically include buttons for executing or applying the user settings as well as a button for canceling the command without affecting the page. Commands panels do not have such buttons and rely on the system options for closing and opening the panel.

If you're using the Flash components—particularly the pushbutton one—you may notice that their appearance seems off. Text in the pushbutton, for example, is horizontally cut off. You can correct this by changing the movie's `scaleMode` in your ActionScript with this code:

```
Stage.scaleMode = "noScale";
```

This code will also keep your movie from being rescaled by the user.

How does Fireworks know whether an extension is a command or a Commands panel? By where it is stored. Commands are in the Configuration/Commands folder while Commands panels are in—you guessed it—the Configuration/Commands Panel folder.

Tip

If you're packaging your Fireworks extensions with the Extension Manager, use the `destination` attribute of the `file` tag to direct your command or Commands panel into the proper folder. For example, the following places a fictitious extension called `EdgeMaker` into the Commands panels folder:

```
<file source="EdgeMaker" destination =
"$fireworks/configuration/command panels/"/>
```

Fireworks API Overview

The Fireworks API employs both *static* methods and properties, as well as *instance* methods and properties. A static method or property (also called a *class* method or property) is associated with the object itself, rather than an instance or copy of the object. As the name implies, an instance method or property is associated with an instance of the object. Instance methods and properties can therefore use the `this` keyword.

Examining Nonstandard Data Types

Because Fireworks deals with graphics-related objects—for example, masks and specific Fireworks settings, such as resolution, that aren't commonly accessed with JavaScript—some common ways to format this data are required. Macromedia provides guidelines for formatting colors, file URLs, masks, matrices, points, rectangles, and resolution.

Colors

Colors are specified in the Hexadecimal RGB (red-green-blue) color model, which is one of the models accessible from the Color Mixer panel in Fireworks. This is the standard method for defining colors in HTML, and is formatted "#RRGGBB," where each color channel is written with a hexadecimal number. For example, pure red is #FF0000. Additionally, you can specify an alpha channel by adding an extra hexadecimal number in the format #RRGGBBAA.

Note

If the alpha channel value is not specified, Fireworks automatically assumes that the alpha channel is fully opaque. For example, a solid red fill color with a hexadecimal value of #FF0000 is interpreted by Fireworks to have a value of #FF0000FF.

File URLs

Fireworks specifies filenames and pathnames in scripts as file URLs. For example, the Windows path to the Fireworks Commands folder

```
C:\Program Files\Macromedia\Fireworks 4\Configuration\Commands
```

looks like this when written as a file URL:

```
file:///C|Program%20Files/Macromedia/Fireworks%204/Configuration/
Commands
```

Note that all slashes are forward slashes, and that the pipe character (|) replaces the colon after the drive letter, and the %20 escape code is substituted for the space.

On a Mac, the path to the Commands folder would be written like this (if the hard drive were named Grover):

```
Grover:Applications:Macromedia Fireworks
4:Configuration:Commands
```

As a file URL, it's written like this:

```
file:///Grover/Applications/Macromedia%20Fireworks%204/
Configuration/Commands
```

Again, %20 is substituted for a space, and forward slashes are used.

Tip   When you're writing scripts to be cross-platform, use the platform property of the fw object to determine whether your script is running on Windows or Macintosh, and write file URLs appropriately.

Masks

Alpha masks are defined using the following properties:

✦ maskBounds specifies a rectangle, which is the area of the mask.

✦ Choose from five types of masks with maskKind: rectangle, oval, zlib compressed, rle compressed, or uncompressed.

✦ maskEdgeMode is either "hard" or "antialiased".

✦ The value for featherAmount is a number between 0 and 1,000, representing the feather value in pixels. A value of 0 means no feathering.

✦ For rectangle and oval masks, the maskData value is ignored. For other masks, maskData should contain 8-bit mask data in hexadecimal format.

Masks are specified in the format {maskBounds: **rectangle**, maskKind: **string**, maskEdgeMode: **string**, featherAmount: **int**, maskData: **hex-string**}.

Matrices

In programming, computer graphics are described using a three-by-three array of numbers called a *matrix*. In Fireworks, the format for a matrix is {matrix: [*float, float, float, float, float, float, float, float, float*]}. Discussion of matrices is beyond the scope of this book.

Points

Specify a point in the format {x: *float*, y: *float*}. For example, when the Pen tool is used, the placement of the initial point is coded like this:

```
fw.getDocumentDOM().addNewSinglePointPath({x:124, y:37},
{x:124, y:37}, {x:124, y:37}, true);
```

In this example, all three point coordinates are the same and correspond to the preceding Bezier control point, the point itself, and the following Bezier control point.

Note   In the previous example, and throughout the book, the code fw. getDocumentDOM() is used to refer to the current active document in Fireworks.

Rectangles

Define a rectangle {left: *number*, top: *number*, right: *number*, bottom: *number*}. If, for example, I draw a rectangle 100×50 pixels, starting at the upper-left corner (0, 0 coordinates), the code looks like this:

```
fw.getDocumentDOM().addNewRectanglePrimitive({left:0, top:0,
right:100, bottom:50}, 0);
```

Another function, addNewRectangle(), takes the same arguments. Elements created with addNewRectangle() are closed paths in rectangle form; if one corner is dragged, the path is reshaped. Objects created with addNewRectanglePrimitive(), however, are true rectangles. If a corner is dragged, the object rescales, remaining a rectangle.

Resolution

The format for specifying resolution with the Fireworks API is {pixelsPerUnit: *number*, units: ["inch" or "cm"]. Setting the resolution of the current document to 72 dpi is accomplished with this code:

```
fw.getDocumentDOM().setDocumentResolution({pixelsPerUnit:72,
units:"inch"})
```

Looking at Global Methods

Global methods are always available for use in Fireworks scripts. The user interaction functions are helpful in debugging code and in guiding the user. The two file output functions — WRITE_HTML() and write() — are only available during an exporting operation.

alert(*message*)

The alert() method displays a simple dialog box (see Figure 26-2) to the user with a Fireworks title, a *message,* and an OK button. The message can be a text string, or the contents of a variable, or the result of a JavaScript statement. The alert() dialog box must be dismissed before the user can continue; this type of dialog box is referred to as *modal.*

All Done!

OK

Figure 26-2: The alert() method is a simple way to tell the user something.

For example, the following code informs the user that the batch process job is completed:

```
alert("All done!");
```

Note   After discovering that the JavaScript engine in Fireworks does not display UTF-8 characters correctly, Macromedia developed a special version of the alert() function to be used in Flash commands. The MMAlert() function works exactly the same as the standard alert() function, except it is only valid in Flash commands. If you are using the fwapi wrapper object, fwapi.alert() has been engineered to actually use MMAlert() under the hood.

confirm(*message*)

The confirm() method displays a string in a modal dialog box and waits for the user to select either the OK or Cancel button, as shown in Figure 26-3. The function returns *true* if OK is selected and *false* if the user clicks Cancel.

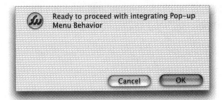

Figure 26-3: Use the `confirm()` method to get a confirmation from a user during an export or batch processing procedure.

The following code asks whether the user is ready to proceed with a particular operation; if not, the operation is not carried out:

```
function doConfirm(curBeh) {
  var message = "Ready to proceed with integrating " + curBeh;
  if (confirm(message)) {
  doFile(curBeh)
  }
}
```

fw.yesNoDialog(*text*)

Looking for an alternative to the standard OK/Cancel alert? Fireworks also offers a dialog box with Yes and No buttons, shown in Figure 26-4. If the user selects Yes, the function returns *true*; if No is selected, *false* is returned. Unlike the other messaging alternatives, the `yesNoDialog()` function is not a global method, but a method of the Fireworks object and so the syntax is slightly different than the others, as shown in this example:

```
var theAns = fw.yesNoDialog("File not found. Continue processing?");
if (theAns != true) {
  fw.closeDocument(newDoc, false);
  fw.openDocument(gThePath, false);
  return;
}
```

Note To offset a problem with UTF-8 characters, Macromedia has developed a special version of this function to be used in Flash commands, `MMYesNoAlert()`. The `MMYesNoAlert()` function also takes one argument but instead of returning a Boolean, returns string values *true* or *false*.

prompt(*caption, text*)

The `prompt()` method enables the user to enter information in a modal dialog box (see Figure 26-5) that can be incorporated in the JavaScript code or HTML output.

The `prompt()` dialog box includes a text field (with a default value) and OK and Cancel buttons. If OK is selected, the contents of the text field are returned; otherwise null is returned.

Figure 26-4: The Yes/No dialog box gives a slightly different interface.

Figure 26-5: The user can type text into the dialog box that's provided with the `prompt()` method.

In this example, the code lets the user select the exported slice's basename during the script's runtime:

```
function getName() {
 var baseName = ""
 prompt("Enter the basename for the slice now being ù
exported.", baseName)
}
```

Note   Currently, the `prompt()` method is the only native mechanism available to Fireworks extension authors for gathering parameters from a user. Some extension creators use multiple prompts or a single prompt with comma-separated values in order to get user input. One other possible route for advanced extensions is to open a parameter form in Dreamweaver and use its values to run a Fireworks command.

WRITE_HTML(arg1[, arg2, . . ., argN])

The `WRITE_HTML()` method converts each argument to a string and outputs the string to the currently open HTML file during export. This method is available only when exporting. The arguments are written one after the other, which enables you to easily concatenate text and variables. To create an end-of-line character, use \n, which is automatically converted to Carriage Return Line Feed (CR LF) for Windows and Carriage Return for Macintosh systems. Quotations within the string should be escaped by prefacing them with the backslash character; therefore, they will be interpreted as part of the string, rather than as quotations.

For example, the following code writes out the ⟨title⟩ tag for an HTML page using a supplied filename and the first ⟨meta⟩ tag:

```
WRITE_HTML("<title>", exportDoc.filename, "</title>\n");
WRITE_HTML("<meta name=\"description\" content=\"Fireworksù
 Splice HTML\">\n");
```

If the filename were MuseumPiece, the following code would be output:

```
<title>MuseumPiece</title>
<meta name="description" content="Fireworks Splice HTML">
```

write(*arg1[, arg2, . . ., argN]*)

The write() method is exactly the same as the WRITE_HTML() method. Macromedia recommends that WRITE_HTML() be used instead of write() to avoid confusion with the document.write() method of JavaScript.

Exploring the Fireworks Global Object

The Fireworks global object enables you to manage files, initiate a find-and-replace operation, report errors in a localized language, and uncover almost any detail about documents or the current application settings. The key global object is fireworks, which can be abbreviated as fw. Note that the object is written in lowercase. The fireworks object and its associated methods and properties are extremely valuable and used throughout commands, templates, and scriptlets alike.

Note In previous versions, the App object was the primary global object and, although Fireworks 4 still supports the App object for backwards compatibility, the object itself has been deprecated and should not be used in future development.

fw

The fw object accesses information about the Fireworks application as it is installed on the user's system. Through the fw object, the programmer can determine the operating system being used; where specific folders, such as Commands or Templates, are located; and what files are currently open, among many other items.

Two of the most powerful methods of the fw object are the getPref() and setPref() pair. With these two methods, you can control virtually every aspect of Fireworks' interface by setting and restoring options.

Properties

Most of the properties of the fw object are read-only—you can get them, but you can't set them—except for batchStatusString, dismissDialogWhenDone, progressCountCurrent, and progressCountTotal.

appBatchCodeDir

This property returns the pathname to the Batch Code folder.

appDir

This property returns the pathname to the folder containing Fireworks.

appExportSettingsDir

This property returns the pathname to the Export Settings folder.

appFavoritesDir

This property returns the pathname to the URL Libraries folder.

appHelpDir

This property returns the pathname to Fireworks' Help folder.

appHtmlCodeDir

This property returns the pathname to the HTML Code folder.

appJsCommandsDir

This property returns the pathname to the Commands folder.

appJsExtensionsDir

This property returns the pathname to the JSExtensions folder.

appMacCreator

A Macintosh identifies which application a particular file belongs to by its Creator code. On a Mac, the appMacCreator property returns Fireworks' Creator code of MKBY.

appMacJsfFileType

A Mac identifies the file type of a particular document by its embedded File Type code. On Macintosh systems, TEXT is the File Type code for text files. Because Fireworks commands and scriptlets are text files, the appMacJsfFileType property returns the string TEXT.

appPatternsDir

This property returns the pathname to the Patterns folder.

appPresetsDir

This property returns the pathname to the Presets folder.

appSettingsDir

This property returns the pathname to the Configuration folder.

appStylesDir

This property returns the pathname to the Styles folder.

appSymbolLibrariesDir

This property returns the pathname to the Libraries folder.

appTexturesDir

This property returns the pathname to the Textures folder.

appXtrasDir

This property returns the pathname to the Plug-ins folder.

batchStatusString

The `batchStatusString` property — which is not read-only — is used to display the current string in the Batch Progress dialog box. You can establish a new message in the dialog box by setting this property to the desired string. For example, the following code from the `BatchTemplate.jst` file displays the filename of each file as it is being processed:

```
fw.batchStatusString = Files.getFilename(sourceDocumentPath);
```

dismissBatchDialogWhenDone

If you display the Batch Progress dialog box, you can cause it to be dismissed automatically by setting the `dismissBatchDialogWhenDone` property — which is obviously *not* read-only — to *true* at some point in the code, as in the following:

```
fw.dismissBatchDialogWhenDone = true;
```

documentList

The `documentList` property returns an array object with a Document object for every document currently open in Fireworks.

The following code makes the first Fireworks document active and brings it to the front for editing:

```
var editFirst = fw.documentList[0].makeActive();
```

platform

The platform property returns win if Fireworks is running on a Windows system and mac if Fireworks is running on a Macintosh.

progressCountCurrent

When a batch process is running, the dialog box keeps track of how many files have been completed, displaying something like "1 of 6 files processed." The progressCountCurrent property—which is not read-only—represents the first number in this message and is used in a loop that increments the number each time a file is completed.

progressCountTotal

The progressCountTotal property is not read-only and represents the second number in the Batch Progress dialog box—the total number of files to be processed. This value can be set from the number of documents selected in the dialog box, which is presented at the beginning of the operation; the chooseScriptTargetDialog() method returns such a list. Therefore, to determine the total number of files to be processed, use code similar to this:

```
var theDocList = fw.chooseScriptTargetDialog(PNG);
fw.progressCountTotal = theDocList.length;
```

Methods

The functions associated with the fw object are all extremely useful. With them, you can do everything from opening a specific file, to altering any Fireworks preferences, or even closing Fireworks itself.

Note   All the fw methods are static.

chooseScriptTargetDialog(*formatlist*)

Similar to locateDocDialog(), the chooseScriptTargetDialog() method displays the same dialog box so that the user can select the files to be targeted for an operation. Unlike locateDocDialog(), here the formatlist is a required argument and no maximum number of documents can be specified. In this example, file formats are limited to BMP files:

```
var theFiles = fw.chooseScriptTargetDialogù
("kMoaCfFormat_TIFF")
```

Tip   To restrict the resulting dialog box from the chooseScriptTargetDialog() method to multiple file types, use the same array structure as locateDocDialog().

findOpenDocument(*pathname*)

The findOpenDocument() method checks to see whether Fireworks already has the given pathname open in a document window. If so, that Document object is returned. If not, it returns null. Usually, `findOpenDocument()` takes the pathname argument from an array of filenames, as in the following code:

```
theDocList = fw.chooseScriptTargetDialog(fw.getPref("PNG"));
for (var i = 0; i < theDocList.length; i++) {
 theDoc = fw.findOpenDocument(theDocList[i]);
 if theDoc == null {
 alert("No file found");
 }
}
```

getPref(*prefname*) and setPref(*prefname, prefval*)

The `getPref()` and `setPref()` methods enable you to read—and alter—the current program settings for almost every aspect of Fireworks. From the default fill color to the *x* and *y* coordinates for the Edit Gradient dialog box, these two methods provide a powerful peek into the program.

The `prefname` and `prefval` arguments are set keywords contained in the Fireworks MX Preferences file.

See Chapter 25 for more about the Fireworks MX Preferences file and specific preference settings.

locateDocDialog(*maxnumdocs* [, *formatlist*])

The `locateDocDialog()` method presents users with a dialog box that enables them to choose one or more files. The `maxnumdocs` argument tells Fireworks whether to use the standard Open dialog box to open a single file, or to use the Open Multiple Files dialog box for loading more than one file. Use 1, 0, or –1 to open the standard Open dialog box and any number higher than 1 to specify the Open Multiple Files dialog box. The number used as an argument does not limit the number of files that can be opened in any other way.

The `formatlist` argument is an optional list of acceptable file types to open. If `formatlist` is omitted, then all files will be listed. The `formatlist` argument is in the form of an array. For example, to specify just the PNG and TIFF file formats for a single file dialog box, use the following code:

```
var formats = [ "PNG", "kMoaCfFormat_TIFF" ];
var theFiles = fw.locateDocDialog(1, formats);
for (f in theFiles) {
 alert(theFiles[f]);
}
```

The resulting dialog box also permits the user to select All Readable Files and All Files.

The `locateDocDialog()` method returns an array of filenames, or, if the dialog box is canceled, it returns null.

Tip

You can also access whatever file types the user's system has available by determining the MultiFileBatchTypes setting with code like this:

```
var thePrefs = fw.getPrefs(MultiFileBatchTypes);
var theFile = fw.locateDocDialog(1,thePrefs);
```

Table 26-1 details the formatlist arguments.

Table 26-1
Fireworks formatlist Arguments

Argument	Document	Filename Extension	Mac File Type Code
ADOBE AI3	Adobe Illustrator	.ai	UMsk
Fireworks JavaScript	Fireworks JSF	.jsf	TEXT
kMoaCfFormat_BMP	Microsoft Bitmap	.bmp	BMP
kMoaCfFormat_FreeHand7and8	Macromedia FreeHand 7.0 or 8.0	.fh7 or .fh8	AGD3
kMoaCfFormat_GIF	GIF image	.gif	GIF
kMoaCfFormat_JPEG	JPEG image	.jpg or .jpeg	JPEG
kMoaCfFormat_PICT	Macintosh Picture	.pict, .pic, or .p	PICT
kMoaCfFormat_RTF	Rich Text Format	.rtf	RTF
kMoaCfFormat_Text	Plain text file	.txt	TEXT
kMoaCfFormat_TIFF	TIFF image	.tif or .tiff	TIFF
PNG	PNG image	.png	PNGf
PS30	Photoshop Document (3.0 or higher)	.psd	8BIM

openDocument(*pathname[, openAsUntitled]*)

The openDocument() method opens the specified file in the pathname argument. Because openDocument() opens another instance of an already opened file, the openDocument() method is often used in conjunction with findOpenDocument(). If the file cannot be opened, openDocument() returns null. If the optional openAsUntitled argument is set as *true*, the document is opened in a new Untitled window.

quit()

The `quit()` method, when invoked, closes Fireworks. No further confirmation is offered, unless an open document has been modified, but not saved. You can use the `confirm()` global method to create a confirmation routine in this way:

```
if (confirm("Ready to Quit?")) {
 fw.quit();
}
```

Document

The Document object in Fireworks is similar to the Document object in JavaScript. Both deal with a document on a precise, exacting level. You use the Fireworks Document object to define the export parameters, as well as the basis for a find-and-replace operation.

Because this object is mostly concerned with a specific document, it has no static properties and only two static methods: `findExportFormatOptionsByName()` and `makeGoodNativeFilePath()`.

Properties

The Document object has numerous properties that enable you to determine whether a file is open and whether it's been modified, gather the current filename, and much more.

Because all the Document object properties work with a specific document, you must associate them with a specific instance of the Document object and not the Document object itself. To get an instance of the Document object, use the `getDocumentDOM()` function, as in this code:

```
var theDoc = fw.getDocumentDOM();
```

Now the properties of the current document are accessible. To see the current background color, for example, your script would include this code:

```
var theDoc = fw.getDocumentDOM();
alert(theDoc.backgroundColor);
```

backgroundColor

This property is the background color of the document.

backgroundUrl

This property is the relative or absolute URL for the Background link.

brushes

The brushes property is read-only and contains an array of Brush objects available for use in the document. The Brush object has properties, such as antiAliased, diameter, and flowRate, that enable you to control aspects of the strokes used in a document. For a complete list of Brush object properties and values, see Macromedia's Extending Fireworks documentation.

currentFrameNum

This is the current frame selected in the Frames panel.

currentLayerNum

This is the current layer selected in the Layers panel.

defaultAltText

If a single or sliced image doesn't have alt text specified, it is given this default.

exportFormatOptions

This is identical to exportOptions (detailed next). It is included for backward compatibility with Fireworks 2 scripts.

exportOptions

Although all the properties of any object are important, certainly the most complex—and arguably the most useful—property of the Fireworks Document object is exportOptions. The exportOptions property returns an object that contains the current export settings. Most of the export settings are expressed as a number, rather than as a string. For example, the following code

```
var theFormat = theDoc.exportOptions.exportFormat
```

returns a 0 if the format is GIF and a 1 if it is JPEG. Several settings—paletteInfo, paletteEntries, and frameInfo—are expressed as arrays.

Table 26-2 details the exportOptions settings.

Table 26-2 exportOptions **Settings**	
Setting	**Possible Values**
animAutoCrop	True | False
animAutoDifference	True | False
applyScale	True | False

Setting	Possible Values
colorMode	0 (Indexed), 1 (24-bit color), or 2 (32-bit color). "Indexed" is default.
crop	True | False
cropBottom	From 0 to the Image Height minus 1
cropLeft	From 0 to the Image Width minus 1
cropRight	From 0 to the Image Width minus 1
cropTop	From 0 to the Image Height minus 1
ditherMode	0 (None), 1 (2×2), or 2 (Diffusion). Default is None.
ditherPercent	0 to 100. 100 is the default value.
exportFormat	0 (GIF), 1 (JPEG), 2 (PNG), 3 (Custom, including TIFF and BMP), or 4 (GIF-Animation)
frameInfo (array)	
delayTime	(Previous) 0100000
frameHidden	True | False
frameName	Text: the name of the frame shown in the Frames panel.
gifDisposalMethod	0 (Unspecified), 1 (None), 2(Background), or 3
interlacedGIF	True | False
jpegQuality	1 to 100. 80 is the default.
jpegSmoothness	0 to 8. 0 is the default.
jpegSubsampling	0 to 4. 1 is the default.
localAdaptive	True | False
lossyGifAmount	0 to 100. 0 is the default.
macFileCreator	"XXXX" (a Macintosh Creator code, Fireworks is "MKBY")
macFileType	"XXXX" (a Macintosh File Type code, used to choose format if exportFormat = Custom)
name	Text-Name of Setting
numCustomEntries	0–256 (default is 0)
numEntriesRequested	0–256 (default is 128)
numGridEntries	0–256 (default is 6)
optimized	True | False

Continued

Table 26-2 *(Continued)*	
Setting	**Possible Values**
paletteEntries (array)	
colorstring1 colorstring2 etc.	Red-Green-Blue-Alpha numbers where each number is in the range 0–255. Example: "255 0 0 255". If Alpha is 0, the color is transparent.
paletteInfo (array)	
colorLocked	True | False
colorModified	True | False
colorSelected	True | False
colorTransparent	True | False
colorDeleted	True | False
paletteMode	"adaptive" (default), "custom", "grid", "monochrome", "Macintosh", "Windows", "exact", or "Web 216".
paletteTransparencyType	0 (None), 1 (Index), 2 (IndexAlpha), or 3 (RGBA). Default is None.
percentScale	1–100000 (default is 100)
progressiveJPEG	True | False
savedAnimationRepeat	0–1000000 (default is 0)
sorting	"none" (default), "luminance", or "popularity"
transparencyIndex	0–255, or –1 if none
useScale	True | False
webSnapAdaptive	True | False
webSnapTolerance	Always set to 14
xSize	–100000 to 100000
ySize	–100000 to 100000

The useScale and applyScale settings of the Document object are dependent on each other to determine the type of scaling that is actually used. The following rules determine the scaling type:

✦ If useScale is *false*, and applyScale is *false*, no scaling is done on export.

✦ If useScale is *true*, then percentScale is used, regardless of the setting of applyScale.

✦ If useScale is *false* and applyScale is *true*, then xSize and ySize are used to determine the scaling in the following manner:

- If the value is positive, the value is used as specified for the *x* or *y* axis.

- If the value is zero, the *x* or *y* axis varies without limit.

- If the value is negative, the *x* or *y* axis varies, but it may be no larger than the absolute value of the specified number.

Note that if one value is positive and one is negative, the positive value is always used.

ExportSettings

The ExportSettings object has properties such as htmlDestination ("same", "one up", "custom", "clipboard") and shimGeneration ("none", "transparent", "internal", "nested tables"). See the Extending Fireworks documentation for a complete list of the properties and associated values of the ExportSettings object.

filePathForRevert

The filePathForRevert property returns the pathname from which the Revert operation reads — in other words, the file opened to create the current document. Use filePathForRevert to determine an original pathname for non-Fireworks native files or documents opened as "Untitled." This property returns null if the document was newly created and not read from a file.

filePathForSave

The filePathForSave property finds and sets the filename of the current document. This property is essential for creating backup files. If the file has never been saved, the result is null. The following code relies on the filePathForSave property to store a filename for later use during a backup operation:

```
function saveName(theDoc) {
  var sourcePath
  if (theDoc.filePathForSave != null) {
  sourcePath = theDoc.filePathForSave
  }
}
```

fills

The fills property is read-only and contains an array of Fill objects available for use in the document. The Fill object has properties like gradient and pattern. See the Extending Fireworks documentation for a complete list of Fill object properties and values.

frameCount

This is the number of frames in the document.

frameLoopingCount

Possible values for the frameLoopingCount property are

✦ 0: Loop forever

✦ 1: Don't loop (just play once)

✦ 2 or more: Loop this number of times

frames

The frames property is read-only and is an array containing the Frame objects in the document. The Frame object has properties such as layers and delay. Refer to Extending Fireworks for a complete list of Frame object properties and acceptable values.

gammaPreview

The gammaPreview property can be either *true* or *false*. On a Windows machine, *true* indicates that View ⇨ Macintosh Gamma is enabled. On a Mac, *true* indicates that View ⇨ Windows Gamma is enabled.

gradients

The gradients property is read-only and is an array that contains the Gradient objects that are available to the document. See Extending Fireworks for a list of Gradient object properties and values.

gridColor

This is the color in which the grid is displayed, which can also be set in the Grid dialog box.

gridOrigin

This is the point that corresponds to the grid origin. You can also set the origin of the grid by dragging it from the intersection of the horizontal and vertical rulers.

gridSize

This is the horizontal and vertical grid size for the document. The horizontal grid size is gridSize.x and the vertical grid size is gridSize.y.

guides

The guides property is read-only, and it corresponds to the Guides object. The Guides object has properties such as color and locked. See Extending Fireworks for a complete list of Guides properties and values.

height

This is the height of the document in pixels.

isDirty

It's often necessary to determine whether a file has been modified before deciding how to act on it. The isDirty property returns *true* if the document has been modified since the last save, or if it has never been saved; otherwise, the property returns *false*.

isPaintMode

This property is read-only. It returns *true* if the document is in paint-mode editing and *false* if it is not.

isSymbolDocument

This read-only property returns *true* if the document is a Graphic Symbol or Button Symbol, and *false* if not. The Symbol-editing window is an open document like any other.

isValid

The isValid property returns *true* if the current document is still open and *false* if it has been closed.

lastExportDirectory

This is the target folder for the last export operation, expressed as a file URL.

lastExportFile

This is the target file for the last export operation, expressed as a file URL.

layers

This read-only property is an array containing the Layer objects in the document. Properties of the Layer object include sharing and layerType. Refer to Extending Fireworks for a complete list of properties and values.

left

The left property is a value in pixels that specifies how far from the left border of the canvas the farthest-left object is located.

mapType

The type of image map that the document creates. Possible values are client, server, or both.

matteColor

The Matte color value for the document, also specified in the Optimize panel.

onionSkinAfter

This is the number of frames after the current frame to be displayed using onion skinning. This value is also specified in the Onion Skinning dialog box, accessed from the Frames panel.

onionSkinBefore

This is the number of frames before the current frame to be displayed using onion skinning.

pathAttributes

This property corresponds to the PathAttrs object, which has properties such as `brush` and `fill`. See Extending Fireworks for a complete list of properties and values.

pngText

The `pngText` property is the text contained in a Fireworks document.

resolution

This is the document's print resolution setting. Possible values are between 1 and 5,000.

resolutionUnits

This is the measurement unit for the document's print resolution setting (`resolution` property). It can be either `"inch"` or `"cm"`, for inches or centimeters, respectively.

textures

The `textures` property is read-only and is an array of Texture objects available to the document. The Texture object has one read-only property, `name`, which contains the name of an associated texture.

top

The `top` property is how far in pixels the topmost object is from the top of the document.

useMatteColor

This can be either *true* or *false*. When *true,* the Matte color specified in the Optimize panel or defined in the `matteColor` property is used when exporting.

width

This is the width of the document in pixels.

Methods

The Document object methods provide a great deal of functionality. These functions activate, save, and close files — and more. The `findExportFormatOptions()` and `makeGoodNativeFilePath()` methods are static, and the rest are instance methods.

exportTo(pathname [, exportOptions])

The actual export operation is handled by the `exportTo()` method. The full pathname argument is mandatory, and if the optional `exportOptions` argument is omitted, the current export settings are used. Should `exportOptions` be specified, they are used without affecting the document's `exportOptions` property. The `exportTo()` method returns *true* if it is successful.

findExportFormatOptionsByName(*name*)

You use this static method to access any preset Export Settings. If an Export Setting is preset with the given name, a Document object is returned with the same settings as the `exportOptions` property. If there is no preset by the given name, null is returned.

makeActive()

Use the `makeActive()` method to make the referenced document the active one in Fireworks. The active document is then brought to the front of all other documents.

makeGoodNativeFilePath(*pathname*)

To make sure that a given pathname ends in a proper Fireworks .png extension, the `makeGoodNativeFilePath` static method is applied. When used, it converts any filename extension to .png. For example, the following code snippets all return `"file:///images/logo.png"` as the filename:

```
var theFile =ù
 Document.makeGoodNativeFilePath("file:///images/logo.ping")
var theFile =ù
 Document.makeGoodNativeFilePath("file:///images/logo.bmp")
var theFile =ù
 Document.makeGoodNativeFilePath("file:///images/logo")
```

save([okToDoSaveAs])

The `save()` method is used to store the document in its default location. If the optional okToDoSaveAs argument is *true,* then the user will be prompted for a file location if the document has never been saved. If okToDoSaveAs is *false* and the file has never been saved, the operation will fail and return *false.* Upon a successful save, the document's dirty flag is cleared. The `save()` method returns *true* if the save operation completes successfully, and *false* otherwise.

Tip
To force a Save As dialog box to appear, set the `fw.filePathForSave` property to null before calling `Document.save()`.

saveCopyAs(*pathname*)

To store a duplicate of the current document, use the `saveCopyAs()` method. You must use the full pathname: for example, `"file:///images/logo.png"`. With this method, neither the `filePathForSave` nor the `isDirty` property is affected.

Errors

To help keep the user informed when something goes wrong, the Fireworks API includes an Errors object. Each property of the Errors object returns a string localized for the language of the program. For example, the code

```
var theError = Errors.EFileIsReadOnly;
```

returns "File is locked" in English. Table 26-3 lists all the Errors properties and their messages in English.

Table 26-3	
Errors Properties	
Property	*English Message*
`EAppAlreadyRunning`	An internal error occurred. Fireworks is optimizing an image.
`EAppNotSerialized`	An internal error occurred.
`EArrayIndexOutOfBounds`	An internal error occurred.
`EBadFileContents`	Unsupported file format.
`EBadJIsVersion`	This script does not work in this version of Fireworks.
`EBadNesting`	An internal error occurred.
`EBadParam`	A parameter was incorrect.
`EBadParamType`	A parameter was not the correct type.
`EBadSelection`	The selection was incorrect for this operation.
`EBufferTooSmall`	An internal error occurred.
`ECharConversionFailed`	An internal error occurred.
`EDatabaseError`	An internal error occurred.
`EDeletingLastMasterChild`	A symbol must contain at least one object.
`EDiskFull`	The disk is full.

Property	English Message
EDuplicateFileName	Filename is already in use.
EFileIsReadOnly	File is locked.
EFileNotFound	The file was not found.
EGenericErrorOccurred	An error occurred.
EGroupDepth	An internal error occurred.
EIllegalThreadAccess	An internal error occurred.
EInternalError	An internal error occurred.
ELowOnMem	Memory is nearly full.
ENoActiveDocument	This command requires an active document.
ENoFilesSelected	At least one file must be selected for scripts to operate.
ENoNestedMastersOrAliases	Although symbols may contain other symbols, a symbol cannot contain a copy of itself. Symbols may not contain Instances or other Symbols.
ENoNestedPasting	The JavaScript contains a paste step, which would create an endless loop.
ENoSliceableElems	No paths were found. Objects were cut.
ENoSuchElement	An internal error occurred.
ENotImplemented	An internal error occurred.
ENotMyType	An internal error occurred.
EOutOfMem	Fireworks is low on memory.
EResourceNotFound	An internal error occurred.
ESharingViolation	An internal error occurred.
EUnknownReaderFormat	Unknown file type.
EUserCanceled	An internal error occurred.
EuserInterrupted	An internal error occurred.
EWrongType	An internal error occurred.

Find

Within the Fireworks API, a separate Find object exists for running a find-and-replace operation. To link the Find object to a particular document, use the MakeFind() method to make the Find object and specify the criteria. Just as the Fireworks find-and-replace facility is capable of searching four different types of elements — text, font, color, and URLs — the findParms argument can take four different array forms.

For example, a text Find and Replace operation that searches for "FW" using the Whole Word option, and replaces it with "Fireworks" is defined with code like this:

```
var findParms = {
whatToFind: "text",
find: "FW",
replace: "Fireworks",
wholeWord: true,
matchCase: false,
regExp: false
};
var theFinder = Document.makeFind(findParms);
```

Note the use of quotation marks and parentheses to delineate the parameters.

Different properties are available depending on the type of Find and Replace operation, specified with the whatToFind() method. Table 26-4 details the four types of Find parameters: text, font, color, and URL.

Generating Errors on Purpose

If you're programming in Fireworks, it's helpful to gain a full understanding of the errors a user might encounter. When users report a problem, most often they mention the error code generated, if any. Fireworks does a terrific job of avoiding numeric error codes that are only meaningful to someone who has a decoding manual.

The Errors collection, as documented in Extending Fireworks, is presented only as an alphabetized list of the properties:

```
EAppAlreadyRunning, EAppNotSerialized, EArrayIndexOutOfBounds,
EBadFileContents, EBadJsVersion, EBadNesting, EBadParam,
EBadParamType, EBadSelection, EBufferTooSmall,
ECharConversionFailed, EDatabaseError, EDeletingLastMasterChild,
EDiskFull, EDuplicateFileName, EFileIsReadOnly, EFileNotFound,
EGenericErrorOccurred, EGroupDepth, EIllegalThreadAccess,
EInternalError, ELowOnMem, ENoActiveDocument, ENoFilesSelected,
ENoNestedMastersOrAliases, ENoNestedPasting, ENoSliceableElems,
ENoSuchElement, ENotImplemented, ENotMyType, EOutOfMem,
EResourceNotFound, ESharingViolation, EUnknownReaderFormat,
EUserCanceled, EUserInterrupted, EWrongType
```

The Error messages presented in Table 26-3 are the errors coded for the English release of the program. So how does a programmer uncover what the messages are in his or her own language? I used Fireworks itself — and a little macro magic — to help decipher the Error properties.

I often use Microsoft Word whenever I need to massage text from one format to another. In this situation, I needed to take the comma-delimited list from Extending Fireworks and ultimately put it into a code that would generate a visible error message. The syntax for my error generator was

```
var theError = Errors.errorCode
alert(theError)
```

where *errorCode* was one of the 37 properties. To accomplish this, first I used Microsoft Word's Find and Replace feature to convert every comma-and-space combination (which separated the properties) into a paragraph return. This gave me a one-property-per-line list. Next, I used Word's Macro Recorder feature to add the necessary text before — `var theError = Errors.` — and after — `alert(theError)` — each property. So what was

```
EAppAlreadyRunning
EAppNotSerialized
EArrayIndexOutOfBounds
```

became

```
var theError = Errors.EAppAlreadyRunning
alert(theError)
var theError = Errors.EAppNotSerialized
alert(theError)
var theError = Errors.EArrayIndexOutOfBounds
alert(theError)
```

and so on until all properties were converted. I then saved this file as a standard text file with a .jsf extension, thus creating a Fireworks command. Upon running the command, each error was reported in sequence and could be copied and included in Table 26-3.

Table 26-4
Find Object Properties and Methods

Type of Find	Property or Method	Possible Values
text	whatToFind	"text"
	find	"Any text string"
	replace	"Any text string"
	wholeWord	(True | False)
	matchCase	(True | False)
	regExp	(True | False)

Continued

Table 26-4 *(continued)*		
Type of Find	*Property or Method*	*Possible Values*
font	whatToFind	"font"
	find	"fontname-to-find"
	replace	"fontname-to-replace"
	findStyle	(–1 to 7) where –1 means (StyleAnyStyle), 0 (StylePlain), 1 (StyleBold), 2 (StyleItalic), 3 (StyleBoldItalic), 4 (StyleUnderline), 5 (StyleBoldUnderline), 6 (StyleItalicUnderline), or 7 (StyleBoldItalicUnderline)
	replaceStyle	(–1 to 7) as described under findStyle
	findMinSize	(0–9999)
	findMaxSize	(0–9999)
	replaceSize	(0–9999, or –1 for "same size")
color	whatToFind	"color"
	find	RGB Alpha values 0–255
	replace	RGB Alpha values 0–255
	fills	(True | False)
	strokes	(True | False)
	effects	(True | False)
URL	whatToFind	"url"
	find	"url-to-find"
	replace	"url-to-replace"
	wholeWord	(True | False)
	matchCase	(True | False)
	regExp	(True | False)

Note   When defining color strings for use in the color Find and Replace operation, defining a few key variables to reuse again and again, such as the following, is often easier:

```
var kSolidWhite = "255 255 255 255";
var kSolidBlack = "0 0 0 255";
var kTransparent = "255 255 255 0";
var kRed = "255 0 0 255";
var kGreen = "0 255 0 255";
var kBlue = "0 0 255 255";
```

Files

The Files object of the Fireworks API is robust and covers more than 20 functions that permit you to perform almost any file operation. All the Files methods are static and must be called from the Files object itself, except for close(), readline(), and write(). No properties are associated with the Files object.

close()

As you might suspect, this Instance method closes the associated file. Although close() is not necessary because all files opened or created as a File object are closed when the script terminates, the close() method enables you to control access to a file within a script.

copy(*sourcePathname, destinationPathname*)

To quickly copy a file to a new location — including on another drive — use the copy() method. This function fails if the file named in the destinationPathname argument already exists. In other words, copy() won't overwrite a file. You can't copy folders with this function.

createDirectory(*pathname*)

Needing new folders (directories) when running batch procedures is not uncommon; the createDirectory() method handles this procedure for you. If the folder creation was successful, the function returns *true;* if not, it returns *false.*

createFile(*pathname[, mactype [, maccreator]]*)

To create a new file of any type, use the createFile() method. This method fails if the file already exists. The mactype (file type) and maccreator (associated application) arguments are necessary for properly making a new permanent file on a Macintosh system.

Cross-Reference See Chapter 14 for Fireworks-related Macintosh File Type codes.

deleteFile(*pathname*)

To remove a file or directory, use the deleteFile() method. If the deletion is successful, *true* is returned. *False* is returned if the pathname supplied in the argument does not exist, or if the file or directory could not be deleted.

deleteFileIfExisting(*pathname*)

Rather than run a separate function to see whether a file exists before removing it, you could use the deleteFileIfExisting() method. With this method, in addition to returning *true* if the file is successfully removed, *true* is also returned if the supplied pathname does not exist. The only circumstance in which *false* is returned is if the found file could not be removed.

enumFiles(*pathname*)

The enumFiles() method returns an array of pathnames for every file specified in the argument. The pathname argument should not, however, point to a file; if it does, enumFiles() returns just the single pathname for the file.

exists(*pathname*)

You can check the existence of either a file or directory with the exists() method. *True* is returned unless the file or directory does not exist or the supplied pathname is invalid.

getDirectory(*pathname*)

To extract just the folder — or directory — portion of a pathname, use getDirectory(). This code returns file:///images/winter:

```
var theFolderName =ù
  Files.getDirectory("file:///images/winter/seasonal.png");
```

getExtension(*filename*)

To retrieve just the filename extension, use the getExtension() method. If the filename has no extension, an empty string is returned. This code returns .png:

```
var theExt = Files.getExtension("logo.png");
```

getFilename(*pathname*)

The parallel function to getDirectory() is getFilename(), which extracts a filename from a fully qualified pathname. This code returns seasonal.png:

```
var theFileName =ù
  Files.getFilename("file:///images/winter/seasonal.png");
```

getLastErrorString()

If the last call to a method in the Files object resulted in an error, getLastErrorString() returns text describing the error. If the last call succeeded, this method returns null. The following example code returns an error if a copy operation was unsuccessful:

```
if (Files.copy(sourcePath, destPath) == false) {
  return Files.getLastErrorString();
}
```

The error returned is taken from the Fireworks API Errors object, described later in this chapter. Note that getLastErrorString() is dedicated to errors committed by methods of the Files object; the Errors object is used for displaying error messages resulting from other situations.

getTempFilePath*([dirname])*

The `getTempFilePath()` method returns a pathname in the system temporary files directory. This function does not create a file; it simply returns a unique pathname that does not conflict with any existing file. If the `dirname` argument is given (and is not null), the pathname will indicate a file in the given directory rather than in the temporary files directory. The `dirname` argument is taken literally, and no other path information is appended.

On a Windows system, `getTempFilePath()` generally returns `file:///C|/windows/TEMP/00000001`, depending on your system settings; on a Macintosh it returns `file:///Macintosh%20HD/Temporary Items/00000001`, where Macintosh HD is the name of your Startup Disk.

isDirectory(*pathname*)

To verify that a supplied pathname is a directory and not a file, use the `isDirectory()` method. If the pathname is not a valid directory, *true* is returned.

makePathFromDirAndFile(*dirname, filename*)

Often, during a batch operation, Fireworks is called upon to take a directory from one source and a filename from another and put them together to store a file. That is exactly what `makePathFromDirAndFile()` does. The directory is specified in the first argument and the filename in the second, as shown in this example:

```
var dirname = "file:///fireworks";
var filename = "borg.png";
theNewFile = Files.makePathFromDirAndFile(dirname, filename)
```

In this example, `file:///fireworks/borg.png` is returned.

open(*pathname, wantWriteAccess*)

A basic function of the Files object, the `open()` method opens a specified file for reading or writing. To write to a file, the `wantWriteAccess` argument must be *true*. If `open()` is successful, a `Files` object is returned, otherwise `null` is returned. The `open()` method is intended for use with text files.

readline()

Text files are often read in one line at a time; in Fireworks, this function is handled by the `readline()` Instance method. The lines are returned as strings without the end-of-line character. Null is returned when the end-of-file is reached (or if the line is longer than 2,048 characters).

rename(*pathname, filename*)

Use the `rename()` method to change a full pathname to a new one. For example, the following code

```
Files.rename("file:///images/logo.png", "newlogo.png");
```

renames the file logo.png to newlogo.png and returns
`file:///images/newlogo.png`.

setFilename(*pathname, filename*)

The `setFileName()` method replaces a filename in a pathname with another
specified filename. For instance, the code

```
Files.setFilename("file:///images/logo.png", "newlogo.png" );
```

returns `file:///images/newlogo.png`. Note that this function does not affect
the file on disk in any way, but is just a convenient way to manipulate pathnames.
Whereas `setFileName()` appears to perform the same operation as `rename()`,
only `rename()` actually alters the name of the file on the drive.

swap(*pathname, pathname*)

Fireworks provides numerous methods for moving files around during an export
operation; the `swap()` method switches the contents of one pathname for the
contents of another. This function is helpful when you need to exchange a source
file for a backup file.

The `swap()` method has two limitations: First, you can only swap files, not folders.
Second, both files to be swapped must be on the same drive.

write(*string*)

To insert text in a file, use this Instance method. No end-of-line characters are
automatically appended after each string; it's necessary to attach a \n to generate a
proper end-of-line character, as in the following code:

```
theString = "Log Report\n";
theFile.write(theString);
```

Dissecting Hotspot Objects

Hotspots — alternatively known as image maps — are one of two types of Web
objects in Fireworks. Along with slices, hotspots enable a wide range of user
interactivity to occur. The Fireworks API hotspot objects are, for the most part,
read-only properties that enable you to gather any needed bit of information about
image maps embedded in the Fireworks document.

Because hotspots and slices employ many of the same mechanisms, several
Fireworks API objects — exportDoc, BehaviorInfo, and BehaviorsList — listed under
Hotspot Objects, are also valid for use with slices.

exportDoc

The exportDoc object is available for use in all the exporting templates —
slices.htt, metafile.htt, and Servermap.mtt. However, exportDoc cannot be outside
of these files. All of its properties are read-only and relate to the current document
and its Document properties, detailed in Table 26-5.

Table 26-5		
exportDoc Properties		
Property	**Possible Value**	**Description**
altText	Text	The text string set as the ALT text for the document.
backgroundColor	Hexadecimal String	String that is the hex color for the document canvas.
BackgroundIsTransparent	True | False	True if the canvas or the export settings are set to transparent GIF.
backgroundLink	URL	The relative or absolute URL for the Background Link.
docID	Number	A number assigned to each document to identify HTML created from it. This number does not change, but multiple Save As commands can result in multiple documents with the same docID.
docSaveName	Text	The filename that was used when the document was saved, such as nav.gif. Path information is not included.
emptyCellColor	Text	The empty table cell color string.
enptyCellContents	Number	Specifies what belongs in empty cells. Values are 1 (nothing), 2 (spacer image), and 3 (nonbreaking space).
EmptyCellUsesCanvasColor	True | False	If *true,* empty cells inherit the value of backgroundColor. If *false,* they receive the value of emptyCellColor.

Continued

Table 26-5 *(continued)*

Property	Possible Value	Description
filename	Relative URL	Simple URL for the exported image, relative to the HTML output: for example, images/Button.gif. In slices.htt, this property is the image basename plus the base extension: for example, Button_r2_c2.gif.
generateHeader	True | False	*True* if an HTML file is exported, *false* if the HTML output is sent to the clipboard.
hasAltText	True | False	*True* if alternate text has been specified in the HTML Properties dialog box.
hasBackgroundLink	True | False	*True* if a Background Link has been set through the HTML Properties dialog box.
height	Number	Height of the exported image in pixels. In slices.htt, it is the total height of the output images.
htmlOutputPath	URL	The complete file URL to which the HTML is being written.
imagename	Text	The image basename, without a filename extension—for example, Button.
IncludeHTMLComments	True | False	If *True,* then comments are left in the HTML. If *False* then all nonessential comments are removed.
numFrames	Number	The number of frames in a file.
pathBase	Pathname without filename extension	The filename with the extension removed—for example, images/Button.

Property	*Possible Value*	*Description*
pathSuffix	Filename Extension	The filename extension. For example, .gif.
startColumn	Number	Indicates the column of the slice when generating HTML for a single slice. Used only in metafile.htt.
startRow	Number	Indicates the row of the slice when generating HTML for a single slice. Used only in metafile.htt.
style	Text	HTML style used for export, such as "Dreamweaver," "Generic," or "FrontPage."
width	Number	Width of the export image in pixels. In slices.htt, it is the total width of the output images.

Image maps

Two objects relate to image maps: ImageMap and ImageMapList. Not only can you uncover the shape and number of coordinates of a hotspot by using these two objects, but you can also determine what, if any, Behaviors are linked to them.

ImageMap object

Like several of the Fireworks API extensions, most of the work with the ImageMap object is handled through an array. Each element in the ImageMap array represents one hotspot in the current document. Get a particular ImageMap object with code like this:

```
var theHotspot = imagemap[0];
```

Properties

The properties of the ImageMap object are all read-only instance properties and are detailed in Table 26-6.

Table 26-6
ImageMap Instance Properties

Property	Possible Value	Description
altText	Text	The specified alternative text.
behaviors	A BehaviorsList object (described later in this chapter)	Details regarding the Behavior attached to the hotspot.
hasAltText	True | False	Returns *true* if alternative text has been specified.
hasHref	True | False	Returns *true* if the hotspot has a URL assigned.
hasTargetText	True | False	Returns *true* if the hotspot has a target specified.
href	Relative or Absolute URL	The assigned URL.
numCoords	1 for circle, 2 for rectangle, and any number for polygon	The number of coordinates used to describe the hotspot in HTML.
radius	Number	The radius of the circle area hotspot.
shape	Circle, rectangle, or polygon	The type of hotspot.
targetText	An HTML frame name	The specified target.

Note   The ImageMap object has one other property associated with it: Behaviors. Because the BehaviorInfo object can also work with slice objects, it is described in detail in the following section.

Methods

The only ImageMap methods are those concerned with gathering the *x* and *y* coordinates for the hotspot, xCoord() and yCoord().

Both xCoord() and yCoord() work identically. Each gets one coordinate, in pixels, for the index point. These methods are used together in conjunction with the numCoords property to list the coordinates for the entire image map, as shown in this code:

```
for (var j=0; j<curImagemap.numCoords; j++) {
 if (j>0) WRITE_HTML(",");
 WRITE_HTML(curImagemap.xCoord(j), ",", curImagemap.yCoord(j));
}
```

ImageMapList object

The ImageMapList object is an array of ImageMap objects, describing the areas in an image map. The ImageMapList object has only one property, `numberOfURLs`, and it is a read-only, static property.

The `numberOfURLs` property is important because it contains the number of hotspots in a particular image map. As such, `numberOfURLs` is often used to loop through an ImageMap object array, as with this code:

```
var i = 0;
while (i < imagemap.numberOfURLs) {
 hasImagemap = true;
 }
 i++;
```

If no image maps are in the document, the `numberOfURLs` returns zero.

Behaviors

Behaviors, in Fireworks, are effects that are exported as JavaScript code to be included in an HTML page. A Behavior is attached to a Web object (a hotspot or a slice) and triggered by a specific user event, such as a mouse click or rolling over an image. Two objects deal with Behaviors: BehaviorsList and BehaviorInfo.

BehaviorInfo

All the properties of the BehaviorInfo object are read-only, and no methods are associated with the BehaviorInfo object.

Although the Behaviors panel lists four main Behavior groups — Simple Rollover, Swap Image, Set Nav Bar, and Set Text of Status Bar — from the BehaviorInfo object perspective, there are six different Behaviors: Status Message, Swap Image, Button Down, Swap Image Restore, Button Highlight, and Button Restore. Only four possible events are recognized: `onMouseOver`, `onClick`, `onMouseOut`, and `onLoad`.

Table 26-7 lists the BehaviorInfo object properties and their possible values.

Table 26-7
Properties for the BehaviorInfo Object

Property	Possible Value	Description
action	1 (Status Message), 2 (Swap Image), 4 (Button Down), 5 (Swap Image Restore), 6 (Button Highlight), 7 (Button Restore), or 9 (pop-up menu)	The type of Behavior.
downHighlight	True | False	For Button Highlight Behaviors, returns *true* if there is a highlight image.
event	0 (onMouseOver), 1 (onClick), 2 (onMouseOut), or 3 (onLoad)	The event that triggers the Behavior.
hasHref	True | False	For Swap Image Behaviors, returns *true* if the swap image swaps in an external file as opposed to a Fireworks frame.
hasStatusText	True | False	For Status Message Behaviors, returns *true* if the status text is not empty.
hasTargetFrame	True | False	For Swap Image Behaviors, returns *true* if the swap image swaps in another frame in the Fireworks file, as opposed to an external file.
horzOffset	Number	If action has a value of 9 (pop-up menu), then the horzOffset property is the menu's horizontal pixel offset.
href	A file URL	For Swap Image Behaviors, the URL for the swap image file for an external file swap image.
preload	True | False	For Swap Image Behaviors, returns *true* if the image is going to be preloaded.
restoreOnMouseout	True | False	For Swap Image Behaviors, returns *true* if the original image is to be restored onMouseOut.

Property	Possible Value	Description
statusText	Text string	The text used in the Status Message Behavior.
targetColumnNum	Number	For Swap Image Behaviors, the column in the slices table that will be swapped.
targetFrameNum	Number (0 to number of frames minus 1)	For Swap Image Behaviors, if hasTargetFrame is *true*, this is the frame number that will be swapped. The first frame is 0.
targetRowNum	Number	For Swap Image Behaviors, the row in the slices table that will be swapped.
vertOffset	Number	If action has a value of 9 (pop-up menu) then the vertOffset property is the menu's vertical pixel offset.

BehaviorsList object

The one property of the BehaviorsList object, numberOfBehaviors, is used in the same fashion as numberOfURLs is used with the ImageMap object, to determine how many Behaviors are included in the current document. In the following code, the numberOfBehaviors property is used to loop through the array of Behaviors:

```
for (var I=0; i<theCurBehaviors.numberOfBehaviors; i++) {
 var curBehavior = theCurBehaviors[i];
 if (curBehavior.action == kActionRadioGroup) {
  groupName = curBehavior.groupName;
 }
}
```

Looking at Slice Objects

Slices make it possible to divide one graphic into several different files, each of which you can save separately with its own export settings or Behaviors. Two objects relate directly to slices: SliceInfo and Slices.

SliceInfo object

The SliceInfo object enables you to examine every aspect of the separate slices of an overall image.

Properties

All properties of the SliceInfo object are read-only, and are detailed in Table 26-8.

Table 26-8
Properties of the SliceInfo Object

Property	Possible Values	Description
altText	Text	The alternative text for this slice.
behaviors	A BehaviorsList object	The BehaviorsList object describing any Behaviors attached to the current slice.
cellHeight	Number in pixels	The height of the current HTML table row.
cellWidth	Number in pixels	The width of the current HTML table column.
downIndex	Number	The index for this slice, if it is a multiple file export down button.
getFrameFileName (frameIndex)	Number	Returns the basename for the slice on the designated frame.
hasAltText	True | False	Returns *true* if the slice has an alternative text description.
HasHref	True | False	Returns *true* if the slice has a URL.
HasHtmlText	True | False	Returns *true* if the slice is a text-only slice.
HasImage	True | False	Returns *true* if the current slice includes an image; text-only slices return *false*.
HasImagemap	True | False	Returns *true* if hotspots are associated with the current slice.
HasTargetText	True | False	Returns *true* if a target is specified for the current slice.
Height	Number in pixels	The height of the image in the slice, including row spans.
Href	URL	The URL for the current slice.
HtmlText	Text	The text string for a text-only slice.
Imagemap	An ImageMapList object	The ImageMapList object describing any hotspots attached to the current slice.

Property	Possible Values	Description
ImageSuffix	Filename extension	The filename extension for the image in the current slice, including the period.
IsUndefined	True | False	Returns *true* if the current slice does not have a user-drawn slice associated with it. Fireworks automatically generates slices to cover these undefined cells.
Left	Number in pixels	The left side of the cell in pixels, starting at 0.
NestedTableSlices	Slices object (detailed later in this chapter)	Slices object describing a nested table that occupies the current table cell. Returns null if the cell doesn't contain a nested table.
setFrameFileName (frameIndex)	Integer, starting with zero	Looks at the specified frame and sets the filename for the slice, without path information. If you set its name to " " (empty string), the image won't export.
skipCell	True | False	Returns *true* if the table cell for the current slice is included in a previous row or column span.
targetText	HTML frame name	The specified target for the current frame.
top	Number in pixels	The top of the cell in pixels, starting at 0.
width	Number in pixels	The width of the image in the slice, including column spans.

Methods

The SliceInfo object has two methods associated with it: getFrameFileName() and setFrameFileName(). Both are instance methods.

getFrameFileName(*frame*)

The getFrameFileName() method reads the filename for the slice and frame. The returned name does not include any path information, such as folder or filename extension. For example, using the Fireworks defaults, the name of the first slice for a file named newLogo.gif, would be newLogo_r1_c1. The first frame in an image file is 0; generally all slices in frame 0 are named. For frames 1 and higher, only slices that are rollovers or that are targeted by a swap image are named.

The following code shows how the getFrameFileName() method is used, both with a constant and with a variable:

```
var curFile = SliceInfo.getFrameFileName(0);
for (var curFrame = 0; curFrame < exportDoc.numFrames;ù
 curFrame++) {
 var curFile = SliceInfo.getFrameFileName(curFrame);
// processing code for each slice goes here
 }
```

setFrameFileName(*frame, filename*)

To change the filename of a slice, use the setFrameFileName() method. Specify the frame number and the new name of the slice in the two arguments, as in the following code:

```
SliceInfo.setFrameFileName(swapFrame, fileName);
```

Note　An interesting side effect of setFrameFileName() is that this method determines which image is written. By default, Fireworks sets it up so that all slices on frame 0 are named, and no other frames are named. If a Swap Image Behavior uses a slice at row 2, column 3 on frame 2, the export templates set the frame filename, so that that image gets written. You can also set slices on frame 0 to an empty string, and they won't get written. This is how the "Don't export undefined slices" option gets implemented.

Slices object

The Slices object is an array of SliceInfo objects. Because slices exist in a table, each slice can be identified by its location in the row and column structure. A two-dimensional array holds these row and column values and marks each instance of a slice object. For example, the slice in the first row, first column position is slices[0][0]. To process all the individual slices, use code similar to the following:

```
var curRow;
var curCol;
for (curRow = 0; curRow < Slices.numRows; curRow++) {
for (curCol=0; curCol < Slices.numColumns; curCol++) {
var curSlice = Slices[curRow][curCol];
// do whatever processing with curSlice.
}
}
```

Notice how you must use both the numRows and numColumns static properties to properly loop through all the slices. Once the individual slice has been identified by its two-dimensional array, the properties of the instance slice can be read.

Several of the static properties of the slices object—doShimEdges, doShimInternal, and doSkipUndefined—refer to options. These options are all set in the HTML Properties dialog box. To find out if the user has selected the No Shims option, use code like this:

```
if (Slices.doShimInternal || Slices.doShimEdges) {
//create shim code here
}
```

Table 26-9 details the static properties of the Slices object.

Table 26-9
Properties of the Slices Object

Property	Possible Values	Description
demoindex	Integer, starting with zero	The index for each file generated for a multiple-file button export.
doDemoHTML	True | False	Returns *true* for a rollover, multiple-file button export.
doShimEdges	True | False	Returns *true* if the Table Shims option is set to Transparent Image in Document Properties.
doShimInternal	True | False	Returns *true* if the Table Shims option is set to Shims from Image in Document Properties.
doSkipUndefined	True | False	Returns *true* if the Export Undefined Slices is not enabled in Document Properties.
imagesDirPath	Relative URL	Path to the folder used to store the images in the sliced table. If the images and the HTML file are in the same folder, returns an empty string.
numColumns	Number	The total number of columns, excluding the shim column, in the HTML table.
numRows	Number	The total number of rows, excluding the shim column, in the HTML table.
shimPath	Relative URL	Path to the GIF file used for shims; for example, images/shim.gif.

Accessing the Fireworks API

The addition of the History panel to Fireworks had a major effect on the Fireworks API. In order to display each user action as a separate repeatable step, each action had to be accessible as a separate function. The Fireworks API JavaScript functions can be categorized in three groups: Document functions, History panel functions, and general Fireworks functions. With these functions, you can programmatically repeat virtually every Fireworks command.

The Fireworks JavaScript API — as well as all the other Fireworks methods and properties — is documented in the Extending Fireworks manual from Macromedia. Rather than repeat the information found in that resource, the balance of this chapter focuses on how to best apply that information.

Document functions

As noted previously, the Fireworks extensibility model relies heavily on the Document Object Model (DOM). In the Fireworks API, every Document function requires the DOM of a specific document in order to work correctly. The getDocumentDOM() function is used to retrieve the DOM in one of two ways. First, the function can be written out for every action, like this:

```
fw.getDocumentDOM.align(top);
```

This method is used in the History panel, as you can see by selecting any action, clicking the Copy Selected Steps to Clipboard button, and then pasting your clipboard in any text editor. Although it's perfectly suited for single-line functionality, spelling out the entire function call each time is considered too wordy for general programming, and this syntax is often used:

```
var theDOM = fw.getDocumentDOM();
```

Once this variable is declared and set to the DOM, all future references to the DOM use the variable instead. For example, a series of statements could read:

```
var theDOM = fw.getDocumentDOM();
theDoc.addNewOval({left:20, top:20, right:100, bottom:50});
theDOM.applyStyle(stylename, 0);
theDOM.setDocumentCanvasSizeToDocumentExtents(true);
fw.exportDocumentAs(theDOM, exportPath, exportOptionsGif);
fw.closeDocument(theDOM, false);
```

The variable used here, the DOM, is completely arbitrary, and you can feel free to choose your own.

The Fireworks API Document functions are, by far, the largest, most comprehensive group of functions. The quickest way that I've found to code a specific action is through the Copy Selected Steps to Clipboard button found on the History panel. Follow these steps to avoid searching through the Extending Fireworks manual for a likely function:

1. Perform the desired action — such as drawing an oval, or adding new frames.

2. If necessary, open the History panel by choosing Window ⇨ History.

3. Select the steps in the History panel that represent your action(s).

4. Click the Copy Selected Steps to Clipboard button.

5. In your favorite text editor, paste the steps.

The steps copied from Fireworks will include all the code necessary to replicate your action, exactly. Usually, the next step in creating a command is to generalize the parameters, so that the command can be applied in many circumstances. For example, when an oval is created in a Fireworks document, the Fireworks-generated code looks like this:

```
fw.getDocumentDOM.addNewOval({left:20, top:20, right:100,
bottom:50});
```

When I've finished incorporating the function into a command, the same code looks like this:

```
theDOM.addNewOval({left:theLeft, top:theTop, right:theRight,
bottom:theBottom});
```

In addition to substituting a variable for the `getDocumentDOM()` function, I've done the same for Fireworks' absolute numbers for the left, top, right, and bottom values. These new variables can then be altered by a user prompt, or another programming function.

Fireworks functions

One group of API functions is generically referred to as the Fireworks functions. These functions are concerned with general document manipulation — creating, exporting, saving, closing, and reverting — as well as executing Find and Replace operations and controlling floater accessibility. You'll also find the often used `getDocumentDOM()` function in this category.

 The general Fireworks functions must be prefaced with either `fireworks` or `fw` — the initial `fireworks` and `fw` are interchangeable.

The getDocumentDOM() function isn't the only way to access the Document Object Model of a document. Both createDocument() and createFireworksDocument() return the DOM when they are used in this manner:

```
var theDOM = fw.createDocument();
var theDOM =
fw.createFireworksDocument({x:400,y:500},{pixelsPerUnit:72,unit
s,"inch"},"#ffffff");
```

These two functions serve exactly the same purpose — to make a new document — but differ in that fw.createDocument() uses the current defaults, whereas with createFireworksDocument(), the size, resolution, and canvas color must be expressly stated.

Several functions in this category are used for connecting to files outside of Fireworks. With the browseDocument() function, you can view any HTML or other compatible file in the user's primary browser. One possible use for the browseDocument() function is to display a help file or programmatically preview an exported file in the browser. Two other functions aid in saving Fireworks files: browseForFileURL() and browseForFolderURL(). The browseForFileURL() function displays an Open or Save dialog box and returns a file URL like this:

```
file:///C|images/clientlogo.gif
```

Note On a Macintosh, the drive letter (here, C) would be replaced by the drive name.

The browseForFolder() function, on the other hand, returns a path to a folder. This function is useful when you want to store a group of generated graphics in a common folder and will be naming them programmatically. The browseForFolderURL() function returns a string like this:

```
file:///C|images
```

Note that the final forward slash is not provided; it's up to the programmer to add that character when saving files.

History panel functions

As you might suspect from the name, the History panel functions are concerned solely with the operations of that particular Fireworks floating palette. These functions enable you to programmatically execute every function capable with the History panel, including the following functions:

✦ Clear all History steps.

✦ Find the number of current steps.

✦ Replay selected steps.

Although these functions might appear arcane at first glance, the History panel functions greatly extend the automation possibilities of Fireworks. As an example, I built a Repeat History command, which enables the user to repeat any series of selected steps — or just the last action taken — any number of times. The Repeat History command uses the History panel functions almost exclusively.

Here's the code for the entire command:

```
var theSteps = fw.historyPalette.getSelection();
  if (theSteps.length == 0) {
    alert("No steps selected.\nPlease select at least one step
and repeat command.");
  } else {
  var theNum = prompt("Repeat History\nEnter the Number of
Repetitions Desired");
  for (i=0;i < parseInt(theNum);++i) {
    fw.historyPalette.replaySteps(theSteps);
  }
}
```

The first line uses the History panel function to get the array of steps currently selected in the History panel:

```
var theSteps = fw.historyPalette.getSelection();
```

Next, a check is made to see whether any steps are selected. If no actions are selected in the History panel, the user is asked to select one or more steps, and then to reissue the following command:

```
if (theSteps.length == 0) {
    alert("No steps selected.\nPlease select at least one step
and repeat command.");
  }
```

Because at least one step has been chosen, the user is then asked with the following function for the number of times the selected steps should be repeated:

```
var theNum = prompt("Repeat History\nEnter the Number of
Repetitions Desired");
```

The number of desired repetitions is stored in the variable, theNum, as a string. The next — and final — bit of code alters that string to a number and then replays the selected steps for the requested number of times.

```
for (i=0;i < parseInt(theNum);++i) {
    fw.historyPalette.replaySteps(theSteps);
  }
```

The Repeat History command is useful when combined with the Fireworks Clone or Duplicate command. If, for example, I wanted to make 10 stars, each rotated 5 degrees from one another, I would create the initial star, clone it, and then with the

Modify ➪ Transform ➪ Numeric Transform command, rotate the clone 5 degrees. Next, I would select the Clone and Rotate steps from the History panel and issue the Repeat History command, specifying 10 repetitions. A starburst effect is created.

On the CD-ROM You'll find the Repeat History command on the CD-ROM that accompanies this book, under Additional Extensions ➪ Joseph Lowery.

Summary

Fireworks includes a comprehensive — to say the least — JavaScript API that allows scripted access to almost all the application's features. Keep the following points in mind when you use Fireworks:

✦ Fireworks provides scripting access to almost every feature of the program.

✦ Full-featured user interfaces can be crafted in Flash and used to create Fireworks commands and command panels.

✦ Nonstandard data types, such as colors, masks, and points, must be formatted correctly within your scripts.

✦ Five global methods are always available: `alert()`, `confirm()`, `prompt()`, `WRITE_HTML()`, and `write()`. Use these methods to display dialog boxes and receive user input, and to write text or HTML into exported documents.

✦ Fireworks provides five global objects that are always available:

  • The `fw` object provides access to many features of Fireworks itself, such as preferences and the platform that Fireworks is running on.

  • The Document object provides access to individual documents, enabling you to change layers, set export options, or find out if a document has been changed since it was opened.

  • The Errors object enables your scripts to provide meaningful error messages, regardless of which localized version of Fireworks they run on.

  • The Files object can be used to copy files, create folders, and perform many other file-related tasks.

  • The Find object provides access to Fireworks' search-and-replace functionality.

✦ Objects such as BehaviorInfo, BehaviorsList, exportDoc, ImageMap, and ImageMapList provide control of exporting options within HTML export templates.

✦ Modifying Fireworks' built-in commands is a good way to begin building your own scripts.

✦   ✦   ✦

Appendixes

Appendix A is a Web primer, a place to get a good grounding on the ways of the Web. Appendix B is a handy reference guide to productivity-boosting keyboard shortcuts on both Macintosh and Windows systems. Appendix C introduces the material on the accompanying CD-ROM.

A Web Primer

If you grew up in graphics using Photoshop, you're savvy with alpha channels and gradients, but the subtleties of Internet protocols and HTML code may have escaped you. With Fireworks you can make HTML and JavaScript as easily as GIFs and JPEGs, so you may find yourself creating whole Web sites — or at least prototypes — directly in Fireworks. A good grounding in the ways of the Web enables you to take full advantage of these powerful Fireworks features.

Note   A significant portion of becoming truly Web-savvy is just knowing what the acronyms mean. Although your eyes may glaze over at the mere mention of protocol suites, the ideas behind these lofty-sounding technical terms are actually fairly simple. Don't let unfamiliar technobabble deter you.

Formatting for the Web

Hypertext Markup Language, or HTML, is the page description language of the World Wide Web. Viewed in a browser, an HTML document such as the one shown in Figure A-1 is a formatted and readable page similar to a page in a printed magazine, complete with an assortment of typefaces and styles, images, and even multimedia such as streaming audio or movies.

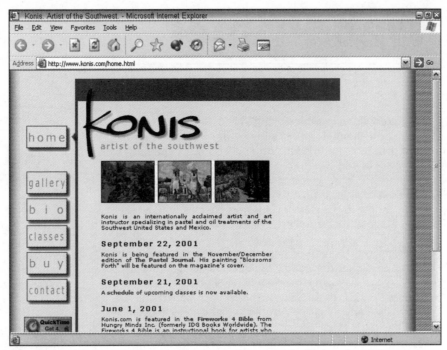

Figure A-1: Viewed in a browser, an HTML document is displayed with formatting such as typefaces and styles.

But opening an HTML document in a text editor reveals the HTML code itself: formatting specifications called tags that tell the browser how to display text and how to link to media such as images and movies.

To view a Web page as HTML code, open it in your Web browser and proceed as follows:

✦ If you are using Netscape Navigator or Communicator, choose View ➪ Page Source.

✦ If you are using Microsoft Internet Explorer, choose View ➪ Source.

✦ If you are using another browser, look for commands similar to the preceding, or consult the browser's documentation.

Typically, the HTML code for the current page appears in your text editor or a special HTML code window, and resembles the code in Figure A-2.

Figure A-2: Viewed in a text editor, the HTML document from Figure A-1 takes on an entirely different appearance.

If what you see is Greek to you, don't worry. The seeming complexity of HTML hides a very simple structure.

Investigating tags and attributes

You can identify tags in HTML code by the angle brackets (<>) that surround them. Everything in an HTML document is either a tag, or is contained inside a tag. Tags specify whether a passage of text is a heading, or a paragraph, or how that passage should be formatted. For example, to display *We Got the Funk* in bold text, you would surround it with the Bold tag, which is a letter *b*, like so:

```
<b>We Got the Funk</b>
```

Note the forward slash (/) in the previous code that marks the second tag as a closing tag. This convention is repeated again and again in HTML, although some tags don't require a closing tag.

An opening and closing tag pair says "anything within me is *this*." For example, the `<title></title>` pair says, "anything within me is the title." The `<b></b>` pair shown previously says, "anything within me is bold."

Many tags can also have attributes that modify the formatting of the tag further; a tag that says "insert a table here" (the `<table>` tag) can have attributes that specify the width of the table, how thick the border should be, and more. Attributes are just placed within a tag. So a plain, bare-minimum opening `<table>` tag is as follows:

```
<table>
```

A `<table>` tag that specifies that the table should be 400-pixels wide and have a 3-pixel border appears as follows:

```
<table width="400" border="3">
```

Although almost one hundred different HTML tags exist, the overwhelming majority of Web pages are created using only a handful of them.

Knowing the top ten tags

HTML has all kinds of tags to meet the needs of all kinds of people, creating all kinds of pages. Fortunately for the beginning Web designer, not all of them are necessary to build almost everything on the Web today. A basic understanding of the ten most commonly used tags takes a lot of the mystery out of a page of HTML code, and Web pages in general. As you take a look at each of these super-tags, you can build a simple example Web page in order to place the tags in context.

Note   Don't worry about remembering every tag and all of its attributes. This section is primarily meant to demystify the underlying code structure of the World Wide Web. Even the most advanced HTML coders frequently consult an HTML reference guide to refine their work.

The HTML tag: <html></html>

The `<html>` tag simply says, "everything within me is HTML." Every HTML document starts with the opening `<html>` tag, and ends with the closing `</html>` tag. Web browsers generally ignore anything in the page that's not within the `<html>` tag. Why? It's not HTML. The HTML tag never takes any attributes.

Tip   XML (Extensible Markup Language) documents also contain an `<xml></xml>` tag pair that encloses all the XML. Similarly, SMIL (Synchronized Multimedia Integration Language) documents have a `<smil></smil>` pair that holds all the SMIL code. These languages also use the / in their tags to specify closing tags.

Starting to build a Web page by adding the `<html>` tag looks like this:

```
<html>
</html>
```

The head tag: <head></head>

You can think of the `<head>` tag as a Web page's way of introducing itself to the browser. It's behind-the-scenes info that isn't displayed in the browser window itself. The `<head>` tag contains the title of the page and indexing information for search engines. Adding the `<head>` tag into our example Web page gives us this (new code is shown in bold text):

```
<html>
<head>
</head>
</html>
```

Note   Other things you might find in a `<head>` tag are script functions that are referenced by scripts in the body of the page (within a `<script>` tag) and CSS (Cascading Style Sheets) formatting information (contained in a `<style>` tag).

The title tag: <title></title>

The `<title>` tag simply contains the plain-language title of the page. This tag is very important because search engines often give the title a lot of weight when they index a page. In other words, if a user searches for *Pokemon,* the list of sites he receives from a search engine is more likely to contain sites with Pokemon in the title than sites that mention Pokemon in the body text but not in the title. The `<title>` tag always goes inside the `<head>` tag and should always be the first one following the opening `<head>` tag; otherwise, some search engines won't find it. Adding a title to our Web page appears as follows:

```
<html>
<head>
<title>An Example Page</title>
</head>
</html>
```

The meta tag: <meta></meta>

The `<meta>` tag enables you to store information about the page within the page itself. Think of `<meta>` tags as fields in a database. You can add as many `<meta>` tags to a page as you like, giving each one a unique name (the type of data) and content (the data). The most commonly used meta names are *description,* which contains a description of the page that some search engines show after the title in their results; and *keywords,* which contains keywords — separated by commas — that search engines use to index your page in their databases. Accurate and descriptive keywords in a keywords `<meta>` tag lead to more interested users finding your page. Use as many as you like, but the first 16 are often given special weight, and repeating keywords (spamming the index) may cause a search engine not to index your page. There are also other `<meta>` tags in use, such as ones that contain the page's author. Now our example page is as follows:

```
<html>
<head>
```

```
<title>An Example Page</title>
<meta name="description" content="A Web page built as anù
 example of the most common tags and where they go.">
<meta name="keywords" content="HTML, code, examples, learning,ù
 tags, markup languages, hypertexts, Web designs, Webù
 authoring">
<meta name="author" content="Derren Whiteman">
</head>
</html>
```

Tip   Make your keywords plural. If you include the keyword mp3s, then Web surfers
looking for mp3 or mp3s will find your page. Include common misspellings, too.

The body tag: <body></body>

The <body> tag is where the stuff you actually see in the browser window lives.
Text, images, plug-ins, Java applets — it's all contained in the <body> tag. The
<body> tag immediately follows the <head> tag. The <body> tag almost always has
some attributes that specify the background color and the text color of the page;
otherwise, the page is displayed in the user's default colors (which vary from user
to user). Colors in HTML are usually specified in RGB color, written in hexadecimal
notation. In this example, use a white (#FFFFFF) background and black (#000000)
text, so the code for our example page now looks like this:

```
<html>
<head>
<title>An Example Page</title>
<meta name="description" content="A Web page built as anù
 example of the most common tags and where they go.">
<meta name="keywords" content="HTML, code, examples, learning,ù
 tags, markup languages, hypertexts, Web designs, Webù
 authoring">
<meta name="author" content="Derren Whiteman">
</head>
<body bgcolor="#FFFFFF" text="#000000">
</body>
</html>
```

Now that it has a <body>, our example page could be displayed in a Web browser,
but the only thing that would be shown would be the white background color.

The paragraph tag: <p></p>

Each opening and closing set of <p> tags contains a paragraph. Paragraphs can
contain text, images, and just about anything that can appear on a Web page.
Browsers leave a line space between paragraphs. You can add an align attribute to
a paragraph tag to specify that it be aligned left, center, or right, as in the example
code. If you leave the align attribute out, the paragraph is aligned left.

```
<html>
<head>
<title>An Example Page</title>
```

```
<meta name="description" content="A Web page built as anù
 example of the most common tags and where they go.">
<meta name="keywords" content="HTML, code, examples, learning,ù
 tags, markup languages, hypertexts, Web designs, Webù
 authoring">
<meta name="author" content="Derren Whiteman">
</head>
<body bgcolor="#FFFFFF" text="#000000">
<p>Here is a paragraph full of text.</p>
<p align="right">Here is a right-aligned paragraph full
 of text.</p>
</body>
</html>
```

Tip   A closing </p> tag is not required by Web browsers, but using one anyway is good practice. XML, SMIL, and other HTML-like languages always require a closing tag, and the HTML 4 specification demands closing tags for complete compliance.

Viewed in a browser, as shown in Figure A-3, our Web page finally has some content.

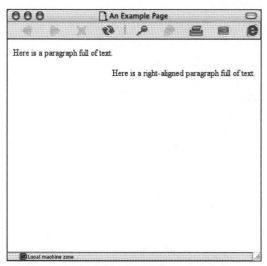

Figure A-3: Browsers leave a line of space between paragraphs and align them according to the <p> tag's align attribute.

The anchor tag: <a></a>

The <a> (anchor) tag is the heart of the World Wide Web because it's used to make hyperlinks. What kind of hypertext would you have without hyperlinks? Making a link is easy: Simply surround text or images that you would like to make into a link with an opening and closing <a> tag and give the tag an href attribute as follows:

```
<a href="http://www.google.com">Search at Google!</a>
```

The href attribute tells the browser what page to go to when the user clicks on *Search at Google!* Links are usually underlined and displayed in dark blue. Adding a link to the word *text* in our example page gives us the following:

```
<html>
<head>
<title>An Example Page</title>
<meta name="description" content="A Web page built as anù
 example of the most common tags and where they go.">
<meta name="keywords" content="HTML, code, examples, learning,ù
 tags, markup languages, hypertexts, Web designs, Webù
 authoring">
<meta name="author" content="Derren Whiteman">
</head>
<body bgcolor="#FFFFFF" text="#000000">
<p>Here is a paragraph full ofù
 <a href="http://www.dictionary.com">text</a>.</p>
<p align="right">Here is a right-aligned paragraph fullù
 of text.</p>
</body>
</html>
```

The previous code looks like Figure A-4 when shown in a browser.

Figure A-4: Links are underlined by default.

The image tag: <img>

The <img> tag is the way you tell a browser, "display this particular image file at this point in the page." Note that there is no closing tag for an <img> tag because it doesn't wrap around other tags or content. It's an image, plain and simple. Although you don't have to put the width and height of the image as width and height attributes, doing so enables pages to load faster. An alt attribute is also a good idea; it provides alternative text for text-only browsers, users who have turned images off in their browsers, and visually impaired Web surfers. You can place an <img> tag within other tags, typically within paragraphs or tables, and you can wrap an <a> tag around it to make the image into a link.

Images are placed in Web pages as illustrations, obviously, but they are also the only reliable way to put certain types of formatting into a page, and thus are often used for titles, logos, and so on. In our example page, we will use one image as an illustration, and one as a page title.

Typically, image files are stored near the HTML file they belong to, either in the same folder, or in their own nearby folder, often called *images* or something similar. The ones for our example page are in the same folder, so the src attributes just contain their names, like so:

```
<html>
<head>
<title>An Example Page</title>
<meta name="description" content="A Web page built as anù
  example of the most common tags and where they go.">
<meta name="keywords" content="HTML, code, examples, learning,ù
  tags, markup languages, hypertexts, Web designs, Webù
  authoring">
<meta name="author" content="Derren Whiteman">
</head>
<body bgcolor="#FFFFFF" text="#000000">
<p><img src="example_title.gif" width="400" height="50"ù
  alt="An Example Page"></p>
<p>Here is a paragraph full ofù
  <a href="http://www.dictionary.com">text</a>.</p>
<p align="right">Here is a right-aligned paragraph fullù
  of text.</p>
<p><img src="mona.gif" width="125" height="160" alt="Aù
  generic placeholder image of the Mona Lisa."></p>
</body>
</html>
```

And the result resembles Figure A-5.

Figure A-5: The `<img>` tag causes the browser to display an image file, such as this Mona Lisa, within a Web page.

You can also use an image from another folder or anywhere on the Web by supplying a valid URL to that image in the `href` attribute.

The font tag: `<font></font>`

Plain text can get pretty boring. Placing a `<font>` tag around text enables us to alter its formatting and specify a typeface with the face attribute, and a color with the color attribute. Colors are specified with RGB color names in hexadecimal notation, however which fonts you can use bears special attention. Fonts are typically specified with a list, such as "Arial, Helvetica, sans serif" because the user must actually have the font you specify on his or her system. If not, then the browser goes to the second choice on the list, then the third, and so on. The options *serif* or *sans serif* should always be the last choices in your font lists. These generic terms tell the browser to use a default serif (such as Times Roman) or sans serif font (such as Helvetica).

Tip   You can also use Bitstream's Dynamic Fonts to download any font with your page. They're viewable natively in Netscape 4+ and with the addition of a small ActiveX Control in IE 4+.

I'm going to bend the rules and go a bit beyond 10 tags by also introducing you to two related tags: To make text bold, wrap it in `<b>` tags; to make it italicized, wrap it in `<i>` tags.

With the addition of `<font>`, `<b>`, and `<i>` tags, our example page now looks as follows:

```
<html>
<head>
<title>An Example Page</title>
```

```
<meta name="description" content="A Web page built as anù
  example of the most common tags and where they go.">
<meta name="keywords" content="HTML, code, examples, learning,ù
  tags, markup languages, hypertexts, Web designs, Webù
  authoring">
<meta name="author" content="Derren Whiteman">
</head>
<body bgcolor="#FFFFFF" text="#000000">
<p><img src="example_title.gif" width="400" height="50"ù
  alt="An Example Page"></p>
<p><font face="Verdana, Helvetica, sans-serif"ù
  color="FF0000"><i>Here</i> is a <b>paragraph</b> full ofù
  <a href="http://www.dictionary.com">text</a>.</font></p>
<p align="right">Here is a right-aligned paragraph fullù
  of text.</p>
<p><img src="mona.gif" width="137" height="190" alt="Aù
  generic placeholder image of the Mona Lisa."></p>
</body>
</html>
```

Figure A-6 shows what our example page now looks like in a browser.

Figure A-6: The <font>, <b>, and <i> tags make the first paragraph of text look quite different from the second.

The table tag: <table></table>

The <table> tag was originally developed so that tables of data — similar to what you find in a spreadsheet — could be more easily displayed in Web pages. These days, it's more commonly used as a way of providing a formatting skeleton for an entire Web page, where elements such as text and images are placed within table cells so that they can appear at an approximate point on a page. The <table> tag is probably the hardest of the top ten tags to grasp just by looking at it, which is why table tags are often created in visual editors, rather than by hand-coding.

Stretching the 10-tag limitation again, the ⟨table⟩ tag always contains two helpers: the ⟨tr⟩ (table row) tag and the ⟨td⟩ (table data) tag. The ⟨tr⟩ tag simply says, "everything within me is a table row." The ⟨td⟩ tag, which always goes within a ⟨tr⟩ tag, is a table cell. Columns aren't specified; they're implied by the number of cells in a row. An empty table with two rows and three columns would appear as follows:

```
<table>
<tr> <td></td> <td></td> <td></td> </tr>
<tr> <td></td> <td></td> <td></td> </tr>
</table>
```

Note that the string of three ⟨td⟩⟨/td⟩ pairs in each row implies the columns. If all tables were completely empty, formatting tables by hand would be much simpler, but after you start to fill them with things, they're a little harder to grasp at first glance. Wrapping the content in a table with three rows and two columns gives us this:

```
<html>
<head>
<title>An Example Page</title>
<meta name="description" content="A Web page built as anù
 example of the most common tags and where they go.">
<meta name="keywords" content="HTML, code, examples, learning,ù
 tags, markup languages, hypertexts, Web designs, Webù
 authoring">
<meta name="author" content="Derren Whiteman">
</head>
<body bgcolor="#FFFFFF" text="#000000">
<table width="500" border="0">
  <tr>
    <td colspan="2"><img src="example_title.gif" width="400"ù
height="50" alt="An Example Page"></td>
  </tr>
  <tr>
    <td> </td>
    <td> </td>
  </tr>
  <tr>
    <td><p><img src="mona.gif" width="125" height="160"ù
alt="A generic placeholder image of the Mona Lisa."></p></td>
    <td><p><font face="Verdana, Helvetica, sans-serif"ù
color="FF0000"><i>Here</i> is a <b>paragraph</b> full ofù
<a href="http://www.dictionary.com">text</a>.</font></p>
        <p align="right">Here is a right-aligned paragraphù
full of text.</p>
    </td>
  </tr>
</table>
</body>
</html>
```

The finished example page, shown in Figure A-7, includes a title, indexing information, formatted text, a hyperlink, an image, and a table — all created with the most commonly used tags.

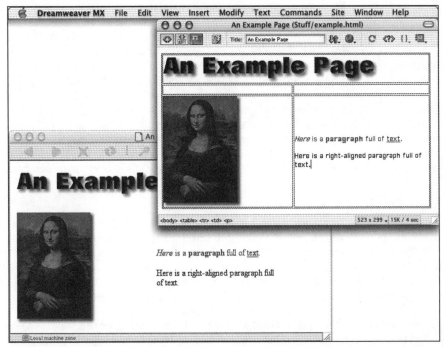

Figure A-7: Looking at the example page in Dreamweaver shows the structure that the `<table>` tag provides. Behind Dreamweaver is the same page in Internet Explorer.

Tip   If you're still hungry for even more tags, the next ones to learn might be `<style>`, `<form>`, `<script>`, and the comment tag. Consult an HTML reference such as Rob Schluter's HTML Tag List at `http://www.home.zonnet.nl/robschluter/htmltaglist/`.

Looking at the Web Browser Variety Show

On an ideal Web, there would be a minimum set of things you could ask any Web browser to do and be guaranteed that they would all do those things in a similar fashion, and do them well. If you stick to authoring for the feature set of Netscape Navigator 3.0, you can pretty much expect most browsers to provide most of the goods, but that still leaves you bumping up against different bugs in individual browsers or browser versions. If you author for a more current Web standard such as CSS 2 (Cascading Style Sheets 2.0), then you find browser support to often be sporadic and buggy. Either way, testing your work in as many browsers as possible is highly recommended, early in the design phase and often.

Examining the browsers

Different projects may require you to target different audiences with different types of browsers. For example, if you're authoring a site that provides tips for using Windows 2000, you can expect the overwhelming majority of your audience to be using Internet Explorer 5 running on Windows 2000 because Internet Explorer 5 is included with Windows 2000. An online magazine for Web professionals might have an audience that's using very current versions of IE or Navigator running on both Windows and Macintosh. A general shopping site probably targets just about anybody, including users of multiple versions of Macintosh, Windows, and AOL browsers. Being familiar with the capabilities and quirks of the browsers you're targeting and — as always — testing, testing, testing, avoids ugly surprises later.

Netscape Navigator (Communicator)

Navigator 1, 2, and 3 are virtually nonexistent now, but Navigator 3 is a good browser to target and test with if you're looking to build a site for a wide audience. It was the first "mature" browser, gained a wide audience, and its feature set was mimicked by browsers that came later. For the most part, if your page works well in Navigator 3, it may not need more than a little tweaking to look very much the same in later versions of Navigator, in Internet Explorer, or in other browsers such as Opera.

Although Navigator 4.x has dwindled in popularity because of the wait for version 6 of Navigator, it remains the most popular non-Microsoft browser, and the trickiest to develop for. It supports some CSS features, including layers, but not to World Wide Web Consortium (W3C) standards. It contains a widely known bug that causes it not to reload a page without CSS formatting if the user resizes the browser window. Navigator 4.x is available for Windows, Macintosh, OS/2, Linux, and many, many other UNIX platforms. Keep in mind that browser plug-ins are platform dependent, and most exist only in Windows and Macintosh versions. When combined with a complete Internet suite, it's called Netscape Communicator, but the browser component is still the same.

Tip   Visit the World Wide Web Consortium at http://www.w3.org.

Netscape's long-awaited update to Navigator 4 is Navigator 6, a completely new product based on the open source work of the Mozilla.org team. Netscape 6 provides excellent support for HTML 4 and CSS 1 standards, but has received only lukewarm product reviews. The open source status of the major components of Netscape 6 suggests that the HTML rendering engine — called *Gecko* — is likely

The Wonders of a Mac with Virtual PC

A Macintosh with Virtual PC installed is the ideal testing computer for any Web design shop because you can run multiple versions of every Netscape, Microsoft, and AOL browser for Windows, Macintosh, and Linux, and also the WebTV viewer, all on the same machine (without multiple hard drive partitions or rebooting). The key to this is getting around IE and AOL for Windows' insistence that there be only one version of their browser on each Windows computer. Virtual PC circumvents this problem by enabling you to maintain multiple configurations, each corresponding to a different virtual boot drive—just a file on your hard disk, really—for the Virtual PC application. Each configuration can contain a different Windows or Linux version, configuration, and browser (and/or set of installed browser plug-ins). In fact, all the screen captures in this book were taken on one Macintosh computer, running multiple versions of Windows, and about 10 different browser versions.

to be built into a range of software and hardware products such as other Web browsers or set-top boxes. Web professionals should definitely keep an eye on these developments.

Microsoft Internet Explorer

IE 1 and 2 were very limited in their feature sets and not widely used, and can be ignored completely. IE 3 includes some basic CSS features, but they are poorly implemented and in a completely different way than IE 4, so targeting CSS at IE 3 is not recommended. The Windows version doesn't support image swaps, but if you use them, the user will not see any errors. Keep this in mind if you create complex image swaps that appear to do nothing when viewed or tested in IE 3.

Note　If a Web design feature doesn't work for a particular browser, but that browser doesn't display an error upon encountering the code, it is said that it "fails without error." It's good to know common Web design terms like this.

Internet Explorer 4 for Windows generally renders HTML pages very well, and supports—albeit incompletely—a number of advanced Web technologies. Its reputation is marred by its forced integration with Windows and its refusal to play nice with a Netscape browser installed on the same machine. IE 5 for Windows improved standards support, but many Web developers still target the feature set of IE 4 (although testing in IE 5 is still recommended). IE 5.5 for Windows introduced a new range of Microsoft-specific HTML extensions, recalling the bad old days when browser manufacturers competed mainly in new ways to encourage Web developers to create pages that would work only in one brand of browser.

Tip　IE 3 is rarely used now, but the feature set survives in many AOL browsers based on it.

Internet Explorer for Macintosh is an entirely different animal from the Windows versions, with different development teams, codebases, and rendering engines. IE 3 and 4 for Macintosh have nice user interfaces, but are — frankly — lousy browsers. However, IE 5.*x* for Macintosh is a completely different story. It continues the Macintosh IE tradition of an excellent user interface, but adds one of the most standards-compliant rendering engine of any shipping browser, code-named *Tasman* by Microsoft, and available only in Macintosh versions of IE 5.x (see Figure A-8).

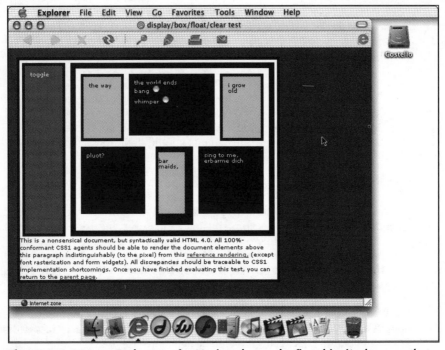

Figure A-8: Internet Explorer 5.x for Macintosh was the first shipping browser that could properly render the W3C's "CSS acid test," a document that tests for full compatibility with the CSS 1.0 specification. Type "about:tasman" in the Address bar of IE 5.x for Macintosh to see a special version of the acid test that substitutes the developer's names for the placeholder text in the real version.

Note   Find the W3C's CSS Acid Test online at `http://www.w3.org/Style/CSS/ Test/current/sec5526c-test.htm`.

As far as plug-in and scripting support in IE, the Windows and Macintosh versions are entirely different as well. IE for Windows uses Windows-only technologies such as ActiveX and VBScript, although it has basic support for Netscape plug-ins and excellent JavaScript support as well. The Mac version uses Netscape plug-ins and JavaScript exclusively, although its support for both in the 3 and 4 versions is the worst of any major browser. However, the support for plug-ins and JavaScript in IE 5.x for Macintosh is excellent. Remember that browser plug-ins are platform-dependent, but Macintosh versions of all major plug-ins are available.

Note UNIX versions of Internet Explorer also exist, but they are not widely used or promoted.

America Online

AOL 3, 4, and 5 browsers are modified versions of Microsoft's Internet Explorer, but, unfortunately, the version numbers do not always correspond. In other words, an AOL 6 browser may be based on IE 3.02, IE 4.x, or IE 5.5. The major modification to keep in mind is that AOL browsers are single-window—they do not allow a second window to be opened. AOL also caches and recompresses images, which can cause artifacts to appear in some JPEGs. Images are also limited to 640×480 in size.

Tip For more about authoring for AOL see AOL's Webmaster page at `http://webmaster.aol.com`.

WebTV

WebTV has not exactly taken the world by storm, and its users remain a very small minority of the Web. Accessing the Web with a TV and a set-top box may be much more popular in the future, though, and future devices will no doubt learn some lessons from WebTV, so it is an interesting study for any Web developer.

WebTV renders Web pages in a fairly unique way in order to account for the very low resolution of TV screens. The major point to note is that its "browser window" is fixed at 544-pixels wide and 378-pixels tall. If your page is wider, it is squeezed to fit. If your page is longer, the user scrolls (a lot) to see the rest. WebTV only allows one browser window, and supports frames in a unique way: Your frameset is converted to a table and then squeezed to fit into 544 pixels. WebTV enables you to use any font you want to as long as it's 14-pixel bold sans serif. Flash is Flash 2.0, and RealAudio is 3.0. One thing that WebTV does very well is play back MIDI files—in a software synthesizer based on technology from Beatnik, Inc.

There's no substitute for actually viewing your work as a WebTV user would see it. Thankfully, the WebTV people offer a free WebTV Viewer for Windows or Macintosh that goes a long way toward helping you make your pages WebTV-savvy. You can find it at `http://developer.msntv.com` and view it in Figure A-9.

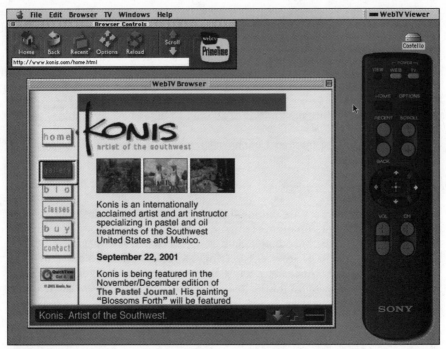

Figure A-9: The Web page from Figure A-1 is revisited in the WebTV Viewer 2.0 for Macintosh.

Understanding cross-platform concerns

The Web can be surprisingly cross-platform when you consider that Netscape browsers act similarly on Windows, Macintosh, and Linux, but you need to keep a few major caveats in mind if you want your Web pages to look similar on different platforms.

Fonts

Before the Web existed, computer-based publishing was primarily print publishing. Choosing a font in a computer program has therefore traditionally meant choosing a point (pt) size. Displaying a 12pt font on a pixel-based computer display requires that the computer convert points, which are $\frac{1}{72}$ of an inch, into pixels (px), the smallest dots a computer monitor can display.

Figure A-10 shows a Web page displayed on a Macintosh, where the specified 10pt font is displayed as a 10px font because the Mac assumes the standard 72 dpi.

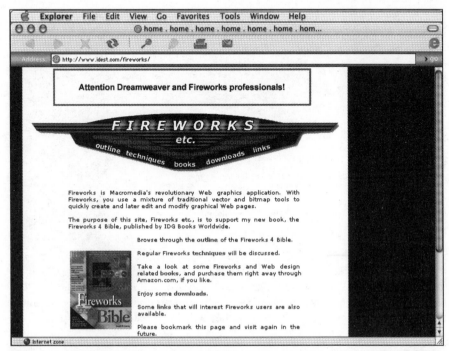

Figure A-10: Mac OS uses a value of 72 dpi to convert points into pixels, so fonts appear smaller in Mac OS browsers than they do in their Windows counterparts.

Figure A-11 shows the same Web page on a Windows computer, where the specified 10pt font is displayed as a 12px font because Windows assumes 96 dpi.

Note   Internet Explorer 5 for Macintosh introduced a new feature to improve the cross-platform display of fonts: It has a resolution preference that is set to the Windows standard of 96 dpi by default. However, it also sets the default font size to 16 points so that users who don't change the settings will actually see text at a *larger* size than their Windows-using counterparts.

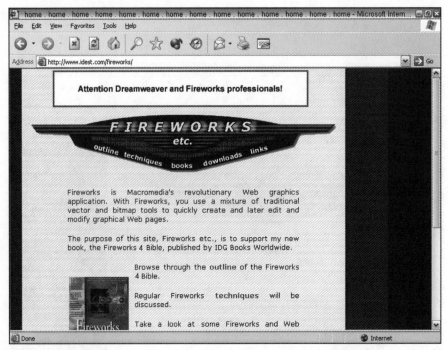

Figure A-11: Windows uses a value of 96 dpi to convert points into pixels, so fonts appear bigger in Windows browsers than they do in their Mac OS counterparts.

Form widgets

Form widgets are provided by a computer's operating system, not by the browser, and so look different on each platform, and are often differently sized as well, as shown in Figure A-12. Web authors need to be aware of this and allow for it in their designs, leaving extra space as necessary and testing on other platforms whenever possible. One common mistake is to mix form widgets with image buttons that resemble the form widgets on your particular operating system. Mac OS X form widgets are very different than those on other operating systems — they appear as translucent glass — and can really change the look of your page.

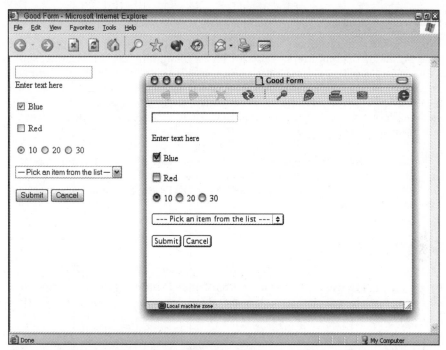

Figure A-12: Form widgets look different and are even slightly different sizes on each operating system.

Understanding Protocols

Information travels across the Internet according to the specifications of a protocol suite called TCP/IP (Transmission Control Protocol/Internet Protocol). A protocol suite is, quite simply, a collection of protocols, or agreements on how to do something. TCP/IP contains over a hundred of them, but let's look at just the most commonly used ones here.

HTTP and HTTPS

HTTP, or Hypertext Transfer Protocol, carries requests for HTML pages from Web browsers to servers, and carries HTML pages back from servers to browsers. As you may well imagine, this function is fairly common on the World Wide Web. When a browser and server want to talk privately — during an e-commerce transaction, for example — they use the HTTPS protocol instead: Hypertext Transfer Protocol Secure. When a browser is using HTTPS, a closed lock or similar icon is displayed for the user and information is encrypted before it's sent. All Web browsers support HTTP; most support HTTPS. An HTTP URL is written http://www.opensrs.com. An HTTPS URL is similar, except it uses an https:// prefix.

FTP

FTP (File Transfer Protocol) enables files to be copied between computers — even different kinds of computers — and for basic file manipulation functions, such as listing a folder of files on a remote computer. Browsers support rudimentary FTP, but a dedicated FTP Client such as WS FTP for Windows or Interarchy for Macintosh is needed to take full advantage of the control that FTP enables. Many FTP servers enable anonymous guest logins, where your e-mail address is your password and you have limited privileges. An FTP URL appears as follows: `ftp://ftp.panic.com`.

Tip It may seem as if *ftp* is specified twice in the URL `ftp://ftp.panic.com`, but that is not the case. The first `ftp` is the protocol, and the second `ftp` is the name of panic.com's FTP server. In the same way, HTTP servers are often named `www`, as in `http://www.panic.com`.

SMTP and POP

SMTP, or Simple Mail Transfer Protocol, enables different computers on a network to route e-mail to each other. POP, or Post Office Protocol, is a newer method for receiving mail. E-mail clients such as Netscape Messenger or Microsoft Outlook Express use SMTP and POP to send and receive e-mail.

NNTP

NNTP (Network News Transfer Protocol) is used by Internet news readers to query news servers, and by news servers to deliver news messages. NNTP is responsible for the Usenet news we all know and love. An NNTP URL appears as: `news://forums.macromedia.com/macromedia.fireworks`.

Note Other protocols use prefixes that are the same as their names — `ftp://` for FTP, for example — but NNTP URLs use the `news://` prefix.

RTSP

RTSP, or Real-Time Streaming Protocol, is perhaps the sexiest Internet protocol, enabling for the efficient transfer of streaming multimedia files such as audio or video over the Internet. The real-time refers to the fact that audio and video files need to get to the client in a timely fashion so as not to interrupt the presentation. An example of server software that sends information using RTSP is QuickTime Streaming Server. All that's needed is the QuickTime Player (see Figure A-13) to receive it. An RTSP URL starts with an `rtsp://` prefix.

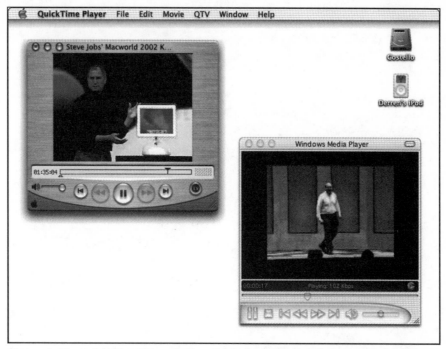

Figure A-13: QuickTime Player (left) and Windows Media Player both use RTSP to receive streaming multimedia (in this case, video) over the Internet.

✦　　✦　　✦

Keyboard Shortcuts

◆   ◆   ◆   ◆

In This Appendix

Saving time with
keyboard shortcuts

Selecting Fireworks
tools the fast and
easy way

Learning the
top ten shortcuts

◆   ◆   ◆   ◆

Fireworks includes a full complement of keyboard shortcuts to cut down on the time and trouble it takes to
access commonly used commands. The default keyboard
shortcuts in Fireworks MX are part of the Macromedia
Common UI and are similar to the defaults found in many
other Macromedia applications. We'll go menu by menu in
the first of the tables that follow. In Table B-12, you'll find
keyboard shortcuts for the Fireworks tools that will aid in
quickly selecting commonly used tools. In Table B-13, you'll
find my Top Ten Fireworks Keyboard Shortcuts.

Note

In the tables throughout this appendix, commands or tools
listed in **bold** text are new or have changed menu, or
panel, locations in Fireworks MX.

The Application Menu

You can find application-specific commands such as
Preferences and Quit in the Application menu on Mac OS X,
also known as the Fireworks menu. Fireworks menu commands are listed in Table B-1.

Table B-1
Fireworks Menu Commands (Mac OS X only)

Command	Keystroke
About Fireworks	n/a
Keyboard Shortcuts	n/a
Preferences	Command+U
Services	n/a
Hide Fireworks	Command+H
Hide Others	n/a
Show All	n/a
Quit Fireworks	Command+Q

The File Menu

The File menu contains commands for file handling and import and export functions. Table B-2 details its keyboard shortcuts.

Table B-2
File Menu Keyboard Shortcuts

Command	Windows	Macintosh
New	Ctrl+N	Command+N
Open	Ctrl+O	Command+O
Open Recent ⇨ Your Recently Opened Documents	n/a	n/a
Reconstitute Table	n/a	n/a
Scan ⇨ Twain Acquire	n/a	n/a
Scan ⇨ Twain Select	n/a	n/a
Scan ⇨ Your Photoshop Acquire Plug-Ins (Macintosh only)	—	n/a
Close	Ctrl+W	Command+W
Save	Ctrl+S	Command+S

Command	Windows	Macintosh
Save As	Ctrl+Shift+S	Command+Shift+S
Save a Copy	n/a	n/a
Revert	n/a	n/a
Import	Ctrl+R	Command+R
Export	Ctrl+Shift+R	Command+Shift+R
Export Preview	Ctrl+Shift+X	Command+Shift+X
Update HTML	n/a	n/a
Export Wizard	n/a	n/a
Batch Process	n/a	n/a
Preview in Browser ⇨ Preview in Primary Browser	F12	F12
Preview in Browser ⇨ Preview in Secondary Browser	Shift+F12	Shift+F12
Preview in Browser ⇨ Set Primary Browser	n/a	n/a
Preview in Browser ⇨ Set Secondary Browser	n/a	n/a
Page Setup	n/a	n/a
Print	Ctrl+P	Command+P
HTML Setup	n/a	n/a
Exit (Windows only)	Ctrl+Q	—

The Edit Menu

The Edit menu enables you to select, duplicate, or remove objects. Cut, Copy, and Paste are standard on all programs; others, such as Paste Attributes, are unique to Fireworks. Table B-3 details the Edit menu's keyboard shortcuts.

Table B-3 Edit Menu Keyboard Shortcuts		
Command	Windows	Macintosh
Undo	Ctrl+Z	Command+Z
Redo	Ctrl+Y	Command+Y

Continued

Table B-3 *(continued)*

Command	Windows	Macintosh
Insert ➪ New Button	n/a	n/a
Insert ➪ New Symbol	Ctrl+F8	Command+F8
Insert ➪ Hotspot	Ctrl+Shift+U	Command+Shift+U
Insert ➪ Slice	Alt+Shift+U	Option+Shift+U
Insert ➪ Empty Bitmap	n/a	n/a
Insert ➪ Bitmap Via Copy	n/a	n/a
Insert ➪ Bitmap Via Cut	n/a	n/a
Insert ➪ Layer	n/a	n/a
Insert ➪ Frame	n/a	n/a
Libraries ➪ Animations	n/a	n/a
Libraries ➪ Bullets	n/a	n/a
Libraries ➪ Buttons	n/a	n/a
Libraries ➪ Themes	n/a	n/a
Libraries ➪ Other	n/a	n/a
Find and Replace	Ctrl+F	Command+F
Cut	Ctrl+X	Command+X
Copy	Ctrl+C	Command+C
Copy as Vectors	n/a	n/a
Copy HTML Code	Ctrl+Alt+C	Command+Option+C
Paste	Ctrl+V	Command+V
Clear	Backspace	Delete
Paste as Mask	n/a	n/a
Paste Inside	Ctrl+Shift+V	Command+Shift+V
Paste Attributes	Ctrl+Alt+Shift+V	Command+Option+Shift+V
Duplicate	Ctrl+Alt+D	Command+Option+D
Clone	Ctrl+Shift+D	Command+Shift+D
Crop Selected Bitmap	n/a	n/a
Crop Document	n/a	n/a
Preferences	Ctrl+U	Command+U
Keyboard Shortcuts	n/a	n/a

Note The last two menu items in Table B-3 are found on Windows and Mac OS 9 only. On Mac OS X, these items are in the Application menu, which is covered in Table B-1.

The View Menu

With the commands on the View menu, you can zoom in or out on your work, or view a grid or guides to assist with layout. Table B-4 details the View menu's keyboard shortcuts.

Table B-4		
View Menu Keyboard Shortcuts		
Command	*Windows*	*Macintosh*
Zoom In	Ctrl+Equals (=)	Command+Equals (=)
Zoom Out	Ctrl+Minus (-)	Command+Minus (-)
Magnification ⇨ 6%	n/a	n/a
Magnification ⇨ 12%	n/a	n/a
Magnification ⇨ 25%	n/a	n/a
Magnification ⇨ 50%	Ctrl+5	Command+5
Magnification ⇨ 66%	n/a	n/a
Magnification ⇨ 100%	Ctrl+1	Command+1
Magnification ⇨ 150%	n/a	n/a
Magnification ⇨ 200%	Ctrl+2	Command+2
Magnification ⇨ 300%	Ctrl+3	Command+3
Magnification ⇨ 400%	Ctrl+4	Command+4
Magnification ⇨ 800%	Ctrl+8	Command+8
Magnification ⇨ 1600%	Ctrl+6	Command+6
Magnification ⇨ 3200%	n/a	n/a
Magnification ⇨ 6400%	n/a	n/a
Fit Selection	Ctrl+Alt+Zero (0)	Command+Option+Zero (0)
Fit All	Ctrl+Zero (0)	Command+Zero (0)
Full Display	Ctrl+K	Command+K

Continued

Table B-4 *(continued)*

Command	Windows	Macintosh
Macintosh Gamma (Windows only)	n/a	—
Windows Gamma (Macintosh only)	—	n/a
Hide Selection	Ctrl+L	Command+L
Show All	Ctrl+Shift+L	Command+Shift+L
Rulers	Ctrl+Alt+R	Command+Option+R
Grid ➪ Show Grid	Ctrl+Alt+G	Command+Option+G
Grid ➪ Snap To Grid	Ctrl+Alt+Shift+G	Command+Option+Shift+G
Grid ➪ Edit Grid	n/a	n/a
Guides ➪ Show Guides	Ctrl+Semicolon (;)	Command+Semicolon (;)
Guides ➪ Lock Guides	Ctrl+Alt+Semicolon (;)	Command+Option+ Semicolon (;)
Guides ➪ Snap to Guides	Ctrl+Shift+Semicolon (;)	Command+Shift+ Semicolon (;)
Guides ➪ Edit Guides	n/a	n/a
Slice Guides	Ctrl+Alt+Shift+ Semicolon (;)	Command+Option+ Shift+Semicolon (;)
Slice Overlay	n/a	n/a
Hide Edges	F9	F9
Hide Panels	F4	F4
Status Bar (Windows only)	n/a	—

The Select Menu

The Select menu contains objects you can insert into your documents. Table B-5 details the items available on the Select menu and their keyboard shortcuts.

Table B-5		
Select Menu Keyboard Shortcuts		
Command	*Windows*	*Macintosh*
Select All	Ctrl+A	Command+A
Deselect	Ctrl+D	Command+D
Superselect	n/a	n/a
Subselect	n/a	n/a
Select Similar	n/a	n/a
Select Inverse	Ctrl+Shift+I	Command+Shift+I
Feather	n/a	n/a
Expand Marquee	n/a	n/a
Contract Marquee	n/a	n/a
Border Marquee	n/a	n/a
Smooth Marquee	n/a	n/a
Save Bitmap Selection	n/a	n/a
Restore Bitmap Selection	n/a	n/a

The Modify Menu

The Modify menu lists commands for altering existing selections. Its keyboard shortcuts are detailed in Table B-6.

Table B-6		
Modify Menu Keyboard Shortcuts		
Command	*Windows*	*Macintosh*
Canvas ⇨ Image Size	n/a	n/a
Canvas ⇨ Canvas Size	n/a	n/a
Canvas ⇨ Canvas Color	n/a	n/a
Canvas ⇨ Trim Canvas	Ctrl+Alt+T	Command+Option+T
Canvas ⇨ Fit Canvas	Ctrl+Alt+F	Command+Option+F

Continued

Table B-6 *(continued)*

Command	Windows	Macintosh
Canvas ➪ Rotate 180°	n/a	n/a
Canvas ➪ Rotate 90° CW	n/a	n/a
Canvas ➪ Rotate 90° CCW	n/a	n/a
Animation ➪ Animate Selection	Alt+Shift+F8	Option+Shift+F8
Animation ➪ Settings	n/a	n/a
Animation ➪ Remove Animation	n/a	n/a
Symbol ➪ Convert to Symbol	F8	F8
Symbol ➪ Edit Symbol	n/a	n/a
Symbol ➪ Tween Instances	Ctrl+Alt+ Shift+T	Command+Option +Shift+T
Symbol ➪ Break Apart	n/a	n/a
Pop-up Menu ➪ Add Pop-up Menu	n/a	n/a
Pop-up Menu ➪ Edit Pop-up Menu	n/a	n/a
Pop-up Menu ➪ Delete Pop-up Menu	n/a	n/a
Mask ➪ Reveal All	n/a	n/a
Mask ➪ Hide All	n/a	n/a
Mask ➪ Paste as Mask	n/a	n/a
Mask ➪ Group as Mask	n/a	n/a
Mask ➪ Reveal Selection	n/a	n/a
Mask ➪ Hide Selection	n/a	n/a
Mask ➪ Disable Mask	n/a	n/a
Mask ➪ Delete Mask	n/a	n/a
Selective JPEG ➪ Save Selection as JPEG Mask	n/a	n/a
Selective JPEG ➪ Restore JPEG Mask as Selection	n/a	n/a
Selective JPEG ➪ Settings	n/a	n/a
Selective JPEG ➪ Remove JPEG Mask	n/a	n/a
Flatten Selection	Ctrl+Alt+ Shift+Z	Command+Option +Shift+Z
Merge Down	Ctrl+E	Command+E
Flatten Layers	n/a	n/a
Transform ➪ Free Transform	n/a	n/a

Command	Windows	Macintosh
Transform ⇨ Scale	n/a	n/a
Transform ⇨ Skew	n/a	n/a
Transform ⇨ Distort	n/a	n/a
Transform ⇨ Numeric Transform	Ctrl+Shift+T	Command+Shift+T
Transform ⇨ Rotate 180°	n/a	n/a
Transform ⇨ Rotate 90° CW	Ctrl+9	Command+9
Transform ⇨ Rotate 90° CCW	Ctrl+7	Command+7
Transform ⇨ Flip Horizontal	n/a	n/a
Transform ⇨ Flip Vertical	n/a	n/a
Transform ⇨ Remove Transformations	n/a	n/a
Arrange ⇨ Bring to Front	Ctrl+Shift+ Up Arrow	Command+Shift+ Up Arrow
Arrange ⇨ Bring Forward	Ctrl+Up Arrow	Command+Up Arrow
Arrange ⇨ Send Backward	Ctrl+Down Arrow	Command+ Down Arrow
Arrange ⇨ Send to Back	Ctrl+Shift+ Down Arrow	Command+Shift+ Down Arrow
Align ⇨ Left	Ctrl+Alt+1	Command+Option+1
Align ⇨ Center Vertical	Ctrl+Alt+2	Command+Option+2
Align ⇨ Right	Ctrl+Alt+3	Command+Option+3
Align ⇨ Top	Ctrl+Alt+4	Command+Option+4
Align ⇨ Center Horizontal	Ctrl+Alt+5	Command+Option+5
Align ⇨ Bottom	Ctrl+Alt+6	Command+Option+6
Align ⇨ Distribute Widths	Ctrl+Alt+7	Command+Option+7
Align ⇨ Distribute Heights	Ctrl+Alt+9	Command+Option+9
Combine Paths ⇨ Join	Ctrl+J	Command+J
Combine Paths ⇨ Split	Ctrl+Shift+J	Command+Shift+J
Combine Paths ⇨ Union	n/a	n/a
Combine Paths ⇨ Intersect	n/a	n/a
Combine Paths ⇨ Punch	n/a	n/a
Combine Paths ⇨ Crop	n/a	n/a
Alter Path ⇨ Simplify	n/a	n/a

Continued

Table B-6 *(continued)*		
Command	**Windows**	**Macintosh**
Alter Path ⇨ Expand Stroke	n/a	n/a
Alter Path ⇨ Inset Path	n/a	n/a
Alter Path ⇨ Hard Fill	n/a	n/a
Alter Path ⇨ Anti-Alias Fill	n/a	n/a
Alter Path ⇨ Feather Fill	n/a	n/a
Group	Ctrl+G	Command+G
Ungroup	Ctrl+Shift+G	Command+Shift+G

The Text Menu

The Text menu enables you to change the formatting options for text objects or to convert them to paths. Table B-7 details Text menu keyboard shortcuts.

Table B-7 Text Menu Keyboard Shortcuts		
Command	**Windows**	**Macintosh**
Font ⇨ Your Font List	n/a	n/a
Size ⇨ Other	n/a	n/a
Size ⇨ Smaller	Ctrl+Shift+comma (,)	Command+Shift+ comma (,)
Size ⇨ Larger	Ctrl+Shift+period (.)	Command+Shift+ period (.)
Size ⇨ 8 to 120	n/a	n/a
Style ⇨ Plain	n/a	n/a
Style ⇨ Bold	Ctrl+B	Command+B
Style ⇨ Italic	Ctrl+I	Command+I
Style ⇨ Underline	n/a	n/a
Align ⇨ Left	Ctrl+Alt+Shift+L	Command+Option+ Shift+L
Align ⇨ Centered Horizontally	Ctrl+Alt+Shift+C	Command+Option+ Shift+C

Command	Windows	Macintosh
Align ➪ Right	Ctrl+Alt+Shift+R	Command+Option+ Shift+R
Align ➪ Justified	Ctrl+Alt+Shift+J	Command+Option+ Shift+J
Align ➪ Stretched	Ctrl+Alt+Shift+S	Command+Option+ Shift+S
Align ➪ Top	n/a	n/a
Align ➪ Centered Vertically	n/a	n/a
Align ➪ Bottom	n/a	n/a
Align ➪ Justified Vertically	n/a	n/a
Align ➪ Stretched Vertically	n/a	n/a
Editor	n/a	n/a
Attach to Path	Ctrl+Shift+Y	Command+Shift+Y
Detach from Path	n/a	n/a
Orientation ➪ Rotate Around Path	n/a	n/a
Orientation ➪ Vertical	n/a	n/a
Orientation ➪ Skew Vertical	n/a	n/a
Orientation ➪ Skew Horizontal	n/a	n/a
Reverse Direction	n/a	n/a
Convert to Paths	Ctrl+Shift+P	Command+Shift+P
Check Spelling	Shift+F7	Shift+F7
Spelling Setup	n/a	n/a

The Commands Menu

Fireworks commands are written in JavaScript and can be added to Fireworks by the user to customize the feature set. Although the Commands menu does not include any keyboard shortcuts, it is included here (see Table B-8) for the sake of completeness and for those using this section as a command reference.

Cross-Reference For more about Fireworks commands, see Chapter 19.

Table B-8
Commands Menu Keyboard Shortcuts

Command	Windows	Macintosh
Manage Saved Commands	n/a	n/a
Manage Extensions	n/a	n/a
Run Script	n/a	n/a
Creative ➪ Add Arrowheads	n/a	n/a
Creative ➪ Add Picture Frame	n/a	n/a
Creative ➪ Convert to Grayscale	n/a	n/a
Creative ➪ Convert to Sepia Tone	n/a	n/a
Creative ➪ Fade Image	n/a	n/a
Creative ➪ Twist and Fade	n/a	n/a
Data-Driven Graphics Wizard	n/a	n/a
Document ➪ Distribute to Layers	n/a	n/a
Document ➪ Hide Other Layers	n/a	n/a
Document ➪ Lock Other Layers	n/a	n/a
Document ➪ Reverse Frames	n/a	n/a
Panel Layout Sets ➪ 1024×768/1152×768/ 1280×1024/800×600/Your Panel Layout Sets	n/a	n/a
Panel Layout Sets ➪ Save Panel Layout	n/a	n/a
Reset Warning Dialogs	n/a	n/a
Resize Selected Objects	n/a	n/a
Web ➪ Create Shared Palette	n/a	n/a
Web ➪ Select Blank ALT Tags	n/a	n/a
Web ➪ Set ALT Tags	n/a	n/a

The Filters Menu

Filters are plug-in image manipulation tools (usually Photoshop-compatible) that expand the capabilities of Fireworks. Table B-9 details the standard filters that are included with Fireworks. Your Filters menu has additional options if you have installed third-party plug-ins.

Table B-9
Filters Menu Keyboard Shortcuts

Command	Windows	Macintosh
Repeat Filter	Ctrl+Alt+Shift+X	Command+Option+Shift+X
Adjust Color ⇨ Auto Levels	n/a	n/a
Adjust Color ⇨ Brightness/Contrast	n/a	n/a
Adjust Color ⇨ Curves	n/a	n/a
Adjust Color ⇨ Hue/Saturation	n/a	n/a
Adjust Color ⇨ Invert	Ctrl+Alt+Shift+I	Command+Option+Shift+I
Adjust Color ⇨ Levels	n/a	n/a
Blur ⇨ Blur	n/a	n/a
Blur ⇨ Blur More	n/a	n/a
Blur ⇨ Gaussian Blur	n/a	n/a
Other ⇨ Convert to Alpha	n/a	n/a
Other ⇨ Find Edges	n/a	n/a
Sharpen ⇨ Sharpen	n/a	n/a
Sharpen ⇨ Sharpen More	n/a	n/a
Sharpen ⇨ Unsharp Mask	n/a	n/a
Eye Candy 4000 LE ⇨ Bevel Boss	n/a	n/a
Eye Candy 4000 LE ⇨ Marble	n/a	n/a
Eye Candy 4000 LE ⇨ Motion Trail	n/a	n/a
Alien Skin Splat LE ⇨ Edges	n/a	n/a

The Window Menu

The Window menu manages document windows and also Fireworks panels. Through this menu you can open, close, arrange, bring to the front, or hide all of Fireworks' windows. Table B-10 details the Window menu keyboard shortcuts.

Tip   All the commands for the various panels and inspectors are toggles. Select once to view a floating window; select again to hide it.

Table B-10
Window Menu Keyboard Shortcuts

Command	Windows	Macintosh
New Window	Ctrl+Alt+N	Command+Option+N
Toolbars ⇨ Main (Windows only)	n/a	—
Toolbars ⇨ Modify (Windows only)	n/a	—
Tools	Ctrl+F2	Command+F2
Properties	Ctrl+F3	Command+F3
Answers	Alt+F1	Option+F1
Optimize	F10	F10
Layers	F2	F2
Frames	Shift+F2	Shift+F2
History	Shift+F10	Shift+F10
Styles	Shift+F11	Shift+F11
Library	F11	F11
URL	Alt+Shift+F10	Option+Shift+F10
Color Mixer	Shift+F9	Shift+F9
Swatches	Ctrl+F9	Command+F9
Info	Alt+Shift+F12	Option+Shift+F12
Behaviors	Shift+F3	Shift+F3
Find and Replace	Ctrl+F	Command+F
Project Log	n/a	n/a
Align	n/a	n/a
Sitespring	n/a	n/a
Cascade	n/a	n/a
Tile Horizontal	n/a	n/a
Tile Vertical	n/a	n/a
Your Open Documents List	n/a	n/a

The Help Menu

The Help menu offers access to Fireworks' online manual, tutorial, and even the Fireworks Web site. Table B-11 details its keyboard shortcuts.

Table B-11		
Help Menu Keyboard Shortcuts		
Command	*Windows*	*Macintosh*
About Balloon Help (Mac OS 9 only)	—	n/a
Show Balloons (Mac OS 9 only)	—	n/a
Fireworks Help	—	Command+?
Welcome	n/a	n/a
What's New	n/a	n/a
Using Fireworks	F1	—
Manage Extensions	n/a	n/a
Fireworks Support Center	n/a	n/a
Macromedia Online Forums	n/a	n/a
Online Registration	n/a	n/a
Print Registration	n/a	n/a
About Fireworks (Windows only)	n/a	—

Tip Mac OS 9 users can display the About Fireworks dialog box by choosing Apple Menu ⇨ About Fireworks.

The Tools Panel

As well as providing keyboard shortcuts for menu commands, Fireworks also enables you to use the keyboard to change the active tool quickly and easily. Hover your cursor over a particular tool and Fireworks displays the name of the tool, as well as its keyboard shortcut. Table B-12 describes each tool's keyboard shortcut.

Note Some of the keyboard shortcuts act as a toggle between tools that are similar. For example, V (or Zero) toggles between the Pointer and the Select Behind tools.

Table B-12
Tools Keyboard Shortcuts

Button	Name	Shortcut
	Pointer	V or Zero
	Select Behind	V or Zero
	Subselection	A or 1
	Scale	Q
	Skew	Q
	Distort	Q
	Crop	C
	Export Area	C
	Marquee	M
	Oval Marquee	M
	Lasso	L
	Polygon Lasso	L
	Magic Wand	W
	Brush	B

Button	Name	Shortcut
	Pencil	B
	Eraser	E
	Blur	R
	Sharpen	R
	Dodge	R
	Burn	R
	Smudge	R
	Rubber Stamp	S
	Eyedropper	I
	Paint Bucket	G
	Gradient	G
	Line	N
	Pen	P
	Vector Path	P
	Redraw Path	P

Continued

	Table B-12 *(continued)*	
Button	*Name*	*Shortcut*
	Rectangle	U
	Rounded Rectangle	U
	Ellipse	U
	Polygon	U
	Text	T
	Freeform	O
	Reshape Area	O
	Path Scrubber (+)	n/a
	Path Scrubber (-)	n/a
	Knife	Y
	Rectangle Hotspot	J
	Circle Hotspot	J
	Polygon Hotspot	J
	Slice	K

Button	Name	Shortcut
	Polygon Slice	K
	Hand	H, or press and hold spacebar
	Zoom	Z

The Top Ten Fireworks Keyboard Shortcuts

Of course, you'll want to learn universal keyboard shortcuts, such as Open, Save, and Close (see Table B-2), and Cut, Copy, and Paste (see Table B-3). But after you have those down, Table B-13 contains my recommendations for the most useful Fireworks-specific keyboard shortcuts, presented with the tools first, and then going across the menus from left to right.

Table B-13 Top Ten Fireworks Keyboard Shortcuts		
Command	**Windows**	**Macintosh**
Pointer/Select Behind Tool	V or Zero	V or Zero
Text Tool	T	T
View ⇨ Magnification ⇨ 50%, 100%, 200%, 400%	Ctrl+5, 1, 2, 4	Command+5, 1, 2, 4
Edit ⇨ Duplicate	Ctrl+Alt+D	Command+Option+D
Select ⇨ Deselect	Ctrl+D	Command+D
Modify ⇨ Transform ⇨ Numeric Transform	Ctrl+Shift+T	Command+Shift+T
Modify ⇨ Align ⇨ Center Vertical	Ctrl+Alt+2	Command+Option+2
Modify ⇨ Align ⇨ Center Horizontal	Ctrl+Alt+5	Command+Option+5
Modify ⇨ Group	Ctrl+G	Command+G
Text ⇨ Check Spelling	Shift+F7	Shift+F7

✦   ✦   ✦

What's on the CD-ROM

This appendix provides you with information on the contents of the CD-ROM that accompanies the *Fireworks MX Bible*. For the latest and greatest information, please refer to the ReadMe file located at the root of the CD. The CD-ROM contains the following:

    ◆ Fully functioning trial versions of Macromedia's Fireworks MX, Dreamweaver MX, Flash MX, and FreeHand 10

    ◆ Fireworks-compatible filters from the leading manufacturers of such tools, Alien Skin Software and Auto FX Software

Also included, from some of the finest designers working with Fireworks today, are a wide range of commands, strokes, gradients, textures, and custom HTML templates designed to make your work more productive. Finally, you'll also find several sample graphics from the book for you to inspect, modify, and experiment with at your leisure.

System Requirements

Make sure that your computer meets the minimum system requirements listed in this section. If your computer doesn't match up to most of these requirements, you may have a problem using the contents of the CD.

For Windows 98SE, Windows 2000, Windows NT4 (with SP 6 or later), Windows Me, or Windows XP:

✦ PC with a Pentium II processor running at 300 Mhz or faster

✦ At least 96 MB of total RAM installed on your computer; for best performance, we recommend at least 128 MB

✦ Ethernet network interface card (NIC) or modem with a speed of at least 28,800 bps

✦ A CD-ROM drive

For Macintosh:

✦ A G3 or faster processor running OS 9.1 or later, or OS X 10.1 or later

✦ At least 96 MB of total RAM installed on your computer; for best performance, we recommend at least 128 MB

Using the CD-ROM

The CD-ROM is a "hybrid" CD-ROM, which means that it contains one section for Windows and one section for Macintosh. Your operating system automatically chooses the correct section.

Several files, primarily the Macromedia trial programs and the additional commercial programs, are compressed. Double-click these files to begin the installation procedure. Most other files on the CD-ROM are not compressed and can simply be copied from the CD-ROM to your system by using your file manager. A few of the Fireworks extensions that include files that must be placed in different folders are also compressed.

Where possible, the file structure of the CD-ROM replicates the structure that Fireworks MX sets up when it is installed. For example, textures are found in the Fireworks MX/Settings/Textures folder on both the CD-ROM and the folder that the Fireworks MX installer creates on your computer.

Within the Extensions folder, you'll find some commands packed in Macromedia .mxp format. Double-click these files to install them using the Extension Manager. For more details on using the Extension Manager, see Chapter 19.

What's on the CD

The *Fireworks MX Bible* companion CD-ROM contains a host of programs and auxiliary files to assist you in your exploration of Fireworks, as well as in your Web-page design work in general. A description of the files and programs on the CD-ROM follows.

Fireworks MX, Dreamweaver MX, Flash MX, and FreeHand 10 demos

If you haven't had a chance to work with Fireworks (or Dreamweaver, Flash, or FreeHand), the CD-ROM offers fully functioning trial versions of these key Macromedia programs for both Macintosh and Windows systems. Each of these demos can be used for 30 days; they cannot be reinstalled for additional use time.

To install a demo, simply double-click its installer icon in the main folder of the CD-ROM and follow the installation instructions on your screen.

Caution   The trial versions of the Macromedia programs are very sensitive to system date changes. If you alter your computer's date, the program "times out" and is no longer functional.

The full Fireworks version comes with a wonderful assortment of styles. To sample this work, visit the Fireworks Web site at `www.macromedia.com/software/fireworks/`.

Additional programs

Fireworks MX is definitely one program that "plays well with others." Virtually any third-party Photoshop-compatible plug-in can be used as a Fireworks Effect — good news if you're a Photoshop user or have Photoshop-compatible filters from another application. Several of the leading filter developers have generously loaned their programs for inclusion on this CD-ROM.

In addition to the filters described in this section, the world-renowned color specialist, Pantone, has contributed a program, ColorWeb Pro, in a trial version to help ease the transition for designers from the world of print to the Web. We are including the full software product along with a QuickTime movie that briefly demos ColorWeb. To activate the software, users must call Pantone to purchase the serial number. The product will not function without purchasing it through Pantone.

Filters from Alien Skin

Alien Skin Software has contributed a trial version of three different filter collections: Xenofex, EyeCandy 4000, and their newest offering, Splat!. Xenofex is a collection of inspirational special effects that energize any graphics project. Realistic natural phenomena and sophisticated distortions have never been easier to create. Eye Candy 4000 from Alien Skin, is a terrific collection of 23 effects applicable to any Fireworks image including Smoke, Marble, Melt and Corona. Splat! adds frames, textures, edges, borders, mosaics and more to Fireworks graphics. Alien Skin's Web site can be found at `www.alienskin.com/`.

Filters from Auto FX

Auto FX Software has contributed a trial version of one of its finest plug-in packages called DreamSuite Series One. DreamSuite Series One is a collection of 18 different plug-ins that offer a wide variety of effects such as Chisel, Crackle, Crease, PhotoBorder, and Liquid Metal. Along with DreamSuite Series One, Auto FX offers DreamSuite Series Two, DreamSuite Gel Series, Photo/Graphic Edges, and AutoEye. The filters in these packages offer effects that aren't available in other plug-in packages making them unique. Auto FX Software's Web site is `www.autofx.com/`.

ColorWeb Pro from Pantone

Many new Web designers are not new to design at all and bring a rich history — as well as a client list — from their print backgrounds. One constant in print color reproduction is the Pantone Color System. Many clients require that all of their graphics, whether intended for print or for the Internet, conform to a specific selection of Pantone colors. The ColorWeb Pro application translates Pantone colors into their RGB equivalents. Find more information by visiting Pantone's Web site at `www.pantone.com/`.

Cross-Reference   Chapter 7 teaches a special technique for using ColorWeb Pro with Fireworks.

Fireworks extensions

Fireworks is blessed with a robust community that not only creates great artwork and utilities, but also shares them. The CD-ROM includes numerous extensions — commands, styles, and textures — from the Fireworks community. Not only can these tools ease your workflow, but they can also vary and enhance your designs.

Fireworks commands

With the availability of the Fireworks graphics engine through the Flash user interface, Fireworks commands are really taking off. Commands are undeniably powerful, whether they are used to automate tedious production or produce fun effects. You can access a Fireworks JavaScript command from anywhere by choosing Commands ➪ Run Script. Flash commands should be installed using the Extension Manager. The CD-ROM has numerous examples in the Extensions folder.

Fireworks styles and textures

Part of the power of Fireworks is the capability to extend both its image-creating capabilities and its HTML output. Making a set of textures available is as simple as copying a folder from one location to another. For the textures included with this CD-ROM, you simply need to copy the images in any of the Textures folders found under the various contributors' names to the equivalent Fireworks folder and then relaunch Fireworks. The *Fireworks MX Bible* companion CD-ROM includes more than 50 new textures.

Tip You can also use an individual texture without having to copy it to your Textures folder by selecting Other from the Textures list in Fireworks and then choosing the texture from another folder on your computer.

Gradients, strokes, and image libraries

Fireworks also gives you the capability to add many other components of an image, such as the stroke or gradient fill. For your graphic-creation pleasure, the CD-ROM includes a useful compendium of various gradient fills, strokes, and image libraries, each in their own self-named folder. Although these are fairly simple to create in Fireworks, why reinvent the wheel when you have so much other work to do? Included in this collection is a wide variety of dotted and dashed strokes as well as an arrowhead library.

Fireworks MX Bible examples

Example images used in the *Fireworks MX Bible* can be found in the Examples folder of the CD-ROM, organized by the chapter in which they appear in the book. You'll find examples of everything from alpha transparency to a pseudo banner ad that conforms to industrywide specifications.

Web resource directory

The Web is a vital resource for any Web designer, whether a seasoned professional or a beginner. The CD-ROM contains an HTML page with a series of links to resources on the Web; the series contains general, as well as Fireworks-specific references.

Shareware programs are fully functional, trial versions of copyrighted programs. If you like particular programs, register with their authors for a nominal fee and receive licenses, enhanced versions, and technical support. *Freeware programs* are copyrighted games, applications, and utilities that are free for personal use. Unlike shareware, these programs do not require a fee or provide technical support. *GNU software* is governed by its own license, which is included inside the folder of the GNU product. See the GNU license for more details.

Trial, demo, or evaluation versions are usually limited either by time or functionality (such as being unable to save projects). Some trial versions are very sensitive to system date changes. If you alter your computer's date, the programs will "time out" and will no longer be functional.

eBook version of *Fireworks MX Bible*

The complete text of this book is on the CD in Adobe's Portable Document Format (PDF). You can read and search through the file with the Adobe Acrobat Reader (also included on the CD).

Troubleshooting

If you have difficulty installing or using any of the material on the companion CD, try the following solutions:

✦ **Turn off any anti-virus software that you may have running.** Installers sometimes mimic virus activity and can make your computer incorrectly believe that it is being infected by a virus. (Be sure to turn the anti-virus software back on later.)

✦ **Close all running programs.** The more programs you're running, the less memory is available to other programs. Installers also typically update files and programs; if you keep other programs running, installation may not work properly.

✦ **See the ReadMe:** Please refer to the ReadMe file located at the root of the CD-ROM for the latest product information at the time of publication.

If you still have trouble with the CD, please call the Customer Care phone number: (800) 762-2974. Outside the United States, call 1 (317) 572-3994. You can also contact Customer Service by e-mail at techsupdum@wiley.com. Wiley Publishing Inc. will provide technical support only for installation and other general quality control items; for technical support on the applications themselves, consult the program's vendor or author.

✦   ✦   ✦

Index

Continued

Continued

Wiley Publishing, Inc.
End-User License Agreement

5. Limited Warranty.

(a) WPI warrants that the Software and Software Media are free from defects in materials and workmanship under normal use for a period of sixty (60) days from the date of purchase of this Book. If WPI receives notification within the warranty period of defects in materials or workmanship, WPI will replace the defective Software Media.

(b) WPI AND THE AUTHOR OF THE BOOK DISCLAIM ALL OTHER WARRANTIES, EXPRESS OR IMPLIED, INCLUDING WITHOUT LIMITATION IMPLIED WARRANTIES OF MERCHANTABILITY AND FITNESS FOR A PARTICULAR PURPOSE, WITH RESPECT TO THE SOFTWARE, THE PROGRAMS, THE SOURCE CODE CONTAINED THEREIN, AND/OR THE TECHNIQUES DESCRIBED IN THIS BOOK. WPI DOES NOT WARRANT THAT THE FUNCTIONS CONTAINED IN THE SOFTWARE WILL MEET YOUR REQUIREMENTS OR THAT THE OPERATION OF THE SOFTWARE WILL BE ERROR FREE.

(c) This limited warranty gives you specific legal rights, and you may have other rights that vary from jurisdiction to jurisdiction.

6. Remedies.

(a) WPI's entire liability and your exclusive remedy for defects in materials and workmanship shall be limited to replacement of the Software Media, which may be returned to WPI with a copy of your receipt at the following address: Software Media Fulfillment Department, Attn.: Fireworks MX Bible, Wiley Publishing, Inc., 10475 Crosspoint Blvd., Indianapolis, IN 46256, or call 1-800-762-2974. Please allow four to six weeks for delivery. This Limited Warranty is void if failure of the Software Media has resulted from accident, abuse, or misapplication. Any replacement Software Media will be warranted for the remainder of the original warranty period or thirty (30) days, whichever is longer.

(b) In no event shall WPI or the author be liable for any damages whatsoever (including without limitation damages for loss of business profits, business interruption, loss of business information, or any other pecuniary loss) arising from the use of or inability to use the Book or the Software, even if WPI has been advised of the possibility of such damages.

(c) Because some jurisdictions do not allow the exclusion or limitation of liability for consequential or incidental damages, the above limitation or exclusion may not apply to you.

7. U.S. Government Restricted Rights. Use, duplication, or disclosure of the Software for or on behalf of the United States of America, its agencies and/or instrumentalities "U.S. Government" is subject to restrictions as stated in paragraph (c)(1)(ii) of the Rights in Technical Data and Computer Software clause of DFARS 252.227-7013, or subparagraphs (c) (1) and (2) of the Commercial Computer Software - Restricted Rights clause at FAR 52.227-19, and in similar clauses in the NASA FAR supplement, as applicable.

8. General. This Agreement constitutes the entire understanding of the parties and revokes and supersedes all prior agreements, oral or written, between them and may not be modified or amended except in a writing signed by both parties hereto that specifically refers to this Agreement. This Agreement shall take precedence over any other documents that may be in conflict herewith. If any one or more provisions contained in this Agreement are held by any court or tribunal to be invalid, illegal, or otherwise unenforceable, each and every other provision shall remain in full force and effect.

M